MODERN WIRELESS COMMUNICATION

TECHNOLOGY AND APPLICATION

1G TO 5G

MODERN WIRELESS COMMUNICATION

TECHNOLOGY AND APPLICATION

1G TO 5G

A. GANESAN

Former Deputy General Manager BSNL,
Visiting Professor, SRM University, Chennai
Visiting Professor, Manipal University.

ESWAR PRESS

THE SCIENCE & TECHNOLOGY BOOK PUBLISHERS
"Archana Arcade" No. 27, Natesan Street
T. Nagar, Chennai - 600 017. INDIA Ph: 2432 3659 / 4286 7431
E-mail:yempeyes@md3.vsnl.net.in/eswarpress@airtelmail.in

Modern Wireless Communication - Technology and Application — 1G to 5G

ESWAR PRESS
ARCHANA ARCADE
NO. 27, NATESAN STREET
T. NAGAR, CHENNAI - 600 017.
Email : yempeyes@md3.vsnl.net.in
Ph : 044 - 2432 3659

ISBN : 81 – 7874 – 091 – 5

Published by
M. Periyasamy
Eswar Press, No. 27, Natesan Street, T. Nagar, Chennai - 17

Page Layout and Diagrams by
HiKey Media, greendurai@yahoo.com

I dedicate

this book

to my parents

Dr. A. Kalanidhi
Former Vice Chancellor Anna University

No.19, Second Street,
East Abhiramapuram,
Mylapore, Chennai – 600 004
☎044-2499 7222, 9841099044
kalanidhi48@yahoo.com

FOREWORD

The book on "***Modern Wireless Communication-Technology and application 1G to 5G***" by *Prof. A. Ganesan* is a comprehensive book describing the developments of communication technology including wireless technology covering from the first Generation networks to the fifth generation communication network. The author has put in good amount of work and presented the topics like GSM, CDMA, WCDMA, LTE etc giving a fair treatment to help the readers familiarized with the details of each technology to the core.

Prof. A. Ganesan has included his vast practical experience in presenting the development of every phase of the telecom network right from the manual switch to the latest like Intelligent Network and wireless communication. He has covered extensively the IEEE wireless standards for WiFi, WiMAX and Bluetooth including network structure, transmission techniques, protocols used and security tools. Mention is to be made of the presentation of 3GPP Evolution and releases and Multimedia Communications which are very relevant in the present day context of emerging new trends in wireless communication with good amount of illustrations.

This book is suitable to be prescribed as a text book for students of engineering of any Technology Universities. Besides, it serves the cause of researchers in the field too. 1G to 5G, the technology has been well drafted and presented for the readers to have first hand information on the communication engineering.

I compliment Prof Ganesan for presenting a technology on communication engineering to help student community and the telecom engineers as a whole.

A. Kalanidhi

No.18, Second Street
East Abhiramapuram
Mylapore, Chennai - 600 004
☎044-2499 1222, 9841099044
kalanithi48@yahoo.com

Dr. A. Kalanidhi
Former Vice Chancellor Anna University

FOREWORD

The book on "Modern Wireless Communication-Technology and application 1G to 5G" by Prof. A. Ganesan is a comprehensive book describing the developments of communication technology including wireless technology covering from the first Generation networks to the fifth generation communication network. The author has put in good amount of work and presented the topics like GSM, CDMA, WCDMA, LTE etc giving a fair treatment to help the readers familiarized with the details of each technology to the core.

Prof. A. Ganesan has included his vast practical experience in presenting the development of every phase of the telecom network right from the manual switch to the latest like Intelligent Network and wireless communication. He has covered extensively the IEEE wireless standards for WiFi, WiMAX and Bluetooth including network structure, transmission techniques, protocols used and security tools. Mention is to be made of the presentation of 3GPP Evolution and releases and Multimedia Communications which are very relevant in the present day context of emerging new trends in wireless communication with good amount of illustrations.

This book is suitable to be prescribed as a text book for students of engineering of any Technology Universities. Besides, it serves the cause of researchers in the field too. 1G to 5G the technology has been well drafted and presented for the readers to have first hand information on the communication engineering.

I compliment Prof. Ganesan for presenting a technology on communication engineering to help student community and the telecom engineers as a whole.

ए. सुब्रमणियन, B.E., M.Tech., I.T.S.
मुख्य महाप्रबंधक
चेन्नई टेलीफोन
A. SUBRAMANIAN,
B.E., M.Tech., I.T.S.
Chief General Manager
Chennai Telephones

भारत संचार निगम लिमिटेड
(भारत सरकार का उद्यम)
BHARAT SANCHAR NIGAM LIMITED
(A Government of India Enterprises)
BSNL 3G)))) Faster than your thoughts BSNL LiVE

78, पुरसैवाक्कम हाई रोड,
चेन्नई - 600 010.
78, Purasawalkam High Road,
Chennai - 600 010
दूरभाष / Phone : का./Off : 2642 6000
2642 5959
फैक्स / Fax : 2641 4600
ई- मैल E-mail : cgm_chennai@bsnl.co.in

FOREWORD

It is with great pleasure that I had gone through the present work on "**Modern Wireless communication- Technology and application 1G to 5G"** by Shri. A. Ganesan.

Shri. A. Ganesan is a prolific writer on the subject matter of telecommunications, who has taken keen interest in understanding and communicating the development in the field of telecommunications.

He has been bestowed with Gold Medal in Mathematics from Madras University and got Degree in Electronics and Telecommunication Engineering from Institution of Electronics and Telecommunications Engineer (INDIA).

Shri A Ganesan is recipient of 'BHARAT SANCHAR SEVA PATHAK' from BSNL. After retirement from BSNL, he has involved himself in Teaching profession as Visiting Prof., Dept. of ECE, SRM University, Chennai and Manipal University and thereby continuing his service to society at large and student community in particular. It is worth to mention here he has submitted his papers on various subjects in National and International Seminars in the field of telecommunications.

His experience in the then Department of Telecommunications (presently BSNL) has been most fruitful not only to the organization in which he has served, but also to entire telecom fraternity by way of his various books on special subject matters in the field of telecommunications.

This presentation will serve not only professionals to update their knowledge but also to the student community to understand the growth from the earlier days.

I am sure that this book will be of immense use to one and all in the field of telecommunications.

Date : 23/07/2012
Place : Chennai

(A.SUBRAMANIAN)

Regd & Corporate Office : Bharat Sanchar Bhavan, Harish Chandra Mathur Lane, Janpath, New Delhi - 110 001. Website : www.bsnl.co.in

PREFACE

Over recent years the wireless Industry has been growing fast with its focus shifting from voice centric to the data-oriented services and the shift is characterized by convergence of technologies to achieve the goal of enabling customers to access "any type of service from anywhere using any device". The growth of mobile communication technology has seen quantum leap in many instances in the past decade, advanced concepts over taking the conventional one. To understand the phenomenal growth, it is but natural that one has to understand the roots and the branches of the communication techniques to further study the latest developments in wireless communication.

With this idea in mind, the first four chapters cover - the basics of access technologies such as wireless in local loop, optical fiber, the modulation and coding, first generation mobile technology standards, and the fundamentals of well known second generation technologies namely GSM and CDMA which are dealt with in detail including traffic calculation and authentication algorithms

While explaining the further developments such as GPRS, EDGE, Mobile Broadband, 3G network and Migration path to 4G, care has been taken to elucidate important technical details in each technology for the readers to understand the concept/technology in a cogent manner. It is indeed unavoidable to not to refer to wireless standards such as CDMA, WiMAX, OFDM, MIMO repeatedly in many chapters when writing a content on wireless technology evolution.

The content of the book is aimed to cover the syllabus of Engineering departments of the universities for an under-graduate / post-graduate course in wireless technology. The book can also serve as a guide/reference material for the students to pursue their research work in the field of communication systems. Having said that, the book is for everyone – students or practicing engineers who are interested in keeping themselves abreast of the latest developments in the field of wireless technology.

This book is an outcome of consolidated efforts of gathering information from different sources, varied write-ups of many academicians' and educational websites and compiling those valuable information into a presentable form useful to readers. Every care has been taken to present the topics with accuracy and correctness, from the available references

I am highly indebted to my students and learned colleagues for providing necessary stimulus for writing this book. I am grateful to those persons whose writings and works have helped me in the preparation of the book. I am equally grateful to reviewers of the manuscript who helped me by offering extremely valuable suggestions and thus contributed to enhance the standard of the book. I thankfully acknowledge the assistance provided my friends, colleagues and my daughter in shaping the articles, chapters and diagrams.

I express my sincere thanks to Sri. A. Subramanian, Chief General Manager, BSNL, Chennai Telephones for his great foreword which has added value to this book. My sincere thanks goes to Dr. A. Kalanidhi, former Vice Chancellor, Anna University, Chennai for his encouraging foreword that has enhanced the grade of this book.

I profusely thank the publisher Sri. M. Periasamy of Eswar Press who has taken keen interest in getting the book printed in a best possible format and shape. I owe my gratitude to HiKey Media for the neat professional work done in formatting the pages and diagrams.

I shall feel amply rewarded if the book proves helpful to those who pursue their study and intend to do research in wireless technologies. I look forward for suggestions to improve the presentation and content.

— A. Ganesan

CONTENTS

4. SECOND GENERATION MOBILE SYSTEMS (GLOBAL SYSTEM FOR MOBILE COMMUNICATION (GSM))

5. GENERAL PACKET RADIO SERVICE (GPRS) AND ENHANCED DATA FOR GLOBAL EVOLUTION (EDGE)

8. THIRD GENERATION NETWORK - 3G (CDMA, CDMA-1X AND WCDMA/UMTS)

1 ACCESS TECHNOLOGIES

1.1 INTRODUCTION

Any service provider or organization should strive to provide high quality service in the most economic method available to end-user, the customer. Telecommunication is no exception and therefore it is needed to keep abreast of Technology advancements and innovations to provide the best quality of service at lowest cost possible to the subscriber.

In the last 20-30 years, we have seen switching equipment move from manual boards, to sophisticated electronic digital exchanges now in use. Transmission technology has also advanced thus far to Optical Fibre Cable, Microwave Radio, Satellite Communications etc, and is continuously developing.

Access network, the network between local exchange and customers, in the Telecom Network accounts for a major portion of resources both in terms of capital and manpower. At present the access network represents approximately 45 to 50% of the total capital investment in the telecom network. It is therefore a very substantial portion of total network and must be given due attention. If this access network is properly maintained, most of the problems in the telecom network could be avoided.

The local external Network or the local Loop also needs adopting newer technologies. By embracing newer technology in the field of External plant, we can maintain a high QOS (Quality of Service) and reduce the cost to the subscriber.

The Radio in Local Loop, i.e, wireless in Local Loop, better known as WLL, can provide, if not better service than Wire line, but an equivalent Local Loop Service at Lower cost.

1.1.1 Access Technologies - Different Types

- Cable Network (2W Copper Local Loop)
- DSL
- ADSL
- Cable Modems
- Optical Fiber Technologies
- wireless

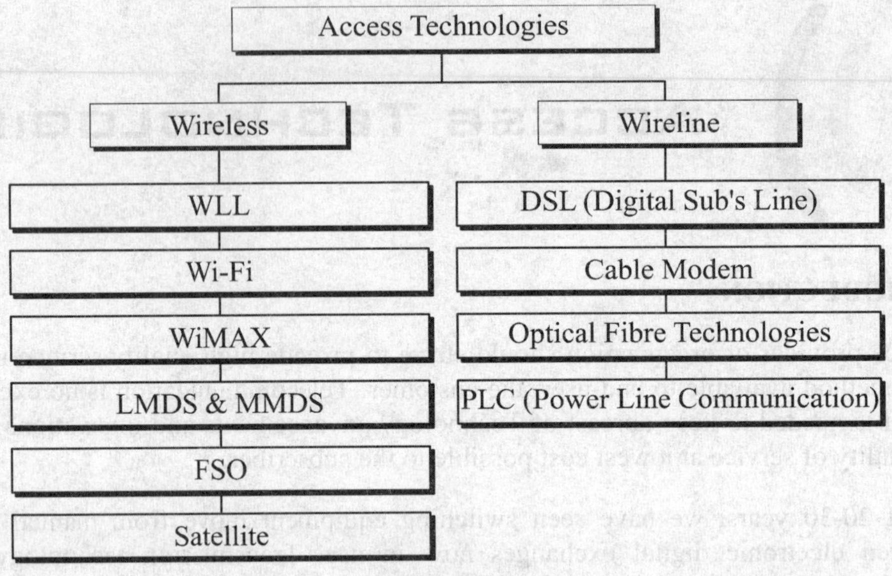

Fig. 1.1

1.1.2 Wireless Access Networks

- Wireless Personal Area Network (WPAN / Bluetooth) (IEEE 802.15)
- Wireless Local Area Network (WLAN / WiFi) (IEEE 802.11)
- Wireless Metropolitan Area Network (WMAN / Wi Max) (IEEE 802.16)
- Fixed Broadband Wireless Access (LMDS/MMDS)
- Cellular Mobile Telephony (GSM-GPRS, EDGE / CDMA 2000 1x EVDO, EVDV) (3G-UMTS / WCDMA

1.1.3 New Access Technologies Under Wireless Category

- Free Space Optics
- Local Multipoint Distribution Service
- Multichannel Multipoint Distribution Service

1.1.4 Free Space Optic FSO (Free Space Optics)

- Also known as FSP (Free Space Photonics) or Optical wireless
- Enables optical transmission of data through open space at near infrared wavelengths (Tera Hz)
- Offers 10 Mbps-2 Gbps over few kilometers
- FSO is optical, wireless, point-to-point, line-of-sight broadband technology, an alternative to fiber optic cable systems
- Speed is comparable to fiber optic transmissions

- Transmits up to 1.25 Gbps at distance of 4 miles (6.4 kilometers) in full-duplex mode
- Uses low-powered infrared (IR) beam sent through open air by transceivers
- Uses unlicensed higher frequency
- Currently FSO uses two different wavelengths, but expect worldwide standard in near future

Several advantages of FSO

- Significantly less expensive than fiber optic or leased lines
- Much faster installation, days or weeks compared to months for fiber optic cables
- Transmission speed can be scaled to meet user's needs; from 10 Mbps to 1.25 Gbps
- Security is key advantage; not easy to intercept or decode

1.1.5 LMDS (Local Multipoint Distribution System)

- Broadband wireless access technology operating in the 28-GHz and 31-GHz ranges
- Voice, data and video
- Data rate in the range of 100s of Mbps
- Available from 2001
- Line-of-sight technology

1.1.6 MMDS -Multichannel Multipoint Distribution System

- In 1998, FCC allowed MMDS frequency to provide two-way services such as wireless Internet access along with voice and video transmissions
- Similar to LMDS, MMDS can transmit video, voice, or data signals at 1.5 Mbps downstream and 300 Kbps upstream at distances up to 35 miles
- Mounted MMDS hub uses point-to-multipoint architecture
- By using lower frequencies, MMDS signals travel longer distances and provide service to cells that are up to 35 miles across
- Pizza box (13 x 13 inch) directional antennas are mounted at receiving location
- Cable runs from antenna to MMDS wireless modem
- Converts analog signal to digital and may be attached to single computer or LAN

Advantages

- *Signal strength*— low frequency MMDS RF signal travels farther and with less interference than high-frequency LMDS RF signals
- *Cell size*— seven times larger than area covered by LMDS transmitters
- *Cost*— MMDS is less expensive than LMDS

Disadvantages

- *Requires direct line-of-sight*— makes installation difficult and eliminates locations blocked by taller obstructions
- *Shared signals*— decreased speed and throughput since users share same radio channel
- *Security*— Unencrypted transmissions may be intercepted and read
- *Limited markets*— available in limited areas in USA

1.1.7 Satellite Technologies

- Uses VSAT (very Small Aperture Terminals) & DTH (Direct To Home) terminals
- C, Ku & Ka bands are used for services involving fixed terminals
- L band is used for mobile services
- Offers data rates 9.6 Kbps for a handheld terminal and 60 Mbps for a fixed VSAT terminal
- Future will support up to 155 Mbps

1.1.8 The Economics of Wire-Line Versus Wireless

- The cost of installing or maintaining wire-line system broadly depends on the cost of labour (Laying Ducts, digging Manholes) where as cost of wireless depends on cost of subscriber unit, which tends to fall over time, with increasing economics of scale.
- Cost of wire-line is more due to use of copper a costly metal in U/G cables whereas WLL is independent of this factor.
- Cost of wire-line system critically depends on the distance and the penetration levels achieved. These factors are not applicable in WLL.
- If a subscriber moves to a different operator in case of wire-line system, the investment is lost, whereas in the case of WLL, the subscriber unit in such case is simply removed and installed elsewhere.
- The cost of wire-line system is incurred, even prior to Marketing to the users, whereas much of the cost of WLL is not incurred until the users subscribe the Network.

Sometimes called radio in the loop or fixed radio access, WLL is a system which connects subscriber to the public switched telephone network using radio signal as a substitute for copper for all or part of the connection between the subscriber and the switch. This includes cordless access system, proprietary fixed access and fixed cellular system.

1.2 PRESENT NETWORK AND LIMITATIONS

At present customer access network predominantly employs technologies based on twisted copper pairs. The copper pairs have limited transmission capacity and hence pose a major constraint to the modernization programme. Also the copper based local network is considered to be responsible for most of the faults in telecom network. The obvious reasons are congestion of underground facilities, complex network planning and limitation of copper cables to handle digital signals leading to a network inappropriate for extending broadband integrated services digital network (ISDN).

Introduction of Digital Technology coupled with radio transmission and optical fibre cable has revolutionized Telecom network world wide. The implementation of the above technologies in the access network can be as follows:

a) Using Radio in the access network (WILL technology), LMDS.

b) Using fibre in the access network (FITL technology)

c) Exploring the existing copper network for higher band width (HDSL, ADSL, VDSL Technologies).

1.3 REQUIREMENTS FOR WIRELESS LOCAL LOOP SYSTEM

A Wireless Local Loop (WLL) system is meant as a replacement for the traditional copper twisted-pair local loop. The WLL system is expected to provide a superior alternative to buried cable. The main purpose of the WLL system is as a substitute for a wired local loop for providing fixed telephone access. The WLL must, in general, provide all services supported today by the wired local loop, and also those that are likely to emerge in the near future. Further, it must provide these with the same, or better, quality.

The requirements of a WLL system can be broadly divided into five categories services, capacity, PSTN connectivity, cost and maintainability.

1.3.1 Services

The WLL system must provide wire line voice quality, preferably using digital technology. It must support all commercial devices that connect to a standard two-wire wire line interface, such as fax machines, modems, videophones, etc. It should support data transmission at the same bit rates as the conventional wire line system (28.8 kbps and higher). It should also be capable of providing narrow band ISDN and 64 kbps data interface to the subscriber. This is especially important in view of the explosive growth in internet connectivity. Taking advantage of the Access network, the network between local exchange and customers, in the Telecom Network accounts for a major portion of resources both in terms of capital and manpower. At present the access network represents approximately 45 to 50% of the total capital investment in the telecom network. It is therefore a very substantial portion of total network and must be given due attention. If this access network is properly maintained, most of the problems in the telecom network could be avoided.

1.3.2 Bandwidth Requirements

The IT revolution has created a heavy thirst for huge amount of data channels and high band width requirements in addition to voice telephony. The service requirements of customers may be categorized as follows:

a) *Multitype services*— POTS, ISDN (BR), High speed data, Video conferencing and video on demand, VPN etc

b) *Medium type services*— POTS, ISDN (BR), leased lines and video on demand

c) Only POTS services.

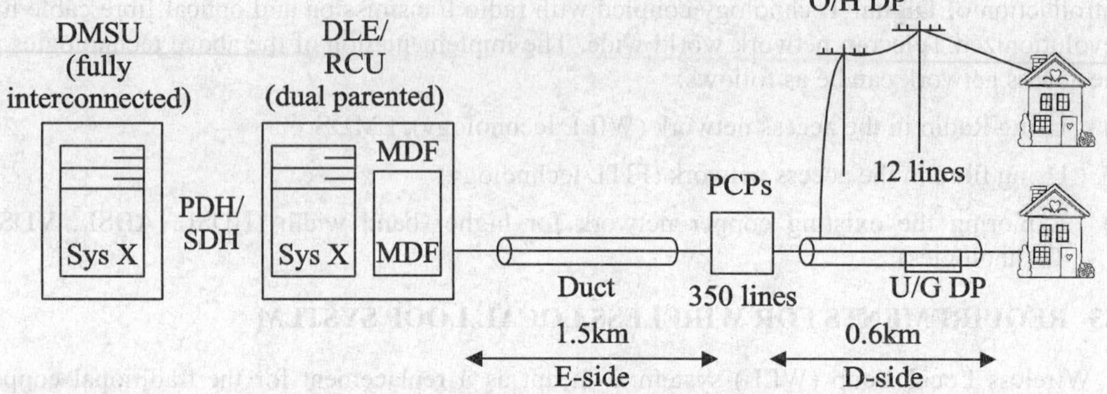

Fig. 1.2: Copper Access Network

Table 1.1: Service/Network Options

Services	*Access Network*
Bulk telephony/Private circuits	Copper pairs/Fibre
Mobile/Niche telephony	GSM/Fixed radio
Metropolitan/Business services	Fibre access/SDH
Broadcast TV/Telephony	HFC/Copper pairs
Broadcast TV only	Satellite
Long distance/Internet	Indirect access
Value-added service providers	Leased lines

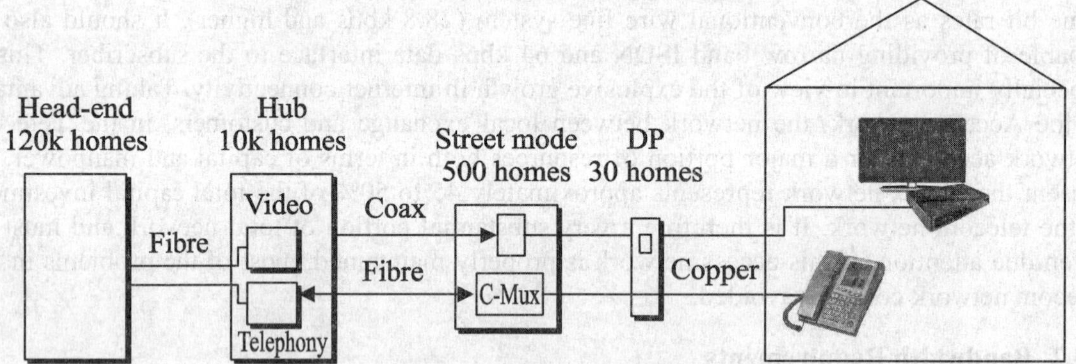

Fig. 1.3: Cable TV Network

1.4 MARKET DYNAMICS

The choice of access technology is crucial to the survival of operators since access is such a dominant part of overall costs. That choice will, however, be dependent on a number of factors, best summarised through the use of the Porter diagram of competitive forces in Figure 1.5. New entrants have been discussed in Section 1.2.2, with many new niche operators selecting specific technology to support their overall strategy. The new technologies available are discussed in Section 1.4.

1.5 DEPLOYMENT OF RADIO

Radio communication has been employed as a replacement for copper based cables in the long distance media for several years. More recent developments of digital radio and advances in microelectronic circuits have given rise to "*Wireless in local loop (WILL)*". It involves using radio to replace the wired link between PSTN switch and the subscriber. WILL is generally used as a "*last mile solution*" to deliver basic phone services expeditiously where none existed before. It shall facilitate cordless telephony for residential as well as commercial complexes where people are highly mobile. It is also used in remote areas where it is uneconomical to lay cables and for rapid development of telephone services.

Table 1.2

System	***Macro cellular***			***Micro cellular***		
Technology	***GSM***	***DAMPS***	***CDMA***	***CT2***	***DECT***	***PHS***
Frequency (MHz)	890-915 935-960	824-849 869-894	824-849 869-894	864-868	1880-1900	1895-1918.1
Cell Size	Large	Large	Large	Small	Small	Small
Multiple Access	TDMA	TDMA	CDMA	FDMA	TDMA	TDMA
RF Channel Spacing	200 KHz	30 KHz	1250 KHz	100 KHz	1728 KHz	300 KHz
Voice Channel/ Carrier	8	3	25 - 45	1	12	4
Modulation	GMSK	PIE/ 4-QPSK	CDMA	2 LEVEL FSK	GFSK	PIE/ 4-QPSK

GSM Global System for Mobile Communication
DAMPS Digital Advanced Mobile Phone Services
CDMA Code Division Multiple Access
CT2 Cordless Telephony-2
DECT Digital Enhanced Cordless Technology
PHS Personal Handiphone Service

The radio technology is able to offer the same level of service quality as that provided by wireline technology. The technology employed shall depend upon various radio access techniques like FDMA, TDMA, CDMA.

Basically two types of technology options are available for wireless in local loop;. The first one based on cellular mobile telephone system can be adopted for fixed wireless in local loop application. These systems have Macro cell architecture with cell radius of tens of kilometers (typically 10-20 kms). The second type based on Micro cell architecture are extension of cordless telephone systems. These systems have cell radius of few hundred meters (typically 50-200 mts.)

The WILL technologies available in different frequency bands and their important parameters are indicated in Table 1.2.

1.5.1 Different Technologies used in WLL System

i) Cor-DECT System – (a) V5.2 interface
(b) R 2 / MF Interface

ii) CDMA system (a) BSC Based V 5.2 interface Billing & Subscriber Management are done by PSTN.
(b) BSC based R 2 / MF Interface Billing & subscriber Management are done by WLL System
(c) *MSC Based*— This will work as an independent PLMN

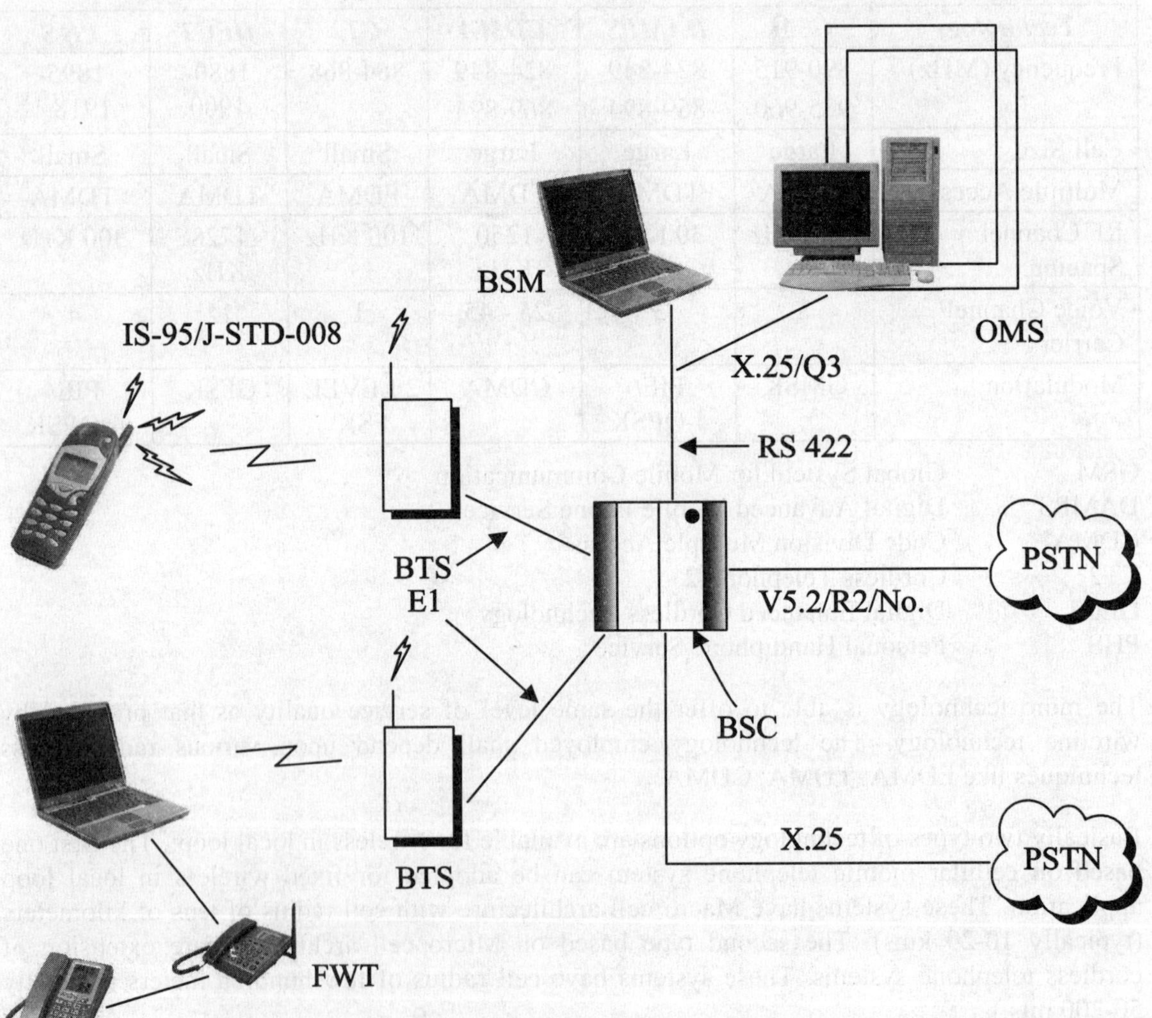

Fig. 1.4: System Configuration CDMA-WLL

1.5.2 Services Offered by WLL

WLL- M is communication system that connects customers to the PSTN network using radio frequency signals instead of conventional copper wires, for the full or part connection between the subscriber and the exchange. This comes with superior voice quality and high speed data capabilities. CDMA is popular with more than 100 million subscribers worldwide and the number keeps on increasing exponentially.

Terminal Types—

- *Fixed Wireless Terminal (FWT)*
- *Hand held terminal*

  Sevice using FWT
- In this case there is a small box fitted with a small antenna at the subscribers premises and a normal telephone instrument is connected to the box. There is no wire connection as in conventional telephone.
- *Service using hand held terminal (WLL-M Service)*

  In this case Subscriber can carry a small handset of CDMA technology There is no antenna or any other equipment at subscribers premises.

1.6 HIGH BITRATES DIGITAL SUBSCRIBER LINE (HDSL)

Even though the fibre will eventually take over the last mile (access portion) of the network, it is felt and generally accepted that it would not be economically justified immediately and would take some more time before it penetrates in the access network. The Telecom Administration has already invested lot in terms of the copper based network and will continue to do so until the fibre becomes more techno-economically feasible. Till such time there is no alternative but to exploit the already buried (but not dead) copper to carry more and more bandwidth.

HDSL is one such technology employing a transmission technique which derives substantial capacity advantage in transporting digital signals in local network over existing copper pairs by providing 64 kbps channels supporting voice, fax and data services with an improved transmission performance. In other words HDSL is able to convert the copper pairs into high speed digital line carriers what were essentially individual voice telephone line carriers. HDSL technology promises the following advantages:

a) Subscriber connectivity over a distance of 4.5 Kms on 0.5 mm copper pairs carrying 2.048 Mbps data.

b) Remote power feeding over copper wires from exchange to subscribers.

c) There is no need for any cable conditioning or selection of pairs.

d) Possible to extend the range of operation to 9 Kms over a single repeater.

HDSL Technology can prove very useful in subscriber access network utilizing the already buried copper pair cables. Recently some new technologies, Asymmetric Digital subscriber line

(ADSL) and Very high speed Digital subscriber line (VDSL) have come up with promise to implement digital TV broadcast, video on demand, interactive distance learning and homeshopping on the existing copper lines. ADSL can carry 6 Mbps signal over 3.5 Kms (approx) and VDSL can carry 26 Mbps to 52 Mbps over a distance of 600-1000 meters (approx.). VDSL may find its use in business applications within a building. DIAS is very popular in many countries and also in India were a single telephone line is used for simultaneous telephone and Internet facilities.

Table 1.3: DSL Technologies

Technology	*ITU-T Standard*	*Distance*	*Downstream Data Rate*	*Upstream Data Rate*
ADSL	G992.1	3.5 Kms	8 Mbps	640 Kbps
2 Wire High-speed DSL	G-991.2	3.0 Kms	2312 Kbps	2312 Kbps
4 Wire High-speed DSL	G-991.2	3.0 Kms	4624 Kbps	4624 Kbps
Very High-speed DSL	G-993.1	300 Mts	52 Mbps	6-26 Mbps
Very High-speed DSL	G-993.1	700 Mts	26 Mbps	26 Mbps

1.7 FIBRE IN LOCAL LOOP (FITL)

Copper cables in the access network have a number of limitations which should be overcome for providing a reliable access network. The limitations of copper cables in the access network are:

a) The old and worn out cables have poor insulation which results in cross talk.

b) Water seepage during rainy season is the major cause for faults in copper cables.

c) The local loop is vulnerable to electromagnetic interception and hence misuse

d) The limitations on loop length and unpredictable growth of demand restricts the quick expansion capability and ease in network flexibility

e) Large size of copper cable calls for more space for leading in cable at MDF and congestion in duct.

f) Copper pairs are bandwidth limited and are not able to support new broad band services.

In order to overcome the limitations of copper cable and to be able to support value broad band services like data, cable video, HDTV and increased use of computer which require bandwidth on demand, optical fibre is introduced in the local loop.

1.7.1 Advantages of Optical Fibre in the Loop

a) Impact of environmental factors is almost negligible on optical fibre cable.

b) Optical fibre cables are not susceptible to electromagnetic interference.

c) Because of fibre's unlimited bandwidth capacity upgradation is very simple as it can be effected by simply changing the end terminal equipment. Repeated digging and laying additional cable is not required.

d) Small size of fibre avoids congestion in ducts and crowding at MDF.

e) Due to inherent wide bandwidth capability optical fibre cable can support narrow band and broad band ISDN services. They can also support video transmission.

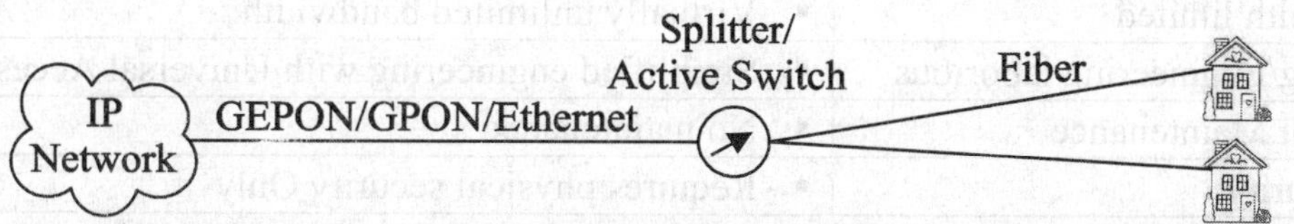

Includes fiber to both individual houses and to apartment blocks (aka FTTH)

(a) FTTH (Home)

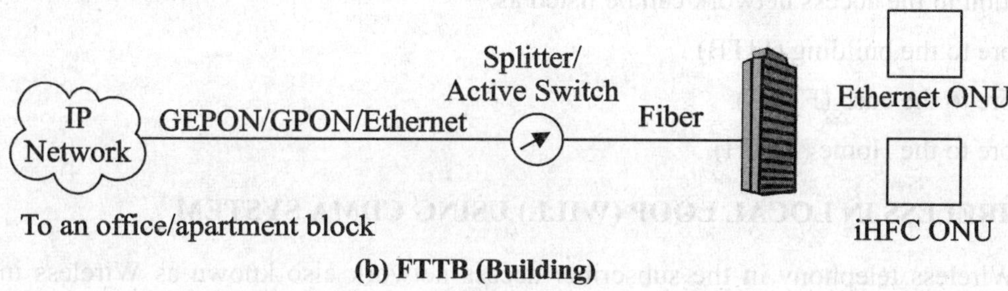

To an office/apartment block

(b) FTTB (Building)

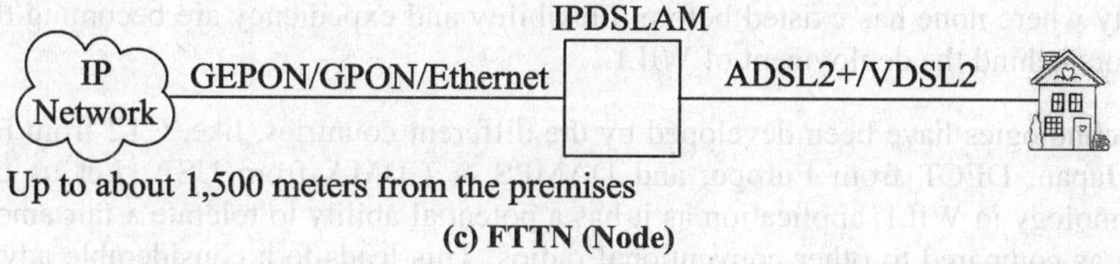

Up to about 1,500 meters from the premises

(c) FTTN (Node)

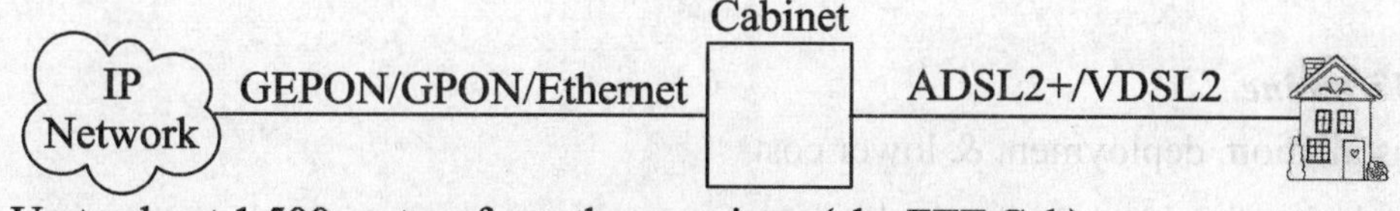

Up to about 1,500 meters from the premises (aka FTT Cab)

(d) FTTC (Curb)

Fig. 1.5: FTTx Options

The advantages offered by FITL and limitations of copper access network can be tabulated as:-

Table 1.4

Copper Access Network Limitations/Challenges	*FITL Advantages*
▪ Bandwidth limited	▪ Virtually unlimited bandwidth
▪ Planning/Engineering laborious	▪ Simplified engineering with Universal Access
▪ Constant Maintenance	▪ No maintenance
▪ No Security	▪ Requires physical security Only
▪ High Attenuation	▪ Fibres offer very low loss

The long term objective of FITL is to take the fibre right upto the subscriber premises or else extend the fibre as close to the subscriber as possible. The various approaches depending upon penetration in the access network can be listed as:

a) Fibre to the building (FITB)

b) Fibre to the curb (FTTC)

c) Fibre to the Home (FTTH)

1.8 WIRELESS IN LOCAL LOOP (WILL) USING CDMA SYSTEM

Fixed Wireless telephony in the subscriber access network also known as Wireless in Local Loop (WILL) is one of the hottest emerging market segments in global telecommunications today. WILL is generally used as "the last mile solution" to deliver basic phone service expeditiously where none has existed before. Flexibility and expediency are becoming the key driving factors behind the deployment of WILL.

Different technologies have been developed by the different countries, like, CT2 from France, PHS from Japan, DECT from Europe, and DAMPS & CDMA from USA. Let us discuss CDMA technology in WILL application as it has a potential ability to tolerate a fair amount of interference as compared to other conventional radios. This leads to a considerable advantage from a system point of view.

Advantages

i. ***Over Wire Line***

- Easy installation, deployment & lower cost
- Quick solution for developing telephones infrastructure
- Mobility & flexibility
- Ease in operation, administration and maintenance
- Reduces the distance
- More bandwidth can be utilized
- No handoffs occur
- Call drop is less than 2%

ii. Over Mobile

- Bigger coverage area
- Improved signal and reduced interference
- Higher capacity

- ***No Reuse of Frequency***

  Fixed to fixed links (using directional antennas on both ends)

  Mobile to fixed links (using directional antennas on one end)

iii. Use of CDMA for WLL

- Large Capacity (a) efficient use of spectrum
- High quality service (a) error detection & correction.
  (b) diversity against fading in air.

iv. Market

- Capable of developing good quality speech and performance equivalent to wire line
- Support Fixed Subs. Unit (FSU), mobile set, modem, FAX, ISDN, Internet.
- Supports more than 28.8 kbps data rates
- Higher service demand
- Limited mobility support
- Voice, data, customer calling services, mobility

1.8.1 Technical Specification of CDMA WLL

- Frequency Band : 824-849 MHz (uplink)
  869-894 MHz (DN-Link)
- RF Spacing : 1.25 MHz
- Duplex Separation : 45 MHz
- Multiple Access Method : Code Division Multiple Access
- Duplex Method : FDD Access Channels per carrier per sector
  : 40 Chls (3 sectors)
- Voice Coding : 8/13 Kbps QCELP
  8Kbps EVRC
- BTS trans power : Upto 20 watts
- Coverage – In rural : 25 Km radius
  – In urban : 5 Km radius.

1.8.2 Spread Spectrum Principle

Originally Spread spectrum radio technology was developed for military use to counter the interference by hostile jamming. The broad spectrum of the transmitted signal gives rise to "Spread Spectrum". A Spread Spectrum signal is generated by modulating the radio frequency (RF) signal with a code consisting of different pseudo random binary sequences, which is inherently resistant to noisy signal environment. We will be studying more on this topic in coming chapters.

A number of Spread spectrum RF signals thus generated share the same frequency spectrum and thus the entire bandwidth available in the band is used by each of the users using same frequency at the same time.

On the receive side, only the signal energy with the selected binary sequence code is accepted and original information content (data) is recovered. The other users signals, whose codes do not match contribute only to the noise and are not "de-spread" back in bandwidth. This transmission and reception of signals differentiated by "codes" using the same frequency simultaneously by a number of users is known as Code Division Multiple Access (CDMA) Technique as opposed to conventional method of Frequency Division Multiple Access and Time Division Multiple Access.

Figure 1.6 explains that how the base band signal of 9.6 Kbps is spread using a Pseudo-random Noise (PN) source to occupy entire bandwidth of 1.25 Mhz. At the receiving end this signal will have interference from signals of other users of the same cell, users of different cells and interference from other noise sources. All these signals get combined with the desired signal but using a correct PN code the original data can be reproduced back. CDMA channel in the trans and receive direction is a FDD (Frequency Division Duplexing) channel. More of CDMA concept and working are explain in detail in forth coming chapters.

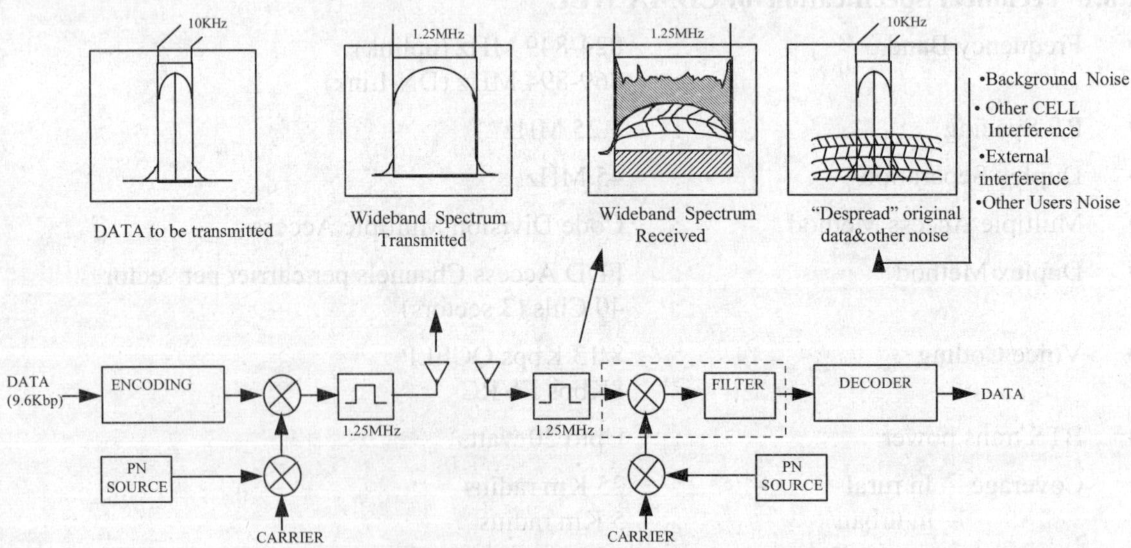

Fig. 1.6: CDMA Access - A Concept

1.8.3 Different Codes used in CDMA

The different types of codes used for identification of traffic channels and users identification etc. are as follows:

Walsh Code— In CDMA the forward traffic channels are separated by unique "Walsh" code. All such codes are orthogonal to each other. The individual subscriber can start communication using one of these codes. These codes are *traffic channel codes* and are used for orthogonal spreading of the information in the entire bandwidth. Orthogonality provides nearly perfect isolation between the multiple signals transmitted by the base station

The basic concept behind creation of the code is as follows:-

a) Repeat the function right
b) Repeat the function below
c) Invert the function diagonally

Seed 0	0 0	0 0	0 0
	0 1	0 1	0 1
		0 0	1 1
		0 1	1 0

Long Code— The long pseudo random noise (PN) sequence is based on 2^{42}characteristic polynomial. Reverse traffic channels (Mobile to Base) are separated by this long code and the data in the forward direction (Base to Mobile) is scrambled. The PN codes are generated using linear shift registers. The long code is unique for the subscribers and is known as users address mask. It repeats every 41 days (at a clock rate of 1.2288 Mcps)

PN offset (Masking)

- Masking will cause the generator to produce the same sequence but offset in time.
- Masking provides the shift in time for PN codes.
- Different masks correspond to different time shifts.
- ESN are used as masks for users on the traffic channels.

Short Code— The short pseudo random noise (PN) sequence is based on 2^{15} characteristic polynomial. This short code differentiates the cells & the sectors in a cell. It also consists of codes for I & Q channel feeding the modulator. Each cell uses different PN offsets. It repeats every 26.67 msec (at a clock rate of 1.2288 Mcps)

1.8.4 Characteristics of CDMA

Less (Optimum) Power Per Cell

Power Control Methods— As we have already seen that in CDMA the entire bandwidth of 1.25 MHz, is used by all the subscribers served in that area. Hence they all will be transmitting on the same frequency using the entire bandwidth but separated by different codes. At the receiving end the noise contributed by all the subscribers is added up. To minimize the level of interfering signals in CDMA, very powerful power control methods have been devised and are listed below:

1) Reverse link open loop power control
2) Reverse link closed loop power control
3) Forward link power control

The objective of *open loop power control in the reverse link* (Mobile to Base) is that the mobile station should adjust its transmit power according to the changes in its received power from the base. Open loop power control attempts to ensure that the received signal strength at the base station from different mobile stations, irrespective of their distances from the base station, should be same.

In *Closed loop power control in reverse link,* the base station provides rapid corrections to the mobile stations' open loop estimates to maintain optimum transmit power by the mobile stations. The base station measures the received signal strength from the mobile connected to it and compares it with a threshold value and a decision is taken by the base every 1.25ms to either increase or decrease the power of the mobile.

In *forward link power control* (Base to Mobile) the cell(base) adjusts its power in the forward link for each subscriber, in response to measurements provided by the mobile station so as to provide more power to the mobile who is relatively far away from the base or is in a location experiencing more difficult environment.

These power control methods attempt to have an environment which permits high quality communication (good S/N) and at the same time the interference to other mobile stations sharing the same CDMA channel is minimum. Thus more numbers of mobile stations are able to use the system without degradation in the performance. Apart from the capacity advantage thus gained, power control extends the life of the battery used in portables and minimizes the concern of ill effects of RF radiation on the human body.

Seamless Hand-off— CDMA provides soft hand-off feature for the mobile crossing from one cell to another cell by combining the signals from both the cells in the transition areas. This improves the performance of the network at the boundaries of the cells, virtually eliminating the dropped calls.

No Frequency Planning— A CDMA system requires no frequency planning as the adjacent cells use the same common frequency. A typical cellular system with a repetition rate of **7** and a CDMA system is shown in the following figures which clearly indicates that in a CDMA network no frequency planning is required.

High Tolerance to Interference— The primary advantage of spread spectrum is its ability to tolerate a fair amount of interfering signals as compared to other conventional systems. This factor provides a considerable advantage from a system point of view.

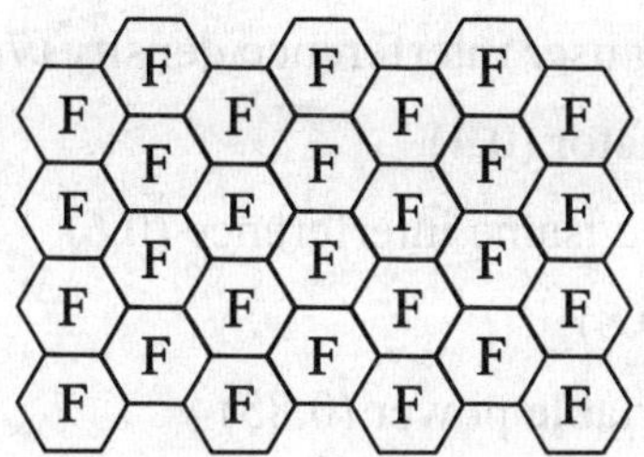

Fig. 1.7: CDMA Frequency Reuse

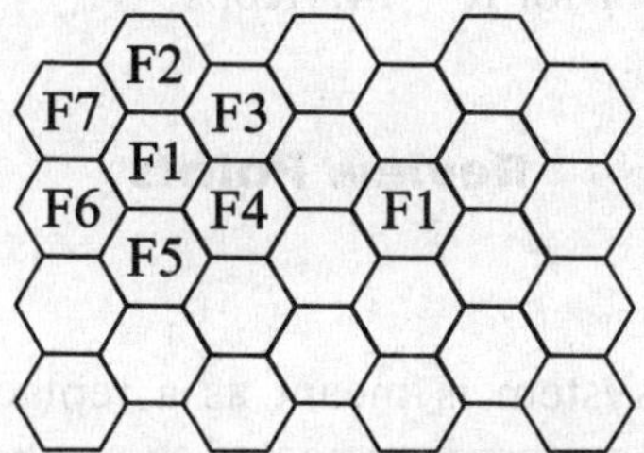

Fig. 1.8: Frequency Reuse of 7

Multiple Diversity— Diversity techniques are often employed to counter the effect of fading. The greater the number of diversity techniques employed, the better the performance of the system in a difficult propagation environment.

CDMA has a vastly improved performance as it employs all the three diversity techniques in the form of the following:

a) *Frequency Diversity*— A wide band RF signal of 1.25 Mhz being used.

b) *Space Diversity*— Employed by way of multipath rake receiver.

c) *Time Diversity*— Employed by way of symbol interleaving, error detection and correction coding.

1.9 CAPACITY CONSIDERATIONS

Let us discuss a typical CDMA wireless in local loop system consisting of a single base station located at the telephone exchange itself, serving a single "cell". In order to increase the number of subscribers served the cell is further divided into "sectors". These sectors are served by directional antennas.

CDMA Capacity

$$N = \frac{W/R}{Eb/lo} \times \frac{1}{d} \times \frac{1}{1+f} \times n \times g$$

Where N = calls per sector

W = Spread spectrum Bandwidth (1.25 MHz)

R = data rate (9.6 kbps or 14.4 kbps)

Eb/Io=		Bit energy/ other user interference density (7dB)
d	=	Voice activity factor (0.4)
f	=	other interference/ same interference (0.6)
n	=	loading factor (0.8)
g	=	reduction for variable power (0.85)
N	=	27 users per sector for R = 9.6Kbps 18 users per sector for R = 14.4Kbps

Review Points

Wireless Local Loop (WLL)

A Wireless Local Loop (WLL) system is meant as a replacement for the traditional copper twisted-pair local loop. The WLL system is expected to provide a superior alternative to buried cable. The main purpose of the WLL system is as a substitute for a wired local loop for providing fixed telephone access. The WLL must, in general, provide all services supported today by the wired local loop, and also those that are likely to emerge in the near future. Further, it must provide these with the same, or better, quality.

Bandwidth Requirements of Customers

The IT revolution has created a heavy thirst for huge amount of data channels and high band width requirements in addition to voice telephony. The service requirements of customers may be POTS, ISDN (BR), High speed data, Video conferencing and video on demand, VPN etc

Radio Technology

The radio technology is able to offer the same level of service quality as that provided by wireline technology. The technology employed shall depend upon various radio access techniques like FDMA, TDMA, CDMA.

High Bitrates Digital Subscriber Line (HDSL)

There is no alternative but to exploit the already buried (but not dead) copper to carry more and more bandwidth. HDSL is one such technology employing a transmission technique which derives substantial capacity advantage in transporting digital signals in local network over existing copper pairs by providing 64 kbps channels supporting voice, fax and data services with an improved transmission performance.

Fibre in Local Loop (FITL)

In order to overcome the limitations of copper cable and to be able to support value broad band services like data, cable video, HDTV and increased use of computer which require bandwidth on demand, optical fibre is introduced in the local loop. Advantages of Optical Fibre in the loop are impact of environmental factors is almost negligible on optical fibre cable and Optical fibre cables are not susceptible to electromagnetic interference.

CDMA System

CDMA technology is used in WILL application as it has a potential ability to tolerate a fair amount of interference as compared to other conventional radios. This leads to a considerable advantage from a system point of view besides easy installation, deployment & lower cost, mobility & flexibility, more bandwidth can be utilized and call drop is less than 2%. Salient features of CDMA WLL are Frequency Band- 824-849 MHz (uplink) and 869-894 MHz (DN-Link). The RF Spacing is 1.25 MHz and Multiple Access Method used is Code Division Multiple Access The Voice Coding achieved is 8/13 Kbps QCELP. Different codes used in CDMA are Walsh Code, Short Code and Long Code. CDMA has a vastly improved performance as it employs all the three diversity techniques viz., Frequency Diversity, Space Diversity, and Time Diversity.

Review Questions

1. What are the disadvantages of wireline connection?
2. What are the advantages of wireless connection?
3. State the limitations of the present telephone networks?
4. Mention the bandwidths used in different wireless systems.
5. Write the parameters of Technical Specifications of WLL system.
6. Write down the advantages of optical fibre in local loop.
7. Write note on Spread Spectrum Principle.
8. What are the technical features of HDSL service?
9. Mention few special characteristics of CDMA-WLL.
10. Write about codes used in CDMA WLL and what is PN offset masking?

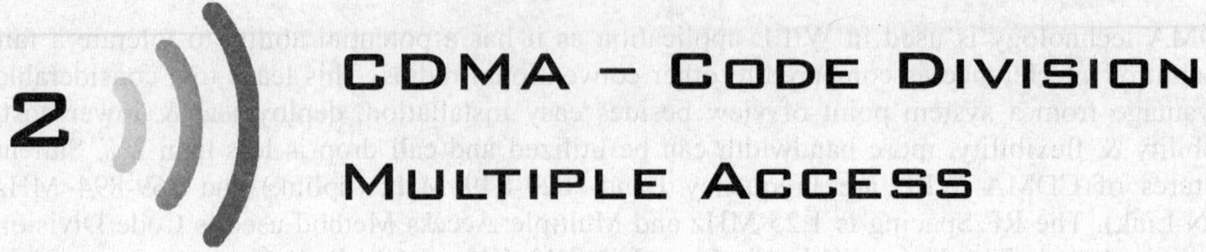

2 CDMA – Code Division Multiple Access

2.1 CDMA TECHNOLOGY

2.1.1 Introduction

The world is demanding more from wireless communication technologies than ever before. More people around the world are subscribing to wireless services and consumers are using their mobiles more frequently. Add in exciting Third-Generation (3G) wireless data services and applications – such as wireless email, web, digital picture taking/sending and assisted-GPS position location applications- and wireless networks are asked to do much more than just a few years ago. And these networks will be asked to do more tomorrow.

This is where CDMA technology fits in, CDMA consistently provides better capacity for voice and data communications than other commercial mobile technologies, allowing more subscribers to connect at any given time, and it is the common platform on which 3G technologies are built.

CDMA is a "spread spectrum" technology, allowing many users to occupy the same time and frequency allocations in a given band/space. As its name implies, CDMA assigns unique codes to each communication to differentiate it from others in the same spectrum.

The CDMA air interface is used in both 2G and 3G network. 2G CDMA standard are branded CDMA One and include IS-95A and IS-95B. CDMA is the foundation for 3G services: the two dominant IMT-2000 standards, CDMA 2000 and WCDMA, are based on CDMA.

CDMA One is the family of IS-95 CDMA Technologies

CDMA One describes a complete wireless system based on the TIA/EIA IS-95 CDMA standard, including IS-95A and IS95B revisions. It represents the end-to-end wireless system with all the necessary specifications that govern its operation. CDMA One provides a family of related services including cellular, PCS and fixed wireless (wireless in local loop).

2.1.2 IS-95 History

The idea for using the form of modulation known as direct sequence spread spectrum (DSSS) for a multiple access system for mobile telecommunications came from a California based company called Qualcomm in the 1980s. Previously DSSS had been mainly used for military or covert communications systems as the transmissions were hard to detect, jam and eavesdrop.

The system involved multiplying the required data with another data stream with a much higher data rate. Known as a spreading code, this widened the bandwidth required for the transmission, spreading it over a wide frequency band. Only when the original spreading code was used in the reconstruction of the data, would the original information be reconstituted. It was reasoned that by having different spreading codes, a multiple access system could be created for use in a mobile phone system.

In order to prove that the new system was viable a consortium was set up and Qualcomm was joined by US network operators Nynex and Ameritech to develop the first experimental code division multiple access (CDMA) system. Later the team was expanded as Motorola and AT&T (now Lucent) joined to bring their resources to speed development. As a result the new standard was published as IS-95A in 1995 under the auspices of the Cellular Telecommunications Industry Association (CTIA) and the Telecommunications Industry Association (TIA). As part of the development of CDMA an organisation called the CDMA Development Group (CDG) was formed from the founding network and manufacturers. Its purpose is to promote CDMA and evolve the technology and standards, although today most of the standards work is carried out by 3GPP2.

It then took a further three years before Hutchison Telecom became the first organisation to launch a system. The IS95 system was widely deployed in North America, and the Asia Pacific region, but there were also networks in South America, Africa, and the Middle East as well as some in Eastern Europe.

With the success of the initial IS95 format, improvements were made and the standard was upgraded to IS95B. The main improvement was that this provided for an increased data rate of 115 kbps as data traffic was starting to be carried.

The basic CDMA system was later further improved and evolved into a 3G system carrying much higher data rates and introducing new improvements. The 3G migration of IS95 was given the brand name cdma2000, and was available in a variety of flavours including cdma2000 1x, cdma2000 1x ev-do (evolution data only or data optimised) and another version was termed cdma2000 1x ev-dv (evolution data and voice), although this version was never seriously deployed.

2.1.3 CDMA within IS-95

The CDMA or code division multiple access system used for IS-95 is very different to other multiple access schemes used in previous cellular systems. However it offers a number of advantages and as a result has been widely used in many cellular technologies.

Note on CDMA— CDMA, Code Division Multiple Access, is a multiple access scheme used by many 3G cellular technologies, and other forms of wireless technology. It uses a process called Direct Sequence Spread Spectrum where spreading codes are used to spread a signal out over a given bandwidth and then reconstituting the data in the receiver by using the same spreading code. By supplying different spreading codes to different users, several users are able to utilises the same frequency without mutual interference.

The advantage of using CDMA over FDMA and TDMA is that it enables a greater number of users to be supported. The improvement in efficiency is hard to define as it depends on many factors including the size of the cells and the level of interference between cells and several other factors.

Unlike the more traditional cellular systems where neighbouring cells use different sets of channels, a CDMA system re-uses the same channels. Signals from other cells will be appear as interference, but the system is able to extract the required signal by using the correct code in the demodulation and signal extraction process. Often more than one channel is used in each cell, and this provides additional capacity because there is a limit to the amount of traffic that can be supported on each channel.

Table 2.1: IS95 Specification Summary

Parameter	*Details*
Multiple Access Scheme	CDMA
Channel bandwidth	1.25 MHz
Data rate	14.4 kbps - IS-95A 115 kbps - IS-95B

2.1.4 IS-95 Summary

IS-95, cdmaOne was a revolutionary system for cellular telecommunications. It paved the way for the other CDMA based 3G systems that were to follow around the globe. It enabled greater levels of spectrum efficiency to be gained while also allowing many other improvements to be introduced. IS-95 itself evolved into the variety of cdma2000 schemes including 1x, 1x ev-do, and the plans were ultimately to migrate onto a 4G system known as UMB - Ultra-Mobile Broadband. However IS-95 proved to be a winner in many areas of the globe, particularly in the Americas and the Far East.

2.2.2 CDMA2000 Leads the 3G Revolution

CDMA2000 represents a family of ITU-approved, IMT-2000 (3G) standards and includes CDMA2000 1X and CDMA2000 1xEV technologies. They deliver increased network capacity to meet growing demand for wireless services and high-speed data services. CDMA2000 1X was the world's first 3G technology commercially deployed (October 2000).

2.2.3 CDMA Deployments

CDMA is the fastest growing wireless technology and it will continue to grow at a faster pace than any other technology. It is the platform on which 3G advanced services are built.

2.3 COMMUNICATION SYSTEM FOR CELLULAR MOBILE

CDMA cellular mobile communication system has emerged as a superior option in many north American countries in late 1980s and has lot of new features.

2.3.1 Standardization of the technologies

Various aspects are taken into account for standardization and the important steps in standardising the CDMA are

1) Conforming to IS95A/B and CDMA2000 1X, making full use of the technical advantages of CDMA;
2) The No.7 signaling system completely conforms to the related technical specifications stipulated by the Ministry of Information Industry and passed tests;
3) Strictly abiding by the country's mobile communications trade standards for CDMA mobile communication networks;
4) Strictly abiding by various CDMA technical specifications and protocols laid by the Ministry of Information Industry;
5) The first system that provides GB ISO4.0 and IOS2.x A interfaces. In addition, it supports the IS634 standard, and is compatible with the CDMA base station systems of multiple manufacturers;
6) The kernel network supports the ANSI41-E protocol, and is compatible with the ANSI41 series protocols;
7) In the aspect of WIN, the system supports IS-771 and IS-826 and various related national WIN standard protocols corresponding to these standards;
8) Providing flexible supports to different frequency bands to facilitate the network operators' selection;
9) The interface with fixed network is air interface or SS7.

2.3.2 Superior Performances

- The partial separated and modularized system design integrates network entities, such as MSC, VLR, HLR AUC, SC and VM respectively;
- The modularized architecture satisfies flexibly and reliably different requirements for configuration and capacity expansion;
- BSS adopts internally the packet transmission mode, which enhances the E1 utilization;
- Supporting various soft and hard handoff modes;
- Supporting large number of subscribers;
- Flexible and stable accounting and network management;
- High security and reliability, and perfect operation and maintenance system;
- All the service functions required by CDMA 2000 1X can be realized by means of addition of hardware entities and software upgrading of the system.

2.3.3 Easy Maintenance

- Friendly graphic operation and maintenance tools in both Chinese and English;
- Universal Windows interface and on-line help;
- Well-equipped system maintenance functions;

- Multiple communication modes are supported to realize remote/local maintenance, extremely reliably and conveniently.

Based on the above analysis, we can come to the following conclusion: The early stage investment of this system appears a little bit high, but, in the long run, considering the transition to cellular network and expansion for new services, this scheme undoubtedly the best choice. Therefore, this scheme is best suited to build up cellular mobile communication systems.

Services - Voice, Data, Customer Calling Services, Mobility

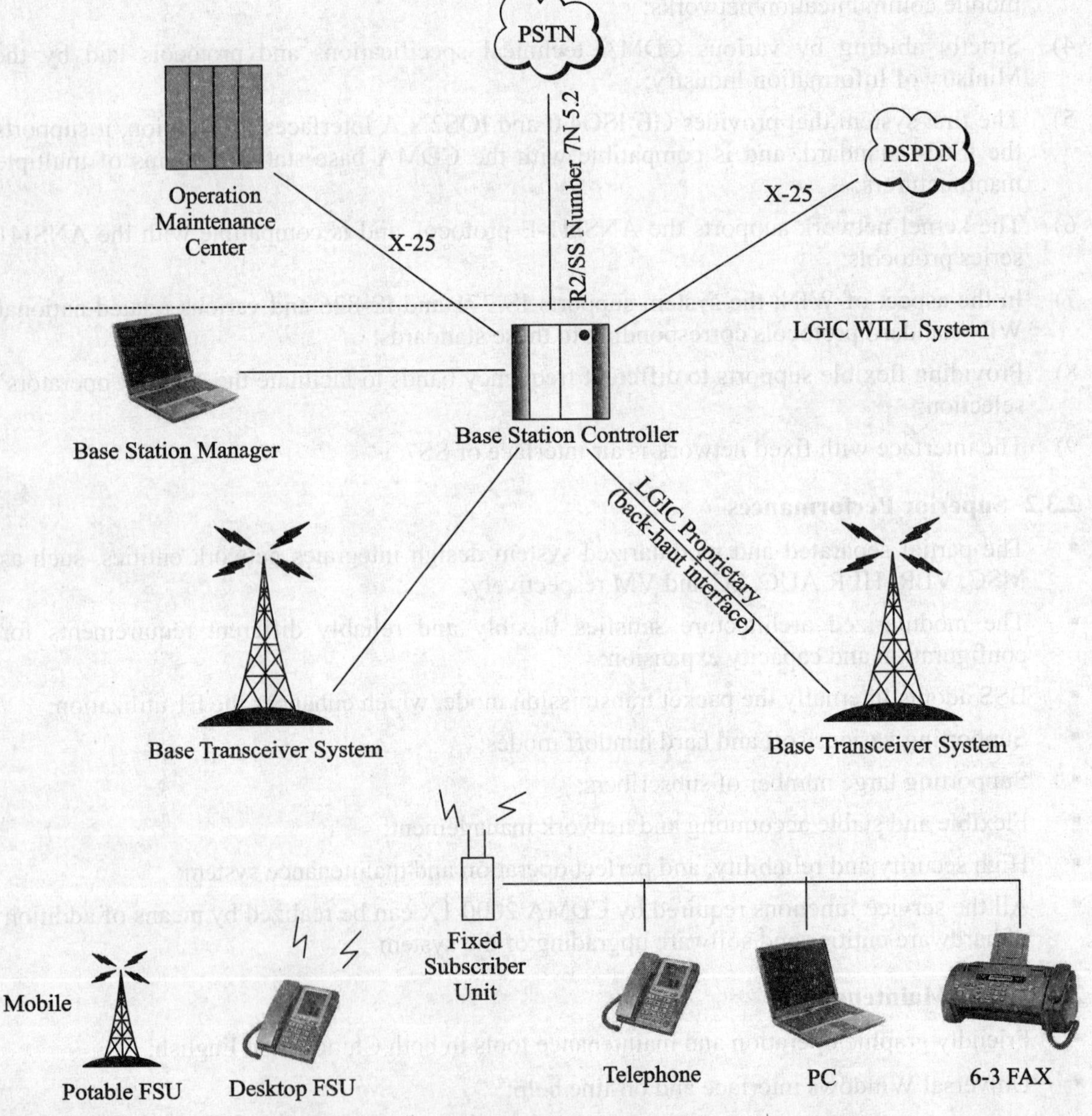

Fig. 2.1: CDMA2000

2.3.4 Advantages

- Easy installation, deployment & lower cost
- Quick solution for developing telephones infrastructure.
- Mobility & flexibility
- Ease in operation, administration & maintenance.
- Reduces the distance
- More bandwidth can be utilized
- Call drop is less than 2%
- Bigger coverage area
- Improved signal and reduced interference
- Higher capacity a) efficient use of spectrum
- High quality service a) error detection & correction.
  b) diversity against fading in air.
- Supports more than 28.8 kbps data rates
- Higher service demand
- Limited mobility support

2.3.5 Technical Specification of CDMA

▪ Frequency Band	:	824-849 MHz (uplink)
	:	869-894 MHz (DN-Link)
▪ RF Spacing	:	1.25 MHz
▪ Duplex Separation	:	45 MHz
▪ Multiple Access Method	:	Code Division Multiple Access
▪ Duplex Method	:	FDD
▪ Access Channels per carrier per sector	:	40 Chls (3 sectors)
▪ Voice Coding	:	8/13 Kbps QCELP 8Kbps EVRC
▪ BTS trans power	:	Upto 20 watts
▪ Power requirements For BSC		
▪ Coverage – In rural	:	25 Km radius
– In urban	:	5 Km radius.

2.3.6 CDMA Cellular Mobile Communication System

1) Telecom services,
2) Data services,
3) Supplementary services,

4) Short message service, and

5) IN service.

2.4 CDMA - 2000 1X TECHNOLOGY FOR CELLULAR MOBILE COMMUNICATION SYSTEM

Main service Evolution of CDMA Networks first deployment of CDMA in commercial cellular systems was in 1994-95 only with IS-95 A as air-interface standard and IS-41 in core network; the complete network known as *cdmaOne*. Next evolutionary step was use of IS-95B air interface standard which supported maximum data rate up-to 64 kbps to a user. Further in CDMA 2000 1x version many of the limitations of earlier IS-95 standard were overcome and new features were added. As a result CDMA 2000 1x has a higher voice capacity and better handling of packet data services.

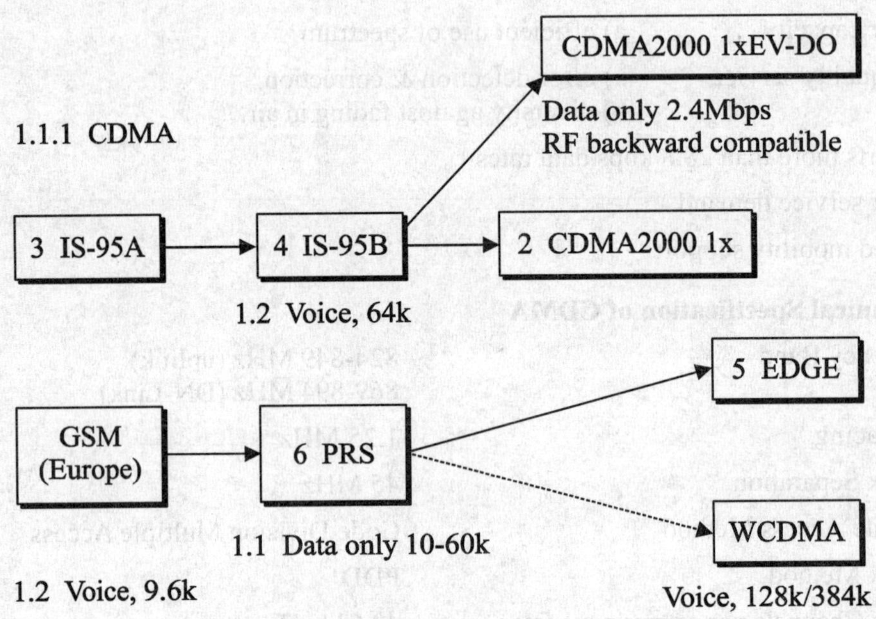

Fig. 2.2: Transition to CDMA

2.4.1 Salient Features of CDMA 2000 1X

- Backward Compatibility with IS-95A & IS-95B
- Support for High data rates on same 1x Carrier
- Support for Simple IP and Mobile IP functionality for seamless mobility for data services.
- Higher capacity for voice communication
- Increased battery life
- Faster forward Power control (relative to IS-95)
- New Radio Configuration to support high data rates and more voice capacity.

2.5 ARCHITECTURE OF CDMA 2000 1X NETWORK

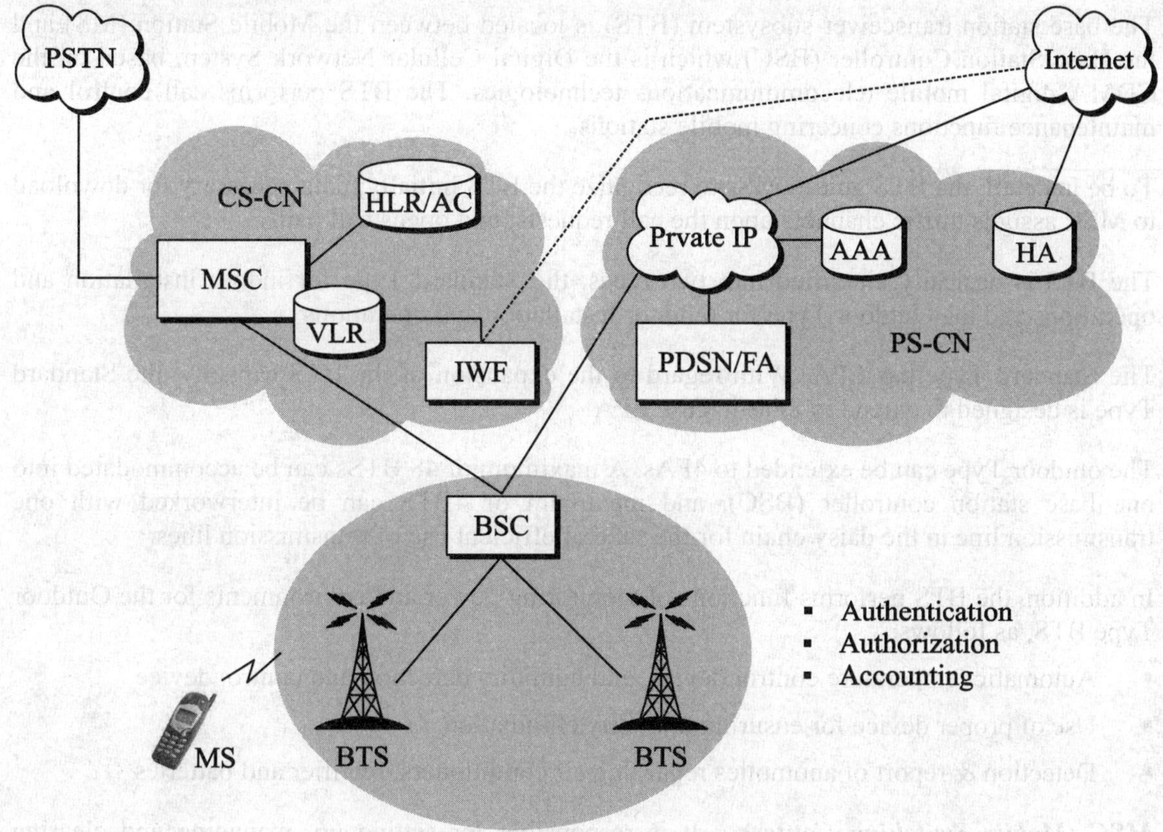

Fig. 2.3: CDMA2000 1x Architecture

CDMA 2000 1x Network Architecture is divided in to three parts. (Fig. 2.3)

- CS-CN (Circuit Switched Core Network)
- PS-CN (Packet Switched Core Network)
- RAN (Radio Access Network)

Circuit Switched Core Network— This section is dedicated for voice communication and also for wireless authentication. This section includes four parts

- MSC (Mobile Switching Center)
- HLR (Home Location Register)
- VLR (Visitor Location Register)
- AUC (Authentication Center)

BTS - Base Transceiver Subsytem

The base station transceiver subsystem (BTS) is located between the Mobile Station (MS) and the Base Station Controller (BSC) which is the Digital Cellular Network System based on the CDMA digital mobile telecommunications technologies. The BTS performs call control and maintenance functions concering mobile stations.

To be in detail, the BTS guides MSs to recognize the BTS initially; data necessary for download to MSs: assigns traffic channels upon the call requests; and opens call paths.

The BTS is basically classified into two types: the Standard Type for indoor installation and operations and the Outdoor Type for outdoor installation and operations.

The Standard Type has LPA. With regard to the expansion of the BTS capacity, the Standard Type is designed to extend to 8Fas in case LPA.

The outdoor Type can be extended to 4FAs. A maximum of 48 BTSs can be accommodated into one base station controller (BSC), and maximum of 4BTS can be interworked with one transmission line in the daisy chain for the sake of efficient use of transmission lines.

In addition, the BTS performs functions of monitoring power and environments for the Outdoor Type BTS, as follows:

- Automatic temperature control device, and humidity detection and control device
- Use of proper device for ensuring humidity elimination
- Detection & report of anomolies regarding air conditioners, rectifier and batteries.

MSC (Mobile Switching Center)— It is responsible for setting up, managing and clearing connections as well as routing the calls to the proper user & provides the network interfaces, the charging function and the function of processing the signaling. MSC get data for call handling from 3 databases: VLR/HLR/AUC.

HLR (Home Location Register)— It is a static database. When a user applies for mobile service, all data about this subscriber will be stored in HLR. It have information of a subscriber like ESN, MDN, IMSI, MIN, service information and valid term. It also stores the mobile subscriber location (MSC/VLR address), to set up the call.

VLR (Visitor Location Register)— VLR is a dynamic database used by MSC for information index. It stores all related information of mobile subscribers that enter its coverage area, which enables MSC to set up incoming and outgoing calls. It stores the subscriber parameters which includes subscriber number, location area identity (LAI), user's status, services which subscriber can use and so on. When the subscriber leaves this area, it should register in another VLR, and the previous VLR will delete all the data about this subscriber. VLR can be built together with the MSC or set separately.

AUC (Authentication Center)— It is an entity to prevent illegal subscribers from accessing CDMA network. It can generate the parameter to confirm the subscriber's identity. At the same time it can encrypt user's data according to user's request. AUC can be built separately or together with HLR.

Packet Switched Core Network— To provide better connectivity to the internet a new core network i.e. PS-CN is introduced to the CDMA 2000 1x network. This section includes four parts

- PDSN (Packet Data Serving Node)
- AAA Server
- Home Agent/ Foreign Agent Server

PDSN (Packet Data Serving Node)— Packet Data Serving Node (PDSN) provides the function of routing of data between Radio Access Network (RAN) and internet.

AAA Server— PS-CN also has the responsibility to authenticate, authorise and account for the CDMA 2000 subscribers wishing to obtain packet data services & to fulfil these task PDSN requires support of AAA server.

Authenticate— verifying that the user is valid & allowed to use packet data services.

Authorization— subscription to the service being offered is valid.

Accounting— Accounting for the service used.

Home Agent/ Foreign Agent Server— HA & FA server is used when mobile IP services are supported by CDMA 2000 PDSN. HA can be considered analogous to HLR and FA with VLR.

RAN (Radio Access Network)— As in IS-95 RAN is composed of number of BSCs & BTSs The CDMA 2000 1x RAN is enhanced to support a higher no. of users on air interface or in other words it has a better spectral efficiency relative to IS-95. It is also modified to support the new packet data services on same 1.25 Mhz channel. This is achieved by software up-gradation at BTS and BSC and addition of a new hardware unit called Packet Control Function (PCF) at BSC. The CDMA 2000 1x air interface is very different from IS-95 but still maintains the backward compatibility with IS-95.

2.6 CDMA CHANNELS

Forward Link Channels

- Pilot Channel
- Sync Channel
- Paging Channels
- Traffic Channels

Reverse Link Channels

- Access Channels
- Traffic Channels

Pilot Channel (W0)

The pilot is used by the subs unit to obtain initial system synchronization and to distinguish cell sites. Every sector of every cell site has a unique pilot channel.

- Transmitted constantly.
- Allows the mobile to acquire the system.
- Provides mobile with signal strength comparison.
- Approximately 20% of the radiated power is in the pilot.
- Has unique PN Offset for each cell or sector.

Sync Channel (W32)

Used during system Acquisition stage. Sync channel provides the subscriber unit with network information related to cell site identification, pilot transmit power & cell site PN offset.

- Used by mobile to synchronize with the system
- Transmits sync message with
  - Pilot PN offset - System time
  - Long PN code - System ID
  - Network ID - Paging channel data rate
- Tx at 1200 bps

Paging CHLS (W1-W7)

On this channel base station can page the subs unit and it can send call set-up and traffic channel assignment information.

- Means of communication between base to mobile station.
- Paging CHL data Rates can be 2.4,4.8 or 9.6 Kbps.
- CDMA assignment has 7 paging channel.
- Each paging CHL supports 180 pages per second.
- Total pages/ CDMA RF channel = 1260
- Provides mobile with
  - System Parameter message - Neighbour list
  - Access Parameter list - CDMA Channel list
- Used by base station to :
  - Page mobile - Transmit overhead information
  - Assign mobile to traffic channel

Traffic Channels (W8-W31 & W33-W63)

The traffic channel carries the actual call. That is, the voice and control information between the subs unit & base station.

TX up to 9.6kbps on rate set 1 and up to 14.4kbps on rate set 2.

Access Channel

a) Provides communication from Mobile to base station when mobile is not using traffic Channel. The access channel is used for call origination & for response to pages, orders & registration requests. It is paired with corresponding paging channel.

b) Each Access CHL use long PN code.

c) Base station responds to transmission on a particular Access Channel.

d) Mobile responds to base station message by emitting on Access Channel.

e) Transmits at 4800bps.

2.7 FORWARD LINK TRANSMISSION AND MODULATION SCHEME

It is clear from the figure 2.4 that in the forward direction both the rate sets are supported and the data rate after convolution encoding will be 19.2 Ksps. Then using the PN code the signal is scrambled. In which each symbol coming out of block interleaver is exclusively-ORed with one symbol of scrambling sequence. Power control bits are then punctured at appropriate places. Then this signal is orthogonally spread using one of the walsh codes. At this place the data rate increases to 1.2288 Mcps, which is sent on I & Q channel. All the information is sent on both the quadrature channels and the each quadrature is spread using short PN code. These short PN codes are second layer of coding used to isolate one sector from another. Now this signal is transmitted which will be received and demodulated at the mobile end.

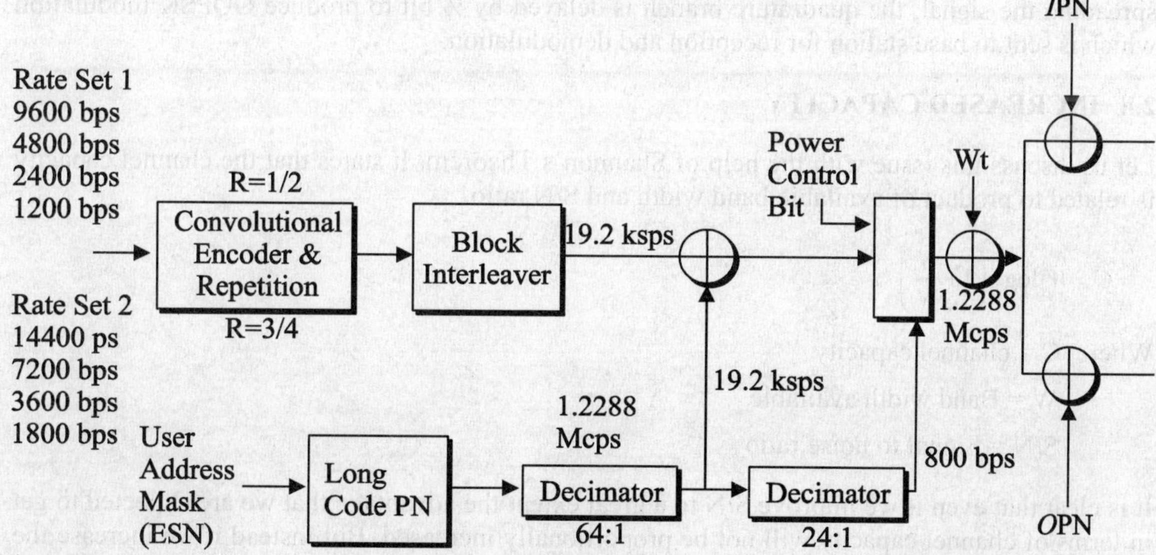

Fig. 2.4: Forward Link Transmission

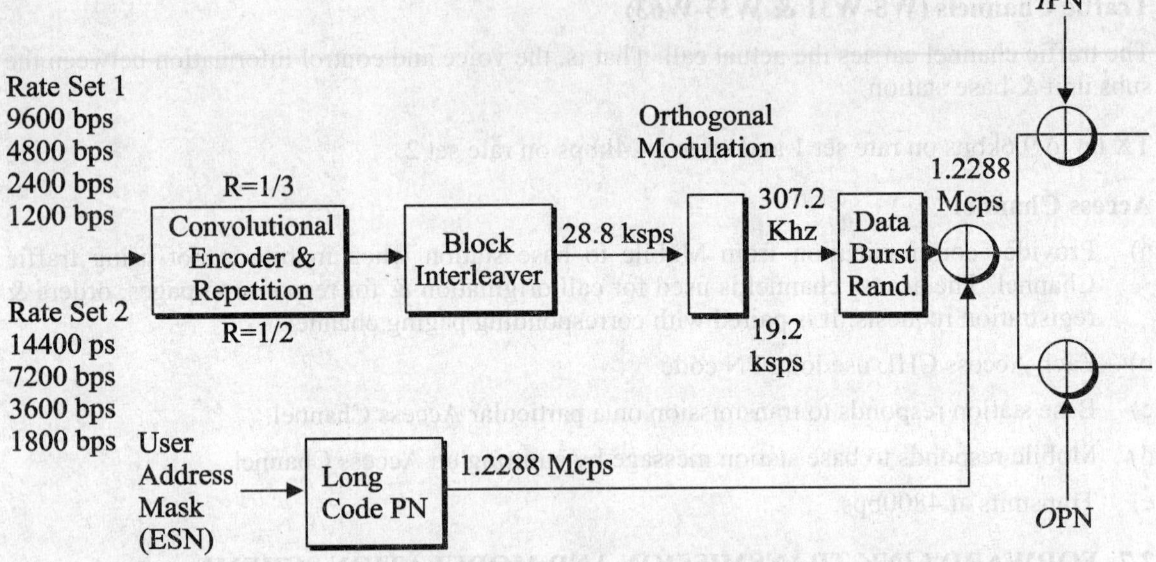

Fig. 2.5: Reverse Link Transmission

In this process also both the rate sets are supported. After convolutional encoding the rates will be 28.8 Ksps. In this case orthogonal modulation is followed by a data burst randomizer that determines when to turn off the mobile transmitter to reduce average transmit power. In order to take advantage of reduced speech activity the vocoder reduces its data rate allowing the transmission of the signal at a lower average level of power. The mobile uses full rates when it transmits, but when redundant information is produced by symbol repetition scheme the data burst randomizer turns off the transmitter pseudo randomly reducing the average transmission power. Then the signal is direct sequence spread using long code and occupies the entire bandwidth. The signal is then sent on I and Q channels and short PN codes are used for spreading the signal, the quadrature branch is delayed by ½ bit to produce OQPSK modulation which is sent to base station for reception and demodulation.

2.8 INCREASED CAPACITY

Let us discuss this issue with the help of Shannon's Theorem. It states that the channel capacity is related to product of available band width and S/N ratio.

$$C = W \log_2 \left(1 + \frac{S}{N}\right)$$

Where C = channel capacity

W = Band width available

S/N = Signal to noise ratio

It is clear that even if we improve S/N to a great extent the advantage that we are expected to get in terms of channel capacity will not be proportionally increased. But instead if we increase the bandwidth (W), we can achieve more channel capacity even at a lower S/N. That forms the basis of CDMA approach, wherein increased channel capacity is obtained by increasing both W & S/N. The S/N can be increased by devising proper power control methods.

2.8.1 Vocoder and Variable Data Rates for Capacity Increase

As the telephone quality speech is band limited to 4 Khz, when it is digitized with PCM its bit rate rises to 64 Kb/s. Vocoding compresses it to a lower bit rate to reduce bandwidth. The transmitting vocoder takes voice samples and generates an encoded speech/packet for transmission to the receiving vocoder. The receiving vocoder decodes the received speech packet into voice samples. One of the important features of the variable rate vocoder is the use of adaptive threshold to determine the required data rate. Vocoders are variable as rate vocoders. By operating the vocoder at half rate on some of the frames the capacity of the system can be enhanced without noticeable degradation in the quality of the speech. This phenomenon helps to absorb the occasional heavy requirement of traffic apart from suppression of background noise. Thus the capacity advantage makes spread spectrum an ideal choice for use in areas where the frequency spectrum is congested.

2.9 CDMA 2000 1X EV-DO

For the requirement of 2 Mbps data rate (By using 3x option) Qualcomm proposed a new standard 1xEV-DO (1x Evolution for Data Optimized) in March of 2000 as another option that supports high-rate data services.

EVDO is optimized for delivering high speed IP wireless data to many mobile and stationary terminals running multiple applications. EVDO is designed for an always on user experience.

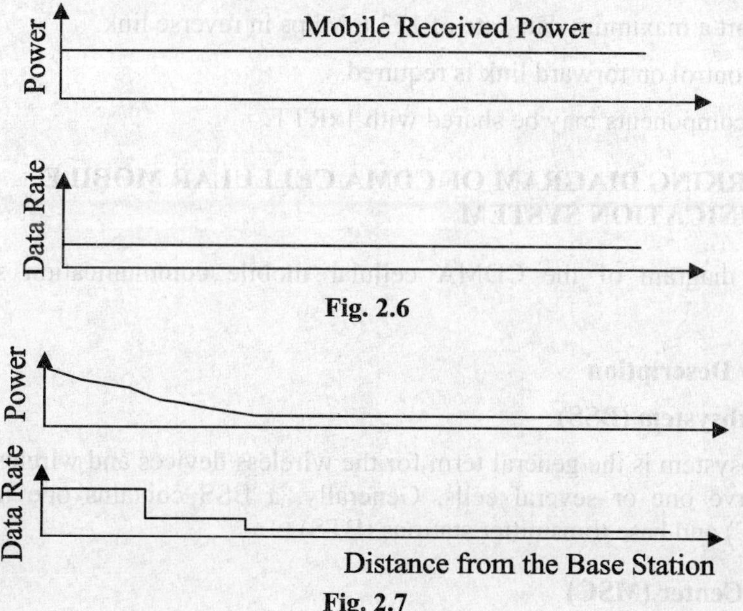

Fig. 2.6

Fig. 2.7

In a classical CDMA 2000 system base station controls its power by using the power control algorithms to provide the mobile a constant data rate and a quality of service for voice applications.

But in EV-DO networks the base station transmits at a fixed power at all the times and controls the rate of data transmission given a constant transmit power.

Since EV-DO is specially designed for packet data services therefore EV-DO designs its air interface to takes advantage of the characteristics of some data services.

Characteristic of Data Rate are

Data rates are mostly asymmetrical— Data rate requirements downstream (on the forward link) are usually higher than those upstream (on the reverse link).

Latency can be tolerated— Data services, unlike voice services, can withstand delays of up to few seconds.

Transmissions are bursty in nature— A burst of data transmission is often followed by a period of inactivity.

Salient Features of EV-DO

- EV-DO uses both CDMA and TDMA.
- Uses its own dedicated 1.25 Mhz carrier.
- It can support a maximum data rate of 2.4 Mbps in forward link.
- It can support a maximum data rate of 153.6 Mbps in reverse link.
- No power control on forward link is required.
- RF system components may be shared with 1xRTT.

2.10 NETWORKING DIAGRAM OF CDMA CELLULAR MOBILE COMMUNICATION SYSTEM

The schematic diagram of the CDMA cellular mobile communication system is shown in Fig. 2.8.

Network Entity Description

Base Station Subsystem (BSS)

Base station subsystem is the general term for the wireless devices and wireless channel control devices that serve one or several cells. Generally, a BSS contains one more base station controllers (BSC) and base transmitter stations (BTS).

Mobile Switch Center (MSC)

MSC is a functional entity that performs control and switching to the mobile stations within the area that it serves, and an automatic connecting device for the subscriber traffic between the CDMA network and other public networks or other MSCs. MSC is the kernel of the CDMA cellular mobile communication system, and it is different from a wired switch in that an MSC must consider the allocation of the wireless resources and the mobility of subscribers, and at least it must implement the follows processing activities:

1) Location Registration processing;

2) Handoff.

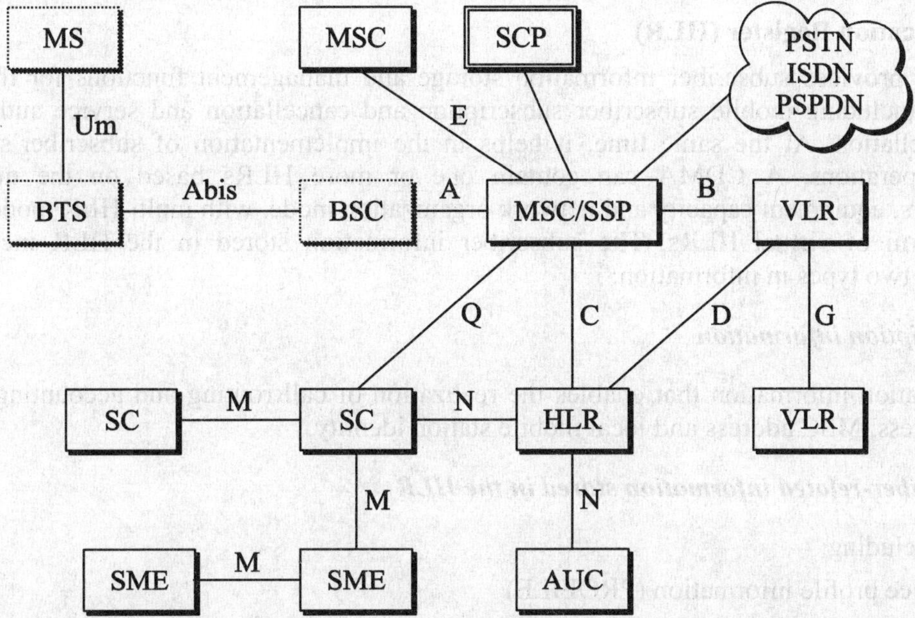

Fig. 2.8: Schematic Diagram of CDMA Cellular Mobile Communication System

Gateway MSC (GMSC)

When a non-CDMA subscriber calls a CDMA subscriber, the call will first be routed to an MSC, which will inquires the corresponding HLR and further route the call to the called party's MSC. This kind of MSC is called Gateway MSC (GMSC). It is up to the network operator to select which MSCs as GMSCs.

Visitor Location Register (VLR)

VLR is responsible for the storage and updating of the subscriber data of mobile stations that roamed to the service area of this VLR. The VLR is generally configured together with the MSC. When the mobile station enters a new location area, the MSC will notice the VLR, which will initiate registration processing to the HLR to update the subscriber location information. The VLR also stores necessary information for the establishment of calls in the database for the MSC to search. One VLR can cover one or more MSC areas. Specifically, the following information is included:

- Service profile information (PROFILE)
- Mobile identification number/international mobile subscriber identity (MIN/IMSI)
- Shared secret data (SSD)

- Electronic serial number (ESN)
- Mobile station authentication data (AUTHEN)
- Mobile station authorization data (AUTHOR)
- Mobile station temporary local directory number (TLDN)
- Mobile station location area information (LAI)

Home Location Register (HLR)

The HLR provides subscriber information storage and management functions for the mobile network, including mobile subscriber subscription and cancellation and service authorization and cancellation. At the same time, it helps in the implementation of subscriber's call and service operations. A CDMA can contain one or more HLRs based on the number of subscribers, equipment capacity and network organization mode, with multi-HLR mode realized in the form of virtual HLRs. The subscriber information stored in the HLR includes the following two types in information:

1. Subscription information

Some location information that enables the realization of call routing and accounting, such as VLR address, MSC address and local mobile station identity.

2. Subscriber-related information stored in the HLR

Mainly including:

- Service profile information (PROFILE)
- Mobile identification number/international mobile subscriber identity (MIN/IMSI)
- Shared secret data (SSD)
- Electronic serial number (ESN)
- Mobile directory number (MDN)

IMSI/MIN and MDN are often used as key for access to the mobile subscriber database.

The HLR also contains the following mobile subscriber information:

- Telecom services
- Data services
- IN services
- Short message service data
- Service restriction (such as roaming restriction)
- Supplementary service parameters

Authentication Center (AUC)

Authentication center is a function entity for the management of authentication information related to the mobile station. It implement mobile subscriber authentication, stores the mobile subscriber authentication parameters, and is able to generate and transmit the corresponding authentication parameters based on the request from MSC/VLR. The authentication parameters in the AUC can be stored in the encrypted form. The authentication center is generally configured together with the HLR. The authentication parameter stored in the AUC include:

1. Authentication key (A_KEY);
2. Share secret data (SSD);
3. Mobile identification number/international mobile subscriber identity (MIN/IMSI);
4. Authentication algorithm (AAV);
5. Accounting (COUNT).

Short Message Center (MC or SC)

As an independent entity in the CDMA cellular mobile communication system, the short message center works in coordination with other entities such as MSC, HLR to implement the reception, storing and transfer of the short messages from CDMA cellular mobile communication system subscribers, and store subscriber-related short message data.

Short Message Entity (SME)

SME is a function entity for synthesis and analysis of short messages.

Operation and Maintenance Center (OMC)

The OMC provides the network operator with network operation and maintenance services, manages the subscriber information and implements network planning, to enhance the overall working efficiency and service quality of the system. Based on the main maintenance functions, there two type of operation and maintenance centers: OMC-S and OMC-R. An OMC-S is mainly used for the maintenance work at the mobile switching subsystem (MSS) side; an OMC-R is mainly used for the maintenance work at the base station subsystem (BSS) side. Of course, for an operation and maintenance system, these two parts are not strictly distinguished from each other. In fact, from the approach of the whole system, the entire CDMA mobile communication system (including MSC/VLR, HLR/AUC, SC, BSC, BTS etc.) should be controlled by a highly efficient operation and maintenance system.

Descriptions of Inter-Entity Interfaces

Interface between MSC and BSS (A-Interface)

In fact, it is the interface between MSC and BSC. Adopting 2Mb/s PCM digital link, the standard protocols for this interface include IS-634, IOS2.4, IOS4.0 etc.

A-interface is mainly used to transmit the following information: (1) BSS management information, (2) Call processing, and (3) Mobility management information.

Interface between MSC and VLR (B-Interface)

This interface is an internal interface, without standard definition. Its functions are as follows:

VLR is the location and management database for subscribers that have roamed into related MSC area. When the MSC needs the subscriber data of the particular MSC area, the MSC is to inquire the VLR; in the case of mobile station location updating, the MSC will request VLR to store the related information; when the user activates the supplementary services or modifies data, the MSC will request the HLR (through VLR) to store the related data.

This interface has no standard definition, and generally uses an internal interface.

CDMA is primarily a voice system, not a data-oriented system. However, data are available to be sent via circuit-switched methods, but the call-processing flow is the same as voice because it still uses a traffic-channel setup for voice transport. The first call processing flowchart is for a mobile-to-land call (origination), shown in Figure The call flows for 2G CDMA are shown next. It is important to note that 2G.

2.11 CALL PROCESSING (Call Flow Chart)

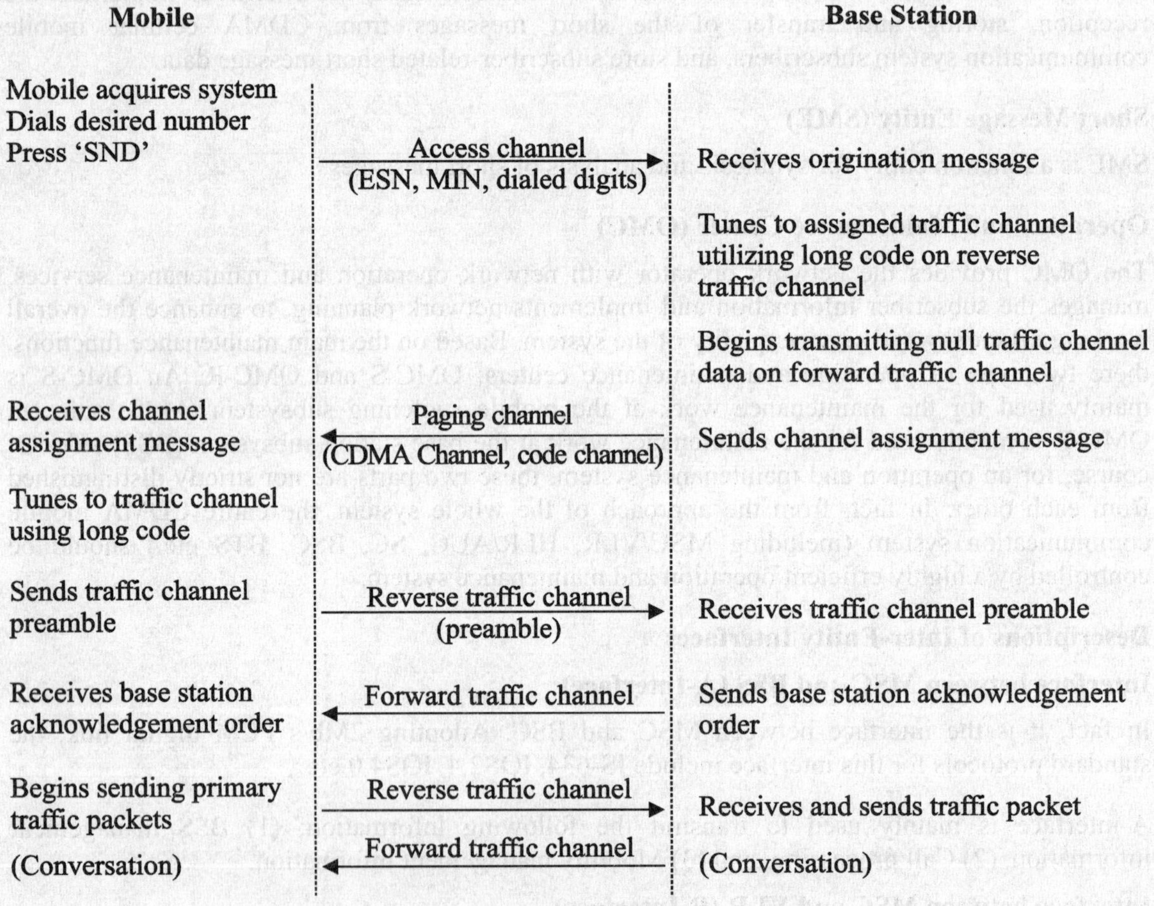

Mobile		Base Station
Mobile acquires system Dials desired number Press 'SND'	Access channel → (ESN, MIN, dialed digits)	Receives origination message
		Tunes to assigned traffic channel utilizing long code on reverse traffic channel
		Begins transmitting null traffic chennel data on forward traffic channel
Receives channel assignment message	← Paging channel (CDMA Channel, code channel)	Sends channel assignment message
Tunes to traffic channel using long code		
Sends traffic channel preamble	Reverse traffic channel → (preamble)	Receives traffic channel preamble
Receives base station acknowledgement order	← Forward traffic channel	Sends base station acknowledgement order
Begins sending primary traffic packets	Reverse traffic channel →	Receives and sends traffic packet
(Conversation)	← Forward traffic channel	(Conversation)

CDMA mobile organization

Fig. 2.9: Mobile Generated Call

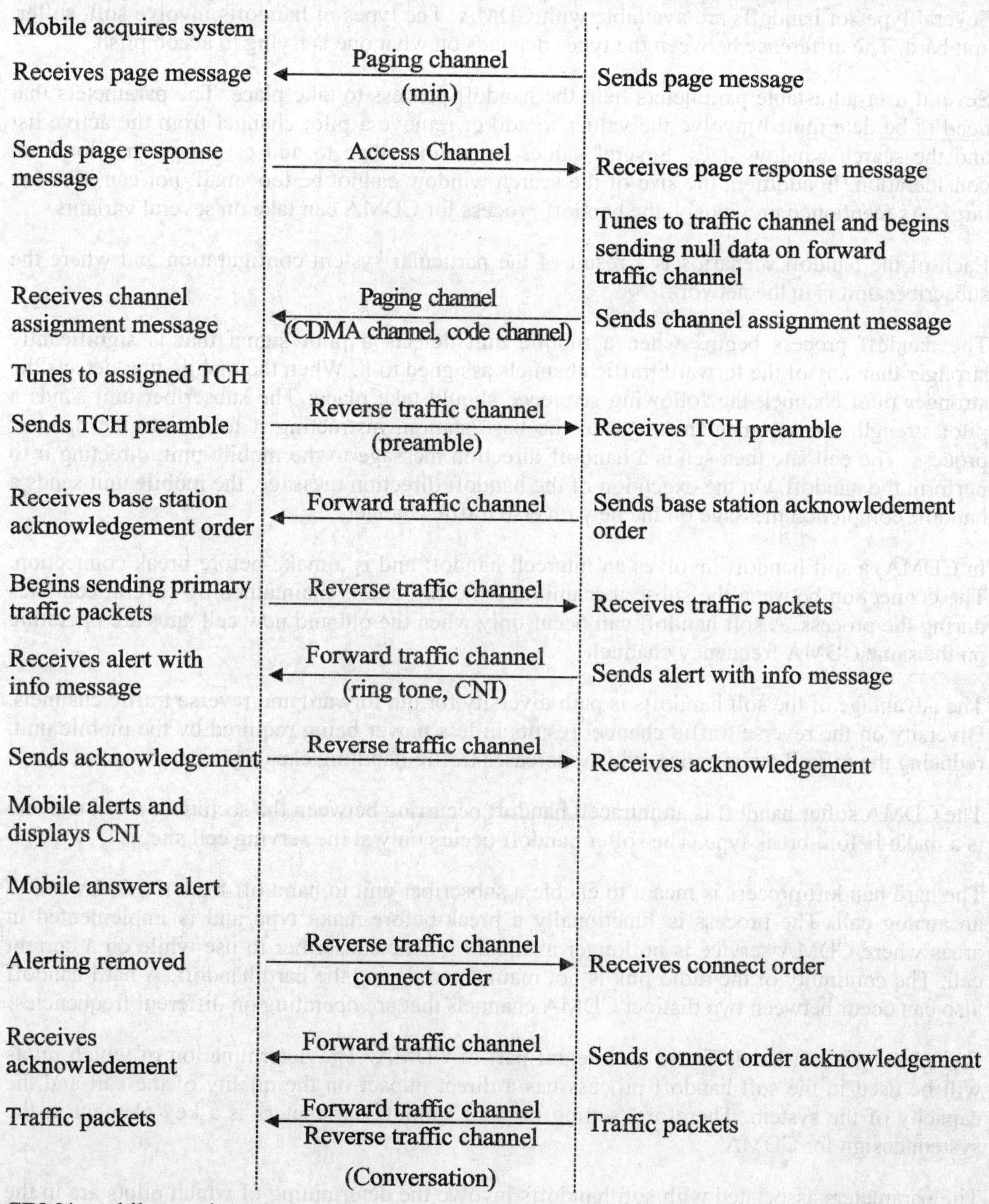

Fig. 2.10: Mobile to Mobile Call

2.12 HANDOFFS

Several types of handoffs are available with CDMA. The types of handoffs involve soft, softer, and hard. The difference between the types depends on what one is trying to accomplish.

Several user-adjustable parameters help the handoff process to take place. The parameters that need to be determined involve the values to add or remove a pilot channel from the active list and the search window sizes. Several values determine when to add or remove a pilot from consideration. In addition, the size of the search window cannot be too small, nor can it be too large. As mentioned previously, the handoff process for CDMA can take on several variants.

Each of the handoff scenarios is a result of the particular system configuration and where the subscriber unit is in the network.

The handoff process begins when a mobile unit detects a pilot signal that is significantly stronger than any of the forward traffic channels assigned to it. When the mobile unit detects the stronger pilot channel, the following sequence should take place: The subscriber unit sends a pilot strength measurement message to the base station, instructing it to initiate the handoff process. The cell site then sends a handoff direction message to the mobile unit, directing it to perform the handoff. On the execution of the handoff direction message, the mobile unit sends a handoff completion message on the new reverse traffic channel.

In CDMA, a soft handoff involves an intercell handoff and is a make-before-break connection. The connection between the subscriber unit and the cell site is maintained by several cell sites during the process. A soft handoff can occur only when the old and new cell sites are operating on the same CDMA frequency channel.

The advantage of the soft handoffs is path diversity for the forward and reverse traffic channels. Diversity on the reverse traffic channel results in less power being required by the mobile unit, reducing the overall interference, which increases traffic-handling capacity.

The CDMA softer handoff is an intracell handoff occurring between the sectors of a cell site and is a make-before-break type. The softer handoff occurs only at the serving cell site.

The hard handoff process is meant to enable a subscriber unit to hand off from a CDMA call to an analog call. The process is functionally a break-before-make type and is implemented in areas where CDMA service is no longer available for the subscriber to use while on a current call. The continuity of the radio link is not maintained during the hard handoff. A hard handoff also can occur between two distinct CDMA channels that are operating on different frequencies.

Soft Handoffs Soft handoffs are an integral part of CDMA. The determination of which pilots will be used in the soft handoff process has a direct impact on the quality of the call and the capacity of the system. Therefore, setting the soft handoff parameters is a key element in the system design for CDMA.

The parameters associated with soft handoffs involve the determining of which pilots are in the Active, Candidate, Neighbor, and Remaining sets. The list of neighbor pilots is sent to the subscriber unit when it acquires the cell site or is assigned a traffic channel.

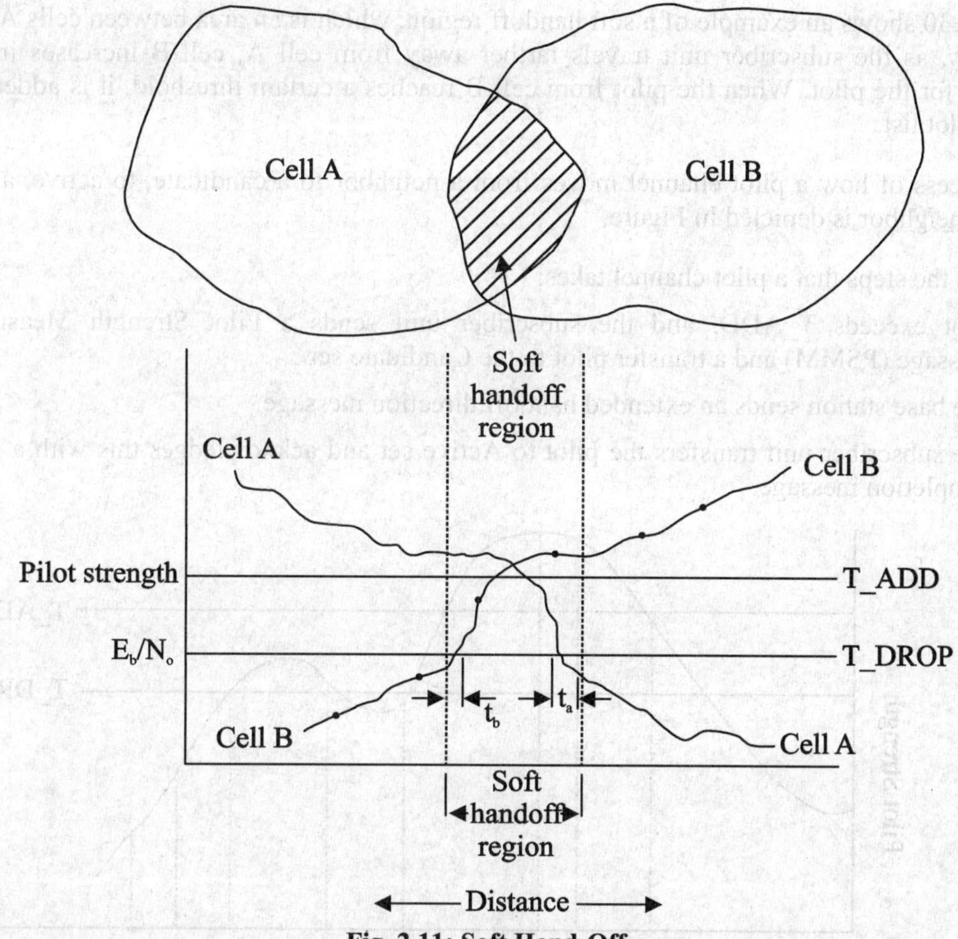

Fig. 2.11: Soft Hand-Off

A brief description of each type of pilot set follows:

1. The Active set is the set of pilots associated with the forward traffic channels assigned to the subscriber unit. The Active set can contain more than one pilot because a total of three carriers, each with its own pilot, could be involved in a soft handoff process.

2. The Candidate set is made up of the pilots that the subscriber unit has reported are of a sufficient signal strength to be used. The subscriber unit also promotes the Neighbor set and Remaining set pilots that meet the criteria to the candidate set.

3. The Neighbor set is a list of pilots that are not currently on the Active or Candidate pilot lists. The Neighbor set is identified by the base station via the Neighbor list and Neighbor list update messages.

4. The Remaining set consists of all pilots in the system that possibly can be used by the subscriber unit. However, the Remaining set pilots that the subscriber unit looks for must be a multiple of Piloting.

Figure 3.30 shows an example of a soft handoff region, which is an area between cells A and B. Naturally, as the subscriber unit travels farther away from cell A, cell B increases in signal strength for the pilot. When the pilot from cell B reaches a certain threshold, it is added to the active pilot list.

The process of how a pilot channel moves from a neighbor to a candidate, to active, and then back to neighbor is depicted in Figure.

Here are the steps that a pilot channel takes:

1. Pilot exceeds T_ADD, and the subscriber unit sends a Pilot Strength Measurement Message (PSMM) and a transfer pilot to the Candidate set.
2. The base station sends an extended handoff direction message.
3. The subscriber unit transfers the pilot to Active set and acknowledges this with a handoff completion message.

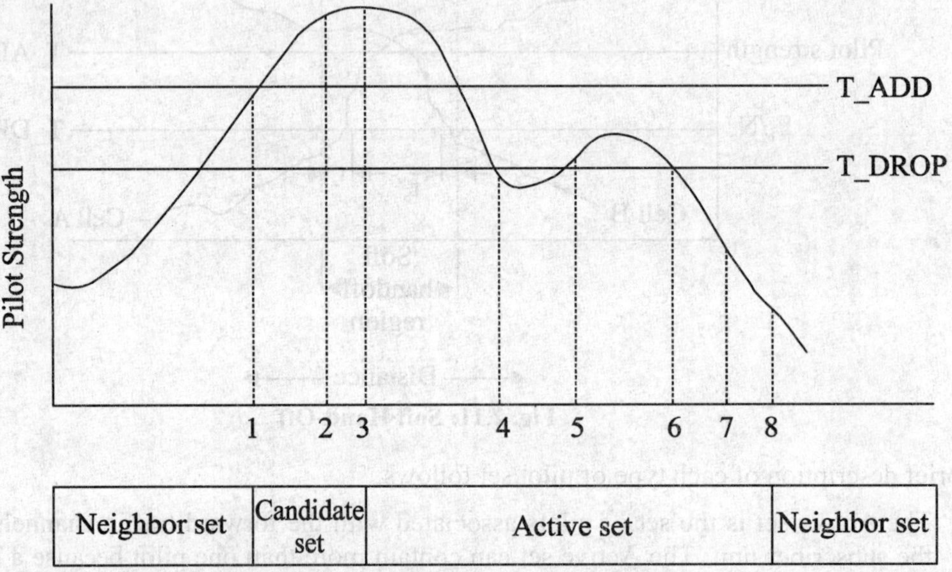

The pilot elevation and demotion process

Fig. 2.12

4. The pilot strength drops below T_DROP, and the subscriber unit begins the handoff drop time.
5. The pilot strength goes above T_DROP prior to the handoff drop time expiring and T_DROP sequences topping.
6. The pilot strength drops below T_DROP, and the subscriber unit begins the hand- off drop timer.
7. The handoff drop timer expires, and the subscriber unit sends a PSMM.
8. The base station sends an extended handoff direction message.

9. The subscriber unit transfers the pilot from the Active set to the Neighbor set and acknowledges this with a handoff completion message.

2.13 RAKE RECEIVER

CDMA mobiles use rake receivers. The rake receiver is essentially a set of four or more receivers (or fingers). One of the receivers constantly searches for different multipath and helps to direct the other three fingers to lock onto strong multipath signals.

- Allows combined reception of up to three different paths.
- Provides searcher receiver to identify changes in path characteristics/new cells.
- Provides both path diversity and frequency diversity.

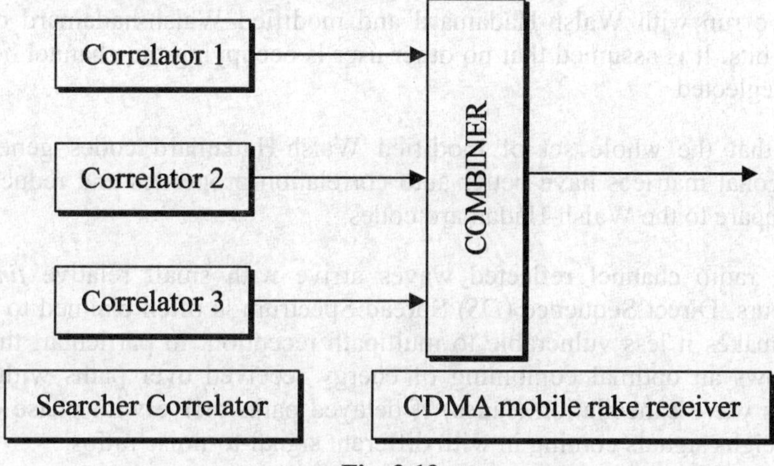

Fig. 2.13

A conventional RAKE receiver uses multipath diversity principle. It collects the energy in the multipath signals instead of suppressing them. RAKE receiver attempts to collect the time shifted versions of the original signal by providing a separate correlation receiver known as finger for each of the multipath signals. Each finger of the RAKE receiver has a separate code generator to generate codes with different phases, where each phase corresponds to a specific multipath.

Fig.2.13 shows the block diagram of such a conventional RAKE receiver. Here matched filter provides the impulse response measurements of the multipath channel profile, from which multipath delays are calculated and provided to different receiver blocks. The code generator of each finger is adjusted to generate a code sequence with a specific phase offset, which corresponds to the detected multipath. The generated code sequence is supplied to the correlator, which despreads the corresponding multipath. The correlation is obtained by multiplying the received sequence chips with corresponding chips of the spreading sequence and summing them up. Delay equalizer provides the time alignment of all the multipaths. Time aligned symbols are send for the maximal ratio combining, in which symbols are multiplied with complex conjugate of the channel estimate and the result of multiplication is summed together into the combined symbol. Finally the bit decision is made using this combined symbol.

Usually, such a RAKE receiver uses Walsh-Hadamard codes for data spreading purpose. These codes, however, cannot guarantee minimum correlation between any two of them. A modified version of that is thus used in the proposed work, as BPSK symbols are used for the simulations. These symbols are spread with the spreading code sequences. Impulse response channel model is used, in which multipath are generated using Rayleigh fading channel characteristics. Noise is generated and added to the multipath. All the multipath are added together to simulate the signal at the receiver. It is assumed that the channel characteristics and the delays are known at the receiver. As the multipath is detected integration process takes place. The integration results are stored for the maximal ratio combining. MRC combines the integration results and sent for bit decisions. The recovered binary data is decoded and probability of error is computed. Simulations have run with Walsh-Hadamard and modified Walsh-hadamard codes for same delays and data bits. It is assumed that no other user is occupying the channel hence multi-user interference is neglected.

It is observed that the whole set of modified Walsh-Hadamard codes generated with the proposed orthogonal matrices have better auto correlation properties and reduces the bit error rates (BER) compare to the Walsh-Hadamard codes.

If, in a mobile radio channel reflected waves arrive with small relative *time delays*, self interference occurs. Direct Sequence (*DS*) Spread Spectrum is often claimed to have particular properties that makes it less vulnerable to multipath reception. In particular, the rake receiver architecture allows an optimal combining of energy received over paths with different time delays. It avoids wave cancellation (fades) if delayed paths arrive with phase differences and appropriately weighs signals coming in with different signal-to-noise ratios.

The rake receiver consists of multiple correlators, in which the received signal is multiplied by time-shifted versions of a locally generated code sequence. The intention is to separate signals such that each finger only sees signals coming in over a single (resolvable) path. The spreading code is chosen to have a very small autocorrelation value for any nonzero time offset. This avoids crosstalk between fingers. In practice, the situation is less ideal. It is not the full periodic *autocorrelation* that determines the crosstalk between signals in different fingers, but rather two *partial correlations*, with contributions from two consecutive bits or symbols. It has been attempted to find sequences that have satisfactory partial correlation values, but the crosstalk due to partial (non-periodic) correlations remains substantially more difficult to reduce than the effects of periodic correlations.

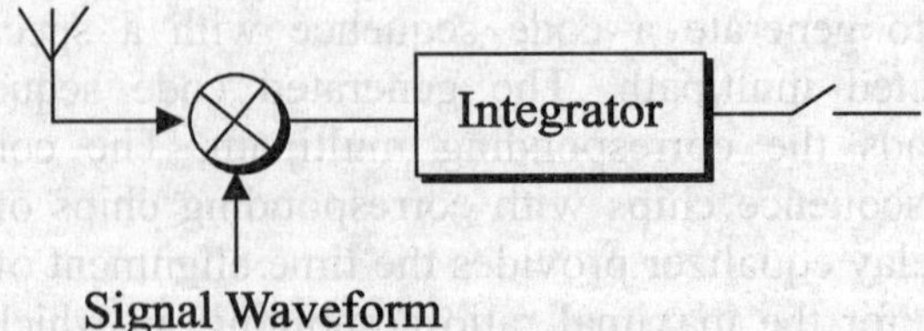

Fig. 2.14: Matched Filter Receiver for AWGN Channel

The rake receiver is designed to optimally detecte a *DS-CDMA* signal transmitted over a *dispersive* multipath channel. It is an extension of the concept of the *matched filter*.

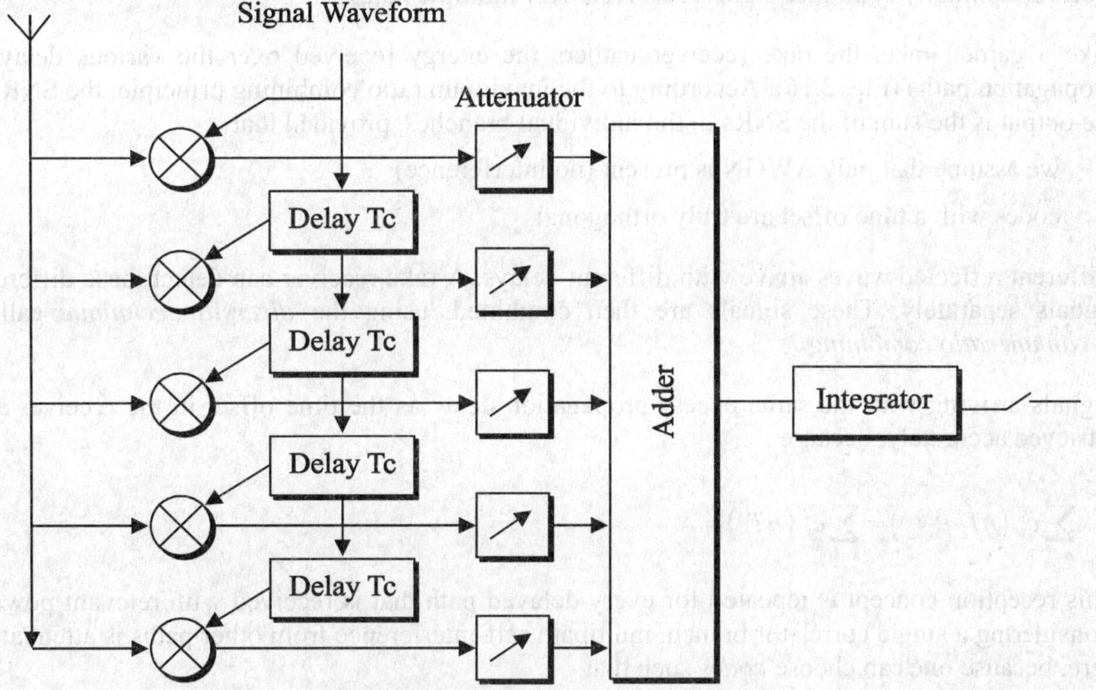

Fig. 2.15: Rake Receiver with 5 Fingers

In the matched filter receiver, the signal is correlated with a locally generated copy of the signal waveform. If, however, the signal is distorted by the channel, the receiver should correlate the incoming signal by a copy of the expected received signal, rather than by a copy of transmitted waveform. Thus the receiver should estimate the delay profile of channel, and adapt its locally generated copy according to this estimate.

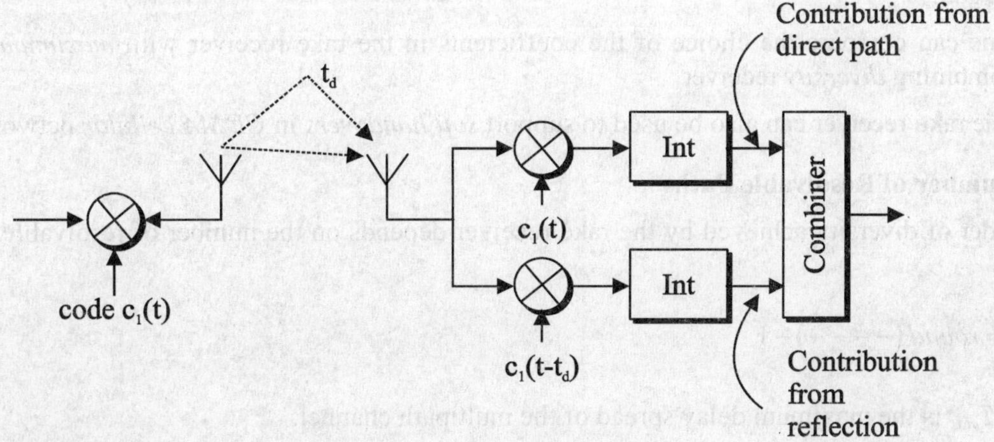

Fig. 2.16: Rake Receiver

In a multipath channel, delayed reflections interfere with the direct signal. However, a DS-CDMA signal suffering from multipath dispersion can be detected by a rake receiver. This receiver optimally combines signals received over multiple paths.

Like a garden rake, the rake receiver gathers the energy received over the various delayed propagation paths (Fig. 2.16). According to the maximum ratio combining principle, the SNR at the output is the sum of the SNRs in the individual branches, provided that

- we assume that only AWGN is present (no interference)
- codes with a time offset are truly orthogonal

Different reflected waves arrive with different delays. A rake receiver can detect these different signals separately. These signals are then combined, using the *diversity technique* called *maximum ratio combining.*

Signals arriving with the same excess propagation delay as the time offset in the receiver are retrieved accurately, because

$$\sum_{n=1}^{N} c_1^2\left(nT_c + t_d\right) = \sum_{n=1}^{N} c_1^2\left(nT_c\right) = N$$

This reception concept is repeated for every delayed path that is received with relevant power. Considering a single correlator branch, multipath self-interference from other paths is attenuated here, because one can choose *codes* such that

$$\sum_{n=1}^{N} c_1\left(nT_c\right) c_1\left(nT_c + t_d\right) \cong 0$$

Rake Facts

- In an interference-free system, each attenuation/amplification coefficient in the Rake receiver is proportional to the received amplitude in the corresponding "bin" of the *delay spread.*
- One can compare the choice of the coefficients in the rake receiver with *maximum ratio* combining *diversity* receiver.
- The rake receiver can also be used to support *soft handovers* in *CDMA cellular* networks.

The Number of Resolvable Paths

The order of diversity achieved by the rake receiver depends on the number of resolvable paths L with

$$L_{T_{chip}}^{T_{max}} = round\left(----\right) + 1$$

where T_{max} is the maximum delay spread of the multipath channel.

Review Points

CDMA

CDMA is a spread spectrum Technology. Many users occupy the same frequency band at the same time. CDMA assigns unique codes to each communication to differentiate.

Advantages of CDMA

Providing flexible support to different frequency band and provides superior performance by way of integrating in a modular design of various network entities like MSC, VLR, HLR etc. Reliability is one of the main quality achieved in CDMA and the capacity expansion is easier as the same frequency band used for all connections.

CDMA WLL

Wireless in Local Loop using CDMA technology is one of the popular access network system used for voice call and data call at more than 28.8 kbps, with high quality service using the spectrum more efficiently. This also provides limited mobility.

CDMA One

Deployment of CDMA in commercial cellular network as IS-95 A was started in 1994-95, with data rate of 64 kbps support. The network was called CDMA one whose advantages include backward compatibility, high data rates, faster forward power control and high capacity for voice communication.

Voice Call

In a forward channel of CDMA, the actual signal (voice/data) is scramble using PN code and the signal is then orthogonally spread using one of the Walsh codes. This data rate is increased to 1.288 Mcps and transmitted over Tx and after receiving in Rx the signal is demodulated.

CDMA 1x EVDO

This system is meeting the requirement of data rate of 3G, i.e. 2Mbps. Qualcomm has proposed this 1x EVDO i.e. Evolution of Data optimised. Instead of base station controlling power using power control Algorithms for a constant data rate, here in the EVDO network BTS transmits at a fixed power at all the times. Maximum data rate supported is 153.6 Mbps.

Rake Receiver

Rack Receiver is a unique mechanism used in CDMA. IT operate with four or more receivers called fingures. This uses the multipath signals received with a time shifted periods at this receiving end, using a newly generated code sequence and a delay suppression mechanism the correlator, despreads the corresponding multipath and finally helps to calculate the combined signal strength of the received signals.

CDMA for Mobile

The CDMA mobile network has major components and they are Mobile Switching Centre, Visiting Location Register, Home Location Register, BTS and Base Station Controller. MSC is the functional entity that controls the switching operations and allocation of radio resources. OMC, the network operation and maintenance centre enables the operation and maintenance of network.

Hand Off

Hand off is the mechanism by which the user is permanently connected to the network without any break even if he moves from one coverage area to another coverage area. May be cell to cell, MSC to MSC and one operator to another operator depending on the situation. The call in progress does not get interrupted. While, the call is handed over from one BTS to another BTS where the signal strength is more. There are hard hand off, where the frequency band in which the call is in progress changes to new frequency band and soft hand off where the frequency band does not change even when the BTS changes.

Review Questions

1. What is the uniqueness of CDMA Technology?
2. Elucidate the main advantages of CDMA system.
3. What different CDMA system used for 3G?
4. Write down the detailed specification for CDMA WLL.
5. Describe the working of Base Transceiver System in CDMA WLL.
6. Explain salient features of CDMA 2000 1x.
7. Draw the schematic diagram of CDMA 1x network and explain the functions of various components.
8. What are the different CDMA radio channels and explain their functions?
9. How a forward traffic channel handles a voice frequency of voice call and transmits on line?
10. Explain the role of Vocoder.
11. What is CDMA 1x EV-DO and explain the salient features of the system?
12. What is a Rake Receiver? Where it is used? Explain the working of rake receiver in CDMA Network.
13. What is the function of VLR in the cellular architecture?
14. Write down the role of OMC and explain its special functions.
15. Draw the call flow chart for mobile initiated call and explain the sequences.
16. What is meant by Hand Off? Write different type of Hand Offs. Explain Soft Hand Off.
17. Explain the sequences with a small sketch to illustrate a hand off (i) between two cells; (ii) between two MSCs in a cellular network.

3 First-Generation Mobile Technology – 1G (Analog)

3.1 FIRST GENERATION (1G) MOBILE

Although the advancement of any technology certainly involves quantum leaps forward from time to time, it is common for major progress also to occur as a result of incremental improvements. For mobile communications technology, advancement has come about in both ways-through occasional revolution and almost certain evolution. Therefore, although this book deals primarily with the technology of first to fourth generation wireless networks, an understanding of earlier systems is important. This understanding provides the appropriate perspective from which to view 3G systems and helps us to understand how solutions for 3G systems have been developed. In other words, it is easier to understand where we are going if we understand where we have been. To help in this understanding, this chapter provides an overview of first-generation (1G) systems.

Cellular communication, referred to as *1G*, is one of the most prolific voice communication platforms that has been deployed within the last two decades. Overall, cellular communication is the form of wireless communication that enables several key concepts to be employed, such as the following:

- frequency reuse
- Mobility of the subscriber
- Handoffs

The cellular concept is employed in many different forms. Typically, when referencing cellular communication, it is usually associated with either the Advanced Mobile Phone System (AMPS) or Total Access Communication Services (TACS) technology. AMPS operates in the 800-MHz band for base-station receiving (821-849 MHz) and transmitting (869-894 MHz). For TACS, the frequency range is 890 to 915 MHz for base-station receiving and 935 to 960 MHz for base-station transmitting.

Many other technologies also fall within the category of cellular communication, and they involve the Personal Communications Service (PCS) bands, including both the domestic U.S. and international bands. In addition, the same concept is applied in several technology platforms that are used currently in the Specialized Mobile Radio (SMR) band (1S-136 and iDEN). However, cellular communication is really used by both the AMPS and TACS bands but is sometimes interchanged with the PCS and SMR bands because of the similarities. However, AMPS and TACS systems are analog-based systems, not digital.

The concept of cellular radio was developed by AT&T at its Bell Laboratories to provide additional radio capacity for a geographic customer service area. The initial mobile systems from which cellular evolved were called mobile telephone systems (MTSs). Later improvements to these systems occurred, and the systems were referred to as improved mobile telephone systems (IMTSs). One of the main problems with these systems was that a mobile call could not be transferred from one radio station to another without loss of communication. This problem was resolved by implementing the concepts of reusing the allocated frequencies of the system. Reusing the frequencies in cellular systems enables a market to offer higher radio traffic capacity. The increased radio traffic enables more users in a geographic service area than with the MTS or IMTS systems.

Cellular radio was a logical progression in the quest to provide additional radio capacity for a geographic area. The cellular system, as it is known today, has its primary roots in the MTS and the IMTS. Both MTS and IMTS are similar to cellular with the exception that no handoff takes place with these networks.

Cellular systems operate on the principle of frequency reuse. Frequency reuse in a cellular market enables a cellular operator to offer higher radio traffic capacity. The higher radio traffic capacity enables many more users in a geographic area to use radio communication than are available with an MTS or IMTS system.

The cellular systems in the United States are broken into Metropolitan Statistical Areas (MSAs) and Rural Statistical Areas (RSAs). Each MSA and RSA has two different cellular operations that offer service. The two cellular operations are referred to as A-band and B-band systems. The A-band system is the nonwireline system, and the B-band is the wireline system for the MSA or RSA.

3.2 VARIOUS 1G SYSTEMS

Numerous mobile wireless systems have been deployed throughout the world. Each of the various 1G wireless systems has its own unique advantages and disadvantages depending on the spectrum available and the services envisioned for delivery. 1G mobility systems are defined as analog systems and typically are referred to as an *AMPS* or *TACS* system. It is important to note that analog systems use digital signaling in many aspects of their networks, including the air interface. However, the analog reference applies to the method that the information content is transported over; that is, no CODEC is involved.

Table 2.1 represents the popular 1G wireless mobility service offerings that have been deployed. As mentioned previously, the two most prolific 1G systems deployed in the world are AMPS and TACS.

All the 1G systems shown in the table use a Frequency Division Multiple Access (FDMA) scheme for radio system access. However, the specific channel bandwidth that each uses is slightly different, as is the typical spectrum allocations for each of the services. The channel bandwidths are as follows:

Table 3.1: 1G Systems

	AMPS	*NAMPS*	*TACS*	*NMT450*	*NMT900*	*C450*
Base Tx, MHz	869-894	869-894	935-960	463-465	935-960	461-466
Base Rx, MHz	824-849	824-849	890-915	453-458	890-915	451-456
Multiple access method	FDMA	FDMA	FDMA	FDMA	FDMA	FDMA
Modulation	FM	FM	FM	FM	FM	FM
Radio channel spacing	30 kHz	10 kHz	25 kHz	25 kHz	12.5 kHz	30 kHz (b) 10 kHz (m)
Number of channels	832	2496	1000	200	1999	222 (b) 444 (m)
CODEC	NA	NA	NA	NA	NA	NA
Spectrum allocation	50 MHz	50 MHz	50 MHz	10 MHz	50 MHz	10 MHz

- AMPS is the cellular standard that was developed for use in North America. This type of system operates in the 800- MHz frequency band. AMPS systems also have been deployed in South America, Asia, and Russia.
- Narrow-Band AMPS (NAMPS) is a product that is used in parts of the United States, Latin America, and other parts of the world. NAMPS is a cellular standard that was developed as an interim platform between 1G and 2G systems and was developed by Motorola. Specifically, NAMPS is an analog radio system that is very similar to AMPS, with the exception that it uses 10-kHz-wide voice channels instead of the standard 30-kHz channels. The obvious advantage with this technology is the capability to deliver, under ideal conditions, three times more capacity than regular AMPS.

NAMPS is able to achieve this smaller bandwidth through changing the format and methodology for Supervisory Audio Tone (SAT) and control communications from the cell site to the subscriber unit. In particular, NAMPS uses a sub carrier method and a digital color code in place of SAT. These two methods make it possible to use less spectrum while communicating the same amount of or even more information at the same time and increasing the capacity of the system with the same spectrum.

AMPS operates in the 800-MHz band for base-station receiving (821-849 MHz) and transmitting (869-894 MHz). For TACS, the frequency range is 890 to 915 MHz for base-station receiving and 935 to 960 MHz for base-station transmitting. AMPS was first commercially introduced in Chicago in the year 1983.

3.3 AMPS: ADVANCED MOBILE PHONE SYSTEM

- Analog Cellular Mobile System.
- Working Frequency range is 800 MHz
- Number of Duplex voice Channels -832

- Number of Control Channels -21
- Channel spacing -30 KHz

3.3.1 Technical Specification

Forward Channel (Down Link) – Base station to Mobile

Reverse Channel (Up Link) – Mobile to Base Station Down

Voice Channel

Base Frequency (Down Link) 869 MHz to 894 MHz (25MHz)

Mobile Frequency (Up Link) 824 MHz to 849 MHz (25 MHz)

Frequency separation between Base Freq and Mobile Freq -45 MHz

Control Channel

Base Freq 879.390 – 879.990

600 KHz – 21 Control Chl

Mob Freq. 834. 390 – 834.990

600 KHz – 21 Control Channels

Forward Control Channel - Base Frequency Channels in will be 25MHz / 30 KHz = 832

Reverse Control Channel- Mobile Frequency channels will be 25 MHz/ 30 KHz = 832

For one cell site number of channels are 832/7=120 or 832/12=69

That is to say, in case of 7 cell cluster 120 channels per cell and for 12 cell cluster 69 channels per cell

3.3.2 Control Channel Functions

1. To keep track of mobile phone
2. To know which is 'ON' which is 'OFF'
3. Keep track of phone no for authentication and billing
4. Detect and prevent fraudulent use
5. Ready to set up calls
6. To page the location of the Cell
7. Ready to transfer calls from cell to cell
8. To carry the information about signal strength

3.3.3 Voice Channel – Functions

- For talking-voice call
- For Control messages system uses voice channel ocassionally

(ie. While there is a conversation by adopting a method called In channel, out of bound signaling with FSK 8 KHz deviation or a total freq. shift of 16 KHz)

Mobile Phone Identification is another function:

Mobile Identification Number MIN – 10 digit is stored in Number assignment Module NAM and NAM is programmable (IMEI IN GSM)

Electronic Serial Number (ESN) – 32 bit No. assigned by the Manufacturer – not changeable MIN and ESN decides authentication & billing

Station Class Mark (SCM)-Indicates the class according to Power Level

- Cl. I + 6 dbw (4W)
- Cl. II + 2 dbw (1.6W)
- Cl. III – 2 dbw (600 MW)

System Identification Number (SID)- to indicate mobile is at home location or Roaming

3.3.4 Working of the System

Mobile Turns – On

- Scans all control channels – Picks up strongest signal.
- SID (Site ID) found indicates the cell site
- System Transmits in forward control channel every 0.8 sec.
- Collision occurs when two mobiles use the same channel.
- Reverse channel transmits MIN & ESN.
- In turn 'ON' condition Mobile continuously (periodically at 46 ms) checks control signal from Cell site.

Out Going Call

- Digits dialed – sent – along with MIN & ESN in control channel
- Then forwarded to MSC – return paging message with voice channel number and power level
- Supervisory Audio Tone (SAT) for continuity and monitoring purpose sent at frequencies 5.9, 6 or 6.03 KHz

Incoming Call

- Mobile site (SID) is known in MSC, MIN is given is given by caller,
- MIN, allotted Voice Channel No. and power level sent on Control Channel to Mobile.
- Mobile confirms by sending ESN in return message
- ESN-MIN match checked (authentication) in MSC
- Call established - conversation begins
- SAT sent on Voice Channel

Hand Off

- Power level of adjacent cell checked
- Signal strength greater from adjacent cell means hand off ordered.
- Voice channel is active only during conversation.
- Mobile is given new channel no. new attenuation code and new SAT frequency
- After confirmation Mobile switches to new cell site, conversation continues.

3.3.5 Disadvantages of AMPS

AMPS is not very private and security is not there. Ordinary FM is used for transmission of speech – that can be picked up by any FM receiver and no security means no protection.

3.4 OTHER 1G SYSTEMS

- TACS is a cellular band that was derived from the AMPS technology. TACS systems operate in both the 800- and 900-MHz band. The first system of this kind was implemented in England. Later these systems were installed in Europe, Hong Kong, Singapore, and the Middle East. A variation of this standard was implemented in Japan, called JTACS.
- Nordic Mobile Telephone (NMT) is the cellular standard that was developed by the Nordic countries of Sweden, Denmark, Finland, and Norway in 1981. This type of system was designed to operate in the 450 and 900-MHz frequency bands. These are noted as NMT450 and NMT900. NMT systems also have be deployed throughout Europe, Asia, and Australia.

The basic service offering for 1G systems was and is voice communication. These systems have been extremely successful, and many of them are still in service offering 1G services only.

ETACS is European first generation analog mobile system working with 935-960 Mhz for Down Link and 890-915 Mhz range for Up Link the channel Bandwidth is 25 Khz and no.of Channel is 1000.

3.4.1 Comparative Study of First Generation Mobile Systems

		AMPS	ETACS
1.	Multiple Access	FDMA	FDMA
2.	Duple Xing	FDD	FDD
3.	Channel B/W	30 KHz	25 KHz
4.	Traf. Chl per RF	1	1
5.	Reverse Chl. Freq	824 – 849	890 – 915
6.	Forward Chl Freq	869 – 894	935 – 960
7.	Voice Modulation	FM	FM

8.	Peak deviation Voice Chl	12 KHz	10·KHz
	Control. Chl	8 KHz	6 KHz
9.	Chl coding for data transmission	BCH (40, 28) FC	40, 28 FC
	BCH	48, 36 RC	48, 36 RC
10.	Data rate on control chl.	10 Kbps	8 Kbps
11.	Spectral efficiency	0.33 bps/Hz	0.33 bps/Hz
12.	Number of channels	832	1000
13.	Number of Contl. channels	21	42
14.	Sys. Id / Area ID	SID	AID
15.	Mobile Id.	MIN	
16.	Electronic Serial No.	ESN	
17.	Voice Modulation Access Code	VMAC Tones on Freq 5970	
18.	Supervisory Audio Tone	SAT 6000 or 6030 Hz	

3.4.2 Defficiencies of 1G Systems

Numerous mobile wireless systems have been deployed throughout the world. Each of the various 1G wireless systems has its own unique advantages and disadvantages depending on the spectrum available and the services

1G systems, however, suffer from a number of difficulties. Some of these difficulties were addressed by adding technology to the network, and some have required the implementation of 2G technology. The biggest problem that led to the introduction of 2G technology was the fact that 1G systems had limited system capacity. This became a serious issue as the popularity of mobile communications grew to a level that far exceeded anyone's expectations. Other problems included the fact that the technologies in question addressed only the air interface, and other interfaces in the network were not specified (at least not initially), which meant limited roaming, particularly between networks that were supplied by different vendors. The technologies did not initially include security mechanisms, which allowed sufficient room for fraud. Finally, some limitation in the technologies led to the problem of "lost mobiles," where a subscriber is located at one mobile switching center (MSC), and the network thinks that the subscriber is elsewhere.

Nevertheless, it is worth emphasizing the popularity of these technologies and the fact that, in some cases, they have been the foundation on which 2G and 3G technologies have been built.

3.5 GENERAL 1G SYSTEM ARCHITECTURE

A generic 1G cellular system configuration is shown in Figure 3.1. The configuration involves all the high-level system blocks of a cellular network. Many components consist of each of the blocks shown in Figure 3.1. The individual system components of a cellular network will be covered in later chapters of this book.

Referring to Figure 3.1, the mobile communicates with the cell site through the use of radio transmissions. The radio transmissions use a full-duplex configuration, which involves separate transmit and receive frequencies for the mobile and the cell sites. The cell site transmits on the frequency to which the mobile unit is tuned, whereas the mobile unit transmits on the radiofrequency to which the cell-site receiver is tuned.

The cell site acts as a conduit for the information transfer, converting the radio energy into another medium. The cell site sends and receives information from the mobile and the mobile telephone system office (MTSO), also called the mobile switching office (MSO). The MTSO is connected to the cell site either by leased T1IEllines or through a microwave system. The cellular system is made up of many cell sites that all interconnect back to the MTSO.

The MTSO processes the call and connects the cell-site radio link to the Public Switched Telephone Network (PSTN). The MTSO performs a variety of functions involved with call processing and is effectively the brains of the network. The MTSO maintains the individual subscriber records, the current status of subscribers, call routing information, and billing information, to mention a few items.

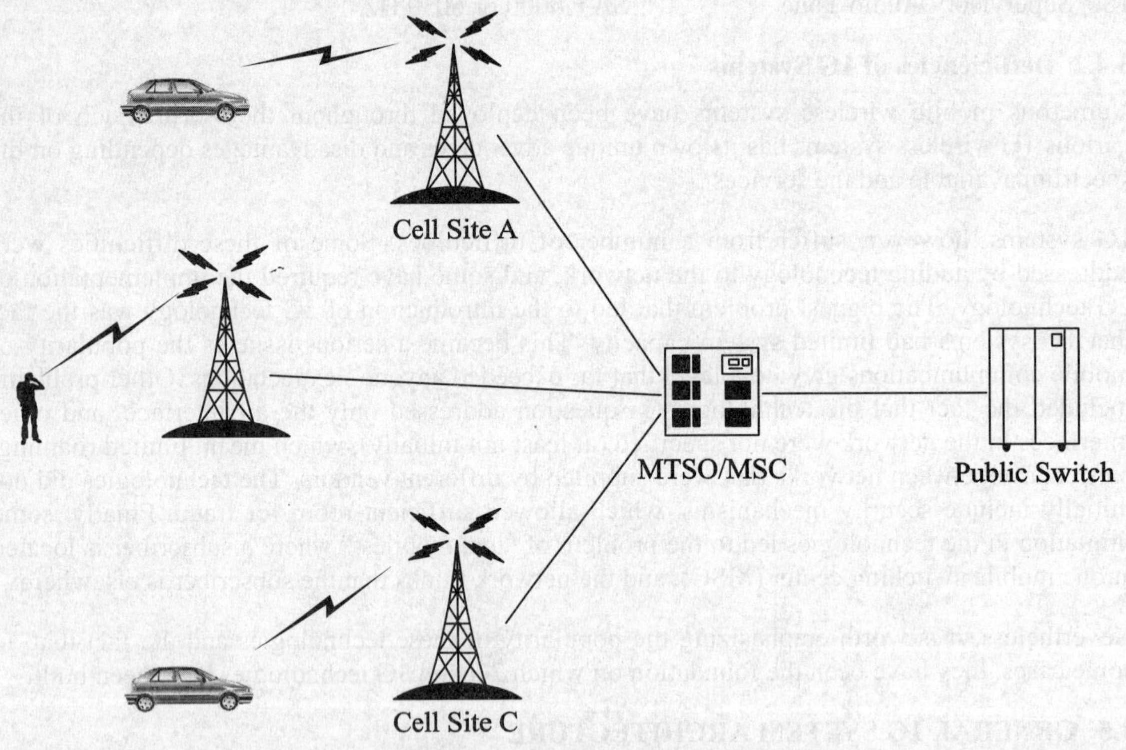

Fig. 3.1: 1G System Configuration

3.5.1 Typical MTSO Configuration

Figure 3.2 shows a generic MTSO configuration. The MTSO is the portion of the network that interfaces the radio world with the PSTN. Mature systems often have multiple MTSO locations, and each MTSO can have several cellular switches located within each building.

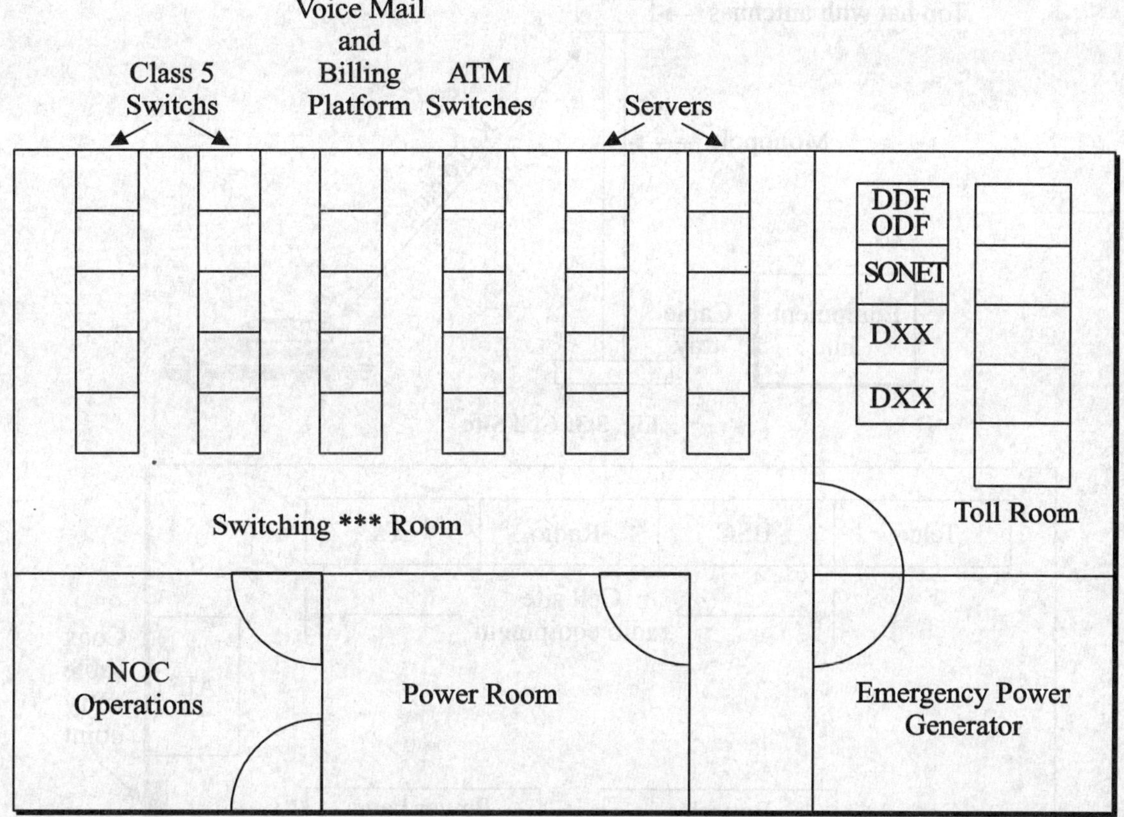

Fig. 3.2: MTSO Configuration

3.5.2 1G BTS (Cell Site) Configuration

Figure 3.3 is an example of a generic cell-site configuration that is a monopole site. The site has an equipment hut associated with it that houses the radio transmission equipment. The monopole, which is next to the equipment hut, supports the antennas used for the cell site at the very top of the monopole. The cable tray, which is between the equipment hut and the monopole, supports the coaxial cables that connect the antennas to the radio transmission equipment.

The radio transmission equipment used for a cellular base station, located in the equipment room, is shown in Figure 3.4. The equipment room layout is a typical arrangement in a cell site. The cell-site radio equipment consists of a base site controller (ESe); a radio bay; and the amplifier, Tx, bay. The cell-site radio equipment is connected to the antenna interface frame (AlF) that provides the receiver and transmit filtering. The AIF then is connected to the antennas on the monopole via coaxial cables that are located next to the AIF bay.

With new versions of equipment the radio bay, Tx bay, and AIF along with the controller can be found to be located in one cabinet.

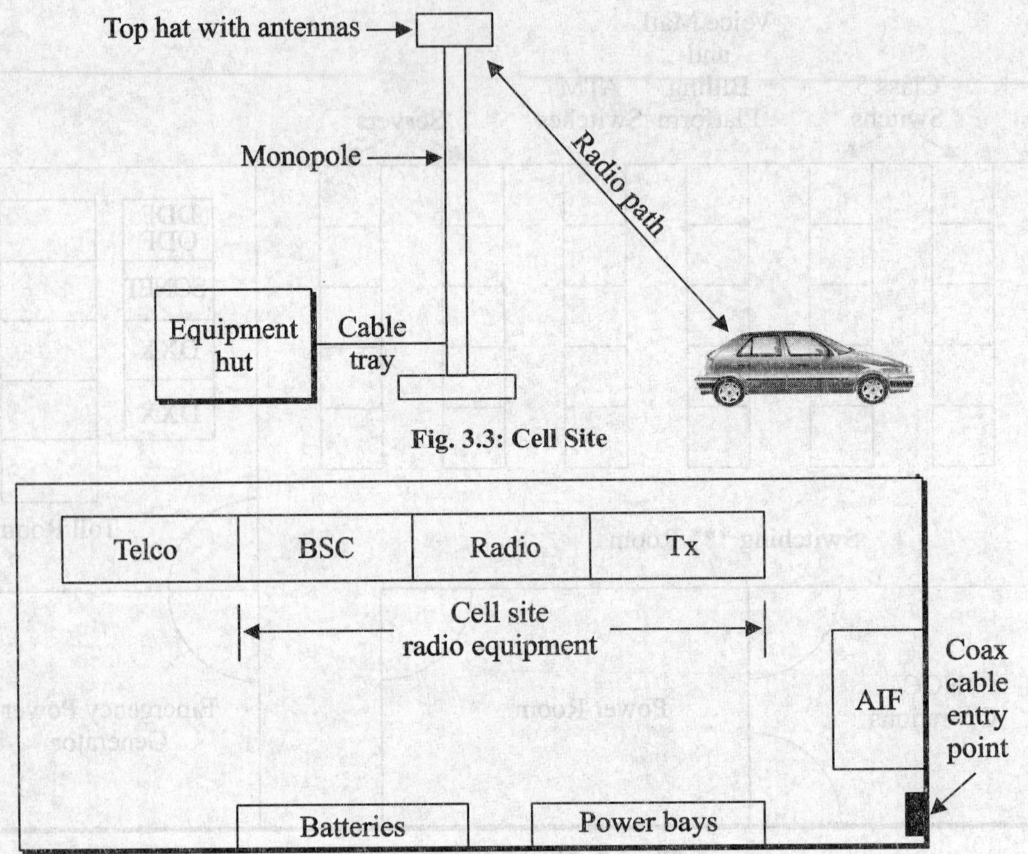

Fig. 3.3: Cell Site

Fig. 3.4: Radio Equipment Room

The cell site is also connected to the MTSO through the Telco bay. The Telco bay provides either TIIEI leased lines or a microwave radio link connection. The power for the cell site is secured through the use of power bays and rectifiers that convert ac electricity to dc. Batteries are used in the cell site in the event of a power disruption to ensure that the site continues to operate until power is restored or the batteries are exhausted.

3.5.3 AMPS Call Setup Scenarios

Several general call scenarios can occur, and they pertain to all cellular systems. A few perturbations of the call scenarios are discussed here that are driven largely by fraud-prevention techniques employed by individual operators. Numerous algorithms are used throughout the call setup and processing scenarios that are not included in Figures 3.5, 3.6, and 3.7. However, the call scenarios presented in these figures provide the fundamental building blocks for all call scenarios used in cellular.

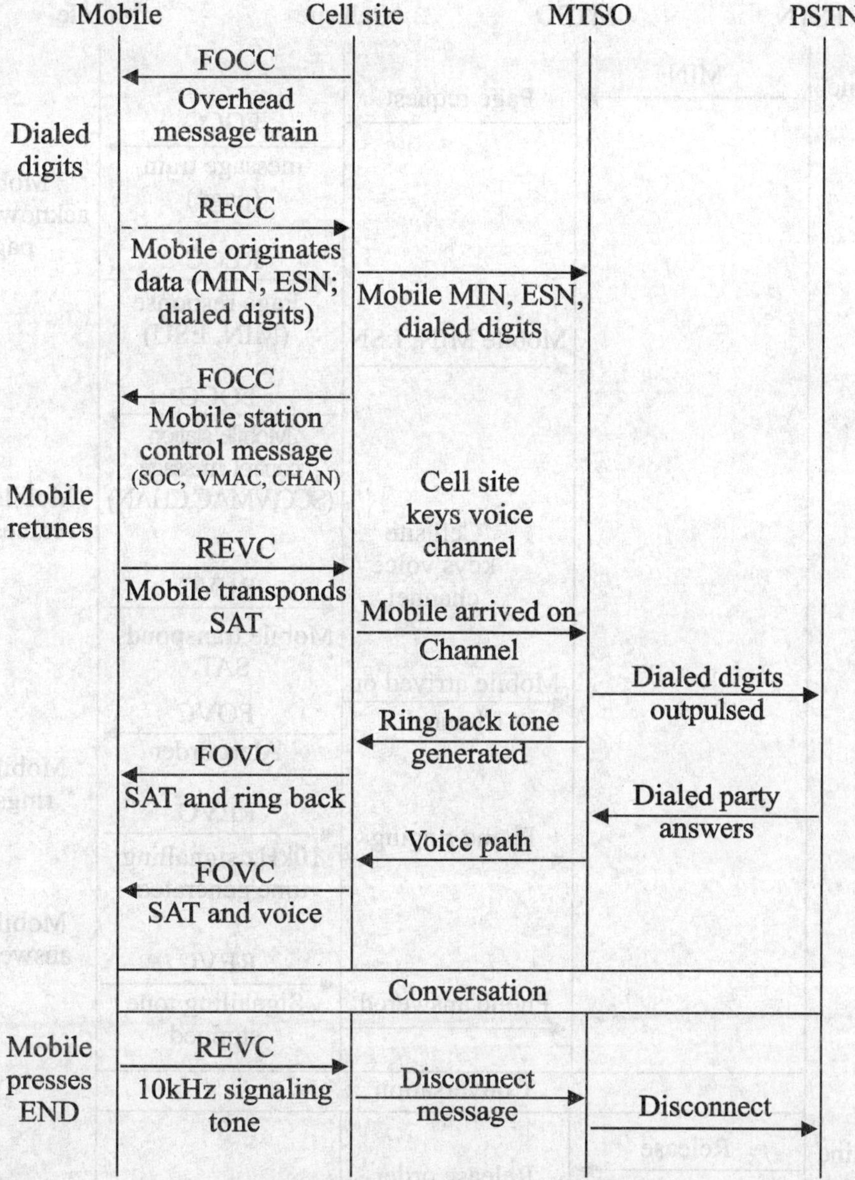

Fig. 3.5: Mobile to Landline Call Setup

3.5.4 Handoff

The handoff concept is one of the fundamental principles of this technology. Handoffs enable cellular to operate at lower power levels and provide high capacity. The handoff scenario presented in Figure 3.8 uses a simplified process. A multitude of algorithms are invoked for the generation and processing of a handoff request and an eventual handoff order. The individual algorithms depend on the individual vendor for the network infrastructure and the software loads used.

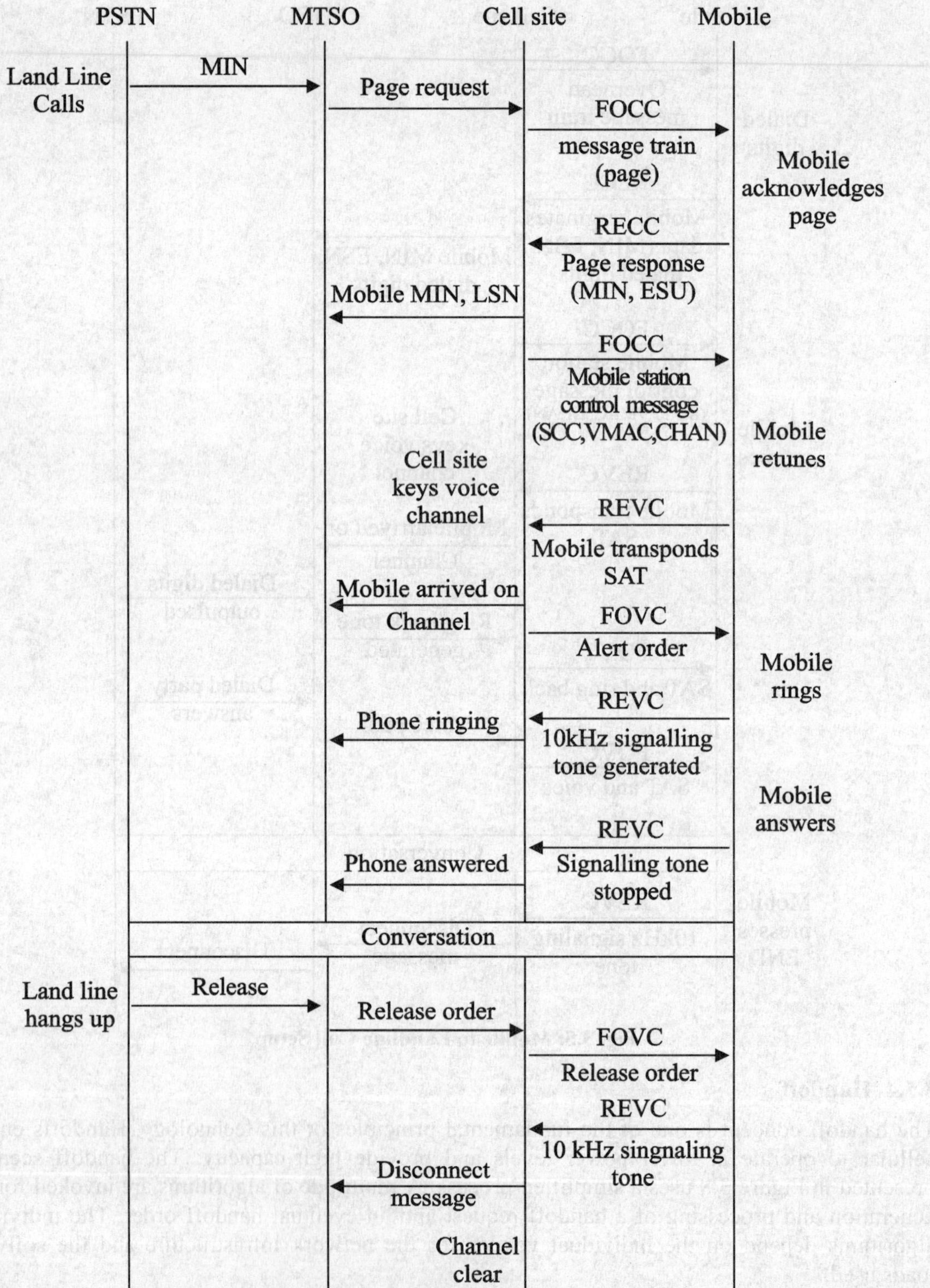

Fig. 3.6: Landline to Mobile Call Set Up

Handing off from cell to cell is fundamentally the process of transferring the mobile unit that has a call in progress on a particular voice channel to another voice channel, all without interrupting the call. Handoffs can occur between adjacent cells or between sectors of the same cell site. The actual need for a handoff is determined by the quality of the radiofrequency (RF) signal received from the mobile unit into the cell site

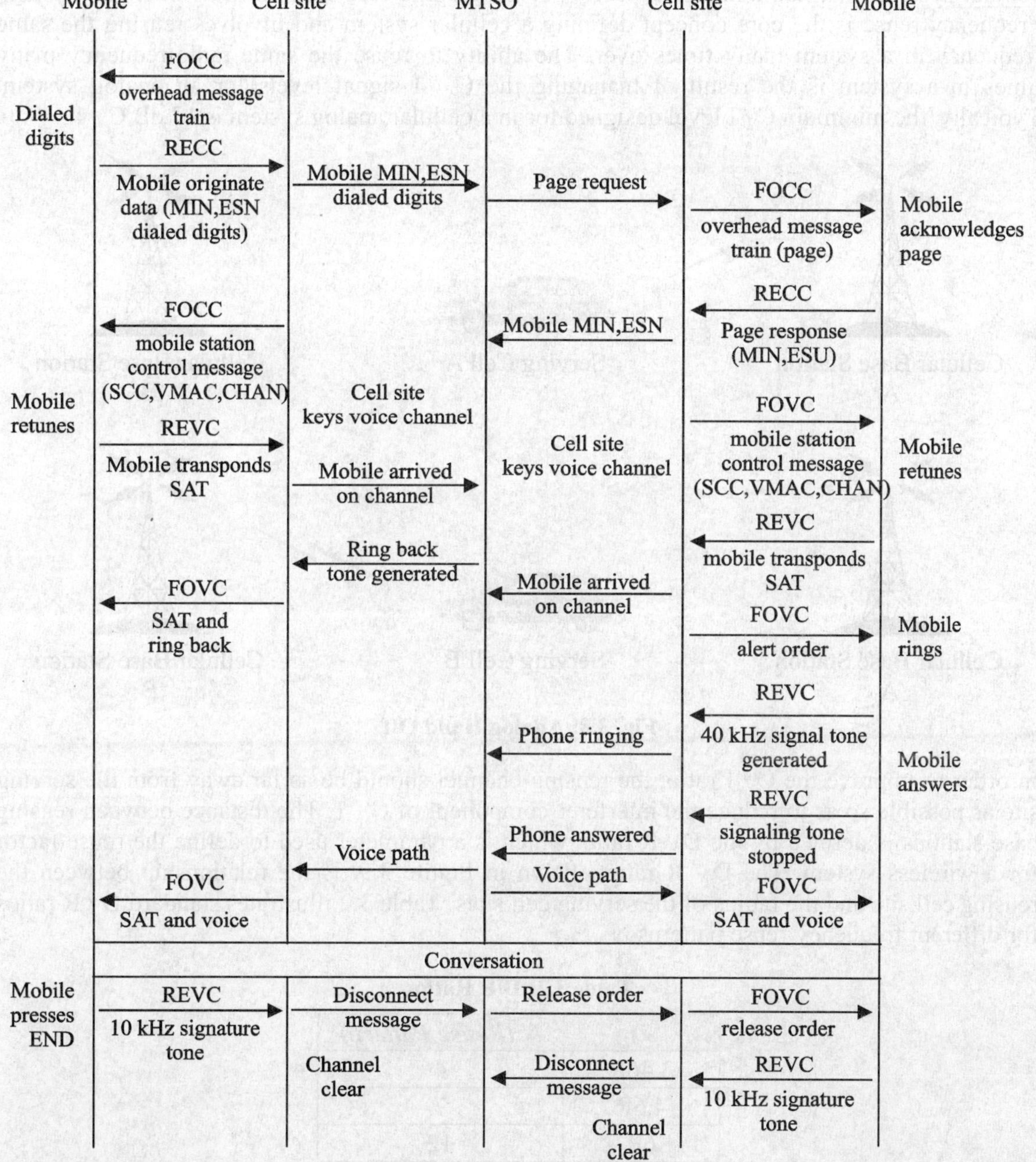

Fig. 3.7: Mobile to Mobile Call

As the mobile unit transverses the cellular network, it is handed off from one cell site to another cell site, ensuring that call quality is maintained for the duration of the conversation.

3.5.5 Frequency Reuse

The concept and implementation of frequency reuse were an essential element in the quest for cellular systems that had a higher capacity per geographic area than an MTS or IMTS system. Frequency reuse is the core concept defining a cellular system and involves reusing the same frequency in a system many times over. The ability to reuse the same radiofrequency many times in a system is the result of managing the C / I signal levels for an analog system. Typically, the minimum C / I level designed for in a cellular analog system is 17 dB C / 1.

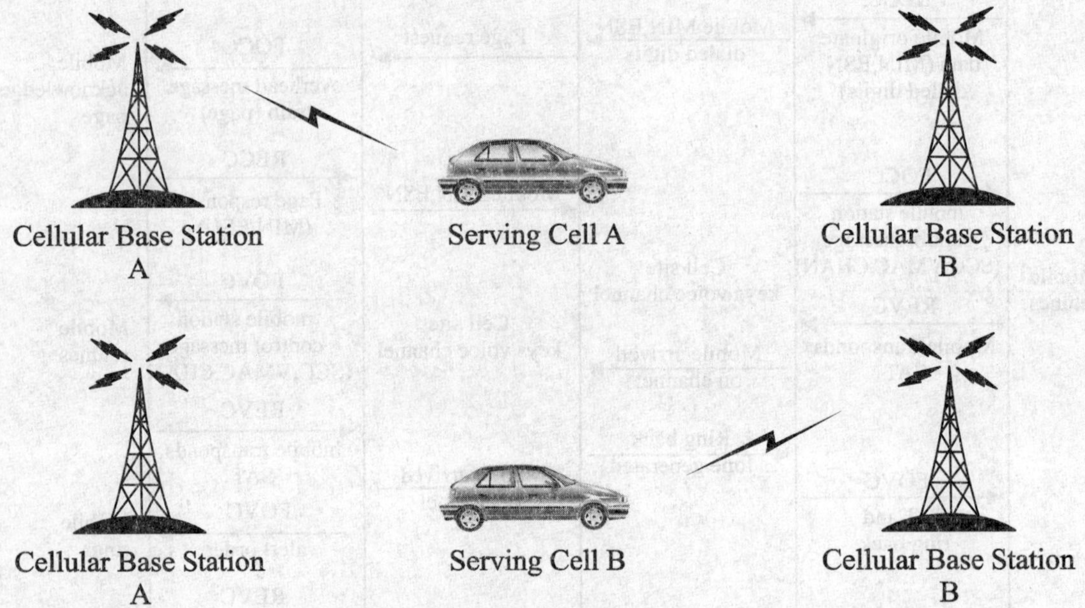

Fig. 3.8: Analog Hand Off

In order to improve the C / I ratio, the reusing channel should be as far away from the serving site as possible so as to reduce the interferer component of C / 1. The distance between reusing base stations is defined by the D / R ratio, which is a parameter used to define the reuse factor for a wireless system. The D / R ratio, shown in Figure 3.9, is the relationship between the reusing cell site and the radius of the serving cell sites. Table 3.2 illustrates standard D / R ratios for different frequency-reuse patterns N

Table 3.2: D/R Ratios

D	*N (Reuse Pattern)*
3.46R	4
4.6R	7
6R	12
7.55R	19

As the D / R table implies, several frequency-reuse patterns are currently in use throughout the cellular industry. Each of the different frequency-r use patterns has it advantages and disadvantages. The most common frequency-reuse pattern employed in cellular is the N = 7 pattern, which is shown in Figure 3.10.

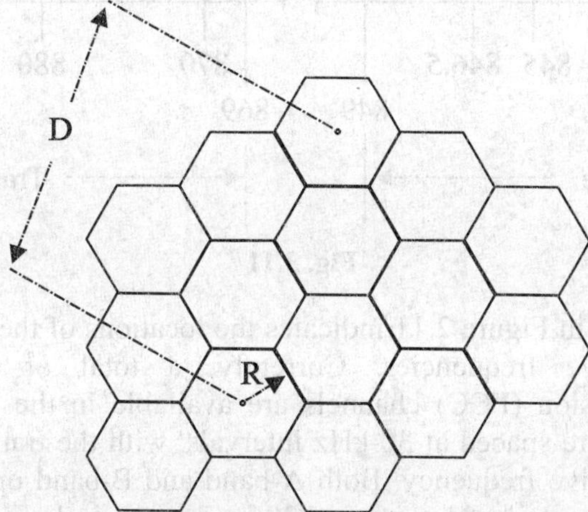

Fig. 3.9: D/R Ratio

The frequency-reuse pattern ultimately defines 'the maximum amount of radios that can be assigned to an individual cell site. The N = 7 pattern can assign a maximum of 56 channels that are deployed using a three-sector design.

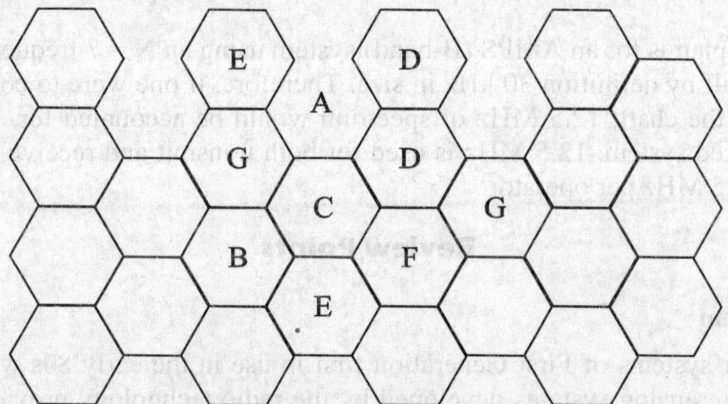

Fig. 3.10: N=7 Frequency Reuse

3.5.6 Spectrum Allocation

Cellular systems have been allocated a designated frequency spectrum within which to operate. Both the A-band and B-band operators are allowed to use a total of 25 MHz of radio spectrum for their systems.

The 25 MHz is divided into 12.5 MHz of transmit frequencies and 12.5 MHz of receive frequencies for each operator. The cellular spectrum is shown in Figure 3.11.

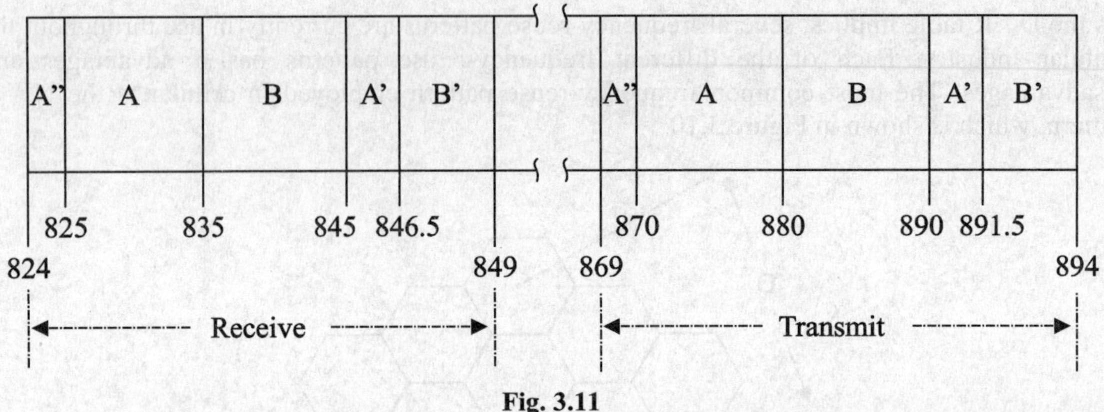

Fig. 3.11

The spectrum chart shown in Figure 2.11 indicates the locations of the A-band and B-band cell-site transmit and receive frequencies. Currently, a total of 832 individual Federal Communications Commission (FCC) channels are available in the United States. The radio channels used in cellular are spaced at 30-kHz intervals, with the transmit frequency operating at 45 MHz above the receive frequency. Both A-band and B-band operators have available to them a total of 416 radio channels: 21 setup and 395 voice channels.

3.5.7 Channel Band Plan

A channel band plan is essential in any wireless system, especially one that reuses the spectrum at defined intervals. The channel band plan is a method of assigning channels, or fixed bandwidth, to a given amount of an RF spectrum that is then grouped in a local fashion.

The channel band plan is for an AMPS (B-band) system using an N = 7 frequency-reuse pattern. The channels are all by definition 30 kHz in size. Therefore, if one were to count the individual channels listed in the chart, 12.5 MHz of spectrum would be accounted for. Since the cellular system is a duplexed system, 12.5 MHz is used for both transmit and receive, whereas the total spectrum used is 25 MHz per operator.

Review Points

1G Cellular System

The major cellular systems of First Generation first in use in the early 80s wee AMPS, TACS and PCS. There are analog systems developed by the radio technology provided by Bell Labs. There were no roaming or no hand off. The instruments very bulky in nature.

Frequency Ranges

It is a must for those who study the 1G system to remember the various 1G systems and their frequency bands allotted as given in the table.

AMPS

Advanced Mobile Phone Systems used in America was using a spectrum in the range of 820 MHz. There were uplink and downlink in two different ranges separated by 45MHz. The bandwidth of the channel was only 30 KHz and there were only 395 voice channels and 21 control channels.

Disadvantages

No security and anybody having a FM receiver can tap the call. Quality of speech rendered by FM was of poor rate, Because of narrow bandwidth (30 KHz) the interference was more. Capacity expansions were very much restricted.

Architecture of 1G System

The radio transmission uses a full deplex configuration which involves separate transmit and receive frequency bands. The call sites act as conduct for the transfer of information. A mobile telephone system office (MTSO) processes the calls and connect cell site radio link to Public Switched Telephone Network.

Review Questions

1. Mention the earlier types of 1G cellular mobile communication in 1980s.
2. What are drawbacks of analog cellular systems?
3. Write down the frequency bands used by various 1G mobile system.
4. What is FDMA in 1G system?
5. Write down the characteristics and specification of AMPS.
6. Write down the functions of voice channel and control channel.
7. Mention the disadvantages of AMPS.
8. Compare the AMPS and ETACS systems.
9. Draw the diagram for the network architecture of AMPS and explain the working.
10. Draw flow chart and explain sequence of call set up for a Mobile to Landline call.
11. Explain the sequence in call set up in the case of Mobile to Mobile call.
12. Explain frequency reuse theory and hand off conditions.
13. What is channel band plan?

4 Second Generation Mobile Systems (Global System for Mobile Communication (GSM))

4.1 INTRODUCTION

Group Speciale' Mobile or Global System for Mobile Communication is an European initiative and GSM is a second generation (2G) digital system which uses Frequency Division Multiplexing (FDM) and Time Division Multiplexing (TDM). It is most successful digital mobile system initiated and standardized by European Telecommunication Standards Institute (ETSI). The major aim on introduction of GSM was to overcome the deficiencies of First Generation Analog System.

4.1.1 GSM Background

The Joint West-European venture of specifying the GSM system started within the CEPT Organization, where the cooperative work in the different areas of telecommunications was formally adopted in the form of recommendations. However, it was a national decision whether or not each recommendation, or set of recommendations, for a given service should be implemented by the administration of each country.

There was a need, however, for a more demanding obligation as far as the GSM was concerned. The system needed to include the concept of international roaming, and success in one country would therefore depend upon the system rollout in other countries. The development and production of system equipment would require large industrial investments that could hardly be justified unless the different national markets evolved somewhat simultaneously. A memorandum of understanding was thus prepared during mid-1987 and signed by the first 12 countries in September 1987.

The GSM system specification work was later transferred to ETSI, an organization controlling standardization and the MOU, which served as an adequate forum for discussions on pure operational matters. The main purpose of the GSM-MOU was to provide a framework for all the necessary measures to be taken by the signatories together to ensure the opening of a commercial service in their respective countries by 1991. Also, the network operators would plan the progressive implementation of the networks in each country so that transport routes between the countries of the signatories could be brought early into the coverage of the respective systems, Priority for coverage would be given to all capital cities including the principal airport by 1991, introduction of special services by 1993, and the full European roaming market by 1995, as shown in Table 4.1.

4.1.2 GSM Operational Requirements

A list of operational requirements was developed that consisted of the following:

- High audio quality and link integrity;
- High spectral efficiency;
- Identical system in all countries (European harmonization and standardization);

Table 4.1: Milestones for a GSM System

Year	*Occurrence*
Mid-1991	Capitals; Voice, emergency calls, call forwarding and barring
Mid-1993	Intercapitol roaming; Short message services (SMS), FAX and call holding
Mid-1995	European roaming; Real-time information, call waiting and conference calls

4.2 GSM TECHNOLOGY AND COVERAGE

4.2.1 Coverage Area

- Introduction of GSM network in any area involves extensive planning.
- Coverage Area-total geographical area to be covered by service provider
- And the area is divided into number of cells and one coverage area is thus formed by a cluster of cells-the number of cells in a single cluster may be 7 or 12 or 19 etc.
- Cell area is the area covered by one specific cell

Planning of GSM network involves,

- Cell Planning with Cluster of cells
- Frequency reuse scheme
- Channel assignment
- Cell splitting
- Capacity constraints
- Trunking efficiency
- Roaming

Cell Site / Coverage area is determined by

- Radio Transmitter Power
- Height and location of antenna
- Type of antenna
- Topography
- Radio Receiver Sensitivity

4.2.2 GSM Technology Offering

- Clarity of speech and elimination of interference noise
- Free from interception and tapping as encryption is used
- Roaming – anywhere in the world
- TDMA Technology used for improving spectrum efficiency
- Full flexibility and interoperability
- Better 'hand off' condition
- More expanded services and features
- Easy cell splitting Technique

GSM Network provides-Telephony, Short message Transmission, Video Tex, Tele Tex, Video Tex and Fax, Teleservice, includes Mobile Telephony Service, Emergency calling, Facsimile.

Bearer Service includes Data Service at 9.6 Kbps Limited to Layers 1,2,3 of OSI

Supplementary Service is Digital in nature and has Call Diversion, Caller Id, call transfer, SMS and Closed user group (160)

4.2.3 Basic Requirements

Basic Requirements to be met are:

- Mobile stations can be used from anywhere in the world
- Enable to offer even latest service like ISDN
- All facilities offered to PSTN Subscribers must be available
- Different type of mobiles, viz vehicle mounted handheld or fixed station.
- Capability for encryption to prevent eavesdropping
- Entire frequency band 890 – 915 MHz for UL
  935 – 960 MHz for DL to be used
- High level of frequency spectrum
- Compatibility to inter work with PSTN /PSPDN
- Different charging structures
- Compatibility of signaling system
- Protection of signaling inform and control information.

4.2.4 GSM Advantages

1. Spectral efficiency by selecting appropriate technologies for efficient modulation, channel coding, inter leaving equalization and speech coding.
2. Capacity-High capacity network in terms of traffic in given geographical area using given bandwidth. Different techniques like frequency reuse, cell splitting and sectorisation.

3. Speech quality is comparatively very good due to defining of air – interface and speech coding techniques.
4. Security is improved
   - by authentications using SIM
   - by encryption
   - IMSI (International Mobile Subscriber Identity
5. Compatibility to inter work with PSTN /PSPDN
6. Different charging structures

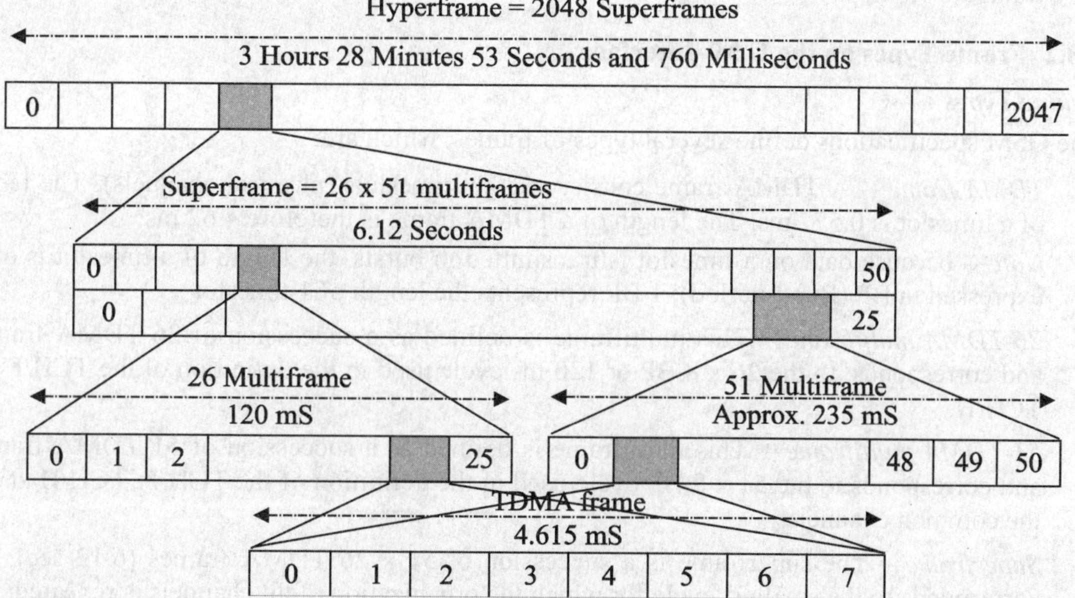

Fig. 4.1: GSM Radio Interface - Cycles

4.3 TECHNICAL PARAMETERS FOR GSM

4.3.1 GSM - Multiframe Structure

- Uses Multiple Access Technologies FDMA and TDMA
- Spacing interval (or bandwidth of a channel) of 200 KHz using FDMA
- Eight Logical Channels derived by using TDMA
- Each Terminal is allotted - 2 way Traffic channel for speech (one for Up link and one for Down link) and separate 2 way control channel
- Multi frame (MF) of 120 ms
- Number of frames 26 in a MF
- 24 frames for information bit
- 2 frames for Associated Control Channel (ACCH)

- Frame duration 4.615 ms
- Multi frame duration 120 s
- One channel has 156.25 bits
- One Time slot (channel) duration is 577 micro seconds
- Bit rate (transmission) 271 Kbps
- Bit duration is 3.69 micro seconds
- Speech transmission rate is 22.8 Kbps (after channel coding)
- Voice rate 13 kbps
- Data rate 9.6 kbps

4.3.2 Frame Types on the U M -Interface

Frame Types

The GSM specifications define several types of frames, which are:

- *TDMA frame*— A TDMA frame consist of eight timeslots (physical channels). The length of a timeslot is 0.577 ms. The length of a TDMA frame is therefore 4.62 ms.

  Note— because data on a timeslot is transmitted in bursts, the length of a timeslot is often expressed in BP (Burst Period); 1 BP represents the length of 1 timeslot.
- *26-TDMA multiframe*— This multiframe is defined as a succession of 26 TDMA frames, and corresponds, to the 26 x 8 BP or 120 ms cycle used in the definition of the TCH/F and TCH/H.
- *51-TDMA multiframe*— This multiframe is defined as a succession of 51 TDMA frames, and corresponds to the 51 x 8 BP cycle used in the definition of the TCH/F, TCH/H and of the common channels.
- *Superframe*— The superframe is a succession of 51 x 26 TDMA frames (6.12 sec), and corresponds to the smallest cycle for which the organization of all channels is repeated.
- *Hyperframe*— The hyperframe is the numbering period. It is 2048 x 51 x 26 x 8 BP long, or 3 hours, 28 minutes, 53 seconds and 760 milliseconds. It is a multiple of all previously cited cycles, and determines all the cycles in the transmission of the radio path. It is in particular the smallest cycle for frequency hopping and for ciphering.

The different frames are depicted in the figure 4.1 on the opposite page.

4.3.3 GSM Radio Spectrum

- Two cellular bands each 25 MHz (for UL and DL separately)
- The forward and reverse frequency bands of 25 MHz is divided into number of individual chls and numbered as AFRCN (Absolute Radio Frequency Chl Numbers)
- AFRCN is always a pair of channels separated by 45MHz
- There are 125 such channels possible but 200 khz is used for guard band and hence effective channels are only 124 in the total 25 MHz spectrum available for allocation to operators.

- AFRCN 1 is thus 890.2 Mhz paired with 935.2 Mhz
- AFRCN 2 is thus 890.4 Mhz paired with 935.4 Mhz and so on.
- 200 KHz channel bandwidth is further divided by TDMA in to 8 time slots (TS)
- so that simultaneously 8 subscribers can use one AFRCN
- 270.8333 kbps/8 users and each user data gets 33.854 kbps
- but actual user data is 22.8 as guard time occupies balance bits
- no. of bits per TS is 156.25 bits and time duration of 576.9 micro sec

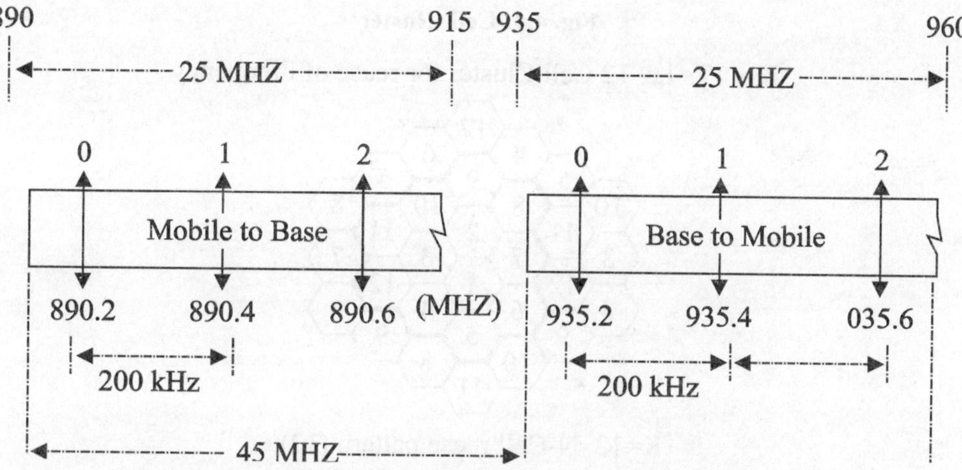

Fig. 4.2: Channel layout and frequency bands of operation

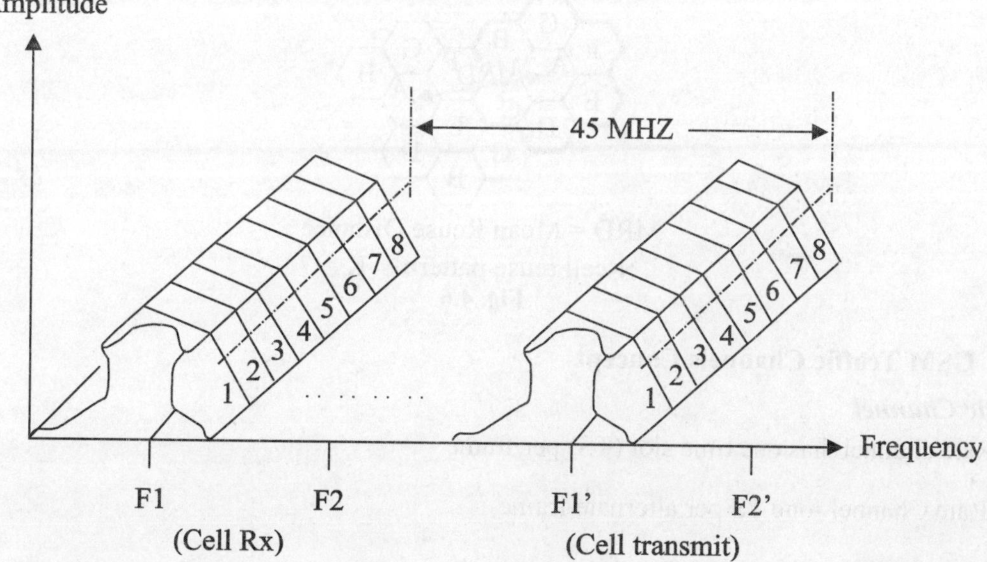

Fig. 4.3: Typical TDMA / FDMA frame structure

Cluster of 4 cells

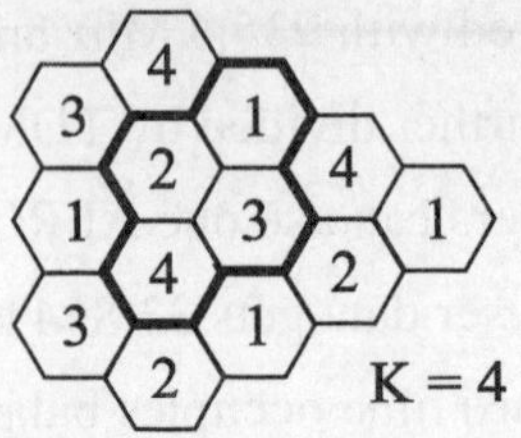

N Cell Reuse Pattern (4)

Fig. 4.4: Cell Cluster

K = 12, i.e. 12 Cell Cluster for reuse of Frequency

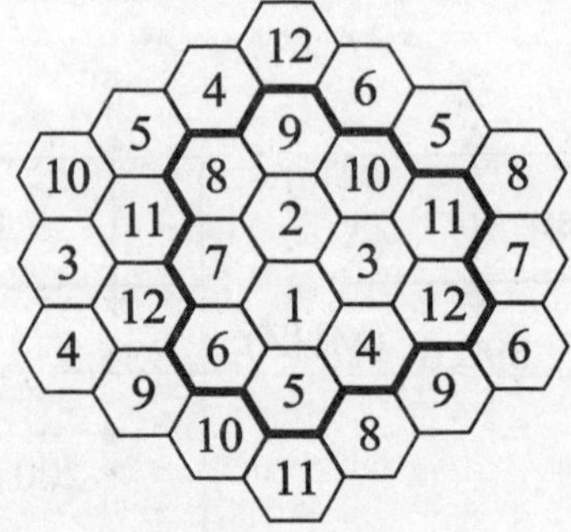

K=12, N-Cell reuse pattern (12)

Fig. 4.5: Cell Formation for Frequency Reuse Pattern

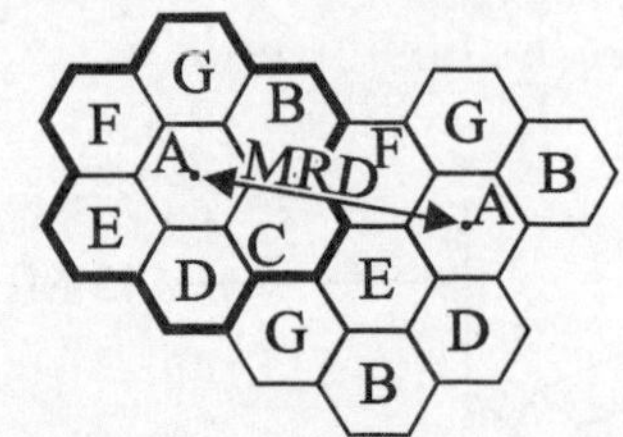

MRD = Mean Reuse Distance

N-cell reuse pattern K = 7

Fig. 4.6

4.3.3 GSM Traffic Channels Concept

Traffic Channel

Full Rate channel has one time slot (TS) per frame

Half Rate Channel -one TS per alternate frame

One Multiframe has 26 consecutive frames.

26th frame – Idle Frame when used as full rate

13th and 26th frame –Slow associated control channel (SACCH)
TS0 NOT USED FOR TCH DATA, but used for broadcast channel

Full rate speech (TCH)- 13 kbps
22.8 kbps when error correction coding added

Full rate Data (TCH) - 9.6 kbps
22.8 kbps when error correction coding added

Half rate speech (TCH)- 6.5 kbps
11.4 kbps when error correction coding added

Half rate data (TCH)- 4.8 kbps
11.4 kbps when error correction coding added

(BCH) (CCCH) (DCCH)

4.4 GSM SYSTEM

A GSM system is basically designed as a combination of three major subsystems: the network subsystem, the radio subsystem, and the operation support subsystem. In order to ensure that network operators will have several sources of cellular infrastructure equipment, GSM decided to specify not only the air interface, but also the main interfaces that identify different parts. There are three dominant interfaces, namely, an interface between MSC and the base Transceiver Station (BTS), and an Um interface between the BTS and MS.

4.4.1 GSM Network Architecture

Every telephone network needs a well-designed structure in order to route incoming call to the correct exchange and finally to the called subscriber. In a mobile network, this structure is of great importance because of the mobility of all its subscribers. In the GSM system, the network is divided into the following partitioned areas:

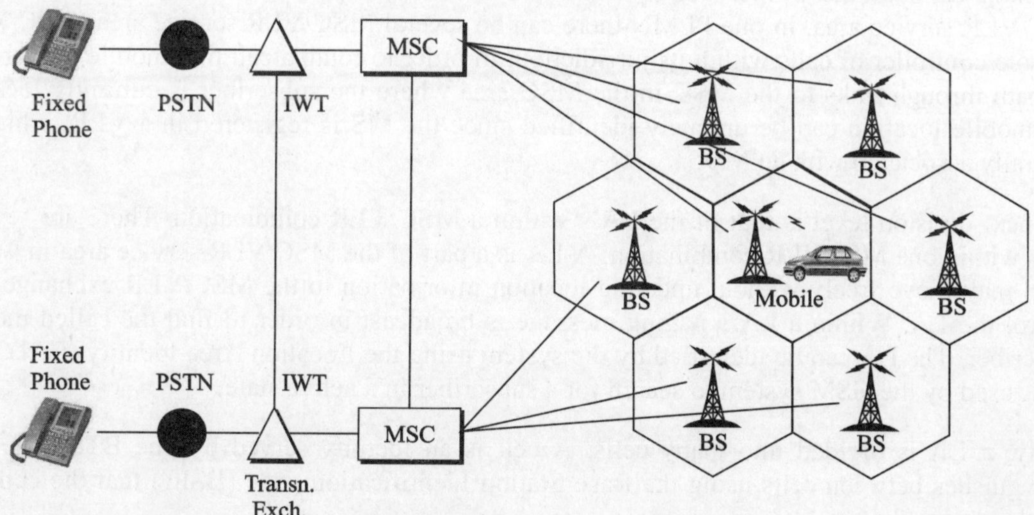

Fig. 4.7: GSM General Architecture

GSM service area; PLMN service area; MSC service area; Location area and Cells.

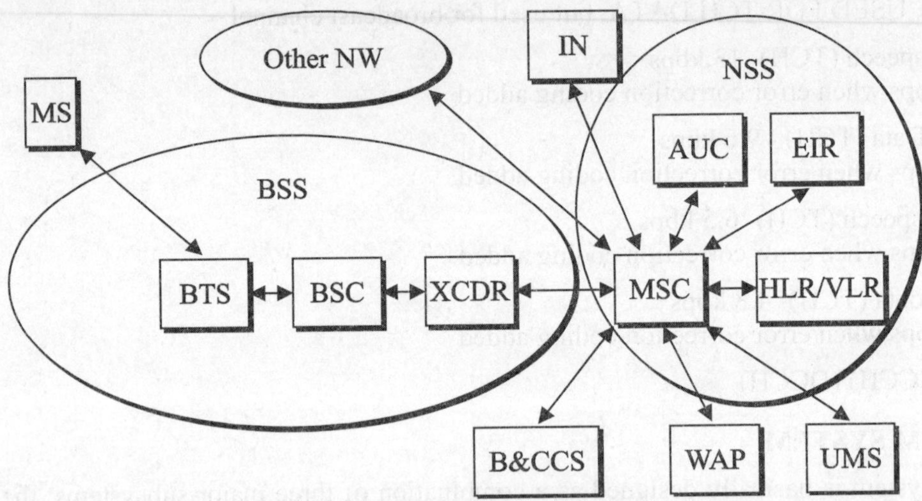

Fig. 4.8: GSM Network Diagram

The GSM service is the total area served by the combination of all member countries where a mobile can be serviced. The next level is the PLMN service area. There can be several within a country, based on its size. The links between a GSM/PLMN network and other PSTN, ISDN, or PLMN network will be on the level of international or national transit exchange. All incoming calls for a GSM/PLMN network will be routed to a gateway MSC. A gateway MSC works as an incoming transit exchange for the GSM/PLMN. In a GSM/PLMN network, all mobile-terminated calls will be routed to a gateway MSC. Call connections between PLMNs, or to fixed networks, must be routed through certain designated MSCs called a gateway MSC. The gateway MSC contains the interworking functions to make these connections. They also route incoming calls to the proper MSC within the network. The next level of division is the MSC/VLR service area. In one PLMN there can be several MSC/VLR service area. MSC/VLR is a role controller of calls within its jurisdiction. In order to route a call to a mobile subscriber, the path through links to the MSC in the MSC area where the subscriber is currently located. The mobile location can be uniquely identified since the MS is registered in a VLR, which is generally associated with an MSC.

The next division level is that of the LA's within a MSC/VLR combination. There are several LA's within one MSc/VLR combination. A LA is a part of the MSC/VLR service area in which a MS may move freely without updating location information to the MSC/VLR exchange that control the LA. Within a LA a paging message is broadcast in order to find the called mobile subscriber. The LA can be identified by the system using the Location Area Identity (LAI). The LA is used by the GSM system to search for a subscriber in a active state.

Lastly, a LA is divided into many cells. A cell is an identity served by one BTS. The MS distinguishes between cells using the Base Station Identification code (BSIC) that the cell site broadcast over the air.

Mobile Station

The MS includes radio equipment and the man machine interface (MMI) that a subscribe needs in order to access the services provided by the GSM PLMN. MS can be installed in Vehicles or can be portable or handheld stations. The MS may include provisions for data communication as well as voice. A mobile transmits and receives message to and from the GSM system over the air interface to establish and continue connections through the system.

Different type of MSs can provide different type of data interfaces. To provide a common model for describing these different MS configuration, "reference configuration" for MS, similar to those defined for ISDN land stations, has been defined.

Each MS is identified by an IMEI that is permanently stored in the mobile unit. Upon request, the MS sends this number over the signaling channel to the MSC. The IMEI can be used to identify mobile units that are reported stolen or operating incorrectly.

Just as the IMEI identities the mobile equipment, other numbers are used to identity the mobile subscriber. Different subscriber identities are used in different phases of call setup. The Mobile Subscriber ISDN Number (MSISDN) is the number that the calling party dials in order to reach the subscriber. It is used by the land network to route calls toward an appropriate MSC. The international mobile subscribe identity (IMSI) is the primary function of the subscriber within the mobile network and is permanently assigned to him. The GSM system can also assign a Temporary Mobile Subscriber Identity (TMSI) to identity a mobile. This number can be periodically changed by the system and protect the subscriber from being identified by those attempting to monitor the radio channel.

Functions of MS

The primary functions of MS are to transmit and receive voice and data over the air interface of the GSM system. MS performs the signal processing function of digitizing, encoding, error protecting, encrypting, and modulating the transmitted signals. It also performs the inverse functions on the received signals from the BS.

In order to transmit voice and data signals, the mobile must be in synchronization with the system so that the messages are the transmitted and received by the mobile at the correct instant. To achieve this, the MS automatically tunes and synchronizes to the frequency and TDMA timeslot specified by the BSC. This message is received over a dedicated timeslot several times within a multiframe period of 51 frames. We shall discuss the details of this in the next chapter. The exact synchronization will also include adjusting the timing advance to compensate for varying distance of the mobile from the BTS.

The MS monitors the power level and signal quality, determined by the BER for known receiver bit sequences (synchronization sequence), from both its current BTS and up to six surrounding BTSs. This data is received on the downlink broadcast control channel. The MS determines and send to the current BTS a list of the six best-received BTS signals. The measurement results from MS on downlink quality and surrounding BTS signal levels are sent to BSC and processed within the BSC. The system then uses this list for best cell handover decisions.

MS keeps the GSM network informed of its location during both national and international roaming, even when it is inactive. This enables the System to page in its present LA.

The MS includes an equalizer that compensates for multi-path distortion on the received signal. This reduces inter-symbol interface that would otherwise degrade the BER.

Finally, the MS can store and display short received alphanumeric messages on the liquid crystal display (LCD) that is used to show call dialing and status information. These messages are limited to 160 characters in length.

Power Levels

These are five different categories of mobile telephone units specified by the European GSM system: 20W, 8W, 5W, 2W, and 0.8W. These correspond to 43-dBm, 39-dBm, 37-dBm, 33-dBm, and 29-dBm power levels. The 20-W and 8-W units (peak power) are either for vehicle-mounted or portable station use.

The MS power is adjustable in 2-dB steps from its nominal value down to 20mW (13 dBm). This is done automatically under remote control from the BTS, which monitors the received power and adjusts the MS transmitter to the minimum power setting necessary for reliable transmission.

SIM Card

As described in the first chapter, GSM subscribers are provided with a SIM card with its unique identification at the very beginning of the service. By divorcing the subscriber ID from the equipment ID, the subscriber may never own the GSM mobile equipment set. The subscriber is identified in the system when he inserts the SIM card in the mobile equipment. This provides an enormous amount of flexibility to the subscribers since they can now use any GSM-specified mobile equipment. Thus with a SIM card the idea of "Personalize" the equipment currently in use and the respective information used by the network (location information) needs to be updated. The smart card SIM is portable between Mobile Equipment (ME) units. The user only needs to take his smart card on a trip. He can then rent a ME unit at the destination, even in another country, and insert his own SIM. Any calls he makes will be charged to his home GSM account. Also, the GSM system will be able to reach him at the ME unit he is currently using.

The SIM is a removable SC, the size of a credit card, and contains an integrated circuit chip with a microprocessor, random access memory (RAM), and read only memory (ROM). It is inserted in the MS unit by the subscriber when he or she wants to use the MS to make or receive a call. As stated, a SIM also comes in a modular from that can be mounted in the subscriber's equipment.

When a mobile subscriber wants to use the system, he or she mounts their SIM card and provide their Personal Identification Number (PIN), which is compared with a PIN stored within the SIM. If the user enters three incorrect PIN codes, the SIM is disabled. The PIN can also be permanently bypassed by the service provider if requested by the subscriber. Disabling the PIN code simplifies the call setup but reduces the protection of the user's account in the event of a stolen SIM.

International Mobile Subscriber Identity

An IMSI is assigned to each authorized GSM user. It consists of a mobile country code (MSC), mobile network code (MNC), and a PLMN unique mobile subscriber identification number (MSIN). The IMSI is not hardware-specific. Instead, it is maintained on a SC by an authorized subscriber and is the only absolute identity that a subscriber has within the GSM system. The IMSI consists of the MCC followed by the NMSI and shall not exceed 15 digits.

Temporary Mobile Subscriber Identity

A TMSI is a MSC-VLR specific alias that is designed to maintain user confidentiality. It is assigned only after successful subscriber authentication. The correlation of a TMSI to an IMSI only occurs during a mobile subscriber's initial transaction with an MSC (for example, location updating). Under certain condition (such as traffic system disruption and malfunctioning of the system), the MSC can direct individual TMSIs to provide the MSC with their IMSI.

Mobile Station ISDN Number

The MS international number must be dialed after the international prefix in order to obtain a mobile subscriber in another country. The MSISDN numbers is composed of the country code (CC) followed by the National Significant Number (N(S)N), which shall not exceed 15 digits.

The Mobile Station Roaming Number (MSRN)

The MSRN is allocated on temporary basis when the MS roams into another numbering area. The MSRN number is used by the HLR for rerouting calls to the MS. It is assigned upon demand by the HLR on a per-call basis. The MSRN for PSTN/ISDN routing shall have the same structure as international ISDN numbers in the area in which the MSRN is allocated. The HLR knows in what MSC/VLR service area the subscriber is located. At the reception of the MSRN, HLR sends it to the GMSC, which can now route the call to the MSC/VLR exchange where the called subscriber is currently registered.

International Mobile Equipment Identity

The IMEI is the unique identity of the equipment used by a subscriber by each PLMN and is used to determine authorized (white), unauthorized (black), and malfunctioning (gray) GSM hardware. In conjunction with the IMSI, it is used to ensure that only authorized usera are granted access to the system. An IMEI is never sent in cipher mode by MS.

Base Station System

The BSS is a set of BS equipment (such as transceivers and controllers) that is in view by the MSC through a single A interface as being the entity responsible for communicating with MSs in a certain area. The radio equipment of a BSS may be composed of one or more cells. A BSS may consist of one or more BS. The interface between BSC and BTS is designed as an A-bis interface. The BSS includes two types of machines: the BTS in contact with the MSs through the radio interface and the BSC, the latter being in contact with the MSC. The function split is basically between transmission equipment, the BTS, and managing equipment at the BSC. A BTS compares radio transmission and reception devices, up to and including the antennas, and also all the signal processing specific to the radio interface. A single transceiver within BTS supports eight basic radio channels of the same TDM frame. A BSC is a network component in the PLMN that function for control of one or more BTS. It is a functional entity that handles common control functions within a BTS.

A BTS is a network component that serves one cell and is controlled by a BSC. BTS is typically able to handle three to five radio carries, carrying between 24 and 40 simultaneous communication. Reducing the BTS volume is important to keeping down the cost of the cell sites.

An important component of the BSS that is considered in the GSM architecture as a part of the BTS is the Transcoder/Rate Adapter Unit (TRAU). The TRAU is the equipment in which coding and decoding is carried out as well as rate adoption in case of data. Although the specifications consider the TRAU as a subpart of the BTS, it can be sited away from the BTS (at MSC), and even between the BSC and the MSC.

The interface between the MSC and the BSS is a standardized SS7 interface (A-interface) that, as stated before, is fully defined in the GSM recommendations. This allows the system operator to purchase switching equipment from one supplier and radio equipment and the controller from another. The interface between the BSC and a remote BTS likewise is a standard the A-bis. In splitting the BSS functions between BTS and BSC, the main principle was that only such functions that had to reside close to the radio transmitters/receivers should be placed in BTS. This will also help reduce the complexity of the BTS.

Functions of BTS

As stated, the primary responsibility of the BTS is to transmit and receive radio signals from a mobile unit over an air interface. To perform this function completely, the signals are encoded,

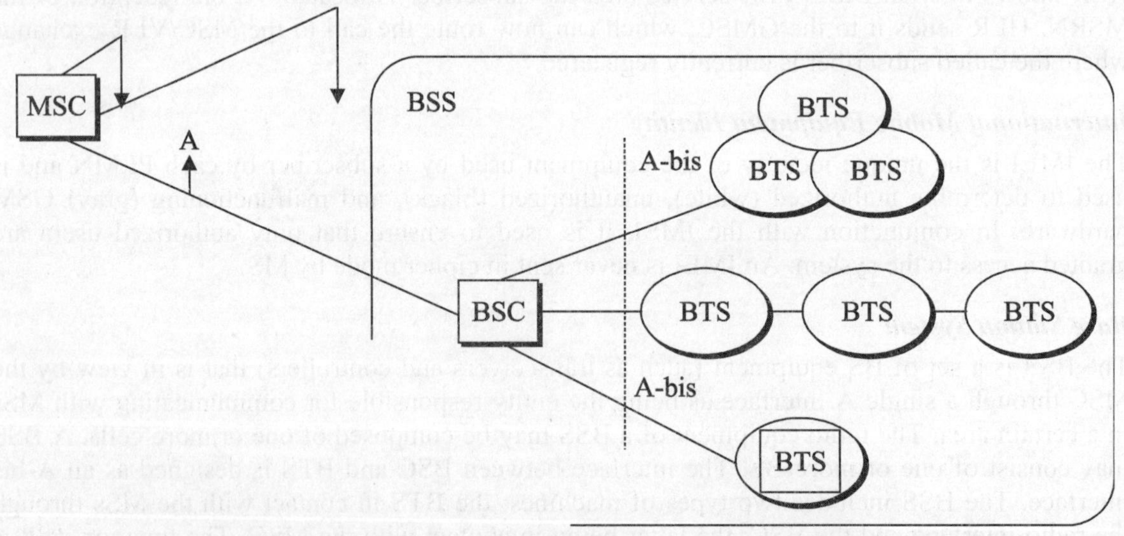

MSC: Mobile Switching Centre BSS: Base Station System
BSC: Base Station Controller BTS: Base Transceiver Station

Fig. 4.9: BSS Block Schematic

encrypted, multiplexed, modulated, and then fed to the antenna system at the cell site. Transcoding to bring 13-kbps speech to a standard data rate of 16 kbps and then combining four of these signals to 64 kbps is essentially a part of BTS, though, it can be done at BSC or at MSC. The voice communication can be either at a full or half rate over logical speech channel. In order to keep the mobile synchronized, BTS transmits frequency and time synchronization signals over frequency correction channel (FCCH and BCCH logical channels. The received signal from the mobile is decoded, decrypted, and equalized for channel impairments.

Random access detection is made by BTS, which then sends the message to BSC. The channel subsequent assignment is made by BSC. Timing advance is determined by BTS. BTS signals the mobile for proper timing adjustment. Uplink radio channel measurement corresponding to the downlink measurements made by MS has to be made by BTS.

BTS-BSC Configurations

There are several BTS-BSC configurations: single site; single cell; single site; multicell; and multisite, multicell. These configurations are chosen based on the rular or urban application. These configurations make the GSM system economical since the operation has options to adapt the best layout based on the traffic requirement. Thus, in some sense, system optimization is possible by the proper choice of the configuration. These include omni directional rural configuration where the BSC and BTS are on the same site; chain and multidrop loop configuration in which several BTSs are controlled by a single remote BSC with a chain or ring connection topology; rural star configuration in which several BTSs are connected by individual lines to the same BSC; and sectorized urban configuration in which three BTSs share the same site amd are controlled by either a collocated or remote BSC.

In rural areas, most BSs are installed to provide maximum coverage rather then maximum capacity.

Transcoder

Depending on the relative costs of a transmission plant for a particular cellular operator, there may be some benefit, for larger cells and certain network topologies, in having the transcoder either at the BTS, BSC or MSC location. If the transcoder is located at MSC, they are still considered functionally a part of the BSS. This approach allows for the maximum of flexibility and innovation in optimizing the transmission between MSC and BTS.

The transcoder is the device that takes 13-Kbps speech or 3.6/6/12-Kbps data multiplexes and four of them to convert into standard 64-Kbps data. First, the 13 Kbps or the data at 3.6/6/12 Kbps are brought up to the level of 16 Kpbs by inserting additional synchronizing data to make up the difference between a 13-Kbps speech or lower rate data, and then four of them are combined in the transcoder to provide 64 Kpbs channel within the BSS. Four traffic channel can then be multiplexed on one 64-Kpbs circuit. Thus, the TRAU output data rate is 64 Kpbs. Then, up to 30 such 64-Kpbs channels are multiplexed onto a 2.048 Mpbs if a CEPT1 channel is provided on the A-bis interface. This channel can carry up to 120-(16x 120) traffic and control signals. Since the data rate to the PSTN is normally at 2 Mbps, which is the result of combining 30-Kbps by 64-Kbps channels, or 120- Kbps by 16-Kpbs channels.

Base Station Controller

The BSC, as discussed, is connected to the MSC on one side and to the BTS on the other. The BSC performs the Radio Resource (RR) management for the cells under its control. It assigns and release frequencies and timeslots for all MSs in its own area. The BSC performs the intercell handover for MSs moving between BTS in its control. It also reallocates frequencies to the BTSs in its area to meet locally heavy demands during peak hours or on special events. The BSC controls the power transmission of both BSSs and MSs in its area. The minimum power level for a mobile unit is broadcast over the BCCH. The BSC provides the time and frequency synchronization reference signals broadcast by its BTSs. The BSC also measures the time delay of received MS signals relative to the BTS clock. If the received MS signal is not centered in its assigned timeslot at the BTS, The BSC can direct the BTS to notify the MS to advance the timing such that proper synchronization takes place. The functions of BSC are as follows.

The BSC may also perform traffic concentration to reduce the number of transmission lines from the BSC to its BTSs, as discussed in the last section.

Switching Subsystems: Mobile Switching Center and Gateway Switching Center

The network and the switching subsystem together include the main switching functions of GSM as well as the databases needed for subscriber data and mobility management (VLR). The main role of the MSC is to manage the communications between the GSM users and other telecommunication network users. The basic switching function of performed by the MSC, whose main function is to coordinate setting up calls to and from GSM users. The MSC has interface with the BSS on one side (through which MSC VLR is in contact with GSM users) and the external networks on the other (ISDN/PSTN/PSPDN). The main difference between a MSC and an exchange in a fixed network is that the MSC has to take into account the impact of the allocation of RRs and the mobile nature of the subscribers and has to perform, in addition, at least, activities required for the location registration and handover.

The MSC is a telephony switch that performs all the switching functions for MSs located in a geographical area as the MSC area. The MSC must also handle different types of numbers and identities related to the same MS and contained in different registers: IMSI, TMSI, ISDN number, and MSRN. In general identities are used in the interface between the MSC and the MS, while numbers are used in the fixed part of the network, such as, for routing.

Functions of MSC

As stated, the main function of the MSC is to coordinate the set up of calls between GSM mobile and PSTN users. Specifically, it performs functions such as paging, resource allocation, location registration, and encryption.

Specifically, the call-handling function of paging is controlled by MSC. MSC coordinates the set up of call to and from all GSM subscribers operating in its areas. The dynamics allocation of access resources is done in coordination with the BSS. More specifically, the MSC decides when and which types of channels should be assigned to which MS. The channel identity and related radio parameters are the responsibility of the BSS, The MSC provides the control of interworking with different networks. It is transparent for the subscriber authentication procedure. The MSC supervises the connection transfer between different BSSs for MSs, with an active call, moving from one call to another. This is ensured if the two BSSs are connected to the same MSC but also when they are not. In this latter case the procedure is more complex, since more then one MSC in involved. The MSC performs billing on calls for all subscribers based in its areas. When the subscriber is roaming elsewhere, the MSC obtains data for the call billing from the visited MSC. Encryption parameters transfers from VLR to BSS to facilitate ciphering on the radio interface are done by MSC. The exchange of signaling information on the various interface toward the other network elements and the management of the interface themselves are all controlled by the MSC. Finally, the MSC serves as a SMS gateway to forward SMS messages from Short Message Service Centers (SMSC) to the subscribers and from the subscribers to the SMSCs. It thus acts as a message mailbox and delivery system.

Visiting Location Register

The VLR is collocated with an MSC. A MS roaming in an MSC area is controlled by the VLR responsible for that area. When a MS appears in a LA, it starts a registration procedure. The MSC for that area notices this registration and transfers to the VLR the identify of the LA where the MS is situated. A VLR may be in charge of one or several MSC LA's. The VLR constitutes the databases that support the MSC in the storage and retrieval of the data of subscribers present in its area. When an MS enters the MSC area borders, it signals its arrival to the MSC that stores its identify in the VLR. The information necessary to manage the MS is contained in the HLR and is transferred to the VLR so that they can be easily retrieved if so required.

Data Stored in VLR

The data contained in the VLR and in the HLR are more or less the same. Nevertheless the data are present in the VLR only as long as the MS is registered in the area related to that VLR. Data associated with the movement of mobile are IMSI, MSISDN, MSRN, and TMSI. The terms permanent and temporary, in this case, are meaningful only during that time interval. Some data are mandatory, others are optional.

Home Location Register

The HLR is a database that permanently stores data related to a given set of subscribers. The HLR is the reference database for subscriber parameters. Various identification numbers and addresses as well as authentication parameters, services subscribed, and special routing information are stored. Current subscriber status including a subscriber's temporary roaming number and associated VLR if the mobile is roaming, are maintained.

The HLR provides data needed to route calls to all MS-SIMs home based in its MSC area, even when they are roaming out of area or in other GSM networks. The HLR provides the current location data needed to support searching for and paging the MS-SIM for incoming calls, wherever the MS-SIM may be. The HLR is responsible for storage and provision of SIM authentication and encryption parameters needed by the MSC where the MS-SIM is operating. It obtains these parameters from the AUC.

The HLR maintains record of which supplementary service each user has subscribed to and provides permission control in granting services. The HLR stores the identification of SMS gateways that have messages for the subscriber under the SMS until they can be transmitted to the subscriber and receipt is knowledge.

Some data are mandatory, other data are optional. Both the HLR and the VLR can be implemented in the same equipment in an MSC (collocated). A PLMN may contain one or several HLRs.

Authentication Center

The AUC stores information that is necessary to protect communication through the air interface against intrusions, to which the mobile is vulnerable. The legitimacy of the subscriber is established through authentication and ciphering, which protects the user information against unwanted disclosure. Authentication information and ciphering keys are stored in a database within the AUC, which protects the user information against unwanted disclosure and access.

In the authentication procedure, the key Ki is never transmitted to the mobile over the air path, only a random number is sent. In order to gain access to the system, the mobile must provide the correct Signed Response (SRES) in answer to a random number (RAND) generated by AUC.

Also, Ki and the cipher key Kc are never transmitted across the air interface between the BTS and the MS. Only the random challenge and the calculated response are transmitted. Thus, the value of Ki and Kc are kept secure. The cipher key, on the other hand, is transmitted on the SS7 link between the home HLR/AUC and the visited MSC, which is a point of potential vulnerability. On the other hand, the random number and cipher key is supposed to change with each phone call, so finding them on one call will not benefit using them on the next call.

The HLR is also responsible for the "authentication" of the subscriber each time he makes or receives a call. The AUC, which actually performs this function, is a separate GSM entity that will often be physically included with the HLR. Being separate, it will use separate processing equipment for the AUC database functions.

Equipment Identify Register

EIR is a database that stores the IMEI numbers for all registered ME units. The IMEI uniquely identifies all registered ME. There is generally one EIR per PLMN. It interfaces to the various HLR in the PLMN. The EIR keeps track of all ME units in the PLMN. It maintains various lists of message. The database stores the ME identification and has nothing do with subscriber who is receiving or originating call. There are three classes of ME that are stored in the database, and each group has different characteristics.

- *White List*— contains those IMEIs that are known to have been assigned to valid MS's. This is the category of genuine equipment.
- *Black List*— contains IMEIs of mobiles that have been reported stolen.
- *Gray List*— contains IMEIs of mobiles that have problems (for example, faulty software, wrong make of the equipment). This list contains all MEs with faults not important enough for barring.

Interworking Function

The IWF, which in essence is a part of MSC, provides the subscriber with access to data rate and protocol conversion facilities so that data can be transmitted between GSM Data Terminal Equipment (DTE) and a land-line DTE.

GSM provides a wide range of data services to its subscribers. The GSM system interfaces with the various forms of public and private data networks currently available. It is the job of the IWF to provide this interfacing capability. Networks to which IWF presently provides interface are as follows.

- PSTN;
- ISDN;
- Circuit-switched public data networks (CSPDN);
- Packet-switched public data networks (PSPDN).

The IWF, which in essence is a part of MSC, provides the subscriber with access to data rate and protocol conversion facilities so that data can be transmitted between GSM Data Terminal Equipment (DTE) and a land-line DTE. It will also allocate a modem from its "modem bank" when required. This will be the case when the GSM DE exchanges data with a land DE connected via an analog modem, through a narrowband PSTN circuit. The IWF also provides direct-connect interfaces for customer-provided equipment such as X.25 Pads. In order to achieve this interconnection, the IWF has to convert protocols between the GSM PLMN and the connecting network. Different protocol conversions may be required for signaling and traffic messages. This may include data rate adaptation and the addition of signaling bits reformatting. Additionally, as previously stated, this may also require an audio modem for transmission through a narrowband telephone link. Figure 4.10 provides the setup for IWF and its interface configuration with PSTN and ISDN users. AGSM interface with modems of different rates for PSTN connection is shown in table.

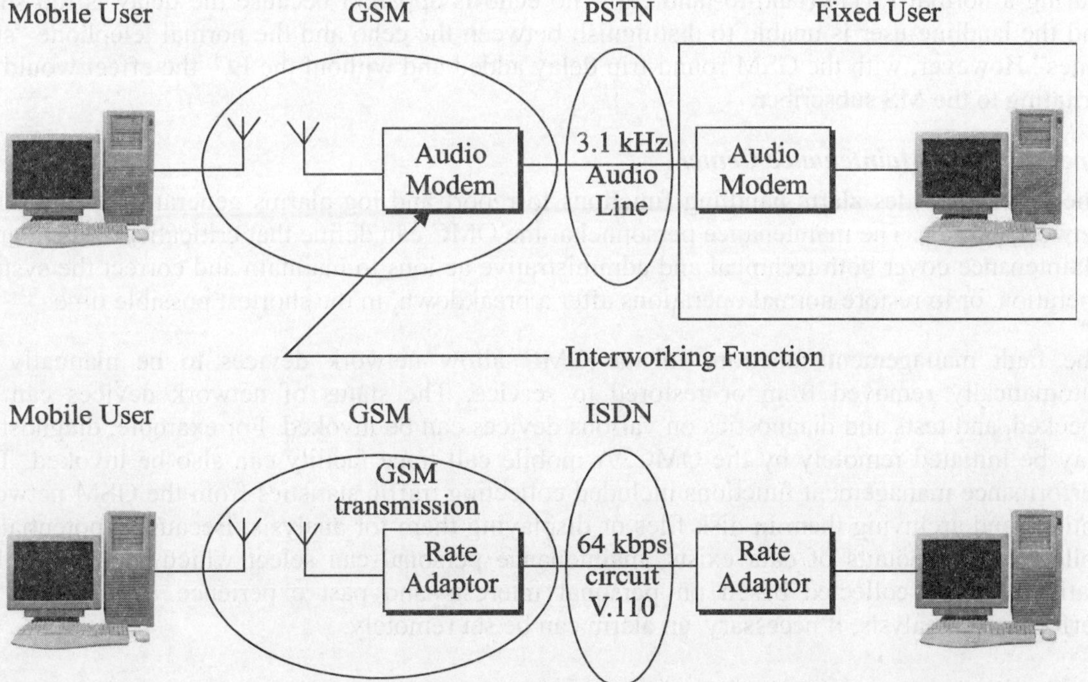

Fig. 4.10: Inter Working Function-GSM, PSTN, ISDN

Table 4.2: Modem Types for a PSTN Interface

Modem Type	*Data Rate (Bps)*	*Transmission Mode*
V.21	300	Asynchronous
V.22	1200	Asynchronous/Synchronous
V.22bis	2400	Synchronous
V.23	1200/75	Asynchronous
V.26ter	2400	Synchronous
V.32	4800/9600	Synchronous

Echo Canceler

EC is used on the PSTN side of the MSC for all voice circuits. The EC is required at the MSC PSTN interface to reduce the effect of GSM delay when the mobile is connected to the PSTN circuit. The total round-trip delay introduced by the GSM system, which is the result of speech encoding, decoding and signal processing, is of the order of 180 ms. Normally this delay would not be an annoying factor to the mobile, except when communicating to PSTN as it requires a two-wire to four-wire hybrid transformer in the circuit. This hybrid is required at the local switching office because the standard local loop is a two-wire circuit. Due to the presence of this hybrid, some of the energy at its four-wire receive side from the mobile is coupled to the four-wire transmit side and thus retransmitted to the mobile. This causes the echo, which does not effect the land subscriber but is an annoying factor to the mobile. The standard EC cancels about 70 ms of delay.

During a normal PSTN (land-to-land call), no echo is apparent because the delay is too short and the landline user is unable to distinguish between the echo and the normal telephone "side tones" However, with the GSM round-trip delay added and without the EC, the effect would be irritating to the MS subscriber.

Operation and Maintenance Center

The OMC provides alarm-handling functions to report and log alarms generated by the other network entities. The maintenance personnel at the OMC can define that criticality of the alarm. Maintenance cover both technical and administrative actions to maintain and correct the system operation, or to restore normal operations after a breakdown, in the shortest possible time.

The fault management functions of the OMC allow network devices to be manually or automatically removed from or restored to service. The status of network devices can be checked, and tests and diagnostics on various devices can be invoked. For example, diagnostics may be initiated remotely by the OMC. A mobile call trace facility can also be invoked. The performance management functions included collecting traffic statistics from the GSM network entities and archiving them in disk files or displaying them for analysis. Because a potential to collect large amounts of data exists, maintenance personal can select which of the detailed statistics to be collected based on personal interests and past experience. As a result of performance analysis, if necessary, an alarm can be set remotely.

The OMC provides system change control for the software revisions and configuration data bases in the network entities or uploaded to the OMC. The OMC also keeps track of the different software versions running on different subsystem of the GSM.

4.4.2 Call Processing

In this we discuss the call processing aspect and look into specifics case of a mobile originated (MO) call and a mobile terminated (MT) call and also RF channel.

4.4.3 RF Channel Overview

RF channel play important role in call processing case. These are basically three types of RF control channel.

1. *Broadcast control channel*— The broadcast channels are points to multipoint channel, which are defined only for down-link direction (BTS to mobile station). They are divided into:

   BCCH (Broad cast control channel— BCCH acts as a beacon. It informs the mobile about system configuration parameters (e.g. LAI, CELLDENTY, NEIGHBOURING Cell identity). Using this information MS choose the best cell to attach to.

   BCCH is always transmitted on full power and it is never frequency hopped.

   FCCHC frequency correction channel— MS must tune to FCCH to listen to BCCH. FCCH transmits a constant frequency shift of the radio carrier that is used by the MS for frequency correction.

   SCH (synchronization channel)— SCH is used to synchronize the MS in time. SCH carries TDMA frame number and BSIC (Base Station Identity Code)

2. *Common control channels*— Common control channels are specified as point to multi-point, which operate only in one direction either in up-link or down-link direction.

   PCH (Paging Channel)— PCH is used in down-link direction for sending paging message to MS whenever there is incoming call.

   RACH (Random Access Channel)— RACH is used by the MS to request allocation of a specific dedicated control channel (SDCCH) either in response to a paging message or for call origination/registration from the MS. this, is an up-link channel and operate in point to point mode.

   AGCH (Access Grant Channel)— AGCH is a logical control channel which is used to allocated a specific dedicated control channel (SDCCH) to MS when MS request for a channel over RACH. AGCH is used in downlink direction.

3. *Dedicated Control Channel*— dedicated control channel are full duplex, point to point channel. They are used for signalling between the BTS and certain MS. They are divided into: -

i) *SACCH (Slow Associated Control Channel)*— the SACCH is a duplex channel, which is always allocated to TCH or SDCCH. The SACCH is used for

- Radio link supervision measurements.
- Power control.
- Timing advance information.

In 26 frame traffic multi-frame 13th frame (frame no 12) is used for SACCH.SACCH is used only for non-urgent procedures.

ii) *FACCH (Fast Associated Control Channel)*— FACCH is requested in case the requirement of signaling is urgent and signaling requirement can not be met by SACCH. This is the case when hand-over is required during conversation phase. During the call FACCH data is transmitted over allocated TCH instead of traffic data. This is marked by a flag known as stealing flag.

iii) *SDCCH (Stand Alone Dedicated Control Channel)*— The SDCCH is a duplex, point to point channel which is used for signaling in higher layer. It carries all the signaling between BTS & MS when no TCH is allocated to MS. The SDCCH is used for service request, location updates, subscriber authentication, ciphering, equipment validation and assignment of a TCH.

4.4.4 Mobile Originated (MO) Call

There are four distinct phase of a mobile originated call-

- Setup phase.
- Ringing phase.
- Conversation phase.
- Release phase.

Out of these phases the setup phase is the most important phase and includes authentication of the subscriber, Ciphering of data over radio interface, validation of mobile equipment, validation of subscriber data at VLR for requests service and assignment of a voice channel on A-interface by MSC. Whenever MS wants to initiate on outgoing call or want to send an SMS it requested for a channel to BSS over RACH. On receiving request from MS, BSS assigns a stand-alone dedicated control channel (SDCCH) to MS over access grant channel (AGCH). Once a SDCCH has been allocated to MS all the call set up information flow takes place over SDCCH.

A connection management (CM) entity initiates a CM Service Request message to the network. Network tries to establish an MM connections between the MS and the network and upon successful establishment of MM connection a CM Service Accept message is received by MS from the network. MS now sends a Call Set up Request to the network which contains the dialed digits (DD) of the called party. As the call setup message is received at the MSC/VLR certain check are performed at MSC/VLR like- whether the requested service is provisioned for the subscriber or not, whether the dialed digits are sufficient or not, any operator determined barring (ODB) does not allow call to proceed further etc. As these checks are performed at

MSC/VLR a Call Proceeding Message is sent from the network towards the MS. After all the checks are successfully passed MSC sends Assignment command to the BSS which contains a free voice channel on A-interface On getting this message BSS allocates a free TCH to the MS and informs the MS to attach to if MS on attaching to this TCH informs the BSS about it. On receiving a response from the BSS, MSC switches the speech path toward the calling MS. Thus at the end of Assignment the speech path is through from MS to MSC. It is important to note that at this stage mobile has not connected user connection as yet. MS at this stage does not listen anything.

After assignment MSC sends a network set-up message to the PSTN requesting that a call be set up. Included in the message are the MS dialed digits (DD) and details specifying which trunk should be used for the call. The PSTN may involve several switching exchanges before finally reaching the final local exchange responsible for applying the ringing tone to the destination phone. The local exchange will generate the ringing tone oyer the trunk, or series of trunk (if several intermediate switching exchange are involved), to the MSC. At this point in time MS will hear ringing tone. The PSTN notifies the MSC with a network-alerting message when this event occurs. MSC informs the MS that the destination number is being alerted. It is important to note that this is primarily a status message to the MS. The MS hears the ringing tone from the destination local exchange through the established voice path.

When the destination party goes off hook, PSTN informs the MSC of this event. At this point, MS is connected to the destination party and billing is started. MSC informs the MS that connection has been established and MS acknowledges the receipts of the connect message.

Under normal condition, the termination of a call is MS initiated or network initiated. In this scenario, we have assumed that MS initiates the release of the call by pressing "end" button and MS send a disconnect message to the MSC. The PSTN party is notified of the termination of the call by a release message from the MSC. The end- to- end connection is terminated. When MSC is left with no side task (e.g. charging indication etc.) to complete a release message is sent to the MS. MS acknowledges with a release complete message. All the resources between MSC and the MS are released completely.

4.4.5 Mobile Terminated (MT) Call

The different phases of a mobile terminated call are

- Routing analysis
- Paging.
- Call setup.
- Call release.

The phases of mobile terminated (MT) call are similar to a mobile originated (MO) call except routing analysis and paging phase. Call to a mobile subscriber in a PLMN first comes to gateway MSC (GMSC). GMSC is the MSC, which is the capable of querying HLR for subscriber routing information. GMSC need not to be part of home PLMN, though it is normal practice to have GMSC as part of PLMN in commercially deployed networks.

GMSC opens a MAP (Mobile Application Part) dialogue towards HLR and Send / Routing / Info-Request (SRI request) specific service message is sent to HLR. SRI request contains MS1SDN of the subscriber. HLR based on location information of this subscriber in its database, opens a MAP dialogue towards VLR and sends Provide / Roaming / Number-request (PRN request)to the VLR. VLR responds to PRN request with PRN response message, which carries an MSRN (mobile subscriber roaming number), which can be used for routing toward visiting MSC in the network. HLR returns MSRN to GMSC (MSC that queried HLR) in SRI response message. On getting MSRN the GMSC routes the call towards VMSC The purpose of this entire exercise is to locate where, the terminating mobile subscriber is.

The MSRN received at GMSC is in international format (Country Code + Area Code + subscriber number). Normally, based on the routing info at GMSC, the call may be routed out of the GMSC towards VMSC of the terminating subscriber, in which case appropriate signaling protocol (MF or ISUP) depending on the nature of connecting of GMSC with subsequent exchange along the route will apply. If at VMSC the terminating mobile subscriber is found to be free (idle), paging is initiated for terminating mobile subscriber. MSC uses the LAI provided by the VLR to determine which BSS's should page the MS. MSC transmit a message to each of these BSS requesting that a page be performed. Included in the message is the TMSI of the MS. Each of the BSS's broadcasts the TMSI of the mobile in a page message on paging channel (PCH).

When MS detects its TMSI broadcast on the paging channel, it responds with a channel request message over Random Access Channel (RACH). Once BSS receives a channel request message, it allocates a stand-alone Dedicated Control Channel (SDCCH) and forwards this channel assignment information to the MS over Access Grant Channel (AGCH). It is over this SDCCH that the MS communicates with the BSS and MSC until a traffic channel assigned to the MS. MS transmits paging response message to the BSS over the SDCCH. Included in this message is MS TMSI and LAI. BSS forwards this paging response message to the MSC. Now Authentication and Ciphering phases are performed to check the authenticity of MS and encrypt data over radio interface.

On the network side after paging is initiated, while waiting for paging response, a defensive timer called, “Early ACM” timer is run at MSC to avoid network timeouts. On successfully getting paging response, a setup message is constructed to be sent towards terminating MS. In case paging fails due to authentication failure or when the subscriber is out of radio-coverage, the call is cleared.

In case CLIP is not subscribed by the terminating mobile subscriber, calling number is not included in set-up message. In case CLIP is subscribed and PI value in calling number parameter indicates “presentation allowed” the number is included in the set-up message. In case CLIP is subscribed but PI received in calling number parameter indicates “presentation restricted” then number is included only if CLIRO is also subscribed to.

MS on receiving the set-up message performs compatibility Checking before responding to the set-up message - it is possible that MS might be incompatible for certain types of call set-ups. Assuming that MS passes compatibility checking, it acknowledges the call setup with set-up confirm message. After getting set-up confirm message from the MS, MSC performs assignment phase (similar to one discussed in MO call) and a voice path is established from MSC to the MS. MS begins altering the user after it receives the traffic channel assignment. MS send alerting message to the MSC. MSC upon receiving the alerting indication from the MS, begins generating an audible ringing tone to the calling party and sends a network alerting via GMSC to the PSTN. Prior to this the calling party heard silence.

At this point in the call, MS is alerting the called party by generating on audible tone. One of the three events can occur-calling party hangs-up, mobile subscriber answers the phone, or the MSC times out waiting for the mobile subscriber to the answer the call. Since radio traffic channel is a valuable resource, GSM does not allow a MS to ring forever.

In the present scenario we have assumed that the mobile subscriber answers the phone. The MS in response to this action stops alerting and sends a connect message to the MSC. MSC removes the audible tone to the PSTN and connects the PSTN trunk to BSS trunk (terrestrial channel) and sends a connect message via GMSC to the PSTN. The caller and the called party now have a complete talk path. This event typically marks the beginning of the call for billing purposes. MSC sends a connect acknowledge message to the MS.

The release triggered by the landline user is done in similar way as the release triggered by mobile user. MSC receives a release message from the network to terminate end-to-end connection. PSTN stops billing the calling landline subscriber. MSC sends a disconnect message towards the MS and MS responds by a Release message. MSC release the connection to the PSTN and acknowledges by sending a Release Complete message to PSTN. Now the voice trunk between MSC and BSS is cleared, traffic channel (TCH) is released and the resources are completely released.

The mobile-to-mobile call scenario is a combination of phases encountered in mobile originated (MO) and mobile terminated (MT) call.

On receipt of the CM Service Request, the MSC optionally may invoke authentication of the mobile. Typically, an MSC is configured to authenticate a mobile whenever it performs an initial location update and every N transactions thereafter (every N calls). Next, the MSC initiates ciphering so that the voice and data sent over the air are encrypted. Since it is the BSS that performs the encryption and decryption, the MSC needs to pass the cypher key (Kc) to the BSS. The BSS then instructs the MS to start ciphering. The MS, of course, generates the Kc independently so that it is not passed over the air. Once the MS has started ciphering, it informs the BSS, which, in turn, informs the MSC.

Next, the MS sends a Setup message to the MSC. This includes further data about the call, including information such as the dialed number and the required bearer capability. Once the MSC has determined that it has received sufficient information to connect the call, it lets the MS know by sending a Call Proceeding message.

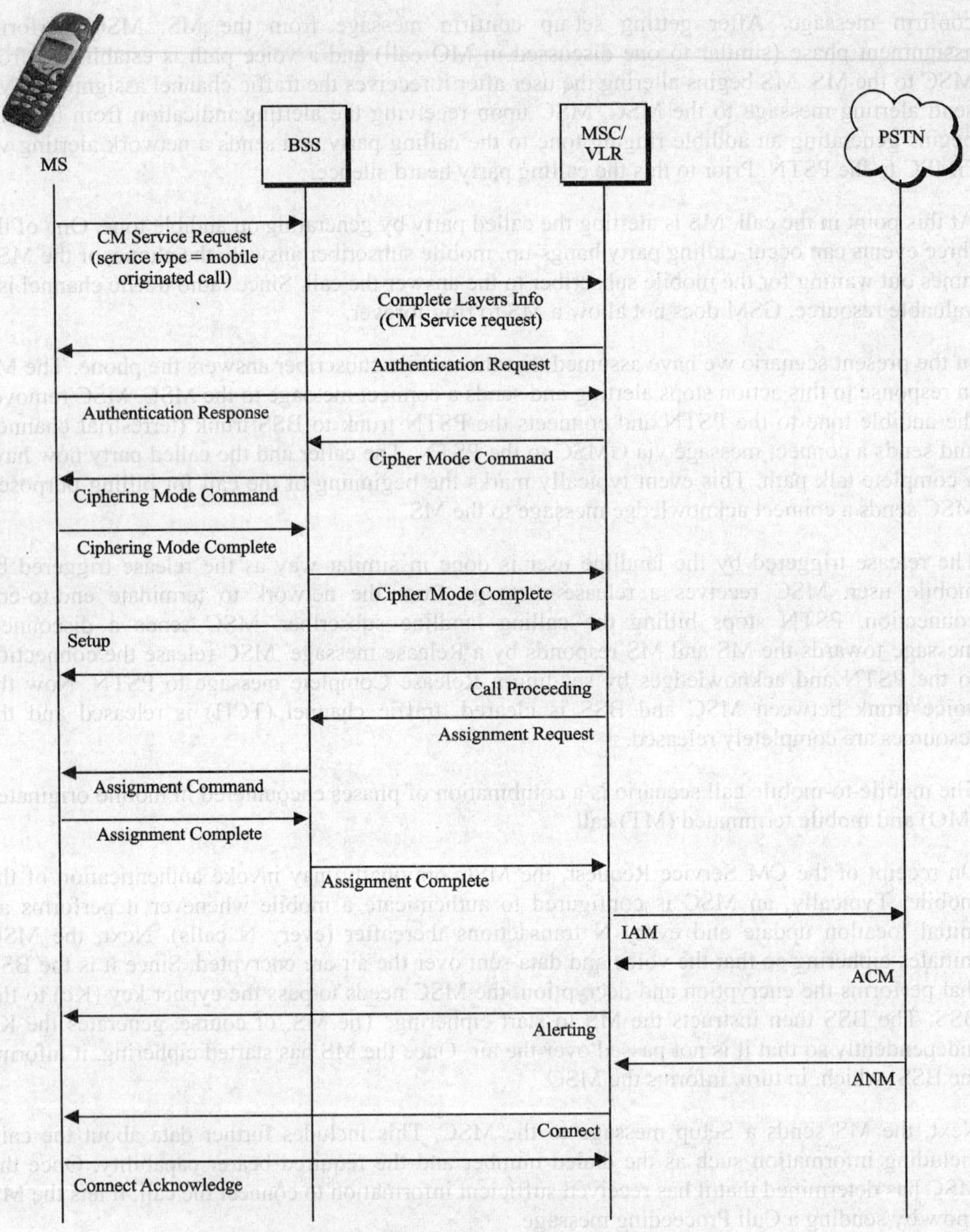

Fig. 4.11: Call Flow Diagram-Mobile to Landline

Next, using the Assignment Request message, the MSC requests the seizure of a circuit between the MSC and ESS. That circuit will be used to carry the voice to and from the MS. At this point, the BSS sends an Assignment Command message to the MS, instructing the MS to move from the SDCCH to a TCH. Further signaling between the MS and the network now will occur on the FACCH associated with the assigned TCH. The MS responds with an Assignment Complete message, indicating that it has moved to the assigned TCH. On receipt of this message, the BSS sends an Assignment Complete message to the MSC, which indicates that a voice path is now available from the MS through to the MSC.

On receipt of the Assignment Complete message from the BSS, the MSC initiates the call setup toward the PSTN. This starts with issuance of an Initial Address Message (lAM). A subsequent receipt of an Address Complete Message (ACM) From the destination end indicates that the destination phone is now ringing. The MSC informs the MS of this fact by sending an Alerting message. In addition, the ACM triggers a one-way path to be opened from the distinction PSTN switch through to the MS, and the ring back tone heard at the MS is actually being generated at the destination PSTN switch.

On answer at the called phone, an Answer Message (ANM) is returned. This leads the MSC to open a two-way path to the MS and also causes the MSC to send a Connect message to the MS. On receipt of 1, he Connect message, the MS responds with a Connect Acknowledge message. The two parties are now in conversation, and from a billing perspective, the clock is now ticking.

The MSRN is a number that appears to the PSTN as a dialable number. Thus it can be used to route a call through any intervening network between the GMSC and the visited MSCNLR. In fact, this is exactly what the GMSC does. It routes the call to the MSCNLR by sending an lAM, with the MSRN as the called-party number. On receipt of the lAM, the MSC/VLR recognizes the MSRN and knows the IMSI for which the MSRN was allocated. At this point, the MSRN can be returned to the pool for use with another call.

Next, the MSC requests the BSS to page the subscriber using the Paging Request message, which indicates the location area in which the subscriber should be paged. The BSS uses the PCB to page the MS.

4.5 LOCATION UPDATE

When an MS is first turned on, it must first "camp on" a suitable cell. This largely involves scanning the air interface to select a cell with a suitably strong received signal strength and then decoding the information broadcast by the BTS on the BCCH. Generally, the MS will camp on the cell with the strongest signal strength, provided that the cell belongs to the home Public Land Mobile Network (HPLMN) and provided that the cell is not barred. The MS then registers with the network, which involves a process known as location updating, as shown in Figure 4.10.

The sequence begins with a channel request issued by the MS on the RACH. This includes an establishment cause, such as location updating, voice-call establishment, and emergency-call establishment. In the example in Figure 4.12, the cause is location updating.

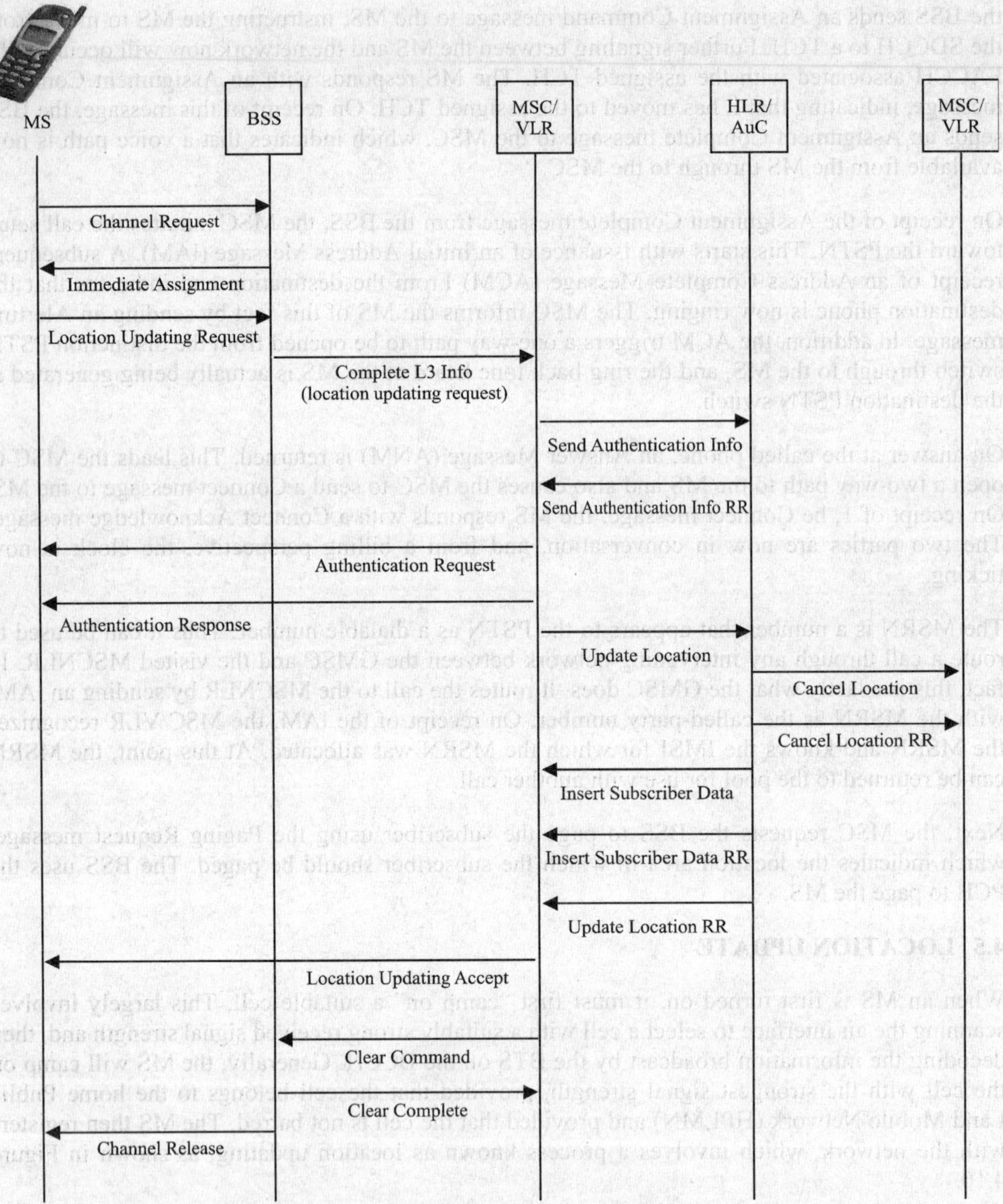

Fig. 4.12: GSM Location Update

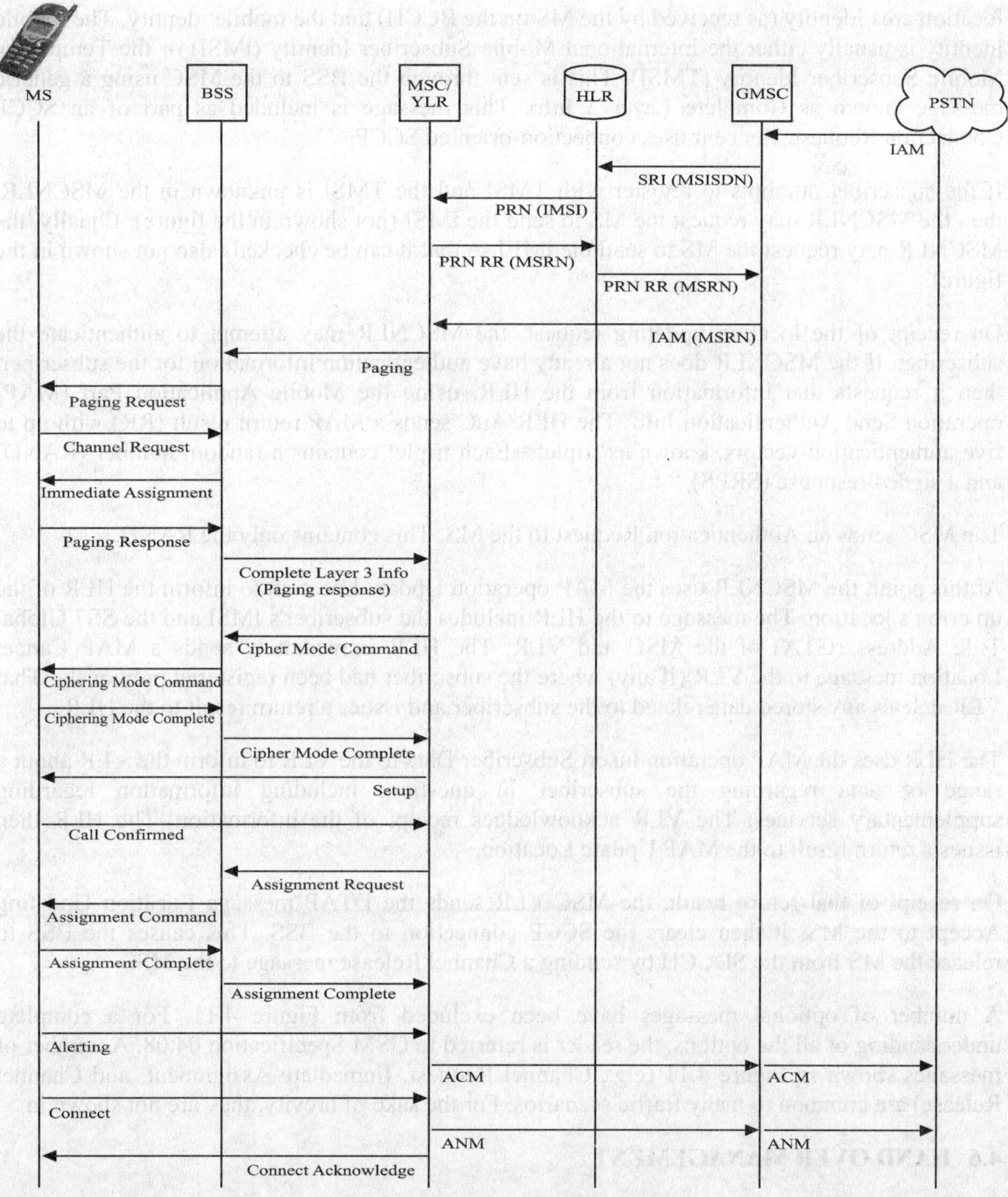

Fig. 4.13: Landline to Mobile Call

The BSS allocates an SDCCH for the MS to use. It instructs the MS to move to the SDCCH by sending an immediate assignment message on the AGCH. The MS then moves to the SDCCH and sends the location updating request. This contains a set of information including the location area identity (as received by the MS on the BCCH) and the mobile identity. The mobile identity is usually either the International Mobile Subscriber Identity (lMSI) or the Temporary Mobile Subscriber Identity (TMSI). This is sent through the BSS to the MSC using a generic message known as Complete Layer 3 Info. This message is included as part of an SCCP Connection Request. Hence it uses connection-oriented SCCP.

If the subscriber attempts to register with TMSI and the TMSI is unknown in the MSCNLR, then the MSCNLR may request the MS to send the IMSI (not shown in the figure). Equally, the MSCNLR may request the MS to send the IMEI so that it can be checked (also not shown in the figure).

On receipt of the location updating request, the MSCNLR may attempt to authenticate the subscriber. If the MSCNLR does not already have authentication information for the subscriber, then it requests that information from the HLR, using the Mobile Application Part (MAP) operation Send Authentication Info. The HLR/AuC sends a MAP return result (RR) with up to five authentication vectors, known as triplets. Each triplet contains a random number (RAND) and a signed response (SRES).

The MSC sends an Authentication Request to the MS. This contains only the RAND.

At this point, the MSCNLR uses the MAP operation Update Location to inform the HLR of the up crib r's location. The message to the HLR includes the subscriber's IMSI and the SS7 Global Title Address (GTA) of the MSC and VLR. The HLR immediately sends a MAP Cancel Location message to the VLR (if any) where the subscriber had been registered previously. That VLR deletes any stored data related to the subscriber and issues a return result to the HLR.

The HLR uses the MAP operation Insert Subscriber Data to the VLR to inform the VLR about a range of data regarding the subscriber in question, including information regarding supplementary services. The VLR acknowledges receipt of the information. The HLR then issues a return result to the MAP Update Location.

On receipt of that return result, the MSC/VLR sends the DTAP message Location Updating Accept to the MS. It then clears the SCCP connection to the BSS. This causes the BSS to release the MS from the SDCCH by sending a Channel Release message to the MS.

A number of optional messages have been excluded from Figure 4.11. For a complete understanding of all the options, the reader is referred to GSM Specification 04.08. A number of messages shown in Figure 4.11 (e.g., Channel Request, Immediate Assignment, and Channel Release) are common to many traffic scenarios. For the sake of brevity, they are not shown in

4.6 HAND OVER MANAGEMENT

A handover (also known as a handoff) is the process by which a call in progress is transferred from a radio channel in one cell to another radio channel either in the same cell or in a different cell. A handover can occur within a cell, between cells of the same BTS, between cells of different BTSs connected to the same BSC, between cells of different BSCs, or between cells of different MSCs. Not only can a handover occur between TCHs, but a handover is also possible from an SDCCH on one cell to an SDCCH on another cell. It is also possible from an SDCCH on one cell to a TCH on another cell. The most common, however, is a handover from TCH to TCH.

The main aim of handover is to avoid losing a call is progress when MS leaves the radio coverage of the call in charge.

Handovers can be classified as

- Internal handover within one cell.
- Internal handover between cells.
- External handover.

The hand-over process may be thought of as consisting of three phases-

1. Recognition that handover is required.
2. Decision of a target cell.
3. Execution of the handover.
   - Allocation and connection of new channel.
   - Reallocation and release of old channel.

The BSS is wholly responsible for first phase. However MSC may trigger BSS to do so through certain, BSSMAP procedure. MSC participates with BSS in execution of phase 2 and 3.

4.6.1 Type of Handovers

- *Rescuer handover* are done to avoid losing a call in progress when MS leaves the radio coverage area of the cell in charge. These are the most common types of handover. The handover decision is triggered by the averaged measurement reports given by the MS, for the beacon frequencies of the adjacent cells given to it by the BSS.
- *Confinement handover* is an handover triggered with the goal of optimizing the interface level. The BSC divides the frequencies in a cell into five interference bands based on interference level on each of them.
- *Traffic hand-overs* are aimed at reducing the congestion in congested cell by handing over some call from one cell to less congested one.

The hand-over procedure provides interface between the call control entities, MAP procedure and the BSSMAP procedure to realize the handover. The handover are further categorized into:

- Intra MSC handover.
- Inter MSC handover.

The intra MSC handover procedure operates as detailed below.

- BSS- A generates the HANDOVER REQUIRED message to MSC containing a list of cells in order of preference to which MS is to be hand-over.

- MSC on getting this message send a HANDOVER REQUEST message to the target BSS i.e. BSS-B.
- BSS-B an receiving handover request messages takes all necessary action for giving radio access to the MS in the new cell and gives a HANDOVER REQUEST ACK to MSC with a handover reference number.
- The HANDOVER REQUEST ACK message contains a HANDOVER COMMAND message, which is to be transparently passed on by the MSC to BSS-A.
- MS now accesses the radio resources of BSS-B with a HADOVER ACCESS on getting which BSS-B verifies the reference number and sends HADOVER DETECT to MSC.
- When MS starts successfully communicating with BSS-B, BSS-B sends HANDOVER COMPLETE message to MSC.
- MSC now release the resources held on BSS-A by sending it a CLEAR COMMAND.

Note— When handover procedure is operational all the message meant for the MS are queued up and are delivered only after the handover is complete. In case handover procedure fails the queued up message meant for the MS are delivered once MS is back in communication with the old BSS.

4.6.2 Inter MSC Handover

Inter MSC handover is required when the target cell belongs to other MSC service area. The successful handover in this case requires a circuit between two MSC's. Inter MSC hand over procedure acquires a circuit between the two MSC's using MAP-E interface.

The handover procedure operates as detailed below-

- MSC-A, on receipts of HANDOVER REQUIRED message from BSS-A, sends a MAP_PREPARE_HANDOVER message to MSC-B containing HANDOVER REQUEST message.
- On receipts of this message MSC-B acquires a handover number from its VLR and returns it to MSC-A in MAP_PREPARE_HANDOVER_REQUEST_resp. message. This message also contains HANDOVER REQUEST ACK containing in turn HANDOVER COMMAND to be given by BSS-A to the MS.
- On getting this message MSC-A diais handover number to obtain a circuit between two MSC's.
- MSC-A on receipt of ACM (ISUP) message from MSC-B sends the HANDOVER COMMAND to BSS-A.
- MSC-B passes the HANDOVER DETECT and HANDOVER COMPLETE message received from the BSS-B to MSC-A.
- After getting HANDOVER COMPLETE from BSS-B over E interface MSC-A initiates the release of radio resources towards BSS-A.

4.6.3 Inter BSC Hand Over

On receipt of the page, the MS attempts to access the network using a Channel Request message on the RACH. The BSS responds with an Immediate Assignment message, instructing the MS to move to an SDCCH. The MS moves to the SDCCB and, once there, indicates to the network that it is responding to the page. The ESS passes the response to the MSC. Refer Figure 4.14.

At this point, the MSC optionally may authenticate the MS (not shown). It then will proceed to initiate ciphering, which is done in the same manner as was described previously for a mobile-originated call. Once ciphering is started, the MSC sends a Setup message to the MS. This is similar to the Setup message that is sent from an MS for a mobile-originated call, including information such as the calling-party number and the required bearer capability.

On receipt of the Setup message, the MS sends a Call Confirmed message to the MSC, indicating that it has the information it needs to establish the call. The Call Confirmed message acts as an instruction to the MSC to establish a path through to the MS. Therefore, the MSC begins the assignment procedure, which establishes a circuit between the MSC and the BSS and a TCH between the BSS and the MS (rather than an SDCCH). Further signaling between the MS and the network now will use the FACCH associated with the TCH to which the MS has been assigned.

Once established on the TCH, the MS starts ringing to alert the user and informs the network by sending the Alerting message to the MSC. This triggers the MSC to open a one-way path back to the original caller, generate a ring-back tone, and send an ACM back to the originating PSTN switch via the GMSC.

Once the called user answers, the MS sends a Connect message to the MSC. This triggers the MSC to send and ANM back to the originating switch and to open a two-way path. Finally, it sends Connect Acknowledge to the MS, and conversation begins.

Depending on the source (the original cell) and the target (the destination cell) involved in the handover, the handover may be handled completely within a BSS or may require the involvement of an MSC. In the case where a handover occurs between cells of the same BSC, the BSC may execute the handover and simply inform the MSC after the handover has taken place. If, however, the hand over occurs between BSCs, then the MSC must become involved because no direct interface exists between BSCs.

A handover in GSM is known as a mobile-assisted handover (MAHO). This means that it is the network that decides if, when, and how a handover should take place. The MS, however, provides information to the network to enable the network to make the decision.

Recall that GSM is a TDMA system, with eight time slots per frame in, the case offer speech. This means that the MS is transmitting for one-eighth of the time and receiving for one-eighth of the time. In fact, at the BTS, a given time slot on the uplink is three time slots later than the corresponding downlink time slot, which means that the MS is not required to receive and transmit simultaneously. We note that this offset is specified at the BTS rather than at the MS because the distance of the MS from the BTS influences the exact instant at which the MS should transmit. For example, when an MS is close to the BTS, it should transmit slightly later than if it were farther from the BTS. This variation is known as time alignment and is controlled by the BSS. In other words, the BSS periodically instructs the MS to change its time alignment as necessary.

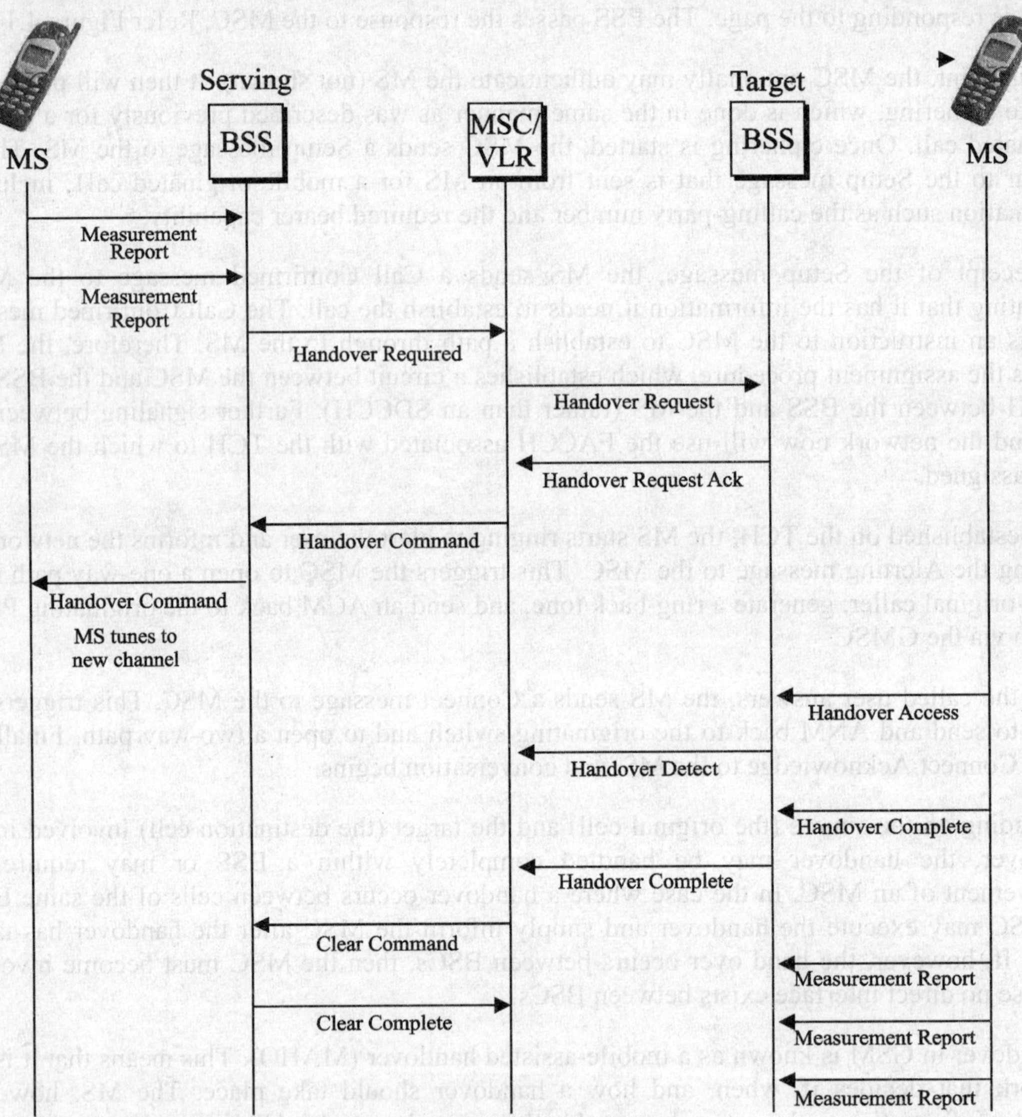

Fig. 4.14: Inter BSC Hand Over

Nonetheless, it is clear that for most of the time the MS is neither transmitting nor receiving. During this time, the MS has the opportunity to tune to other carrier frequencies and determine how well it can receive those signals. It then can relay that information to the network to allow the network to make a determination as to whether the MS would be better served by a different cell. Because of frequency reuse, it is possible that a number of nearby cells might be using the same BCCR frequency. Therefore, it is not sufficient for the MS simply to report signal strength for specific frequencies. Rather, the MS must be able to synchronize to the BCCR of neighboring cells and decode the information being transmitted. Exactly which frequencies the MS should check for are specified in system information messages transmitted by the BTS on the BCCR and the SACCH. The MS sends measurement reports to the BSS on the SACCR as often as possible. These reports include information on how well the MS can "hear" the serving cell, as well as information about signal-strength measurements on up to six neighboring cells. Specifically, for the serving cell, the MS reports the RXLEV (an indication of received signal strength) and the RXQUAL (an indication of the bit error rate on the received signal). For neighboring cells, the MS reports the BSIC, the BCCR frequency, and the RXLEV.

In addition to the measurements reported by the MS, the BTS itself makes measurements regarding the RXLEV and RXQUAL received from the MS. These measurements and those from the MS are reported to the BSC. Based on its internal algorithms, the BSC makes the decision as to whether a handover should occur and, if so, to which cell.

Figure shows an inter-BSC handover. In this case, it is not sufficient for the Base to handle the handover autonomously-it must involve the MSC. Therefore, once the serving BSC determines that a handover should take place, it immediately sends the message Handover Required to the MSC. This message contains information about the desired target cell (or the cells in the preferred order) plus information about the current channel that the MS is using. The MSC analyzes the information and identifies the target BSC associated with at least one of the target cells identified by the source BSC. It then sends a Handover Request message to the target BSC. This contains, among other items, information about the target cell, the type of channel required, and in the case of a speech or data call, the circuit to be used between the MSC and the target BSC.

If the target BSC can accommodate the handover (if resources are available), then it allocates the necessary resources and responds to the MSC with the Randover Request Acknowledge message. This message contains a great deal of information regarding the cell and channel to which the MS is to be transferred, such as the cell identity, the exact channel to be used (including the type of channen, synchronization information, the power level to be used by the MS when accessing the new channel, and a handover reference. The MSC then sends the Randover Command message to the serving BSC. This message is used to relay the information received from the target BSC. On receipt of the Handover Command message from the MSC, the serving BSC passes the information to the MS in a Handover Command message over the air interface.

On receipt of the Handover Command message, the MS releases existing RF connections, tunes to the target channel, and attempts to access that channel. On access, it may send a Handover Access message to the target BSS. It will do so if it was commanded to do so in the Handover Command message. If the Handover Access message is received by the target BSS, then it sends a Handover Detect message to the MSC. When the MS has established all lower-layer connections on the target channel, it sends a Handover Complete message to the target BSC, which, in turn, sends a Handover Complete message to the MSC. At this point, the MS again starts taking measurements of neighboring cells. Meanwhile, the MSC instructs the old ESC to release all radio and terrestrial resources related to the MS.

4.7 GSM INTERFACES

Interfaces

For the connection of the different nodes in the GSM network, different interfaces are defined in the GSM specifications. The GSM interfaces discussed in this lesson are:

Air interface or U m - interface

The Air Interface is the interface between the BTS (Base Transceiver Station) and the MS (Mobile Station). The air interface is required for supporting:

- Universal use of any compatible mobile station in a GSM network
- A maximum spectral efficiency

A bis-interface

The A bis -interface is the interface between the BSC (Base Station Controller) and the BTS. The interface comprises traffic and control channels. Functions implemented at the A bis -interface are:

- Voice-data traffic exchange
- Signaling exchange between the BSC and the BTS
- Transporting synchronization information from the BSC to the BTS

A-interface

The A-interface is the interface between the BSC and the MSC.

4.7.1 The U M -Interface

Introduction

One of the most important interfaces is the U m or Air interface. This interface is thoroughly specified to achieve a full compatibility between mobile stations of various manufacturers and networks of different operators.

FDMA and TDMA Methods

To achieve a high spectral efficiency in the cellular network a combination of FDMA (Frequency Division Multiple Access) and TDMA (Time Division Multiple Access) is used. The FDMA part involves the division by frequency of the 25 MHz bandwidth into 124 carrier frequencies spaced 200 KHz for GSM-900. For GSM-1800 the frequency spectrum of the 75 MHz bandwidth is divided into 374 carrier frequencies spaced 200 KHz. One or more frequencies are assigned to each BTS. Each of these carrier frequencies is then divided in time, using a TDMA scheme to increase the number of channels' per carrier frequency.

Each carrier frequency channel carries eight time-division multiplexed physical channels. A physical channel is determined by the carrier frequency (or a number of carrier frequencies and a defined hopping sequence) and the timeslot number. A mobile station can transmit speech data only during its assigned timeslot.

Uplink and Downlink

In the frequency range specified for the GSM-900 mobile radio networks, 124 frequency channels with a bandwidth of 200 KHz are available for both the uplink and downlink direction. The uplink (mobile station to BTS) uses the frequencies between 890 MHz and 915 MHz and the downlink (BTS to mobile station) uses the frequencies between 935 MHz and 960 MHz. The duplex spacing, the spacing between the uplink and downlink channel, is 45 MHz.

GSM-1800 uses a similar scheme. The difference is that for GSM-1800 the uplink uses the frequencies between 1710 MHz and 1785 MHz and the downlink the frequencies between 1805 MHz and 1880 MHz. The duplex spacing is 95 MHz.

4.7.2 Types of Logical Channels

- Traffic channel
- Broadcast channels
- Common control channel
- Dedicated control channels

Traffic Channels:

- TCH/F
- TCH/H

Logical Channels on the U M -Interface

Logical Channels

One or more logical channels can be transmitted on a physical channel. There are different types of logical channels. The type of logical channel is determined by the function of the information transmitted over it.

The following types of logical channels are defined:

- Traffic channels
- Broadcast channels
- Common control channels
- Dedicated control channels

Note that the first channel type carries speech and data, and the other types control information (signaling).

4.7.3 Traffic Channels

The traffic channels are used to send speech or data services. There are two types of traffic channels. They are distinguished by their transmission rates.

The following traffic channels are provided:

- *TCH/F (Traffic CHannel Full rate)*— The TCH/F carries information at a gross bit rate of 22.8 kbit/s (after channel coding). The net (or effective) bit rate at the TCH/F is for speech 13 kbit/s and for data 12, 6 or 3.6 kbit/s (before channel coding). The transmission rates of the data services allow services which are compatible to the existing, respectively, 9.6, 4.8 and 2.4 kbit/s PSTN and ISDN services.
- *TCH/H (Traffic CHannel Half rate)*— The TCH/H carries information at a gross bit rate of 11.4 kbit/s. The net bit rate at the TCH/H is for speech 5.6 kbit/s and for data 6 or 3.6 kbit/s.

A TCH/F or a TCH/H may also be used to send signaling information (for example call forwarding and short messages), in that case a small portion of the time slot is used.

Broadcast Channels:

- BCCH
- FCCH
- SCH
- CBCH

Common Control Channels:

- PCH
- AGCH
- RACH

Dedicated Control Channels

- SACCH
- FACCH
- SDCCH

4.7.4 Broadcast Channels

The information distributed over the broadcast channels helps the mobile stations to orient themselves in the mobile radio network.

The broadcast channels are point-to-multipoint channels which are only defined for the downlink direction (BTS to the mobile station). They are divided into:

- *BCCH (Broadcast Control CHannel)*— Via the BCCH the mobile station is informed about the system configuration parameters (for example Local Area Identification, Cell Identity and Neighbor Cells). Using this information the mobile stations can choose the best cell to attached to the BCCH is also known as beacon.
- *FCCH (Frequency Correction CHannel)*— To communicate with the BTS the mobile station must tune to the BTS. The FCCH transmits a constant frequency shift of the radio frequency carrier that can be used by the mobile station for frequency correction.

- *SCH (Synchronization CHannel)*— The SCH is used to time synchronize the mobile stations. The data on this channel carries the TDMA frame number and the BSIC (Base Station Identity Code).
- *CBCH (Cell Broadcast CHannel)*— The CBCH is used for the transmission of generally accessible information (Short Message Service messages) in a cell, which can be polled by the mobile station.

4.7.5 Common Control Channels

Common control channels are specified as point-to-multipoint channels which only operate in one direction of transmission, either in the uplink or downlink direction. The following channels are provided:

- *PCH (Paging CHannel)*— The PCH is used in the downlink direction for paging the mobile stations.
- *AGCH (Access Grant CHannel)*— The AGCH is also used in the downlink direction. A logical channel for a connection is allocated via the AGCH if the

4.7.7 Network Attachment Process

Network attachment is the process of selecting an appropriate cell (radio frequency) by the mobile station to provide the available services, and making its location known to the network.

The process starts when the mobile is switched on, and ends when the mobile station enter the idle mode. In idle mode the mobile station does not have a traffic channel allocated to make or receive a call, but the Public Land Mobile Network (PLMN) is aware of the existence of the mobile station within the chosen cell.

For normal service, the mobile station has to camp on a suitable call, tune to that cell's control channel. The choice of such a suitable cell for the purpose of normal service is referred to as "normal camping".

The network attachment process consists of the following tasks:-

- *Cell Identification*— When Mobile Station is switched on, it attempts to make contact with a GSM PLMN by performing following actions.
  - ✓ Measure the BCCH channel.
  - ✓ Search for a suitable call.

  The Mobile Station measure the signal strength of the BCCH (Broadcast Control Channel) channels received. It stores a list information about 30 of these BCCH channels, such as signal strength and the frequency corresponding.

- *PLMN Selection*— The particular PLMN to be contacted can be selected either in one of the following modes:

  Automatic mode— In automatic mode, the station will choose which PLMNs to try by itself. The automatic mode is based on the existence of the preferred list, which is stored- in a non-volatile memory in the SIM. This list includes a number of PLMN identities in order of preference and is under control of the. user. The most preferred is usually the home PLMN. The list is filled in by the user through a mechanism to be specified by the mobile station manufacturer. The automatic mode is normally used when the mobile station operates on its home PLMN (that is the PLMN the mobile station is subscribed to).

Manual mode— In manual mode, the user is presented a list containing all found PLMNs. The user chooses one of the PLMNs from the list.

- *Cell selection*— The mobile station attempts to find a suitable cell by passing through the list in descending order of received signal strength; the first BCCH channel which satisfies a set of requirements. The requirement that a cell must satisfy before a mobile station can be provide service from it, are:

  1. It should be a cell of the selected PLMN.

     The mobile station checks whether the cell is part of the selected PLMN.

  2. It should not be "barred".

     The PLMN operator may decide not to allow mobile stations to access certain cells. These cells may, for example, only be used for handover traffic. Barred cell information is broadcast on the BCCH to instruct mobile stations not to access these cells.

  3. The radio path loss between the mobile station and the selected BTS must be below a threshold set by the PLMN operator.

  4. It should not be in an LA which is in list of "forbidden LA's for roaming".

No Suitable Cell Found

If the mobile station is unable to find a suitable cell to access, it attempts to access a cell irrespective of the PLMN identity, and enters a "limited service" state in which it can only attempt to make emergency calls.

When successfully camped on a cell the mobile station regularly looks to see if there is a better cell in terms of a cell-re-selection criterion, and if there is, the better cell is selected-. Also if one of the other criteria changes, (e.g. the current serving cell becomes based), or there is downlink signaling failure, a new cell is selected.

4.8 CAPACITY INCREASING METHODS

4.8.1 Frequency Reuse

In a frequency reuse concept frequencies used in a given cell are simultaneously reused a few cells away.

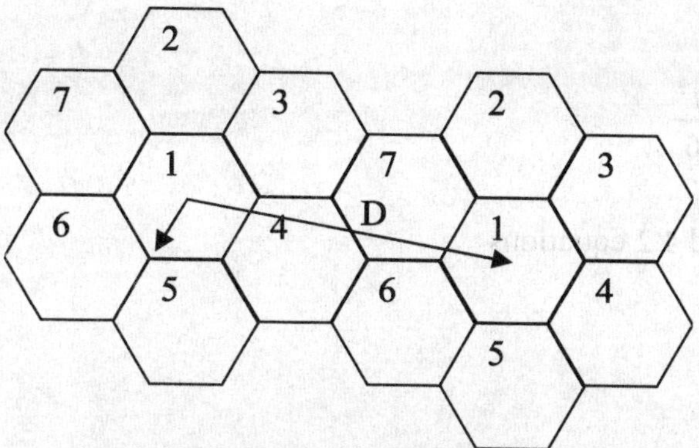

Fig. 4.15: Frequency Reuse Pattern, N= 7

As shown in Fig.4.15 the available set of frequencies can be distributed among a cluster of seven cells. Fig. 4.16 shows the distribution of available set of frequencies among four cells. These seven or four set of different frequencies (a cluster size of seven or four) can be reused after a certain distance. The distance kept between the cells using the same frequency should be sufficient enough to keep the cochannel interference to an acceptable level. This concept of frequency reuse is the key to high capacity of a cellular system.

Let us- discuss the cell separation considerations. We assume a cellular system having a cell radius "*R*" and a cochannel separation distance "*D*". The cluster size (N) assumed is equal to 7. A cochannel interference reduction factor "*q*" can-tie defined as

$$q = \frac{D}{R} \tag{4.1}$$

The cell separation distance "*D*" depends upon the *C/I*. Where "*C*" is the received carrier power from the desired transmitter and "*I*" is the cochannel interference received from all the interfering cells. For a seven cell reuse pattern the number of cochannel interfering cells shall be six in. number. Hence

$$I = {}_{m=1}^{m=6}\sum I_m$$

Where *Im* is the interference due to m[th] interferer. Assuming a path loss of 40 dB/decade

i.e. Loss proportional to (distance)

we get

–4

$C \alpha R$

and $I = {}^{m=6}\sum I_m \alpha .6D_{m=1}^{-4}$

also

$$\frac{C}{I} = \frac{C}{\sum^{6} I_m} = \frac{R-4}{6D^{-4}} = \frac{q^4}{6} \tag{4.2}$$

Combining both 4.1 and 4.2 equations

we get

$$D = q.R = R\left(6C/I\right)^{-4} \tag{4.3}$$

Higher values of "*q*" reduce Cochannel interference. But higher "*q*" means higher value of "*N*" i.e. less number of channels per cell, leading to less traffic handling capacity of the system. The lower values of "*q*" (lower "*N*") increase Cochannel interference but the system can handle large traffic.

Based upon the mean opinion score in any analog system, for an acceptable voice quality, the value of C/I has been found to be equal to 18dB. If we are to use a seven cell reuse pattern and an omnidirectional antenna at the cell site, the value of "*q*" can be calculated from Table 4.3 which will be typically 4.6. If the carrier to interference ratio (C/I) is greater than 18dB throughout the cell coverage area, the system is said to be properly designed. But here we have assumed the distance of the mobile units from the interfering cells to be uniformly equal to "*D*" in all the cases. But in worst case when the mobile moves to the boundary of the cell the distance "*D*" reduces to "*D-R*" and C/I drops down to even 14.47 dB and hence a frequency reuse pattern of 7 (N=7) in such cases will not be sufficient to meet the C/I criteria of 18 dB or more. Similarly the value of q, N and C/I obtained corresponding to various values of cluster size are indicated below:

Table 4.3

q	***N***	***C/I (Worst Case)***	***Remarks (Voice quality)***
4.6	7	14.47	Not good
5.2	9	19.78	Acceptable
6.0	12	22.54	Acceptable

Hence either frequency reuse pattern of 9 or 12 can be used. But this shall mean reduced traffic handling capacity. In order to take care of this problem we may use directional antennas (sectored cell) instead of a omni directional cell. Using directional antennas the number of interferers is reduced because of front to back ratio of antenna coming into picture. For a seven cell system the number of cochannel interferers reduces from six to two, if we change from a single cell pattern to a three sectored cell pattern. Typically if a three sectored cell pattern is used, Cochannel C/I interference improves from 14.47dB in worst case to 24.5dB and then it meets the requirement of 18dB in the entire coverage area. A frequency reuse pattern of four is normally used for urban application where we get more number of carriers per cell instead of using a seven cell frequency reuse pattern which is not suitable to handle a large traffic. For urban application if a frequency reuse pattern of four and a three sector cell is used then C/I becomes 20dB in worst cases (refer fig. 4.15).

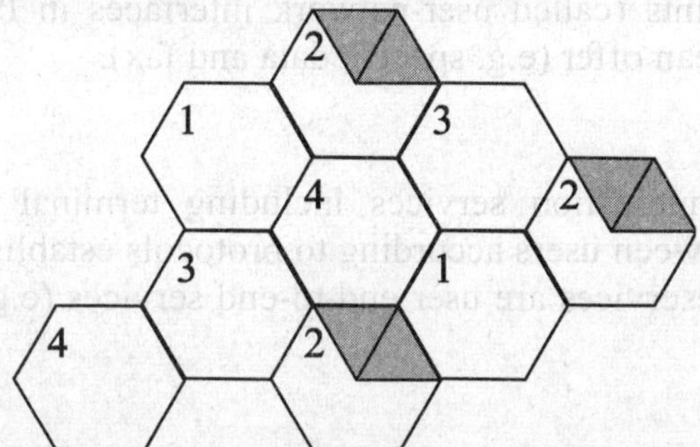

Fig. 4.16: Frequency Reuse Pattern, N=4 and a Three Sectored Cell

Hand-Off

When the mobile unit travels along a path it crosses different cells. Each time it enters into a different cell associated with different frequency, control of the mobile is taken over by the other base station, and Hand Off occurs between the two base stations. Decision for Hand Off is taken based upon the

a) Receive signal strength information, if it is below a threshold value

b) Carrier to interference ratio information, if it is less than 18dB in normal circumstances. (for analog systems)

The hand offs can be delayed, forced or controlled as per the network requirement to increase the call handling capacity and have minimum number of call, dropping cases.

4.8.2 Cell Splitting

When the number of users reaches a saturation in a startup cell and no more spare frequency is available then the start up cell is split. Usually the startup cell splits in four smaller cells and traffic increases by four and thereby more number of subscribers can be served.

After *n* splits the traffic will be

$Tn = To\ (4)^n$ and the power will be reduced and

$Pn = \text{P0} - \text{n(12)dB}$.

Hence cell splitting with lower transmission power in the resulting cells also improves the capacity of the cellular system.

4.9 GSM SERVICES

4.9.1 Types of Services

The ETSI Standards define the telecommunication services in the same way as ISDN (Integrated Services Digital Network) does. Different types of services are distinguished: bearer services, tele-services and supplementary services.

Bearer Services

Bearer services are telecommunication services providing the capability of transmission of signals between access points (called user-network interfaces in ISDN). The bearer services describe what the network can offer (e.g. speech, data and fax).

Teleservices

Teleservices are telecommunication services including terminal equipment functions, that provide communication between users according to protocols established by agreement between network operators. The teleservices are user end-to-end services (e.g. emergency call and short message service).

Supplementary Services

Supplementary Services modify or supplement a basic telecommunication service. Consequently, they cannot be offered to a customer as a stand-alone service. They must be offered together or in association with a basic telecommunication service. The same supplementary service may be applicable to a number of telecommunication services. Most supplementary services are directly inherited from a fixed network, with minor modifications (when needed) to adapt to mobility. Examples of supplementary services are calling line identification and call waiting.

4.9.2 Supplementary Services

Supplementary Services Management

Administrative functions can be performed by both the mobile subscriber or network to control Supplementary Services. These functions include:

- *Provisioning*— The service provider makes an service available for a subscriber.
- *Invoking*— The service required is invoked by the subscriber (for. example by pressing a specific button) or automatically by the network or terminal as a result of a particular condition (e.g. calling number identification for each incoming call).

Applicability of Supplementary Services

An operation is effective on those basic services (within the basic service group) that have been provisioned, and for which the supplementary service is applicable.

Supported Supplementary Services

In interworking situations with CSPDN and PSPDN these services can only be used during call setup (e.g. call forwarding services) When a call is established between a mobile station and a Public Data network (PDN), the MS acts; as a data network terminal and can consequently only use the services that are supported by the relevant PDN. (PDN supplementary services are outside the scope of GSM).

4.9.3 Line Identification Services

- Calling Line Identification Presentation (CLIP)
- Calling Line Identification Restriction (CLIR)

- Connected Line Identification Presentation (COLP)
- Connected Line Identification Restriction (COLR)

Line Identification Services

Calling Line Identification Presentation (CLIP)

The CLIP service allows the called party to receive the line identity of the calling party. The network delivers the calling line identity to the called party at call set-up time, regardless of the terminal capacity to handle the information. The CLIP service may not be applicable if least one of the two parties is not an ISDN or GSM PLMN subscribe (depends on national network specific rules).

Calling Line Identification Restriction (CLIR)

The CLIR service enables the calling party to restrict presentation of its line identity to the called party. For inter-network calls, when the CLIR service is invoked, the originating network provides the destination network with a notification that the line identity of the calling party is not allowed to be presented to the called party.

Normally CLIR takes precedence over CLIP. However, depending on national regulations, some networks may define categories of subscribers that have the ability to override the presentation restriction (CLIR) and have the calling line identity presented (e.g. the police).

Connected Line Identification Presentation (COLP)

The COLP service allows the calling party to' receive the line identity of the connected party. This service is not a dialling check, but the calling subscriber receives the full connected line identity as used in a full ISDN/GSM environment, i.e including all the information necessary to unambiguously connected party. The network delivers the connected line identity to the calling party regardless of the terminal capability to handle the information.

Connected Line Identification Restriction (COLR)

The COLR service allows the connected party to prevent presentation of its line identity to the calling party. The network automatically invokes the COLR service for each incoming call at set- up phase. When the COLR service is invoked, the destination network provides the originating network with a notification that the line identity of the connected party is not allowed to be presented to the calling party. This also applies to inter-network calls.

Normally COLR takes precedence over COLP. However, depending on national regulations, some networks may define categories of subscribers that have the ability to override the presentation restriction (COLR) and. have the connected line identity presented (e.g. the police).

4.9.4 Call Offering Services

- Call Forwarding Unconditional (CPU)
- Call Forwarding on Mobile Subscriber Busy (CFB)
- Call Forwarding in Mobile Subscriber Not Reachable (CFNRc)

Call Offering Services

Call Forwarding Unconditional (CFU)

This service permits a called mobile subscriber to have the network send all incoming calls (or just those associated with a specific basic service group), addressed to its directory number, to another directory number. The ability of the served mobile subscriber (i.e. the 'forwarding subscriber' or the 'called subscriber') to originate calls is unaffected: If this service is activated, calls are forwarded no matter what the condition of the termination.

Call Forwarding on Mobile Subscriber Busy (CFB)

This service permits a called mobile subscriber to have the network send all incoming calls (or just those associated with a specific, basic service group), that reach a busy signal, to another directory number.

If the served mobile subscriber is connected to an active call and has another call on hold the subscriber can alternate between the two calls, or disconnect either the active call, the held call, or both calls. Again no new call can be accepted, except when using the CW service.

Multiparty Supplementary Services

- Multi Party Service (MPTY)
- Multi Party Supplementary Services

4.9.5 Multi Party Service (MPTY)

This service provides a mobile subscriber with the ability to have a multi-connection call, i.e. a simultaneous communication with more, than one, party.

A pre-condition for the MPTY service is that the served mobile subscriber is in control of one active call and one call on hold, both calls having been answered. In this situation the served mobile subscriber can request the network to begin the MPTY service, Once a MPTY call is active, remote parties may be added, disconnected or separated.

What MPTY can do

During a multi-party call, the served mobile subscriber is able to:

- Put the connection to multi-party on hold. The served mobile subscriber may make a new call (to a potential participant) or process a Call Waiting request. While the multi-party call is on hold, the remote parties in that call can still communicate with each other.
- Add another party, to which a private communication has been established previously (see above). By again invoking the MPTY service, the network joins the active call and the MPTY call on hold together, resulting in an active multi-party call again.
- Separate a remote party. Explicitly choose one remote party to have a private conversation with. This results in that remote party being removed from the multi-party call which is placed on hold, and the conversation between the served mobile subscriber and the designated remote party being a normal active call. Again, while on hold, the participants of the MPTY call can still communicate with each other. The separated party can be added again to the MPTY call or released.

- Disconnect the entire MPTY call or disconnect remote parties on a one at a time basis.

4.9.6 Charging Supplementary Services

Advice of Charge (Information) (AOCI)

This service permits the mobile station to display an accurate estimate of the size of the bill which will eventually be levied in the Home PLMN (HPLMN).

Advice of Charge (Charging) (AOCC)

This service allows the mobile subscriber to indicate the charge that will be made for the use of telecommunication services. It is intended for applications where the user is generally not the subscriber but is known to the subscriber, and where the user pays the subscriber, rather than the Service Provider.

The charge information is based as closely as possible on the charge that will be levied on the subscriber's bill in the Home PLMN (HPLMN).

4.9.7 Call Restriction Services

Barring Outgoing Calls

- All Outgoing Calls (Baoc)
- Outgoing International Calls (BOIC)
- Outgoing International Calls ex Home (BOIC-exHC)

Barring Incoming Calls

- All Incoming Calls (BAIC)
- Incoming Calls, Roaming Outside Home (BIC-Roam)

Call Restriction Services

The Call Restriction supplementary services allow the possibility for a mobile subscriber to bar certain categories of outgoing or incoming calls at the subscriber's access. The group of Call Restriction Services includes two supplementary services:

- Barring outgoing calls
- Barring incoming calls

Types of Calls Barred

The mobile subscriber can select the categories of calls to be barred. The following categories are defined:

- All outgoing calls (BAOC)
- Outgoing international calls (BOIC)
- Outgoing international calls except those directed to the home PLMN country (BOIC- exHC)
- All incoming calls (BAIC)
- Incoming calls when roaming outside the home PLMN country (BIC-Roam)

4.10 TRAFFIC CALCULATION METHODS

As with any mobile communications technology, traffic calculation and system dimensioning for GSM begin with an estimation of how much traffic demand there will be and from where it will come. In other words, one must estimate the traffic demand in the coverage of each cell. This is rather an inexact science. One certainly can acquire demographic data such as population density, average household income, and so on. One also can acquire data related to vehicular traffic in order to estimate traffic demand for cells that cover roads. Based on these factors and others (such as how many competing operators exist), one makes an estimate ofthe peak traffic demand per cell. This estimate may well be incorrect. Fortunately, however, time is an ally. In a new network, traffic demand grows gradually, which provides the operator with sufficient time to monitor usage and more accurately predict traffic demand over time.

Because all GSM traffic is circuit-switched, network dimensioning is a relatively straightforward process once traffic demand per cell is specified. The process largely involves determining the amount of traffic to be carried in the busy hour and dimensioning the network according to Erlang tables.

The air interface, which represents the scarcest resource in the network, is dimensioned with the highest blocking probability. Typically, network designers dimension the air interface according to a 2 percent blocking probability (Erlang B). For a oneTRX cell with seven TCRs (BCCR, CCCR, and SDCCHl4 are sharing time slot 0), the cell can accommodate approximately 2.9 Erlangs. For a two-TRX cell with 14 TCHs (time slot 0 on one carrier is used for BCCR and CCCR and time slot 1 is used for SDCCH/8), the cell can accommodate approximately 8.2 Erlangs. For a three-TRX cell with 22 TCRs (one time slot is allocated for SDCCHl8), the cell can accommodate approximately 14.9 Erlangs. It is important to note that the traffic-carrying capacity of each cell must be calculated independently.

Other interfaces in the network usually are dimensioned at much lower blocking probabilities. For example, the A interface typically would be designed for a 0.1 percent blocking probability. Similar blocking would apply to other network-intemal interfaces such as the interface between the MSC and IWF. Typically, interfaces to other networks, such as the PSTN, are dimensioned at slightly higher blocking probabilities-such as 0.5 percent. Of course, the choice of blocking probability for any interface is a balance between cost and quality. The lower the blocking probability, the higher is the quality, and the higher is the cost. The higher the lower blocking probability, the lower is the quality, and the lower is the cost.

4.11 GSM NETWORK PLANNING

4.11.1 The planning covers service area, traffic demand, estimation of cell radius and software tools for network planning

I. Service Area

- Estimation of traffic demand
- Available frequency resources
- Evolving an optimum coverage scheme of placing the cells over the entire service area so as to provide complete mobility to the subscribers.

II. Traffic Demand Estimation

- Population distribution
- Car usage distribution
- Income level distribution
- Land usage distribution
- Telephone usage distribution

III. Estimation of Cell Radius

- ✓ Service Area
  - Terrain conditions
  - Density of foliage
  - Man made structures
- ✓ Signal level at an unit distance from base station
- ✓ Signal strength decay per decade of distance.

IV. Mobile Radio Network Planning Software Tools

- Propagation Predictions based upon various propagation models e.g OKUMARA-HATA, WALFISCH-IKEGAMI or special external models written by the users
- Interference analysis
- Automatic frequency planning
- Coverage analysis by contour plots
- Comparison with actual radio field measurements
- Efficient tool to load, analyze and display system performance evaluation

4.11.2 GSM Cell Planning Requirement

- Provision of required Capacity
- Optimum use of the available frequency spectrum
- Minimum number of cell sites
- Provision of adequate Coverage of the given area, for a minimum specified level of interference
- Provision of easy and smooth expansion of the network in future

4.11.3 GSM Planning Process

1. Capacity Planning
2. Coverage Planning
3. Parameter Planning
4. Equipment Planning
5. Optimization

I. ***Basic Planning***

- Say the service provider wants to launch his network with 20 sites or for 10,000 subscribers in a city
- The following assumptions are made in the planning process :
  - ✓ 25 mE average traffic per subscriber
  - ✓ Grade of Service 2%
  - ✓ Mobile to Mobile traffic 10%
  - ✓ Mobile to PSTN traffic 70%
  - ✓ Land to Mobile traffic 20%
  - ✓ Average to cell duration 90 seconds

Traffic capacity of 2 carrier with 15 TCHs = 8.2E (approximately 1330 subscribers). A 2/2/2 site will have a capacity of about 990 subscribers.

II. ***Example***

- 1/1/1 sites (350 subs per site) 7000 subscribers.
- 2/2/2 sites (990 subs per site) 19800 subscribers.
- 1/1/1 sites....10000/350 30 sites.
- 2/2/2 sites....10000/990 11 sites.

III. ***Example***

For 10000 capacity, at 25mE traffic, the total traffic is 250E. We assume a hypothetical distribution of traffic as shown below:

Table 4.4

Urban high density	20	50E	6	2
Urban	30	75E	10	3
Industrial	15	37.5E	5	2
Suburban	25	62.5E	7	3
Highways	5	12.5E	2	1
Quasi open	5	12.5E	2	1
Total	100	250E	32	12

- We may choose 2/2/2 sites for first 3area types and 1/1/1 sites for the rest.

Frequency Assignment for 12 Sectors (four-cell repeat)

Table 4.5

3A	*4A*	*IB*	*2B*	*3B*	*4B*	*1C*	*2C*		*3C*	*4C*
3	4	5	6	7	8	9	10		11	12
15	16	17	18	19	20	21	22		23	24
27	28	29	30	31	32	33	34		35	36
39	40	41	42	43	44	45	46		47	48
51	52	53	54	55	56	57	58		59	60
63	64	65	66	67	68	69	70		71	72
75	76	77	78	79	80	81	82		83	84
87	88	89	90	91	92	93	94		95	96
99	100	101	102	103	104	105	106		107	108
11	112	113	114	115	116	117	118		119	120
23	124									

- es a total of 18 sites. After customer's approval, site selection is done.

4.11.3 Cell Planning

I.

- What is the area to be covered?
- How many sites are required for this area ? (cell radius of 1km means an approximate coverage area of 3 Sq.kms).
- Do we need so many sites? Can some sites be bigger?
- Decide number of sites based on capacity and coverage requirements.
- Divide city into clutter types such as:
  - ✓ Urban
  - ✓ Suburban
  - ✓ Quasi Open
  - ✓ Water
- Identify "search areas" covering all clutter types.
- Customer selects a few sample sites.

II.

- Survey sites with reference to
  - ✓ Clutter heights
  - ✓ Vegetation levels
  - ✓ Obstructions
  - ✓ Sector orientation
  - ✓ Building strength and other Civil requirements

- Prepare Power budgets
- Conduct Propagation tests
- Calculate coverage probabilities
- Verify against predictions and modify planning tool parameters
- Prepare final coverage map

4.11.4 RF Link Budget Table

Table 4.6

Transmitting End	***MS***	***BTS***
Tx RF Output	33 dBm	43 dBm
Body Loss	-2.0 dB	0 dB
Combiner Loss	0 dB	0 dB
Feeder Loss (@2dB/100m)	0 dB	1.5 dB
Connector Losses	0 dB	2 dB
Tx Antenna Gain	0 dB	17.5 dB
EIRP	31 dBm (A)	57 dBm(C)
Receiving End	***BTS***	***MS***
Rx sensitivity	-107 dBm	-102 dBm
Rx. Antenna gain	17.5 dB	0 dB
Diversity Gain	3 dB	0 dB
Connector Loss	2 dB	0 dB
Feeder Loss	1:5 dB	0 dB
Interference Degradation-Margin	3 dB	3 dB
Body Loss	0 dB	3 dB
Duplexer Loss	0 dB	0 dB
Rx Power	-121 dBm	-96 dBm
Fade Margin	4 dB	4 dB
Required Isotropic Rx Power	-117 dBm(B)	-92 dBm(D)
Maximum Permissible Path	148dB	149 dB

4.11.5 Propagation Loss

- $L_{FS} = 10\log\left[\left(\frac{4\pi d}{\lambda}\right)^2\right]$
- $L_{FS} = 32.44 + 20\log(f) + 20\log(d)$
  Where f = frequency in MHz; d = distance in Kms

- $L_{FS} = L_0 + 10\gamma \log(d)$

  Where is the SLOPE of the attenuation characteristic

Multipath Environment

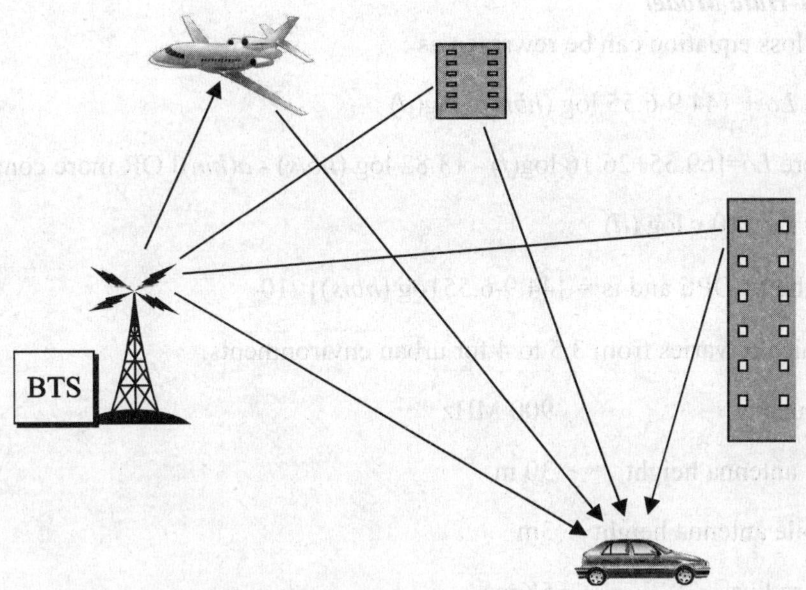

Fig. 4.17

Propagation Models

I. Okumara Model

The Okumara tests are valid for :

- 150-2000 Mhz
- 1-100 Kms
- BTS heights of 30 -100 meters
- MS antenna height, typically 1.5 m (1-10m)
- The results of Okumara tests were graphically represented

II. Hata Model

The basic equation for the 150-1000 MHz band is given by

Lp=69.55+ 26.16 log(f) -13.82 log ($hbts$) - a (hm) + {44.9- 6.551og($hbts$)} log(d)

Where f = frequency in MHz

$Hbts$ = BTS antenna height in meters (30-100m)

d = distance in Kms (1 to 20 Kms)

hm = mobiIe antenna height in meters (l-10m)

$a(hm)$ = correction for mobile height if hm is >1.5 meters

= 3.2 [log(11.75hm)-4.97 for Dense urban and

= {1.1 log(f)-0.7} hm-{1.56 log (f)-0.8} for Urban areas

III. Okumara-Hata Model

The path loss equation can be rewritten as :

- $Lp = Lo + \{44.9\text{-}6.55 \log (hbts)\} \log(d)$

  Where Lo=[69.55+26.16 log(f) - 13.82 log ($hbts$) - a(hm)] OR more conveniently

- $Lp = Lo + 10\, y \log (d)$

  γ is the SLOPE and is = {44.9-6.551og ($hbts$)} /10

  γ typically varies from 3.5 to 4 for urban environments.

- Frequency 900 MHz
- BTS antenna height 30 m
- Mobile antenna height 3m
- Cell radius 5Kms
- Also calculate the Attenuation slope for this site.
- Lp = [69.55+26.16 log(f) - 13.82 log ($hBTS$) - a (hm)]+ [44.9 - 6.55 log ($hBTS$)] log(d).
- $a(hm)$ ={ 1.1 log (f) -0.7 } hm - {1.56 log (f) -0.8}

  26.16 log (f) = 77.28dB

  13.82 log($hSTS$) = 20.41dB

  [44.9 - 6.551og ($hSTS$)] log (d) = 24.62 dB

  a(hm) = 3.81dB

  $\therefore$ Path Loss Lp =69.55 + 77.28 - 20.41 + 24.62 - 3.81 = 147.23dB.

Attenuation Slope γ = [44.9 - 6.55 log ($hSTS$)]/10 =35.225/10 =3.5225.

The receive signal strength RSS is given by :

$RSS = ERP\text{-} \{Lo + 10\, \gamma \log(d)\}$.

The distance d can be calculated from :

$d = 10^{[ERP - Lo - RSS]/10\gamma}$

Or, from the equation for *RSS*,

Log (d) =[ERP - RSS - Lo]/10γ

ie. d = antilog [ERP - RSS - Lo)/10γ]

Lo = 69.55 + 26.16 log (f) - 13.82 log($hbts$) - a(hm).

Example

Calculate the cell radius for a site that has:

Frequency: 900 MHz BTS height: 30meters

Mobile height: 3 meters BTS ERP: 55dBm

Expected RSS at the cell boundary (d=R) = -75 dBm.

Lo = 122.61 dB; γ =3.5 (calculated in the previous example).

122.61 - 75+35 log (d) =55 dBm.

log (d) = 7.39/35 =0.2111

Therefore d= antilog (0.2111) =1.62 Kms.

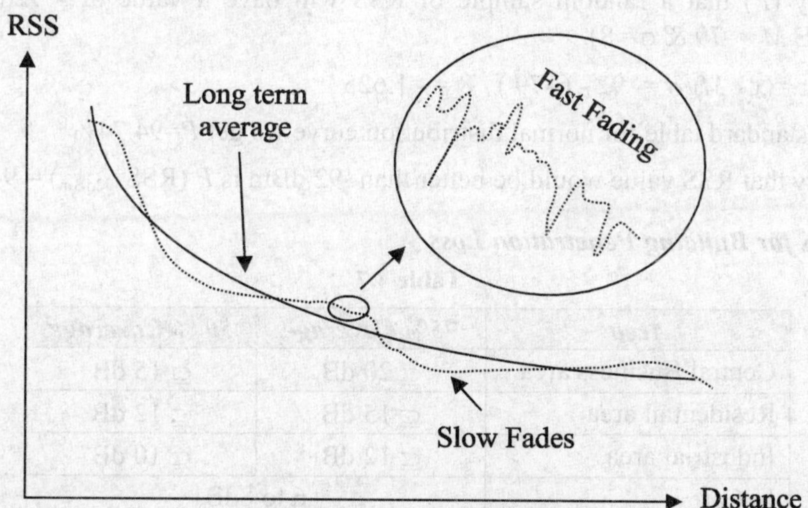

Fig. 4.18: Signal Variations

Standard Deviation

Example

The RSS values obtained from a drive test in a BTS area in a city

- 80 dBm, - 79 dBm, - 77 dBm, -82.5 dBm, - 84.35 dB - 78.65 dBm

- Mean RSS "M" = -79.97 dBm
- Standard deviation σ = 6.068

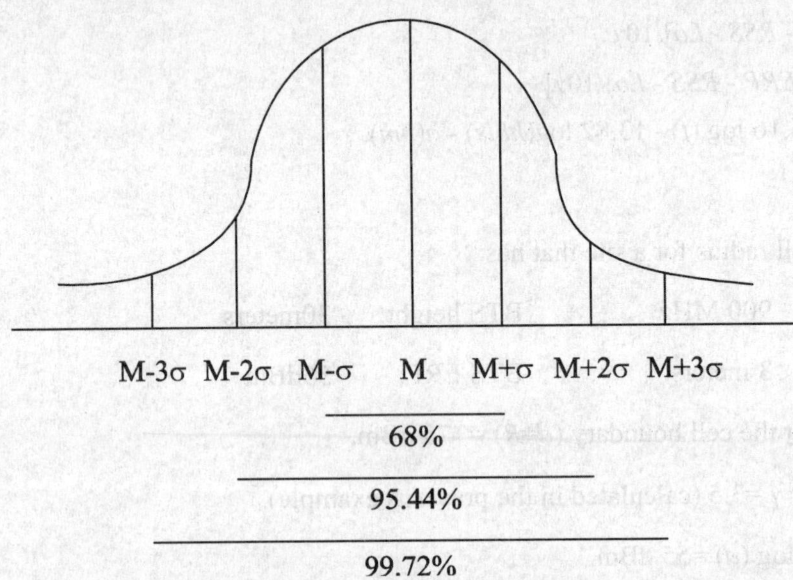

Fig. 4.19: Confidence Interval

Probability

- Probability (*P*) that a random sample of RSS will have a value of - 92dBm or better (ASSUME M= -79 & σ= 8)
- Compute $z = (x - M)/\sigma = -92 - (-79) / 8 = -1.625$
- Refer the standard table for normal distribution curve we get *P*=94.74%
- Probability that RSS value would be better than -92 dBm is P ($RSS_{<92dBm}$) = 94.74%

Typical Values for Building Penetration Loss

Table 4.7

Area	*75% Coverage*	*50 % Coverage*
Central Business area	⊆ 20 dB	⊆ 15 dB
Residential area	⊆ 15 dB	⊆ 12 dB
Industrial area	⊆ 12 dB	⊆ 10 dB
In Car	6 to 8dB	

- If the minimum RF signal strength for 90 % coverage on the street is, say - 92 dBm, then for 75 % in building coverage in a central business area, we should have a signal level of -72 dBm on the road;

  This shall provide - 92 dBm inside the building.

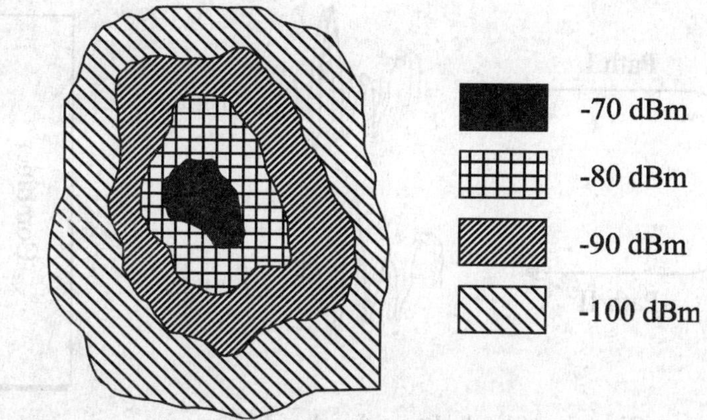

Fig. 4.20: Coverage Plots

4.13 MOBILE ANTENNAS

4.13.1 Antenna Considerations

- Uniform coverage in a cell
- Space availability
- Several antenna sites may be needed
- In - building penetration is a must
- Building acts as a RF shield & hence decreases coverage
- Building reflects signals & provide coverage to those areas where LOS would have failed. Such additional paths improve in-building penetration
- Antenna at a very high point may not meet in-building coverage requirements

4.13.2 Diversity Antenna Systems

- Diversity is used to combat the effects of multi path fading.
- In general we have the following types of Diversity.
- In the Time Domain: Interleaving
- In the Frequency Domain: Frequency Hopping
- In the Spatial Domain: Space Diversity

A Diversity antenna System essentially has:

- Two or More, antenna
- A combiner circuitry

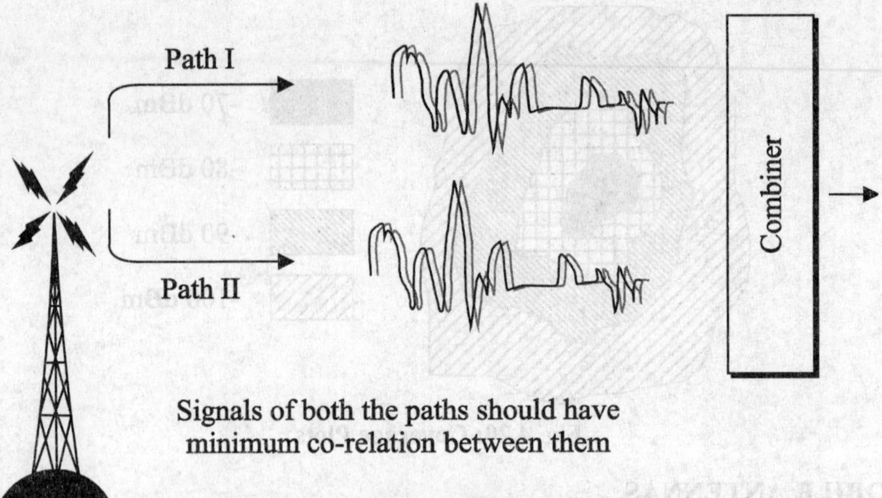

Fig. 4.21: Diverse Propagation Paths

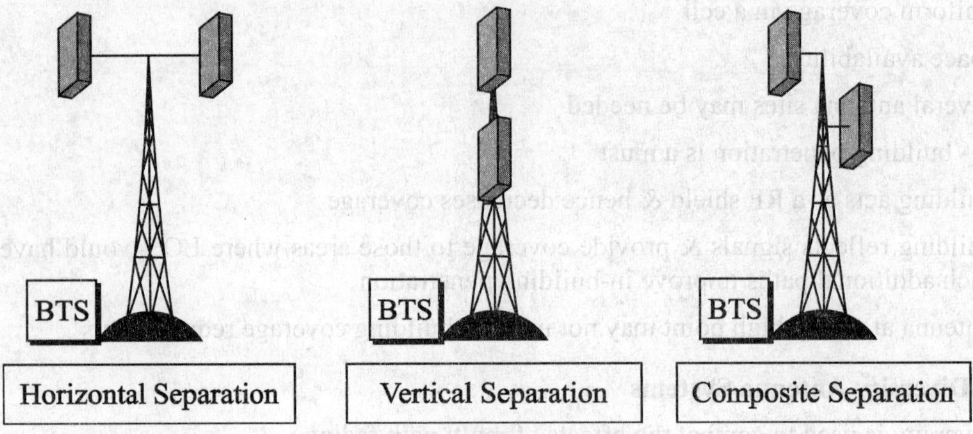

Fig. 4.22: Antenna Diversity

4.13.3 Antenna Spacing

Table 4.8

Separation	D/λ	*900Mhz*	*1800Mhz*
Horizontal	10	3.3m	1.7m
Vertical	17	5.7m	2.8m

- Figures given in the table are for minimum required separation.
- If space is not a constraint, larger separation is always recommended.
- Horizontal separation is preferred because it provides low correlation values.
- However, horizontal separation suffers from angular dependence

- Vertical separation does not suffer much from angular dependence. It also requires minimum supporting fixtures and does not occupy a lot of space
- But, as the distance increase, the correlation between the RF signals at the antenna points increase rapidly, thereby negating the very advantage of space diversity.

4.13.4 Coverage Area Capacity

I. Capacity Planning- Required TCH Channels

- Number of Subscribers to be served 150 Subscribers
- Average traffic per subscriber 25mE Traffic per
- Grade of service GoS = 2%

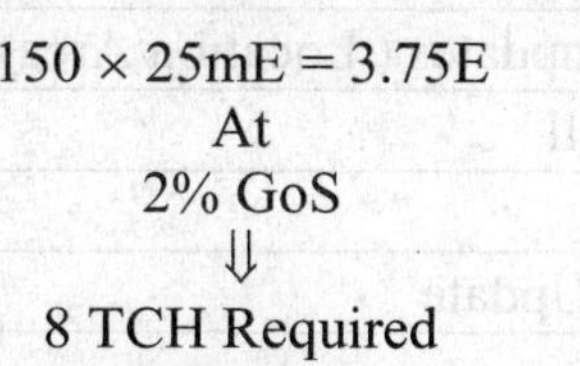

150 × 25mE = 3.75E
At
2% GoS
⇓
8 TCH Required

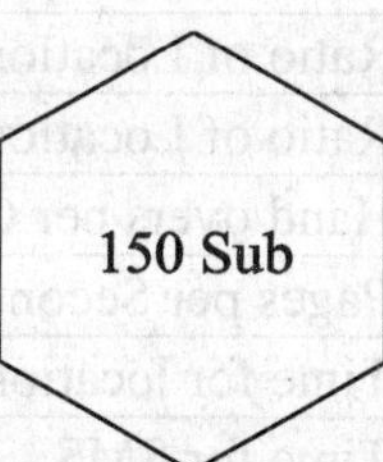

II. Capacity Planning- TCH Channels Required

- Number of Subscribers to be served 200 Subscribers
- Average traffic per subscriber 25mE Traffic per
- Grade of service GoS = 2%

200 × 25mE = 5.0E
At
2% GoS
⇓
10 TCH Required

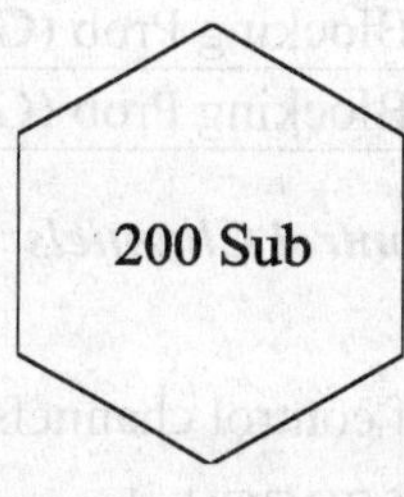

III. Capacity Planning - TCH Channels Required

- Number of Subscribers to be served 300 Subscribers
- Average traffic per subscriber 25mE Traffic per
- Grade of service GoS = 2%

300 × 25mE = 7.5 E
At
2% GoS
⇓

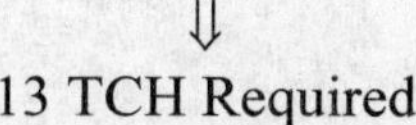

13 TCH Required

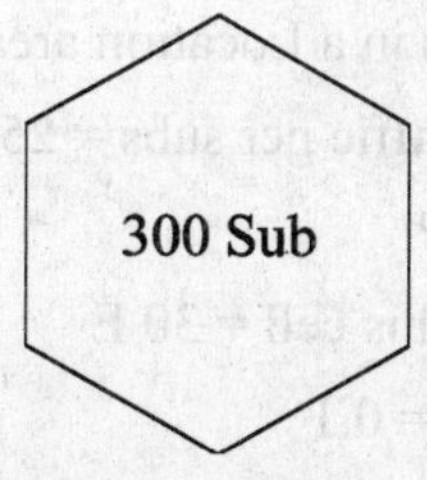

Control Channel Configuration

1. Combined Time Slot: (TS0 of BCCH Carrier)

   1 BCCH +3 CCCH + 4 SDCCH

2. Non Combined Time Slot:

   (1 BCCH + 9 CCCH) in one time slot (TS 0)

   8 SDCCH in one time slot (any time slot)

Typical Call Parameters

Table 4.9

Parameter	*Value*
Call Duration	T=120 sec
Ratio of SMS per call	S=0.1
Ratio of Location updates (Non Location Area)	L=2
Ratio of Location updates (Location Area)	L=7
Hand overs per Call	H=2.5
Pages per Second	P=3
Time for location Update	T_{LU}=4sec
Time for SMS	T_{SMS}=6sec
Call set up time	Tc=S sec
Guard time for SDCCH	Tc= 4 sec
Blocking Prob (GOS) for TCHs	<2%
Blocking Prob (GOS) for SDCs	<1%

Planning of Control Channels

What is needed:

- Number of control channels
- Number of SDCCH channels
- Whether a combined or non combined time slot is needed

Calculations - Example 1

Given that:

- 40000 subs in a Location area
- Average traffic per subs = 25 mE
- Calculate P
- Traffic in this cell = 30 E
- SMS ratio = 0.1
- Other parameters assumed as given in the "Table"

Example 2

Step 1: Calculate P (Pages per second) :

- 40000 subs in a Location area

- Average traffic per subs = 25 mE
- Hence total traffic E=40,000 × 25 mE= 1000 E
- Average Call Duration = 120 sec.

Hence the call rate (Calls/hour) = E ÷ (120/3600)

- Calls/hour = 1000 ÷ (120/3600) = 30,000
- Average number of mobile terminated calls = 20 % = 6,000
- Assume two pages per cell. Hence number of pages / Hr=12,000
- Number of pages per second = 12000/3600 = 3.333

Example 3

Step 2: Calculate NPCH (Number of Paging Channels) :

- $N_{PCH} = P/(2 \times 4 - 25)$
- $N_{PCH} = 3.333/(2 \times 4.25) = 0.392$

Step 3 : Calculate N_{AGCH} (Number of AGCH Channels) :

For this we need λ values

- $\lambda_{call} = e \div (120/3600) = 900$ calls/hr in the cell
- $\lambda_{SMS} = \lambda_{call} \times SMS = 900 \times 0.1 = 90$
- $\lambda_{LU} = \lambda_{call} \times L = 900 \times 7 = 6300$
- $\lambda_{AGCH} = (\lambda_{call} + \lambda_{SMS} + \lambda_{LU})/3600 = (900 + 90 + 6300)/3600 = 2.025$ /second
- $N_{AGCH} = 2.025/(2 \times 4.25) = 0.2382$

Example 4

Step 4 : Calculate N_{PAGCH} (Number of PAGCM Channels) :

$N_{PAGCH} = (N_{PCH} + N_{AGCH})$ / UCCCH

Where UCCCH is the % utilization of control channels

Typically, UCCCH= 0. 33

$N_{PAGCH} = (0.2382 + 0.392) / 0.33 = 1.909$ blocks N_{AGCH}

This means we need a minimum of 2 CCCH blocks

Example 5

Step 5: Calculate SDCCH Requirement:

We need SDCCH channel during Call set-up, Location updates & SMS.

Hence Erlang offered for SDCCH Channel

$\{\lambda_{call} \times T_C + \lambda_{LU} \times (T_{LU} + T_g) + \lambda_{SMS} + T_g)\}/3600$

We Know that

$T_g = 4$, $T_C = 5$, $T_{LU} = 4$, $T_{SMS} = 6$ seconds from the "table"

$\therefore$ SDCCH Channel Erlang = ($900 \times 5 + 6300 \times 9 + 90 \times 10$)/3600 = 17.25 E

Example 6

Step 6 : Calculate SDCCH Channels :

From Erlang Tables with GoS =1 % & E = 17.25 we see that

SDCCH Channels = 27

- Each Time slot accommodates =8 SDCCH Channels
- Hence we need 3 independent Time slots & one Combined Time slot to accommodate 27 SDCCH Channels

Control Channel Planning

TS 0 = Combined time slot (BCCH + 4 SDCCH).........f_{BCCH}

TS 1 = SDCCH (8 SDCCH, Channels).......f_{BCCH}

TS 1 & TS 2 (16 SDCCH Channels),..........f_x any other freq. in the cell

Example 7

Step 7 : Number of RF Carriers need

Cell Traffic = 30 E
At
2% GoS
⇓
39 TCH Required

Time slots required for traffic channels = 39

Time slots required for control channels = 4

Total Time slots required 39 + 4 = 43

So RF Carriers needed = 43 / 8 = 5.375 = 6 (say)

Review Questions

1. Write down special features offered by GSM Technology.
2. Basic requirements to be met by 2nd Generation Network?
3. What are the major advantages of GSM?
4. Write note on Technical specification prescribed by GSM.
5. Elucidate radio spectrum utilization in 2G (GSM)
6. What is AFRCN? Derive the AFRCN number for frequencies 891.2 MHz, 893.4 MHz, 935.4 MHz also find out the DL/UL frequency pair.
7. The user data is 33.854 kbps - derive this by simple calculation for a voice call / data call.
8. Explain TDMA and FDMA with relevant sketches. How these multiplexing is implemented in GSM?
9. What is a coverage area? How many cells can be there in one cluster?
10. What is a frequency reuse method? why this technique is used in cellular network?
11. Explain the GSM working by drawing a neat diagram with its architecture and all the component blocks.
12. Write a detailed note on Base Station Subsystem and explain the functions of BTS and BSS.
13. What is MSC? What are the main functions of MSC?
14. Write note on VLR and HLR.
15. Draw call flow chart for Mobile originates call to PSTN.
16. What is meant by hand over? How this call hand-over is handled by BTS-BSC-MSC?

5 GENERAL PACKET RADIO SERVICE (GPRS) AND ENHANCED DATA FOR GLOBAL EVOLUTION (EDGE)

5.1 GPRS

GPRS (General Packet Radio Service) is the world's most ubiquitous wireless data service, available now with almost every GSM network. GSM system (2G) with GPRS capability is sometimes also known as 2.5G. GPRS is a connectivity solution based on Internet Protocols that supports a wide range of enterprise and consumer applications. Theoretical maximum speeds of up to 171.2 kilobits per second (kbps) are achievable with GPRS using all eight timeslots at the same time. This is about three times as fast as the data transmission speeds possible over today's fixed telecommunications networks and ten times as fast as current Circuit Switched Data services on GSM networks. Practically with throughput rates of up to 40 kbit/s, users have a similar access speed to a dial-up modem, but with the convenience of being able to connect from anywhere. GPRS customers enjoy advanced, feature-rich data services such as colour Internet browsing, e-mail on the move, powerful visual communications such as video streaming, multimedia messages and location-based services.

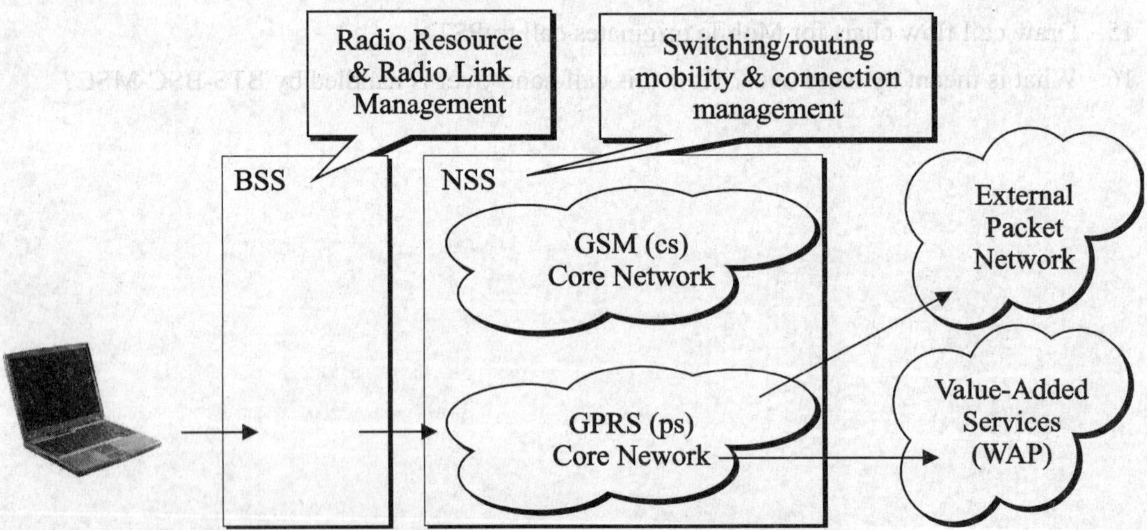

Fig. 5.1: GPRS General Configuration

5.1.1 GPRS Standardization

The ETSI (European Telecommunications Standardization Institute) does the standardisation work for GPRS. E2E3 GPRS & EDGE, Ver2 28.02.2008 2 of 6

Key Points

GPRS uses a packet-based switching technique, which will enhance GSM data services significantly, especially for bursty Internet/intranet traffic.

Some application examples:

- Bus, train, airline real-time information
- Locating restaurants and other entertainment venues based on current Location
- Lottery
- E-commerce
- Banking
- E-mail
- Web browsing

The main advantages of GPRS for users:

- Instant access to data as if connected to an office LAN
- Charging based on amount of data transferred (not the time connected)
- Higher transmission speeds

The main advantages for operators:

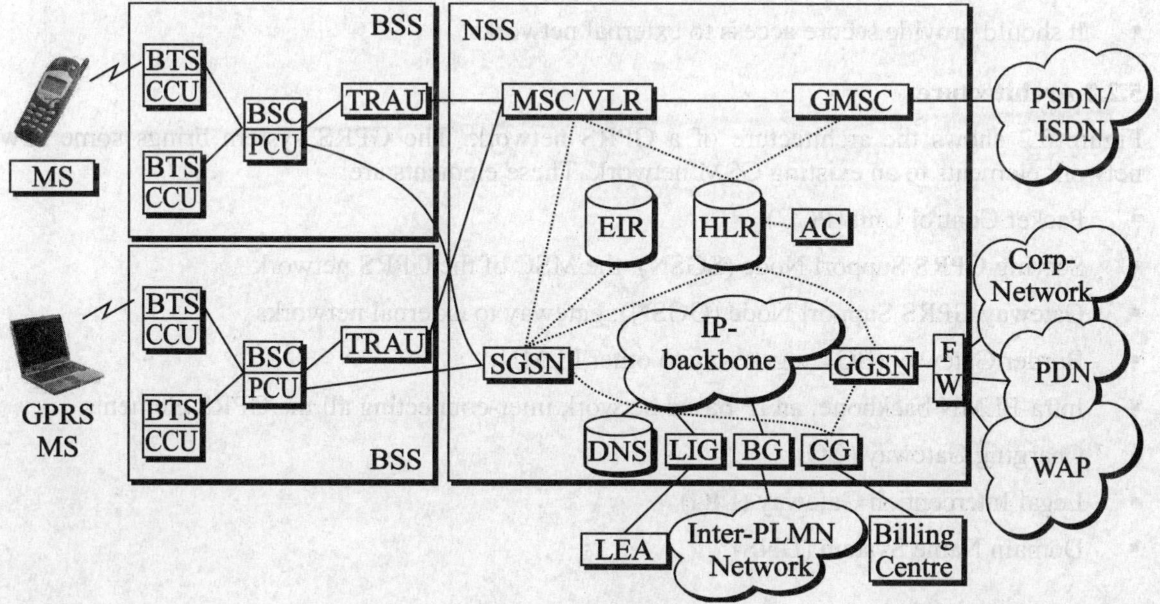

Fig. 5.2: Architecture

- Fast network roll-out with minimum investment
- Excess voice capacity used for GPRS data
- Smooth path to 3G services.

In circuit switching, each time a connection is required between two points, a link between the two points is established and the needed resources are reserved for the use of that single call for the complete duration of the call. In packet switching, the data to be transferred is divided up into packets, which are then sent through the network and re-assembled at the receiving end.

5.2 GPRS NETWORK

The GPRS network acts in parallel with the GSM network, providing packet switched connections to the external networks by way of up grading the existing 2G platform to suit data transmission.

5.2.1 The requirements of a GPRS network

- The GPRS network must use as much of the existing GSM infrastructure with the smallest number of modifications to it.
- Since a GPRS user may be on more than one data session, GPRS should be able to support one or more packet switched connections.
- To support the budgets of various GPRS users, it must be able to support different Quality of Service (QoS) subscriptions of the user.
- The GPRS network architecture has to be compatible with future 3rd and 4th generation mobile communication systems.
- It should be able to support both point-to-point and point-to-multipoint data connections.
- It should provide secure access to external networks.

5.2.2 Architecture

Figure 5.2 shows the architecture of a GPRS network. The GPRS system brings some new network elements to an existing GSM network. These elements are:

- Packet Control Unit (PCU)
- Serving GPRS Support Node (SGSN): the MSC of the GPRS network
- Gateway GPRS Support Node (GGSN): gateway to external networks
- Border Gateway (BG): a gateway to other PLMN
- Intra-PLMN backbone: an IP based network inter-connecting all the GPRS elements
- Charging Gateway (CG)
- Legal Interception Gateway (LIG)
- Domain Name System (DNS)

5.2.3 Firewalls

Firewalls used wherever a connection to an external network is required. Not all of the network elements are compulsory for every GPRS network.

5.2.4 Packet Control Unit (PCU)

The PCU separates the circuit switched and packet switched traffic from the user and sends them to the GSM and GPRS networks respectively. It also performs most of the radio resource management functions of the GPRS network. The PCU can be either located in the BTS, BSC, or some other point between the MS and the MSC. There will be at least one PCU that serves a cell in which GPRS services will be available. Frame Relay technology is being used at present to interconnect the PCU to the GPRS core.

5.2.5 Channel Codec Unit (CCU)

The CCU is realised in the BTS to perform the Channel Coding (including the coding scheme algorithms), power control and timing advance procedures.

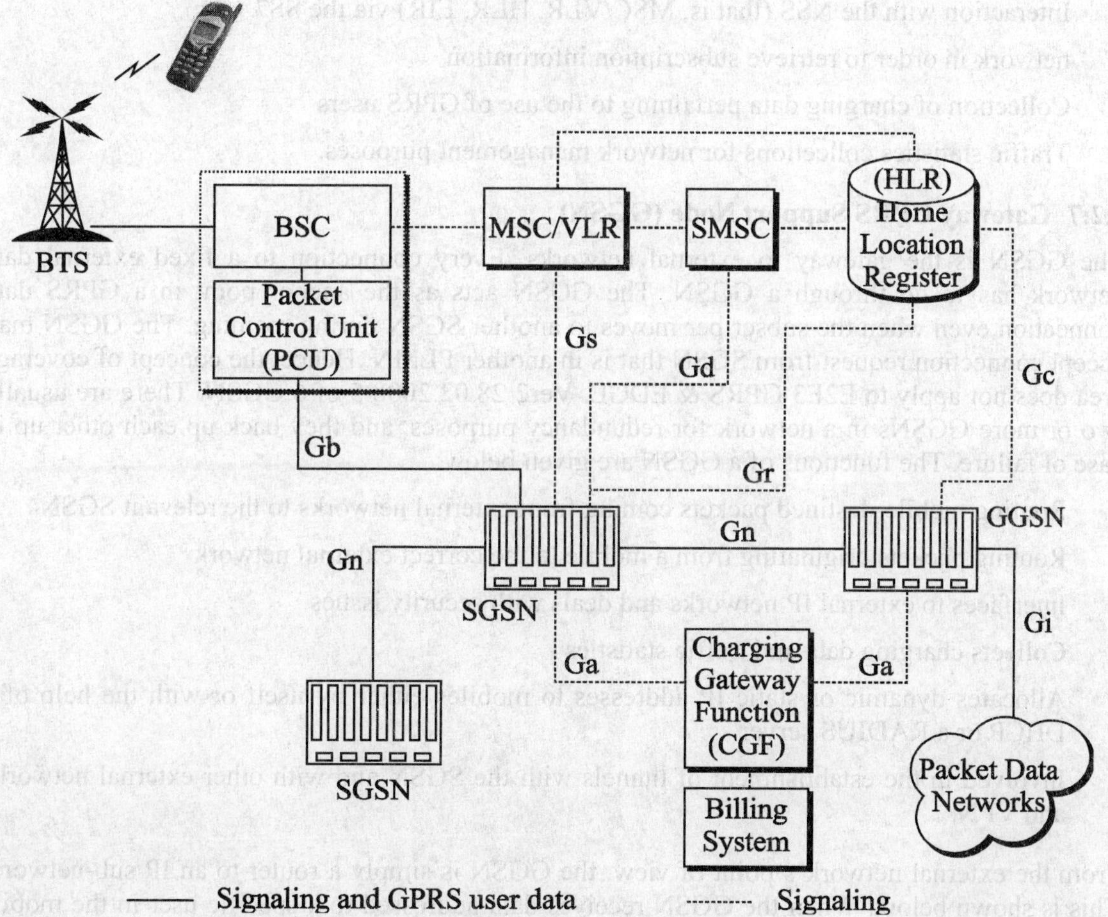

Fig. 5.3: GPRS Block Schematic

5.2.6 Serving GPRS Support Node (SGSN)

The SGSN is the most important element of the GPRS network. The SGSN of the GPRS network is equivalent to the MSC of the GSM network. There must atleast one SGSN in a GPRS network. There is a coverage area associated with a SGSN. As the network expands and the number of subscribers increases, there may be more than one SGSN in a network. The SGSN has the following functions:

- Protocol conversion (for example IP to FR)
- Ciphering of GPRS data between the MS and SGSN
- Data compression is used to minimise the size of transmitted data units
- Authentication of GPRS users
- Mobility management as the subscriber moves from one area to another, and possibly one SGSN to another
- Routing of data to the relevant GGSN when a connection to an external network is required
- Interaction with the NSS (that is, MSC/VLR, HLR, EIR) via the SS7
- network in order to retrieve subscription information
- Collection of charging data pertaining to the use of GPRS users
- Traffic statistics collections for network management purposes.

5.2.7 Gateway GPRS Support Node (GGSN)

The GGSN is the gateway to external networks. Every connection to a fixed external data network has to go through a GGSN. The GGSN acts as the anchor point in a GPRS data connection even when the subscriber moves to another SGSN during roaming. The GGSN may accept connection request from SGSN that is in another PLMN. Hence, the concept of coverage area does not apply to E2E3 GPRS & EDGE, Ver2 28.02.2008 5 of 6 GGSN. There are usually two or more GGSNs in a network for redundancy purposes, and they back up each other up in case of failure. The functions of a GGSN are given below:

- Routing mobile-destined packets coming from external networks to the relevant SGSN
- Routing packets originating from a mobile to the correct external network
- Interfaces to external IP networks and deals with security issues
- Collects charging data and traffic statistics
- Allocates dynamic or static IP addresses to mobiles either by itself or with the help of a DHCP or a RADIUS server
- Involved in the establishment of tunnels with the SGSN and with other external networks and VPN.

From the external network's point of view, the GGSN is simply a router to an IP sub-network. This is shown below. When the GGSN receives data addressed to a specific user in the mobile network, it first checks if the address is active. If it is, the GGSN forwards the data to the SGSN serving the mobile. If the address is inactive, the data is discarded. The GGSN also routes mobile originated packets to the correct external network.

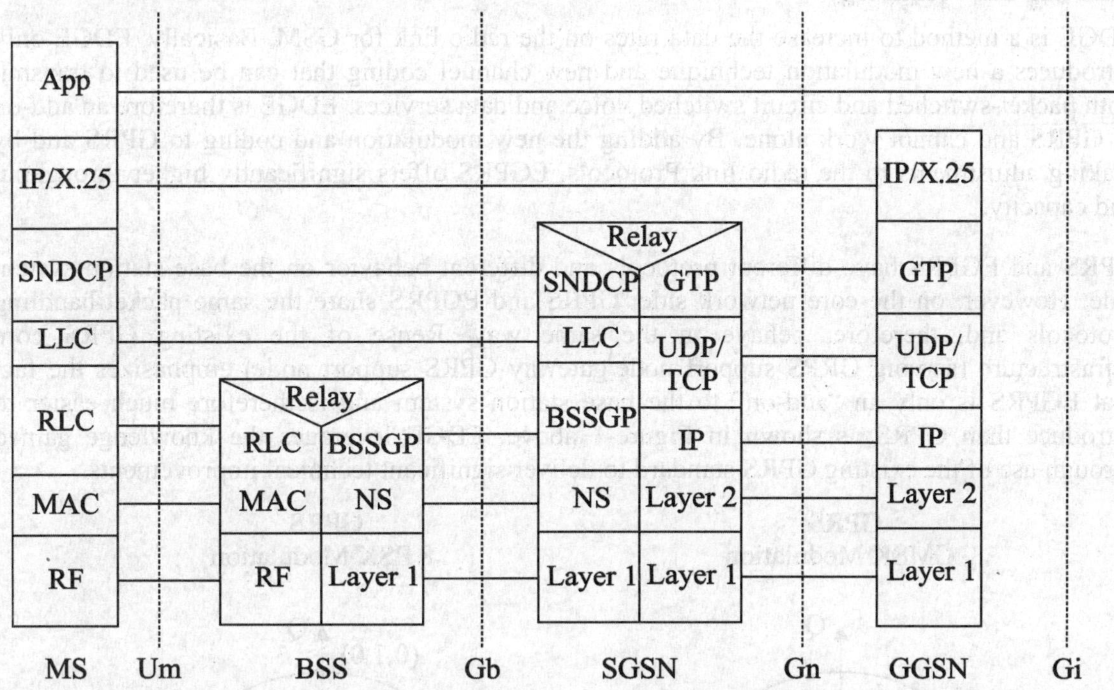

Fig. 5.4: Interfaces and Functions

5.2.8 GPRS MS (Mobile Station/Handset)

Different GPRS MS classes were introduced to cope with the different needs of future subscribers. The mobiles differ in their capabilities.

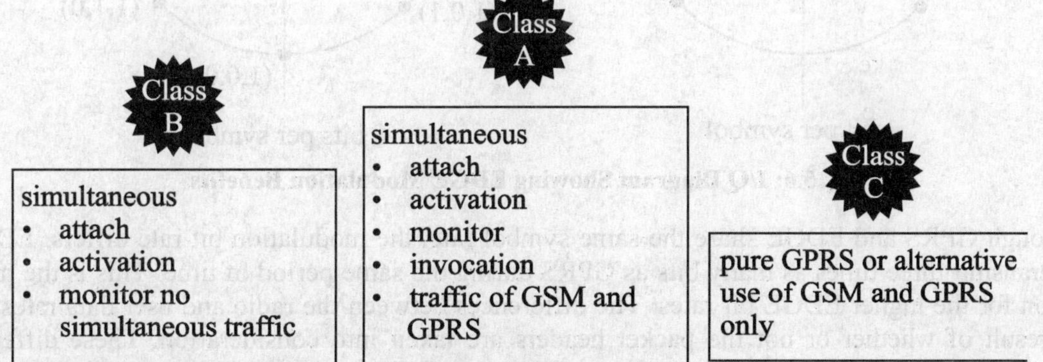

Fig. 5.5: Classes of service

5.3 ENHANCED DATA FOR GLOBAL EVOLUTION (EDGE)

5.3.1 EDGE Technology

EDGE is a method to increase the data rates on the radio link for GSM. Basically, EDGE only introduces a new modulation technique and new channel coding that can be used to transmit both packet-switched and circuit switched voice and data services. EDGE is therefore an add-on to GPRS and cannot work alone. By adding the new modulation and coding to GPRS and by making adjustments to the radio link Protocols, EGPRS offers significantly higher throughput and capacity.

GPRS and EGPRS have different protocols and different behavior on the base station system side. However, on the core network side, GPRS and EGPRS share the same packet-handling protocols and, therefore, behave in the same way. Reuse of the existing GPRS core infrastructure (serving GRPS support node/gateway GPRS support node) emphasizes the fact that EGPRS is only an "add-on" to the base station system and is therefore much easier to introduce than GPRS as shown in Figure-1 above. EDGE leverages the knowledge gained through use of the existing GPRS standard to deliver significant technical improvements.

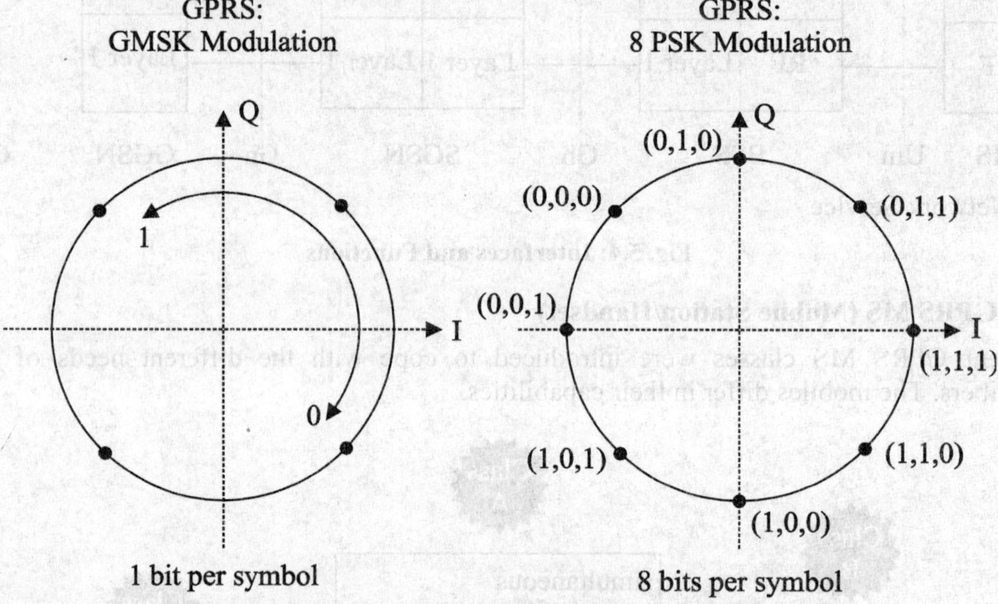

Fig. 5.6: I/Q Diagram Showing EDGE Modulation Benefits

Although GPRS and EDGE share the same symbol rate, the modulation bit rate differs. EDGE can transmit three times as many bits as GPRS during the same period of time. This is the main reason for the higher EDGE bit rates. The differences between the radio and user data rates are the result of whether or not the packet headers are taken into consideration. These different ways of calculating throughput often cause misunderstanding within the industry about actual throughput figures for GPRS and EGPRS. The data rate of 384 kbps is often used in relation to EDGE. The International Telecommunications Union (ITU) has defined 384 kbps as the data rate limit required for a service to fulfill the International Mobile Telecommunications-2000

(IMT-2000) standard in a pedestrian environment. This 384 kbps data rate corresponds to 48 kbps per time slot, assuming an eight-time slot terminal

5.3.2 EDGE Modulation Technique

The modulation type that is used in GSM is the Gaussian minimum shift keying (GMSK), which is a kind of phase modulation. This can be visualized in an I/Q diagram that shows the real (I) and imaginary (Q) components of the transmitted signal (Figure 3) below. Transmitting a zero bit or one bit is then represented by changing the phase by increments of + p or - p. Every symbol that is transmitted represents one bit; that is, each shift in the phase represents one bit.

To achieve higher bit rates per time slot than those available in GSM/GPRS, the modulation method requires change. EDGE is specified to reuse the channel structure, channel width, channel coding and the existing mechanisms and functionality of GPRS and HSCSD. The modulation standard selected for EDGE, 8-phase shift keying (8PSK), fulfills all of those requirements. 8PSK modulation has the same qualities in terms of generating interference on adjacent channels as GMSK. This makes it possible to integrate EDGE channels into an existing frequency plan and to assign new EDGE channels in the same way as standard GSM channels. The 8PSK modulation method is a linear method in which three consecutive bits are mapped onto one symbol in the I/Q plane. The symbol rate, or the number of symbols sent within a certain period of time, remains the same as for GMSK, but each symbol now represents three bits instead of one. The total data rate is therefore increased by a factor of three. The distance between the different symbols is shorter using 8PSK modulation than when using GMSK. Shorter distances increase the risk for misinterpretation of the symbols because it is more difficult for the radio receivers to detect, which symbol it, has received. Under good radio conditions, this does not matter. Under poor radio conditions, however, it does. The "extra" bits will be used to add more error-correcting coding, and the correct information can be recovered. Only under very poor radio environments is GMSK more efficient. Therefore the EDGE coding schemes are a mixture of both GMSK and 8PSK.

5.3.3 Coding Schemes

For GPRS, four different coding schemes, designated CS1 through CS4, are defined. Each has different amounts of error-correcting coding that is optimized for different radio environments. For EGPRS, nine modulation coding schemes, designated MCS1 through MCS9, are introduced. These fulfill the same task as the GPRS coding schemes. The lower four EGPRS coding schemes (MSC1 to MSC4) use GMSK, whereas the upper five (MSC5 to MSC9) use 8PSK modulation.

A packet sent with a higher coding scheme (less error correction) that is not properly received, can be retransmitted with a lower coding scheme (more error correction) if the new environment requires it. This is not possible with GPRS.

5.3.4 Packet Handling

Another improvement that has been made to the EGPRS standard is the ability to retransmit a packet that has not been decoded properly with a more robust coding scheme. For GPRS, re segmentation is not possible. Once packets have been sent, they must be retransmitted using the original coding scheme even if the radio environment has changed. This has a significant impact on the throughput, as the algorithm decides the level of confidence with which the link adaptation (LA) must work. As a result, the link adaptation for GPRS requires careful selection of the coding scheme in order to avoid retransmissions as much as possible. With EGPRS, resegmentation is possible. Packets sent with little error protection can be retransmitted with more error protection, if required by the new radio environment. The rapidly changing radio environment has a much smaller effect on the problem of choosing the wrong coding scheme for the next sequence of radio blocks because re segmentation is possible. Therefore, the EGPRS link-controlling algorithm can be very aggressive when selecting the modulation coding schemes.

5.4 GSM/GPRS/EDGE TRAFFIC DIMENSIONING

GSM voice circuit-switched traffic dimensioning is a relatively straightforward process, once traffic demand per cell is specified. The process largely involves determining the amount of traffic to be carried in the busy hour and dimensioning the network according to an Erlang B table using a 2 percent Grade of Service eGOS) as the reference or dimensioning objective.

For a GSM channel, referred to as a TRX, there are a total of 8 time slots, TCHs, each capable of carrying an individual traffic at full rate and, of course, up to 16 at half-rate, assuming full deployment for the individual radio carrier. However, when dimensioning a GSM cell or sector, it is important to remember that there are other elements that need to be included that comprise the BSC and other core network elements in addition to the backhaul method:

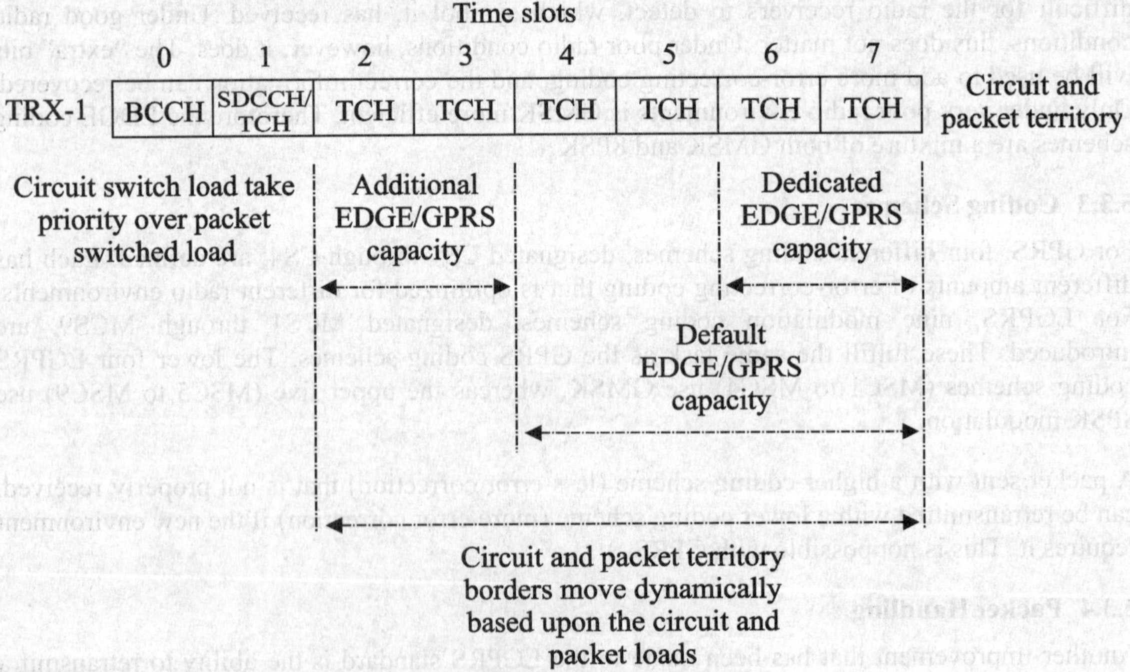

Fig. 5.7: GSM Channel Configuration

As discussed previously, the introduction of both GPRS and EDGE into a GSM network puts some additional pressure on radio dimensioning. Two primary methods are used for dimensioning a GPRSIEDGE network with GSM: estimation or standard uniform configuration.

The estimation method uses existing traffic and factors into a growth rate that then determines the number of TCHs needed for data and the number of TCHs needed for voice. Because data and circuit-switched traffic typically have different busy hours, a dedicated data slot and shared default data slots are used. The dedicated TCHs are used for data and only data, whereas the shared slots can be used for both voice and data, with voice having priority over data at all times.

An important thing to remember is that multiple users can be assigned to the same TCH, but the lowest speed, CS, will determine the speed to all the users. Figure 5.7 is an illustration of a channel configuration used for a GSM / GPRS / EDGE site.

Addressing Window

The packets in GPRS are numbered from 1 to 128. Since the number of packets is limited to 128 and the addressing window is 64, the packet sending process can run out of addresses after 64 packets. In EGPRS, the addressing numbers have been increased to 2048 and the window has been increased to 1024 in order to minimize the risk for stalling. This, in turn, minimizes the risk for retransmitting low-layer capability frames and prevents decreased throughput.

5.5 EDGE-NETWORK PLANNING AND OPTIMIZATION

GPRS networks are able to handle higher bit rates than GSM networks, but the data rates still fall short of what is required to make existing GSM networks deliver services at a speed comparable to that promised by third-generation networks. The delay in the deployment of third-generation systems led to the emergence of a technology known as EDGE. This was capable of delivering services similar to those of third-generation networks, yet with implementation on the existing second-generation networks (e.g. GSM).

EDGE stands for 'enhanced data rates for GSM evolution'. The enhancement from GSM was to GPRS (i.e. voice and packet), while further enhancement of GPRS led to EDGE networks, as shown in Figure 5.8. The fundamental concept remains the same, i.e. voice, CS data and PS data being carried, and the network architecture is the same as in a GPRS network. Enhancement of HSCSD is known as ECSD (enhanced circuit-switched data), while enhancement of GPRS is known as EGPRS.

EGPRS implementation has a major effect on protocol structure (e.g. on layer 1 or layer 2). The modulation and coding schemes are quite different in EGPRS (this is explained later in the chapter).

In ECSD, though user data rates do not go beyond 64 kbps, fewer time slots are required to achieve this compared HSCSD. The architecture of ECSD is based on HSCSD transmission and signalling, thus having minimal impact on existing specifications.

Focus on EDGE network planning aspects from the EGPRS perspective is described below.

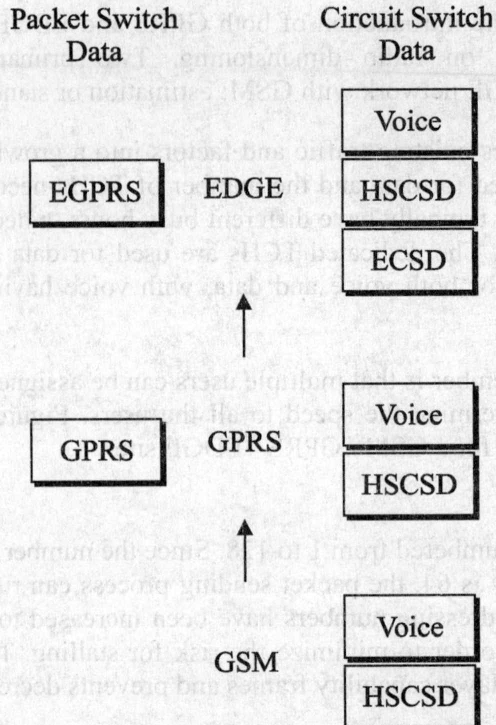

Fig. 5.8: EDGE Evolution

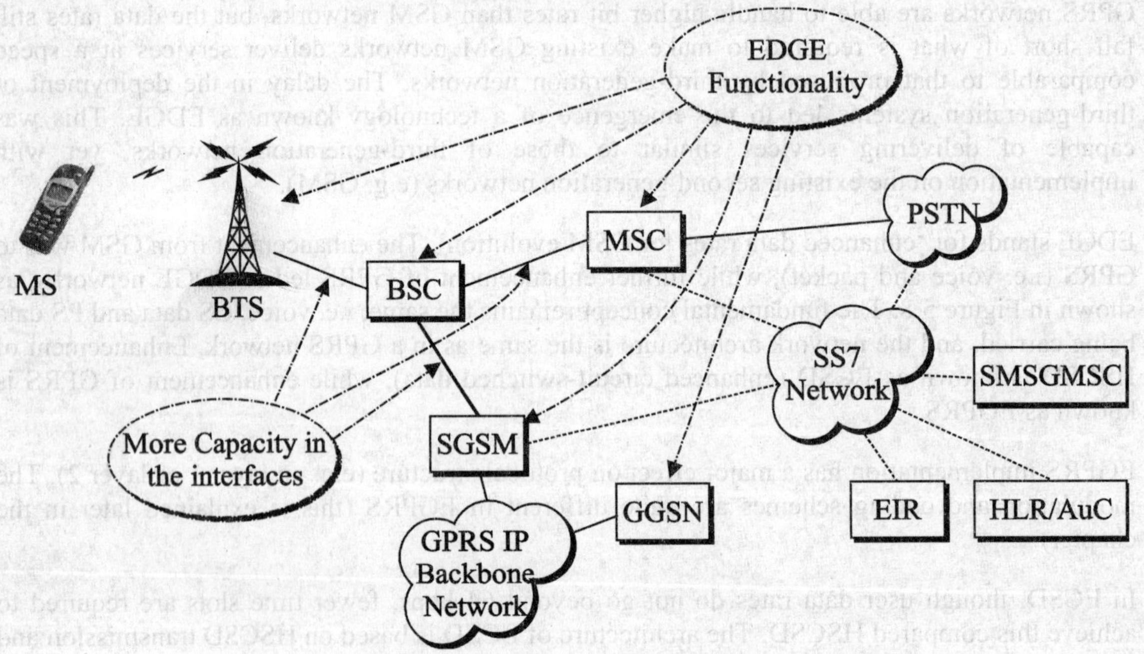

Fig. 5.9: EDGE Funcationality

5.5.1 The EDGE System

As shown in Figure 5.9, the EDGE system is quite similar to the GPRS system (compare with Figure 5.3), but with the capability *for* higher data rates. The most important change the new modulation scheme. In GSM and GPRS, the GMSK modulation scheme was used

In GMSK modulation, only one bit per symbol is used. In an EDGE network, octagonal phase-shift keying (8-PSK) modulation is used which enables a threefold higher gross data rate of 59.2 kbps per radio time slot by transmitting three bits per symbol. GMSK is a constant-amplitude modulation while 8-PSK has variations in the amplitude. This amplitude variation changes the radio performance characteristics, so hardware changes in the base stations are mandatory.

5.5.2 EDGE Network Planning

The radio network planning process is similar to that for GSM and GPRS networks. However, because of minor hardware and software changes in the existing network, that lead major changes in network performance, the network planning parameters change quite a bit. Owing to increased bit rates, transmission planning undergoes a major change with introduction of the concept of a dynamic A-bis interface. In contrast, core network planning virtually the same as for a GPRS network.

5.5.3 Radio Network Planning-Modulation and Coding Schemes

As already mentioned, the EDGE system is an enhancement to the existing GPRS system. There are nine modulation and coding schemes (MCS-l to MCS-9) that provide different throughputs, as shown in Table 5.1. The MCS scheme carries data from 8.8 kbps to 59.2 Kbps on the existing GSM carrier of 270.833 kbps. For coding schemes MCS-l to MCS-4, modulation is still GMSK; for MCS-5 to MCS-9 it is 8-PSK.

Based on this coding scheme, a data rate of 473 kbps (8 bits x 59.2 kbps) can be achieved.

Though GMSK is a more robust scheme, 8-PSK gives more data throughput. However, the increased data rate comes at the price of decreased sensitivity of the system. This has an impact on network planning. Another advantage in EDGE networks is that the switching between different coding schemes can take place easily, which was not possible in a GPRS network. When data transmission takes place in a GPRS coding scheme, it is not possible to switch the coding scheme on more reception failure, so the re-transmission takes place with exactly the same protection as for its initial transmission. In EGPRS, it is possible to change the MCS, i.e. the data block can be sent again but with better protection than for its initial transmission. This is done through a process called link adaptation.

One more observation on the coding scheme is that the new set of GMSK coding is being used, e.g. CS-1 is equivalent to 8 kbps in GPRS networks, with similar changes in coding schemes CS-2,CS-3 and CS-4. These changes are to provide incremental redundancy support, as will now be explained.

Table 5.1: Modulation and Coding Scheme in EDGE

MCS	*Modulation*	*User rate (kbps)*
1	GMSK	8.8
2	GMSK	11.2
3	GMSK	14.8
4	GMSK	17.6
5	8-PSK	22.4
6	8-PSK	29.6
7	8-PSK	44.8
8	8-PSK	54.4
9	8-PSK	59.2

5.5.4 Link Adaptation and Incremental Redundancy

As the propagation conditions change with time and region, the quality of the signal changes. Because of this, the modulation and coding schemes change all the time. Link adaptation is used for maximizing the throughput per channel and changing the coding scheme depending upon the channel conditions. Basically, this leads to provision of the highest throughput possible with the lowest amount of delay. This gives better link quality and makes EDGE a more efficient system. Link adaptation (LA) algorithms are responsible for link adaptation. These algorithms activate the LA feature based on bit-error probability (BEP) measurements.

Incremental redundancy (IR) improves the throughput and is done by automatically adapting the total amount of transmitted redundancy to the radio channel conditions. This is achieved using two techniques: ARQ (automatic repeat request) and FEC (forward error correction). In the GPRS system, when errors are detected in the RLC blocks, re-transmissions requested and provided until the correct information reaches the destination. FEC provides the redundant user information that is used by the receiver to correct errors caused by radio channel disturbances. However, in an EDGE system, not all the redundant information is sent immediately. Only a small amount is send at first. If decoding is then successful, this saves a lot of capacity; if decoding is unsuccessful, then the normal ARQ process takes place. Because the LA algorithm selects the amount of redundancy for each individual transmission, this process basically reduces the number of re-transmissions and subsequent delays. The re-transmission mechanism in EDGE is more efficient (than in GPRS networks) I by virtue of the IR phenomenon.

LA operates always on a first-sent block or a re-transmitted block, and upon receiving BEP measurements will change the MCS according to the condition of the network. IR is a specific re-transmission algorithm also known as 'hybrid ARQ II' (it includes puncturing, I storage and soft combining at the receiving end) that if enabled together with LA will allow I a change in MCS within the family. In order to change MCS during re-transmission, LA should be enabled. Note that ETSI specifications make IR mandatory only for the MS as receiving side, not for the BTS.

5.5.5 Channel Allocation

Channel allocation in EDGE networks is nearly the same as in GPRS networks. BCCH, PCH, RACH, AGCH are the signalling channels, while PACCH is the only associated channel when the physical resources are assigned. Channel allocation algorithms are responsible for assignment of the channels to mobile stations. The EDGE base station should be capable of being synchronized with the existing GSM base stations. This will maximize the efficiency as both the base stations can be configured as one sector instead of two, thereby making only one BCCH necessary for the operation. Moreover, an increase in data rates leads to an increased signalling requirement for a given traffic and applications.

5.6 SMART RADIO CONCEPT

Implementation of the smart radio concept enhances the performance of the radio link, both in the uplink and downlink directions, by the use of diversity methods described later in the chapter.

5.6.1 Radio Network Planning Process

The basic process of radio network planning remains the same as in GPRS networks. However, because of the changes in the modulation and coding schemes, there are some changes in the coverage, capacity, and parameter planning of EDGE radio networks.

5.6.2 Coverage Planning

The link budget has a direct impact on coverage. As the EDGE network focuses more on, PS data, the delay tolerance becomes a critical factor in defining system quality level. Some factors that affect link budget calculations specifically in EDGE are noted below.

5.6.3 Incremental Redundancy

Use of IR in coordination with LA not only makes re-transmission more efficient but also optimizes the performance of the system. It reduces the required CII by at least 3 dB. Link budgets are calculated for a given modulation and coding scheme for a specific BLER. The BLER value affects directly the gain due to IR. In fact, the higher the BLER, the higher the IR gain.

5.6.4 Body Loss

When a mobile comes near to the human body, the signal level goes down. This is known as body loss. In GSM 900, this loss is typically 3 dB. No body loss is taken into account for packet data services in an EDGE network.

5.6.6 Diversity Effects

Use of diversity schemes generally has a positive impact on link performance, thereby increasing the area covered by individual sites. Both uplink and downlink diversity schemes are possible. However, smart radio concepts can be used to increase the coverage performance of an EDGE network drastically.

In uplink diversity, multiple antennas are used so as to cancel the correlated noise received at the antennas. Reduction of noise leads to a gain in the signal level. When there is no noise, the system allows the signal to flow without noise reduction. In the downlink direction, two transmitters are used and the signal is transmitted through two uncorrelated paths in bursts with slight delays. The transmitted power increases substantially with the use of two transmitters. Transmission of the signal over two different paths with delay reduces the effects of fast fading. Thus, the link performance and coverage can be increased substantially in EDGE radio networks as compared with GSM or GPRS radio networks.

5.6.7 Received Signal Strength

Signal strength in radio networks can be expressed in relation to interference signals. There are three parameters that specify this: Eb/No, Es/No, and C/N. Both Es/No and C/N can be expressed in terms of Eb/No, which is the ratio of available bit energy to the noise spectral density (also known as the signal-to-noise ratio). Es/No is the ratio of energy-per-symbol to noise. For a GPRS system (with GMSK modulation) this ratio is unity, while for EDGE systems (8-PSK modulation) it is Eb/No + 4.77 dB (as three bits is one symbol). C/N is the ratio of total received power to total noise. The following are useful relationships:

Eb/No(dB) = Es/No - 4.77

C/N(dB) = Eb/No + 6.07

Link budget calculations can be done by using MCS and BLER. However, received signal strength can be calculated for some specified data rates as well. Es/No can be used for throughput (per time slot) calculations in a cell. As seen in earlier chapters, the received signal strength is dependent upon the transmitted signal strength, losses, antenna heights and gains (TX and RX) and distance travelled by the signal. Loss in the signal strength gives the cell range. Thus, relationship between energy-per-symbol limited by noise can be plotted with respect to the cell range. Link level simulations with the above calculations can give the throughput per time slot for each coding scheme.

5.7 CAPACITY PLANNING

Capacity planning for EDGE networks is quite similar to that for GPRS networks, but the increase in throughput per radio time slot in EDGE changes some aspects of the planning. A brief overview of these concepts and their effects on throughput per radio time slot is given below.

The territory aspects (i.e. dedicated, default, CSW, etc.) stand the same for EDGE networks. Dedicated territory is specifically for PS traffic, CSW territory for CS traffic; default territory can be used for PS traffic if the CS traffic is not using it (CS traffic has a priority over PS traffic for default territory). The number of time slots that are assigned in each of these territories can be changed dynamically based on the load conditions.

The concept of frequency re-use is similar to that of GSM/GPRS radio networks. The re-use pattern defines the number of cells that can be used within a cluster in a manner such that no two neighboring cells have the same frequency. A frequency re-use of 3/9 means that each frequency is used only once in three sites/cluster, wherein each site is three sectored. A frequency re-use of 1/3 will have a higher value of interference and thus would degrade the throughput per radio time slot. Thus, a higher frequency re-use value will give a higher throughput and less delay. However, the spectral efficiency is higher in cases of lower frequency re-use as fewer frequencies are being used. Time-slot capacities have a larger dynamic range compared with GPRS radio networks. The number of time slots available is fewer than the number of users in a cell (or network). This means that several users will be using same time slot, reducing the throughput per user. Thus, the higher the number of users (per time slot), the lower will be the throughput (per user) and the higher the delay. PS traffic can be allocated to the BCCH TRX or non-BCCH TRX. Since the spectrum efficiency is usually the same for BCCH and non-BCCH cases, the TSL capacity remains constant on the BCCH layer, making the BCCH layer more suitable for achieving high throughput. Usually, the frequency re-use patterns have been found to be more stringent on non-BCCH TRXs, hence BCCH TRXs are better at giving higher throughput. Enabling of frequency hopping does not have a major impact on capacity or quality of the EGPRS radio network.

Capacity planning dimensioning requires inputs related to cell configuration and traffic behavior. This mainly includes the number of transceivers, definition of EDGE territories (number of time slots in CSW, dedicated and default territories), CS and PS traffic, etc. The outputs of capacity planning mainly include the amount of PS traffic, maximum, minimum and average PS load, available time slots of CS traffic, blocking rate, etc. Capacity Planning based on this dimensioning is done on a cell basis to make sure that required capacity is available for CS and PS traffic, apart from signalling. Traffic types determine the signalling needs. Unlike in GPRS networks where short messages increase the resource (PRACH/PAGCH) requirements for channel set-up, EDGE networks do not face such a problem because of enhanced data rates. However, in EDGE networks, signalling requirements may be greater. This is because, if more and more users are able to get attached to the network using the same time slot even when the net load is constant (i.e. more users per time slot means less throughput per user), a decrease in TCH utilization would take pIace during a TBF. If this TCH utilization remains constant, more signalling channels are required, reducing the number of users getting connected to the network.

Thus, the steps involved in the dimensioning of an EDGE radio network can be summarized as follows:

- CS and PS territories are identified. For the PS territory, the number of time slots in the default and dedicated modes should be defined.
- Total traffic load inclusive of CS and PS should be defined.
- Delay versus load factor should be studied.
- Rate reduction factor/parameter must be calculated.
- Number of TRXs required for supporting the traffic is calculated.

Outputs of Dimensioning can be

- number of time slots required for voice traffic
- number of time slots required for data traffic

- number of time slots in default and dedicated territories
- average and maximum PS load
- average and minimum user throughput
- number of TRXs required supporting the above parameters.

Parameters in Planning

Apart from the parameters that have been discussed in earlier chapters, there are few additional parameters in EDGE radio networks. The most important ones are related to link , adaptation and incremental redundancy.

Once EGPRS has been enabled; the initial coding scheme is selected. LA parameters are dependent on the modulation and coding scheme selections, for both initial transmission and re-transmissions. Although the MCS selections are based on the BTS parameters, the MCS used for the transmission is based on the BLER limits. However, MCS for both transmissions and re-transmissions can be affected by the mobile station memory.

Parameters related to multi-BCF and common BCCH assume importance in an EDGE radio network. As mentioned before, EDGE-capable and non-EDGE-capable transceivers in a one sector can be configured to have only one BCCH. TBF parameter setting makes it possible for TBFs of GPRS and EDGE radio networks to be multiplexed dynamically on one time slot. However, this scenario should be avoided, as the performance suffers in both the uplink and downlink. In the UL, GPRS performance suffers owing to the large amount of 8-PSK re-transmissions taking place, while in the DL, it is due to the GMSK modulation being used where 8-PSK is carrying higher data rates for EDGE.

Parameters related to delay and throughput assume importance owing to higher sub scriber expectations from an EDGE network.

5.8 TRANSMISSION NETWORK PLANNING

The transmission network planning process for an EDGE network is similar to the existing GSM Network. However, owing to the higher data rates, there is a new functionality called 'dynamic Abis'. Thus, the following concepts assume importance in the design of an EDGE transmission network:

- dynamic Abis
- dimensioning of dynamic Abis
- dimensioning of the PCU/BSc.

5.8.1 A-bis

The interface between the base station and the BSC is known as the Abis interface, as show in Figure. In GSM/GPRS networks this interface is 'static'. As we know in GSM/GPRS networks the transceiver channels are mapped onto the A-bis PCM time slots.

Each TCH uses two bits of PCM frame, and these two bits together are known as PCM sub-time slots. This is 'static' in nature because each TRX reserves its full capacity from the A-bis interface constantly even if there are no active users in the air-interface. This make dimensioning of the Abis interface straightforward compared to that in EDGE networks.

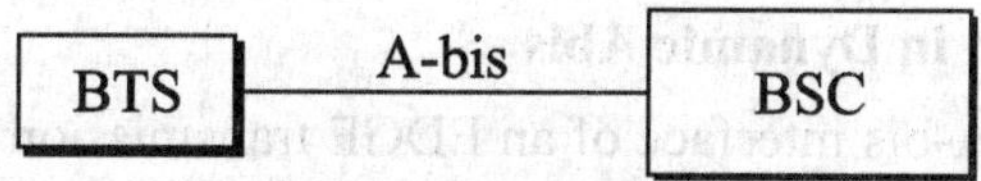

Fig. 5.10: Abis Interface

5.8.2 Dynamic A-bis Functionality in EDGE Networks

Turning now to EDGE networks, octagonal phase-shift keying (8-PSK) changes data rates from as low as 8.8 kbps to 59.2kbps, i.e. from coding scheme MCS-1 to MCS-9. Although s voice signals are still carried in 16 kbps A-bis channels, for data this proves insufficient especially beyond coding scheme MCS-2. To carry more than 16 kbps traffic in the air interface, the data traffic needs more that 16 kbps A-bis channels - probably 32, 48, 64 or 80 kbps. This data traffic is not there all the time, so the concept of 'dynamic' Abis carne into being. Figure shows an example of 'static' and 'dynamic' A-bis.

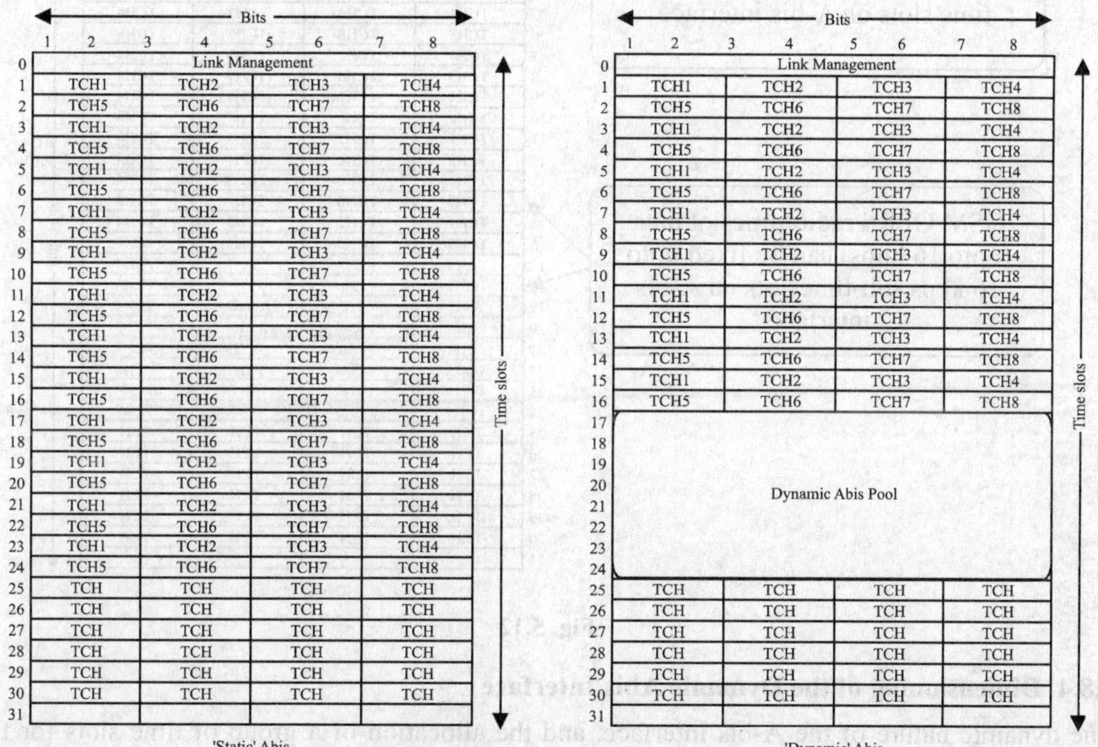

'Static' Abis (Bits 1–8; Time slots)

Time slot	Bits 1–2	Bits 3–4	Bits 5–6	Bits 7–8
0	Link Management			
1	TCH1	TCH2	TCH3	TCH4
2	TCH5	TCH6	TCH7	TCH8
3	TCH1	TCH2	TCH3	TCH4
4	TCH5	TCH6	TCH7	TCH8
5	TCH1	TCH2	TCH3	TCH4
6	TCH5	TCH6	TCH7	TCH8
7	TCH1	TCH2	TCH3	TCH4
8	TCH5	TCH6	TCH7	TCH8
9	TCH1	TCH2	TCH3	TCH4
10	TCH5	TCH6	TCH7	TCH8
11	TCH1	TCH2	TCH3	TCH4
12	TCH5	TCH6	TCH7	TCH8
13	TCH1	TCH2	TCH3	TCH4
14	TCH5	TCH6	TCH7	TCH8
15	TCH1	TCH2	TCH3	TCH4
16	TCH5	TCH6	TCH7	TCH8
17	TCH1	TCH2	TCH3	TCH4
18	TCH5	TCH6	TCH7	TCH8
19	TCH1	TCH2	TCH3	TCH4
20	TCH5	TCH6	TCH7	TCH8
21	TCH1	TCH2	TCH3	TCH4
22	TCH5	TCH6	TCH7	TCH8
23	TCH1	TCH2	TCH3	TCH4
24	TCH5	TCH6	TCH7	TCH8
25	TCH	TCH	TCH	TCH
26	TCH	TCH	TCH	TCH
27	TCH	TCH	TCH	TCH
28	TCH	TCH	TCH	TCH
29	TCH	TCH	TCH	TCH
30	TCH	TCH	TCH	TCH
31				

'Dynamic' Abis (Bits 1–8; Time slots)

Time slot	Bits 1–2	Bits 3–4	Bits 5–6	Bits 7–8
0	Link Management			
1	TCH1	TCH2	TCH3	TCH4
2	TCH5	TCH6	TCH7	TCH8
3	TCH1	TCH2	TCH3	TCH4
4	TCH5	TCH6	TCH7	TCH8
5	TCH1	TCH2	TCH3	TCH4
6	TCH5	TCH6	TCH7	TCH8
7	TCH1	TCH2	TCH3	TCH4
8	TCH5	TCH6	TCH7	TCH8
9	TCH1	TCH2	TCH3	TCH4
10	TCH5	TCH6	TCH7	TCH8
11	TCH1	TCH2	TCH3	TCH4
12	TCH5	TCH6	TCH7	TCH8
13	TCH1	TCH2	TCH3	TCH4
14	TCH5	TCH6	TCH7	TCH8
15	TCH1	TCH2	TCH3	TCH4
16	TCH5	TCH6	TCH7	TCH8
17–24	Dynamic Abis Pool			
25	TCH	TCH	TCH	TCH
26	TCH	TCH	TCH	TCH
27	TCH	TCH	TCH	TCH
28	TCH	TCH	TCH	TCH
29	TCH	TCH	TCH	TCH
30	TCH	TCH	TCH	TCH
31				

Fig. 5.11: 'Static' and 'Dynamic' Abis

A group of these dynamic A-bis channels is known as a 'dynamic A-bis pool' (DAP). A DAP consists of a minimum of one time slot, while the maximum may depend on the system capability within one PCM.

With EDGE transceivers, the BSC allocates A-bis capacity for data calls from the EGPRS dynamic pool (EDAP) when needed, i.e. when MCS-3 or higher is used. Standard GPRS (non-EGPRS) calls using CS-2, CS-3 and CS-4 can also use EDA resources when allocated in EGPRS territory (EDGE transceivers).

5.8.3 Time-Slot Allocation in Dynamic Abis

Time-slot allocation in the A-bis interface of an EDGE transmission network is almost the same as in GSM/GPRS networks. Traffic channels on the A-bis still occupy 16 kbps sub-time slot for voice, and data rates up to 16 kbps. However, for data rates above 16 kbps, one master sub-time slot of 16 kbps and up to four sub-time slots from the DAP are required, as shown in Figure. The requirements for signalling channels for TRXs and BCF are the same as in GSM/GPRS networks. The pilot bits for synconisation can be accommodated in the TSO or TS31 (or any other time slot).

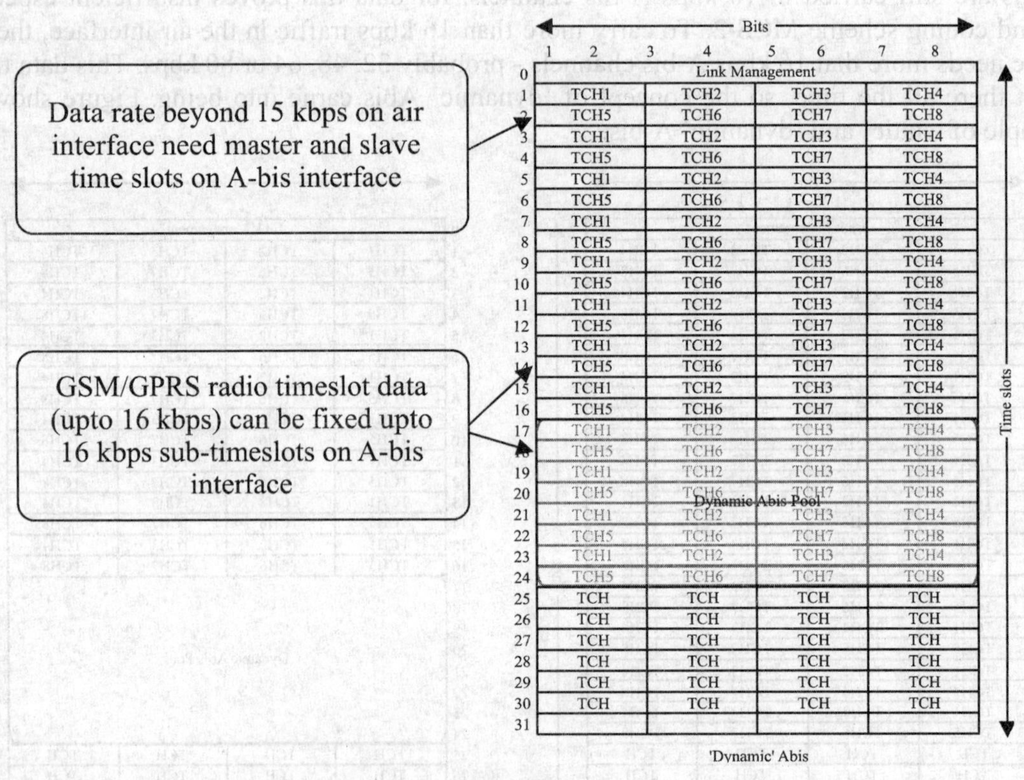

Fig. 5.12

5.8.4 Dimensioning of the Dynamic Abis Interface

The dynamic nature of the A-bis interface, and the allocation of a group of time slots for the DAP, changes the static capacity calculation of GSM/GPRS networks. In the latter, the A-bis interface allocates the whole capacity for the transceiver irrespective of usage; that makes the capacity calculations simpler, because knowledge of the number of TRXs and the signalling rate leads to the amount of capacity required on the A-bis interface.

Before we look into DAP dimensioning, it should be remembered that DAP is used only for packet data for an MCS scheme greater than 2. Also, for each of the coding schemes, the number of required traffic channels will vary from none in MCS-l (or CS-l) to four in MCS-8/9, as shown in Figure . (Designers should refer to specific product information and the system capabilities before they design the pool.) Also, the number of A-bis channels will increase when signalling is added to it, which again depends upon the system being used in the network. The A-bis channels that are present in the pool are also known as 'slaves'.

Based on the requirements of mobile subscribers, the sub-time slots from the pool are requested. The number of time slots allocated to the pool is usually in whole numbers one, two, three, four or more time slots - depending on the DAP handling capacity of the system. Obviously, the number of time slots allocated to the DAP cannot be more than 30 (if TSO and TS3l are 'reserved' for management purposes).

Table 5.2: Transmission Requirement for EGPRS Coding Schemes at the A-bis Interface

Coding scheme	*Bit rate (bps)*	*Min. A-bis PCM allocation*
CS-1	8000	■
CS-2	12000	■
CS-3	14400	■
CS-4	20000	■■
MCS-1	8800	■
MCS-2	11200	■
MCS-3	14800	■
MCS-4	17600	■■
MCS-5	22400	■■
MCS-6	29600	■■
MCS-7	44800	■■
MCS-8	54400	■ ■■■
MCS-9	59200	■ ■■■

Dimensioning of dynamic A-bis means dimensioning of the pool. Once the number of time slots required for DAP is known, the remaining process becomes similar to dimensioning/planning of GSM/GPRS transmission networks. The main idea behind DAP dimensioning is to find the number of time slots that can be assigned to a pool in such a manner that the Abis interface does not become a limitation for the air interface throughput. Thus the main inputs for this would be the number of radio time slots required for PS traffic (i.e. dedicated and default territory in an EDGE radio network), me capacity of radio time slots, blocking that could take place on the Abis interface, etc.

Based on these inputs and the number of PCM time slots available for the pool, the required' number of PCM time slots can be calculated. Obviously, limitations and capability of the equipment needs to be taken into consideration. So:

$$B(n, N, p) = \sum_{x=N=l}^{n} P(x)$$

where B is the blocking probability of the DAP, N is the number of time slots available in the pool, p is the utilisation of EDGE channels in the air interface, and n is the number of traffic channels used in the air interface.

This dimensioning will result in outputs such as the maximum throughput possible on the air-interface with A-bis acting as a bottleneck, and the number of time slots required to 'low maximum possible throughput on the air interface to be carried on the A-bis.

5.8.5 The Impact of Dynamic Abis on Transmission Network Design

Assume that there is a base station site having a configuration of 3 + 3 + 3. When operating in the GSM mode, using 16 kbps signalling, the required number of PCM time slots per transceiver is 2.25 (two for traffic and 0.25 for 16 kbps signalling). This means that total number of time slots required for these nine TRXs is 9 x 2.25 = 20.25; i.e. 21time slots approximately. This would mean that, of 32 time slots, TSO and TS31 along, with these 21 are used' (23 in total), leaving nine time slots available for possible future grades. In an EDGE network, these nine time slots might be used for the DAP, if they are sufficient.

Now consider this EDGE network using the MCS-9 coding scheme; i.e. each user logging the network for PS services requires four A-bis channels, or one full additional timeslot, apart from the master sub-time slot on the PCM. This means that at a given time only nine users can use the system at a maximum rate of 59.2 kbps. As soon as a tenth subscriber logs on to the network also requesting the MCS-9 scheme, the system starts sharing its resources. This means that although access will be given to this tenth subscriber, the request will be downgraded to lower coding schemes like MCS-6 or MCS-7. Also, the coding scheme of the existing subscribers logged on may be downgraded to MCS-6 or MCS-7, in order to accommodate this new subscriber. So the throughput on the air-interface goes down because of the limitation on the Abis interface. In this case it would be advisable to have, more time slots in the pool, implying more PCMs required per site, with additional CO Thus, the number of time slots planned for DAP should be a balance between the desirable throughput and cost.

5.9 CORE NETWORK PLANNING

Both CS and PS core network planning remain similar to what was described in Chapters 4 and 5. The major change in the packet core section is enhanced capacities of the BSC and GSN to cater to higher data rates on the radio network. Dimensioning of the packet core network mainly involves the PCV, the Gb interface and the SGSN, as follows:

- *PCU dimensioning:*

  Number of transceivers that can be supported by one PCV

  Amount of (data) traffic that can be handled by one PCU

  Number of traffic channels that can be handled by one PCU

- *Gb interface dimensioning:*

  Minimum number of Gb interfaces required between the PCV and SGSN, Uplink and downlink traffic calculations for the frame relay links
- *SGSN dimensioning:*

  Number of subscribers

  Processing capacity of the SGSN

  Gb interface capacity.

5.9.1 Network Optimisation

Optimization of an EDGE network will focus mainly on the radio and transmission networks owing to the increased data rate on the air-interface and the introduction of the dynamic feature on the A-bis interface. Usually, optimization of radio and transmission networks is performed separately, but this scenario changes owing to the fact that the dynamic Abis if not properly planned, may become a bottleneck for the air interface throughput. There are three main steps, as shown in Figure. The 'conventional' radio network optimization process will be quite similar to that explained in earlier chapters for SM/GPRS networks. Transmission network optimization remains similar also, except for optimizing the A-bis capacity so that it does not become a bottleneck for the air-interface.

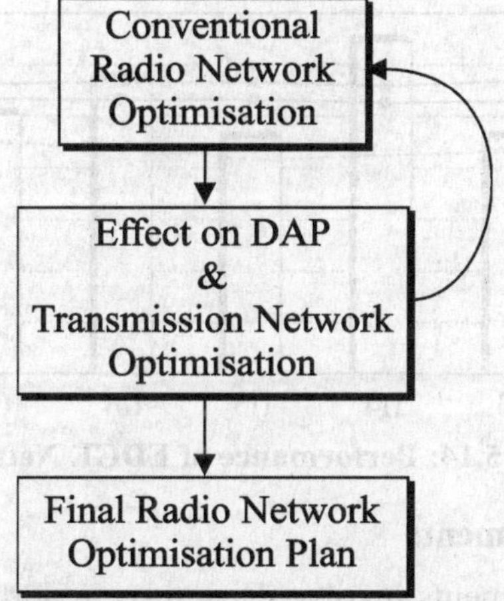

Fig. 5.13: Network Optimization

5.9.2 Radio Network Optimization

Coverage, capacity and quality can be improved by using the standard principles of optimization that have been described earlier for GSM/GPRS. The main focus in EDGE radio I network optimization will be on throughput, which affects the capacity and coverage directly. One important point to remember is that, since EDGE implementation will generally be on top of an existing GPRS network, it is essential that throughput improvement i_' measured and analysed with respect that of the GPRS network.

5.9.3 Transmission Network Optimization

The optimization process is similar to that in GSM networks, however, there are two extra factors that need to be considered during the EDGE optimization process: the dynamic nature of the A-bis interface, and the air-interface throughput changes due *to* bottleneck created by the A-bis. As there is a pool of time slots reserved for packet data, it will always be the case that the number of packet service users increases in the network. Though the pool itself will be dynamic, the number of time slots that will be used for the pool will be static; so once it is figured out that the required time slots (in the pool) need to be increased, some optimization will be required. The situation is more severe if the number of PCMs required per base station also needs to be increased.

5.10 KEY PERFORMANCE INDICATORS

The major extra KPls relate to the definitions of the EDGE territory, BLER (block error rate), MCS schemes used, BCCH usage, etc. These parameter settings define the initial throughput. Adjustments to these settings (apart from those in the GSM/GPRS network) will permit maximization of throughput.

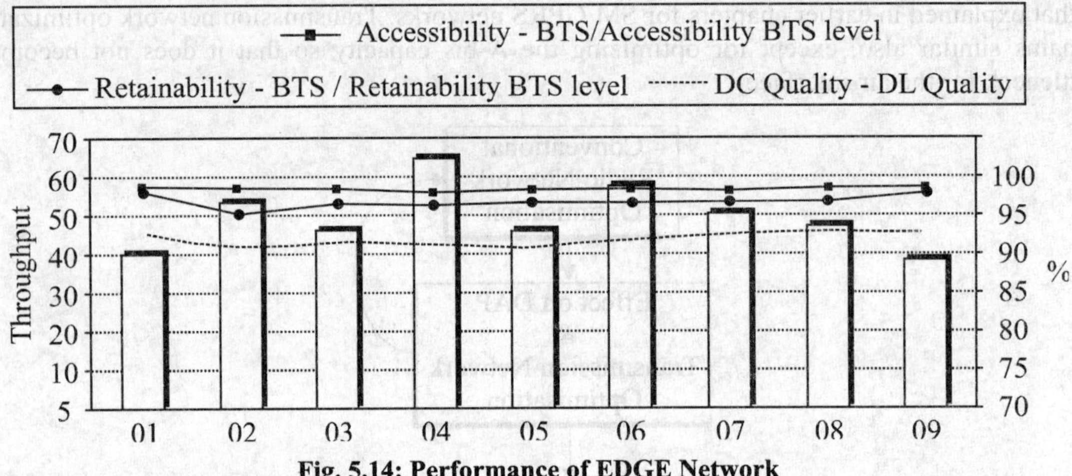

Fig. 5.14: Performance of EDGE Network

5.10.1 Performance Measurements

As usual, performance measurements involve drive tests, reports from the network management system (NMS), and network planning tools. However, the focus will be on throughput ill an EDGE network, and the key areas of performance measurement will therefore be at the air interface and the Abis interface. For the air interface, the interest will be on capacity, coverage and quality; while for the A-bis interface it will be on the variation of throughput with respect to modulation and coding schemes. One such example of performance based on accessibility, retain ability, quality (ARQ) and peak traffic is shown in Figure 5.14.

As stated earlier , performance indicators like the ability of mobile stations to get access to the cell (accessibility), DCR (retainability), call quality in the downlink IDL-quality), etc. need to be measured. Figure shows an example of BTS performance measurements.

Table 5.3

Date	BTS ID	Accessibility (BTS level)	Retainability (BTS level)	(dB) UL Quality	(dB) DL Quality	TCH Erlang
MIO6/03	8TS1	98.61	99.05	92.73	72.01	0.55
MIO7/03	8TS1	98.21	96.49	91.35	91.23	0.68
MIO8/03	8TS1	66.18	100.00	99.11	99.33	2.06
MIO9/03	8TSI			100.00	95.62	0.11

Measurement of the Abis throughput capacity with respect to the coding schemes used by mobile subscribers will be critical in adjusting the boundaries of the dynamic pool. The example in Figure shows the variation of the pool with respect to modulation and ling schemes.

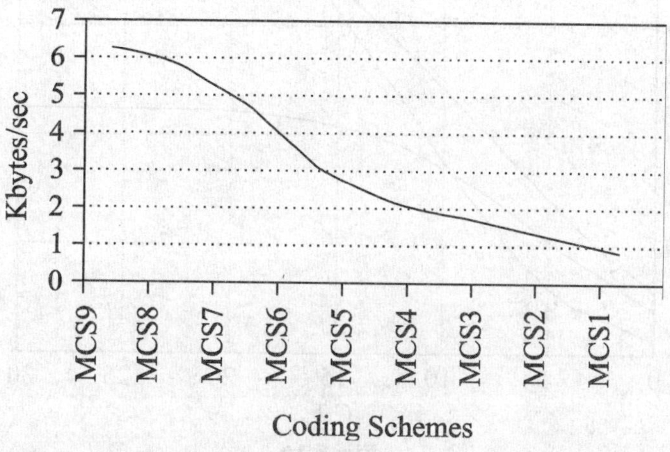

Fig. 5.15

Performance of an EDGE network will usually be in terms of the underlying GPRS ark. The achieved mean throughput values and delay values in an EDGE network are better than for the GPRS network, even when the load is higher. The measurement information serves not only to increase coverage and capacity, but also the quality of service experienced by end-users, which will be closely observed in EDGE networks. The optimum value of QoS will depend ultimately on traffic requirements. Interactive traffic has more stringent quality requirements than background traffic. Spectrum efficiency will playa big role in achieving this. The tradeoff between the number of transceivers and interference levels (i.e. between higher throughput and more users) is a delicate issue. Final optimization plans will be similar to those for GSM/GPRS networks, but with stringent QoS requirements guiding the results.

5.10.2 Improvement of Throughput in EDGE Networks

QoS depends on the service required, but higher throughput will be the main QoS-fulfilling requirement in an EDGE network. Throughput on the air interface and coverage (both at hot spots and cell edges) will be the main focus in the planning as well as optimization of the radio network. Throughput is dependent upon a number of factors such as C II, handovers, MCS changes, etc. An increase in the C/I ratio will result in increased throughput (shown in the simulation in Figure). Measurement at the cell edges will be critical, and here performance improvement can be achieved by using concepts such as antenna tilts, power increase/decrease, etc.

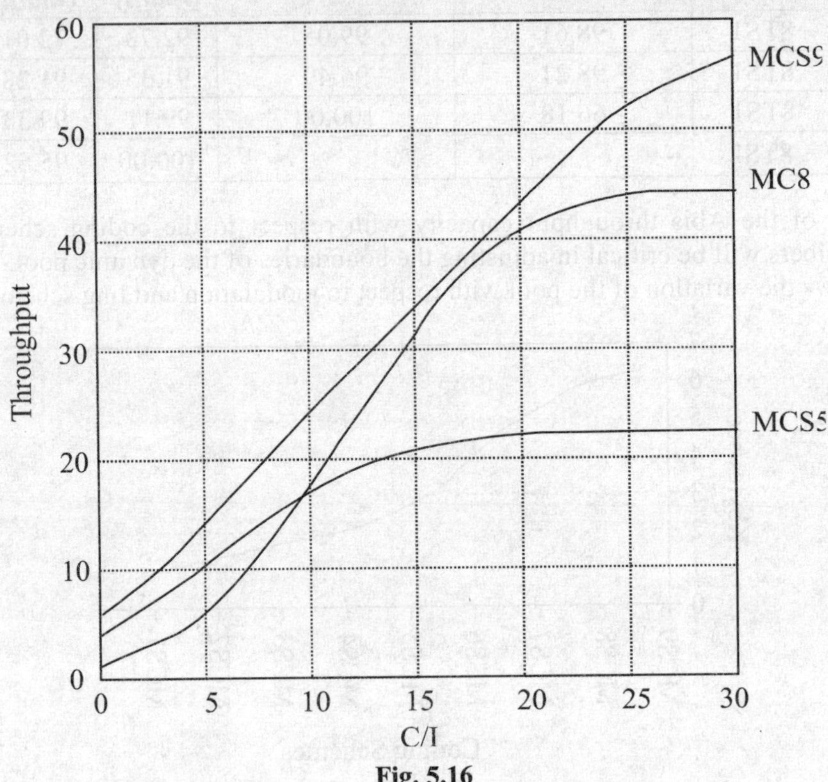

Fig. 5.16

Increasing the number of handovers will also decrease throughput, so optimization of the neighbors to reduce unnecessary handovers can be one possible solution to increase throughput. Throughput also decreases with the number of MCS changes from higher throughput MCS to lower-throughput MCS. Optimization can be achieved by parameter auditing after observing the C/I and receiver level statistics against MCS changes.

Review Questions

1. What is GPRS? Mention the maximum theoretical speed of data rate in GPRS.
2. Write down the main advantages of GPRS.
3. Differentiate between circuit switching and packet switching.
4. What are the requirements of GPRS network?
5. Draw a sketch showing the components of GPRS network and explain the functions of the new components viz. SGSN and GGSN
6. What is EDGE? How the GPRS network to EDGE network?

7. Write above EDGE modulation technique.
8. Explain how network planning and optimization is done in the case of EDGE network.
9. Write about Radio network planning process.
10. What are the important points to be taken care of while doing capacity planning.
11. What is A-bis? Write about the dynamic functionality in EDGE.
12. Discuss the points to be considered for network optimization (RN and Trans)
13. Evaluate the key performance indicators in EDGE network.

6 GSM Security Algorithms and Features

6.1 GSM SECURITY

GSM security algorithms are used to provide authentication and radio link privacy to users on a GSM network.

GSM uses three different security algorithms called A3, A5, and A8. In practice, A3 and A8 are generally implemented together (known as A3/A8).

An A3/A8 algorithm is implemented in Subscriber Identity Module (SIM) cards and in GSM network Authentication Centres. It is used to authenticate the customer and generate a key for encrypting voice and data traffic, as defined in 3GPP TS 43.020 (03.20 before Rel-4). Development of A3 and A8 algorithms is considered a matter for individual GSM network operators, although example implementations are available.

An A5 encryption algorithm scrambles the user's voice and data traffic between the handset and the base station to provide privacy. An A5 algorithm is implemented in both the handset and the base station subsystem (BSS).

6.2 3GPP CONFIDENTIALITY AND INTEGRITY ALGORITHMS UEA2 AND UIA2

The GSM Association, having cooperated in the development of the 3GPP Confidentiality and Integrity Algorithms UEA2 and UIA2 ("The UEA2 & UIA2 Algorithm"), has been granted distribution rights to the Algorithms that have been developed through the collaborative efforts of the 3GPP Organisational Partners.

The UEA2 and UIA2 Algorithm specifications are available below and may be used only for the development and operation of equipment conforming to the UEA2 & UIA2 Algorithm or standards based on it. Every Beneficiary intending to implement and/or use the UEA2 & UIA2 Algorithm must sign a Restricted Usage Undertaking with a Custodian and demonstrate that they satisfy the approval criteria specified in the Restricted Usage Undertaking. A fee of EUR4,000 is chargeable to non-members of the GSM Association wishing to implement and/or use the UEA2 and UIA2 Algorithm.

Specification of the 3GPP Confidentiality and Integrity Algorithms UEA2 & UIA2: UEA2 & UIA2

Document 1— Specifications of the 3GPP Confidentiality and Integrity Algorithms UEA2 & UIA2

Document 2— Specification of the 3GPP Confidentiality and Integrity Algorithms UEA2 & UIA2:

Document 3— Specification of the 3GPP Confidentiality and Integrity Algorithms UEA2 & UIA2: Implementor's Test Data

Document 4— Specification of the 3GPP Confidentiality and Integrity Algorithms UEA2 & UIA2: Design Conformance Test Data

Document 5— Specification of the 3GPP Confidentiality and Integrity Algorithms UEA2 & UIA2: Design and Evaluation report

Every Beneficiary must send to the GSM Association two signed paper copies of the Restricted Usage Undertaking - one copy will be countersigned and returned. Non-GSM Association members must also enclose the Administrative Charge of € 4,000.

6.3 3GPP A5/3 AND GEA3 ALGORITHMS

The GSM Association is a Custodian of the A5/3 encryption algorithms for GSM and EDGE, and the GEA3 encryption algorithm for GPRS, that have been developed through the collaborative efforts of the A5/3 and GEA3 encryption algorithm specifications are available below. They may be used only for the development and operation of GSM, EDGE and GPRS mobile communications and services. Every Beneficiary intending to implement and/or use the algorithms must sign a Restricted Usage Undertaking with a Custodian and demonstrate that they fulfill the approval criteria specified in the Restricted Usage Undertaking. A fee of EUR2,000 is chargeable to non-members of the GSM Association wishing to implement and/or use the A5/3 and GEA3 algorithm specifications.

The A5/3 and GEA3 algorithms are based on the 3GPP ciphering algorithm (F8), for which Mitsubishi holds essential patents. Beneficiaries of the A5/3 and GEA3 algorithms must also be licensed by Mitsubishi Electronic Corporation Japan. Mitsubishi grants royalty-free licenses under those patents under separate written license agreements and subject to other terms and conditions which are believed fair and commercially reasonable. Mitsubishi reserves the right to refuse or withdraw the license to/from the parties that refuse to license, or claim unfair, unreasonable or discriminatory royalty rates for their essential GSM/3G IPRs.

6.4 GSM MILEAGE

The 3GPP specification TS 55.205 contains an example set of algorithms which may be used as the GSM authentication and key generation functions A3 and A8. The algorithms specified in this document are examples that may be used by an operator who does not wish to design his own.

The specification document 3GPP TS 55.205 "Specification of the GSM-MILENAGE Algorithms: An example algorithm set for the GSM Authentication and Key Generation functions A3 and A8" is available here. Download, implementation and use of the example algorithm set is subject to the terms indicated in the document only and is available at no cost.

6.5 SECURITY ACCREDITATION SCHEME

Recent years have been a phenomenal success for GSM, with hundreds of millions of customers worldwide. As the number of customers increase, so too does the importance of network operators' security.

There are numerous security risks faced by every network operator. Suppliers may introduce certain risks, the consequences of which will be borne by the operator, therefore network operators are dependent on their suppliers to control risks, and to provide confidence that adequate security is in place.

As the inherent security of the GSM system is fundamental to its global success, many GSM operators consider carrying out security audits of their key strategic suppliers, whose products have the most impact on the security of their GSM operations. Some GSM operators do not have the resources or expertise to undertake such audits, while other operators commit considerable time and resources to ensuring that adequate security procedures and processes are in place. The conduct of individual audits at all suppliers would impose a significant burden and cost on the industry.

With this in mind, the GSM Association manages the Security Accreditation Scheme (SAS), which is a voluntary scheme whereby suppliers subject their production sites and processes to a comprehensive security audit. The scheme is wholly funded by participating suppliers and a number of benefits accrue to network operators and GSM suppliers alike.

Advantages to Suppliers

- Ability to demonstrate commitment to security and reduction of risks for customers
- Reduced number of individual operator inspections
- Certification from the world's leading wireless industry representative body
- Opportunity to receive a world-class security review of operations
- Provides a uniform approach to security audits

Advantages to Network Operators

- No longer need to invest, in financial or resource terms, in conducting individual audits
- Scheme is conducted by highly qualified individuals at no cost to the operator
- The scheme sets a rigorous security standard demonstrating supplier commitment to the highest levels of security
- Offers peace of mind that suppliers have implemented appropriate security measures

The GSM Association uses its broad reach to publicise those suppliers who have signed up to the scheme, highlighting to members the benefits of acquiring products from GSM Association security certified suppliers, and making an overview of audit results available to all GSM Association members.

Participation in SAS by some of the industry's largest suppliers has played a major role in the success of the scheme to date. The Security Accreditation Scheme is currently open to all smart card suppliers, regardless of location, and the GSM Association welcomes the participation of all interested parties

6.6.1 Mobile Application Security

The market share of mobile user equipment with open operating systems is steadily increasing and will continue to grow rapidly in future. Openness offers clear benefits to customers, device manufacturers, software developers and operators as it facilitates the development of rich and compelling applications. However, openness also presents challenges and risks and malicious applications are likely to increase in number and complexity in the future. Therefore, mobile application related security is a key issue for the mobile industry.

6.6.2 GSM Association Mobile Application Security Initiative

The GSM Association Identified the Need for a More Coordinated Approach to Application Security Across Mobile Operating Systems to Reduce the Risk of Malware Whilst Facilitating Users and Developers. a Dedicated Project Team Embarked on an Industry Initiative to Proactively Define and Promote an Effective Solution Across Open Os Platforms and Operators. From the Outset, the Focus was on Prevention Rather Than Detection and Cure and the Objective was to use Application Certification and Terminal Security Policies to Create an Environment Designed to Reduce the Risk of Malware Impacting on Consumers.

The challenges for the Mobile Application Security Special Project Team (MAS) were many and included the need to:

- Proactively protect mobile users from fraud and malicious applications
- Assure quality and accountability of mobile applications
- Maintain trust in mobile platforms (and avoid similar problems in the Internet world)
- Secure existing and future business
- Protect operators against costs originating from malicious applications
- Facilitate certification processes to reduce barriers for developers
- Ensure consistency across different OS platforms and operators.

Findings Published

In the course of its work, MAS defined a set of aligned terminal and certification programme requirements necessary to limit security risks and to support stakeholder needs. The initiative identified gaps in the existing terminal and certification process implementations and presented its key findings and recommendations to GSMA members and other key stakeholders on a confidential basis.

What's Next?

Although MAS has concluded its work, much remains to be done to ensure the barriers necessary to reduce the risk of malware are erected. Much of the necessary follow on work is already underway in the Open Mobile Terminal Platform (OMTP) and industry players are strongly encouraged to engage in the ongoing activities to further validate and strengthen the countermeasures already identified. The authentication algorithm used in the GSM system is known as the A3 algorithm.

Most GSM network operators utilize a version of the COMP128 algorithm as the implementation of the A3 algorithm.

A3's task is to generate the 32-bit Signed Response (SRES) utilizing the 128-bit random challenge (RAND) generated by the Home Location Register (HLR) and the 128-bit Individual Subscriber Authentication Key (Ki) from the Mobile Station's Subscriber Identity Module (SIM) or the Home Location Register (HLR).

A3 actually generates 128 bits of output. The first 32 bits of those 128 bits form the Signed Response.

The A3 algorithm is implemented in the Subscriber Identity Module (SIM).

6.7 ENCRYPTION IN GSM NETWORKS

The encryption algorithm used in the GSM system is a stream cipher known as the A5 algorithm.

Multiple versions of the A5 algorithm exist which implement various levels of encryption.

- A5/0 utilizes no encryption.
- A5/1 is the original A5 algorithm used in Europe.
- A5/2 is a weaker encryption algorithm created for export and used in the United States.
- A5/3 is a strong encryption algorithm created as part of the 3rd Generation Partnership Project (3GPP).

The stream cipher is initialized with the Session Key (Kc) and the number of each frame. The same Kc is used throughout the call, but the 22-bit frame number changes during the call, thus generating a unique keystream for every frame. The same Session Key (Kc) is used as long as the Mobile Services Switching Center (MSC) does not authenticate the Mobile Station again. In practice, the same Session Key (Kc) may be in use for days.

Authentication is an optional procedure in the beginning of a call, but it is usually not performed. The A5 algorithm is implemented in the Mobile Station (MS).

6.8 KEY GENERATION IN GSM NETWORKS

The key generation algorithm used in the GSM system is known as the A8 algorithm.

Most GSM network operators utilize the a version of the COMP128 algorithm as the implementation of the A8 algorithm.

A8's task is to generate the 64-bit Session Key (Kc), from the 128-bit random challenge (RAND) received from the Mobile Services Switching Center (MSC) and from the 128-bit Individual Subscriber Authentication Key (Ki) from the Mobile Station's Subscriber Identity Module (SIM) or the Home Location Register (HLR).

One Session Key (Kc) is used until the MSC decides to authenticate the MS again. This might take days.

A8 actually generates 128 bits of output. The last 54 bits of those 128 bits form the Session Key (Kc). Ten zero-bits are appended to this key before it is given as input to the A5 algorithm.

The A8 algorithm is implemented in the Subscriber Identity Module (SIM).

6.9 AUTHENTICATION KEY GENERATION IN A GSM NETWORK

Encryption in the GSM network utilizes a Challenge/Response mechanism.

1. The Mobile Station (MS) signs into the network.
2. The Mobile Services Switching Center (MSC) requests 5 triples from the Home Location Register (HLR).
3. The Home Location Register creates five triples utilizing the A8 algorithm. These five triples each contain:
   - A 128-bit random challenge (RAND)
   - A 32-bit matching Signed Response (SRES)
   - A 64-bit ciphering key used as a Session Key (Kc).
4. The Home Location Register sends the Mobile Services Switching Center the five triples.
5. The Mobile Services Switching Center sends the random challenge from the first triple to the Base Transceiver Station (BTS).
6. The Base Transceiver Station sends the random challenge from the first triple to the Mobile Station.
7. The Mobile Station receives the random challenge from the Base Transceiver Station and encrypts it with the Individual Subscriber Authentication Key (Ki) assigned to the Mobile Station utilizing the A3 algorithm.
8. The Mobile Station sends the Signed Response to the Base Transceiver Station.
9. The Base Transceiver Station sends the Signed Response to the Mobile Services Switching Center.
10. The Mobile Services Switching Center verifies the Signed Response.
11. The Mobile Station generates a Session Key (Kc) utilizing the A8 algorithm, the Individual Subscriber Authentication Key (Ki) assigned to the Mobile Station, and the random challenge received from the Base Transceiver Station.
12. The Mobile Station sends the Session Key (Kc) to the Base Transceiver Station.

13. The Mobile Services Switching Center sends the Session Key (Kc) to the Base Transceiver Station.
14. The Base Transceiver Station receives the Session Key (Kc) from the Mobile Services Switching Center.
15. The Base Transceiver Station receives the Session Key (Kc) from the Mobile Station.
16. The Base Transceiver Station verifies the Session Keys from the Mobile Station and the Mobile Services switching Center.
17. The A5 algorithm is initialized with the Session Key (Kc) and the number of the frame to be encrypted.
18. Over-the-air communication channel between the Mobile Station and Base Transceiver Station can now be encrypted utilizing the A5 algorithm.

This process authenticates the GSM Mobile Station (MS) to the GSM network. One known security limitation of GSM networks is that the GSM network is never authenticated by the GSM Mobile Station (MS).

This one-way authentication makes it possible for an attacker to pretend to be a GSM network provider.

6.10 THE A3 AND A8 ALGORITHMS

Most GSM providers use a version of COMP128 for both the A3 authentication algorithm and the A8 key generation algorithm.

Ian Goldberg and David Wagner of the University of California at Berkeley demonstrated that all A8 implementations they looked at, including the few that did not use COMP128, were deliberately weakened. The A8 algorithm takes a 64-bit key, but ten key bits were set to zero. The attack on the A8 algorithm demonstrated by Goldberg and Wagner takes just 2 to 19 queries to the GSM SIM (Subscriber Identity Module), which takes roughly 8 hours.

Josyula R. Rao, Pankaj Rohatgi and Helmut Scherzer of IBM and Stephane Tinguely of the Swiss Federal Institute of Technology have published Partitioning Attacks: Or How to Rapidly Clone Some GSM Cards which shows a method by which COMP128 can be broken in less than a minute.

The COMP128-2 and COMP128-3 algorithms have been developed to address the security issues of COMP128-1. COMP128-2 and COMP128-3 are secret algorithms which have not been subject to cryptanalysis. COMP128-3 fixes the issue where 10 bits of the Session Key (Kc) were set to zero.

GSM network operators are slowly migrating from COMP128 (also known as COMP128-1) to COMP28-2 or COMP128-3. Because the A3 and A8 algorithms are stored in the Subscriber Identity Module, this requires changing the GSM subscribers SIM cards.

6.11 LOCKING AND UNLOCKING

Most GSM Mobile Stations (MS) are sold to be used on a specific GSM network. The Mobile Stations are "locked" to only accept a Subscriber Identity Module (SIM) from the GSM carrier that sold the Mobile Station.

There are several situations where you would want to unlock your Mobile Station. For example, you might wish to switch GSM service providers and keep your current Mobile Station. Or, you may have purchased a new Mobile Station and you want to sell your old Mobile Station to someone who is subscribed to a different GSM service provider. A third situation is if you are travelling extensively in another GSM service providers area and you would like to get local GSM service instead of paying roaming charges.

There are two methods of unlocking Mobile Stations. The first method, which requires no equipment, is to enter the unlock code for your Mobile Station from the keypad. Your GSM service provide will be able to give you this unlock code, but may not be willing to do so. The second method is to use dedicated unlocking hardware which plugs into your Mobile Station and unlocks it. You may purchase this hardware, or send your Mobile Station to an unlocking service which will unlock it for a small fee.

6.12 IMEI

The IMEI (International Mobile Equipment Identity) is a unique 17 or 15 digit code used to identify an individual mobile station to a GSM or UMTS network. The IMEI number provides an important function; it uniquely identifies a specific mobile phone being used on a mobile network. The IMEI is a useful tool to prevent a stolen handset from accessing a network and being used to place calls. Mobile phone owners who have their phones stolen can contact their mobile network provider and ask them disable a phone using its IMEI number. With an IMEI number, the phone can be blocked from the network quickly and easily.

It is important to note that swapping a SIM card will not stop a phone from being banned. IMEI numbers are stored in the phones themselves, not on the SIM cards.

An IMEI is only used to identify the device and does not relate to a specific individual or organization. Other numbers such as the ESN (Electronic Serial Numbers) and MEID (Mobile Equipment Identifiers) can link an individual to a phone. Usually, an IMSI number stored on a SIM card can identify the subscriber on a network.

There are several ways in which you can locate your mobile phone's IMEI number. The IMEI can usually be found on the handset, beneath the battery, sometimes printed on a small white label. Another way to easily locate your IMEI phone is to dial the following sequence of numbers into the handset: *#06#. If you have a Sony Ericsson mobile phone, you can retrieve the IMEI by pressing the following key sequence: right,*, left, left,*, left, *, left.

The Structure of an IMEI Number

IMEI numbers either come in a 17 digit or 15 digit sequences of numbers. The IMEI format currently utilized is AA-BBBBBB-CCCCCC-D:

- AA : These two digits are for the Reporting Body Identifier, indicating the GSMA approved group that allocated the TAC (Type Allocation Code).
- BBBBBB : The remainder of the TAC
- CCCCCC : Serial sequence of the Model
- D : Luhn check digit of the entire model or 0 (This is an algorithm that validates the ID number)

6.13 CENTRAL EQUIPMENT IDENTITY REGISTER (CEIR)

If a mobile handset is lost or stolen, the owner of the device can contact the CEIR (Central Equipment Identity Register) which will blacklist the device in all currently operating switches. This makes the lost or stolen handset unusable. The action of blacklisting stolen mobile handsets is seen as a deterrent to crime. It is possible, however, to change an IMEI with special tools and there are certain mobile networks that do not automatically blacklist handsets registered with the CEIR. Current statistics state that approximately ten percent of IMEI's in use today are not unique or have been reprogrammed (hacked).

Table 6.1: CEIR Classification of Handsets

Color	*Meaning*
White	Valid Mobile Station
Grey	Mobile Station to be tracked
Black	Barred Mobile Station

6.14 PRACTICAL APPLICATIONS

How can I Find My IMEI?

The IMEI (International Mobile Equipment Identity) number can be displayed on most phones by dialing the code *# 06 #.

The IMEI is also usually printed on the compliance plate under the battery.

What is an IMSI?

The IMSI (International Mobile Subscriber Identity) is a unique 15-digit code used to identify an individual user on a GSM network.

The IMSI consists of three components:

- Mobile Country Code (MCC)
- Mobile Network Code (MNC)
- Mobile Subscriber Identity Number (MSIN)

The IMSI is stored in the Subscriber Identity Module (SIM).

What is a TIMSI?

The TIMSI (Temporary IMSI) is a pseudo-random number generated from the IMSI (International Mobile Subscriber Identity) number.

The TIMSI is utilized in order to remove the need to transmit the IMSI over-the-air. This helps to keep the IMSI more secure.

To track a GSM user via the IMSI/TIMSI, an eavesdropper must intercept the GSM network communication where the TIMSI is initially negotiated.

In addition, because the TIMSI is periodically renegotiated, the eavesdropper must intercept each additional TIMSI re-negotiation session.

What are the PIN and PUK?

PIN (Personal Identity Number) is a 4-8 digit access code which can be used to secure your telephone from use.PIN2 (Personal Identity Number 2) is a 4-8 digit access code which can be used to access the priority number memory and cost of calls.The PUK (Personal Unblocking Key) and PUK2 are used to unlock the PIN and PIN 2 codes respectively if your SIM card is blocked.

How Do I Change My PIN and PUK?

Table 6.2

Change SIM Card PIN	** 04 * old PIN * new PIN * new PIN #
Change SIM Card PIN2	** 042 * old PIN2 * new PIN2 *new PIN2 #
Change SIM Card PUK	** 05 * old PUK * new PUK * new PUK #
Change SIM Card PUK2	** 052 * old PUK2 * new PUK2 * new PUK2 #

Note— These codes only work on some mobile stations offered by some providers.

How Do I use CallerID?

Calling Line Identification Presentation (CLIP) affects your reception of CallerID data:

Table 6.3

Activate Incoming (CLIP)	* 30 # SEND
Deactivate Incoming (CLIP)	# 30 # SEND
Verify Incoming (CLIP)	*# 30 # SEND

Calling Line Identification Restriction (CLIR) affects your transmission of CallerID data:

Table 6.4

Activate Outgoing (CLIR)	* 31 # SEND
Deactivate Outgoing (CLIR)	# 31 # SEND
Verify Outgoing (CLIR)	*# 31 # SEND

Note— These codes only work on some service plans offered by some providers.

What is a Subscriber Identity Module (SIM)?

The Subscriber Identity Module (SIM) is a small smart card which contains both programming and information. The A3 and A8 algorithms are implemented in the Subscriber Identity Module (SIM).Subscriber information, such as the IMSI (International Mobile Subscriber Identity), is stored in the Subscriber Identity Module (SIM).

The Subscriber Identity Module (SIM) can be used to store user-defined information such as phonebook entries. One of the advantages of the GSM architecture is that the SIM may be moved from one Mobile Station to another. This makes upgrades very simple for the GSM telephone user.

Review Questions

1. Why GSM security algorithm is required?
2. What are the different security algorithms? Where they are implemented?
3. Write note on 3GPP confidentiality and integrity algorithms.
4. What are 3GPP-A3 and 3GPP-A5 algorithms? Where and how they are used?
5. What is SAS? What SAS is aimed to achieve?
6. Elucidate the advantages of SAS both for operators and for users.
7. Write about Mobile Application Security.
8. What Algorithms used for encryption in GSM networks?
9. What Algorithms used for key generation in GSM network?
10. How do Authentication and key generation work in GSM network?
11. What is meant by locking and unlocking?
12. Write detailed note on IMEI.
13. What is TIMSI? How is this used in mobile network?

7 3GPP Evolution (3GPP Releases)

7.1 INTRODUCTION

The 3rd Generation Partnership Project (3GPP) unites [Six] telecommunications standards bodies, known as "Organizational Partners" and provides their members with a stable environment to produce the highly successful Reports and Specifications that define 3GPP technologies.

These technologies are constantly evolving through - what have become known as - Generations of commercial cellular / mobile systems. 3GPP was originally the standards partnership evolving GSM systems towards the 3rd Generation. However, since the completion of the first LTE and the Evolved Packet Core specifications, 3GPP has become the focal point for mobile systems beyond 3G.

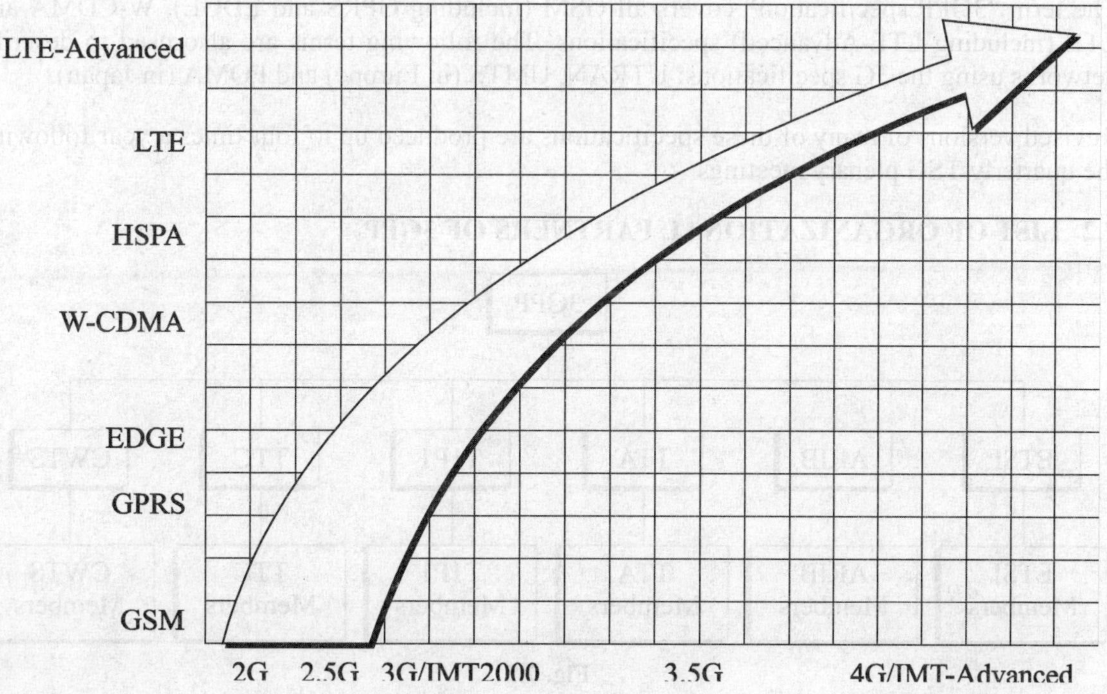

Fig. 7.1: Evolution of Technologies

From 3GPP Release 10 onwards - 3GPP is compliant with the latest ITU-R requirements for IMT-Advanced 'Systems beyond 3G'. The standard now allows for operation at peak speeds of 100 Mbit/s for high mobility and 1 Gbit/s for low mobility communication.

The original scope of 3GPP was to produce Technical Specifications and Technical Reports for a 3G Mobile System based on evolved GSM core networks and the radio access technologies that they support (i.e., Universal Terrestrial Radio Access (UTRA) both Frequency Division Duplex (FDD) and Time Division Duplex (TDD) modes).

The scope was subsequently amended to include the maintenance and development of the Global System for Mobile communication (GSM) Technical Specifications and Technical Reports including evolved radio access technologies (e.g. General Packet Radio Service (GPRS) and Enhanced Data rates for GSM Evolution (EDGE)).

3GPP was created in December 1998 by the signing of the "The 3rd Generation Partnership *Project Agreement*". The latest *3GPP Scope and Objectives document* has evolved from this original Agreement.

The discussions that led to the signing of the 3GPP Agreement were recorded in a series of slides called the *"Partnership Project Description"* that describes the basic principles and ideas on which the project is based. The Partnership Project Description has not been maintained since its first creation but the principles of operation of the project still remain valid.

The term "3GPP specification" covers all GSM (including GPRS and EDGE), W-CDMA and LTE (including LTE-Advanced) specifications. The following terms are also used to describe networks using the 3G specifications: UTRAN, UMTS (in Europe) and FOMA (in Japan).

Revised versions of many of these specifications are produced up to four times a year following the quarterly TSG plenary meetings.

7.2 LIST OF ORGANIZATIONAL PARTNERS OF 3GPP

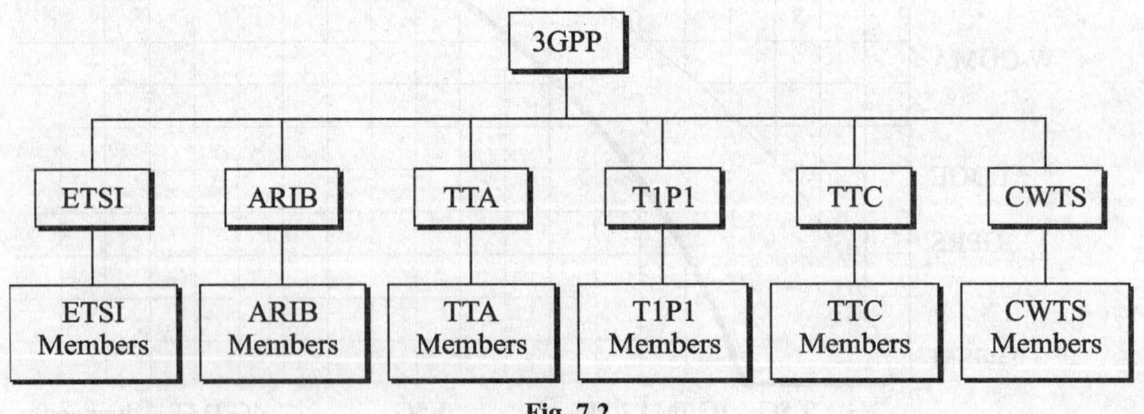

Fig. 7.2

- Association of Radio Industries and Business (ARIB) of Japan
- Telecommunication Technology committee (TTC) of Japan

- European Telecommunication standards Institute
- Standard committee T1 telecommunication
- Telecommunication Technology Association of Korea
- China Wireless Telecommunication standards group of China
- Telecommunication Technology Association of Korea China Wireless Telecommunication standards group of China

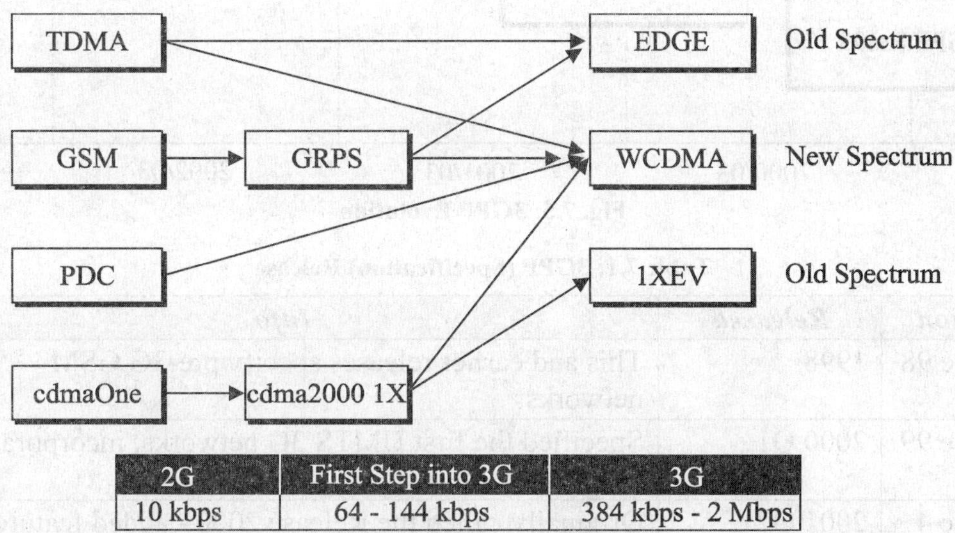

Fig. 7.3: Evolution to 3G

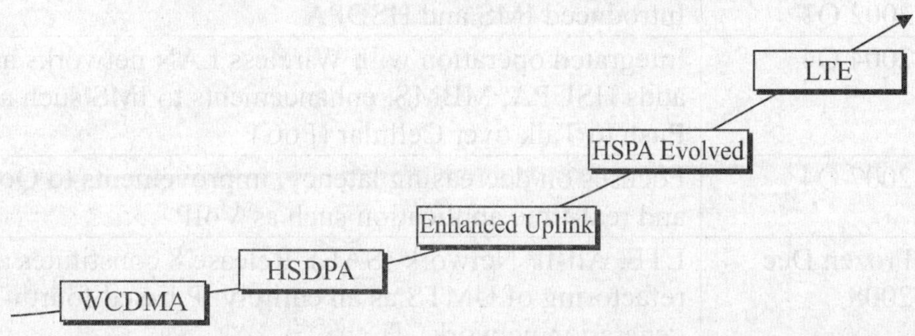

3GPP	R99/1999	R5/2002	R6/2005	R7/2007*	R8/2008**
Peak	0.384 Mbps DL	14 MBps DL	14 Mbps DL	28/42 Mbps DL*	160 Mbps DL
Date Rate	0.064 Mbps	0.384 Mbps	6 Mbps UL	12 Mbps UL	50 Mbps UL
Commercial Availability	2001	2005	2006	2008	2009

* Expected: 28 Mbps with MIMO, 42 Mbps with MIMO + 64 QAM

** Expected: LTE specification ready end 2007

Fig. 7.4: Driven by Data Rate

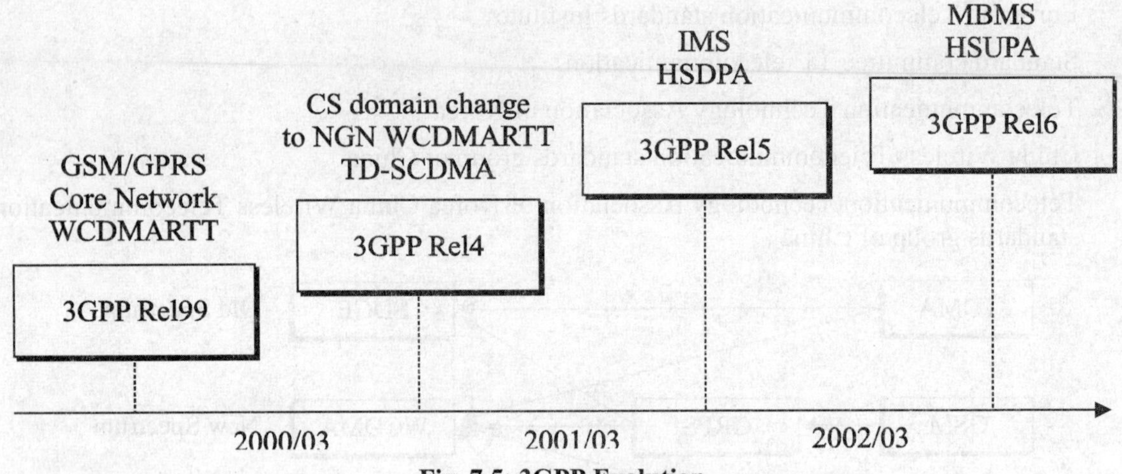

Fig. 7.5: 3GPP Evolution

Table 7.1: 3GPP (Specification) Release

Version	*Released*	*Info*
Release 98	1998	This and earlier releases specify pre-3G GSM networks
Release 99	2000 Q1	Specified the first UMTS 3G networks, incorporating a CDMA air interface.
Release 4	2001 Q2	Originally called the Release 2000 - added features including an all-IP Core Network
Release 5	2002 Q1	Introduced IMS and HSDPA
Release 6	2004 Q4	Integrated operation with Wireless LAN networks and adds HSUPA, MBMS, enhancements to IMS such as Push to Talk over Cellular (PoC)
Release 7	2007 Q4	Focuses on decreasing latency, improvements to QoS and real-time application such as VoIP.
Release 8	Frozen Dec 2008	LTE, All-IP Network (SAE). Release 8 constitutes a refactoring of UMTS as an entirely IP based fourth-generation network.
Release 9	In progress, expected to be frozen in Dec 2009	SAES Enhancements, WiMAX and LTE/UMTS Interoperability
Release 10	In progress	LTE Advanced

Table 7.2: Full Details of the Specifications, their History and Current Status can be found in the 3GPP Specifications Status Database

Year-Month	*Remark*	*Latest Status*	*Specs Directory*	*TSG CN #*	*TSG RAN* #*	*TSG T #*	*TSG SA #*	*TSG GERAN #*	*TSG CT #*
2011-12		StatusList	2011-12		54		54	52	54
2011-09		StatusList	2011-09		53		53	51	53
2011-06		StatusList	2011-06		52		52	50	52
2011-03		StatusList	2011-03		51		51	49	51
2010-12		StatusList	2010-12		50		50	48	50
2010-09		StatusList	2010-09		49		49	47	49
2010-06		StatusList	2010-06		48		48	46	48
2010-03		StatusList	2010-03		47		47	45	47
2009-12		StatusList	2009-12		46		46	44	46
2009-09		StatusList	2009-09		45		45	43	45
2009-06		StatusList	2009-06		44		44	42	44
2009-03		StatusList	2009-03		43		43	41	43
2008-12		StatusList	2008-12		42		42	40	42
2008-09		StatusList	2008-09		41		41	39	41
2008-06		StatusList	2008-06		40		40	38	40
2008-03		StatusList	2008-03		39		39	37	39
2007-12		StatusList	2007-12		38		38	36	38
2007-09		StatusList	2007-09		37		37	35	37
2007-06		StatusList	2007-06		36		36	34	36
2007-03		StatusList	2007-03		35		35	33	35
2006-12		StatusList	2006-12		34		34	32	34

Year-Month	*Remark*	*Latest Status*	*Specs Directory*	*TSG CN #*	*TSG RAN* #*	*TSG T #*	*TSG SA #*	*TSG GERAN #*	*TSG CT #*
2006-09	GERAN henceforward meets synchronously with other TSGs, so no further “delta” directories necessary	StatusList	2006-09		33		33	31	33
2006-06	New at GERAN only.		2006-06					30	
2006-06		StatusList	2006-06		32		32		32
2006-04	New at GERAN only.		2006-04					29	
2006-03		StatusList	2006-03		31		31		31
2006-01	New at GERAN only.		2006-01					28	
2005-12		StatusList	2005-12		30		30		30
2005-11	New at GERAN only.		2005-11					27	
2005-09		StatusList	2005-09		29		29		29
2005-									
2005-09		StatusList	2005-09		29		29		29
2005-08/09	New at GERAN only.		2005-09					26	
2005-06	New at GERAN only.		2005-06					25	
2005-06		StatusList	2005-06		28		28		28
2005-04	New at GERAN only.		2005-04					24	
2005-03	RAN closed and RANnew opened, CN and T closed, CT opened.	StatusList	2005-03	27	27bis, 27	27	27		27
2005-01	New at GERAN only.		2005-01					23	
2004-12		StatusList	2004-12	26	26	26	26		
2004-11	New at GERAN only.		2004-11					22	
2004-09		StatusList	2004-09	25	25	25	25		
2004-08	New at GERAN only.		2004-08					21	

Year-Month	*Remark*	*Latest Status*	*Specs Directory*	*TSG CN #*	*TSG RAN* #*	*TSG T #*	*TSG SA #*	*TSG GERAN #*	*TSG CT #*
2004-06	New at GERAN only.		2004-06					20	
2004-06		StatusList	2004-06	24	24	24	24		
2004-04	New at GERAN only.		2004-04					19	
2004-03		StatusList	2004-03	23	23	23	23		
2004-02	New at GERAN only.		2004-02					18	
2003-12		StatusList	2003-12	22	22	22	22		
2003-11	New at GERAN only.		2003-11					17	
2003-09		StatusList	2003-09	21	21	21	21		
2003-09	New at GERAN only.		2003-09					16	
2003-06	New at GERAN only.		2003-06					15	
2003-06		StatusList	2003-06	20	20	20	20		
2003-04	New at GERAN only.		2003-04					14	
2003-02		StatusList	2003-03	19	19	19	19		
2003-02	New at GERAN only.		2003-02					13	
2002-12, 2002-11		StatusList	2002-12	18	18	18	18	12	
2002-09		StatusList	2002-09	17	17	17	17	11	
2002-06	Rel-5 GERAN features content functionally frozen		2002-06					10	
2002-06	Rel-5 features content functionally frozen (remainder, non-GERAN)	StatusList	2002-06	16	16	16	16		
2002-04			2002-04					9	
2002-03	Rel-5 features content functionally frozen (part)	StatusList	2002-03	15	15	15	15		
2002-02								8	
2001-12									

The table 7.2 leads to information such as:

- Specifications arising from each plenary TSG meeting, including the latest versions of each specification that was not changed at that meeting. i.e. each directory holds a complete set of specifications.
- The month of the meeting and the meeting number

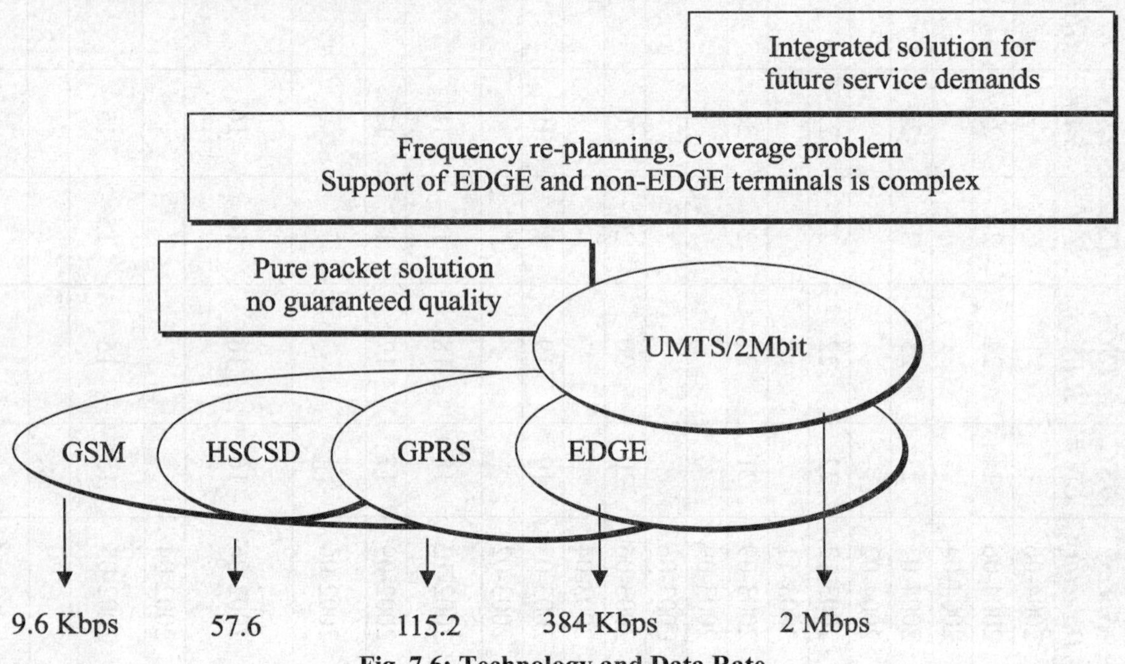

Fig. 7.6: Technology and Data Rate

- The Status List (ZIPped RTF or Word format) summarizing the current version number for every release of every 3GPP specification following each TSG plenary meeting.
- Details of each specification (working group, rapporteur, the Project Manager in MCC (Mobile Competence Centre), the meeting at which it was, or is expected to be, "frozen" (i.e. the point after which only corrections are allowed) - all are in the Status lists.

The first Release of the third generation specifications was essentially a consolidation of the underlying GSM specifications and the development of the new UTRAN radio access network. The foundations were laid for future high-speed traffic transfer in both circuit switched and packet switched modes.

7.3 MAIN COMPONENTS AND FUNCTIONS IN THE ARCHITECTURE

The basic principle is that the MSC is split into an MSC server and a (Circuit-Switched) Media Gateway (CS-MGW), the external interfaces remaining the same as much as possible as for a monolithic MSC. The MSC server provides the call control and mobility management functions, and the CS-MGW provides the stream manipulating functions, i.e. bearer control and transmission resource functions. The same applies to the GMSC, split into a GMSC server and a CS-MGW.

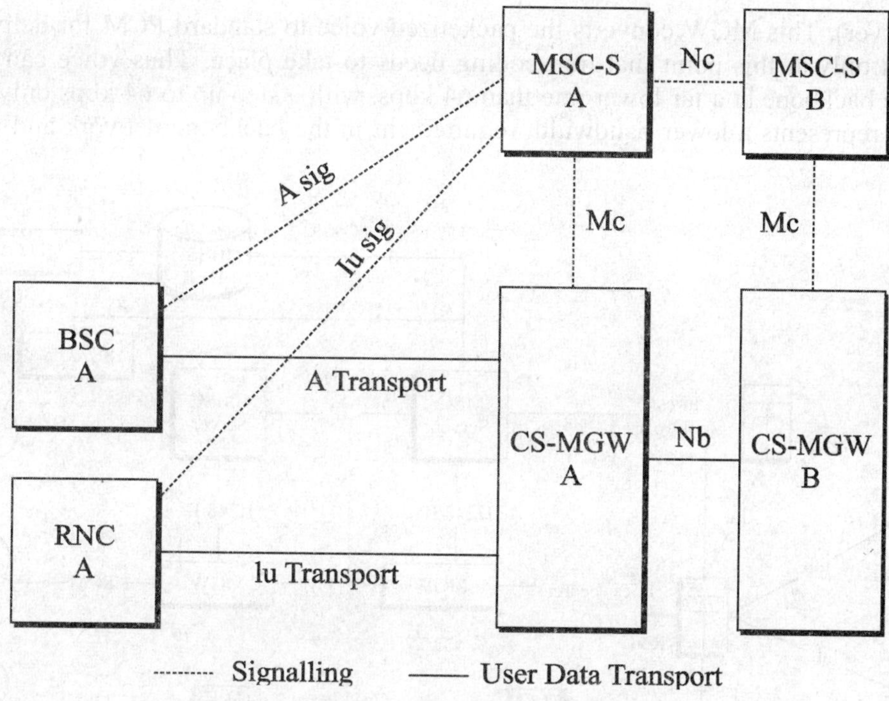

Fig. 7.7: BICC Network Architecture

The 3GPP Release 4 Network Architecture

3GPP Release 4 introduces a significant enhancement to the core network architecture as it applies to the CS domain. Basically, the MSC is broken into constituent parts, and it is allowed to be deployed in a distributed manner, as shown in Figure 7.7. Specifically, the MSC is divided into an MSC server and a media gateway (MGW). The MSC server contains all the mobility management and call-control logic that would be contained in a standard MSC. It does not, however, reside in the media path. Rather, the media path is via one or more MGWs that establish, manipulate, and release media streams (voice streams) under the control of the MSC server.

Control signaling for circuit-switched calls is between the RNC and the MSC server.

The media path for circuit-switched calls is between the RNC and the MGW. As far as the RNC is concerned, these two entities could be the same physical device, as would be the case when the RNC is communicating with a traditional MSC. Typically, an MGW takes calls from the RNC and routes those calls toward their destinations over a packet backbone. In many cases, the packet backbone will be IP-based, such that backbone traffic is Voice over IP (VoIP), as described in more detail in Chapter 10. Given that the PS domain also uses an IP backbone, then only one backbone network is needed, which can mean significant cost savings for the network operator.

At the remote end, where a call needs to be handed off to another network, such as the Public Switched Telephone Network (PSTN), another MGW is controlled by a Gateway MSC server

(GMSC server). This MGW converts the packetized voice to standard PCM for delivery to the PSTN. It is only at this point that transcoding needs to take place. Thus voice can be carried through the backbone at a far lower rate than 64 kbps, with a step up to 64 kbps only at the last point. This represents a lower bandwidth requirement in the backbone network and therefore a lower cost.

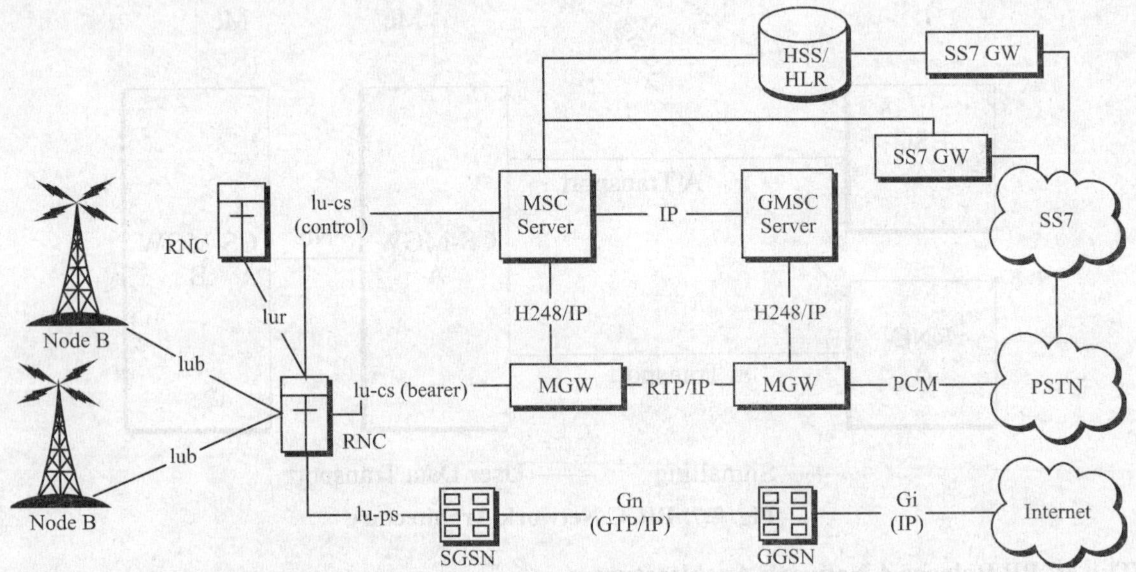

Fig. 7.8: 3GPP Release 4 Distributed Network Architecture

The control protocol between the MSC server or GMSC server and the MGW i.s the International Telecommunications Union (ITU) H.248 protocol. This protocol is also known as MEGACo. The call-control protocol between the MSC server and the GMSC server can be any suitable call-control protocol. The 3GPP standards suggest, but do not mandate, the Bearer Independent Call Control (BICC) protocol, which is based on the ITU-T Recommendation Q.1902.

Figure 7.9 shows an example of a voice-call establishment using this architecture.

For the sake of brevity, the messages are limited to those that relate to call establishment as seen from the core network. Thus the RRC protocol messages between the UE and UTRAN have been omitted.

When the Setup message arrives from the UE, the MSC server performs a call-routing determination. It then responds with a Call Proceeding message to the UE. Based on the call-routing determination, the MSC server chooses an MGW to handle the call. It instructs (Add Request) the MGW to establish a new context and places a termination in that context. The termination in question (1'1) will be on the network side of the MGW. Once the new context is established by the MGW, the MSC server requests the RAN to establish an RAE to handle the call. Once the RAE has been assigned, the MSC server is in a position to establish a media connection between the RNC and the MGW. Therefore, it requests the MGW to add a new termination to the context that has just been established. This new termination (T2) will face toward the RNC. Because the new termination is in the same context as termination 1'1, a path is created from one side of the MGW to the other.

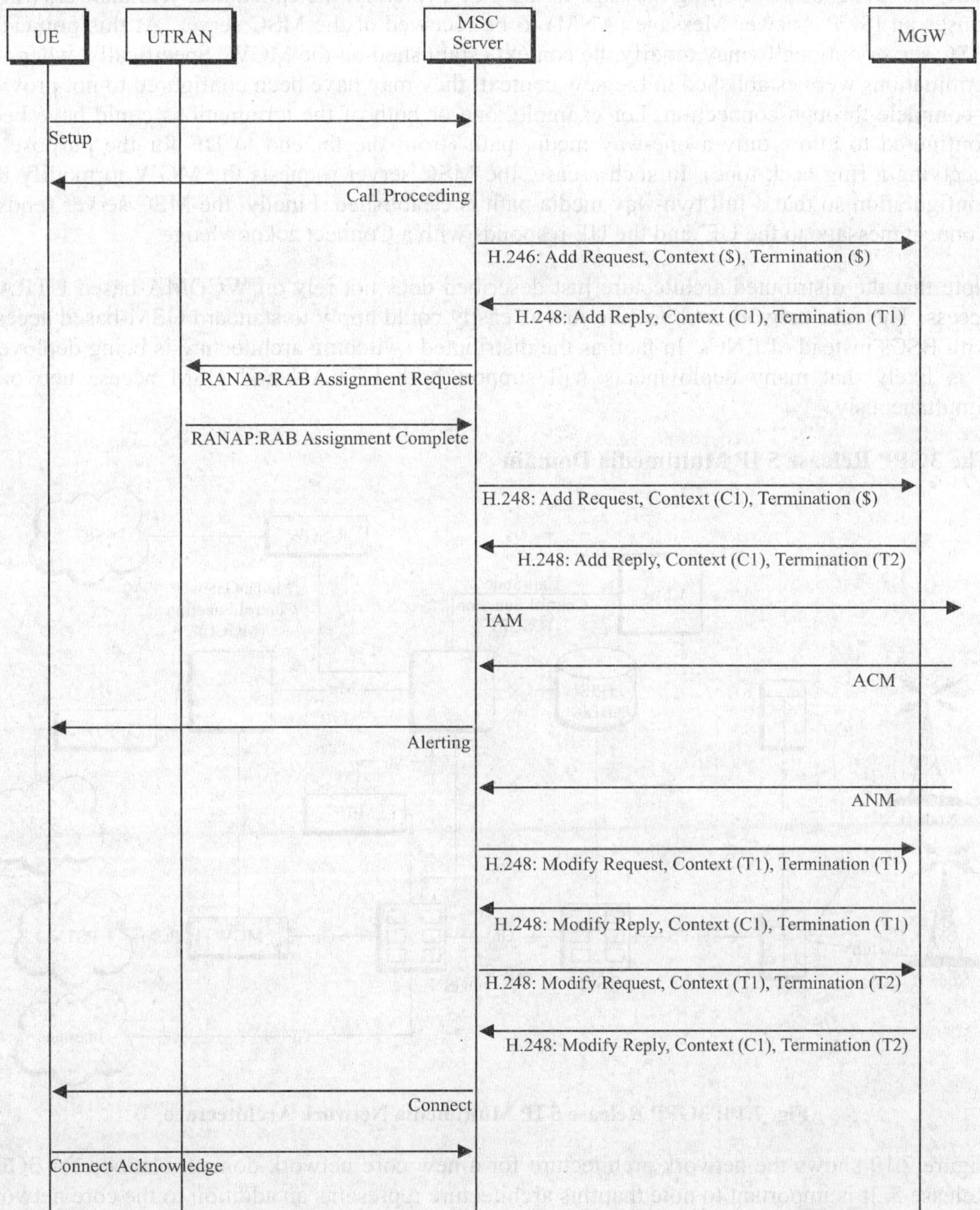

Fig. 7.9: Mobile-originated call with 3GPP Release 4 distributed architecture

The MSC server then sends the ISUP Initial Address Message (lAM) to the called network (such as the PSTN). On receipt of an Address Complete Message (ACM) from the far end, the MSC server sends an Alerting message to the UE. Typically, the called user will answer, which causes an ISUP Answer Message (ANM) to be received at the MSC server. At this point, the MSC server optionally may modify the context established on the MGW. Specifically, when the terminations were established in the new context, they may have been configured to not provide a complete through-connection. For example, one or both of the terminations could have been configured to allow only a one-way media path (from the far end to DE for the purpose of receiving a ring-back tone). In such a case, the MSC server requests the MGW to modify the configuration so that a full two-way media path is established. Finally, the MSC server sends a Connect message to the UE, and the UE responds with a Connect acknowledge.

Note that the distributed architecture just described does not rely on WCDMA-based UTRAN access. The core network architecture just as easily could apply to standard GSM-based access, with BSCs instead of RNCs. In fact, as the distributed switching architecture is being deployed, it is likely that many deployments will support both UTRAN and GSM access networks simultaneously.

The 3GPP Release 5 IP Multimedia Domain

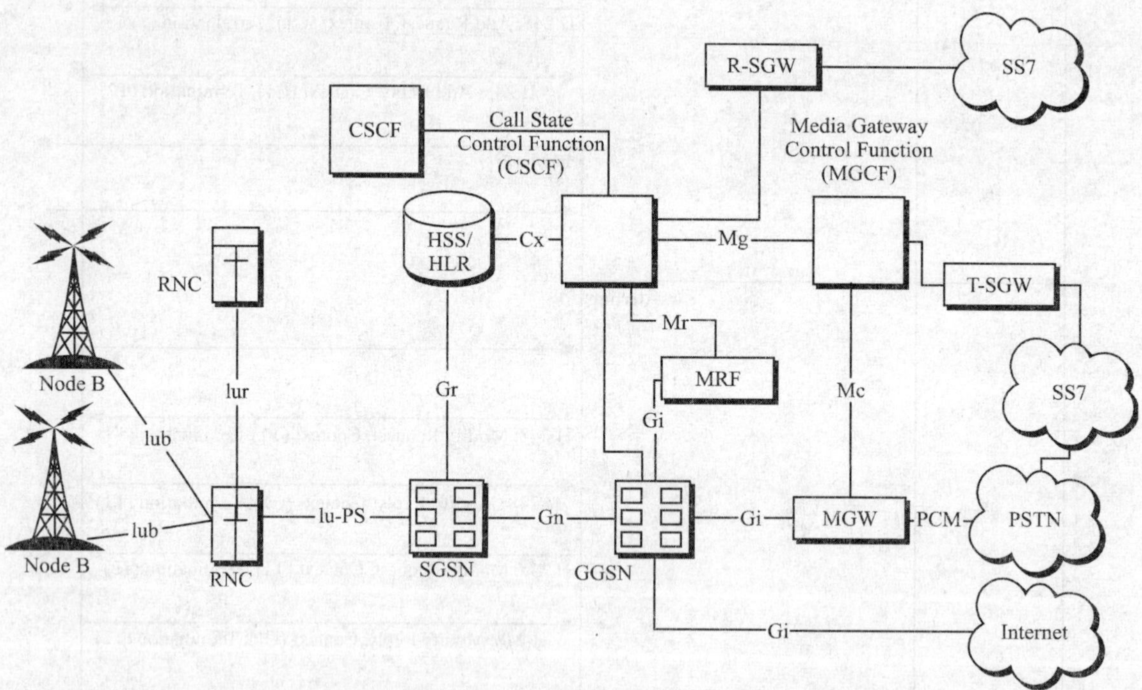

Fig. 7.10: 3GPP Release 5 IP Multimedia Network Architecture

Figure 7.10 shows the network architecture for a new core network domain planned for 3GPP Release 5. It is important to note that this architecture represents an addition to the core network rather than a change to the existing core. Instead, 3GPP Release 5 introduces a new core network domain in addition to the established CS and PS domains. This new domain is available for new user devices that have the capability and the call-model logic needed to take advantage of the new domain. Thus the UTRAN now can be connected to three different logical core network domains-the CS domain, the PS domain, and the IP Alultimedia (IM) domain. When a terminal wants to use the services of the core network, it indicates which domain it wants to use. Existing (pre-Release 5) terminals will continue to request the services of the CS or PS domain. New terminals also will be able to request the services of the 1M domain.

Note that while the 1M domain is a new domain, it uses the services of the PS domain. All 1M traffic is packet-based and is transported using PS domain nodes such as the SGSN and the GGSN.

The 1M domain is based on the Session Initiation Protocol (SIP). In fact, the Call State Control Function (CSCF) of Figure 7.10 is effectively an SIP proxy. The 1M architecture enables voice and data calls to be handled in a uniform manner all the way from the UE to the destination. A complete convergence of voice and data takes place such that voice is simply a type of data with specific QoS requirements. This convergence enables a number of new advanced services. Moreover, the use of SIP means that a great deal of service control can be placed in the UE rather tl1an in the network, making it easier for the subscriber to customize services to meet his or her particular needs.

(G)MSC Server

The MSC Server comprises all the call control and mobility control parts of an MSC. As such, it is responsible for the control of mobile originated and mobile terminated CS domain calls. It terminates the user to network signalling (see in particular TS 24.008) and translates it into the relevant network to network signalling (see in particular TS 29.002). It also contains a VLR.

The MSC Server controls the parts of the call state that pertain to connection control for media channels in a CS-MGW.

A GMSC Server is to a GMSC as an MSC Server is to an MSC.

Circuit Switched - Media Gateway (CS-MGW)

The CS-MGW interfaces the transport part of the UTRAN/BSC with the one of the core network, over Iu or the A interface. It interacts with the (G)MSC server for resource control.

A CS-MGW may also terminate bearer channels from a circuit switched network and media streams from a packet network (e.g., RTP streams in an IP network). As the entity interfacing the access and the core network, the CS-MGW operates the requested media conversion (it contains e.g. the TRAU), the bearer control and the payload processing (e.g. codec, echo canceller, conference bridge). It supports the different Iu options for CS services (AAL2/ATM based as well as RTP/UDP/IP based).

The CS-MGW bearer control and payload processing capabilities also need to support mobile specific functions such as SRNS relocation/handover and anchoring. Current H.248 standard mechanisms are applied to enable this. Further tailoring (i.e packages) of the H.248 may be required to support additional codecs and framing protocols, etc.

Note that no confusion should be made between the CS-MGW defined here and the IP Multimedia CN Subsystem Media Gateway, the IM-MGW, defined in Release 5.

7.3.1 Interfaces and Protocols

Mc Reference Point: (G)MSC Server to CS-MGW

The Mc reference point describes the interfaces between the MSC Server and CS-MGW, and between the GMSC Server and CS-MGW. It supports a separation of call control entities from bearer control entities, and a separation of bearer control entities from transport entities.

It uses the H.248/IETF Megaco protocol, jointly developed by ITU-T and IETF, with the parameters and options specified in TS.29232 ("Media Gateway Controller (MGC) – Media Gateway (MGW) Interface;Stage 3)

It has the following properties:

- flexible connection handling which allows support of different call models and different media processing purposes not restricted to H.323 usage.
- open architecture where extensions/packages definition work on the interface may be carried out.
- dynamic sharing of MGW physical node resources. A physical MGW can be partitioned into logically separate virtual MGWs/domains consisting of a set of statically allocated terminations.
- dynamic sharing of transmission resources between the domains as the MGW controls bearers and manage resources according to the H.248 protocols.

Mobile specific functions such as SRNS relocation/handover and anchoring are also supported.

Nc Reference Point: MSC Server to (G)MSC Server

Over the Nc reference point, the Network-Network based call control is performed. Examples of this are ISUP or an evolvement of ISUP for bearer independent call control (BICC). The protocol used on the Nc interface is specified in TS 29.205: "Application of Q.1900 Series to Bearer Independent circuit-switched core network architecture; Stage 3". In fact, the Nc interface uses ITU's BICC as specified in ITU Rec. Q.1902.x series of recommendations. It supports IP and ATM transports in a bearer-independent manner for the ISDN service set, allowing the physical separation of the call control entities from the bearer control entities, hence the name "Bearer-Independent Call Control".

The interworking between BICC and ISUP shall follow the ITU recommendation Q.1912.1 ("ISUP-BICC Interworking") and Q.19.12.2 ("Interworking between selected signalling systems and BICC").

Nb Reference Point: CS-MGW to CS-MGW

Over the Nb reference point, the bearer control and transport are performed. Different options are possible for user data transport and bearer control, as defined in TS.29.414 ("Core Network

Nb Data Transport and Signalling Transport"). It can be IP bearer control protocol, BICC tunnelling protocol, "AAL type 2 signalling protocol (Q.2630.1-2).

In the case of ATM or IP transport, the passage of compressed speech at variable bit rates is possible through the CS core network.

7.4 SPEECH ENCODING AND DECODING

General speech coding concepts:In a normal MS to MS call configuration, the Speech Signal is first encoded in the originating MS, sent over the Air Interface and on Ater, converted to A-law or □-law ITU-T Rec. G.711 in the local transcoder (TRAU), carried over the fixed network, transcoded again in the distant transcoder, sent over the distant Air Interface and finally decoded in the terminating MS. When the Iu interface is used, the transcoder is in the MSC.

The figure below, extracted from TR 23.977, shows the different types of transcoding taking place for end-to-end calls, in case BICC is used (see first chapter). The end-user is either a PSTN-user (upper part of the figure), or she/he is a GSM/GERAN user (middle part) or she/he is a UMTS-user (lower part). The figure is limited to the infrastructure side of the end-to-end call, i.e. the radio interface and the MSs are not shown.

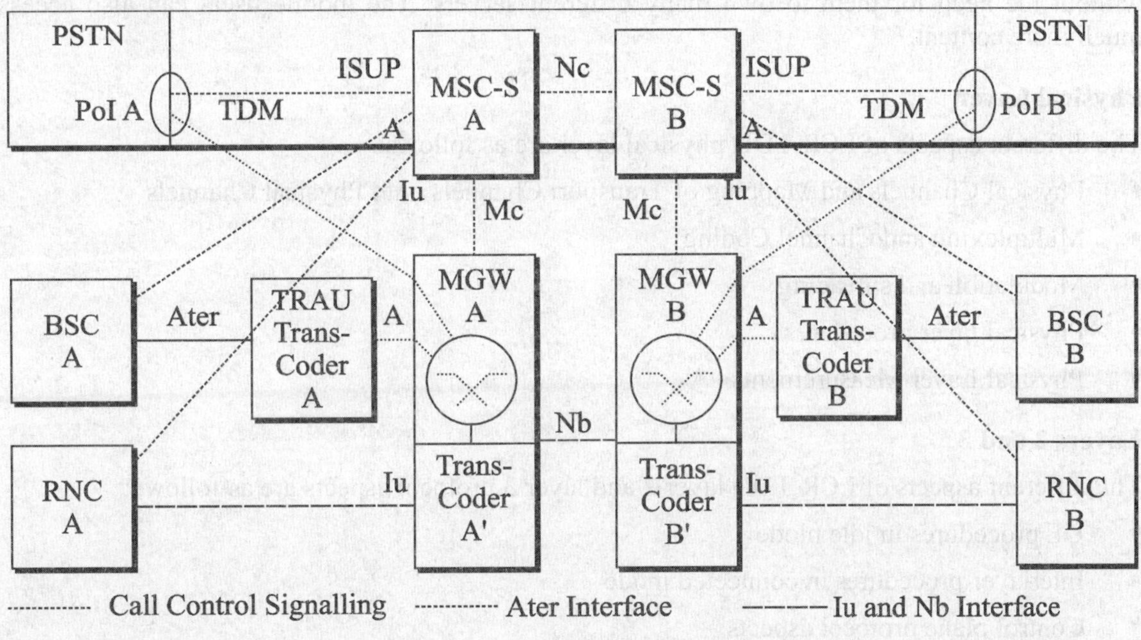

Fig. 7.11: Bearer Independent Core Network with A- and iu-Interfaces

In this configuration, the two speech codecs (coder/decoder pairs) at both ends are said to in "Tandem Operation" as they introduce a double transcoding. The key inconvenience of a tandem configuration is the degradation of the speech quality. This degradation is usually more noticeable when the speech codecs are operating at low rates and in noisy conditions.

Streaming refers to the ability of an application to play synchronised media streams like audio and video streams in a continuous way while those streams are being transmitted to the client over a data network.

The applications which can be built on top of streaming services can be classified into "on-demand" and "live" information delivery. Examples of the first category are music and news-on-demand applications. Live delivery of radio and television programs are examples of the second category.

Streaming over fixed-IP networks is already a major application. While the Internet Engineering Task Force (IETF) and the W3C [Paolo, please put in full "W3C". Is it "World Wide Web Consortium (W3C)" ?] have developed a set of protocols used in fixed-IP streaming services, for 3G systems, the 3G packet-switched streaming service (PSS) fills the gap between 3G MMS, e.g. downloading, and conversational services.

The terminal complexity for a PSS-only mobile is lower than for conversational services: there is no need for media input devices, media encoders and some protocols can be avoided.

This feature enables a multitude of streaming applications to be deployed by content providers, without the need for them to own many different servers. The mobile users can also access much more content.

Physical Layer

The different aspects of LCR TDD physical layer are as follows:

- Physical Channels and Mapping of Transport Channels onto Physical Channels
- Multiplexing and Channel Coding
- Modulation and spreading
- Physical layer procedures
- Physical Layer Measurements

Layers 2 and 3

The different aspects of LCR TDD layer 2 and layer 3 protocol aspects are as follows:

- UE procedures in idle mode
- Interlayer procedures in connected mode
- Control plane protocol aspects
- User plane protocol aspects
- mobility aspects

UE Radio Access Capability

It includes the definition of UE radio access capabilities for low chip rate option.

UTRAN Network iub/iur Protocol Aspects

The following enhancements of the radio frame structure have impacted the Iur/Iub protocols:

- Different frame structure than for high chiprate TDD option;
- Different basic midamble sequences, maximum channel impulse response is scalable (W=8, 9, 12, 16, 21, 32, 64), depending on number of users and environment, including the association between midambles and channelisation codes;
- Use of only one burst type for physical channels except special bursts in DwPCH/UpPCH. Because there is only one burst type in low chip rate TDD option, "burst type" defined as a parameter for physical channel is not necessary;
- Support of different timeslot formats due to different number of bits and L1 control signals and midamble length;
- Support of use of 8PSK for special timeslots/all timeslots per cell;
- Beacon function is provided by DwPCH and P-CCPCH.

In NBAP and RNSAP messages, the information elements referring to time slot information, burst types, and common physical channels were updated to cover both TDD chip rate options.

Three physical channels were added to support the low chip rate TDD option. These are:

DwPCH (Downlink Pilot Channel), UpPCH (Uplink Pilot Channel) and FPACH (Fast Physical Access CHannel). Besides, two physical channels, Primary SCH and Secondary SCH, are not needed in low chip rate TDD option

In NBAP and RNSAP messages, the information elements referring to common physical channels had to be updated to cover both TDD chip rate options. For FPACH and DwPCH, new IEs had to be introduced.

7.5 IMPROVEMENTS OF UMTS AND GSM PRE-RELEASE 4 FEATURES

Multimedia Messaging Service

Acronym	MMS
UID	1818
Main responsibility	T2

The Multimedia Messaging Service (MMS) was first introduced in Release 99. It allows users to send and receive messages exploiting a large array of media types e.g. text of almost unlimited length, images, audio and video clips, while also making it possible to support new content types as they become popular. Multiple media elements can be combined into a composite single message. Messages can be sent either to a mobile phone or to an e-mail address.

Table 7.3: References for "Multimedia Messaging Service"

Document	*Title/Contents*
TP-000078	WI Sheet
Impacted Specifications	
TS 22.140 TS 23.140	Multimedia Messaging (MMS) stage 1 Multimedia Messaging (MMS) stage 2/3
New Dedicated Specifications	
	None

The main new network element of the Multimedia Message Service Environment (MMSE) is the MMS Relay/Server which is responsible for storage and handling of incoming and outgoing messages and for the transfer of messages between different messaging systems. Beside these tasks, the MMS Relay/Server has many other tasks which are described in TS 23.140. Other involved MMS elements are the MMS User Agent and MMS User databases. The functional descriptions of the involved MMS elements are provided in TS 23.140 and for implementation of the MMS User Agent – MMS Relay/Server interface a reference to the WAP Implementation of MMS is given. Whereas the Release 99 specifications only included the concept with little technical details, the Rel-4 document was enhanced significantly.

The following enhancements were introduced in Rel-4:

- The MMS Service Behaviour Description, the MMS Reference Architecture, the Multimedia Messaging framework, Application protocol framework and service primitives, and the Technical realisation of MMS service features were added.
- To enable interoperability of MMS between terminals and MMS network equipment of different manufacturers, the definition of a minimum set of mandatory media formats for the MMS User Agent was introduced. It included AMR for media type Audio, and Baseline JPEG for media type Image. The optional support of several more codecs is specified.
- The service behaviour description and the technical realization of Delivery-report and Read-reply report were introduced.
- Support for streaming in MMS was added.
- As implementation examples for the MM1 interface between MMS User Agent and MMS Relay/Server, WAP implementation and IP implementation of MMS were added as Annexes.
- Support for prepaid services in MMS was added.
- The reply-charging feature was added. This allows a user to take over the charge for the sending of a reply-MM to their submitted MM from the recipient(s). The originating MMS User Agent may define a reply-charging limitation request (e.g. may specify the latest time of submission of the reply-MMs or a maximum size of reply-MMs).
- Support of address hiding was added.

- The interworking with external servers (in particular IP-based) was further defined. An annex was added giving guidance on MM3 principles.
- The addressing scheme was further elaborated.
- The ability of forwarding MMs without prior download was inserted.
- MM7: MMS Relay/Server – MMS VAS Applications was added to the reference architecture. (Please note that a detailed stage 2 and stage 3 description was added in Rel-5)
- An example of Integration with Unified Messaging System (UMS) was added as an annex.
- Charging enhancements: An annex was added describing information of MMs/abstract messages which may be required for inclusion into Call Data Records (CDRs) for MMS for the purpose of Billing and Traceability.
- The support of SMS over MMS was added. For this the encapsulation of a short message (SMS) in a multimedia message (MMS) was specified.
- Handling of MMS-related information on the USIM was specified.

MExE Enhancements Rel-4

The work item MExE enhancements Rel-4 consists of two Building Blocks (BB):

- MExE Rel-4 Improvements and Investigations: Under this BB, several enhancements where introduced in Rel-4 of which the most significant are mentioned in the MExE description below
- MExE Security Analysis Activity: This BB was suggested to carry out an analysis of the MExE security framework and evaluate if it is sufficient to eliminate the risks posed by downloading content and applications. This analysis was performed by SA WG3 (Security) in co-operation with T2-MExE group.

MExE is a feature introduced in GSM Release 98, enhanced in GSM Release 99 to cover the following additional enhancements: SIM MExE certificate management, security clarifications and QoS aspects. Release 4 introduced further enhancements of which the most significant was the introduction of a new small footprint Java classmark (Classmark 3).

In Release 99, UTRAN can only accept or reject a radio access bearer request from the core network. For services that could accept looser QoS requirements than those requested by the CN in the RAB establishment request there exist no means for UTRAN to propose alternative (looser) QoS. For such services the RAB establishment will fail, or alternatively the CN could re-attempt the RAB reestablishment with looser QoS requirements which would significantly increase the setup time.

In Release 4 the Radio Access Bearer setup is enhanced with a QoS negotiation mechanism. This aligns the procedure with the already existing CN solution used in GPRS and it improves the service setup time.

RAB Quality of Service Renegotiation over Iu

WID in RP-000500

Affected RAN3 spec: TS25.413

New dedicated TR: 25.851 (RAB Quality of service negotiation over Iu)

Release 99 also does not allow the UTRAN to renegotiate RAB/QoS parameters for on-going calls/session. Since the UTRAN is responsible for managing the radio resources, it was seen necessary that the UTRAN is able to initiate RAB renegotiation for efficient use of the radio interface.

In Release 4 the management of Radio Access Bearers for on-going calls/session was enhanced such that QoS parameters can be renegotiated by the UTRAN

The intention is also to allow continuation of service through UTRAN initiated QoS renegotiation

RAB Quality of Service Negotiation over Iu during Relocation

WID in RP-010168

Affected RAN3 spec: TS 25.413

In Release 99 no means exists for the UTRAN to propose an alternative QoS for services that could accept looser QoS requirements than those requested by the CN in the relocation request.

In Release 4 the relocation is enhanced such that QoS parameters can be negotiated by the UTRAN during relocation.

PS-Domain handover for real-time services

WID in RP-000127

Affected RAN3 spec: 25.413

New dedicated TR: 25.936 (PS-Domain handover for real-time services)

In Release 99, Relocation for services from PS domain is only optimised for non-real-time services. The R99 mechanism was originally designed for non-real-time services. The principle is that the N-PDUs are forwarded from the source RNC buffers to the target RNC. Data buffering is not adapted to real-time services, and means that interruption may exceed the requirement for real-time services.

In Release 4 the relocation is optimised by utilising a N-PDU duplication mechanism in the RNC/BSS and the execution of relocation is performed after relocation resource allocation.

7.6 EMERGENCY CALL ENHANCEMENTS IN RELEASE 4

7.6.1 Terminal Interfaces

The Feature Rel-4 Terminal Interfaces consists of the following three Building Blocks (BB) which are described in the following sections:

- AT commands enhancements
- Wide Area Data Synchronization
- Terminal local model

7.6.2 Wide Area Data Synchronisation

In Release 99, the concept of Wide Area Synchronisation for 3GPP has been developed to allow data stored in the ME/USIM to be synchronised with the outside world. In Rel-4, SyncML was introduced as the preferred synchronisation mechanism replacing IrMC level 4.

This specification provides a definition of a Wide Area Synchronisation protocols. The synchronization protocol was originally based upon IrMC level 4 in Release 99 which was replaced by SyncML in Rel-4. The document covers Wide Area Network Synchronisation between current and future mobile communication end-user devices, desktop applications and server-based information servers.

7.6.3 Location Services Enhancements

Between Rel99 LCS and Releases 4 LCS, the main difference concerns documentation. The Stage 2 documents are restructured, as shown below.

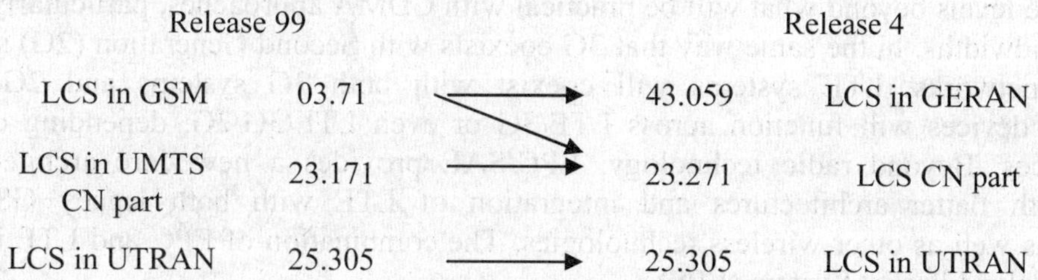

Release 99				Release 4
LCS in GSM	03.71	→	43.059	LCS in GERAN
LCS in UMTS CN part	23.171	→	23.271	LCS CN part
LCS in UTRAN	25.305	→	25.305	LCS in UTRAN

Fig. 7.12: Restructuring of LCS Stage 2 between Release 99 and Release 4

Release 99 and Release 4 are practically identical. The main difference is the support of OTDOA method in LCR TDD (see description of corresponding feature) mode only starting from Release 4.

Also in Rel 4, the "Deferred Location Request" is introduced: in response to this request, the location is provided to the LCS client as soon as the target mobile becomes reachable again. Differed answers triggered by other types of events are considered, but will not be standardised before Release 6.

Lastly, new OSA (Application Programming Interface for Open Access Service) APIs are defined for the LCS.

7.7 INTEROPERABILITY

Rather than emphasizing any one wireless approach, 3GPP's evolutionary plan is to recognize the strengths and weaknesses of every technology and to exploit the unique capabilities of each one accordingly. GSM, based on a TDMA approach, is mature and broadly deployed. Already extremely efficient, there are nevertheless opportunities for additional optimizations and enhancements. Standards bodies have already defined "Evolved EDGE," which will be available for deployment in the 2009 to 2010 timeframe. Evolved EDGE more than doubles throughput over current EDGE systems, halves latency, and increases spectral efficiency. By the end of the decade, because of sheer market momentum, the majority of worldwide subscribers will still be using GSM/EDGE technologies.

Meanwhile, CDMA was chosen as the basis of 3G technologies including WCDMA for the frequency division duplex (FDD) mode of UMTS and Time Division CDMA (TD-CDMA) for the time division duplex (TDD) mode of UMTS. The evolved data systems for UMTS, such as HSPA and HSPA+, introduce enhancements and simplifications that help CDMA-based systems match the capabilities of competing systems, especially in 5 MHz spectrum allocations.

Innovations such as dual-carrier HSPA, explained in detail in the appendix section "Evolution of HSPA (HSPA+)," coordinate the operation of HSPA on two adjacent 5 MHz carriers for higher throughput rates. In combination with MIMO, dual-carrier HSPA will achieve peak network speeds of 84 Mbps.

Given some of the advantages of an OFDM approach, 3GPP has specified OFDMA as the basis of its Long Term Evolution effort. LTE incorporates best-of-breed radio techniques to achieve performance levels beyond what will be practical with CDMA approaches, particularly in larger channel bandwidths. In the same way that 3G coexists with Second Generation (2G) systems in integrated networks, LTE systems will coexist with both 3G systems and 2G systems. Multimode devices will function across LTE/3G or even LTE/3G/2G, depending on market circumstances. Beyond radio technology, EPC/SAE provides a new core architecture that enables both flatter architectures and integration of LTE with both legacy GSM-HSPA networks, as well as other wireless technologies. The combination of EPC and LTE is referred to as the Evolved Packet System (EPS).

LTE is of crucial importance to operators since it provides the efficiencies and capabilities being demanded by the quickly growing mobile broadband market. The cost for operators to deliver data (e.g., cost per Mbyte) is almost directly proportional to the spectral efficiency of the technologies. LTE has the highest spectral efficiency of any specified technology, making it an essential technology as the market matures.

LTE is available in both FDD and TDD modes. Many deployments will be based on FDD in paired spectrum. The TDD mode, however, will be important in enabling deployments where paired spectrum is unavailable.

To address ITU's IMT-Advanced requirements, 3GPP is developing LTE-Advanced, a technology that will have peak rates of more than 1 Gbps. See the appendix section "4G, IMT-Advanced and LTE-Advanced" for a detailed explanation.

Although later sections quantify performance and presents functional details of the different technologies, this section provides a summary intended to provide a frame of reference for the subsequent discussion. Table 7.4 summarizes the key 3GPP technologies and their characteristics.

Table 7.4: Characteristics of 3GPP Technologies

Technology Name	*Type*	*Characteristics*	*Typical Downlink Speed*	*Typical Uplink Speed*
GSM	TDMA	Most widely deployed cellular technology in the world. Provides voice and data service via GPRS/ EDGE.		
EDGE	TDMA	Data service for GSM networks. An enhancement to original GSM data service called GPRS.	70 kbps to 135 kbps	70 kbps to 135 kbps
Evolved EDGE	TDMA	Advanced version of EDGE that can double and eventually quadruple throughput rates, halve latency and increase spectral efficiency.	175 kbps to 350 kbps expected (Single Carrier) 350 kbps to 700 kbps expected (Dual Carrier)	150 kbps to 300 kbps expected
UMTS	CDMA	3G technology providing voice and data capabilities. Current deployments implement HSPA for data service.	200 to 300 kbps	200 to 300 kbps
HSPA	CDMA	Data service for UMTS networks. An enhancement to original UMTS data	1 Mbps to 4 Mbps	500 kbps to 2 Mbps
HSPA+	CDMA	Evolution of HSPA in various stages to increase throughput and capacity and to lower latency.	1.5 Mbps to 7 Mbps	1 Mbps to 4 Mbps
LTE	OFDMA	New radio interface that can use wide radio channels and deliver extremely high throughput rates. All communications handled in IPdomain.	4 Mbps to 24 Mbps (in 2 x 20 MHz)	
LTE-Advanced	OFDMA	Advanced version of LTE designed to meet IMT-Advanced requirements.		

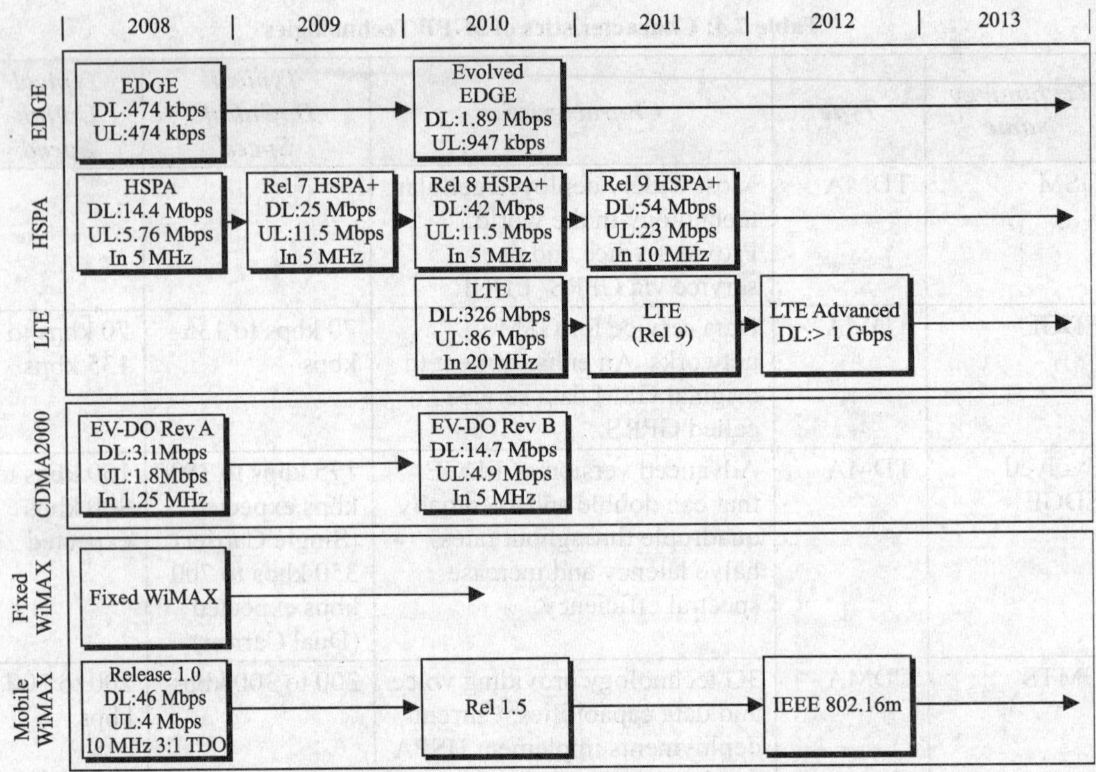

Fig. 7.13: Evolution of TDMA, CDMA and OFDMA Systems

7.8 ADDRESSING MULTIPLE TECHNOLOGIES

The development of GSM and UMTS-HSPA happens in stages referred to as 3GPP releases, and equipment vendors produce hardware that supports particular versions of each specification. It is important to realize that the 3GPP releases address multiple technologies. For example, Release 7 optimized VoIP for HSPA, but also significantly enhanced GSM data functionality with Evolved EDGE. A summary of the different 3GPP releases is as follows:

- *Release 99*— Completed. First deployable version of UMTS. Enhancements to GSM data (EDGE). Majority of deployments today are based on Release 99. Provides support for GSM/EDGE/GPRS/WCDMA radio-access networks.
- *Release 4*— Completed. Multimedia messaging support. First steps toward using IP transport in the core network.

After Release 99, release versions went to a numerical designation instead of designation by year.

- *Release 5*— Completed. HSDPA. First phase of IMS. Full ability to use IP-based transport instead of just Asynchronous Transfer Mode (ATM) in the core network.

- *Release 6*— Completed. HSUPA. Enhanced multimedia support through Multimedia Broadcast/Multicast Services (MBMS). Performance specifications for advanced receivers. WLAN integration option. IMS enhancements. Initial VoIP capability.
- *Release 7*— Completed. Provides enhanced GSM data functionality with Evolved EDGE. Specifies HSPA Evolution (HSPA+), which includes higher order modulation and MIMO. Provides fine-tuning and incremental improvements of features from previous releases. Results include performance enhancements, improved spectral efficiency, increased capacity, and better resistance to interference. Continuous Packet Connectivity (CPC) enables efficient "always-on" service and enhanced uplink UL VoIP capacity, as well as reductions in call set-up delay for PoC. Radio enhancements to HSPA include 64 QAM in the downlink DL and 16 QAM in the uplink. Also includes optimization of MBMS capabilities through the multicast/broadcast, single-frequency network (MBSFN) function.
- *Release 8*— Completed. Comprises further HSPA Evolution features such as simultaneous use of MIMO and 64 QAM. Includes work item for dual-carrier HSPA (DC-HSPA) wherein two WCDMA radio channels can be combined for a doubling of throughput performance. Specifies OFDMA-based 3GPP LTE. Defines EPC.
- *Release 9*— Under development. Likely 2010. Will include HSPA and LTE enhancements including HSPA multi-carrier operation.
- *Release 10*— Under development. Likely 2011. Will specify LTE-Advanced that meets the requirements set by ITU's IMT-Advanced project.

Whereas operators and vendors actively involved in the development of wireless technology are heavily focused on 3GPP release versions, most users of the technology are more interested in particular features and capabilities such as whether a device supports HSDPA. For this reason, the detailed discussion of the technologies in this paper emphasizes features as opposed to 3GPP releases.

7.9 SPECTRUM

Another important aspect of UMTS-HSPA deployment is the expanding number of available radio bands, as shown in Table 7.5, and the corresponding support from infrastructure and mobile-equipment vendors. The fundamental system design and networking protocols remain the same for each band; only the frequency-dependent portions of the radios have to change.

As other frequency bands become available for deployment, standards bodies are adapting UMTS for these bands as well. This includes 450 and 700 MHz. UMTS-TDD equipment is already available for 450 MHz. The 1710-1770 uplink was matched with 2110-2170 downlink to allow for additional global harmonization of the 1.7/2.1GHz band. Meanwhile, the Federal Communications Commission auctioned the 700 MHz band in the United States in January 2008. The availability of this band, the Advanced Wireless Services (AWS) band at 1710-1755 MHz with/2110-2155 MHz in the US, and the forthcoming 2.6 GHz frequency band in Europe are providing operators with wider deployment options. An increasing number of operators are also deploying UMTS at 900 MHz, a traditional GSM band.

As the total amount of available spectrum increases and as technologies simultaneously become spectrally more efficient, total capacity rises rapidly, supporting more subscribers and making many new types of applications feasible.

7.9.1 FDD Bands

The following figure shows the FDD bands defined for 3GPP technologies.

Table 7.5: FDD Bands for 3GPP Technologies

Operating Band	*Band Name*	*Total Spectrum*	*Uplink (MHz)*	*Downlink (MHz)*
Band 1	2.1 GHz	2 x 60 MHz	1920-1980	2110-2170
Band 2	1900 MHz	2 x 60 MHz	1850-1910	1930-1990
Band 3	1800 MHz	2 x 75 MHz	1710-1785	1805-1880
Band 4	1.7/2.1 GHz	2 x 45 MHz	1710-1755	2110-2155
Band 5	850 MHz	2 x 25 MHz	824-849	869-894
Band 6	800 MHz	2 x 10 MHz	830-840	875-885
Band 7	2.6 GHz	2 x 70 MHz	2500-2570	2620-2690
Band 8	900 MHz	2 x 35 MHz	880-915	925-960
Band 9	1700 MHz	2 x 35 MHz	1749.9-1784.9	1844.9-1879.9
Band 10	Ext 1.7/2.1 GHz	2 x 60 MHz	1710-1770	2110-2170
Band 11	1500 MHz	2 x 25 MHz	1427.9-1452.9	1475.9-1500.9
Band 12	Lower 700 MHz	2 x 18 MHz	698-716	728-746
Band 13	Upper 700 MHz	2 x 10 MHz	777-787	746-756
Band 14	Upper 700 MHz Public Safety / Private	2 x 10 MHz	788-798	758-768

7.9.2 TDD Bands

It should be noted that although the support of a new frequency band may be introduced in a particular release, the 3GPP standard also specifies ways to implement devices and infrastructure operating on any frequency band, according to release anterior to the introduction of that particular frequency band. For example, although band 5 (US Cellular Band) was

Table 7.6: TDD Brands for 3GPP Technologies

Operating Band	*Total Spectrum*	*Frequencies (MHz)*
Band 33	20 MHz	1900-1920
Band 34	15 MHz	2010-2025
Band 35	60 MHz	1850-1910
Band 36	60 MHz	1930-1990
Band 37	20 MHz	1910-1930
Band 38	50 MHz	2570-2620
Band 39	40 MHz	1880-1920
Band 40	100 MHz	2300-2400

introduced in Release 6, the first devices operating on this band were compliant with the release 5 of the standard.

7.9.3 Higher Spectrum for More Speed

Different countries have regulated spectrum more loosely than others. For example, operators in the United States can use either 2G or 3G technologies in cellular, Personal Communications Service (PCS), and 3G bands, whereas in Europe there are greater restrictions—although efforts are underway that are resulting in greater flexibility including the use of 3G technologies in current 2G bands.

With the projected increase in the use of mobile-broadband technologies, the amount of spectrum required by the next generation of wireless technology (that is, after 3GPP LTE in projects such as International Mobile Telecommunications (IMT) Advanced) could be substantial given the desire to operate radio channels as wide as 100 MHz. Ideally, this spectrum would fall below 5 GHz. This search for new spectrum is a long-term undertaking, and it may be well into the next decade before any such new spectrum becomes available. Given the expanding size and economic significance of the mobile- computing industry, however, decisions made on new spectrum—especially with respect to global harmonization—will have profound consequences.

As regulators make more spectrum available, it is important that such spectrum be:

1. Harmonized on a regional or global basis.
2. Unencumbered by spectrum caps and other legacy voice-centric spectrum policies.
3. Made available in as wide radio channels as possible (i.e., 10 MHz, 20 MHz and more).
4. Utilized efficiently without causing interference to existing spectrum holders.

Emerging technologies such as LTE benefit from wider radio channels. These wider radio channels are not only spectrally more efficient, but offer greater capacity, an essential attribute because typical broadband usage contributes to a much higher load than a voice user. For instance, watching a YouTube video consumes 100 times as many bits per second on the downlink as a voice call.

Figure 7.14 shows increasing LTE spectral efficiency obtained with wider radio channels, with 20 MHz showing the most efficient configuration.

Of some concern in this regard is that spectrum for LTE is becoming available in different frequency bands in different countries. For instance, initial US deployments will be at 700 MHz, in Japan at 1500 MHz and in Europe at 2.6 GHz. Thus, with some many varying spectrum bands, it will most likely necessitate that roaming operation be based on GSM or HSPA on common regional or global bands.

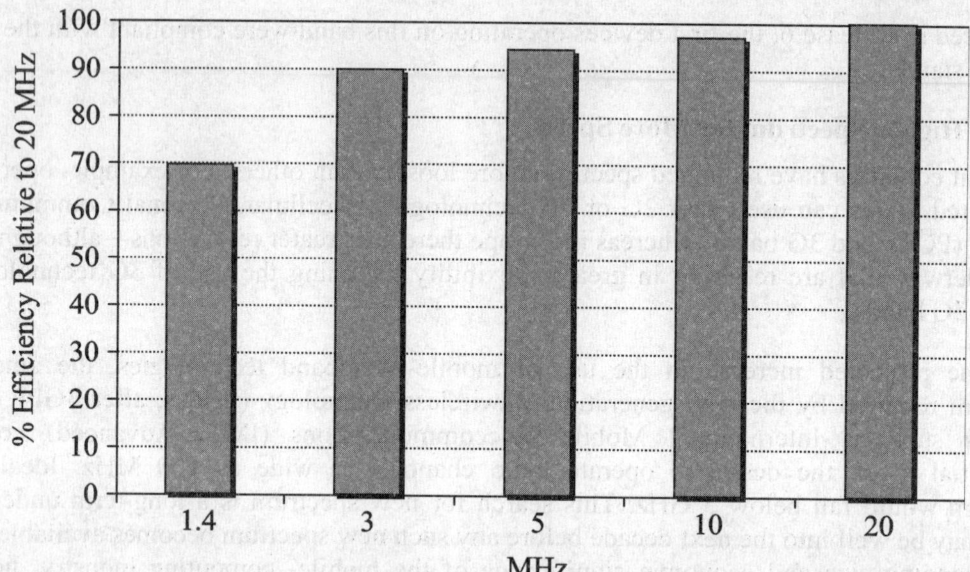

Fig. 7.14: LTE Spectral Efficiency as Function of Radio Chennel Size

7.10 CORE-NETWORK EVOLUTION

3GPP is defining a series of enhancements to the core network to improve network performance and the range of services provided, and to enable a shift to all-IP architectures.

One way to improve core-network performance is by using flatter architectures. The more hierarchical a network, the more easily it can be managed centrally; the tradeoff, however, is reduced performance, especially for data communications, because packets must traverse and be processed by multiple nodes in the network. To improve data performance and, in particular, to reduce latency (delays), 3GPP has defined a number of enhancements in Release 7 and Release 8 that reduce the number of processing nodes and result in a flatter architecture.

In Release 7, an option called one-tunnel architecture allows operators to configure their networks so that user data bypasses a serving node and travels directly via a gateway node. There is also an option to integrate the functionality of the radio-network controller directly into the base station.

For Release 8, 3GPP has defined an entirely new core network, called the Evolved Packet Core, previously called System Architecture Evolution. The key features and capabilities of EPC/SAE include:

- Reduced latency and higher data performance through a flatter architecture.
- Support for both LTE radio-access networks and interworking with GSM-HSPA radio-access networks.
- The ability to integrate non-3GPP networks such as WiMAX.
- Optimization for all services provided via IP.

This paper provides further details in the sections on HSPA Evolution (HSPA+) and EPC/SAE.

7.11 SERVICE EVOLUTION

Not only do 3GPP technologies provide continual improvements in capacity and data performance, they also evolve capabilities that expand the services available to subscribers. Key service advances include Fixed Mobile Convergence (FMC), IMS, and broadcasting technologies. This section provides an overview of these topics, and future chapters provide greater detail on each of these items.

7.11.1 Fixed Mobile Convergence

FMC refers to the integration of fixed services (such as telephony provided by wireline or Wi-Fi) with mobile cellular-based services. Though FMC is still in its early stages of deployment by operators, it promises to provide significant benefits to both users and operators. For users, FMC will simplify how they communicate making it possible for them to use one device (for example, a cell phone) at work and at home where it might connect via a Wi-Fi network or a femto cell. When mobile, users connect via a cellular network. Users will also benefit from single voice mailboxes and single phone numbers, as well as the ability to control how and with whom they communicate. For operators, FMC allows the consolidation of core services across multiple-access networks. For instance, an operator could offer complete VoIP-based voice service that supports access via DSL, Wi-Fi, or 3G. FMC also offloads the macro network from data-intensive applications such as movie downloads.

There are various approaches for FMC, including Generic Access Network (GAN), formerly known as Unlicensed Mobile Access (UMA), femtocells, and IMS. With GAN, GSM-HSPA devices can connect via Wi-Fi or cellular connections for both voice and data. UMA/GAN is a 3GPP technology, and it has been deployed by a number of operators, including T-Mobile in the United States. An alternative to using Wi-Fi for the "fixed" portion of FMC is femtocells. These are tiny base stations that cost little more than a Wi- Fi access point and, like Wi-Fi, femtocells leverage a subscriber's existing wireline- broadband connection (for example, DSL). Instead of operating on unlicensed bands, femtocells use the operator's licensed bands at very low power levels. The key advantage of the femtocell approach is that any single-mode, mobile-communications device a user has can now operate using the femtocells.

7.11.2 IP Multimedia Subsystem

IMS is another key technology for convergence. It allows access to core services and applications via multiple-access networks. IMS is more powerful than GAN, because it supports not only FMC, but also a much broader range of potential applications. In the United States, AT&T has committed to an IMS approach and has already deployed an IMS-based video sharing service. Although defined by 3GPP, the Third Generation

Partnership Project 2 (3GPP2), CableLabs and WiMAX have adopted IMS. IMS is how VoIP will (or could) be deployed in CDMA 2000 EV-DO, WiMAX, HSPA and LTE networks.

IMS allows the creative blending of different types of communications and information, including voice, video, IM, presence information, location, and documents. It provides application developers the means to create applications that have never before been possible, and it allows people to communicate in entirely new ways by dynamically using multiple services. For example, during an interactive chat session, a user could launch a voice call. Or during a voice call, a user could suddenly establish a simultaneous video connection or start transferring files. While browsing the Web, a user could decide to speak to a customer-service representative. IMS will be a key platform for all-IP architectures for both HSPA and LTE.

A new initiative called Rich Communications Suite (RCS), supported by many operators and vendors, builds upon IMS technology to provide a consistent feature set, as well as implementation guidelines, use cases, and reference implementations. RCS uses existing standards and specifications from 3GPP, OMA and GSMA.

Core features include:

- An enhanced phone book (device and/or network based) that includes service capabilities and presence-enhanced contact information.
- Enhanced messaging (supporting text, instant messaging and multimedia) with chat and messaging history.
- Enriched calls that include multimedia content (e.g., video sharing) during voice calls.

Another important new service is support for mobile TV through what is called multicast or broadcast functions. 3GPP has defined multicast/broadcast capabilities for both HSPA and LTE.

7.12 DEVICE INNOVATION

Computing itself is becoming more mobile, and notebook computers and smartphones are now prevalent. In fact, all mobile phones are becoming "smart," with some form of data capability, and leading notebook vendors are now offering computers with integrated 3G (e.g., HSPA) capabilities. Modems are available in multiple formats including USB devices, PC Cards and Express cards.

Computer manufacturers are also delivering new form factors such as netbooks, mobile Internet devices (MID) and smartbooks. The movement to open networks also allows a greater number of companies to develop products that use wireless networks in both vertical-market and horizontal-market scenarios. According to a recent report by Forward Concepts, the global MID-only market is expected to grow from 305,000 shipments in 2008 to 40 million in 2012.[29]

Cellular telephones are becoming more powerful and feature large color touch displays, graphics viewers, still cameras, movie cameras, MP3 players, IM clients, e-mail clients, Push-to-Talk over Cellular (PoC), downloadable executable content capabilities, and ever more powerful browsers. All these capabilities consume data.

Review Questions

1. What is GPP? Who are the organizational partners of 3GPP?
2. List out all the 3GPP recommendations along with the data rates achieved for ul & dl?
3. Compare the different technologies used for mobile network and their data rates.

4. Write about Bearer Independent Core Network Architecture and explain the working by a drawing.
5. What is CS-MGW? Explain in detail.
6. Write note on UTRAN lub / lur protocols and operations.
7. What are the enhancement done in Rel-4 to introduce MS?
8. Tabulate the characteristic of 3GPP Technologies?
9. Write the new features in GPP Rel - 6, 7, 8, 9 and 10.
10. What is meant by Spectrum? Define spectral efficiency. Evaluate the spectral efficiency in LTE.
11. Write note on service evolution in GPP releases.

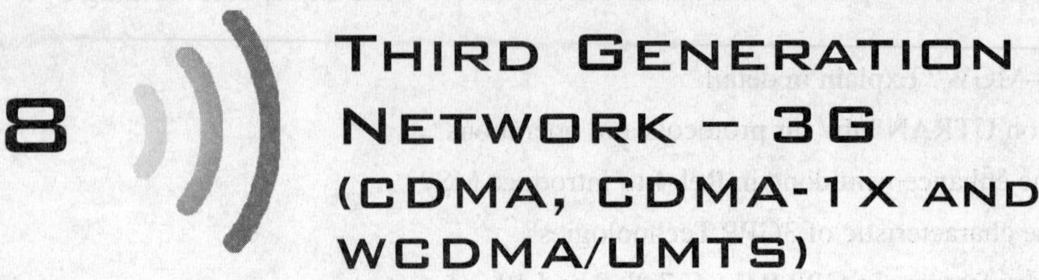

8 Third Generation Network – 3G (CDMA, CDMA-1X and WCDMA/UMTS)

8.1 INTRODUCTION

The emergence of the Third Generation Mobile Technology (Commonly known as 3G), has been the latest innovation in the field of communication. In fact, in the European market few years back the operators have taken license to operate 3G services at quite high cost. After initial teething troubles, the technology is finally taking shape. The architecture and the specification are in place. The products and the network roll outs have started and customer base is growing.

The main aim of global third generation (3G) wireless standards is to address emerging user demands and to provide new services. The concept of 3G wireless technology represents a shift from voice-centric services to multimedia-oriented (voice, data, video, fax) services. In addition, heavy demand for remote access to personalized data is fueling development of applications, such as the Wireless Application Protocol (WAP) and multimedia management, to complement the 3G protocols. Complementary standards, such as Bluetooth, will enable interoperability between a mobile terminal (phone, PDA etc.) and other electronic devices, such as a laptop/desktop and peripherals, providing added convenience to the consumer.

Today, new technologies are quickly emerging that will optimize the transport of data services and offer higher bandwidth in a mobile environment. As a case in point, the increased use of the Internet as an acceptable source for information distribution and retrieval, in conjunction with the increased demand for global mobility has created a need for 3G wireless communications protocols.

The third generation of mobile communications will greatly enhance the implementation of sophisticated wireless applications. Users will be able to utilize personal, location-based wireless information and interactive services.

3G is the next generation of wireless network technology that provides high speed bandwidth (high data transfer rates) to handheld devices. The high data transfer rates will allow 3G networks to offer multimedia services combining voice and data. Specifically, 3G wireless networks support the following maximum data transfer rates:

- 2.05 Mbits/second to stationary devices.
- 384 Kbits/ second for slowly moving devices, such as a handset carried by a walking user.
- 128 Kbits/second for fast moving devices, such as handset in moving vehicles.

These data rates are the absolute maximum numbers. For example, in the stationary case, the 2.05 Mb/second rate is for one user hogging the entire capacity of the base station. This data rate will be far lower if there is voice traffic (the actual data rate would depend upon the number of calls in progress). The maximum data rate of 128 Kbits/second for moving devices is about ten times faster than that available with the current 2G wireless networks. Unlike 3G networks, 2G networks were designed to carry voice but not data. 3G wireless networks have the bandwidth to provide converged voice and data services. 3G services will seamlessly combine superior voice quality telephony, high speed mobile IP services, information technology, rich media, and offer diverse content.

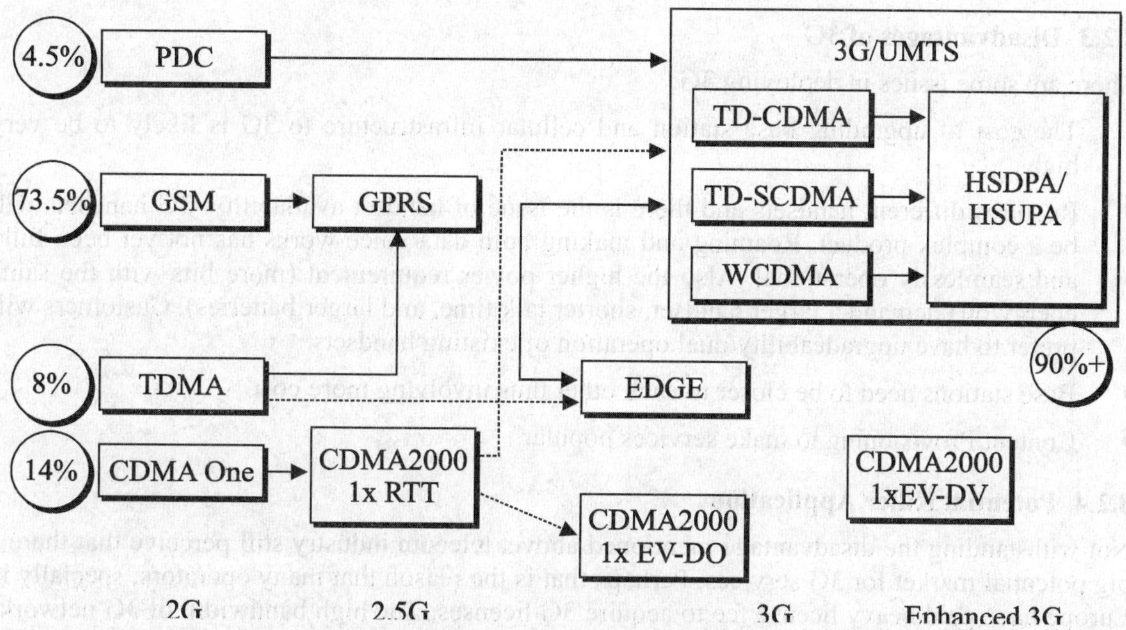

Fig. 8.1: Evolution of 3G

8.2.1 Characteristics of 3G Services

- Always-on connectivity. 3G networks use IP connectivity, which is packet based.
- Multi-media service with streaming audio and video.
- Email with full-fledged attachments such as Power Point files.
- Instant messaging with video/audio clips.
- Fast downloads of large files such as faxes and Power Point files.
- Access to corporate applications.

8.2.2 Advantages of 3G

3G networks offer the users advantages such as:

- New radio spectrum to relieve overcrowding in existing systems.

- More bandwidth, security and reliability.
- Interoperability between service providers.
- Fixed and variable data rates.
- Asymmetric data rates.
- Backward compatibility of devices with existing networks.
- Always-online devices, 3G will use IP connectivity. IP is packet based (not circuit based).
- Rich multimedia services.

8.2.3 Disadvantages of 3G

There are some issues in deploying 3G:

- The cost of upgrading base station and cellular infrastructure to 3G is likely to be very high.
- Requires different handsets and there is the issue of handset availability. 3G handsets will be a complex product. Roaming and making both data/voice works has not yet been fully and seamlessly operational. Also the higher power requirement (more bits with the same energy/bit) demand a larger handset, shorter talk time, and larger batteries). Customers will prefer to have upgradeability/dual operation of existing handsets.
- Base stations need to be closer to each other thus involving more cost.
- Content Provisioning to make services popular.

8.2.4 Potential Killer Applications

Not withstanding the disadvantage mentioned above, telecom industry still perceive that there a big potential market for 3G services, Perhaps that is the reason that many operators, specially in Europe have paid heavy license fee to acquire 3G licenses. The high bandwidth of 3G networks will lead to the creation of new services, some of which we have no idea at this time. The big question is what services will be big revenue markets for the wireless service providers. In 2G networks, the big winners have been short text messaging in GSM networks (In Europe and countries other that USA) and image downloads. Some of the services likely to be big winners in 3G networks are:

- video conferencing
- video messaging
- Mobile Games

The first application is more form business application. The other two are targeted towards the younger generation. MMS (Multi Media Services) are likely to grow very fast. Similarly, as per some estimation, it is felt that gaming industry could be as big as $20-25 billion in near future. In fact, the optimist predict that it will be bigger than Hollywood box office collection. The trend is not restricted to US but is likely to be followed by Asian countries. Presently India and China are perceived as bid market for Mobile Growth (Including 3G).

8.2.5 Architecture

Wideband CDMA (W-CDMA) is compatible with the current 2G GSM networks prevalent in Europe and parts of Asia. W-CDMA will require bandwidth of between 5 Mhz and 10 Mhz, making it a suitable platform for higher capacity applications. It can be overlaid onto existing GSM, TDMA (IS-36) and IS95 networks. Subscribers are likely to access 3G wireless services initially via dual band terminal devices. W-CDMA networks will be used for high-capacity applications and 2G digital wireless systems will be used for voice calls.

The second radio interface is CDMA2000 which is backward compatible with the second generation CDMA IS-95 standard predominantly used in US. The third radio interface, Universal Wireless Communications – UWC-136, also called IS-136HS, was proposed by the TIA and designed to comply with ANSI-136, the North American TDMA standard.

3G wireless networks consist of a Radio Access Network (RAN) and a core network. The core network consists of a packet-switched domain, which includes 3G SGSNs and GGSNs, which provide the same functionality that they provide in a GPRS system, and a circuit-switched domain, which includes 3G MSC for switching of voice calls. Charging for services and access is done through the Charging Gateway Function (CGF), which is also part of the core network. RAN functionality is independent from the core network functionality. The access network provides a core network technology independent access for mobile terminals to different types of core networks and network services. Either core network domain can access any appropriate RAN service; e.g. it should be possible to access a "speech" radio access bearer from the packet switched domain.

3G Technology isn't just a new radio interface. It is lot more from the consideration both the service provider and the customer. Though 3G is primarily based on evolution of second-generation technologies such as GSM/GPRS, the overall picture is quite a bit more complex than that of present 2G. 3G is not just a matter of building a totally new infrastructure, but also entails to have the migration plans in place, both for the short term and the long term. Existing 2G operators need to upgrade their networks to remain competitive.

The 3G terminals will also have new capabilities that 2G terminals do not. Multimedia applications and host of other services based on standard Internet technology will converge cellular telephones and the Internet technologies. Users will be able to download Java based applications on their terminals, just as they do today on the World Wide Web. Nevertheless, the new technology is associated with new security threats and even if security is enhanced, the risk of security lapses will still be there, unless extra precautions are taken.

3G wireless technology introduces new Radio Access Network (RAN) consisting of Node B and RNC network elements. The 3G Core Network consists of the same entities as GSM and GPRS: 3G MSC/VLR, GMSC, HLR/AuC/EIR, 3G-SGSN, and GGSN. IP technology is used end-to-end for multimedia applications and ATM technology is used to provide reliable transport with QoS.

3G wireless solutions allow for the possibility of having an integrated network for circuit-switched and packet-switched services by utilizing ATM technology. The BSC may evolve into an RNC by using add-on cards or additional hardware that is co-located. The carrier frequency (5Mhz) and the bands (2.5 to 5Ghz) are different for 3G wireless technology compared to 2G/2G+ wireless technology. Evolution of BSC to RNC requires support for new protocols such as PDCP, RRC, RANAP, RNSAP and NBAP. Therefore, BTS' evolution into Node B may prove to be difficult and may represent significant capital expenditure on the part of network operators.

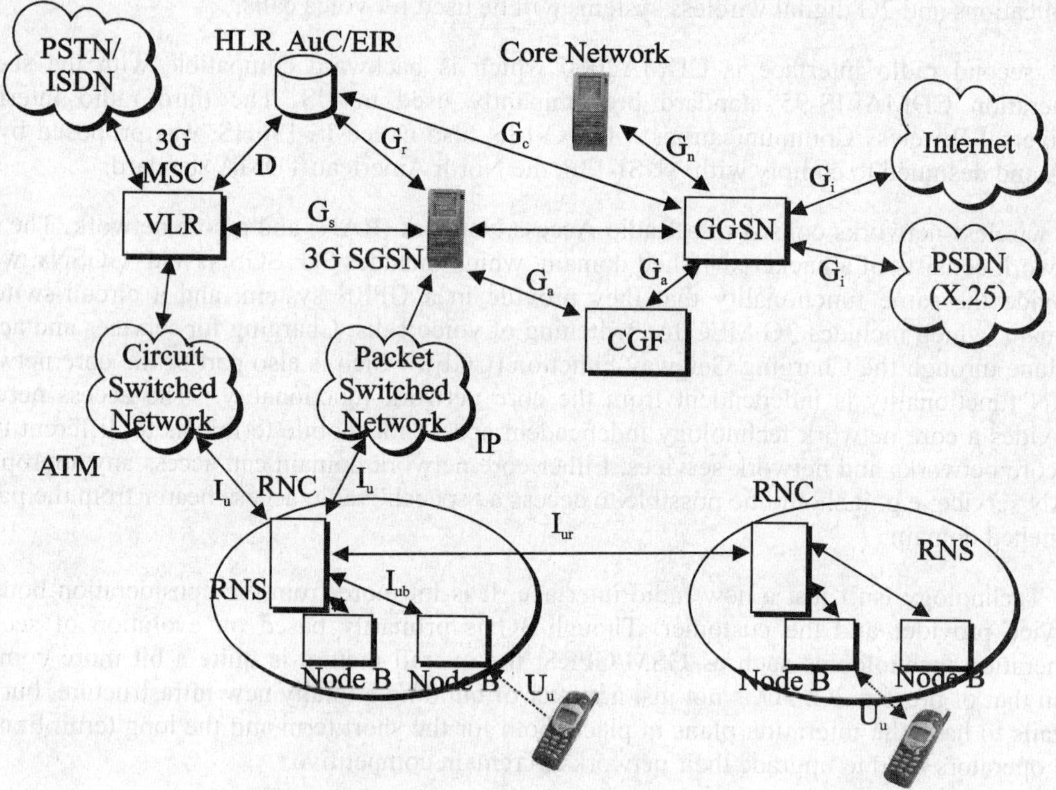

Fig. 8.2: 3G Wireless Network Architecture

MSC evolution depends on the selection of a fixed network to carry the requested services. If an ATM network is chosen, then ATM protocols will have to be supported in 3G MSC along with interworking between ATM and existing PSTN/ISDN networks. The evolution of SGSN and GGSN to 3G nodes is relatively easier. Enhancements to GTP protocol and support for new RANAP protocol are necessary to support 3G wireless systems. ATM protocols need to be incorporated to transport the services. The HLR databases evolve into 3G-HLR by adding 3G wireless user profiles. The VLR database must also be updated accordingly. The EIR database needs to change to accommodate new equipment that will be deployed for 3G wireless systems. Finally, global roaming requires compatibility to existing deployment and graceful fallback to an available level when requested services are not available in the region. Towards this end, the Operator Harmonization Group (OHG) is working closely with 3G Partnership Projects (3GPP and 3GPP2) to come up with global standards for 3G wireless protocols.

8.3 CDMA2000 EVOLUTION

The aim of the CDMA2000 is to provide a migration path from the original cdmaOne / IS-95 system through the CDMA2000 1X format to further high speed formats. These different standards have all been standardised under the IS-format and a diagram of the migration path is given below:

8.3.1 CDMA2000 Formats

The CDMA2000 1X format is the basic 3G standard, but in what is termed CDMA2000 1xEv, there are further developments. There are basically two routes for the evolution that were initially proposed, only one of which was deployed:

- *CDMA2000 1X EV-DO—* The first of these known as CDMA2000 1xEV-DO (EVolution Data Only) or as is becoming more widely known Evolution Data Optimised) is something of a sideline from the main evolutionary development of the standard. It is defined under IS-856 rather than IS-2000, and as the name indicates it only carries data, but at speeds up to 3.1Mbps in the forward direction and 1.8 Mbps in the reverse direction, the speed in the reverse link being upgraded as part of Release A of the standard. The first commercial CDMA2000 1xEV-DO network was deployed by SK Telecom (Korea) in January 2002.
- *CDMA2000 1X EV-DV—* The second is CDMA2000 1X EV-DV (Evolution Data and Voice). The idea was that this system would carry both data and voice services. It was never deployed as the EV-DO system was deployed in preference and there was no requirement for a data and voice service as voice could be carried on DO as either VoIP or by falling back to the CDMA2000 1X format.

8.3.2 CDMA2000 1XRTT and 3XRTT

The CDMA2000 1XRTT and 3XRTT terms refer to what are termed “Radio Transmission Technologies”. The original IS-95 and deployments of CDMA2000 utilised the 1.25 MHz channel spacing. This provided what is effectively the first phase of the 3G development and roll out. However to enhance the performance beyond that possible using the technologies such as 1xEV-DO and 1xEV-DV, the channel bandwidth of 1.25 MHz was deemed insufficient for even higher data rates. Accordingly by increasing the bandwidth, higher data rates were possible. The further evolution of the CDMA2000 system involves utilising channel bandwidths of 3 times the standard 1.25 MHz bandwidth under what was termed 3XRTT. Further bandwidth increases to 5X, 7X and so forth could in theory be contemplated.

For CDMA2000 1XRTT technology, a Spreading Rate 1 (SR1) was used where the signal was spread to occupy a bandwidth of 1.25 MHz. Here the spread rate was the same as that used for IS-95, i.e. 1.2288 Mcps. For 3XRTT technology, Spreading Rate 3 (SR3) was used. Here the spreading rate was 3.6864 Mcps. It was found that if the spreading rate remained the same but the data rate increased, as happens with video downloads and other 3G applications, the processing gain decreased. Accordingly the coverage and signal strength needed to be improved to match the new conditions. By increasing the spreading rate, the performance could be boosted without the need for improvements in coverage.

IS-95 was the first CDMA mobile phone system to gain widespread use and it is found widely in North America. Its brand name is cdmaOne and the initial specification for the system was IS95A, but its performance was later upgraded under IS-95B. It is this later specification that is synonymous with cdmaOne. Apart from voice the mobile phone system is also able to carry data at rates up to 14.4 kbps for IS-95A and 115 kbps for IS-95B.

IS95 / cdmaOne was the fist cellular telecommunications system to use the CDMA - code division multiple access system. Previous systems had used FDMA - frequency division multiple access or TDMA - time division multiple access. With IS-95 being a second generation - 2G system and all the later 3G systems using CDMA as their access.

8.3.3 CDMA 2000 Standard

The acceptance of CDMA 2000 solutions in Asia, North America, and Latin America, which accounted for over four million 3G CDMA2000 users by the end of 2001 and adding more than 1 million new subscribers per month, provides vivid proof of the demand for 3G services and applications. A broad range of color LCD phones and wireless devices are entering the market, including: camera phones, video on Demand phones, Global Positioning System (GPS), and multimedia enabled devices. These new devices, combined with high speed packet data, are opening the door for the creation of a broad array of services that deliver greater choice for consumers and enhance operators' ability to differentiate. The wireless consumer's usage and demands have changed dramatically. The Korean experience demonstrates that the increased capabilities of CDMA200 networks can drive a fundamentally different consumer experience and operator business model.

CDMA2000 is a cost-effective evolutionary technology for CDMA, TDMA and GSM operations. CDMA2000 is an evolution of cdmaOne (IS-95) technology. CDMA2000's development benefited from extensive experience acquired through the operation of cdmaOne systems, as well as the requirements of third generation wireless systems. The result is an efficient and versatile technology. CDMA2000 1X supports both voice and data while CDMA2000 1xEV-DO (Data Optimized) supports data only in 1.25 MHz of spectrum. The objective of this paper is to cover key features of CDMA2000 1X.

The first commercial CDMA2000 network was launched in Korea in October 2000. By the end of 2001 there were 4.2 million commercial subscribers using CDMA2000 in Korea, adding over 800,000 new subscribers per month. As of end of 2001, more than 40 operators wordwide have announced plans for commercial deployment of CDMA2000. Currently there are 93 commercial CDMA2000 terminals manufactured by 20 different manufactures. cdmaOne has been deployed in over 50 countries of five continents and there are over 100 million subscribers worldwide.

8.3.4 Major new Enhancements in CDMA2000

- Nearly doubling the voice capacity – from 14.8 Erlang per sector RF carrier (in 1.25 MHz) to 26.4 Erlang per sector per RF carrier (in 1.25 MHz).
- "Always On" Peak packet data rate of 307 kbps (release A)
- Connectivity to ANSI-41, GSM-MAP, and IP networks.

- Various bands and bandwidths of operation in support of different operator needs: 450, 800, 900, 1700, 1800, 1900, and 2100 MHz.
- Fully backward compatible with cdmaOne systems.
- Improved service multiplexing and QoS management.
- Flexible channel structure in support of multiple services with various QoS and variable transmission rates.

8.4 3GPP RELEASES

The CDMA2000 standard is being supported by "The Third Generation Partnership Project 2," or 3GPP2 organization. It is benefiting from the expertise of specialists from Korean, Japanese, Chinese, and North American standards bodies. The ITU approved the CDMA2000 1X and 1xEV radio access systems as members of the IMT-2000 family of standards.

For the most part, the IS-95 related standards documents were enchanced to provide support for new capabilities and services. CDMA2000 release 0 was published in August 1999, release A in March 2000, and release B is in balloting stage.

Release 0 provides the physical layer details in depth and the key

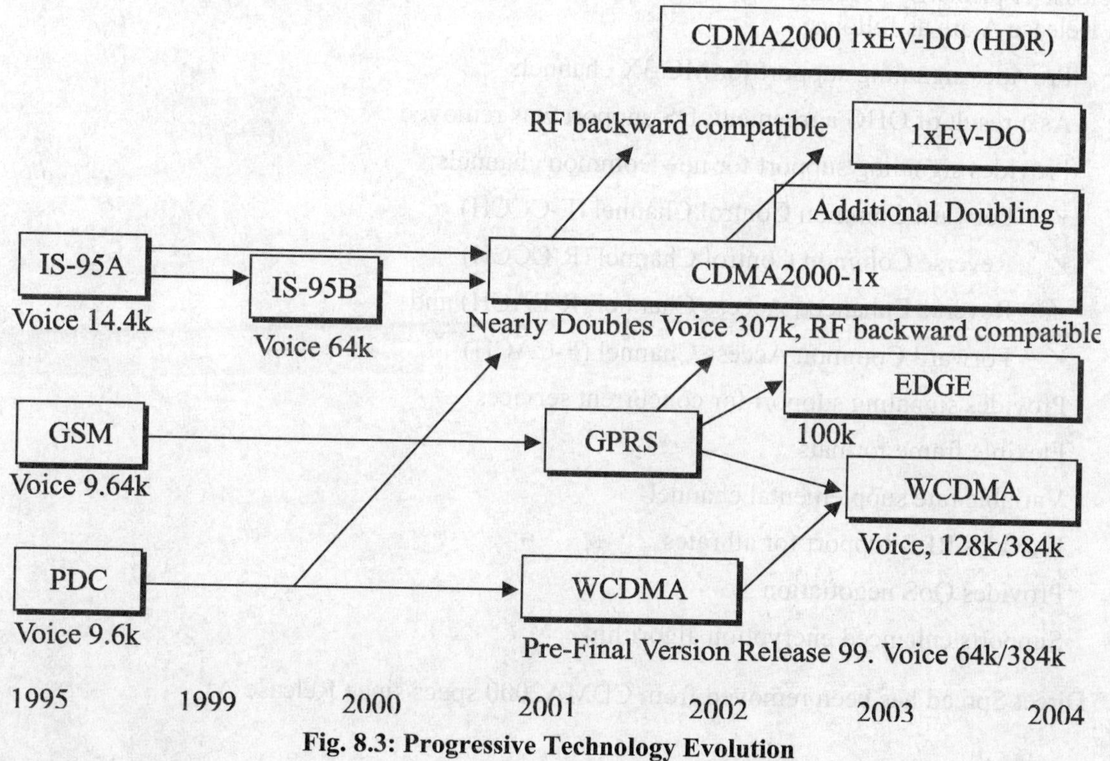

Fig. 8.3: Progressive Technology Evolution

Features of Release 0:

- Provides full physical layer support for all modes
  - ✓ Multiple Carrier 1X
  - ✓ Multiple Carrier 3X
  - ✓ Direct Spread *
- For MC 1X
  - ✓ Provides higher capacity for voice services (approximately twice)
  - ✓ Provides up to 153.6 kbps peak data rate and higher capacity (more than twice) for data services
  - ✓ Provides cleaner structure for mixed services
  - ✓ Reduces battery consumption in idle mode through use of Quick Paging Channel
  - ✓ Includes TIA/EIA-95B as a subset; builds upon IS-95B signaling
- Provides signaling support for new 1X dedicated channels
- Uses IS-95 A Paging Channel and Access Channel for common channel support
- Provides basic MAC support

Release A primarily provides signaling support for a new set of common channels. Key features of Release A are as follows:

- Provides signaling support for MC 3X channels
- As a result of OHG agreement, DS support was removed
- Provides signaling support for new common channels
  - ✓ Forward Common Control Channel (F-CCCH)
  - ✓ Reverse Common Control Channel (R-CCCH)
  - ✓ Reverse Enhanced Access Channel (R-EACH) and
  - ✓ Forward Common Access Channel (F-CACH)
- Provides signaling support for concurrent services
- Flexible frame formats
- Variable rate supplemental channel
- Provides RLP support for all rates
- Provides QoS negotiation
- Supports enhanced encryption algorithm

(* Direct Spread has been removed from CDMA2000 specs since Release A)

8.5 KEY FEATURES OF CDMA

8.5.1 Frequency Bands

The CDMA2000 physical layer includes several modes of operation. This enables the operators to deploy and configure their networks based on their own needs and local regulations. Several options exist for the band of operation and system bandwidth. CDMA2000 networks have been deployed in the 450 MHz, 800 MHz, 1700 MHz, and 1900 MHz, and deployments in IMTS-2000 band are expected in 2002 and 2003. But nothing precludes the deployment of CDMA2000 in other bands, such as 900 MHz and 1800 MHz bands. Spectral efficiency of CDMA2000 permits high traffic deployments in any 1.25 MHz of spectrum.

Initially in the CDMA2000 standards two spreading rates were specified, A 1. 25 MHz full duplex bandwidth referred to as "Spreading Rate 1" (SR1), or "1X" and a 3.75 MHz full duplex bandwidth-referred to as "Spreading Rate 3" (SR3), or "3X". Today the 125 MHz configuration, SRI is predominately being deployed.

8.5.2 Spectrum Requirements

The fundamental spreading rate is 1.2288 Mcps for SR1. It requires 1.25 MHz of bandwidth (625 KHz from the center frequency) when the adjacent RF carriers are nothing but other CDMA carriers. However, It requires 1.8 MHz of bandwidth (900 KHz from the center frequency) when both adjacent RF carriers are narrow band GSM or TDMA carriers.

8.5.3 Battery Life

As mobile phones take the place of wire-line phones, the stand-by time of phones have become an essential customer satisfaction parameter. CDMA2000 major battery life enhancing features include:

- Quick paging channel operation
- Improved reverse link performance
- New common channel structure and operation
- Reverse link gated transmission
- New MAC states for efficient and ubiquitous idle time operation

8.5.4 Synchronization

CDMA2000 is synchronized with the Universal Coordinated Time (UTC). The forward link transmission timing of all CDMA2000 base stations in the world are synchronized within a few microseconds. The base station synchronization can be achieved through several techniques including self-synchronization, radio beep, or through satellite based systems such as GPS, Galileo, or GLONASS. The reverse link timing is based on the received timing derived from the first multi-path component used by the terminal.

There are several benefits to synchronization of all base station in a network. The common time reference improves acquisition of channels and handoff procedures since there is no time ambiguity when looking for and adding a new cell in the active set. It also enables the system to operate some of the common channels in soft-handoff, which improves the efficiency of the common channel operation. In addition, the common network time reference allows to implement very efficient "position location" technique such as gpsOne.

8.5.5 Power Control

The basic frame length is 20 ms divided in to 16 equal power control groups. In addition, CDMA2000 defines a 5 ms frame structure, essentially to support signaling bursts, as well as 40 and 80 ms frames, which offer additional interleaving depth and diversity gains for data services. Unlike IS-95 where Fast Closed Loop Power Control was applied only to the reverse link, CDMA2000 channels can be power controlled at up to 800 Hz in both reverse and forward links. The reverse link power control command bits are punctured into the F-FCH or the F-DCCH (explained in later sections) depending on the service configuration. The forward link power control command bits are punctured in the last quarter of the R-PICH power control slot.

In the reverse link, during gated transmission, the power control rate is reduced to 400 to 200 Hz on both links. The reverse link power control sub-channel may also be divided into two independent power control streams, either both at 400 bps, or one at 200 bps and the other at 600 bps. This allows for independent power control of forward link channels.

In addition to the closed loop power control, the power on the reverse link of CDMA2000 is also controlled through an Open Loop Power Control mechanism. This mechanism inverses the slow fading effect due to path loss and shadowing. It also acts as a safety fuse when the fast power control fails. When the forward link is lost, the closed loop reverse link power control is "freewheeling" and the terminal disruptively interferes with neighboring. In such case, the open loop reduces the terminal output power and limits the impact to the system.

Finally the Outer Loop Power drives the closed loop power control to the desired set point based on error statistics that it collects from the forward link or reverse link. Due to the expanded data rate range and various QoS requirements, different users will have a different outer loop thresholds, thus different users will be received with different power levels at the base station. In the reverse link, CDMA2000 defines some nominal gain offsets based on various channel frame format and coding schemes. The remaining differences will be corrected by the outer loop itself.

8.5.6 Soft Handoff

In parallel to dedicated channel operation, the terminal keeps searching for new cells as it moves across the network. In addition to the active set, neighbor set, and remaining set, the terminal also maintains a Candidate Set.

When a terminal is traveling in a network, the pilot from a new BTS (P2) strength exceeds the minimum threshold TADD for addition in the active set. However, initially its relative contribution to the total received signal strength is not sufficient and the terminal moves P2 to the candidate set. The decision threshold for adding a new pilot to the active set is defined by a linear function of signal strength of the total active set. The network defines the slope and cross point of the function. When strength of P2 is detected to be above the dynamic threshold, the terminal signals this event to the network. Then terminal receives a handoff direction message from the network requesting the addition of P2 in the active set. The terminal now operates in soft-handoff. The strength of serving BTS (P1) drops below the active set threshold, meaning P1 contribution to the total received signal strength does not justify the cost of transmitting P1. The terminal starts a handoff drop timer. The timer expires and the terminal notifies the network moving P1 from the active set to the candidate set. Then P1 strength drops below TDROP and the terminal starts a handoff drop timer, which expires after a set time. P1 is then moved from candidate set to neighbor set. This step-by-step procedure with multiple thresholds and timers ensures that resource is only used when beneficial to the link and pilots are not constantly added and removed from the various lists and therefore, limits the associated signaling.

In addition to intra-system, intra-frequency monitoring, the network may direct terminal to look for base stations on a different frequency or a different system. CDMA2000 provides a framework to the terminal in support of the inter frequency handover measurements. This consists of identity and parameters of the system to be measured. The terminal performs required measurements as allowed by its hardware capability. In case of a terminal with dual receiver structure, the measurement can be done in parallel. In case of a terminal with single receiver, the channel reception will be interrupted when performing the measurement. In this case, during the measurement, a certain portion of a frame will be lost. In order to improve the chance of successful decoding, the terminal is allowed to bias the FL power control loop and boost the RL transmit power before performing the measurement. This method increases the energy per information bit and reduces the risk of losing the link in the interval. Based on measurement reports provided by the terminal, the network then decides whether to handoff a given terminal to a different system of frequency or not. It does not release the resource until it receives confirmation that handoff was successful or the timer expires. This enables the terminal to come back in case it could not acquire the new frequency or the new system.

8.5.7 Transmit Diversity

Transmit diversity consists of de-multiplexing and modulating data into two orthogonal signals, each of them transmitted from a different antenna at the same frequency. The two orthogonal signals are generated using either Orthogonal Transmit Diversity (OTD) or Space-Time Spreading (STS). The receiver reconstructs the original signal using the diversity signals, thus taking advantage of the additional space and/or frequency diversity.

Another transmission option is directive transmission. The base station directs a beam towards a single user or a group of users in a specific location, thus providing space separation in addition to code separation. Depending on the radio environment transmit diversity techniques may improve the link performance by up to 5 dB.

8.6 VOICE AND DATA CHANNELS IN CDMA2000

CDMA2000 forward traffic channel structure may include several physical channels:

- The Fundamental Channel (F-FCH) is equivalent to functionality Traffic Channel (TCH) for IS-95. It can support data, voice, or signaling multiplexed with one another at any rate from 750 bps to 14.4 kbps.

- The Supplemental Channel (F-SCH) support high rate data services. The network may schedule transmission on the F-SCH on a frame by frame basis, if desired.
- Dedicated Control Channel (F-DCCH) is used for signaling or bursty data sessions. This channel allows for sending the signaling information without any impact on the parallel data stream.

The reverse traffic channel structure is similar to the forward traffic channel. It may include R-PICH, a Fundamental Channel (R-FCH), and/or a Dedicated Control Channel (R_DCCH), and one or several Supplemental Channel or channels (R-SCH). Their functionality and encoding structure is the same as for the forward link with data rates ranging from 1 kbps to 1 Mbps (It is important to note that while the standard supports maximum data rate of 1 Mbps, existing products are supporting peak data rate of 307 kbps).

8.6.1 Traffic Channel

The traffic channel structure and frame format is very flexible and in order to limit the signaling load that would be associated with a full frame format parameter negotiation, CDMA2000 specifies a set of channel configurations, it defines a spreading rate and an associated set of frames for each configuration.

The forward traffic channel always includes either a fundamental channel or a dedicated control channel. The main benefit of this multi-channel forward traffic structure is the flexibility to independently set-up and tear down new services without any complicated multiplexing reconfiguration or code channel juggling. The structure also allows different handoff configurations for different channels. For example, the F-DCCH, which carries critical signaling information, may be in soft-handoff while the associated F-SCH operation could be based on a best cell strategy.

8.6.2 Supplemental Channels

One key CDMA2000 1x feature is the ability to support both voice and data services on the same carrier. CDMA2000 operates at up to 16 or 32 times the FCH rate – also referred to as 16x or 32x in Release 0 and A respectively. In contrast to voice calls, the traffic generated by packet data calls is bursty, with small durations of high traffic separated by larger durations of no traffic. It is very inefficient to dedicate a permanent traffic channel to a packet data call. This burstiness impacts the amount of available power to the voice calls, possibly degrading their quality if the system is not engineered correctly. Hence, a key CDMA2000 design issue is assuring that a CDMA channel carrying voice and data calls simultaneously do so with negligible impact to the QoS both.

Supplemental Channels (SCHs) can be assigned and de-assigned at any time by the base station. The SCH has the additional benefit of improved modulation, coding, and power control schemes. This allows a single SCH to provide a data rate of up to 16 FCH in CDMA2000 Release 0 (or 153.6 kbps for Rate Set 1 rates), and up to 32 FCH in CDMA2000 Release A (or 307.2 kbps for Rate Set 1 rates). Note that each sector of a base station may transmit multiple SCHs simultaneously if it has sufficient transmit power and Walsh codes. The CDMA2000 standard limits the number of SCHs a mobile station can support simultaneously to two. This is in addition to the FCH or DCCH, which are set up for the entire duration of the call since they are used to carry signaling and control frames as well as data. Two approaches are possible, individually assigned SCHs, with either finite or infinite assignments, and shared SCHs with infinite assignments.

For bursty and delay-tolerant traffic, assigning a few scheduled fat pipes is preferable to dedicating many thin or slow pipes. The fat-pipe approach exploits variations in the channel conditions of different users to maximize sector throughput. The more sensitive the traffic becomes to delay, such as voice, the more appropriate the dedicated traffic channel approach becomes.

8.6.3 Individually Assigned SCH

In CDMA2000 the most common way to allocate a high-speed link to a user is to assign an SCH to the user. During the assignment, the data being transmitted on the SCH is directed to only that particular user. This type of approach requires signaling which introduces delay. Current implementations require approximately five frames, that is, 100 msec of latency. If the user is moving at a relatively slow speed, it would be possible to change the rate from one SCH assignment to the other in a manner so as to adapt to a changing path loss or shadowing. For example, if the user is moving away from the cell, the assigned SCH rate may be gradually reduced with time as the link quality deteriorates. The delay introduced by signaling, however, is intolerable if one wants to schedule SCH transmissions based on faster changing characteristics of the channel such as Rayleigh fading.

Option A – Infinite Duration

Assign a user an SCH with an infinite duration. This will ensure that the user will not need to go through the signaling process every time it needs to transmit data using the SCH, and no interference will be generated to other users when no data is transmitted because the F-SCH may have discontinuous transmission at any time, for any duration. However, it is a very inefficient approach because the Walsh space is reserved to a user who might be idle most of the time.

Option B – Pseudo-Infinite Assignment

Assign a new SCH for a very large duration to users that need to download a large amount of data, and release that SCH as soon as the user becomes idle. This approach is more efficient than Option A because idle users do not occupy Walsh space for the entire duration of the call. However, every download must bear with an additional delay due to signaling. Another advantage of this approach is that the base station does not need to guess how much data the user has to download; it just de-assigns the SCH when the user is idle. The associated drawback is that the base station does not know when the assignment will end, which makes it hard for the base station to plan the sharing of the sector capacity. There is additional signaling necessary to de-assign SCHs when users become idle.

Option C – Pseudo-Finite Assignment

Same as Option B but in order to let the base station conduct some scheduling, the assignments are stopped before the user is done downloading; it can resume later when the base station gives it a new assignment. This approach allows the base station to do some scheduling as with Option B, with the advantage that the duration is not predetermined. There is again additional signaling involved to de-assign an SCH before it becomes idle; the base station scheduling chops down the previous transmission in pieces.

Option D – Fixed – Assignment Duration

Assign a new SCH for a predetermined duration to users that need to download a large amount of data. This approach is similar to Option C with the difference that since assignments have predetermined duration, no signaling is needed to end the SCH assignment. However, the associated limitation is that the scheduling is less flexible (the duration is fixed).

Shared SCH approach takes a different approach. This option enjoys the benefits of both methods C and D without their drawbacks.

8.6.4 Shared SCH

In this approach, a particular SCH with one fixed rate is assigned to a group of users. This means that all users in the group keep processing the same SCH indefinitely. The key is that the data transmitted on the SCH may be directed to only one of them. When the data is directed to a particular mobile station, it should be able to decode a good frame. At the same time, all other users in the same group will decode an erasure and nothing will be passed to RLP, which will behave as if the frame was a discontinuous transmission.

This method enjoys the benefits of both previous methods because as long as a user can demodulate the same rate, no signaling is involved. At the same time, the same Walsh space can be shared amongst an arbitrarily large number of users. Moreover, this type of SCH assignment being virtually signaling-free, a scheduling algorithm can change the scheduled user every frame, 20 ms. This allows channel-sensitive scheduling. However, the frame size being 20 ms the fading process must stay reasonably slow, so Rayleigh fading-sensitive scheduling is only possible for very low speeds.

The signaling-free assumption is true as long as the user supports the rate of the SCH. If channel conditions change so that the rate cannot be supported anymore, the user would have to be moved to a different SCH group with a lower rate, in which case signaling would be involved. As long as a user can support the SCH rate, no signaling is necessary.

8.7 CODING SCHEMES

CDMA2000 provides the option of using turbo coding or convolution coding on the forward and reverse SCHs. Both coding schemes are optional for both the base station and the mobile station, and the capacity of each is communicated through signaling messages prior to the setup of the call. In addition to peak rate increase and improved rate granularity, the major improvement to the traffic channel coding in CDMA2000 is the support of turbo coding at rate 1/2, 1/3, or 1/4. The turbo code is based on 1/8 state parallel structure and can only be used for supplemental channels and frames with more than 360 bits. Turbo coding provides a very efficient scheme for data transmission and leads to better link performance and system capacity improvements. In general, turbo coding provides a performance gain in terms of power savings over convolutional coding. This gain is a function of the data rate, with higher data rates generally providing more turbo coding gain.

8.8 CDMA2000 BENEFITS

8.8.1 Increased Voice Capacity

Voice continues to be a major source of traffic and revenue for wireless operators today, while packet data traffic is beginning to emerge as a major source of revenue in upcoming years. CDMA2000 1X is the most spectrally efficient technology, delivering the highest voice and packet data throughput using the least amount of spectrum for the lowest cost.

CDMA2000 1X supports 35 traffic channels per sector per RF, (26 Erlangs/sector/RF) using EVRC vocoder. EVRC vocoder first became commercial in 1999. Next generation SMV vocoder is expected to become commercial in 2002. SMV covoder (SMV2 mode) will increase the voice capacity to 45 traffic channel per sector per RF, (35 Erlangs/sector/RF), while maintaining similar voice quality to EVRC.

Voice capacity improvement in forward link is contributed to fast power control, lower code rates (1/4 rate), and transmit diversity (for single path Rayleigh fading). In reverse link capacity improvement is primarily due to coherent reverse link.

8.8.2 Higher Data Throughput

Today's commercial CDMA2000 1X networks (phase 1) support peak data rate of 153.6 kbps. Korean operator, SK Telecom launched first CDMA2000 network in October 2000 and followed by two other Korean operators, KT Freetel and LG Telecom. Commercial handsets based on MSM5100 (CDMA2000 phase 2) are expected in first half of this year, which deliver peak data rate of 307.2 kbps.

CDMA2000 1xEV-DO commercial products will be also become available in first half of 2002. Enabling operators to support peak data rate of 2.4 Mbps (in 1.25 MHz RF Bandwidth).

8.8.3 Summary of CDMA 2000 Features

CDMA2000's development benefited from the extensive experience acquired through several years of operation of cdmaOne systems. Explicit steps were taken to increase voice capacity and data throughput. As a result, CDMA2000 is a very efficient and robust technology. The standard we devised and tested in various spectrum bands, including the new IMT-2000 allocations. In many countries, there is tremendous demand for new services and the operations are looking to provide new services to many more subscribers at reasonable prices. The unique features, benefits and performance of CDMA2000 make it an excellent technology of choice for high voice capacity and high-speed packet data. Due to its optimized radio technology, CDMA2000 allows operators to invest in fewer number of cell sites with faster deployment, and ultimately enabling the service providers to increase revenues with faster Return On Investment (ROI).

8.9 CDMA2000 1X OVERVIEW

There are a number of updates and changes that were introduced to improve the performance of CDMA2000 1X, IS2000 over cdmaOne IS-95. However in all cases backward compatibility is maintained, allowing both IS-95 and CDMA2000 mobiles to access the same base stations. This provided a cost effective upgrade path for both users and operators.

For CDMA2000 1X, several new methods of coding and spreading were used and these enabled much higher capacities to be achieved.

- *Walsh Codes*— The first major change in CDMA2000 1X was that the Walsh Codes used were increased from 64 bits for IS-95 to 128 bits for CDMA2000 1X. In addition to this, CDMA2000 1X used more error coding functions as well and used turbo codes rather than the convolutional codes used for IS-95. This enabled higher speed data to be sent. In addition to this interleaving and symbol repetition were used to provide the various data rates.
- *Turbo codes*— Turbo codes were introduced into CDMA2000 1X. They were a new class of error correction codes that enabled transfer rates over a noisy channel to approach the "Shannon" limit. The turbo coding principle was first proposed in 1993 by Professors Claude Berrou and Alain Glaxieux. Originally their claims that the codes could double throughput for a given power were treated with scepticism, but their findings were eventually proved to be true. Turbo coders use powerful interleavers that reduce the susceptibility of a data stream to random and impulsive noise. By working on "soft" bits from a radio receiver, the Turbo codes enable the decoder to extract the maximum level of data from the noisy signals. Turbo codes require two encoders and two decoders per link. These blocks operate in parallel and work synergistically. They also used an iterative process to reduce the amount of processing required, but despite this they still require more processing power than previous coding systems such as convolutional codes.
- *Spectrum efficiency*— Apart from the improvements in the spreading and channel generation, there were also changes in the air interface itself. The IS-95 forward link used a form of QPSK where the data on both the I and Q channels are the same. However for CDMA2000 1X the I and Q channels were different, and this gave the advantage that half the bandwidth could be used for the same number of chips, or twice the number of chips can be sent in the same bandwidth. While this did make the reception more sensitive to phase errors, other improvements included an improved system of forward power control and forward transmit diversity.
- *Reverse link upgrades*— Similarly there were significant changes on the reverse link where several new channels were added. These included a pilot channel as well as supplemental data channels and a control channel for signalling. Additionally, similar to the forward link the reverse link used Walsh Codes to differentiate between the different channels. A further change was that the format of the carrier modulation was changed. With the reverse link now transmitting multiple channels the use of OQPSK would not prevent zero crossings. To achieve this, the modulation format was changed to a scheme known as Orthogonal Complex Quadrature Phase Shift Keying (OCQPSK). This form of modulation required a number of stages. First the channels to be transmitted were split so that some take the I path

and others take the Q path. Next they were scrambled along with the Walsh code spreading. In the scrambling process the probability of zero crossings was identified and using a scheme known as Orthogonal Variable Spreading Function (OVSF) the probability of zero crossings was reduced. Accordingly the channels were spread with a Walsh Code sequence and summed with the correct gain to produce the I and Q sequences. These were then further spread by a long PN code with its mobile specific long mask to identify the mobile and these I and Q sequences were modulated onto the carrier. Although particularly complicated, this form of modulation did have fewer zero crossings and the power amplifier in the mobile did not have to be run in a linear mode, thereby saving battery power.

Summary

The CDMA2000 1X system gave many significant advantages over the original IS-95 scheme. Enabling higher data rates it also allowed improvements in performance as well as improvements in spectrum efficiency that enabled operators to gain a higher return on the spectrum. Also users saw improvements in performance.

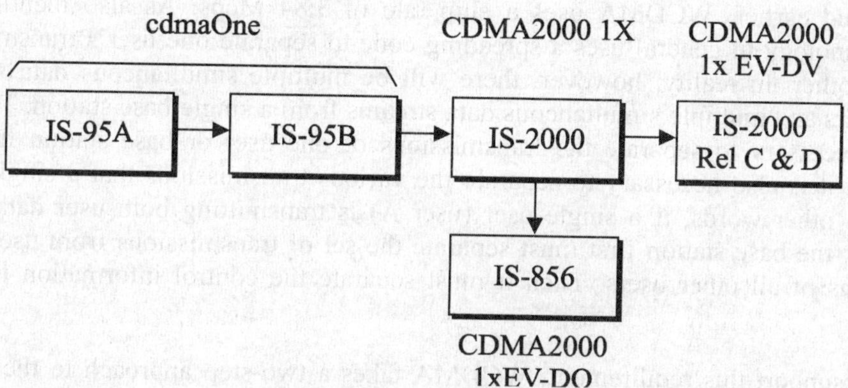

Fig. 8.4: CDMA2000 Evolution

8.10 WCDMA-UMTS

8.10.1 WCDMA-UMTS Frequencies

There are currently six bands that are specified for use for UMTS / WCDMA although operation on other frequencies is not precluded. However much of the focus for UMTS is currently on frequency allocations around 2 GHz. At the World Administrative radio Conference in 1992, the bands 1885 - 2025 and 2110 - 2200 MHz were set aside for use on a world wide basis by administrations wishing to implement International Mobile Telecommunications-2000 (IMT-2000). The aim was that allocating spectrum on a world wide basis would facilitate easy roaming for UMTS / WCDMA users.

Within these bands the portions have been reserved for different uses:

- 1920-1980 and 2110-2170 MHz Frequency Division Duplex (FDD, W-CDMA) Paired uplink and downlink, channel spacing is 5 MHz and raster is 200 kHz. An Operator needs 3

- 4 channels (2x15 MHz or 2x20 MHz) to be able to build a high-speed, high-capacity network.

- 1900-1920 and 2010-2025 MHz Time Division Duplex (TDD, TD/CDMA) Unpaired, channel spacing is 5 MHz and raster is 200 kHz. Transmit and receive transmissions are not separated in frequency.
- 1980-2010 and 2170-2200 MHz Satellite uplink and downlink.

UMTS carrier frequencies are designated by a UTRA Absolute Radio Frequency Channel Number (UARFCN). This can be calculated from:

UARFCN = 5 x (frequency in MHz)

UMTS uses wideband CDMA as the radio transport mechanism. The UMTS channels are spaced by 5 MHz.

8.10.2 The WCDMA Air Interface

As mentioned earlier, WCDMA uses a chip rate of 3.84 Mcps. As also mentioned earlier, CDMA technology in general uses a spreading code to separate one user's transmissions from those of another. In reality, however, there will be multiple simultaneous data streams from multiple users and multiple simultaneous data streams from a single base station. Therefore, not only is it necessary to separate the transmissions of one user or base station from those of another, but it is also necessary to separate the various transmissions that a single user might generate. In other words, if a single user (user A) is transmitting both user data and control information, the base station first must separate the set of transmissions from user A from the transmissions of all other users. Then it must separate the control information from the user data.

In order to support this requirement, WCDMA takes a two-step approach to the transmission from a single user, as shown in Figure 6.1. First, each individual data stream is spread to the chip rate by the application of a spreading code, also known as a channelization code, that operates at the chip rate of 3.84 Mcps. Then the combined set of spread signals is scrambled by the application of a scrambling code, which also operates at the chip rate. The channelization spreads the individual data streams and hence increases the required bandwidth. Since the scrambling code also operates at the chip rate, however, it does not increase the required bandwidth further. At the receiving end, the combined signal is first descrambled by application of the appropriate scrambling code. The individual user data streams then are recovered through application of the appropriate channelization codes. Clearly, it is important that different users employ different scrambling codes. Multiple users, however, can use the same channelization codes, provided, however, that no two transmissions from the same user employ the exact same channelization code.

8.10.3 UPlink Spreading, Scrambling, and Modulation

A physical channel is what carries the actual user data or control information over the air interface. A physical channel can be considered a combination of frequency, scrambling code, and channelization code, and in the uplink, as we shall describe later, the relative phase is also significant. For example, if a given user is transmitting user data and control information, then the user data stream will be carried on one physical channel, and the control information will be carried on a different physical channel.

A number of different physical channels are used in the uplink, with a given type of channel selected according to what the user equipment (UE) is attempting to do-such as simply request access to the network, send a single burst of data, or send a stream of data. These channels are described in further detail later in this chapter. For now, let us focus on the situation where a user is transmitting a stream of data, which would happen in a voice conversation. In such a situation, the terminal normally will use at least two physical channels-a Dedicated Physical Data Channel (DPDCH) and a Dedicated Physical Control Channel (DPCCH). The DPDCH carries the user data, and the DPCCH carries control information. Depending on the amount of data to be sent, a single user can use just a single DPDCH, which will support up to 480 kbps of user data or as many as six DPDCHs, which will support up to 2.3 Mbps of user data.

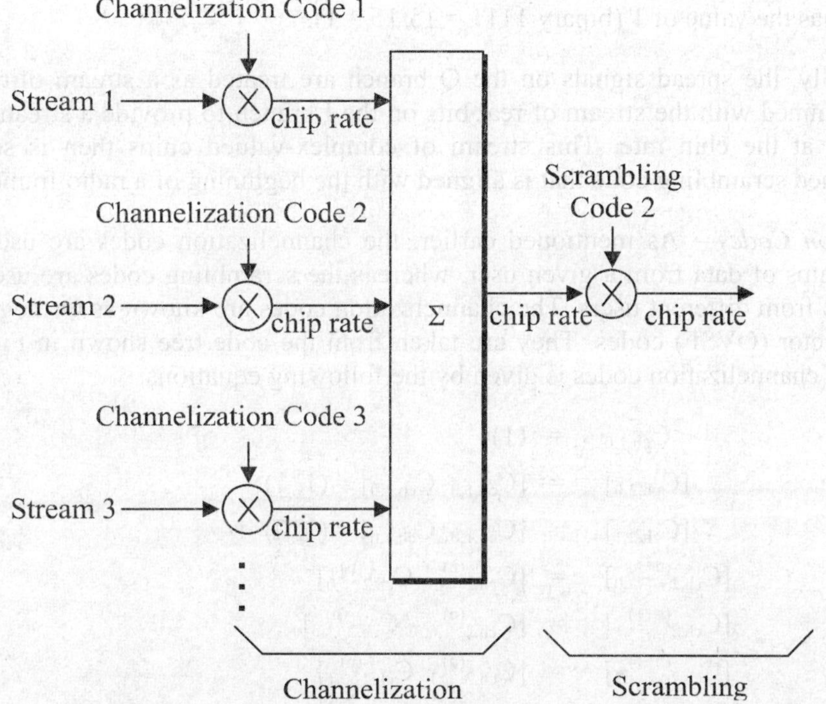

Fig. 8.5: Spreading and Scrambling, basic concept

A DPDCH can have a variable spreading factor. This simply means that the user bit rate does not have to be fixed to a specific value. The spreading factor for a DPDCH can be 4, 8, 16, 32, 64, 128, or 256. These correspond to DPDCH bit rates of 15 kbps (3.84 x 106/256 = 15 x 103) and up to 960 kbps (3.84 x 106/4 = 960 x 103). Of course, these are not the actual user data rates because a significant amount of coding overhead is included in the DPDCH to support forward error correction. In general, the user data rate is approximately half (or less) of the

DPDCH rate. Thus, for example, a DPDCH operating at a spreading rate of 4 will carry data at a rate of 960 kbps. Of this, however, only about 480 kbps will correspond to usable data. The rest is consumed by additional coding required for error correction. If a single user wants to transmit user data at a rate greater than 480 kbps, then multiple DPDCHs can be used (up to a maximum of 6).

Figure 6.2 shows how multiple DPDCHs are handled. Also shown is the DPCCH, which is also sent whenever one or more DPDCHs are sent. The channelization codes (Cd 1 to Cd 6) represent the channelization codes applied to each ofthe six DPDCHs. The channelization code applied to the DPCCH is represented as CC' Each of the DPDCHs is spread to the chip rate by a channelization code. DPDCHs 1,3, and 5 are channelized and weighted by a gain factor bd. These DPDCHs are on the so-called I (in-phase) branch. DPDCHs 2, 4, and 6 plus the DPCCH are on the so-called Q (quadrature) branch. These are also channelized. These spread DPDCHs are also weighted by the gain factor bd, whereas the spread DPCCH is weighted by the gain factor b,_ The two gain factors are specified as 4-bit words that represent steps from a to 1. Thus 0000 = off, 0001 = 1/15,0010 = 2/15, and 1111 = 15/15 = 1. At any given instant, one ofthe two gain factors has the value of 1 (binary 1111 = 15/15 = 1).

Mathematically, the spread signals on the Q branch are treated as a stream ofimaginary bits. These are summed with the stream of real bits on the I branch to provide a stream of complex-valued chips at the chip rate. This stream of complex-valued chips then is subjected to a complex-valued scrambling code that is aligned with the beginning of a radio frame.

Channelization Codes— As mentioned earlier, the channelization codes are used to separate multiple streams of data from a given user, whereas the scrambling codes are used to separate transmissions from different users. The channelization codes are known as Orthogonal Variable Spreading Factor (OVSF) codes. They are taken from the code tree shown in Figure 6.3. The generation of channelization codes is given by the following equations:

$$\begin{aligned}
C_{ch,1,0} &= (1) \\
[C_{ch,2,0}] &= [C_{ch,1,0}\ C_{ch,1,0}] = (1, 1) \\
[C_{ch,2,1}] &= [C_{ch,1,0}\ C_{ch,1,0}] = (1, 0) \\
[C_{ch,2^{(n+1)},0}] &= [C_{ch,2^{(n)},0}\ C_{ch,2^{(n)},0}] \\
[C_{ch,2^{(n+1)},1}] &= [C_{ch,2^{(n)},0} - C_{ch,2^{(n)},0}] \\
[C_{ch,2^{(n+1)},2}] &= [C_{ch,2^{(n)},1}\ C_{ch,2^{(n)},1}] \\
[C_{ch,2^{(n+1)},3}] &= [C_{ch,2^{(n)},1} - C_{ch,2^{(n)},1}], \text{ etc.}
\end{aligned}$$

In general, a given physical channel uses a channelization code that is related to the spreading factor being used for the channel. When only one DPDCH is to be transmitted, then the channelization code is Cch,SF,k> where SF is the spreading factor, and k = SF/4. Therefore, if the spreading factor is 128 (as determined by the user data rate plus coding overhead), then the code to be used shall be Cch,I28,32' The spreading factor for the DPCCH is always 256, and the channelization code is Cc" 256 o.

When more than one DPDCH is to be transmitted (greater than 960 kbps of combined user data and coding overhead), then each DPDCH will have a spreading factor of 4, and the channelization code for each DPDCH will be Cch,4,k' k = 1 for DPDCH1 and DPDCH'2, k = 2 for DPDCH3 and DPDCH4, and k = 3 for DPDCHs and DPDCHG• For example

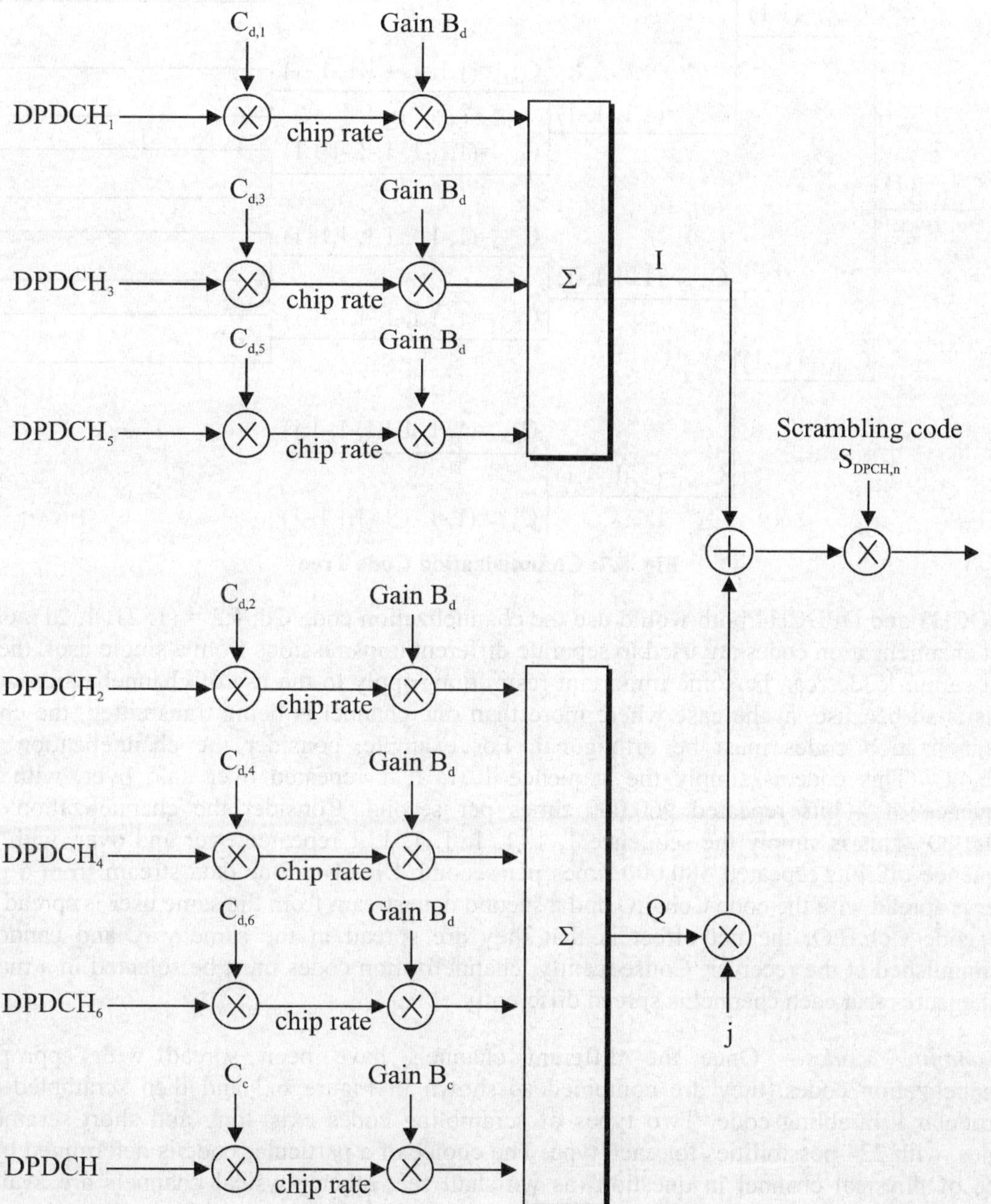

Fig. 8.6: Uplink Channelization and Scrambling

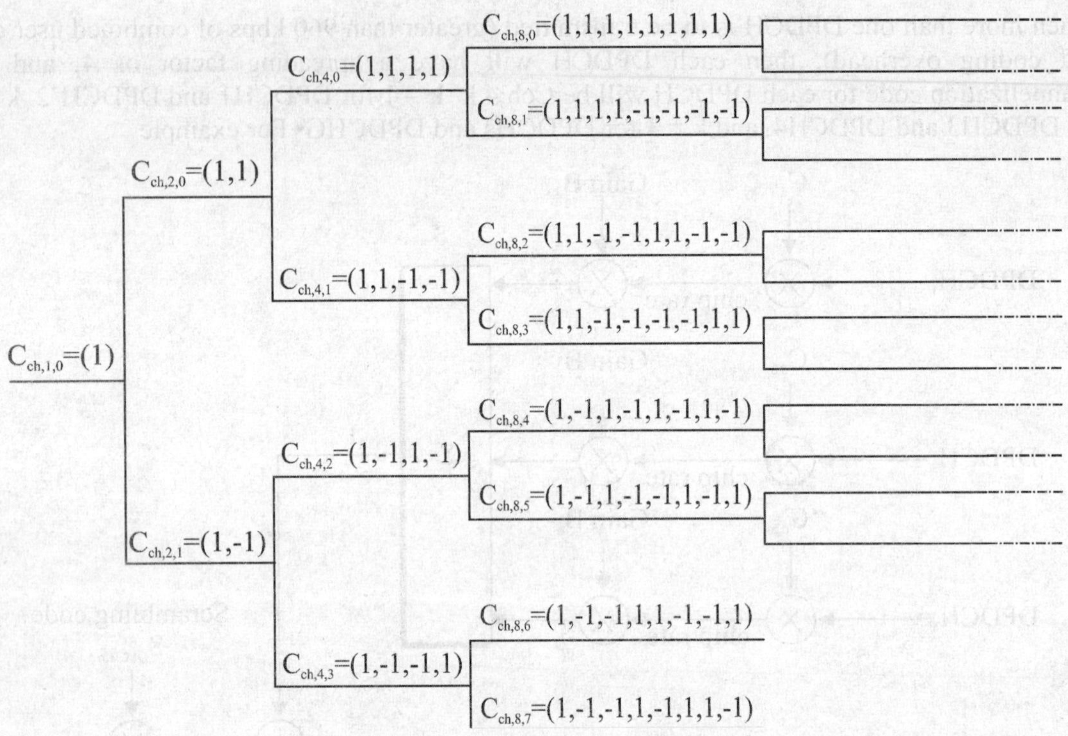

Fig. 8.7: Channelization Code Tree

DPDCH3 and DPDCH4 both would use the channelization code Cd,,4,2 = (1, 21, 1, 21). Given that channelization codes are used to separate different transmissions from a single user, the fact that certain codes can be some important restrictions apply to the use of channelization codes. This is so because, in the case where more than one channel is being transmitted, the chosen channelization codes must be orthogonal. For example, consider the channelization code Cch,4,O' This code is simply the sequence 1, 1, 1, 1 repeated over an.d over, with each sequence of 4 bits repeated 960,000 times per second. Consider the channelization code Cch,B,O' This is simply the sequence 1, 1, 1, 1, 1, 1, 1, 1 repeated over and over, with each sequence of8 bits repeated 480,000 times per second. Clearly, ifone data stream from a given user is spread with the code Cch,4,O and a second data stream from the same user is spread with the code Cch,B,O, the net effect is that they are spread in the same way and cannot be distinguished at the receiver. Consequently, channelization codes must be selected in a manner that ensures that each channel is spread differently.

Scrambling Codes— Once the different channels have been spread with appropriate channelization codes, they are combined as shown in Figure 6.2 and then scrambled by a particular scrambling code. Two types of scrambling codes exist-long and short scrambling codes, with 224 possibilities for each type. The choice of a particular code is determined by the type of physical channel in question (as we shall see, other physical channels are available besides the DPDCH and DPCCH) and by the higher layer that requires the use of a channel in the first place. Depending on higher-layer requirements, a DPDCH or DPCCH can use either a short scrambling code or a long scrambling code.

Clearly, the channelization codes are far from random, and they do not need to have pseudorandom prop ,rtiQ,. Scrambling cod(~" however, must appear to be random and thus must have pseudorandom characteristics. The easiest way to generate a pseudorandom sequence is through the use of a linear feedback shift register such as that shown in Figure 6A. This is basically a set of flip-flops that are clocked at a particular rate, and the output ofthe last flip-flop is copied back into one or more ofthe other flipflops, I 0 sibly after an addition. In Figure 6.4, each of the gain values (g,,) is simply a lor a O. Depending on the values of eachgn (i.e., exactly where the output is fed back), a different output pattern can be achieved. This output pattern can be described by a polynomial and is known as a generator polynomial.

It is possible to produce maximum-length sequences, know~ m-sequ.mces. This means that if a register has m elements, then it can produce a sequence of length 2m 2 1. For example, if a shift register has 10 elements, then it can produce a sequence of length 210 21 (1023). This is a pattern that repeats after every 1023 bits. An m-sequence has a number of properties, including the property that, over the period of the sequence, there will be exactly 2/1/21 ones and 2m21 2 1 zeros.

The long scrambling codes used in WCDMA are known as gold codes and are constructed from the modulo 2 addition of portions of two binary m-sequences. The portions used are segments oflength 38,400. This is due to the fact, as will be explained later in this chapter, that the frame length in WCDMA is 10 ms, which corresponds to 38,400 chips. Because the long scrambling codes are generated from m-sequences, they have pseudorandom characteristics. The short scrambling codes also have pseudorandom characteristics. These, however, are much shorter, at a length of 256 chips. Long scrambling codes are uSFd in the case where the base station uses a rake receiver. Short scrambling ccdes canoe used when the base station uses advanced multiuser detection techniques such as a Parallel Interference Cancellation (PIC) receiver.

Uplink Modulation— WCDMA uses Quadrature Phase Shift Keying (QPSK) modulation in the uplink This technique is depicted in Figure 6.5. The stream of spread and scrambled signals, such as the output shown in Figure 6.2, forms the complex-valued input stream of chips. The real and imaginary parts are separated, with the real part of a given complex chip forming the in-phase (I) branch and the imaginary part forming the quadrature-phase (Q) branch in the modulator.

8.10.4 Downlink Spreading, Scrambling, and Modulation

As is the case for the uplink, a number of channels are used in the downlink. In fact, more channels are defined for the downlink than for the uplink. This is so because the downlink includes pilot channels, synchronization channels, channels used for the bl'oC1dcast of system information, channels used for the paging of subscribers, and so on.

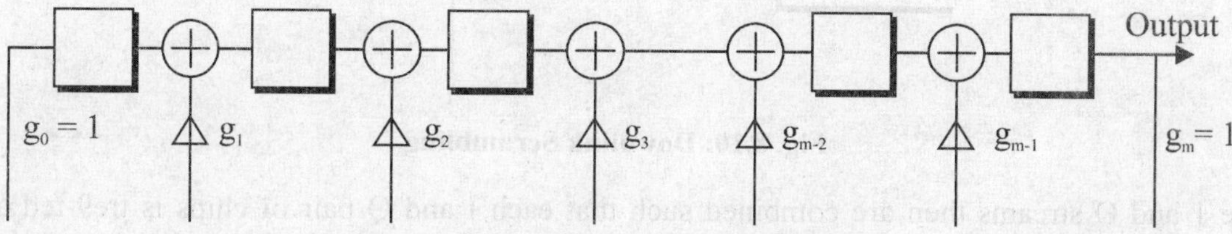

Fig. 8.8: Linear Feedback Shift Register

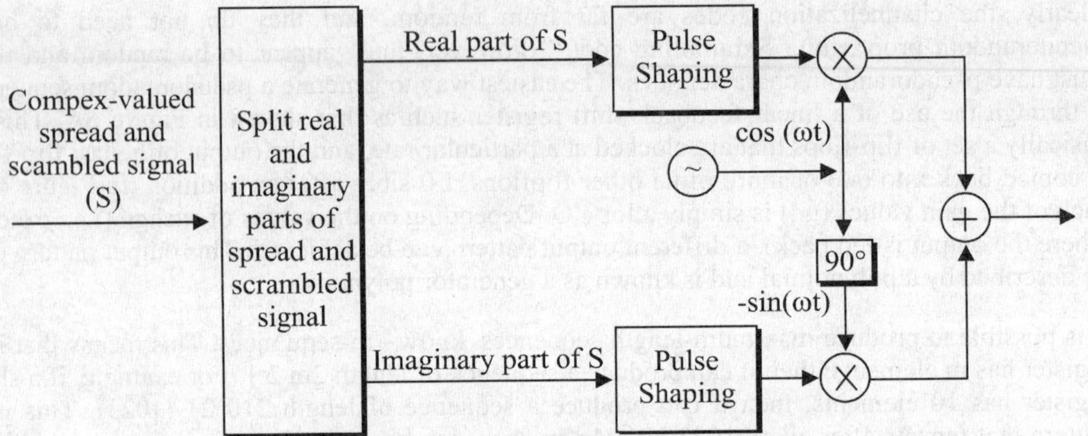

Fig. 8.9: Uplink Modulcation (QPSK)

Downlink Spreading— With the exception ofthe synchronization channels (SCHs), the downlink channels are spread to the chip rate and scrambled, as shown in Figure 6.6. Each channel to be spread is split into two streams-the I branch and the Q branch. The even symbols are mapped to the I branch, and the odd symbols are mapped to the Q branch. The I branch is treated as a stream of real-valued bits, whereas the Q branch is treated as a stream of imaginary bits. Each of the two streams is spread by the same channelization code. The spreading code/channelization code to be used is taken from the same code tree as used in the uplink-i.e., OVSF codes that are chosen to maintain the orthogonality between different channels transmitted from the same base station. The spreading ratp for a given channel depends on the channel in question.

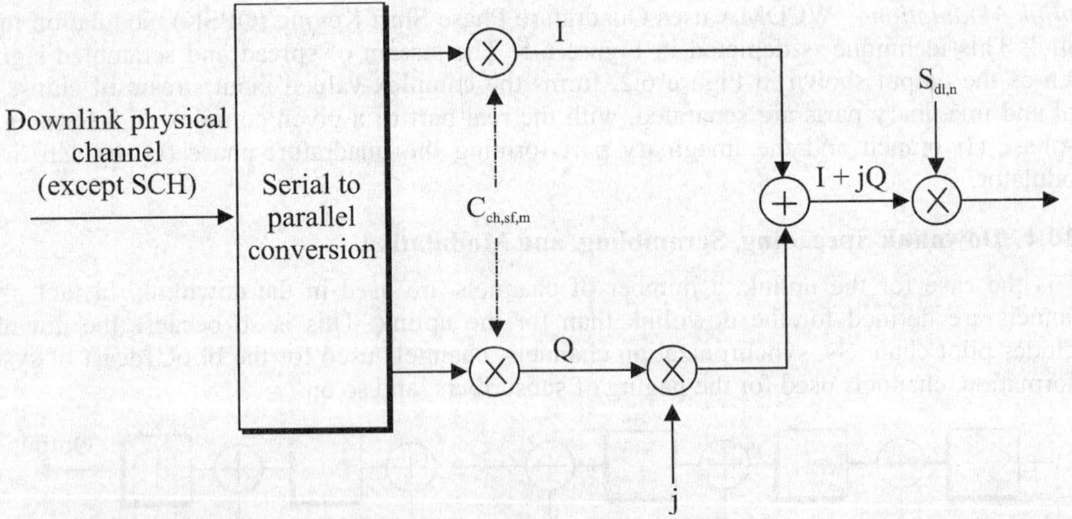

Fig. 8.10: Downlink Scrambling

The 1 and Q streams then are combined such that each I and Q pair of chips is tre9-ted as a single complex value, and the result of combining them is a stream of complexvalued chips.

This stream of chips then is subjected to a complex downlink scrambling code, identified as Sdl.n in Figure 6.6.

On important differeul:e occurs between preading in the uplink and downlink. In the uplink, the data for a given physical channel (such as a single DPDCH) are directed either to the I branch or to the Q branch, as shown in Figure 6.2. Thus, on the uplink, no serial-to-parallel conversion takes place. Therefore, for a spreading factor of, say, 8, the data rate of the physical channel is simply 3,840,00018 = 480 kbps.

On the downlink, however, each channel (with the exception of the synchronization channel) is subjected to a serial-to-parallel conversion, as shown in Figure 6.6. For a given spreading factor, the serial-to-parallel conversion effectively doubles the data rate of the physical channel. In other words, half the channel's data is carried on the I branch and half on the Q branch, and both of these are spread with the same spreading factor.

If, for example, we have a spreading factor of 8, then the data rate on the I channel is 480 kbps, and the data rate on the Q channel is al 0 480 kbps. The net data rate is 960 kbps-twice that achieved on the uplink for the same value of spreading factor. In reality, however, the data rate on the downlink is not quite twice that on the uplink. This is due to the fact, as explained later, that control information is time-multiplexed with a user data on the downlink. This reduces the net throughput for a given downlink data channel. Nonetheless, for a given spreading factor on the downlink, the effective throughput is significantly greater than the corresponding throughput on the uplink for the same spreading factor.

Downlink Scrambling— The downlink scrambling codes are used to separate the transmissions of one cell from those of another. The downlink scrambling codes are gold codes similar to the long scrambling codes used in the uplink. As is the case for the long codes used on the uplink, the codes used on the downlink are limited to a 10-ms duration. There is a total of 218 - 1 (262,143) downlink scrambling codes. Not all these codes are used, however. If all possible codes were to be usable, then one could find a situation where a terminal would have to check a received signal against all 262,143 codes. This could occur, for example, during cell selection. Clearly, checking against so many scrambling codes is impractical.

Therefore, the available downlink scrambling codes are separated into 512 groups.

Each group contains one primary scrambling code and 15 secondary scrambling codes. Thus 512 primary scrambling codes and 7680 secondary scrambling codes exist, for a total of 8192 downlink scrambling codes. Table 6.1 shows the allocation of secondary downlink scrambling codes to primary downlink scrambling codes.

A cell is allocated one, and only one, primary scrambling code, which, of course, has 15 secondary scrambling codes associated with it. A given base station will use its primary scrambling code for the transmission of channels that need to be heard by all terminals in the cell. Thus paging messages need to be scrambled by the cell's primary scrambling code. For that matter, all transmissions from the base station simply can use the cell's primary scrambling code. After all, it is the scrambling code that identifies the cell, whereas the various channelization codes are used to separate the various transmissions (physical channels) within the cell.

Universal Mobile Telecommunications Service (UMTS)

Table 8.1: Allocation of Secondary Scrambling Codes to Primary Scrambling Codes

Primary Scrambling Code Number	*Secondary Scrambling Codes Numbers*
0	1 - 15
16	17 - 31
32	33 - 47
48	49 - 63
8176	8177 - 8191

Table 8.2: Primary Scrambling Code Groups

Primary Scrambling Group Number	**Primary Scrambling Code Numbers**
0	0, 16, 32, 48, 64, 80, 96, 112
1	128, 144, 160, 176, 192, 208, 228, 240
2	256, 272, 288, 304, 320, 336, 352, 368
63	8064, 8080, 8096, 8112, 8128, 8144, 8160, 8176

A cell can, however, choose to use a secondary scrambling code for channels that are directed to a specific user and do not need to be decoded by other users. In general, it is a good idea for all transmissions from a cell to use the cell's primary scrambling code because this helps to minimize interference.

As described earlier, 512 primary scrambling codes are available. These are divided into 64 groups, each consisting of 8 scrambling codes, as shown in Table 6.2.

As mentioned earlier, downlink spreading and scrambling are applied to all downlink physical channels transmitted on a cell, with the exception ofthe SCH. This channel is added to the downlink stream, as shown in Figure 6.7. In fact, as explained later in this chapter, the SCH contains two subchannels-the primary SCH and the secondary SCH. The reason why these are transmitted without scrambling is the fact that they are the first channels decoded by a terminal. If they were scrambled, then the terminal would first have to know the scrambling code of the base station just to synchronize.

Downlink Modulation— As is the case for the uplink, the downlink uses QPSK modulation. The process in the downlink is the same as that shown in Figure 6.5 for the uplink. Each complex-valued chip is split into its constituent real and imaginary parts. The real part is sent on the I branch of the modulator, and the imaginary branch is sent on the Q branch of the modulator.

8.10.5 WCDMA Air-Interface Protocol Architecture

We have already mentioned some ofthe types of physical channels defined in WCDMA. In fact, many different channel types exist, and the various types of channels are defined in a logical hierarchy.

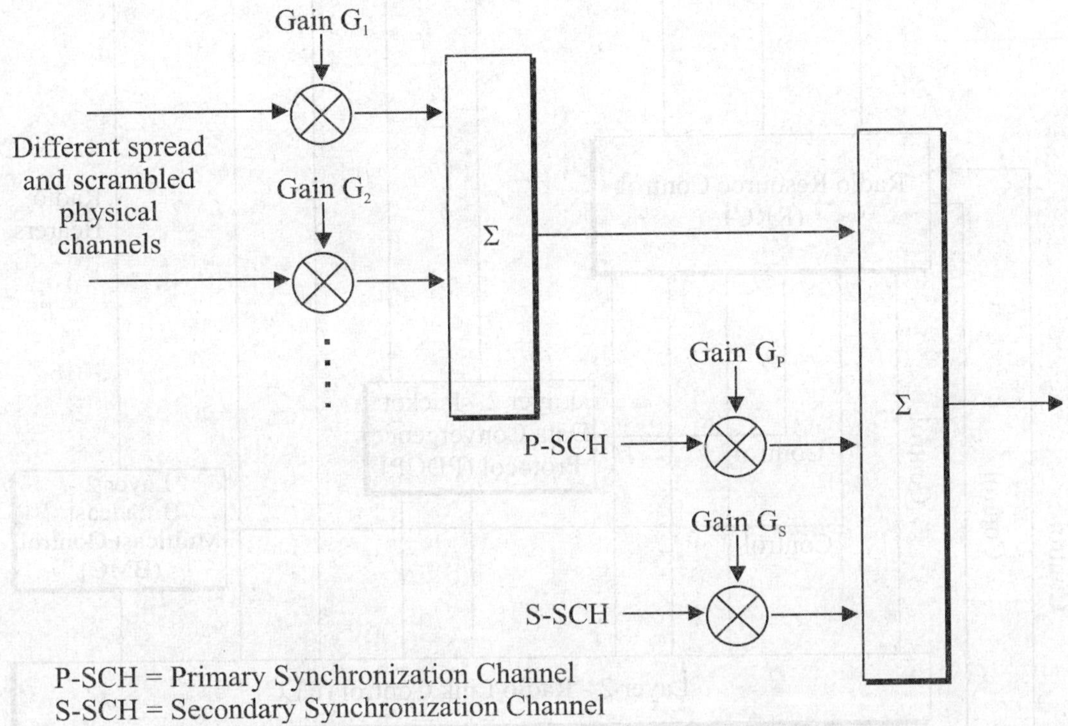

P-SCH = Primary Synchronization Channel
S-SCH = Secondary Synchronization Channel

Fig. 8.11: Downlink Multiplexing of the Synchronization Channel

Figure 6.8 shows the overall logical structure of the WCDMA air interface. At the lowest level, we have the physical layer. The functions of the physical layer include radiofrequency (RF) processing, spreading, scrambling and modulation, coding and decoding for support of forward error correction, power control, timing advance, and soft handover execution. Physical channels, such as those already mentioned, exist at the physical layer and are used for transmission across the RF interface. A given physical channel is defined by a combination of frequency, scrambling code, channelization code, and in the uplink, phase. Some physical channels exist solely for the correct operation of the physical layer. Other physical channels are used to carry information provided to or from higher layers.

Higher layers that want to transmit information across the RF interface pass information to the physical layer through the Medium Access Control (MAC) layer using a number of logical channels. The MAC maps these logical transport channels to channels. The physical layer maps transport channels to physical channels.

Above the MAC layer, we find the Radio Link Control (RLC) layer. Among the services provided by RLC are the following:

- RLC connection establishment and release. A given upper layer may request the use of a certain radio bearer. For each radio bearer, an RLC connection is established between the MS and the network.

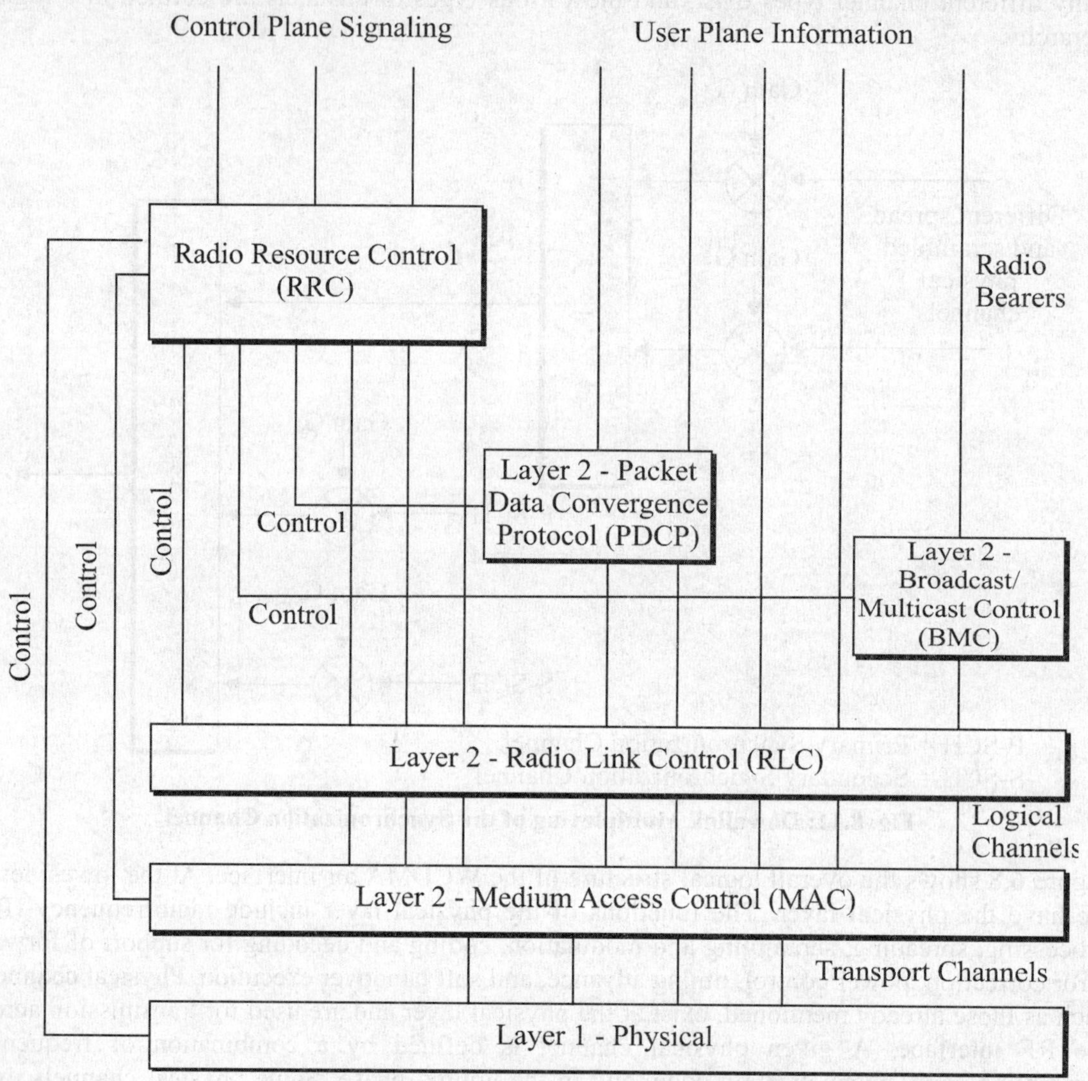

Fig. 8.12: WCDMA air-interface protocol structure

- Error detection. RLC includes a sequence number check function that enables the detection of errors in received protocol data units (PDUs).

II Ensuring error-free delivery through acknowledgments (if the upper-layer protocol has requested an acknowledged service). RLC can request that the peer entity retransmit in the event that a PDU is received incorrectly, lost, or received out of sequence. Note that this type of error correction is different from the error correction that is achieved through coding schemes on the air interface.

- In-sequence delivery. This ensures that PDUs are passed to the upper layer in the correct order.
- Unique delivery. This ens\lres that a given PDU is passed to an upper layer only once, even if erroneously received twice at RLC.
- Quality of service (QoS) management. Upper layers can request a certain QoS.1t is RLC that ensures that the QoS is controlled.

RLC supports both acknowledged and transparent services. With transparent service, any errors in received PDUs will cause the PDU to be discarded, in which case it is up to the upper layer to recover from the loss according to its own capabilities. With acknowledged service, RLC recovers from errors in received data by requesting a retransmission by the peer entity (the DE or the network).

One of the protocols above the RLC layer is the Packet Data Convergence Protocol (PDCP). The main objective of PDCP is to enable the lower layers (RLC, MAC, and the physical layer) to be common regardless of the type or structure of the user data. For example, packet-data transfer from a DE could use either IPv4 or IPv6. One does not want the RLC and lower layers to be different depending on which of those two protocols a subscriber uses. Moreover, if new protocols are introduced, one would want them to be supported by the same radio interface. PDCP meets these objectives by maintaining a standard interface to RLC regardless of the type of user data. PDCP is similar to the Subnetwork Dependent Convergence Protocol (SNDCP) of GPRS. .

In Figure 6.8 we also find Broadcast / Multicast Control (BMC). This is a function that handles the broadcast of user messages across the cell. In other words, BMC supports the cell broadcast function, similar to cell broadcast as defined in GSM. This enables users in a cell to receive broadcast messages, such as traffic warnings and weather information. In GSM, cell broadcast also has been used as a means of informing users of the geographic zone that they are in as part of zone-based tariffing.

One of the most important components depicted in Figure 6.8 is the Radio Resource Control (RRC). RRC can be considered the overall manager of the air interface and, as such, is responsible for the management of radio resources, including determination of which radio resources will be allocated to a given user. As can be seen, all control signaling to or from users passes through RRC. This is necessary so that requests from a user or from the network can be analyzed and radio resources allocated as appropriate. Also, a control interface exists between RRC and each of the other layers. Among the functions performed or controlled by RRC are

- The broadcast of system information.
- The establishment of initial signaling connections between the UE and the network.

When the user and network want to communicate, an RRC connection is first established. It is this RRC connection that is used for the transfer of signaling information between the DE and the network for the purpose of allocation and management of the radio resources to be used.

- The allocation of radio bearers to a UE. A given DE may be allocated multiple radio bearers for the transfer of user data.
- Measurement reporting. RRC determines what needs to be measured, when it should be measured, and how it should be reported.
- Mobility management. It is the RRC that determines when, for example, a call should be handed over. RRC also executes cell res election and location area or routing area updates.
- Quality of Service (QoS) control. The allocation of radio resources has a direct consequence for the QoS perceived by the user. Since RRC controls the allocation of radio resources, it has a direct influence on QoS. The resources allocated by RRC must be aligned with the QoS offered to the subscriber.

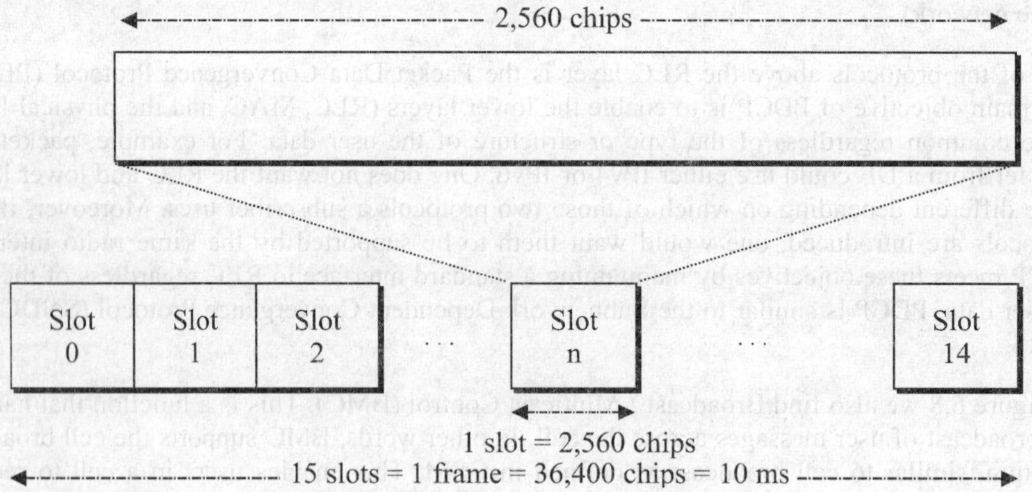

Fig. 8.13: WCDMA Channel Framing Structure

8.10.6 Synchronisation

The level of synchronisation required for the WCDMA system to operate is provided from the Primary Synchronisation Channel (P-SCH) and the Secondary Synchronisation Channel (S-SCH). These channels are treated in a different manner to the normal channels and as a result they are not spread using the OVSFs and PN codes. Instead they are spread using synchronisation codes. There are two types that are used. The first is called the primary code and is used on the P-SCH, and the second is named a secondary code and is used on the S-SCH.

The primary code is the same for all cells and is a 256 chip sequence that is transmitted during the first 256 chips of each time slot. This allows the UE to synchronise with the base station for the time slot.

Once the UE has gained time slot synchronisation it only knows the start and stop of the time slot, but it does not know information about the particular time slot, or the frame. This is gained using the secondary synchronisation codes.

There is a total of sixteen different secondary synchronisation codes. One code is sent at the beginning of the time slot, i.e. the first 256 chips. It consists of 15 synchronisation codes and there are 64 different scrambling code groups. When received, the UE is able to determine before which synchronisation code the overall frame begins. In this way the UE is able to gain complete synchronisation.

The scrambling codes in the S-SCH also enable the UE to identify which scrambling code is being used and hence it can identify the base station. The scrambling codes are divided into 64 code groups, each having eight codes. This means that after achieving frame synchronisation, the UE only has a choice of one in eight codes and it can therefore try to decode the CPICH channel. Once it has achieved this it is able to read the BCH information and achieve better timing and it is able to monitor the P-CCPCH.

8.10.7 UMTS Power Control

As with any CDMA system it is essential that the base station receives all the UEs at approximately the same power level. If not, the UEs that are further away will be lower in strength than those closer to the node B and they will not be heard. This effect is often referred to as the near-far effect. To overcome this the node B instructs those stations closer in, to reduce their transmitted power, and those further away to increase theirs. In this way all stations will be received at approximately the same strength.

It is also important for node Bs to control their power levels effectively. As the signals transmitted by the different node Bs are not orthogonal to one another it is possible that signals from different ones will interfere. Accordingly their power is also kept to the minimum required by the UEs being served.

To achieve the power control there are two techniques that are employed: open loop; and closed loop.

Open loop techniques are used during the initial access before communication between the UE and node B has been fully established. It simply operates by making a measurement of the received signal strength and thereby estimating the transmitter power required. As the transmit and receive frequencies are different, the path losses in either direction will be different and therefore this method cannot be any more than a good estimate.

Once the UE has accessed the system and is in communication with the node B, closed loop techniques are used. A measurement of the signal strength is taken in each time slot. As a result of this a power control bit is sent requesting the power to be stepped up or down. This process is undertaken on both the up and downlinks. The fact that only one bit is assigned to power control means that the power will be continually changing. Once it has reached approximately the right level then it would step up and then down by one level. In practice the position of the mobile would change, or the path would change as a result of other movements and this would cause the signal level to move, so the continual change is not a problem.

8.10.8 Logical Channels

Broadcast Control Channel (BCCH), (downlink). This channel broadcasts information to UEs relevant to the cell, such as radio channels of neighbouring cells, etc.

Paging Control Channel (PCCH), (downlink). This channel is associated with the PICH and is used for paging messages and notification information.

Dedicated Control Channel (DCCH), (up and downlinks) This channel is used to carry dedicated control information in both directions.

Common Control Channel (CCCH), (up and downlinks). This bi-directional channel is used to transfer control information.

Shared Channel Control Channel (SHCCH), (bi-directional). This channel is bi-directional and only found in the TDD form of WCDMA / UMTS, where it is used to transport shared channel control information.

Dedicated Traffic Channel (DTCH), (up and downlinks). This is a bidirectional channel used to carry user data or traffic.

Common Traffic Channel (CTCH), (downlink) A unidirectional channel used to transfer dedicated user information to a group of UEs.

8.10.9 Transport Channels

Dedicated Transport Channel (DCH), (up and downlink). This is used to transfer data to a particular UE. Each UE has its own DCH in each direction.

Broadcast Channel (BCH), (downlink). This channel broadcasts information to the UEs in the cell to enable them to identify the network and the cell.

Forward Access Channel (FACH),(down link). This is channel carries data or information to the UEs that are registered on the system. There may be more than one FACH per cell as they may carry packet data.

Paging Channel (PCH) (downlink). This channel carries messages that alert the UE to incoming calls, SMS messages, data sessions or required maintenance such as re-registration.

Random Access Channel (RACH), (uplink). This channel carries requests for service from UEs trying to access the system

Uplink Common Packet Channel (CPCH), (uplink). This channel provides additional capability beyond that of the RACH and for fast power control.

Downlink Shared Channel (DSCH) (downlink).This channel can be shared by several users and is used for data that is "bursty" in nature such as that obtained from web browsing etc.

8.10.10 Physical Channels

Primary Common Control Physical Channel (PCCPCH) (downlink). This channel continuously broadcasts system identification and access control information.

Secondary Common Control Physical Channel (SCCPCH) (downlink) This channel carries the Forward Access Channel (FACH) providing control information, and the Paging Channel (PACH) with messages for UEs that are registered on the network.

Physical Random Access Channel (PRACH) (uplink). This channel enables the UE to transmit random access bursts in an attempt to access a network.

Dedicated Physical Data Channel (DPDCH) (up and downlink). This channel is used to transfer user data.

Dedicated Physical Control Channel (DPCCH) (up and downlink). This channel carries control information to and from the UE. In both directions the channel carries pilot bits and the Transport Format Combination Identifier (TFCI). The downlink channel also includes the Transmit Power Control and FeedBack Information (FBI) bits.

Physical Downlink Shared Channel (PDSCH) (downlink). This channel shares control information to UEs within the coverage area of the node B.

Physical Common Packet Channel (PCPCH). This channel is specifically intended to carry packet data. In operation the UE monitors the system to check if it is busy, and if not it then transmits a brief access burst. This is retransmitted if no acknowledgement is gained with a slight increase in power each time. Once the node B acknowledges the request, the data is transmitted on the channel.

Synchronisation Channel (SCH) The synchronisation channel is used in allowing UEs to synchronise with the network.

Common Pilot Channel (CPICH) This channel is transmitted by every node B so that the UEs are able estimate the timing for signal demodulation. Additionally they can be used as a beacon for the UE to determine the best cell with which to communicate.

Acquisition Indicator Channel (AICH) The AICH is used to inform a UE about the Data Channel (DCH) it can use to communicate with the node B. This channel assignment occurs as a result of a successful random access service request from the UE.

Paging Indication Channel (PICH) This channel provides the information to the UE to be able to operate its sleep mode to conserve its battery when listening on the Paging Channel (PCH). As the UE needs to know when to monitor the PCH, data is provided on the PICH to assign a UE a paging repetition ratio to enable it to determine how often it needs to 'wake up' and listen to the PCH.

CPCH Status Indication Channel (CSICH) This channel, which only appears in the downlink carries the status of the CPCH and may also be used to carry some intermittent, or "bursty" data. It works in a similar fashion to PICH.

Collision Detection/Channel Assignment Indication Channel (CD/CA-ICH) This channel, present in the downlink is used to indicate whether the channel assignment is active or inactive to the UE.

8.11 UMTS TDD AND FDD

8.11.1 TDD - Time Division Duplex

A communications system requires that communication is possible in both directions: to and from the base station to the remote station. There are a number of ways in which this can be achieved. The most obvious is to transmit on one frequency and receive on another. The frequency difference between the two transmissions being such that the two signals do not interfere. This is known as frequency division duplex (FDD) and it is one of the most commonly used schemes, and it is used by most cellular schemes.

It is also possible to use a single frequency and rather than using different frequency allocations, use different time allocations. If the transmission times are split into slots, then transmissions in one direction take place in one time slot, and those in the other direction take place in another. It is this scheme that is known as time division duplex, TDD, and it is used for UMTS-TDD.

Note on TDD and FDD duplex schemes— In order for radio communications systems to be able to communicate in both directions it is necessary to have what is termed a duplex scheme. A duplex scheme provides a way of organizing the transmitter and receiver so that they can transmit and receive. There are several methods that can be adopted. For applications including wireless and cellular telecommunications, where it is required that the transmitter and receiver are able to operate simultaneously, two schemes are in use. One known as FDD or frequency division duplex uses two channels, one for transmit and the other for receiver. Another scheme known as TDD, time division duplex uses one frequency, but allocates different time slots for transmission and reception.

When using a TDD system, there are a number of characteristics that are pertinent for TDD systems. These characteristics need to be accommodated when developing or using TDD systems.

- *Utilisation of unpaired bands*— Typically there is more traffic in the downlink (network to the mobile) than in the uplink (mobile to network). Accordingly the operator is able to allocate more time to the downlink transmission than the uplink. This is not possible with the paired spectrum required for FDD systems where it is not possible to re-allocate the use of the different bands. As a result of this, it is possible to make very efficient use of the available spectrum.
- *Discontinuous transmission*— In any TDD system it is necessary to switch between transit and receive. This takes a certain amount of time. Not only does it take time for the mobile and the base station to change between transmit and receive in terms of ramping up or down the power, along with the settling of any transients. In addition to this the time is

required between transmit and receive to accommodate the transmission time between the mobile and the base station. As a result a guard band is required.

- *Uplink / downlink interference*— As both uplink and downlink share the same channel there can be interference between the two transmission directions. To overcome this, base stations are synchronised to ensure that they do not transmit when an adjacent base station is receiving, otherwise the better siting and possible higher power level will cause interference.

- *Equivalent conditions for uplink and downlink*— As both uplink and downlink use the same channel, they are subject to the same propagation conditions. With FDD systems using different frequencies for the uplink and downlink there are significant differences. By using the same frequency fading conditions can be counteracted more effectively.

8.11.2 UMTS TDD / FDD Comparison

While UMTS TDD and UMTS FDD are both specified in the same standard and share very many properties, there are naturally some differences.

Table 8.3

Parameter	*UMTS TDD*	*UMTS FDD*
Multiple access method	TDMA, CDMA	CDMA
Duplex method	TDD	FDD
Channel spacing	5 MHz [1]	5 MHz
Carrier chip rate	3.84 Mcps	3.84 Mcps
Time slot structure	15/14 slots/frame	15 slots/frame
Frame length (ms)	10	10
Multirate concept	Multicode, multislot and OVSF[2]	Multicode and OVSF[2]
Burst types	(1) traffic bursts (2) randmo access burst (3) synchronisation burst	N/A
Detection	Coherent based on midamble	Coherent based on pilot symbols
Dedicated channel power control	Uplink: open loop 100 Hz or 200 Hz rate Downlink: closed loop max 800 Hz rate	Rast closed loop 1500 Hz rate
Spreading factors	1 .. 16	4 .. 512

Notes

[1] for TD-SCDMA the channel spacing is 1.6 MHz

[2] OVSF = Orthogonal variable Spreading Factor

8.11.3 UMTS TDD within 3GPP

All the standards for UMTS 3G systems have been defined under the auspices of 3GPP - the third generation partnership project. The standards not only define the FDD systems, but also the TDD system.

In these specifications, it was the original intent of UMTS that the TDD spectrum would be used to provide high data rates in selected areas forming what could be termed 3G hot zones.

8.11.4 UMTS TDD Details

UMTS TDD uses many of the same basic parameters as UMTS FDD. The same 5 MHz channel bandwidths are used. UMTS TDD also uses direct sequence spread spectrum and different users and what can be termed "logical channels" are separated using different spreading codes. Only when the receiver uses the same code in the correlation process, is the data recovered. In W-CDMA all other logical channels using different spreading codes appear as noise on the channel and ultimately limit the capacity of the system. In UMTS TDD, a scheme known as multi user detection (MUD) is employed in the receiver and improves the removal of the interfering codes, allowing higher data rates and capacity.

In addition to the separation of users by using different logical channels as a result of the different spreading codes, further separation between users may be provided by allocating different time slots. There are 15 time slots in UMTS TDD. Of these, three are used for overhead such as signalling, etc and this leaves twelve time slots for user traffic. In each timeslot there can be 16 codes. Capacity is allocated to users on demand, using a two dimensional matrix of timeslots and codes.

In order for UMTS TDD to achieve the best overall performance, the transport format, i.e. the modulation and forward error correction can be altered for each user. The schemes are chosen by the network, and will depend on the signal characteristics in both directions. Higher order forms of modulation enable higher data speeds to be accommodated, but they are less resilient to noise and interference, and this means that the higher data rate modulation schemes are only used when signal strengths are high. Additionally the levels of forward error correction can be changed. When errors are likely, i.e. when signal strengths are low or interference levels are high, Similarly higher levels of forward error correction are needed under low require additional data to be sent and this slows the payload transfer rate. Thus it is possible to achieve much higher data transfer rates when signals are strong and interference levels are low.

8.11.5 UMTS TDD Performance

UMTS TDD is able to support high peak data rates. Release 5 of the UMTS standard provides HSDPA (high-speed downlink packet access). The scheme allows the use of a higher order modulation scheme called 16-QAM (16 point quadrature amplitude modulation), which enables peak rates of 10 Mbps per sector in commercial deployments. The next release increases the modulation to 64-QAM, and introduces intercell interference cancellation (called Generalized MUD) and MIMO (multiple in, multiple out). In combination, these increase the peak rate to 31 Mbps per sector.

Handover or handoff is as important for UMTS as any other form of cellular telecommunications system. As with any other cellular telecommunications system it is essential that UMTS handover is performed seamlessly so that the user is not aware of any change. Any failures within the UMTS handover (or UMTS handoff) procedure will lead to dropped calls which will in turn result in user dissatisfaction and ultimately it may lead to users changing networks, ti ereby increasing the churn rate.

It is worth noting that the two terms UMTS handover and UMTS handoff have the same meaning. UMTS handover tends is the terminology that tends to be used within Europe, whereas UMTS handoff is more likely to be used within North America.

8.12 UMTS HANDOVER TYPES

Within UMTS it is possible to define a number of different types of UMTS handover or handoff. With the advent of generic CDMA technology, new possibilities for effecting more reliable forms of handover became possible, and as a result one of a variety of different forms of handover are available depending upon the different circumstances.

For purely inter W-CDMA technology, there are three basic types of handover:

- *Hard handover*— This form of handover is essentially the same as that used for 2G networks where one link is broken and another established.
- *Soft handover*— This form of handover is a more gradual and the UE communicates simultaneously with more than one Node B or base station during the handover process.
- *Softer handover*— Not a full form of UMTS handover, but the UE communicates with more than one sector managed by the same NodeB.
- *UMTS GSM inter RAT handover*— This form of handover occurs when mobiles have to change between Radio Access Technologies.
- *UMTS GSM inter RAT handover*— This form of handover occurs when mobiles have to change between Radio Access Technologies.

Each of the different types of handover is used on different occasions dependent upon the conditions. Further details of each type of UMTS handover are given in the individual sections below.

8.12.1 UMTS Hard Handover

The name hard handover indicates that there is a "hard" change during the handover process. For hard handover the radio links are broken and then re-established. Although hard handover should appear seamless to the user, there is always the possibility that a short break in the connection may be noticed by the user.

The basic methodology behind a hard handover is relatively straightforward. There are a number of basic stages of a hard handover:

1. The network decides a handover is required dependent upon the signal strengths of the existing link, and the strengths of broadcast channels of adjacent cells.

2. The link between the existing NodeB and the UE is broken.
3. A new link is established between the new NodeB and the UE.

Although this is a simplification of the process, it is basically what happens. The major problem is that any difficulties in re-establishing the link will cause the handover to fail and the call or connection to be dropped.

UMTS hard handovers may be used in a number of instances:

- When moving from one cell to an adjacent cell that may be on a different frequency.
- When moving from one cell to an adjacent cell that may be on a different frequency.
- When implementing a mode change, e.g. from FDD to TDD mode, for example.
- When moving from one cell to another where there is no capacity on the existing channel, and a change to a new frequency is required.

One of the issues facing UMTS hard handovers was also experienced in GSM. When usage levels are high, the capacity of a particular cell that a UE is trying to enter may be insufficient to support a new user. To overcome this, it may be necessary to reserve some capacity for new users. This may be achieved by spreading the loading wherever possible - for example UEs that can receive a sufficiently strong signal from a neighbouring cell may be transferred out as the original cell nears its capacity level.

8.12.2 UMTS Soft Handover

Soft handover is a form of handover that was enabled by the introduction of CDMA. Soft handover occurs when a UE is in the overlapping coverage area of two cells. Links to the two base stations can be established simultaneously and in this way the UE can communicate with two base stations. By having more than one link active during the handover process, this provides a more reliable and seamless way in which to perform handover.

In view of the fact that soft handover uses several simultaneous links, it means that the adjacent cells must be operating on the same frequency or channel as UEs do not have multiple transmitters and receivers that would be necessary if they were on different frequencies.

When the UE and NodeB undertake a soft handover, the UE receives signals from the two NodeBs and combines them using the RAKE receiver capability available in the signal processing of the UE.

In the uplink the situation is more complicated as the signal combining cannot be accomplished in the NodeB as more than one NodeB is involved. Instead, combining is accomplished on a frame by frame basis. The best frames are selected after each interleaving period. The selection is accomplished by using the outer loop power control algorithm which measures the signal to noise ratio (SNR) of the received uplink signals. This information is then used to select the best quality frame.

Once the soft handover has been completed, the links to the old NodeB are dropped and the UE continues to communicate with the new NodeB.

As can be imagined, soft handover uses a higher degree of the network resources than a normal link, or even a hard handover. However this is compensated by the improved reliability and performance of the handover process. However with around 5 to 10% of handovers falling into this category, network operators need to account for it.

8.12.3 UMTS Softer Handover

A form of handover referred to as softer handover is really a special form of soft handover. It is a form of soft handover that occurs when the new radio links that are added are from the same NodeB. This occurs when several sectors may be served from the same NodeB, thereby simplifying the combining as it can be achieved within the NodeB and not require linking further back into the network.

UMTS softer handover is only possible when a UE can hear the signals from two sectors served by the same NodeB. This may occur as a result of the sectors overlapping, or more commonly as a result of multipath propagation resulting from reflections from buildings, etc.

In the uplink, the signals received by the NodeB, the signals from the two sectors can be routed to the same RAKE receiver and then combined to provide an enhanced signal.

In the downlink, it is a little more complicated because the different sectors of the NodeB use different scrambling codes. To overcome this, different fingers of the RAKE receiver apply the appropriate de-spreading or de-scrambling codes to the received signals. Once this has been done, they can be combined as before.

In view of the fact that a single transmitter is used within the UE, only one power control loop is active. This may not be optimal for all instances but it simplifies the hardware and general operation.

8.12.4 Inter-RAT / Intersystem UMTS / GSM Handover

In many instances it is necessary for the UMTS radio access network to handover to the 2G GSM network. These handovers are given a variety of names including Inter-RAT handover as they are handing over between different forms of Radio Access Technology, Intersystem Handover, and UMTS / GSM Handover. These handovers may be required for one of a variety of reasons including:

- Limited UMTS coverage
- UMTS network busy whereas spare capacity is available on GSM network

The most common form of intersystem or inter-RAT handover is between UMTS and GSM. There are two different types of inter-RAT handover:

- *UMTS to GSM handover*— There are two further divisions of this category of handover:
  - ✓ *Compressed mode handover*— Using compressed mode handover the UE uses the gaps in transmission that occur to analyse the reception of local GSM base stations. The UE uses the neighbour list provided by the UMTS network to monitor and select a suitable candidate base station. Having selected a suitable base station the handover takes place, but without any time synchronisation having occurred.

- ✓ *Blind handover*— This form of handover occurs when the base station hands off the UE by passing it the details of the new cell to the UE without linking to it and setting the timing, etc of the mobile for the new cell. In this mode, the network selects what it believes to be the optimum GSM based station. The UE first locates the broadcast channel of the new cell, gains timing synchronisation and then carries out non-synchronised intercell handover.

- *Handover from GSM to UMTS*— This form of handover is supported within GSM and a "neighbour list" was established to enable this occur easily. As the GSM / 2G network is normally more extensive than the 3G network, this type of handover does not normally occur when the UE leaves a coverage area and must quickly find a new base station to maintain contact. The handover from GSM to UMTS occurs to provide an improvement in performance and can normally take place only when the conditions are right. The neighbour list will inform the UE when this may happen.

8.12.5 UMTS Handover Methodology

The decisions about handover are generally handled by the RNC. It continually monitors information regarding the signals being received by both the UE and NodeB and when a particular link has fallen below a given level and another better radio channel is available, it initiates a handover. As part of this monitoring process, the UE measures the Received Signal Code Power (RSCP) and Received Signal Strength Indicator (RSSI) and the information is then returned to the node B and hence to the RNC on the uplink control channel.

CDMA2000 is the evolution of the original IS-95 cdmaOne system. CDMA2000 has a number of evolutions of which the first was CDMA2000 1X, sometimes also called CDMA2000 1XRTT.

CDMA2000 1X which is also standardised as IS-2000 supports circuit-switched voice, and has the capability to provide up and sometimes beyond 35 simultaneous call per sector and as such it doubles the capacity of the original IS-95 networks. It also enables the transmission and reception of data at rates up to 153 kbps in both directions. It was recognized by the International Telecommunications Union (ITU) as an IMT-2000 standard in November 1999.

8.13 PROTOCOLS USED IN 3G

The following is a brief description of each protocol layer in a 3G wireless network infrastructure:

- *Global Mobility Management (GMM)*— protocol that includes attach, detach, security, and routing area update functionality.

- *Node B Application Part (NBAP)*— provides procedures for paging distribution, broadcast system information and management of dedicated and logical resources.

- *Packet Data Convergence Protocol (PDCP)*— maps higher level characteristics onto the characteristics of the underlying radio-interface protocols. PDCP also provides protocol transparency for higher layer protocols.

- *Radio Link Control (RLC)*— provides a logical link control over the radio interface.

- *Medium Access Control (MAC)*— controls the access signaling (request and grant) procedures for the radio channel.
- *Radio resource Control (RRC)*— manages the allocation and maintenance of radio communication paths.
- *Radio Access Network Application Protocol (RANAP)*— encapsulates higher layer signaling. Manages the signaling and GTP connections between RNC and 3G-SGSN, and signaling and circuit-switched connections between RNC and 3G MSC.

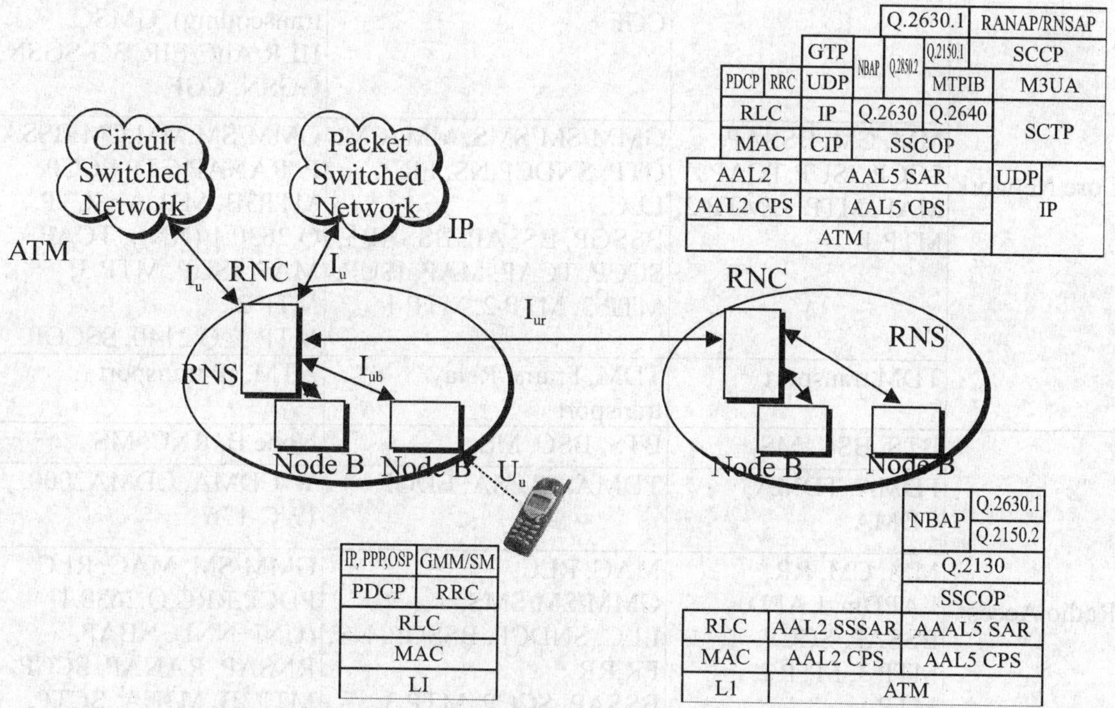

Fig. 8.14: Protocols Used in Node B, RNC and Mobile Handsets

- *Radio Network Service Application Part (RNSAP)*— provides the communication between RNCs.
- *GPRS Tunnel Protocol (GTP)*— protocol that tunnels the protocol data units through the IP backbone by adding routing information. GTP operates on top of TCP/UDP over IP.
- *Mobile Application Part (MAP)*— supports signaling between SGSN/GGSN and HLR/AuC/EIR.
- *AAL2 Signaling (Q.2630.1, Q.2150.1, Q.2150.2, AAL2 SSSAR, and AAL2 CPS)*— protocols suite used to transfer voice over ATM backbone using ATM adaptation layer 2.
- *Sigtran (SCTP, M3UA)*— protocols suite used to transfer SCN signaling protocols over IP network.
- *AAL2 Signaling (Q.2630.1, Q.2150.1, Q.2150.2, AAL2 SSSAR, and AAL2 CPS)*— protocols suite used to transfer voice over ATM backbone using ATM adaptation layer 2.

- *Sigtran (SCTP, M3UA)*— protocols suite used to transfer SCN signaling protocols over IP network.

8.14 COMPARISON OF 2G AND 3G MOBILE NETWORKS

Table 8.4: Comparison between 2G and 3G wireless networks

Feature	*2G*	*2G+*	*3G*
Core Network	MSC/VLR, GMSC, HLR/AuC/EIR	MSC/VLR, GMSC, SGSN, GGSN, HLR/AuC/EIR, CGF	3G MSC/VLR (with added interworking and transcoding), GMSC, HLR/AuC/EIR, 3G-SGSN, GGSN, CGF
	MM, CM, BSSAP, SCCP, ISUP,TCAP, MAP, MTP 3, MTP 2, MTP 1	GMM/SM/SMS, MM, CM, GTP, SNDCP,NS, FR, LLC, BSSGP, BSSAP, BSSAP+, SCCP, TCAP, MAP, ISUP, MTP 3, MTP 2, MTP 1	GMM/SM,MM,CM,BSSAP, RANAP,GTP,SCCP, MTP3B, M3UA, SCTP, Q.2630.1 (NNI), TCAP, MAP, ISUP, MTP 3, MTP 2, MTP 1, Q.2140, SSCOP
	TDM transport	TDM, Frame Relay transport	ATM, IP transport
Radio Access	BTS, BSC, MS	BTS, BSC, MS	Node B, RNC, MS
	FDMA, TDMA, CDMA	TDMA, CDMA, EDGE	W-CDMA, CDMA2000, IWC-136
	MM, CM, RR, LAPDm, LAPD, BSSAP, SCCP, MTP 3, MTP 2, MTP 1	MAC, RLC, GMM/SM/SMS, LLC, SNDCP, BSSGP, NS, FR,RR, BSSAP, SCCP, MTP 3, MTP 2, MTP 1	GMM/SM, MAC, RLC, PDCP,RRC,Q.2630.1 (UNI+NNI), NBAP, RNSAP, RANAP, SCCP, MTP3B, M3UA, SCTP, GTP-U, Q.2140, Q.2130, SSCOP, CIP
Handsets	Voice only terminals	New type of terminal Dual mode TDMA and CDMA Voice and data terminals WAP, no multimedia support	New type of terminal Multiple modes Voice, data and video terminals WAP, multimedia mgmt
Databases	HLR, VLR, EIR, AuC	HLR, VLR, EIR, AuC	Enhanced HLR, VLR, EIR, AuC
Data Rates	Up to 9.6 Kbps	Up to 57.6 Kbps (HSCSD) Up to 115Kbps (GPRS) Up to 384 Kbps (EDGE)	Up to 2Mbps

Feature	2G	2G+	3G
Applications	Advanced voice, Short Message Service (SMS)	SMS, Internet	Internet, multimedia
Roaming	Restricted, not global	Restricted, not global	Global
Compatibility	Not compatible to 3G	Not compatible to 3G	Compatible to 2G, 2G+ and Bluetooth

Table 8.5: Trillium's 3G Wireless Software Solutions

Device Description	*Replaces 2G/2G+*	*Required Protocols*
Node B - Responsible for radio transmission / reception in one or more cells within a service area to/from the mobile handsets.	Base Transceiver Station (BTS)	RLC/MAC. NBAP. AAL2 Signaling.Q.2130. SSCOP
RNC (Radio Network Controller) - Responsible for controlling the use and the integrity of the radio resources.	Base Station Controller (BSC)	PDCP. RLC/MAC. RRC. RANAP. RNSAP. NBAP. AAL2 Signaling. SIGTRAN (SCTP/ M3UA). GTP. Q.2130. SSCOP. Q.2140. MTP3B. SCCP. CIP
3G-SGSN (Serving GPRS Node) - Provides voice and packet data services and management of mobile subscribers.	2G SGSN	RANAP. SCTP/M3UA. GTP. Broadband SS7 (SCCP. MTP3B. Q.2140. SSCOP). CIP. GMM/SM/SMS. MAP. TCAP. MTP 2. MTP 1
3G-GGSN (Gateway GPRS Node) - Provides a gateway interface to external Packet Data Networks (PDN) and manages the routing of the tunneled mobile network protocol data units (PDUs) across the PDN.	2G GGSN	GTP. MAP. TCAP. SCCP. MTP 3. MTP 2. MTP 1
3G-CGF (Charging Gateway Function) - responsible for billing services	2G-CGF	GTP'
3G-MS - The 3G mobile station (handset) enhanced to provide users enhanced voice and data services.	2G-MS	GMM/SM. PDCP. RLC/MAC. RRC
3G-HLR/AuC/EIR -The 3G Home Location Register Database with User Profiles	2G-HLR/AuC/EIR	MAP.TCAP.SCCP.MTP3. MTP 2. MTP 1
3G-MSC/VLR - The 3G Mobile Switching Center and Visitor Location Register Database	2G-MSC/VLR	BSSAP+.ISUP.SCCP.MTP3. MTP 2. MTP 1. RANAP. SCCP. Q.2140. SSCOP. AAL2 Signaling

As mentioned above, although there are many similarities between 2G and 3G wireless networks (and many of the 2G and 3G components are shared or connected through interworking functions), there are also many differences between the two technologies. Table 2 compares the differences between the core network, the radio portion and other areas of the two networks.

Review Points

3G Network

3G is the next generation of wireless network technology that provides high speed bandwidth (high data transfer rates) to handheld devices. 3G networks offer multimedia services combining voice and data and support the following maximum data transfer rates:

- 2.05 Mbits/second to stationary devices.
- 384 Kbits/ second for pedestrian speed

Characteristics of 3G

Always-on connectivity. 3G networks use IP packet based connectivity, Multi-media service with streaming audio and video,Email with full-fledged attachments such as Power Point files, Instant messaging with video/audio clips, Fast downloads of large files such as faxes and Power Point files, Access to corporate applications.

Advantages of 3G

3G networks offer - New radio spectrum to relieve overcrowding in existing systems - more bandwidth, security and reliability -interoperability between service providers - fixed and variable data rates - asymmetric data rates - backward compatibility of devices with existing networks - always-online devices, -rich multimedia services.

Disadvantages of 3G

The cost of upgrading base station and cellular infrastructure to 3G is very high,it requires different handsets and there is the issue of handset availability, 3G handsets will be a complex product , roaming and making both data/voice works has not yet been fully and seamlessly operational. Also the higher power requirement (more bits with the same energy/bit) demand a larger handset, shorter talk time, and larger batteries). Customers will prefer to have upgradeability/dual operation of existing handsets, base stations need to be closer to each other thus involving more cost.

CDMA2000 for 3G

CDMA2000 is a cost-effective evolutionary technology for . CDMA2000 is an evolution of cdmaOne (IS-95) technology. An efficient and versatile technology, CDMA2000 1X supports both voice and data while CDMA2000 1xEV-DO (Data Optimized) supports data only in 1.25 MHz of spectrum. The first commercial CDMA2000 network was launched in Korea in October 2000. By the end of 2001 there were 4.2 million commercial subscribers using CDMA2000 in Korea. CDMA2000 terminals are manufactured by 20 different manufactures.

Major new enhancements that CDMA2000 is offering are nearly doubling the voice capacity – from 14.8 Erlang per sector RF carrier (in 1.25 MHz) to 26.4 Erlang per sector per RF carrier (in 1.25 MHz),always On" Peak packet data rate of 307 kbps (release A),Various bands and bandwidths of operation in support of different operator needs: 450, 800, 900, 1700, 1800, 1900, and 2100 MHz,fully backward compatible with cdmaOne systems, Improved service multiplexing and QoS management and flexible channel structure in support of multiple services with various QoS and variable transmission rates.

Frequency Bands

Initially in the CDMA2000 standards two spreading rates were specified, A 1. 25 MHz full duplex bandwidth referred to as "Spreading Rate 1" (SR1), or "1X" and a 3.75 MHz full duplex bandwidth-referred to as "Spreading Rate 3" (SR3), or "3X". Today the 125 MHz configuration, SRI is predominately being deployed. The fundamental spreading rate is 1.2288 Mcps for SR1. It requires 1.25 MHz of bandwidth (625 KHz from the center frequency) when the adjacent RF carriers are nothing but other CDMA carriers. However, It requires 1.8 MHz of bandwidth (900 KHz from the center frequency) when both adjacent RF carriers are narrow band GSM or TDMA carriers

Power Control

The basic frame length is 20 ms divided in to 16 equal power control groups. In addition, CDMA2000 defines a 5 ms frame structure, essentially to support signaling bursts, as well as 40 and 80 ms frames, which offer additional interleaving depth and diversity gains for data services. In addition to the closed loop power control, the power on the reverse link of CDMA2000 is also controlled through an Open Loop Power Control mechanism.

Transmit Diversity

Transmit diversity consists of de-multiplexing and modulating data into two orthogonal signals, each of them transmitted from a different antenna at the same frequency. The two orthogonal signals are generated using either Orthogonal Transmit Diversity (OTD) or Space-Time Spreading (STS). The receiver reconstructs the original signal using the diversity signals, thus taking advantage of the additional space and/or frequency diversity.

Voice and Data Channels

CDMA2000 forward traffic channel structure may include several physical channels like the Fundamental Channel (F-FCH), Traffic Channel (TCH), the Supplemental Channel (F-SCH), Dedicated Control Channel (F-DCCH) and the reverse traffic channel structure is similar to the forward traffic channel. It may include R-PICH, a Fundamental Channel (R-FCH), and/or a Dedicated Control Channel (R_DCCH), and one or several Supplemental Channel or channels (R-SCH).

Turbo Coding

CDMA2000 provides the option of using turbo coding or convolution coding on the forward and reverse SCHs. Both coding schemes are optional for both the base station and the mobile station, and the capacity of each is communicated through signaling messages prior to the setup of the call. In addition to peak rate increase and improved rate granularity, the major improvement to the traffic channel coding in CDMA2000 is the support of turbo coding at rate $\frac{1}{2}$, $\frac{1}{3}$, or $\frac{1}{4}$.

Review Questions

1. What is the data rates offered by 3G wireless network?
2. Write down advantages and disadvantages of 3G system.
3. Draw a schematic diagram of 3G architecture and explain the working of various blocks.
4. What are new enhancements brought out in 3G by the use of CDMA2000.
5. Write note on various types of channels in CDMA2000.
6. What are points considered for deciding the frequency bands?
7. Write note on power control mechanisms deployed in CDMA2000 system.
8. What is meant by soft handoff and explain how the handoff is effected?
9. Write note on voice and data channels in this system.
10. What is the types of coding used and what are overriding priorities to use this?

9.2.1 Trends in Mobile Broadband

As stated in a Rysavy Research report for CTIA on mobile broadband spectrum demand, "We are at a unique and pivotal time in history, in which technology capability, consumer awareness and comfort with emerging wireless technology, and industry innovation are converging to create mass-market acceptance of mobile broadband."

The market factors contributing to the surging growth in this market are shown in the following figure.

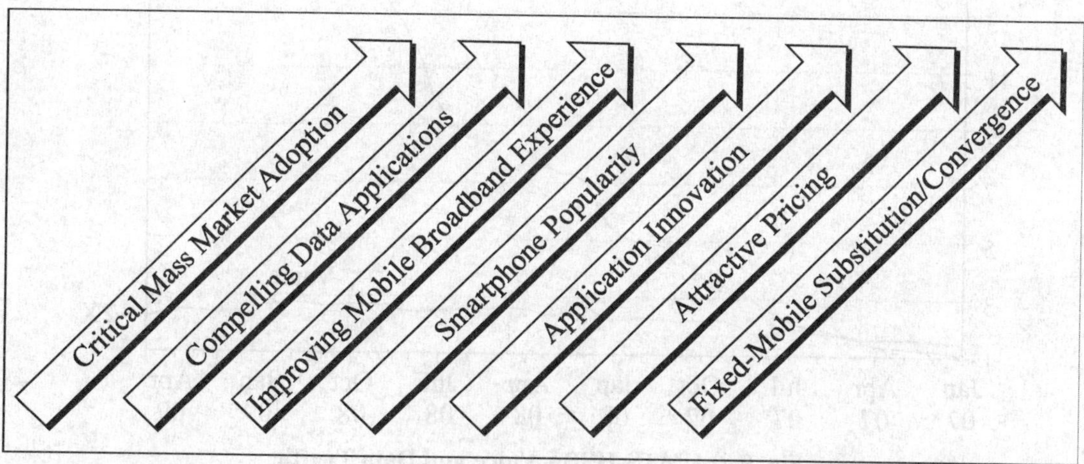

Fig. 9.1: Market Factors Contributing to Growth of Mobile Broadband

As data constitutes a rising percentage of total cellular traffic, it is essential that operators deploy spectrally efficient data technologies that meet customer requirements for performance—especially because data applications can demand significantly more network resources than traditional voice services. Operators have a huge investment in spectrum and in their networks; data services must leverage these investments. It is only a matter of time before today's more than 4 billion cellular customers start taking full advantage of data capabilities. This adoption will offer tremendous opportunities and the associated risks to operators as they choose the most commercially viable evolutionary path for migrating their customers. The EDGE/HSPA/LTE evolutionary paths provide data capabilities that address market needs and deliver ever-higher data throughputs, lower latency, and increased spectral efficiency.

As a consequence, this rich network and device environment is spawning the availability of a wide range of wireless applications and content. Because of its growing size—and its unassailable potential—application and content developers are making the wireless market a high priority. For example, there are now more than 50,000 applications for the Apple iPhone.

Based on one leading UMTS-HSPA infrastructure vendor's statistics, Figure 9.2 compares the rapid growth in wireless data traffic compared to voice traffic across multiple operators. By mid 2009, in HSPA coverage areas worldwide, the volume of data traffic significantly exceeded voice traffic. Operators that are the most aggressive with mobile broadband services are experiencing data growth rates even higher than these average values. Traffic has continued to increase since.

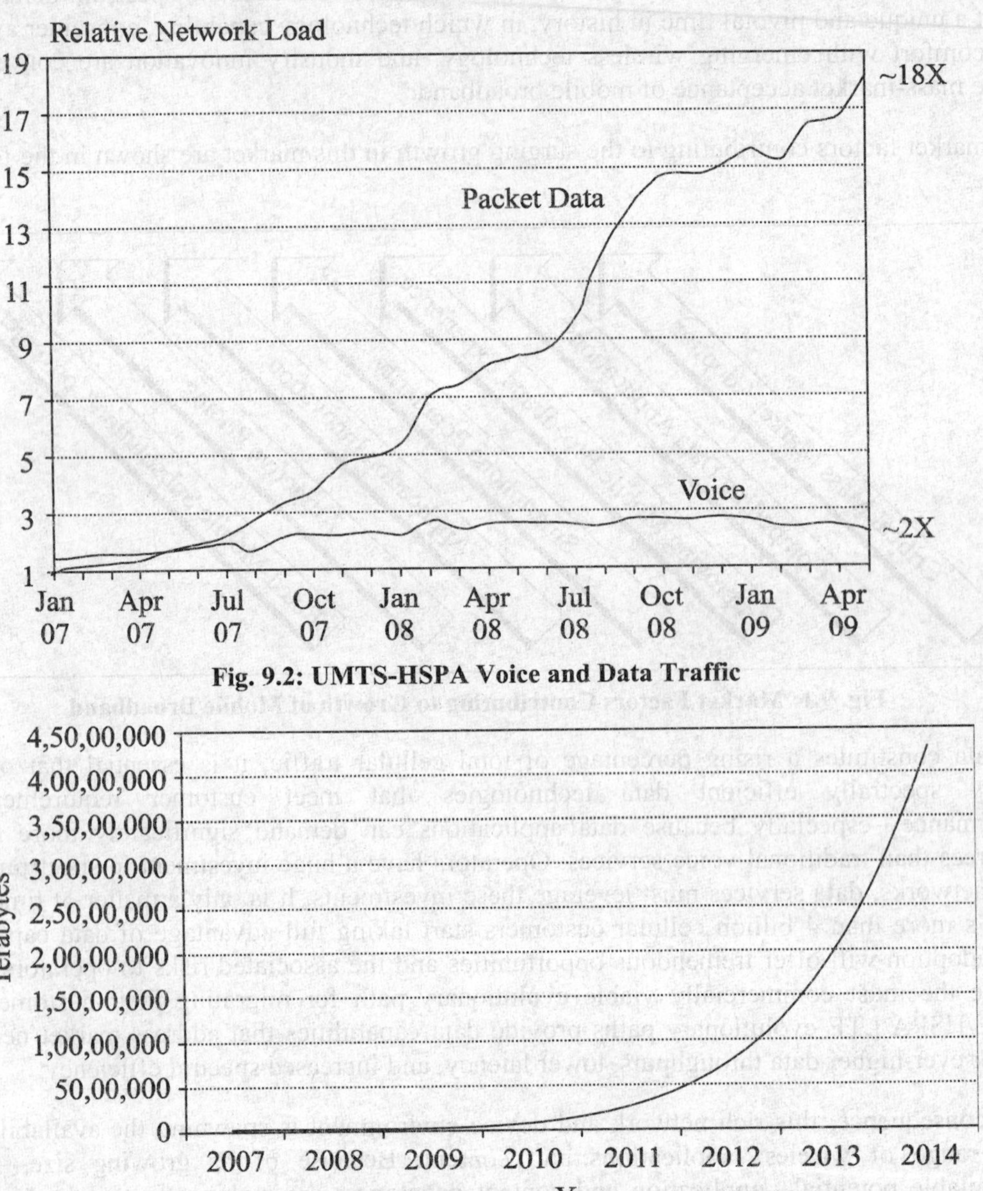

Fig. 9.2: UMTS-HSPA Voice and Data Traffic

Fig. 9.3: Mobile Data Growth in the United States (Source: Chetan Sharma Consulting, 2009)

Over the time, data demands are expected to grow significantly. Figure 9.3 shows a projection by Chetan Sharma of mobile data growth in the US through 2014.

The key for operators is enhancing their networks to support the demands of consumer and business applications as they grow, along with offering complementary capabilities such as IP-based multimedia. This is where the GSM family of wireless-data technologies is the undisputed leader. Not only does it provide a platform for continual improvements in capabilities, but it does so over huge coverage areas and on a global basis.

9.3 EDGE/HSPA/HSPA+ DEPLOYMENT

Three quarters of GSM networks today support EDGE, representing more than 345 networks in approximately 170 countries.

Because of the very low incremental cost of including EDGE capability in GSM network deployments, virtually all new GSM infrastructure deployments are also EDGE-capable and nearly all new mid- to high-level GSM devices include EDGE radio technology.

Meanwhile, UMTS has established itself globally. Nearly all WCDMA handsets are also GSM handsets, so WCDMA users can access the wide base of GSM networks and services. There are more than 336 million UMTS-HSPA customers worldwide spanning 283 commercial networks. Two hundred and sixty four operators in 114 countries offer HSDPA, and 77 of these have HSUPA deployed. Almost all UMTS operators are deploying HSPA for two reasons: first, the incremental cost of HSPA is relatively low and second, HSPA makes such efficient use of spectrum for data that it results in a much lower overall cost per megabyte of data delivered. Already, there are more than 1375 commercial HSPA devices available worldwide from 135 suppliers. Devices include handsets, data cards, modems, routers, laptops, media players and cameras.

Operators have begun deploying evolved HSPA features and HSPA+ launches include:

Telstra (Australia), Mobilkom (Austria), CSL Limited (Hong Kong), Starhub (Singapore). As the technology matures, upgrading to HSPA+ will likely represent a minimal investment for operators in order to significantly boost network performance.

9.4 STATISTICS

A variety of statistics show the rapid growth in wireless data. Chetan Sharma reported that in Q1 2009, the US wireless data market grew 32% over Q1 of 2008 to reach $10B in mobile data revenues, the first time the US market has crossed the $10B milestone.

He also states that 62% of US subscribers were using some form of data service.

Berg Insight reported that in the European Union, 11.6% of broadband links at the end of 2008 were based on HSPA in both mobile and home environments. Pyramid Research projects the number of European mobile broadband users to reach 117 million in 2014, up from 24 million in 2008.

Though most mobile broadband growth today is based on HSPA (with some EV-DO), LTE should see relatively rapid adoption as it becomes deployed starting in 2010. Pyramid Research expects LTE networks to grow more quickly than prior 3G networks, reaching 100 million subscribers in just four years from initial 2010 deployments. According to Juniper Research, there are already in excess of 30 network operator commitments to LTE. According to 3G

Americas (www.3gamericas.org), there are more than 100 operators that have committed or expressed intentions to commit to LTE.

From a device perspective, Informa WCIS projected in June 2009 the following sales growth rate for WCDMA handsets:

2009-307 million, 2010: 416 million, 2011: 564 million, 2012: 736 million, 2013: 927 million

It is clear that both EDGE and UMTS/HSDPA are dominant wireless technologies. And powerful data capabilities and global presence mean these technologies will likely continue to capture most of the available wireless-data market.

9.5 DATA MARKET

By the end of 2013, the global 3G wireless market is expected to include more than 2 billion subscribers, of which 1.6 billion will use 3GPP technologies, representing 80% market share. As data constitutes a rising percentage of total cellular traffic, it is essential that operators deploy spectrally efficient data technologies that meet customer requirements for performance—especially because data applications can demand significantly more network resources than traditional voice services.

9.6 DEPLOYMENT OF HSPA

Almost all UMTS operators are deploying HSPA for two reasons: first, the incremental cost of HSPA is relatively low and second, HSPA makes such efficient use of spectrum for data that it results in a much lower overall cost per megabyte of data delivered. Already, there are more than 1375 commercial HSPA devices available worldwide from 135 suppliers. Devices include handsets, data cards, modems, routers, laptops, media players and cameras. Though most mobile broadband growth today is based on HSPA (with some EV-DO), LTE should see relatively rapid adoption as it becomes deployed starting in 2010. Pyramid Research expects LTE networks to grow more quickly than prior 3G networks

Review Questions

1. What are the different options for managing the bandwidth?
2. Write note on growth of wireless data market.
3. Explain how the deployment of HSPA or HSPA+ has helped customers to enjoy more benefits and operators to develop a data market?

10 Multimedia Communications over Wireless Networks

10.1 MULTIMEDIA

Generally "Multimedia" has no strict definition. But in our context, multimedia indicates the computer technology (multimedia computing) for more efficient communication by using different media types:

- Text
- Audio and speech
- Images
- Graphics
- Video

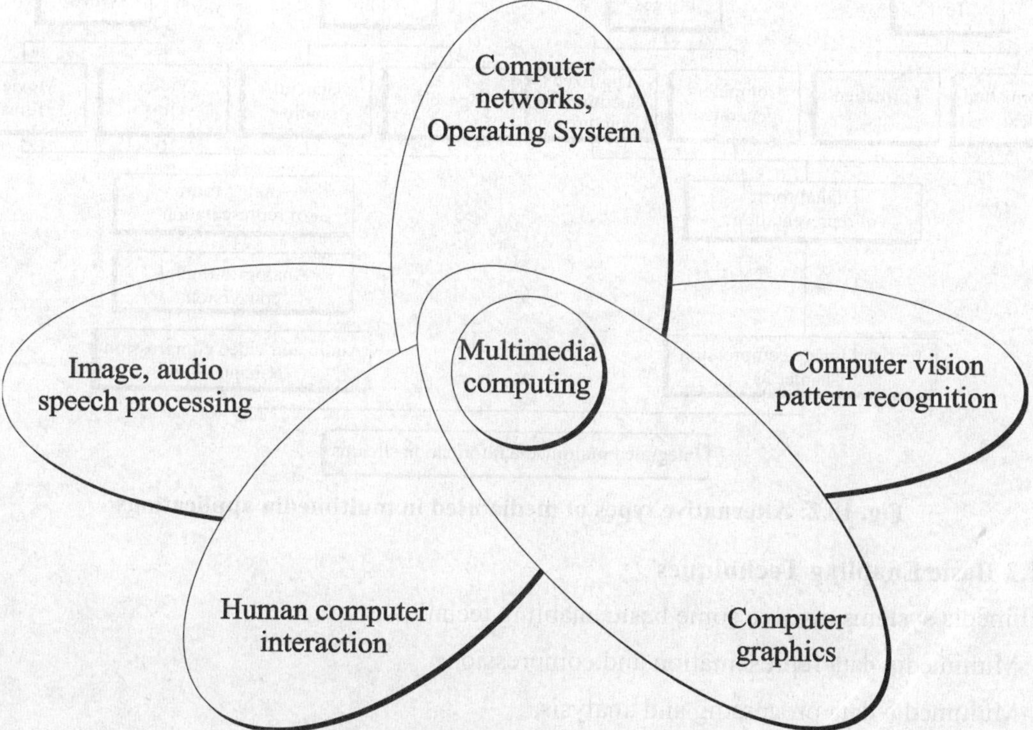

Fig. 10.1: Multimedia is Multidisciplinary

- Multimedia involves more than simple addition of new data types.
- It integrates a wide range of symbol modes simultaneously into a coherent framework.
- The framework is usually denoted as a multimedia system.

10.1.1 Challenges of Multimedia Computing

- Developing a successful multimedia system is non-trivial.
  - ✓ Continuous media types such as video need a lot of space to store and very high bandwidth to transmit.
  - ✓ They also have tight timing constraints.
  - ✓ Automatically analyzing, indexing and organizing information in audio, image and video is much harder than from text.
  - ✓ Multimedia involves many different research areas and needs more complex and more efficient algorithms and hardware platforms.

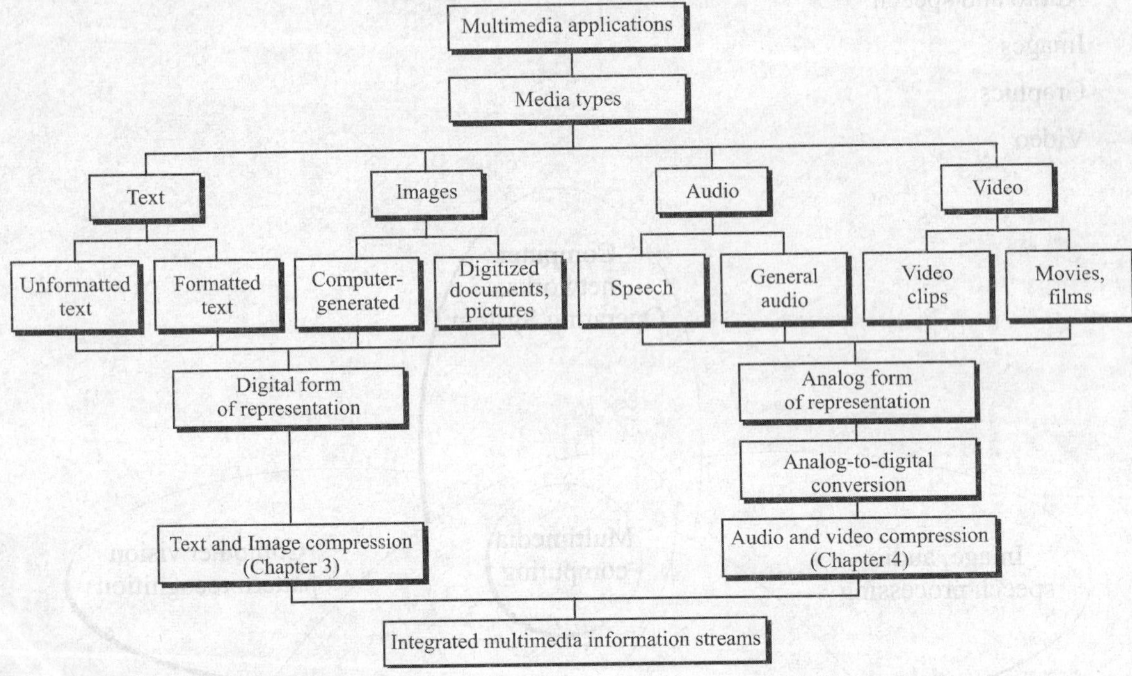

Fig. 10.2: Alternative types of media used in multimedia applications

10.1.2 Basic Enabling Techniques

Multimedia systems involve some basic enabling techniques:

- Multimedia data representation and compression.
- Multimedia data processing and analysis.
- Transmitting multimedia data through communication networks.

- Multimedia database, indexing and retrieval.

10.1.3 Media Delivery

- Transmitting multimedia data across the network is another topic in multimedia computing.
- There are different issues when we transmit video and audio through packet network, such as
  - ✓ Quality of service.
  - ✓ Synchronization.
  - ✓ Error and congestion control.
  - ✓ Session setup and book keeping.

10.1.4 Multimedia Requirements

- To develop schemes for multi-access networks which can provide performance guarantees.
- To develop a distribute route-selection strategy for point-to-point networks.
- Real-time multimedia applications require guaranteed performance communication services, such as throughput, delay, delay jitter and loss rate.
- The characteristics of a source, such as peak and average rate, are known at channel establishment time.
- Channel parameters have to be predicted in live continuous video sources.

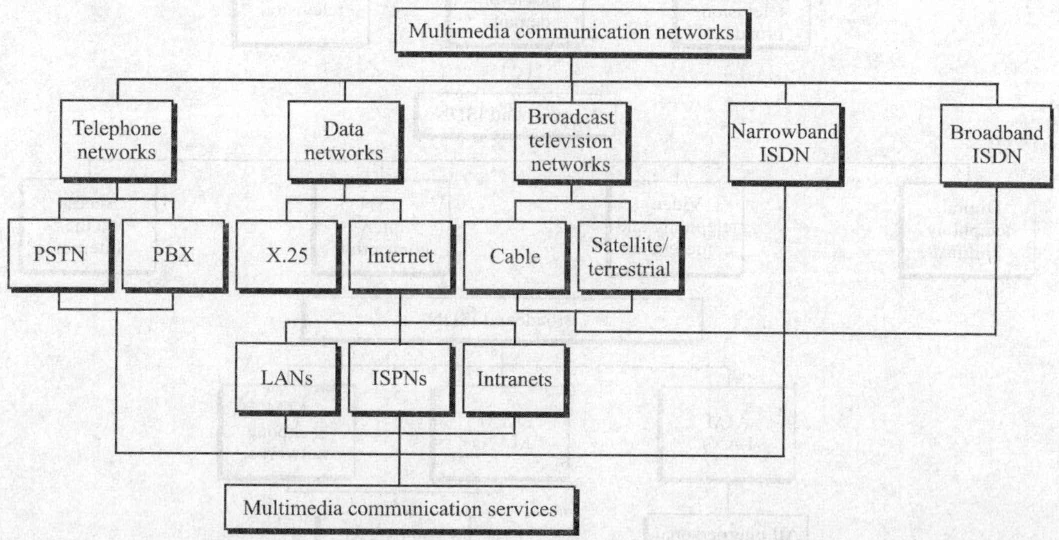

PSTN - Public Switched Telephone Network
PBX - Private Branch Exchange
ISDN - Integrated Services Digital Network
LANs - Local Area Networks
ISPNs - Internet Service Provider Networks

Fig. 10.3: Multimedia Communication Networks

- The possibility for users to select some resources that best meet their needs.
- The possibility to interact with another user whose equipment has differing characteristics.
- The communications network must allow any user to select the service components he/she wants:
- The possibility for users to join in or withdraw from a communication session according to certain policies, such as agreement of all interacting partners before admitting a new user.
- The possibility to set such quality of service parameters as the synchronization tolerance between the service components, the echo sensitivity, the burst sensitivity, and so on.

10.1.7 Multimedia Communications

Different kind of MM communications which are categorized as,

- High-Density File Transfers
- Graphics File Transfers
- Audio File Transfers
- Video File Transfers
- Audio Communication
- Computer-Based Telephony
- Computer-Based Audio Conferencing
- Streaming Audio
- Video Communication
- Video Conferencing
- Streaming of Video

10.2 DIGITIZATION OF INFORMATION

For enabling transmission of video and speech as well different forms of data through selected networks, it is imperative that the information should be converted or more specifically digitized and there are several techniques for digitizing, the images, data , speech or audio and video.

10.2.1 Digitizing Images – Classification

- Image (still picture)
- Computer-generated images (computer graphics)
- Digitized images of documents and/or pictures e.g. fax-scanned files, scanned color-image files
- Graphics
  - ✓ high-level language form: description of attributes of objects

- ✓ bit-map form: actual pixel-images
  - gif: graphical interchange format
  - tiff: tagged image file format
  - srgp: simple raster graphics package
- Digitized Documents
  - ✓ Facsimile (FAX) machine, about 2Mbits/page(black-white/pixel)
- *Pixel resolution*— 8 per mm
- *Line resolution*— 3.85 or 7.7 per mm(100 or 200 lines per inc
- *pixel (or pel)*— picture element
- VGA 640 × 480 =pixels 8-bits/pixel

10.2.2 Digitized Pictures

- *m*-bit per pixel (pixel depth *m*) (pixel depth is number of bits per pixel)
  - ✓ good-quality black-white picture: 8-bit/pixel(256 gray levels)
  - ✓ colored-picture: 24-bit/pixel(R/G/B each 8-bit yielding 16 M colors)
- *Coloring Principles*— How is color produced and represented ?
  - ✓ Color gamut— a whole spectrum of colors
  - ✓ Three primary colors— R (Red), G (Green), B (Blue)
    - all kinds of colors are produced by using different proportions of these primary colors
    - Additive Color Mixing on a black surface
    - Subtractive Color Mixing on a white surface
- *Raster-Scan Principles*— TV Screen or Computer CRT Monitor
  - ✓ NTSC (National Television Standards Committee)-USA
    - 525(active 480) lines/frame & 60-time refresh rate/sec
  - ✓ PAL (Phase Alternation Line)/CCIR/SECAM
    - 625(active 576) lines/frame & 50-time refresh/sec

frame— a complete set of *N* horizontal scan lines

1. *N*=525(NTSC) & 625(PAL/SECAM/CCIR)
2. Refresh rate (Hz) = 60(NTSC) & 50(PAL/SECAM/CCIR)
3. *M* is determined by the aspect ratio

frame refresh rate— Number of frames per second and it must be at least 50 Hz to avoid flickering

10.2.3 Scanning Method

Two important scanning methods followed in digitization are,

Progressive scanning— 1→2→3→...→*N*: one frame (60 or 50 Hz refresh rate)

Interlaced scanning— 1→3→5→...→*N*-1: first half frame (field) (30 or 25 Hz) refresh rate
2→4→6→...→*N*: 2nd half frame (filed) (30 or 25 Hz) refresh rate

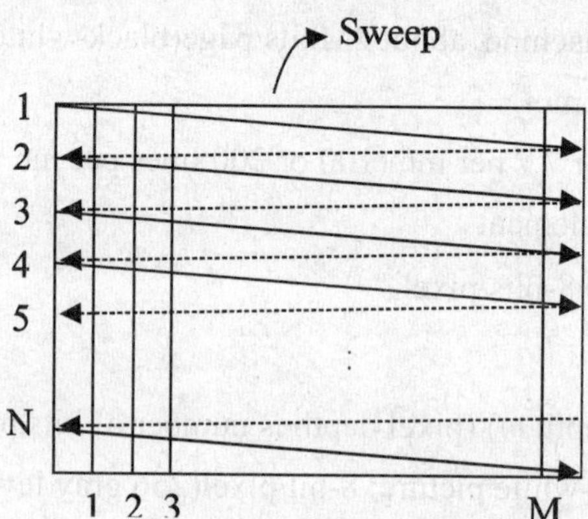

Fig. 10.6: Scanning Order

10.2.4 Raster-Scan Principles

- *Raster*— a finely-focused electro beam
- *Phosphor*— a light-sensitive material that emits light when energized
  - ✓ white-sensitive phosphor— a single electron beam used
  - ✓ color-sensitive phosphor— each pixel comprises a set of three color-sensitive phosphors, one each for R, G, B signals, called phosphor triad
  - ✓ beam signal may be either analog or digital form
- *Pixel Depth*— number of bits per pixel
  - ✓ CLUT (Color Look-Up Table)— 24-bit/pixel yields 2^{24} colors. But eye discriminates between some ranges of colors hence, each pixel value is used as an index on CLUT of 256 colors (compression achieved !)

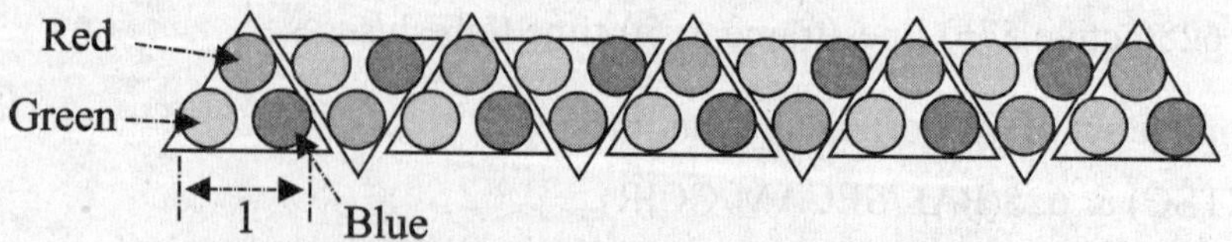

Spot Size: 0.635mm (0.025 inch)

Fig. 10.7

Aspect Ratio— ratio of the screen width to the screen height

- ✓ NTSC, 525 scan lines/frame ⇒ 480(45) data (control) lines
  - 4/3 aspect ratio ⇒ 480 × 4/3(=640) pixels/line
  - 16/9 aspect ratio ⇒ 480 × 16/9(=853.33) pixels/line
- ✓ PAL/CCIR/SECAM 625 lines/frame ⇒ 576(49) data (control) lines
  - 4/3 aspect ratio ⇒ 576 × 4/3(=768) pixels/line
  - 16/9 aspect ratio ⇒ 576 × 16/9(=1024) pixels/line

Table 10.1: Computer Graphics Array

Standard	*Resolution*	*No. of Colours*	*Bytes/frame*
VGA	640 × 480 × 8	256	307.2K
XGA	640 × 480 × 16 1024 × 768 × 8	64K 256	614 4K 786.432K
SVGA	800 × 600 × 16 1024 × 768 × 8 1024 × 768 × 24*	64K 256 16M*	960K 786.432K 2359.296K*

*Note: * Refresh rate: 50-70 Hz*

Example

Derive the time to transmit the following digitized images at both type of networks whose data rates are 64Kbps and 1.5Mbps

a.) 640×480×8 VGA-compatible image

b.) 1024×768×24 SVGA-compatible image

Solution

The size of each image in bit is as follows

a.) VGA image = 640×480×8 = 2.46Mbits

- b.) SVGA image = 1024×768×24 =18.88Mbits

The time to transmit each image is given as follows

at 64Kbps : VGA = 2.46Mbits/64Kbps = $[2.46\times10^6]/[64\times10^3]$ = 38.4 sec.
SVGA = $[18.88\times10^6]/[64\times10^3]$ = 295 sec.

at 1.5Mbps: VGA = 2.46Mbits/1.5Mbps = $[2.46\times10^6]/[1.5\times10^6]$ = 1.64 sec.
SVGA = $[18.88\times10^6]/[1.5\times10^6]$ = 12.59 sec.

10.2.5 Digital Cameras & Scanners

- (Still image cameras) 2-D grid of photo-sites (diode), light-sensitive cells, made of charge-coupled devices (CCD's)

- ✓ level of light intensity on each photosites is converted into a digital value using an AD converter when the shutter is activated
- (Scanners) single-row of photo-sites is exposed in time-sequence with the scanning operation
- How are color images obtained ?
  - ✓ each photosite/pixel is coated with R/B/G filter & the color is determined by the level of it together with 8 neighbors in a 3 × 3 grid structure
  - ✓ use of three separate exposures of a single photosite, say, first R filter, second G filter, and finally B filter
  - ✓ use of three separate image sensors per pixel
- (e.g) TIFF (tagged image file format), TIFF/EP for electronic photography

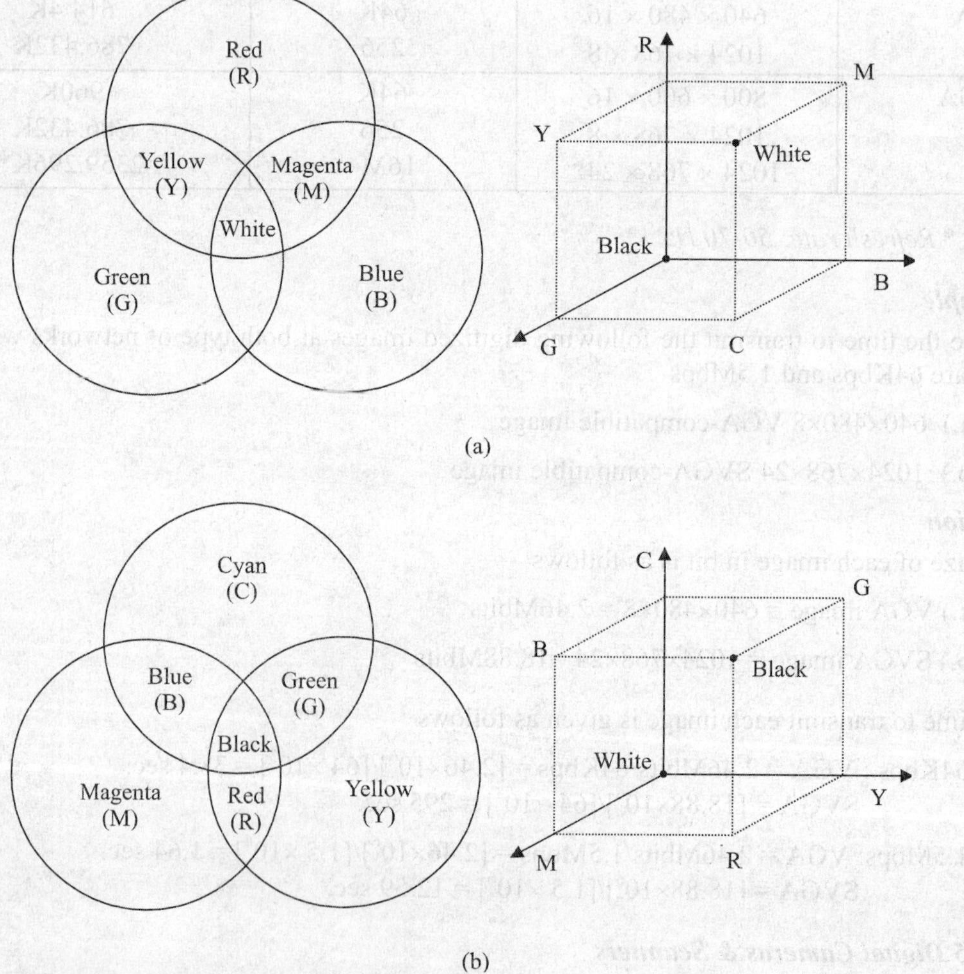

Fig. 10.8: Color derivation principles: (a) additive color mixing; (b) subtractive color mixing

10.2.6 Video (Motion): Broadcast TV

Video Applications

- *Entertainment*— Broadcast TV, VCR/DVD Recordings
- *Interpersonal*— Video Telephony & Videoconferencing
- *Interactive*— Video Clips on PC Windows
- *Scanning Sequences*— Interlaced Scanning

To minimize the amount of tx bandwidth, a frame is divided into two halves called fields

(e.g) 525-line 50-time frame refresh rate/sec.

262.5 odd lines 50-time field rate/sec.

262.5 even lines 50-time field rate/sec.

⇒ In reality,

525-line 25-time frame refresh rate/sec.

10.2.7 Broadcast TV

- Color Signals
  - ✓ Three properties of a color
    - Brightness, Hue (Tint) & Saturation
  - ✓ Color production: an equation of R, G, and B phosphors
    - 0.299 R + 0.587 G + 0.114 B , where, 0.299+0.587+0.114=1
  - ✓ Luminance refers to the brightness of a source, the hue & the saturation called, chrominance characteristics
    - say, luminance $Y_s = 0.299\ R_s + 0.587\ G_s + 0.114\ B_s$
      Y_s: magnitude of luminance signal
      R_s, G_s, B_s: magnitudes of three major colors
  - ✓ Two color difference signals: Blue chrominance C_b and Red chrominance C_r
    - $C_b = B_s - Y_s$, $C_r = R_s - Y_s$
- Chrominance Components
  - ✓ Composite Video Signal for Transmission
    - Y_s, C_b, and C_r signals are combined together and signal differences are scaled down before transmission

In PAL

- Y = 0.299 R + 0.587 G + 0.114 B
- $U(C_b) = 0.493(B-Y) = -0.147R-0.289G+0.437B$
- $V(C_r) = 0.877(R-Y) = 0.615R-0.515G-0.1B$

In NTSC

- $Y = 0.299\ R + 0.587\ G + 0.114\ B$
- $I(C_b) = 0.74(R\text{-}Y)\text{-}0.27(B\text{-}Y) = 0.599R\text{-}0.276G\text{-}0.324B$
- $Q(C_r) = 0.48(R\text{-}Y)\text{+}0.41(B\text{-}Y) = 0.212R\text{-}0.528\text{+}0.311B$

Table 10.2: Digital Video-PC Video Digitization

Digitization Format	***System***	***Spatial Resolution***	***Temporal Resolution***
4:2:2	525-line 625-line	$Y= 640\times480, C_b = 0,= 320\times240$ $Y=768\times576,\ C_b=C_r=384\times288$	60Hz 50Hz
SIF	525-line 625-line	$Y= 320\times240,\ C_b = C_r= 160\times240$ $Y= 384\times288,\ C_b=C_r= 192\times144$	30Hz 25Hz
CIF		$Y= 384\times288,\ C_b = C_r= 192\times144$	30Hz
QCIF		$Y= 192\times144,\ C_b=C_r= 96\times72$	15/7.5Hz
▪ Video captureboard or S/W required ▪ All PC monitors use "progressive (non-interlaced) scanning"			

SIF - Source Intermediate Format

CIF - Common Intermediate Format

QCIF - Quarter Common Intermediate Format

10.3 MULTIMEDIA PROTOCOLS

As in the case of any computer communication system the MM communication also uses various types of protocols.

10.3.1 Multimedia Protocol Specifications

- QoS (Quality of Service) requirements of multimedia streams:
- Throughput:
- The data transmission rate
- Data compression
- High transmission rate like, several Mbps (Megabits per second).
- Transfer Delay:
  - ✓ time between the production of data at the source and its presentation at the sink
- Jitter:
  - ✓ variance of the transfer delay
  - ✓ use of buffers to reduce jitter
- Error Rates:
  - ✓ loss of data in a continuous data transfer

SDP includes description of:

✓ Media to use (codec, sampling rate)

✓ Media destination (IP address and port number)

✓ Session name and purpose

✓ Times the session is active

✓ Contact information

Note— indeed SDP is a data format rather than a protocol.

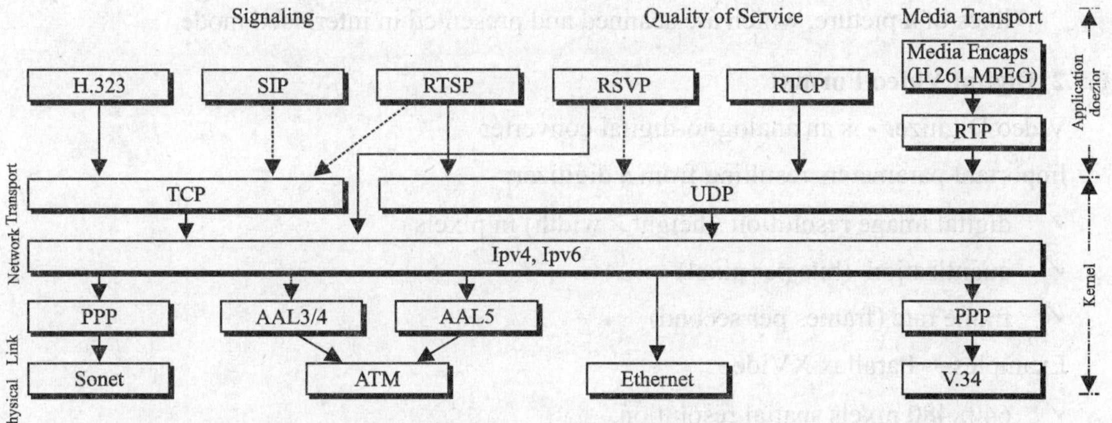

Fig. 10.10: General Protocol Architecture for Multimedia Communication

10.4 MULTIMEDIA NETWORKING APPLICATIONS

Classes of MM applications can be classified as,

1) Streaming stored audio and video
2) Streaming live audio and video
3) Real-time interactive audio and video

Interactive, Real-Time Multimedia applications— IP telephony, video conference, distributed interactive games etc. end-end delay requirements:

Audio— upto 150 msec good, upto 400 msec OK and includes application-level network delays, higher delays noticeable and impair interactivity.

Session initialization— called party be able to advertise its IP address, port number, encoding algorithms.

10.5 VIDEO FORMAT

- NTSC (National Television Systems Committee) TV Format (USA TV Standard)

10.5.1 Analog video format

- Color carrier 4.429 MHz; refresh rate 30 Hz (29.92Hz); 4.2 MHz for luminance, 1.5 MHz for each of the two chrominance channels
- Resolution— 833×635 picture elements
- Refresh Rate— 30 Hz
- Aspect Ratio— 4:3
- Interlaced format
  - ✓ Each frame is composed of two consecutive fields, each containing half the scanning lines of a picture, which are scanned and presented in interlaced mode.

10.5.2 Digital Video Format

- Video Digitizer - is an analog-to-digital converter
- Important parameters resulting from a digitizer:
  - ✓ digital image resolution (height × width) in pixels
  - ✓ quantization (bits per pixel)
  - ✓ frame rate (frames per second)
- Examples— Parallax XVideo
  - ✓ 640×480 pixels spatial resolution;
  - ✓ 24 bits per pixel resolution (16777216 shades of gray or color)
  - ✓ 20 fps; if the image resolution is 320×240 pixels then this video board can provide even 30 fps.
- Output of digital video goes mostly to raster displays which have large video RAM memories. These displays use for presentation of color systems the Color Look Up Table (lut).

10.5.3 High Definition TV (HDTV) Format

- Research on HDTV started in Japan 1968
- Current TV standard
- Resolution
  - ✓ twice as many horizontal and vertical columns and lines than conventional systems (NTSC)
  - ✓ Two resolution systems
    - High 1440 Level with 1,440×1,152 pixels
    - High Level with 1,920×1,152 pixels
- Frame rate— 50 or 60 frames per second
- Aspect Ratio— 16:9

- Interlaced and/or progressive scanning formats
  - ✓ Conventional systems use interlaced (alternation of scanning lines) format
  - ✓ HDTV similar to computer displays, uses progressive scanning

10.6 DIGITAL TRANSMISSION BANDWIDTH

- Bandwidth requirements for Images:
  - ✓ Raw Image Transmission Bandwidth = size of the image = spatial resolution × pixel resolution;
  - ✓ Compressed Image Transmission Bandwidth depends on the compression scheme (e.g., JPEG) and content of the image;
  - ✓ Symbolic Image Transmission bandwidth = size of the instructions and variables carrying graphics primitives and attributes.
- Bandwidth Requirements for Video:
  - ✓ Uncompressed Video Bandwidth:= image size × frame rate;
  - ✓ Compressed Video Bandwidth:= depends on the compression scheme (e.g., JPEG, MPEG) and content of the video (scene changes).
- Example: Assume the following video characteristics - 720,000 pixels per image (frame), 8 bits per pixel quantization, and 60 frames per second frame rate. The *Video Bandwidth*:= 720,000 pixels per frame × 8 bits per pixel × 60 fps
- which results in HDTV data rate of 43,200,000 bytes per second = 345.6 Mbps When we use MPEG compression, the bandwidth goes to 34 Mbps with some loss in image/video quality.

10.7 IP MULTIMEDIA SUB-SYSTEM (IMS)

IMS has been envisaged to summarize all the requirements and basic mechanisms of multimedia communication over wireless networks using NGN (Next Generation Network) technology. Aspects of the IMS architecture, like interworking between mobile/wireless and fixed networks as well as the evolution of the SIP protocol are standardized by the 3GPP, the ETSI-TISPAN and the IETF bodies. By exploiting this concept and through the introduction of some extra core network elements, IMS allows realizations of versatile, mixed-technology, call schemes, such as UMTS-to-WLAN and PSTN-to- Broadband, over native packet switched links. Potentially, every packet switched network is compatible with the IMS architecture and can be integrated within it through a number of logical interfaces implementing different manifestations of the SIP protocol.

10.7.1 IMS Implementation Strategy

IMS will be a gradually built out over the next 10 years and will consist of three key phases:

- *Phase I (2005 – 2008)*— Proof of concepts and field trials focused on leveraging IP within the transport and application level.

- *Phase II (2008 – 2012)*— Significant IMS deployments with a key focus area of converging wire line and wireless solutions beginning on a mass scale with the enterprise and spreading into the residential markets.
- *Phase III (2012 and beyond)*— VoIP becomes the prevalent voice, video and data technology and QoS will be fully monitored and guaranteed.

10.7.2 Enabler Technology

IMS enables services to be delivered in a standardized, well-structured way that truly makes the most of layered architecture. At the same time, it provides a future-proof architecture that simplifies and speeds up the service creation and provisioning process, while enabling legacy interworking. The horizontal architecture of IMS enables operators to move away from vertical 'stovepipe' implementations of new services – eliminating the costly and complex traditional network structure of overlapping functionality for charging, presence, group and list management, routing and provision. NGN is an enabler technology and will continue shaping the future of communications and become the main focal point of industry's efforts towards 4G and its commercial roll-out. IMS is the operator solution to differentiate from commodity priced best-effort data services, offering end-to-end QoS deploying the packet switched IP backbone and network equipment like SGSN (Serving GPRS Support Node) and GGSN(Gateway GPRS Support Node).

10.7.3 Session Border Control in IMS

The IP-Multimedia Subsystem (IMS) defines the functional architecture for a managed IP-based network. It aims to provide a means for carriers to create an open, standards-based network that delivers integrated multimedia services to increase revenue, while also reducing network CapEx and OpEx.

IMS was originally designed for third-generation mobile phones, but it has already been extended to handle access from WiFi networks, and is continuing to be extended into an access-independent platform for service delivery, including broadband fixed-line access. It promises to provide seamless roaming between mobile, public WiFi and private networks for a wide range of services and devices.

The IMS architecture has been designed to enable operators to provide a wide range of real-time, packet-based services and to track their use in a way that allows both traditional time-based charging as well as packet and service-based charging. It has become increasingly popular both with wireline and wireless service providers as it is designed to increase carrier revenues, deliver integrated multimedia services, and create an open, standards-based network.

IMS provides a wide range of session border control, including call access control, reachability and security. It also provides a framework for the deployment of both basic calling services and enhanced services, including

- multimedia messaging
- web integration

- presence-based services
- push-to-talk.

At the same time, it draws on the traditional telecommunications experience of

- guaranteed QoS
- flexible charging mechanisms (time-based, call-collect, premium rates)
- lawful intercept legislation compliance.

Network operators also hope that IMS will cut their CapEx and OpEx through the use of a converged IP backbone and the open IMS architecture.

- The IMS architecture defines many common components (for example, call control and configuration storage) so less development work is required to create a new service as this existing infrastructure can be reused.
- The use of standardized interfaces should increase competition between suppliers; preventing operators from being locked into a single supplier's proprietary interfaces.

As a result, IMS should enable new services to be rolled out more quickly and cheaply, compared with the traditional monolithic design of telephony services.

10.7.4 IMS Architecture

IMS is one of 3GPP's greatest success stories. Originally designed to evolve UMTS networks to deliver Internet Protocol multimedia to mobile users, IMS has become the core component within 3G, cable TV and next generation fixed telecoms networks.

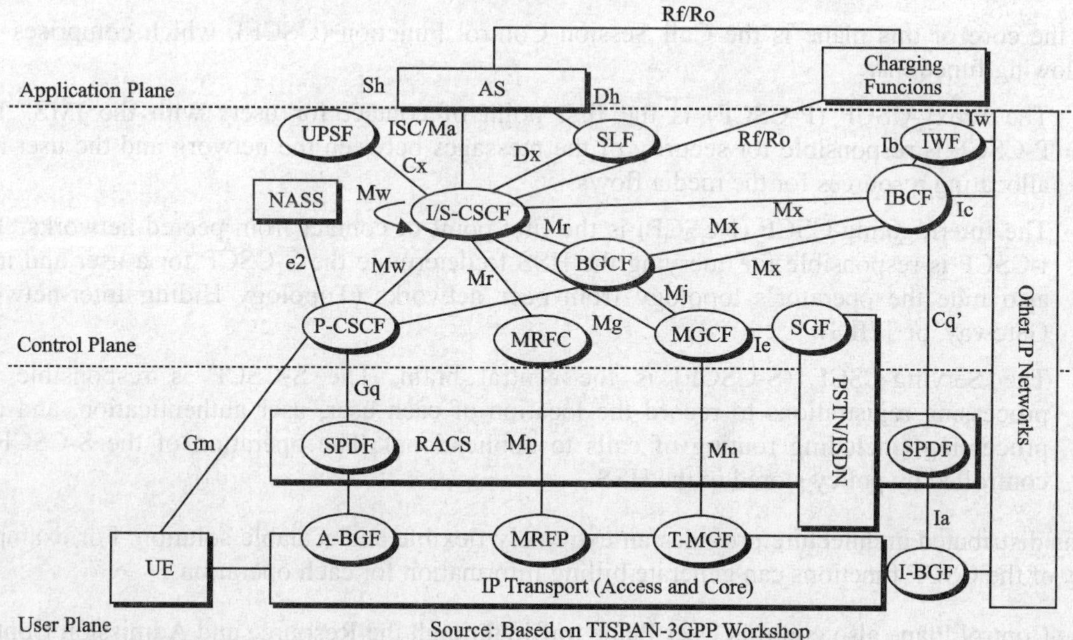

Fig. 10.11: IMS Architecture

The diagram above (Fig. 10.11) shows the IP Multimedia Subsystem architecture.

IMS decomposes the networking infrastructure into separate functions with standardized interfaces between them. Each interface is specified as a "reference point", which defines both the protocol over the interface and the functions between which it operates. The standards do not mandate which functions should be co-located, as this depends on the scale of the application, and a single device may contain several functions.

The 3GPP architecture is split into three main planes or layers, each of which is described by a number of equivalent names: Service or Application Plane, Control or Signaling Plane, and User or Transport Plane.

Application Plane

The application plane provides an infrastructure for the provision and management of services, and defines standard interfaces to common functionality including

- configuration storage, identity management, user status (such as presence and location), which is held by the Home Subscriber Server (HSS)
- billing services, provided by a Charging Gateway Function (CGF)
- control of voice and video calls and messaging, provided by the control plane.

Control Plane

The control plane sits between the application and transport planes. It routes the call signaling, tells the transport plane what traffic to allow, and generates billing information for the use of the network.

At the core of this plane is the Call Session Control Function (CSCF), which comprises the following functions.

- The Proxy-CSCF (P-CSCF) is the first point of contact for users with the IMS. The P-CSCF is responsible for security of the messages between the network and the user and allocating resources for the media flows.
- The Interrogating-CSCF (I-CSCF) is the first point of contact from peered networks. The I-CSCF is responsible for querying the HSS to determine the S-CSCF for a user and may also hide the operator's topology from peer networks (Topology Hiding Inter-network Gateway, or THIG).
- The Serving-CSCF (S-CSCF) is the central brain. The S-CSCF is responsible for processing registrations to record the location of each user, user authentication, and call processing (including routing of calls to applications). The operation of the S-CSCF is controlled by policy stored in the HSS.

This distributed architecture provides an extremely flexible and scalable solution. For example, any of the CSCF functions can generate billing information for each operation.

The Control Plane also controls User Plane traffic through the Resource and Admission Control Subsystem (RACS). This consists of the Policy Decision Function (PDF), which implements local policy on resource usage, for example to prevent overload of particular access links, and Access-RAC Function (A-RACF), which controls QoS within the access network.

User Plane

The User plane provides a core QoS-enabled IPv6 network with access from User Equipment (UE) over mobile, WiFi and broadband networks. This infrastructure is designed to provide a wide range of IP multimedia server-based and P2P services.

Access into the core network is through Border Gateways (GGSN/PDG/BAS). These enforce policy provided by the IMS core, controlling traffic flows between the access and core networks.

Within the User Plane

- the Interconnect Border Control Function (I-BCF) controls transport level security and tells the RACS what resources are required for a call
- the I-BGF, A-BGF Border Gateway Functions provide media relay for hiding endpoint addresses with managed pinholes to prevent bandwidth theft, and implement NAPT and NAT/Firewall traversal for media flows.

10.8 UNICAST IP ROUTING

IMS specification began in 3GPP Release 5 as part of the core network evolution from circuit-switching to packet-switching and was redefined by subsequent Releases 6 and 7.

Initially, IMS was an all-IP system designed to assist mobile operators deliver next generation interactive and interoperable services, cost-effectively, over an architecture providing the flexibility of the Internet.

Standardisers now base their core network evolution on Common IMS. Session Initiation Protocol was selected as the signalling mechanism for IMS, thereby allowing voice, text and multimedia services to traverse all connected networks. 3GPP works closely with experts in the IETF to ensure maximum re-usability of internet standards, preventing fragmentation of IMS standards.

With the adoption of IMS by other industry sectors, the potential of a mass market to bring about substantial economies of scale will provide affordable broadband wireless access regardless of how and where users connect.

The responsibility for producing the Common IMS specifications in 3GPP lies largely with the Services and System Aspects (SA) group.

IP routing protocols have been an essential element of IP networks for many years. However more recently, this technology has been the focus of new development, as routing has evolved to handle the needs of next generation networks. Traditional IP routing protocols have therefore been substantially extended in a number of areas.

- Pre-integrated CLI, XML/web and SNMP management interfaces using MINDLink (Metaswitch) are available via the *embedded*MIND™ product from our partner Go Ahead Software.
- Pre-integrated CLI, web, SNMP, and NETCONF northbound interfaces are available from our partner Tail-f Systems.

IP Stack Integration

The asynchronous, message-based interfaces to the underlying IP transport allow the products to be efficiently integrated in all system architectures. We provide integration with the standard IP stack for each operating system as part of our standard pre-ported N-BASE versions, and with the standard sockets API used by the majority of IP stacks.

Data Plane Integration

For performance reasons, Data Plane functionality is normally closely integrated with the communications hardware, so most chipsets are supplied with their own Layer 1 and Layer 2 drivers. All of Metaswitch's network software products use carefully designed interfaces that can be easily integrated with these drivers. These interfaces are implemented using an asynchronous message-based paradigm, thereby allowing complete flexibility of data plane design. This includes distributed data planes and programming backup data planes when resilience is required.

For some products and environments, Metaswitch is able to supply complete reference data plane implementations.

Integrated Control Plane

Integrated Control Plane is a portable source code product that can be used to implement a MPLS/GMPLS and IP Routing control plane on a huge range of network equipment.

The Integrated Control Plane supports the full range of options described on the MPLS/GMPLS and IP Routing web pages and is suitable for any router, switch, optical or WDM device. It is scalable from embedded customer premises equipment (CPE) to massive devices with control plane function distributed across multiple processors or blades. A wide range of options for high availability are also available. With the first portable, longest standing, and most mature solution in the industry. MPLS solutions are used throughout the world by many of the leading manufacturers of communications equipment.

Benefits of DC-MPLS Include

- Integrated routing and signaling
- Integrated MPLS Transport Solutions
- Integrated Layer 3 VPN Solutions
- Integrated Optical Transport solutions
- Component and OS integration
- Integrated with Configuration Safe Store

- Most mature MPLS solution in the industry
- Most widely deployed solution in the industry
- Backed by a stable, reliable company
- Provides carrier grade scale
- Provides carrier grade high availability

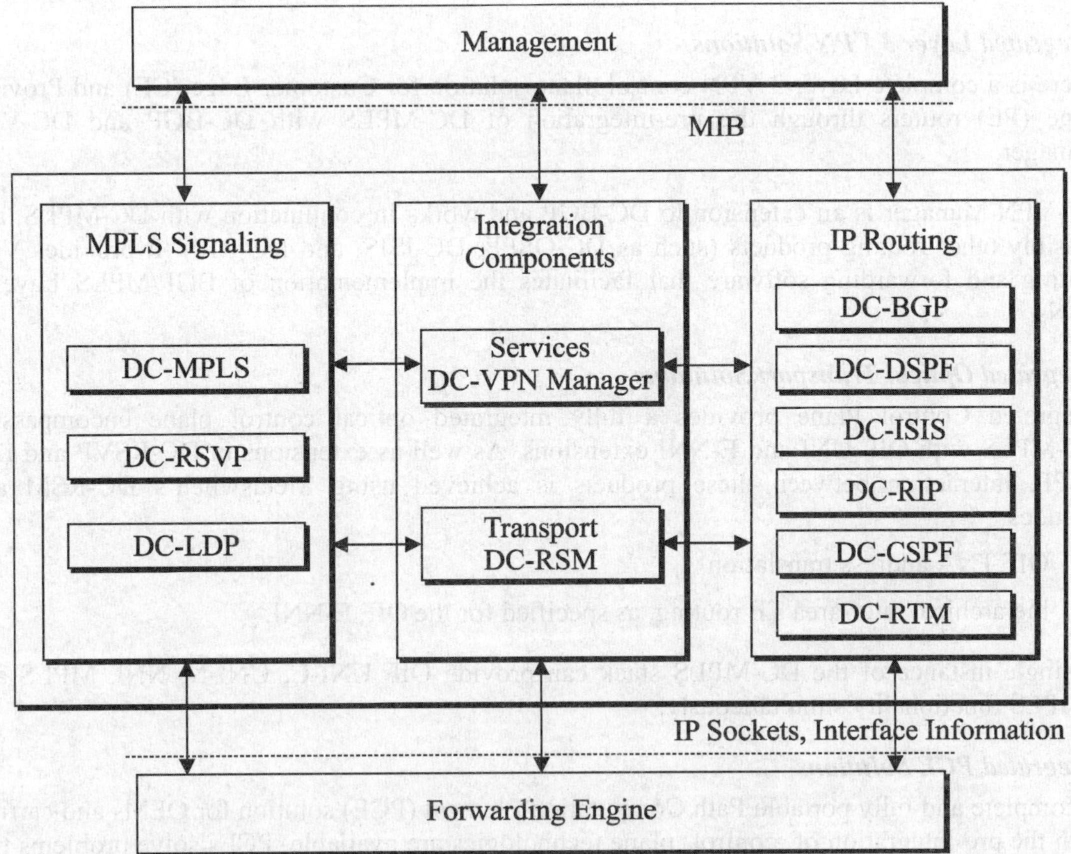

Fig. 10.13: Integrated Control Plane Architecture

The two main components of the Integrated Control Plane are the DC-MPLS and IP Routing product suites.

The Integrated Control Plane includes components that facilitate a rapid time to market for an equipment vendor building virtually any type of networking device. For the majority of vendors, custom integration effort is only required between the control plane and the switch fabric (such as packet IP, packet MPLS, TDM, WDM or other), and between the control plane and the agent managing and controlling the vendor's device.

Integrated MPLS Transport

The Route Selection Manager (DC-RSM) is used for MPLS transport. It mediates between DC-MPLS and DC-OSPF or DC-ISIS to allow automatic calculation of a route (very likely a TE-route) through the network. This includes the logic needed to find diverse paths, for example with Fast Re-Route (RFC4090) and end-to-end restoration (RFC4872). DC-RSM includes support for many packet applications, including traditional IP/MPLS, MPLS-TP and OTN.

Integrated Layer 3 VPN Solutions

There is a complete Layer 3 VPN control plane solution for Customer Edge (CE) and Provider Edge (PE) routers through the pre-integration of DC-MPLS with DC-BGP and DC-VPN Manager.

DC-VPN Manager is an extension to DC-BGP and works in conjunction with DC-MPLS, and possibly other routing products (such as DC-OSPF, DC-ISIS, and DC-RIP). It provides VPN routing and forwarding software that facilitates the implementation of BGP/MPLS Layer 3 VPNs.

Integrated Optical Transport Solutions

Integrated Control Plane provides a fully integrated optical control plane encompassing DC-MPLS with OIF UNI and E-NNI extensions. As well as extensions in DC-RSVP and DC-OSPF, interaction between these products is achieved using Metaswitch's DC-RSM and includes

- OIF TNA address translation
- hierarchical inter-area TE routing, as specified for the OIF E-NNI.

A single instance of the DC-MPLS stack can provide OIF UNI-C, UNI-N, NNI, MPLS and GMPLS functionality simultaneously.

Integrated PCE Solutions

A complete and fully portable Path Computation Element (PCE) solution for OEMs and carriers with the pre-integration of control plane technologies are available. PCEs solve problems that arise for path computation in the next-generation (G)MPLS network, and without needing to replace any existing network hardware.

10.9 IP ROUTING ARCHITECTURE

IP Routing products form part of its suite of IP Routing, MPLS, and VoIP network software products. This entire suite shares the same architecture and coding standards, so that the individual products can be readily integrated to form complete control-plane solutions.

The IP Routing products share the following architecture.

This architecture supports a wide range of applications, including highly-scaled and distributed architectures, and the use of common RTM and CSPF components provides flexible support of multiprotocol devices.

- The Routing Table Manager, DC-RTM, allows routing information to be shared between different Metaswitch network software products, third-party routing products, and static configuration. DC-RTM manages the combined forwarding table and the export of routes under the control of a policy engine.
- DC-CSPF is the Constrained Shortest Path First calculator, which provides traffic engineering support for DC-ISIS and DC-OSPF. This includes disjoint routes for protection switching and extensions for optical switching.

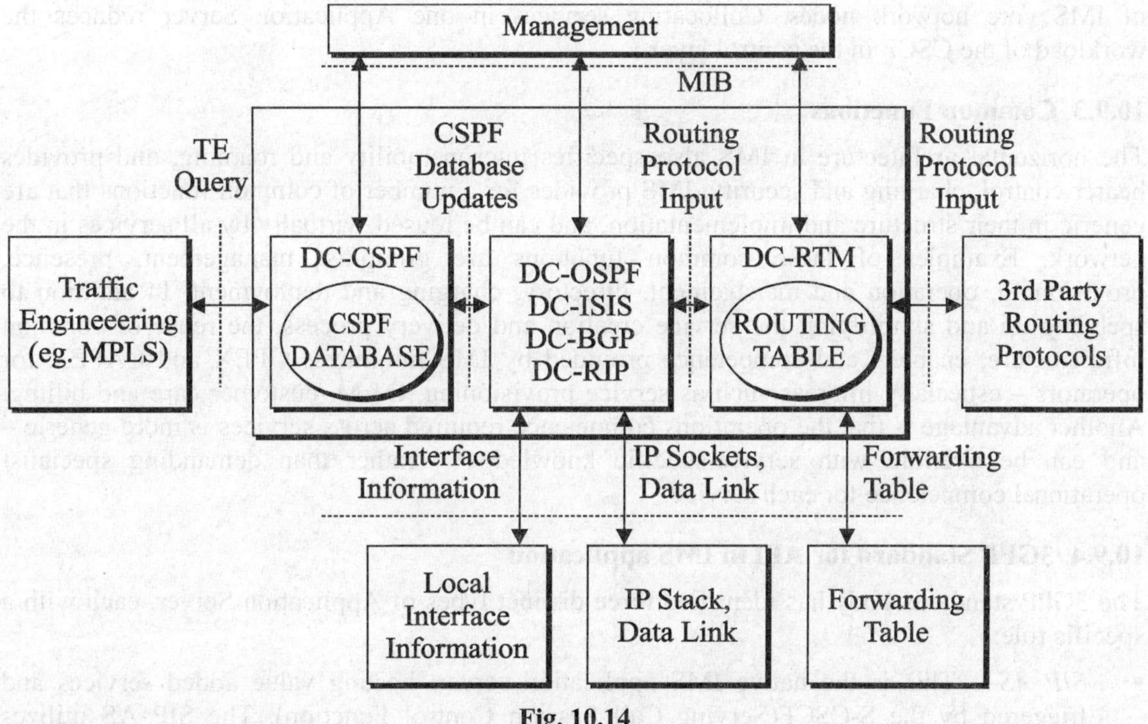

Fig. 10.14

10.9.1 Service Interoperability for Mass Market Services

Terminal-to-terminal interoperability is essential to create convenience and clarity in user's expectations of person-to-person communications services. At the same time, interoperability between operators is necessary to give users the freedom to roam between different networks. IMS enables a single inter-operator relationship to be established and built upon for each service. Today, when one user wishes to access another user's service – for example, to check status or location – routing to the other user's service is service specific, and the requesting user's operator service has to be involved. What's more, there has to be service-specific network-to-network interface, routing, service access point and security in place – and therefore a specific interoperator service agreement as well.

10.9.2 Service Creation and Delivery

In the pre-IMS world, services are specified and supported by a single logical node, or set of nodes, performing specialized features for the service. Each service appears as an island, with its own service-specific node(s). The only possible way to interface between services – for example, for service composition – is through protocols. In the absence of any common service framework, each service may have to be designed and implemented from scratch. With the introduction of the IMS architecture, many functions can be reused for fast service creation and delivery. IMS services are hosted by Application Servers, which means they are implicitly placed in the IMS application layer, and that various aspects of service control are defined. A single Application Server may host multiple services – for example, telephony and messaging. Collocation of multiple services has significant advantages, especially with regard to the loading of IMS core network nodes. Collocating services in one Application Server reduces the workload of the CSCF in the control layer.

10.9.3 Common Functions

The horizontal architecture in IMS also specifies interoperability and roaming, and provides bearer control, charging and security. IMS provides for a number of common functions that are generic in their structure and implementation, and can be reused virtually by all services in the network. Examples of these common functions are group/list management, presence, provisioning, operation and management, directory, charging and deployment. In addition to speeding up and simplifying the service creation and delivery process, the reuse of common infrastructure, enablers and competence provided by IMS minimizes OPEX and CAPEX for operators – especially in areas such as service provisioning, O&M, customer care and billing. Another advantage is that the operations competence required across services is more generic – and can be overlaid with service-specific knowledge – rather than demanding specialist operational competence for each service.

10.9.4 3GPP Standard for API in IMS application

The 3GPP standards body has identified three distinct types of Application Server, each with a specific role:

- *SIP AS*— This is the native IMS application server, hosting value added services and triggered by the S-CSCF(Serving Call Session Control Function). The SIP AS utilizes resources such as the Home SubscriberServer (HSS) or User Profile Server Function (UPSF) to store and lookup the identities and information used in calls and sessions made by subscribers.
- *OSA-SCS*— an Open Service Access - Service Capability Server interfaces with application servers using OSA/Parlay API. SCS(Session Control Server)s allow application servers to view and gain access to IMS and legacy wire line and wireless networks. The SCS allows current service subscribers, which are on legacy wire line and wireless networks, to access the new IMS applications.
- *IM-SSF*— The IM-SSF(IP Multimedia-Service Switching Function) is another gateway server. In this case, the IM-SSF provides networking between IMS and a CAMEL service environment by bridging SIP-ISC and CAP protocols. IMS framework expects the application servers to replace existing TDM and legacy applications.

10.10 MULTIMEDIA BROADCAST MULTICAST SERVICE (MBMS)

Another new service named Multimedia Broadcast Multicast Service (MBMS), defined in 3GPP as "a point-to-multipoint (PTM) downlink bearer service for IP data in the PS domain" offering high speed data rates is going to gain prominence in the NGN-Wireless integration.

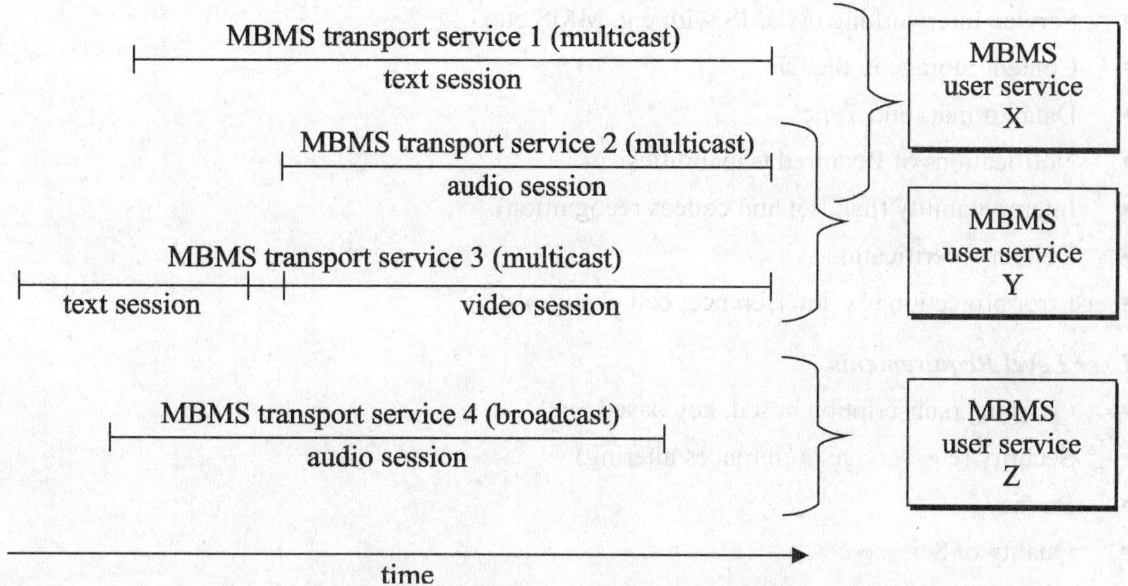

Fig. 10.15: MBMS Service Requirements

Objectives

- Offer high speed Data Rates up to 256 kbit/s
- Enhance UMTS by a more efficient Multicast and Broadcast Mode

Multicast Mode

- Subscription needed
- Authorization needed
- Received by Specific users

Broadcast Mode

- No Subscription
- No Authorization
- Received by All users within the service area
- Service must be enabled locally

An MBMS user service may have:

- More than one Broadcast or Multicast services (not a combination)

- Broadcast or Multicast services with successive media sessions
- Different QoS for each media session
- Different MBMS transport services at different times or in parallel
- Service Classes
- Service Interworking (MBMS with e.g. MMS etc)
- Content Storage in the UE
- Data Formats and Types
- Notifications of Required Capabilities
- Interoperability (handset and codecs recognition)
- Delivery Verification
- Error protection (ex. interference, cell changes etc.)

User Level Requirements

- Charging (subscription based, key based, etc)
- Security (e.g. service preferences altering)
- Privacy
- Quality of Service
- Subscription Preferences

10.10.1 MBMS Architecture

Multimedia Broadcast/Multicast Service (MBMS) is a unidirectional point to multipoint bearer service over cellular networks which are becoming increasingly important as an economic driver for mobile data services, allowing the service provider to efficiently and economically deliver multimedia information to larger populations of users without requiring disproportionate amount of network resources.

MBMS Architecture enables to achieve :

- Reduced cost per bit delivered for broadcast/multicast multimedia services
- Assured QoS for multimedia streaming services
- Ability of serving large groups simultaneously with multimedia content.
- In static PTM (point to multipoint) mode, a common channel (Forward Access Channel)) is mapped to S-CCPCH(Common Pilot Channel) and is configured and transmitted continuously
- If multiple cells in a Node B are supporting the same MBMS service on S-CCPCH, one FACH can be used to transport the service on the Iub interface to serve all cells (option)
- Algorithms for Power handling, admission, load control, congestion control, multiplexing services for optimized performance and spectral efficiency

Multipoint-to-Multipoint services

- Multiparty Video Conferencing
- Multiplayer Games
- Multiparty Messaging

MBMS Features and Services

- Efficient use of Radio & Core Network Resources
- PTM Broacasting and Multicasting Capability
- Different QoS for each Media Session
- Synchronization between media sessions
- Service Interworking (MBMS with MMS etc)
- Streaming over RTP / SRTP (protocols)

10.10.3 Major Advantages

MBMS architecture enables the efficient usage of radio-network and core-network resources with an emphasis on radio interface efficiency. As a result, MBMS offers the following benefits:

- Low cost solution since no new transmission equipment is required
- Uses existing 3G spectrum, therefore, it is ready for deployment immediately
- Lower handset costs since no new receiver is required for MBMS broadcast reception
- Same footprint as 3G, requires no new dedicated sites
- Most 3G service providers could quite easily build their Mobile TV market with MBMS to address the immediate needs with assured increase in ARPU.

10.11 MULTICAST IP ROUTING PROTOCOLS

A complete range of network software products for Core, Edge, Border and IGMP/MLD Proxy multicast routers as well as OLTs, DSLAMs, carrier Ethernet platforms and any other devices driving triple play and next generation services are available. The vendor also provides a complete suite of unicast IP routing products, which includes BGP, IS-IS(-TE), OSPF(-TE) and RIP.

Multicast IP Routing products have been architected from the ground up to support the requirements of modern networks, with scalability, redundancy, traffic engineering and many other features designed into the very first releases of this software.

Multicast Routing Common Features:

- Full mandatory protocol support (as specified in the relevant RFCs and Internet-Drafts).
- Optional enhancements to the protocol for next-generation applications.

- Support for virtual routers.
- Distribution to provide maximum scalability.
- Redundancy so that the software continues to function following hardware/software failure.
- Integration with unicast IP Routing products.
- Full MIB support.

Applications

A "multicast router" can provide a range of different functionality. Multicast IP Routing software is designed for all these applications.

Multicast Core Routers

- Single multicast domain
- Handle multicast routing protocol communication with other multicast routers

Multicast Edge Routers

- Handle IGMP and MLD requests
- Provide core router functionality

Multicast Border Routers

- Bridge multicast domains running the same, or different, internal multicast routing protocols
- Provide core or edge router functionality

Multicast Group Membership Discovery (MGMD) Proxies

- Aggregate group membership requests from downstream hosts
- Forward requests upstream to the designated multicast router
- Examples: IP DSLAMs and OLTs (Optical Line Termination)
- Drives IPTV services

Massively Scaled Routers

- Smart cache technology
- Distributed architecture

Redundant Systems-High Availability Framework, State replication between instances

Architecture

- Multicast IP Routing products share a common architecture to facilitate the integration of the family members

10.12 MPLS AND GMPLS

Since its introduction in the late 1990s, Multi-Protocol Label Switching (MPLS) has evolved into a hugely successful and flexible networking technology.

In its original RFC 3031 guise, the fundamental MPLS concept was to switch packets based upon looking up a label in the packet header. This label is swapped with a different label suitable for the next hop towards the packet's destination. In this form it has been widely deployed on routers and switches, under the IP/MPLS monitor.

Subsequently, Generalized MPLS (GMPLS) expanded the concept of a label to include implicit attributes of the flow, such as wavelength or timeslot. This led to the adoption of GMPLS for circuit as well as packet switching, and it is widely deployed in such roles today.

MPLS and GMPLS naturally allow layering through the process of label stacking. This leads to outer labels being used for transport functions and inner labels to define the service. Thus, the real power of MPLS and GMPLS is the ability to layer any service over any transport, and to combine multiple services over a common transport, while providing appropriate QoS for each service.

MPLS transport provides options for traffic engineering, guaranteed QoS, and fast protection and restoration. It can be used for a variety of technologies including

- Packet transport, including the new MPLS Transport Profile (MPLS-TP) that brings the QoS and OAM capabilities usually associated with optical transport to less expensive packet based equipment
- TDM and WDM transport; this includes the next-generation transports of the Optical Transport Network (OTN), where circuit and packet traffic can be carried efficiently on the same device.

MPLS services include

- Packet IP traffic, including Layer 3 VPNs (a very popular carrier offering)
- Packet Layer 2 traffic (for example the booming Carrier Ethernet market)
- Pseudowires that can carry packet or circuit traffic (which is proving vital for mobile backhaul).

Control Plane

Whilst the underlying MPLS and GMPLS switching operations typically make use of dedicated switching hardware, a control plane is used to program this hardware and to perform a wide range of functions. The control plane is the most widely deployed and most flexible control plane available.

VOIP and IMS

Voice over IP, or more generally multimedia over IP, is the ability to set up interactive messaging, telephony and video conferencing over an IP network. IP Multimedia Subsystem (IMS) is next generation network architecture designed to deliver integrated multimedia services, network convergence, and create an open, standards-based network. The protocols include,

- Session Initiation Protocol (SIP)
- Media Gateway Control Protocol (MGCP)
- MEGACO/H.248
- Diameter

Applications

DC-SIP, DC-Megaco/H.248, DC-MGCP and DC-Diameter have been designed from the outset as the high-performance, scalable solution for demanding applications. DC-SIP, DC-Megaco/H.248 and DC-Diameter are also fully IPv6 compliant.

IMS Functions

- Application Servers
- P/I/S-CSCF
- IBCF
- BGF/I-BGF
- MRFC, MGFC, MRFP, MGF
- Charging functions

Embedded End-Points

- Soft phones
- Mobile phones
- IADs
- Residential Gateways

Gateways between Heterogeneous Networks

- Trunking gateways
- Radio base station
- Media Gateways

Intelligent Network Servers

- Softswitches
- Media Gateway Controllers
- Universal Messaging Systems
- Location Servers
- IP PBXs
- Application Servers

Multimedia Broadcast and Multicast Service

IP Multicast in the UMTS standard has some drawbacks as listed below,

- 1 GTP-Tunnel per Multicast Group Member
- Packet Duplication (Waste of Radio Resources)
- Limited Radio Transmission Efficiency

To overcome these following solution is adopted:

- 1 GTP-Tunnel per Multicast Flow
- Less Amount of Data in the Network
- Efficient Use of Radio Resources

10.13 CHALLENGES AHEAD

Migration of mobile networks to NGN capable of MMS delivery is driven by the enhanced capability of 3G UMTS access networks in the subsequent "releases" of 3GPP beyond 7 and 8 and standardization process is still more elaborate. Speed of this migration will depend on widespread acceptance and appropriation of new services by end-users; but also on the maturity of the newly introduced technologies.There are few challenges to all the players in this transition during the implementation of NGN. Network equipment vendors must provide cost-effective solutions based on a smooth network migration in a competitive way. Network operators have to master the roll-out of new technologies in a controlled and phased mannerand have to introduce a more acceptable pricing policy. Service designers require to develop attractive contents and services needed by the largest subscriber base at affordable cost.

Despite the emergence of new fixed and wireless communication technologies, like the WiFi, WiMAX and xDSL, with high bandwidth rates and seamless conformity to the IP, the capability of the new UMTS technology to deliver its services in a "measurable" way and with user-defined QoS has been identified as the main reason for the success of the new multimedia Wishing to further exploit users arisen awareness about new multimedia communication services and expand possibilities for new profits in the new fixed and wireless network domains, the industry has set a new target, that of creating "ubiquity" in service delivery along with "seamlessness" in keeping steady the "user experience" in terms of service tariffing and QoS satisfaction by fully exploiting the capabilities of NGN and IMS.

Review Points

Challenges

Developing a successful multimedia system has its own challenges like, need for a lot of space to store and very high bandwidth to transmit, have tight timing constraints. Automatically analyzing, indexing and organizing information in audio, image and video is much harder than from text. Multimedia involves many different research areas and needs more complex and more efficient algorithms and hardware platforms.

Enabling Techniques

Some basic enabling techniques required are -Multimedia data representation and compression - Multimedia data processing and analysis-Multimedia database, indexing and retrieval. There are different issues when we transmit video and audio through packet network viz.,Quality of service, Synchronization, Error and congestion control and session setup and book keeping.

Multimedia Communication System Architecture

The system should have the,- the ability to manage dynamically the achieved QoS of each service component, -the possibility for users to select some resources that best meet their needs, -the possibility to interact with another user whose equipment has differing characteristics, the communications network must allow any user to select the service components he/she wants, - the possibility for users to join in or withdraw from a communication session according to certain policies, such as agreement of all interacting partners before admitting a new user and the possibility to set such quality of service parameters as the synchronization tolerance between the service components, the echo sensitivity, the burst sensitivity, and so on

Digitization of Information

Digitizing Images, Graphics, Digitized Documents, Digitized Pictures are the prerequisite for further to proceed for transmission of MM.

Multimedia Protocols

Multimedia protocol specifications include, -QoS (Quality of Service) requirements of multimedia streams, -Throughput (the data transmission rate, data compression,several Mbps), - Transfer Delay ie.,time between the production of data at the source and its presentation at the sink ,- Jitter ie., variance of the transfer delay and use of buffers to reduce jitter,-Error Rates viz., loss of data in a continuous data transfer.

Protocols

Signaling— SIP/SDP (IETF), H.323 (ITU-T)

Media— RTP (IETF's, adopted by ITU-T),

Transport— UDP, TCP, (Stream Control Transmission Protocol – RFC 2960) TRIP - Telephony Routing over IP – ` RSVP - Resource Reservation Setup Protocol and` COPS - Common Open Policy Service.

Multimedia Networking Applications

There are three classes of MM applications viz.,

1) Streaming stored audio and video
2) Streaming live audio and video and
3) Real-time interactive audio and video

Interactive, Real-Time Multimedia applications include -IP telephony, video conference, distributed interactive games etc. The end-end delay requirements are audio: < 150 msec good, < 400 msec, application-level (packetization) and network delays ,higher delays noticeable, impair interactivity.

IP Multimedia Sub System (IMS)

The IP-Multimedia Subsystem (IMS) defines the functional architecture for a managed IP-based network. It aims to provide a means for carriers to create an open, standards-based network that delivers integrated multimedia services. IMS is the basic mechanisms of multimedia communication over wireless networks using NGN (Next Generation Network) technology. Aspects of the IMS architecture, like interworking between mobile/wireless and fixed networks as well as the evolution of the SIP protocol are standardized by the 3GPP, the ETSI-TISPAN and the IETF bodies. IMS allows realizations of versatile, mixed-technology, call schemes, over native packet switched links. Potentially, every packet switched network is compatible with the IMS architecture and can be integrated within it through a number of logical interfaces implementing different manifestations of the SIP protocol.

IMS Architecture

IMS is one of 3GPP's greatest success stories. Originally designed to evolve UMTS networks to deliver Internet Protocol multimedia to mobile users, IMS has become the core component within 3G, cable TV and next generation fixed telecoms networks. IMS specification began in 3GPP Release 5 as part of the core network evolution from circuit-switching to packet-switching and was refined by subsequent Releases 6 and 7. Initially, IMS was an all-IP system designed to assist mobile operators deliver next generation interactive and interoperable services, cost-effectively, over an architecture providing the flexibility of the Internet. Standardisers now base their core network evolution on Common IMS.

Common Functions of IMS

The architecture in IMS also specifies interoperability and roaming, and provides bearer control, charging and security. IMS provides for a number of common functions that are generic in their structure and implementation, and can be reused virtually by all services in the network. Examples of these common functions are group/list management, presence, provisioning, operation and management, directory, charging and deployment. In areas such as service provisioning, O&M, customer care and billing IMS gives a leverage.

Multimedia Broadcast Multicast Service (MBMS)

Another new service is Multimedia Broadcast Multicast Service (MBMS), defined in 3GPP as "a point-to-multipoint (PTM) downlink bearer service for IP data in the PS domain" offering high speed data rates. The objectives are, offer high speed Data Rates up to 256 kbit/s and enhance UMTS by a more efficient Multicast and Broadcast Mode. Multicast Mode requires subscription, and authorization and can be received by specific users only, while Broadcast Mode, no Subscription nor authorization is needed and received by all users. An MBMS user service may have, more than one Broadcast or Multicast services (not a combination), different QoS for each media session, different MBMS transport services at different times or in parallel,

9 Wireless Data Networks and Bandwidth Management

9.1 INTRODUCTION

Although it is true that most 3G systems are now offering throughputs of about 1 Mbps—which is comparable to what many users experience with a basic DSL or cable- modem service—the overall capacity of wireless systems is generally lower than it is with wireline systems. This is especially true when wireless is compared to optical fiber, which some operators in developed countries (such as the U.S.) are now deploying to people's homes. With wireline operators looking to provide 50 to 100 Mbps to either people's homes or businesses via next-generation cable-modem services, very high- speed DSL (VDSL) or fiber—especially for services such as high-definition IP Television (IPTV)—the question becomes, "Is it possible to match these rates using wireless approaches?" The answer is yes from a purely technical perspective, but it is no from a practical point of view. It is only possible to achieve these rates by using large amounts of spectrum, generally more than what is available for current 3G systems, and by using relatively small cell sizes. Otherwise, it simply will not be possible to deliver the hundreds of gigabytes per month that users will eventually be consuming over their broadband connections with wide-area wireless networks. Consider today's high definition (HD) television content that demands 6 to 9 Mbps of continuous connectivity, wherein one subscriber could essentially consume the entire capacity of a WiMAX or HSPA cell sector.

Thus, operators are both deploying and considering multiple approaches for managing bandwidth. These include:

- *More spectrum*— Spectrum correlates directly to capacity, and more spectrum is becoming available globally for mobile broadband.
- *Increased spectral efficiency*— Newer technologies are spectrally more efficient, meanir greater throughput in the same amount of spectrum.
- *More cell sites*— Smaller cell sizes result in more capacity per subscriber.
- *Femtocells*— Femto cells can significantly offload the macro network. Pricing can tocell encourage users to move high-bandwidth activities (e.g., movie downloads connections.
- *Wi-Fi*— Wi-Fi networks offer another means of offloading heavy traffic.
- *Off-peak hours*— Operators can offer lower rates or perhaps fewer res on large data transfers that occur at off-peak hours such as overnight.

- *Quality of service*— By prioritizing traffic, large downloads can occur with lower priority, thus not affecting other active users.

It will take a creative blend of all of the above as well as other measures to make the mobile broadband market successful and to enable it to exist as a complementary solution to wired broadband.

3GPP technologies clearly address proven market needs; hence their overwhelming success. The 3GPP roadmap, which anticipates continual performance and capacity improvements, provides the technical means to deliver on proven business models. As the applications for mobile broadband continue to expand, HSPA, HSPA+, LTE and LTE-Advanced will continue to provide a competitive platform for tomorrow's new business opportunities.

Table 9.1 summarizes the strengths and weaknesses of wireless versus wireline broadband approaches

Table 9.1: Strengths and Weakness of Broadband Approaches

	Strength	*Weakness*
Mobile broadband (EDGE, HSPA, LTE)	▪ Constant connectivity ▪ Broadband capability across extremely wide areas ▪ Good access solution for areas lacking wireline infrastructure ▪ Capacity enhancement via FMC ▪ Excellent voice communications	▪ Lower capacity than wireline approaches ▪ Inability to serve high-bandwidth applications such as IP TV
Wireline broadband (e.g., DSL, DOCSIS, FTTH)	▪ High-capacity broadband at very high data rates ▪ Evolution to extremely high throughput rates	▪ Expensive to deploy new networks, especially in developing economies lacking infrastructure

9.2 WIRELESS DATA MARKET

By May 2009, more than 3.7 billion subscribers were using GSM-HSPA—approaching an astonishing 50 percent of the world's total 6.8 billion population. By the end of 2013, the global wireless market is expected to include more than 2 billion subscribers, of which 1.6 billion Chse 3GPP technologies, representing 80% market share. In 2007, 3G Americas President lifesurson stated, "This level of wireless technology growth exceeds that of almost all other global anging innovations." This growth continues. Clearly, GSM-HSPA has established now conance. Although voice still constitutes most cellular traffic, wireless data worldwide wireless da a significant percentage of revenue per user (ARPU). In the United States, 2009. y more than 26 percent of ARPU, and is projected to hit 30% by the end of

This section exa the rapid growth o ds and deployment, and then provides market data that demonstrates ata.

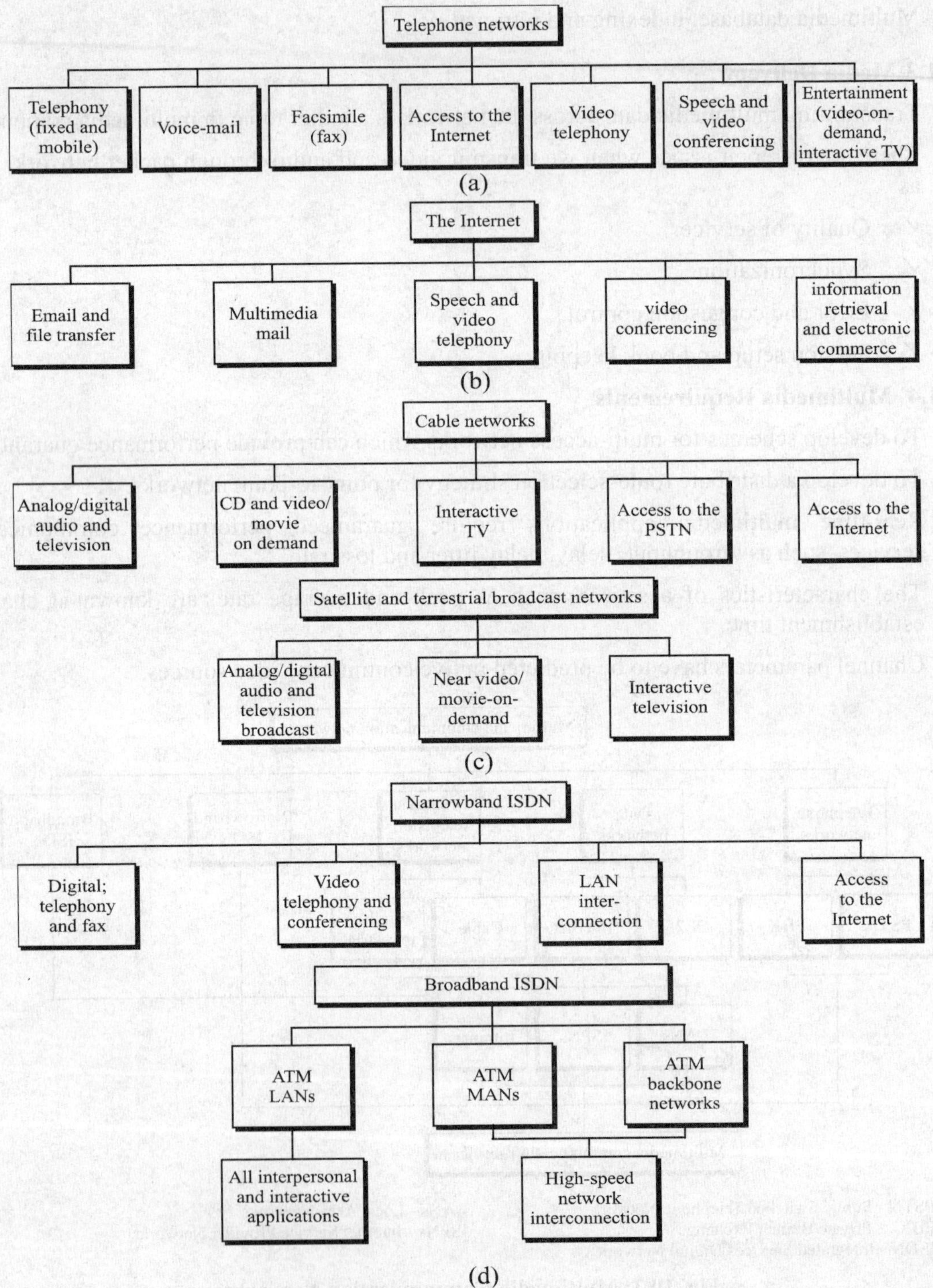

Fig. 10.4: Multimedia Communication Networks and their Services

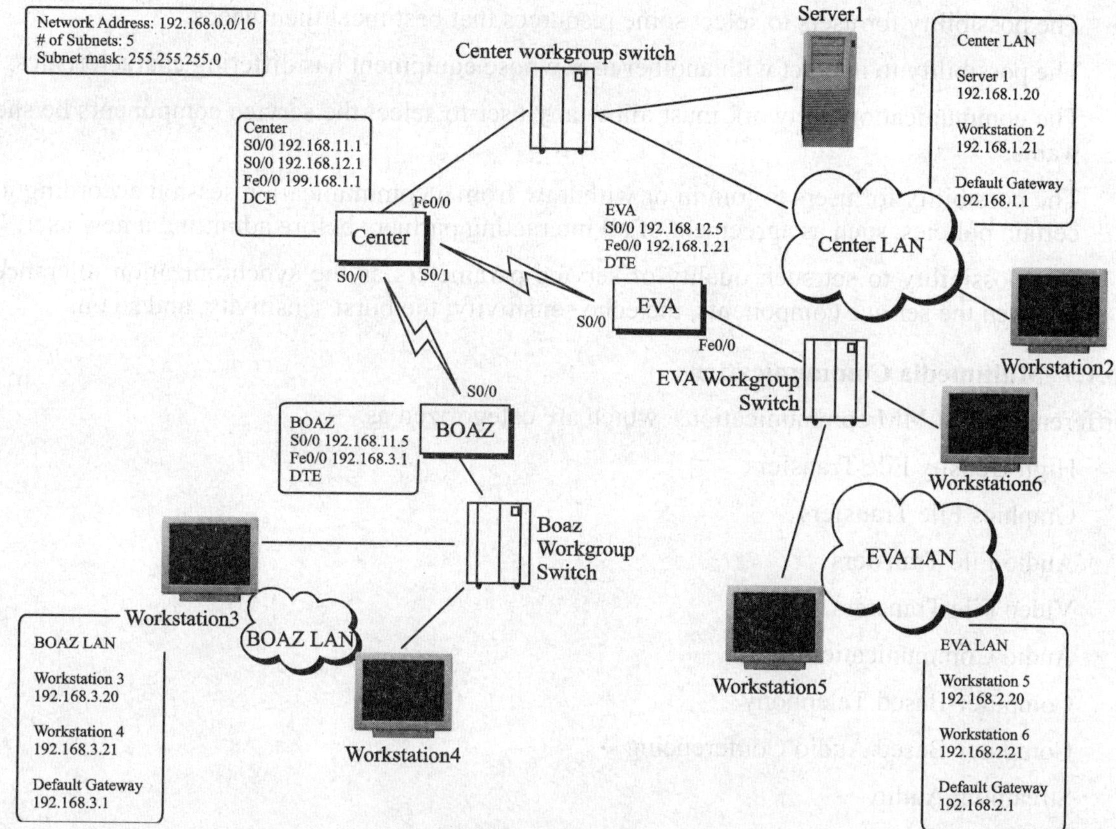

Fig. 10.5: Multimedia System

10.1.5 Multimedia Communication System

There are different methods adopted in multimedia Communication System such as

- LAN Access Method
- Routing
- Frame and Packet Structures
- Packet Discrimination
- Identify packets that require special handling.
- Be capable of accommodating those special requirements.
- Bandwidth Requirement, Reservation and Conservation
- High bandwidth and low latency

10.1.6 Multimedia Communication System Architecture

The MM system architecture must be having,

- The ability to manage dynamically the achieved QoS of each service component

10.3.2 Protocols-Over View

- *Signaling*— SIP/SDP (IETF), H.323 (ITU-T) SIP is adopted by 3GPP;
- *Media*— RTP (IETF's, adopted by ITU-T)
- *Transport*— UDP, TCP, (Stream Control)
- *Transmission Protocol*– RFC 2960)
- *Supporting protocols*— DNS
- *TRIP*— Telephony Routing over IP –discovery and exchange of IP, telephony gateway routing tables between providers
- *RSVP*— Resource Reservation Setup Protocol
- *COPS* —Common Open Policy Service- protocol for supporting policy control over QoS
- *Diameter*— Authentication, Accounting, Authorization
- RTP/RTCP, RTSP, and RSVP are general Multimedia protocols

A general view of the real-time protocols and their major functions are,

The protocols and their application field…

- *stream description*— SDP, SMIL... function: describe the session and content
- *stream control*— RTSP function: remote control the session
- *media transport*— RTP function: send data and metadata
- *resource reservation*— RSVP function: DiffServ

There protocols make sure the communication path offers appropriate guaranties otherwise Best-Effort transmissions may not be successful.

10.3.3 Session Initiation Protocol (SIP)

- SIP is end-to-end, client-server session signaling protocol
- SIP's primarily provide presence and mobility
- Protocol primitives: Session setup, termination, changes

Arbitrary services built on top of SIP, e.g.:

- ✓ Redirect calls from unknown callers to secretary
- ✓ Reply with a webpage if unavailable
- ✓ Send a JPEG on invitation

Features

- Textual encoding (telnet, tcpdump compatible)

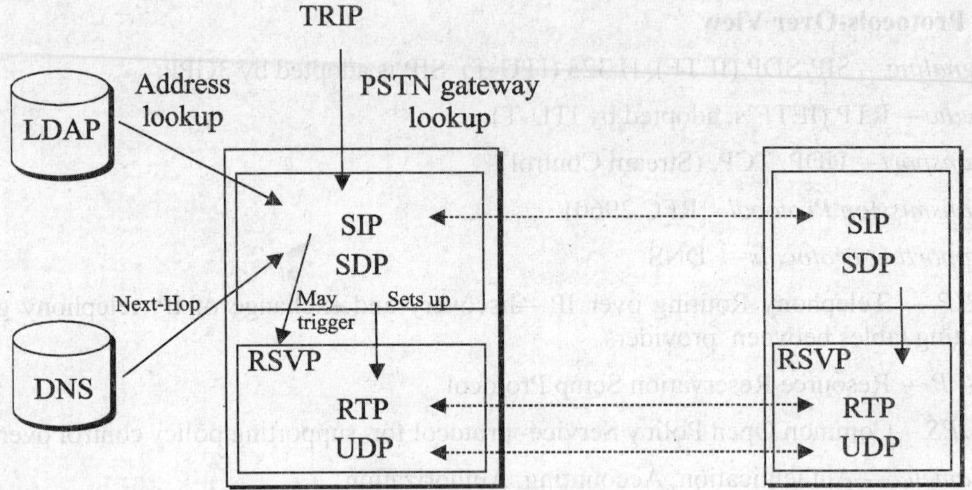

Fig. 10.9: SIP Overview

SIP - General Purpose

Presence Protocol

- SIP is not limited to Internet telephony
- SIP establishes user presence
- SIP messages can convey arbitrary signaling payload: session description, instant messages, JPEGs, any MIME types
- Suitable for applications having a notion of session distributed virtual reality systems, network games, video conferencing, etc.
- Applications may leverage SIP infrastructure (Call Processing, User Location, Authentication)

Instant Messaging and Presence

- SIP for Appliances, SIP is not Transport Protocol or QoS Reservation Protocol or Gateway Control Protocol
- Some argue it may be used for accessing IP-enabled appliances ...
- It does NOT dictate anything such as

  product features and services (color of your phone and distinctive ringing melodies, number of simultaneous calls your phone can handle, don't disturb feature, ...) and network configuration

10.3.4 Session Description Protocol (SDP)

- Used to specify client capabilities
- Example (client can support MPEG-1 video codec, and MP3 codecs)
- Convey sufficient information to enable participation in a multimedia session

A full range of high-function portable Unicast IP Routing software products, including BGP, IS-IS(-TE), OSPF(-TE) and RIP, with options available for both IPv4 and IPv6 networks are provided by the vendor. The vendor also provides a compatible range of Multicast IP Routing software products, including PIM and IGMP/MLD.

10.8.1 Applications

These IP Routing network software products have been designed from the outset to support the most demanding applications.

- Massively Scaled Routers
  - ✓ Incremental ....
  - ✓ Smart cache technology
  - ✓ Distributed architecture
- Redundant Systems
  - ✓ High Availability Framework
  - ✓ State replication between instances
- Edge Routers
  - ✓ BGP/MPLS VPN and Virtual Routers
- Traffic Engineering and QoS
  - ✓ TE extensions
  - ✓ Close MPLS integration
- Optical Networks
  - ✓ Complex constrained routing

Integrated Solutions

The individual products are also available pre-integrated with other products as Integrated Control Plane Solutions, and flexible Component Integration with third-party software allowing rapid development of complete solutions.

IP Version 6

All the products are available with IP version 6 implementation options.

10.8.2 Architecture

IP Routing products share a common architecture to facilitate the integration of the family members. Integration: The N-BASE dramatically reduces our customers' integration effort and time. All network software products (including packet and optical MPLS, IP routing, MGCP/Megaco/H.248, SIP, Diameter, Session Border Controller (SBC), ATM and SNA) are written to the N-BASE APIs, and only ever access local system resources via the N-BASE APIs. For access to local system resources such as the management plane or data plane, the N-BASE provides well-documented, stable APIs (known as "stubs"). These are typically customizable macro interfaces to local system services and use asynchronous, message-based interfaces between the components. This design enables the products to be readily integrated with any operating system and underlying hardware, as well as custom user applications, third-party components, and legacy systems.

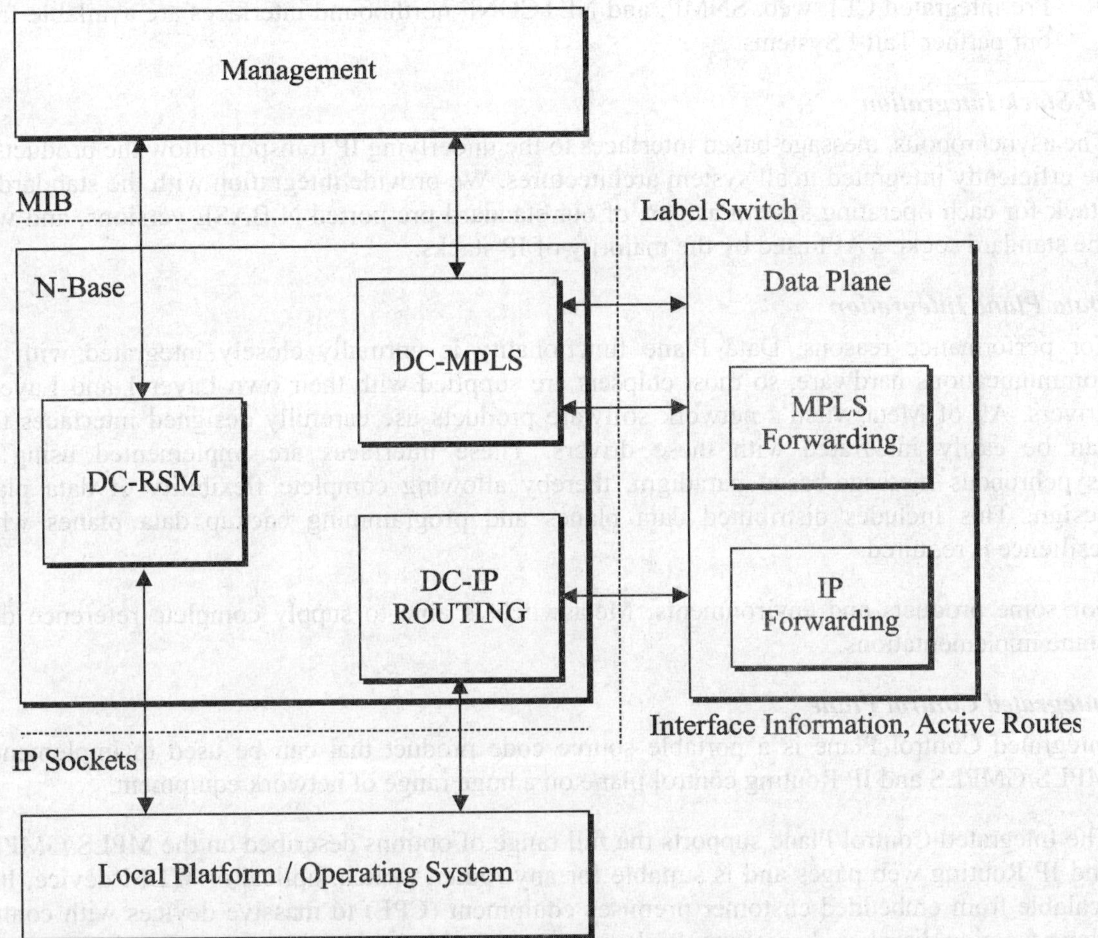

Fig. 10.12: IP Routing Architecture

The above diagram illustrates some of integrated control plane products (DC-RSM, DC-MPLS, and DC-IP Routing) communicating via N-BASE "stubs" (MIB, IP Sockets, Label Switch, Interface Information, and Active Routes) with local system resources (the Management plane, the native IP stack in the Operating System, and Data Plane components).

Management Integration

All network software products use a common interface for management and configuration. This can easily be mapped onto a wide range of management tools and has been used by our customers for integration with CLI, GUI and SMNP management suites.

Fully integrated management solutions:

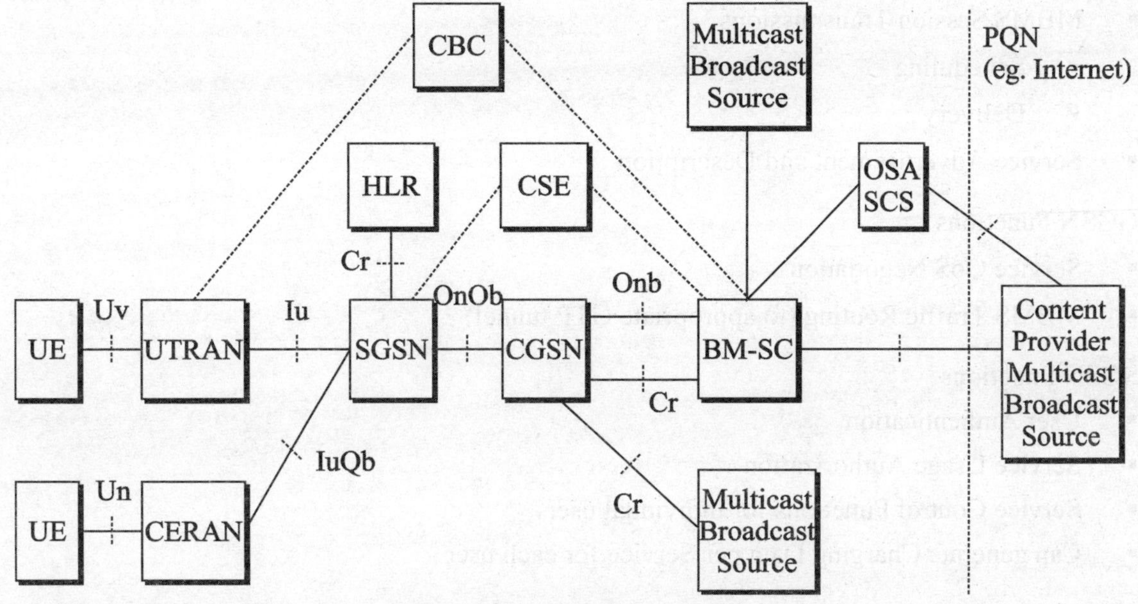

Fig. 10.16: MBMS Architecture

UMTS Main Elements

CN – Core Network

- GGSN (Gateway GPRS Support Node)
- SGSN (Serving GPRS Support Node)

UTRAN – UMTS Terrestial Radio Access Network

- RNC (Radio Network Controller)
- Node-B (Base Stations)

UE – User Equipment

- Terminals (3G mobile phones)

NEW MBMS Element

- BM-SC (Broadcast Multicast Service Center)

BM-SC Functions

- Content Provider Charging (per transmitted data, per QoS, etc)
- MBMS Transport
  - ✓ Service Parameters (e.g. QoS, MBMS service area)
  - ✓ Initiate/Terminate bearer resources
- Authorization and Initiation of MBMS services

- MBMS Session Transmissions
  - ✓ Scheduling
  - ✓ Delivery
- Service Advertisement and Description

GGSN Functions

- Service QoS Negotiation
- MBMS Traffic Routing (to appropriate GTP tunnel)

SGSN Functions

- User Authentication
- Service Usage Authorization
- Service Control Functions for individual users
- Can generate Charging Data per Service for each user

UTRAN Functions

- Delivery of MBMS Data to Designated Service Area
- Support Initiation/Termination of MBMS Transmissions by the CN
- Support intra-RNC, inter-RNC mobility of MBMS receivers
- Transmission of MBMS announcements

UE Functions

- Activation/Deactivation of MBMS Data Reception
- Reception of MBMS Data without Explicit User Request
- Reception of MBMS Service Announcements while Active or Idle
- Support Security Operations

10.10.2 Potential Services in MBMS

Improvement of existing 2G/3G services is achieved by the introduction of MBMS

- Real-Time services (e.g. emergency announcements)
- Location-Based services (e.g. multimedia tourist information)
- Announcement services (e.g. commercial offers, electronic tickets)

Mobile Broadcast services

- Mobile TV
- Visual Radio (FM with other multimedia services)
- Cross Referencing services (e.g. between Mobile TV, Visual Radio)
- Interactive TV/Radio (e.g. voting what to see/listen next)

interoperability (handset and codecs recognition), delivery verification and error protection (ex. interference, cell changes etc.) within the service area.

MBMS Architecture

Multimedia Broadcast/Multicast Service (MBMS) is a unidirectional point to multipoint bearer service over cellular networks which are becoming increasingly important as an economic driver for mobile data services, allowing the service provider to efficiently and economically deliver multimedia information to larger populations of users without requiring disproportionate amount of network resources. MBMS Architecture enables to achieve, reduced cost per bit delivered for broadcast/multicast, assured QoS for multimedia streaming services and ability of serving large groups simultaneously with multimedia content. MBMS architecture enables the efficient usage of radio-network and core-network resources with an emphasis on radio interface efficiency. MBMS offers Low cost solution since no new transmission equipment is required and uses existing 3G spectrum, therefore, it is ready for deployment immediately.

MPLS and GMPLS

Multi-Protocol Label Switching (MPLS) has evolved into a hugely successful and flexible networking technology and the fundamental MPLS concept was to switch packets based upon looking up a label in the packet header. In this form it has been widely deployed on routers and switches, under the IP/MPLS moniter. Generalized MPLS (GMPLS) expanded the concept of a label to include implicit attributes of the flow, such as wavelength or timeslot. This led to the adoption of GMPLS for circuit as well as packet switching, and it is widely deployed in such roles today. MPLS and GMPLS naturally allow layering through the process of label stacking and the real power of MPLS and GMPLS is the ability to layer any service over any transport, and to combine multiple services over a common transport, while providing appropriate QoS for each service.

Review Questions

1. What are the basic enabling technique for MM communication?
2. List the requirements for MM delivery and MM communication system.
3. What are the desired capability of MM communication system?
4. Write a note on digitization of information of various types.
5. What are different scanning principles followed and explain their methods.
6. What is aspect ratio? Give the figures for NTSC & PAL system.
7. Write note on Computer Graphics Array.
8. How are colour images obtained?
9. What is frame refresh rate? What are the properties of colour and how they are illustrated in MM?
10. Write about digitization format SIF, CIF and QCIF. Mention their spatial resolution.
11. Name different protocols used in MM communication.

12. Write note on SIP and SDP protocols.
13. Draw the schematic for the general protocol architecture for multimedia communication and explain the functions of each block.
14. Write note on digital video format.
15. What is IMS? Explain the role of IMS in MM communication with suitable diagram.
16. Explain the functions of application plane and control plane in IMS architecture.
17. What are the main functions of Call Session Control in IMS?
18. Describe the integration plane in IP network.
19. What is MBMS? Explain the main features.
20. Draw the architecture of MBMS and describe the functions of the major components.
21. List out different services offered in MBMS and their features.
22. Write note on MPLS and GMPLS with specific reference to its main features.

11 IEEE 802 Wireless Standards

11.1 INTRODUCTION

The IEEE 802 Standard comprises a family of networking standards that cover the physical layer specifications of technologies from Ethernet to wireless. IEEE 802 is subdivided into 22 parts that cover the physical and data-link aspects of networking. The better known specifications (as in table below) include 802.3 Ethernet, 802.11 Wi-Fi, 802.15 Bluetooth/ZigBee, and 802.16.

All the 802.11 specifications use the Ethernet protocol and Carrier Sense Multiple Access with Collision Avoidance (CSMA/CA) for path sharing. The original modulation used in 802.11 was phase-shift keying (PSK). However, other schemes, such as complementary code keying (CCK), are used in some of the newer specifications. The newer modulation methods provide higher data speed and reduced vulnerability to interference.

Table 11.1: IEEE 802 Specification Listing

802	*Overview*	*Basics of physical and logical networking concepts*
802.1	Bridging	LAN/MAN bridging and management. Covers management and the lower sub-layers of OSI Layer 2, including MAC-based bridging (Media Access Control), virtual LANs and port-based access control.
802.2	Logical Link	Commonly referred to as the LLC or Logical Link Control specification. The LLC is the top sub-layer in the data-link layer, OSI Layer 2. Interfaces with the network Layer 3.
802.3	Ethernet	"Grandaddy" of the 802 specifications. Provides asynchronous networking using "carrier sense, multiple access with collision detect" (CSMA/CD) over coax, twisted-pair copper, and fiber media. Current speeds range from 10 Mbps to 10 Gbps. Click for a list of the "hot" 802.3 technologies.
802.4	Token Bus	Disbanded
802.5	Token Ring	The original token-passing standard for twisted-pair, shielded copper cables. Supports copper and fiber cabling from 4 Mbps to 100 Mbps. Often called "IBM Token-Ring."
802.6	Distributed queue dual bus (DQDB)	"Superseded **Revision of 802.1D-1990 edition (ISO/IEC 10038). 802.1D incorporates P802.1p and P802.12e. It also incorporates and supersedes published standards 802.1j and 802.6k. Superseded by 802.1D-2004." (See IEEE status page.)

802	Overview	Basics of physical and logical networking concepts
802.7	Broadband LAN Practices	Withdrawn Standard. Withdrawn Date: Feb 07, 2003. No longer endorsed by the IEEE. (See IEEE status page.)
802.8	Fiber Optic Practices	Withdrawn PAR. Standards project no longer endorsed by the IEEE. (See IEEE status page.)
802.9	Integrated Services LAN	Withdrawn PAR. Standards project no longer endorsed by the IEEE. (See IEEE status page.)
802.10	Interoperable LAN security	Superseded **Contains: IEEE Std 802.10b-1992. (See IEEE status page.)
802.11	Wi-Fi	Wireless LAN Media Access Control and Physical Layer specification. 802.11a,b,g,etc. are amendments to the original 802.11 standard. Products that implement 802.11 standards must pass tests and are referred to as "Wi-Fi certified."
802.11a		▪ Specifies a PHY that operates in the 5 GHz U-NII band in the US - initially 5.15-5.35 AND 5.725-5.85 - since expanded to additional frequencies ▪ Uses Orthogonal Frequency-Division Multiplexing ▪ Enhanced data speed to 54 Mbps ▪ Ratified after 802.11b
802.11b		▪ Enhancement to 802.11 that added higher data rate modes to the DSSS (Direct Sequence Spread Spectrum) already defined in the original 802.11 standard ▪ Boosted data speed to 11 Mbps ▪ 22 MHz Bandwidth yields 3 non-overlaping channels in the frequency range of 2.400 GHz to 2.4835 GHz ▪ Beacons at 1 Mbps, falls back to 5.5, 2, or 1 Mbps from 11 Mbps max.
802.11d		▪ Enhancement to 802.11a and 802.11b that allows for global roaming ▪ Particulars can be set at Media Access Control (MAC) layer
802.11e		▪ Enhancement to 802.11 that includes quality of service (QoS) features ▪ Facilitates prioritization of data, voice, and video transmissions
802.11g		▪ Extends the maximum data rate of WLAN devices that operate in the 2.4 GHz band, in a fashion that permits interoperation with 802.11b devices ▪ Uses OFDM Modulation (Orthogonal FDM) ▪ Operates at up to 54 megabits per second (Mbps), with fall-back speeds that include the "b" speeds

802	*Overview*	*Basics of physical and logical networking concepts*
802.11h		▪ Enhancement to 802.11a that resolves interference issues ▪ Dynamic frequency selection (DFS) ▪ Transmit power control (TPC)
802.11i		▪ Enhancement to 802.11 that offers additional security for WLAN applications ▪ Defines more robust encryption, authentication, and key exchange, as well as options for key caching and pre-authentication
802.11j		▪ Japanese regulatory extensions to 802.11a specification ▪ Frequency range 4.9 GHz to 5.0 GHz
802.11k		▪ Radio resource measurements for networks using 802.11 family specifications
802.11m		▪ Maintenance of 802.11 family specifications ▪ Corrections and amendments to existing documentation
802.11n		▪ Higher-speed standards -- under development ▪ Several competing and non-compatible technologies; often called "pre-n" ▪ Top speeds claimed of 108, 240, and 350+ MHz ▪ Competing proposals come from the groups, EWC, TGn Sync, and WWiSE and are all variations based on MIMO (multiple input, multiple output)
802.11x		▪ Mis-used "generic" term for 802.11 family specifications
802.12	Demand Priority	Increases Ethernet data rate to 100 Mbps by controlling media utilization.
802.13	Not used	Not used
802.14	Cable modems	Withdrawn PAR. Standards project no longer endorsed by the IEEE.
802.15	Wireless Personal Area Networks	Communications specification that was approved in early 2002 by the IEEE for wireless personal area networks (WPANs).
802.15.1	Bluetooth	Short range (10m) wireless technology for cordless mouse, keyboard, and hands-free headset at 2.4 GHz.
802.15.3 wa	UWB	Short range, high-bandwidth "ultra wideband" link
802.15.4	ZigBee	Short range wireless sensor networks
802.15.5	Mesh Network	▪ Extension of network coverage without increasing the transmit power or the receiver sensitivity ▪ Enhanced reliability via route redundancy ▪ Easier network configuration - Better device battery life

802	Overview	Basics of physical and logical networking concepts
802.16	Wireless Metropolitan Area Networks	This family of standards covers Fixed and Mobile Broadband Wireless Access methods used to create Wireless Metropolitan Area Networks (WMANs.) Connects Base Stations to the Internet using OFDM in unlicensed (900 MHz, 2.4, 5.8 GHz) or licensed (700 MHz, 2.5 – 3.6 GHz) frequency bands. Products that implement 802.16 standards can undergo WiMAX certification testing.
802.17	Resilient Packet Ring	IEEE working group description
802.18	Radio Regulatory TAG	IEEE 802.18 standards committee
802.19	Coexistence	IEEE 802.19 Coexistence Technical Advisory Group
802.20	Mobile Broadband Wireless Access	IEEE 802.20 mission and project scope
802.21	Media Independent Handoff	IEEE 802.21 mission and project scope
802.22	Wireless Regional Area Network	IEEE 802.22 mission and project scope

11.2 IEEE 802.3

802.3 is a standard specification for Ethernet, a method of physical communication in a local area network (LAN), which is maintained by the Institute of Electrical and Electronics Engineers (IEEE). In general, 802.3 specifies the physical media and the working characteristics of Ethernet. The original Ethernet supports a data rate of 10 megabits per second (Mbps) and specifies these possible physical media:

- 10BASE-2 (Thin wire coaxial cable with a maximum segment length of 185 meters)
- 10BASE-5 (Thickwire coaxial cable with a maximum segment length of 500 meters)
- 10BASE-F (optical fiber cable)
- 10BASE-T (ordinary telephone twisted pair wire)
- 10BASE-36 (broadband multi-channel coaxial cable with a maximum segment length of 3,600 meters)

This designation is an IEEE shorthand identifier. The "10" in the media type designation refers to the transmission speed of 10 Mbps. The "BASE" refers to baseband signalling, which means that only Ethernet signals are carried on the medium (or, with 10BASE-36, on a single channel). The "T" represents twisted-pair; the "F" represents fiber optic cable; and the "2", "5", and "36" refer to the coaxial cable segment length (the 185 meter length has been rounded up to "2" for 200).who use the access as a free Internet connection. The activity of locating and exploiting security-exposed wireless LANs is called war driving. An identifying iconography, called war chalking, has evolved. Any entity that has a wireless LAN should use security safeguards such as the Wired Equivalent Privacy (WEP) encryption standard, the more recent Wi-Fi Protected Access (WPA), Internet Protocol Security (IPsec), or a virtual private network (VPN).

11.3 IEEE 802.11 STANDARD

IEE 802.11 is an evolving family of specifications for wireless local area networks (WLANs) developed by a working group of the Institute of Electrical and Electronics Engineers (IEEE). There are several specifications in the family and new ones are occasionally added.

All the 802.11 specifications use the Ethernet protocol and Carrier Sense Multiple Access with Collision Avoidance (CSMA/CA) for path sharing. The original modulation used in 802.11 was phase-shift keying (PSK). However, other schemes, such as complementary code keying (CCK), are used in some of the newer specifications. The newer modulation methods provide higher data speed and reduced vulnerability to interference.

- A family of wireless LAN (WLAN) specifications developed by a working group at the Institute of Electrical and Electronic Engineers (IEEE)
- Defines standard for WLANs using the following four technologies
  - ✓ Frequency Hopping Spread Spectrum (FHSS)
  - ✓ Direct Sequence Spread Spectrum (DSSS)
  - ✓ Infrared (IR)
  - ✓ Orthogonal Frequency Division Multiplexing (OFDM)
- Different Versions are 802.11a, 802.11b, 802.11g, 802.11e, 802.11f, 802.11i

11.4 WIRELESS ETHERNET STANDARDS

- *IEEE 802.11*— The Initial release of the standard capable of transmissions of 1 to 2 Mbps and operates in 2.4 GHz band using either frequency hopping spread spectrum (FHSS) or direct sequence spread spectrum (DSSS).
- *IEEE 802.11a*— Capable of transmissions upto 54 Mbps and operates in 5 GHz band and uses an orthogonal frequency division multiplexing OFDM encoding scheme .
- *IEEE 802.11b*— Capable of transmissions of upto 11 Mbps and operates in 2.4 GHz band and uses only DSSS encoding scheme.
- *IEEE 802.11g*— Capable of transmissions upto 54 Mbps and operates in 2.4 GHz band

11.4.1 802.11 - Transmission

- Most wireless LAN products operate in unlicensed radio bands and the main advantages are
  - ✓ 2.4 GHz is most popular
  - ✓ Available in most parts of the world
  - ✓ No need for user licensing

- Most wireless LANs use spread-spectrum radio technology as it is
  - ✓ Resistant to interference and secure
  - ✓ Two popular methods
    - Frequency Hopping (FH)
    - Direct Sequence (DS)

11.4.2 Basic principles of Spread Spectrum

Spread Spectrum modulation techniques are defined as being those techniques in which:

- The bandwidth of the transmitted signal is much greater than the bandwidth of the original message, and
- The bandwidth of the transmitted signal is determined by the message to be transmitted and by an additional signal known as the Spreading Code.

Two main Spread Spectrum modulation techniques are defined:

Frequency Hopping Spread Spectrum (FHSS) and Direct Sequence Spread Spectrum (DSSS).

By transmitting the message energy over a bandwidth much wider than the minimum required, Spread Spectrum modulation techniques present two major advantages: low power density and redundancy.

Low power density relates to the fact that the transmitted energy is spread over a wide band, and therefore, the amount of energy per specific frequency is very low. The effect of the low power density of the transmitted signal is that such a signal will not disturb (interfere with) the activity of other systems' receivers in the same area and that such a signal can not be detected by intruders, providing a high level of intrinsic security.

Redundancy relates to the fact that the message is (or may be) present on different frequencies from where it may be recovered in case of errors. The effect of redundancy is that Spread Spectrum systems present high resistance to noises and interference, being able to recover their messages even if noises are present on the medium.

WLAN and WBA applications in the unlicensed spectrum use the frequency band known as "2.4 GHz" (ranging from 2.4 GHz to 2.4835 GHz, same as the Industrial, Scientific and Medical - ISM band). The operation in this band is defined by IEEE 802.11.

For licensed spectrum operation, most applications use the so called "sub 11 GHz bands" including frequencies such as 2.5 GHz, 2.6 GHz, 3.5 GHz, 3.6 GHz, 3.8 GHz, etc.

Spread Spectrum modulation techniques are composed of two consecutive modulation processes executed on the carrier signal (Fig. 11.1):

- Process 1 - executed by the spreading code (= the spreading process). It is this spreading process that generates the wide bandwidth of the transmitted signal.
- Process 2 - executed by the message to be transmitted.

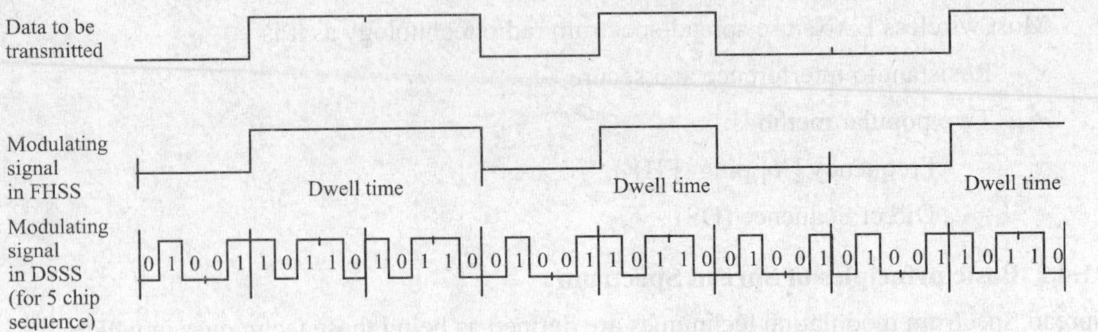

Fig. 11.1: Signals used to modulate the carrier in FHSS and DSSS

Dwell time in FHSS is represented as 3 × data bit duration. Spreading sequence in DSSS is represented as being 5 chip long)

Notes:

1. FHSS— The frequency of the carrier has a different value for each dwell time.
2. DSSS— The frequency of the carrier has a constant, fixed value for each system.

Process 1— Spreading code modulation

The frequency of the carrier is periodically modified (hopped) following a specific sequence of frequencies.

In FHSS systems, the *spreading code* is this list of frequencies to be used for the carrier signal, a.k.a. the "hopping sequence"

The amount of time spent on each hop is known as dwell time and is typically in the range of 100 ms.

Process 2 — Message modulation

The message modulates the (hopping) carrier (FSK), thus generating a narrow band signal for the duration of each dwell, but generating a wide band signal, if the process is regarded over periods of time in the range of seconds.

- *Redundancy* is achieved through the possibility to execute re-transmissions on different carrier frequencies (hops).

Process 1 — Spreading code modulation

For the duration of every message bit, the carrier is modulated (PSK) following a specific sequence of bits (known as chips). The process is known as "chipping" and results in the substitution of every message bit by (same) sequence of chips.

In DSSS systems, the ***spreading code*** is the chip sequence used to represent message bits.

Process 2 — Message modulation

For message bits "0", the sequence of chips used to represent the bit remains as dictated by process1 above. For message bits "1", the sequence of chips dictated by process 1 above, is inverted. In this way message bits "0" and "1" are represented (over the air) by different chip sequences (one being the inverted version of the other one).

Redundancy is achieved by the presence of the message bit on each chip of the spreading code. Even if some of the chips of the spreading code are affected by noise, the receiver may recognize the sequence and take a correct decision regarding the received message bit.

11.4.3 FHSS main parameters

FHSS is defined (in IEEE 802.11) in the 2.4 GHz band as operating over 79 frequencies ranging from 2.402 GHz to 2.480 GHz (country specific bands have different frequencies, defined in IEEE 802.11 and IEEE 802.11.d).

Each of the frequencies is GFSK modulated, with a channel width of 1 MHz.

The rates defined are 1 Mbps and 2 Mbps (there are products in the market operating at 3 Mbps, too)

11.4.4 DSSS main parameters

DSSS is defined (in IEEE 802.11) in the 2.4 GHz band as operating on one of 14 possible carriers (country specific bands have different number of frequencies, defined in IEEE 802.11 and IEEE 802.11.d).

The selected carrier (channel) is PSK modulated with a channel width of 22 MHz.

The rates defined in IEEE 802.11 are 1 Mbps and 2 Mbps.

IEEE 802.11.b adds to DSSS the rates of 5.5 Mbps and 11 Mbps (in the 2.4 GHz band), while keeping the channel width at 22 MHz.

11.4.5 Systems Collocation

The issue: How many independent systems may operate simultaneously without interference?

In *DSSS* systems, collocation could be based on the use of different spreading codes (sequences) for each active system (CDMA = Code Division Multiple Access). On condition that the sequences used are highly distinguishable one from the other one (property known as orthogonality) each receiver will be able to "read" only the information dedicated to it (receiver and transmitter use same spreading code). CDMA could indeed be the solution, but orthogonal pseudo-random sequences are needed. The number of orthogonal pseudo-random sequences is limited and it is a function of the sequence length [number of chips (bits) in the sequence].

Table 11.2

Length of sequence (in chips)	*Number of available sequences*	*Number of possible collocated systems*
15	2	2
31	6	6
63	6	6
255	16	16
1,023	60	60

Actual (IEEE 802.11 and 802.11.a based) DSSS systems use 11 bit long spreading sequences making the use of CDMA impossible. System collocation is therefore based on the fixed allocation of bandwidth to each system (same as in narrow band systems).

For the transmission of 11 Mchips per second (Msymbols per sec), IEEE 802.11 needs a contiguous band of 22 MHz, and defines the need for a minimum distance of 30 MHz between the carrier frequencies of collocated DSSS systems.

As the total available bandwidth in the ISM band is 83.5MHz (2.4GHz - 2.4835GHz) and as the distance between carriers has to be 30 MHz, only 3 DSSS systems may be collocated, without interference. If more than 3 systems are collocated, their contiguous 22 MHz channels will overlap, forcing their users to share the channels. The actual behavior and the amount of actual interference is a function of the overlapping size and signal strength.

For *FHSS* systems, IEEE 802.11 defines 79 different hops for the carrier frequency. Using these 79 frequencies, IEEE 802.11 defines 78 hopping sequences (each with 79 hops) grouped in three sets of 26 sequences each. Sequences from same set encounter minimum collisions and therefore may be allocated to collocated systems. Theoretically, 26 FHSS systems may be collocated, but collisions will still occur in significant amounts. To lower the amount of collisions to acceptable levels, the actual number of FHSS collocated systems should be around 15.

All the above is correct for the case in which the FHSS collocated systems operate independently, without any synchronization among their hopping sequences.

If synchronization is allowed, 79 systems could be collocated (theoretically), each one of them using at any moment in time, one of the 79 available frequencies. However, this would require expensive filters in the radio circuitry. Actual products require about 6 MHz separation allowing the collocation of about 12 systems, without any collision! While such synchronization is not always allowed in the unlicensed band of 2.4 GHz, it is common practice in the licensed bands.

The possibility of having collocated systems without collisions, has a tremendous impact on the aggregate capacity / throughput of the installation as well as its efficiency in terms of bps per Hz (see "Throughput" section, later in this paper).

11.4.6 Narrow band interference

DSSS systems have to be able to receive the energy present in their "working band" which is 22 MHz. The filters included in the radio interface allow all the signals present in the working band to enter the device. A narrow band interference signal (interference present around one single frequency) is accepted by the receiver, and if enough energy is present on it, the interfering signal will totally block the receiver.

FHSS systems work with narrow band signals (located each time around a different carrier frequency) and therefore the filters included in the radio have a much narrower pass band.

A narrow band interference signal present on a specific frequency, will block only one specific hop (or maybe a couple, if the interfering signal has a wider band). The FHSS receiver will not be able to operate at that specific hop, but, after hopping to a different frequency, the narrow filter will reject the interfering signal, and the hopper will execute reception without being disturbed... (In IEEE 802.11 the frequencies for consecutive hops are separated by at least 6 MHz in order to reduce to a minimum the chances of being disturbed by same interference on two consecutive hops).

11.4.7 Throughput

The issue: What amount of data is actually carried by the system (measured in bps).

The RATE of a system is defined as the amount of data (per second) carried by a system WHEN IT IS ACTIVE. As most communications systems are not able to carry data 100% of the time, an additional parameter - the THROUGHPUT - is defined, as the AVERAGE amount of data (per second) carried by the system. The average is calculated over long periods of time. Obviously, the throughput of a system is lower than its rate.

In addition, when looking for the amount of data carried, the overhead introduced by the communication protocol should be considered, too.

(For an Ethernet network for example, the rate is 10 Mbps, but the throughput is 3 Mbps to 4 Mbps only! ... and some of these bits are the header of layer 2, some are the header of layer 3, 4, 5, 6, 7, and only some of these bits (not ALL of them) are the "real" data bits, those bits generated by the application...)

11.4.8 Aggregate throughput of collocated systems

Based on the IEEE 802.11 specifications, the maximum number of DSSS systems that can be collocated is 3. These 3 collocated systems provide an aggregate rate of 3 × 11 Mbps = 33 Mbps, or a net aggregate throughput of about 3 × 7 Mbps = 21 Mbps. Let's note that because of the rigid allocation of sub-bands to systems, collisions between signals generated by collocated systems do not occur, and therefore the aggregate throughput is a linear function of the number of systems.

FHSS systems may be operated with synchronized or non-synchronized hopping sequences, based on the world region and on the allocated spectrum (unlicensed or licensed).

In the non-synchronized case, as the band is allocated in a dynamic way among the collocated systems (they use different hopping sequences which are not synchronized), collisions do occur, lowering the actual throughput.

The greater the number of collocated systems (APs), the greater the number of collisions. For small quantities of collocated APs, each additional AP brings in almost all its net throughput; the amount of collisions added to the system is not significant. When the number of APs reaches about 15, the amount of collisions generated by additional APs is so high that in total they lower the aggregate throughput.

In the synchronized case, collisions are totally eliminated, up to 12 systems can be collocated (see "Systems collocation" section in this paper), and the aggregate rate and throughput is a linear function of the number of collocated systems.

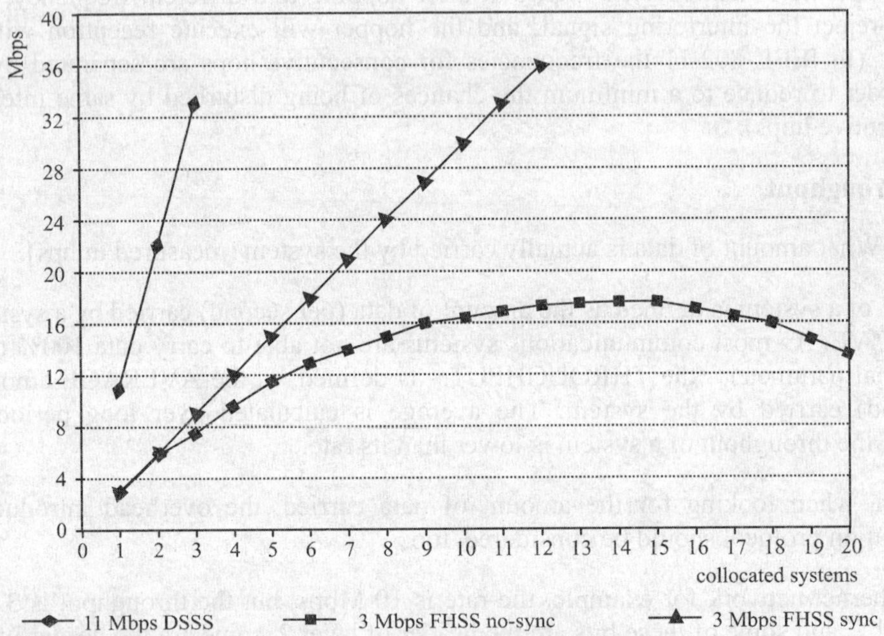

Fig. 11.2: Aggrigate Rate

Studying the graphs above, one can conclude that:

- DSSS systems provide a greater aggregate rate / throughput than non-synchronized FHSS systems. (DSSS systems are always separated in terms of frequencies and never collide; non-synchronized FHSS are not separated in terms of frequencies, collisions occur, and the resultant aggregate rate / throughput is lower)
- Synchronized FHSS systems never collide, and as a result, they provide more or less the same aggregate rate / throughput as DSSS systems. We should mention however, that even if the aggregate numbers are equivalent, the way these capacity is distributed among the users is different: DSSS has the advantage of providing independent users with rates of up to 11 Mbps, while FHSS provides a maximum of 3 Mbps per independent user.

So, if there is no way of synchronizing the APs (because the local radio regulations do not allow synchronization, or because the APs are geographically distributed, e.g. a WLAN in an office space), then, DSSS provides higher aggregate (and individual) rates / throughputs.

However, when synchronization is allowed and possible (e.g. a base station in a cellular deployment, where all the APs are located on same pole, and / or the system is operated in a licensed band), then FHSS would be recommended, as it provides slightly higher aggregate numbers.

11.4.9 Security

The issue: Protecting the transmission against eavesdropping

IEEE 802.11 compliant DSSS systems use one well known spreading sequence of 11 chips, and can modulate one of the 14 channel defined in the standard. As the sequence used is apriori known, the carrier frequency is fixed for a given system, and the number of possible frequencies is limited, it would be quite easy for a listener to "tune in" on the DSSS transmission. Message protection should be achieved by encrypting the data. This option increases the price of the product, while lowering its performance, because of the processing power needed for the encryption process.

In FHSS, the frequencies to be used in the hopping sequence may be selected by the user. In the unlicensed band, any group of 26 frequencies or more (out of the 79 available) is legal. To "tune in", a listener should know the number of frequencies selected in the system, the actual frequencies, the hopping sequence, as well as the dwell time! The FHSS modulation acts as a layer 1 encryption process. There could be no need for application level encryption!

11.4.10 Collocation / Aggregate Rate

a) Figure 11.2 - Signals used to modulate the carrier in FHSS and DSSS (Dwell time in FHSS is represented as 3× data bit duration. Spreading sequence in DSSS is represented as being 5 chip long)

Notes:

1. *FHSS*— The frequency of the carrier has a different value for each dwell time.
2. *DSSS*— The frequency of the carrier has a constant, fixed value for each system.

DSSS biggest advantage over FHSS is its capability to provide rates of up to 11 Mbps. When covering the whole 2.4 GHz band, three systems may be installed, providing an aggregate rate of 33 Mbps. (Overall efficiency: 33Mbps/83.5MHz = 0.39 bits/Hz). Additional systems, if installed, will share the spectrum with the already installed systems, lowering the overall aggregate rate / throughput because of collision occurrences.

In a 2.4 GHz FHSS synchronized environment, up to 12 systems can be collocated, providing an overall aggregate rate of 36 MHz (efficiency: 36Mbps/83.5MHz= 0.43 bits/Hz).

In a licensed FDD FHSS synchronized environment, up to 6 systems may be collocated in a 10.5MHz band, providing an aggregate rate of 18 Mbps (efficiency: 18Mbps/10.5MHz = 1.7 bits/Hz).

b) Contiguous band

IEEE 802.11 DSSS needs 22MHz, contiguous. If such a band is not available, the system can not be operated. FHSS does not require contiguous band for correct operation. If some frequencies are not available (administrative reasons, multipath effects, noises, etc.), FHSS system could be set to use sequences that do not include the unavailable frequencies.

c) Coverage

11 Mbps DSSS and 3 Mbps FHSS, cover more or less the same distances.

d) Near / far problem

Present in DSSS, not critical in FHSS.

e) Multipath sensitivity

DSSS is extremely sensitive, especially when operated at 11Mbps. To minimize multipath effects, point-to-multipoint topology systems have to be limited to small environments such as offices, while long distance systems are restricted to the use of directional antennas, limiting the DSSS technology to point-to-point topology applications.

f) Bluetooth interference

FHSS are significantly less sensitive to Bluetooth interference

11.5 802.11- PHYSICAL LAYER

Physical (PHY) layer is of three categories viz, Infra red, Frequency Hopping Spread Spectrum and Direct Sequence Spread Spectrum (IR, FHSS, DSSS)

11.5.1 Direct Sequence SS

- DSSS (Direct Sequence Spread Spectrum)
  - ✓ Signal is spread by a wide bandwidth pseudorandom sequence (code sequence)
  - ✓ Signals appear as wideband noise to unintended receivers
  - ✓ Not for intra-cell multiple access
  - ✓ Nodes in the same cell use same code sequence

DS systems use a carrier that remains fixed to a specific frequency band. The data signal is spread onto a much larger range of frequencies (at a much lower power level) using a specific encoding scheme. Some of the salient features are listed below:

- Much higher throughput than FH (11 Mbps)
- Better coverage range

- Less resistant to noise (made up for by redundancy – it transmits at least 10 fully redundant copies of the original signal at the same time)
- DBPSK modulation for 1 Mbps (Differential Binary Phase Shift Keying), DQPSK for 2 Mbps (Differential Quadrature PSK)
- Preamble and header of a frame is always transmitted with 1 Mbps, rest of transmission 1 or 2 Mbps
- chipping sequence: +1, -1, +1, +1, -1, +1, +1, +1, -1, -1, -1 (Barker code)
- max. radiated power 1 W (USA), 100 mW (EU), min. 1mW
- Data Scrambling using 8-bit LFSR
- 128-bit Preamble Sync pattern
- 48-bit Header
- Antenna Diversity
- Multipath fading of a signal can inhibit reception
- Multiple antennas can significantly minimize
- Spatial Separation of Orthoganality
- Choose Antenna during Preamble Sync pattern
- Presence of Preamble Sync pattern
- Presence of energy

11.5.2 FHSS (Frequency Hopping Spread Spectrum)

- FH systems use a radio carrier that "hops" from frequency to frequency in a pattern known to both transmitter and receiver.
  - ✓ spreading, despreading, signal strength, typically 1 Mbps
  - ✓ min. 2.5 frequency hops/s (USA), two-level GFSK modulation
  - ✓ 2 & 4GFSK
  - ✓ Data Whitening for Bias Suppression
    - – 32/33 bit stuffing and block inversion
    - – 7-bit LFSR scrambler
  - ✓ 80-bit Preamble Sync pattern
  - ✓ 32-bit Header

The main advantages of this system include

- Easy to implement
  - ✓ Resistance to noise
  - ✓ Limited throughput (2-3 Mbps @ 2.4 GHz)

Infrared method is used in some cases which has

- ✓ 850-950 nm, diffuse light, typ. 10 m range
- ✓ carrier detection, energy detection, synchronization

- Wireless LAN standard defined in the unlicensed spectrum (2.4 GHz and 5 GHz U-NII bands)
- Standards covers the MAC sublayer and PHY layers

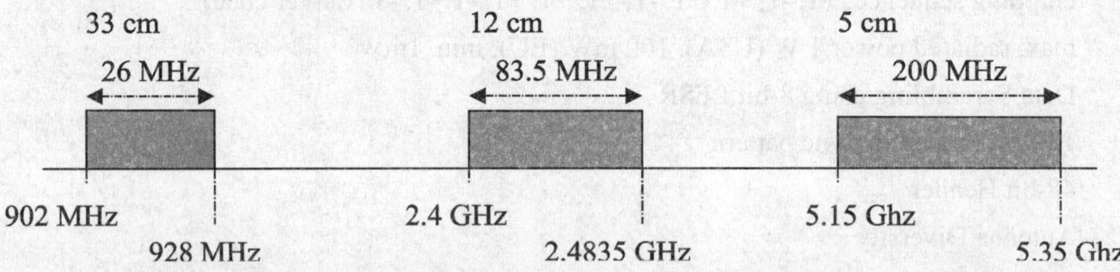

Fig. 11.3: IEEE 802.11 - Different Frequency Ranges and Channel Bandwidth

- Three different physical layers in the 2.4 GHz band are possible such as FHSS. DSSS and IR
- OFDM based Physical layer in the 5 GHz band (802.11 a) is unique

11.5.3 IEEE 802.11b DSSS

- ISM unlicensed frequency band (2.4GHz)
- Channel bandwidth: f_{hgh} -U = 22MHz
- 1 MHz guard band
- Direct sequence spread spectrum in each channel
- 3 non-overlapping channels

Table 11.3: Frequency Ranges in Channel 1 - 11

Channel	f_{low}	f_{high}
1	2.401	2.423
2	2.404	2.428
3	2.411	2.433
4	2.416	2.438
5	2.421	2.443
6	2.426	2.448
7	2.431	2.453
3	2.436	2.458
9	2.441	2.463
10	2.446	2.468
11	2.451	2.473

- Direct Sequence (DSSS)
  - ✓ Using one of 11 overlapping channels, multiply the data by an 11-bit number to spread the 1M-symbol/sec data over 11MHz
    - Requires RF linearity over 11MHz
    - Spreading yields processing gain at receiver
    - Less immune to interference

Spread-Spectrum Communications

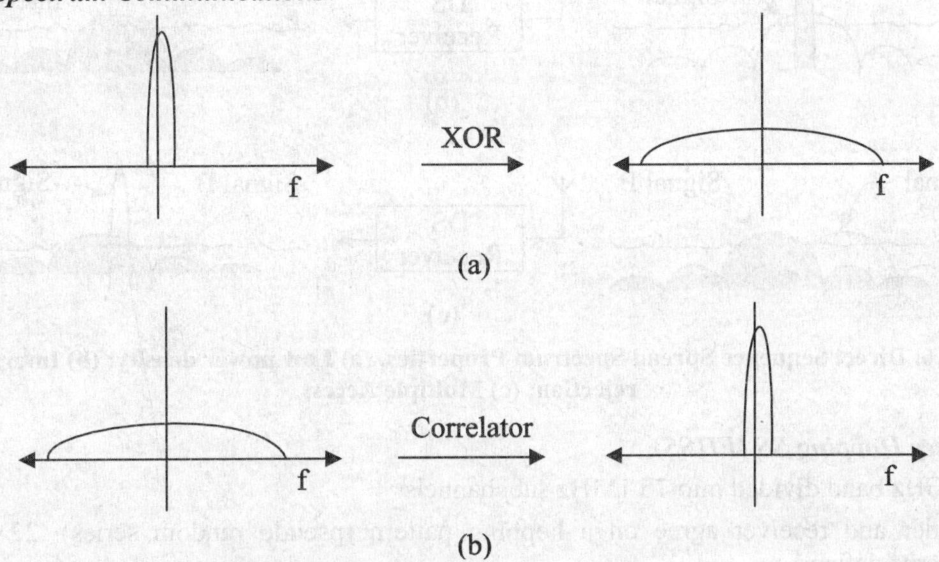

Fig. 11.4: (a) Effect of PN Sequence on Transmit Spectrum; (b) Received Signal is Correlated with PN to Recover Data and Reject Interference

DSSS Barker Code Modulation

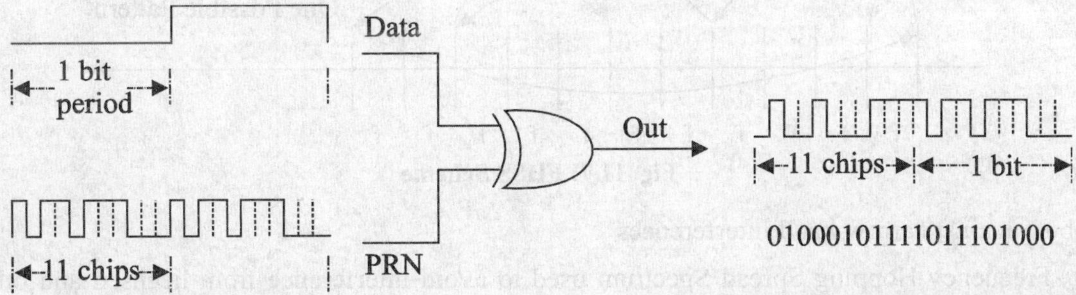

11 Bit Barker Code (PRN):
1 0 1 1 1 0 1 0 0 0

Fig. 11.5: Digital Modulation of Data with PRN Sequence

DSSS Properties

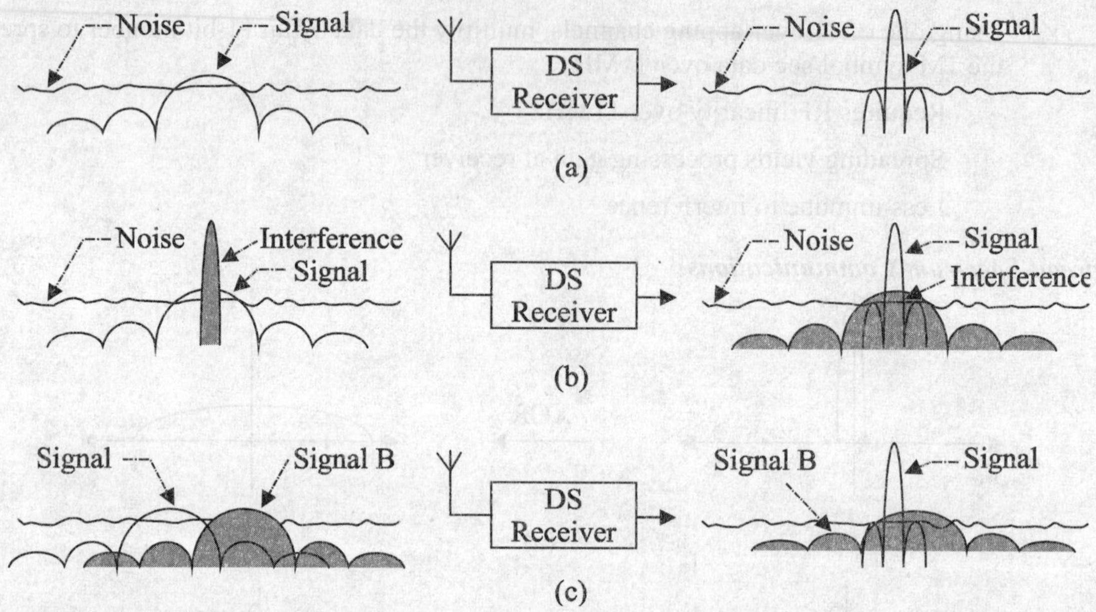

Fig. 11.6: Direct Sequence Spread Spectrum Properties, (a) Low power density; (b) Interference rejection; (c) Multiple Access

Frequency Hopping SS (FHSS)

- 2.4GHz band divided into 75 1MHz subchannels
- Sender and receiver agree on a hopping pattern (pseudo random series). 22 hopping patterns defined
- Different hopping sequences enable co-existence of multiple BSSs

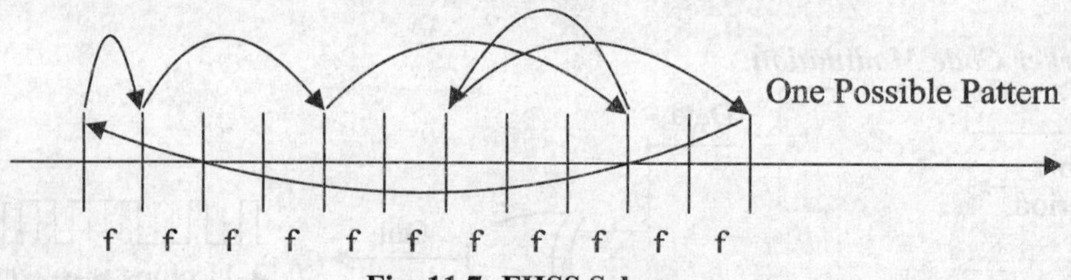

Fig. 11.7: FHSS Scheme

Robust against narrow-band interferences

- Frequency Hopping Spread Spectrum used to avoid interference from licensed and other non-licensed users, and from noise, e.g., microwave ovens
- Frequency Hopping (FHSS) working:
  - ✓ Using one of 78 hop sequences, hop to a new 1MHz channel (out of the total of 79 channels) at least every 400milliseconds
  - ✓ Requires hop acquisition and synchronization
  - ✓ Hops away from interference

Physical Layer enables the following functions in the sequence Preamble Sync, 16-bit Start Frame Delimiter, PLCP Header including 16-bit Header CRC, MPDU, 32-bit CRC

11.5.4 RSSI - Received Signal Strength Indication

- Combination of both
- Clear Channel Assessment
- Require reliable indication that channel is in use to defer transmission
- Use same mechanisms as for Antenna Diversity
- Use NAV information

Table 11.4: Performance, Theoretical Maximum Throughput

	1 Mbit/sec		*2 Mbit/sec*	
MSDU size (bytes)	***DS***	***FH (400 ms hop time)***	***DS***	***FH (400 ms hop time)***
128	0.364	0.364	0.517	0.474
512	0.694	0.679	1163	1.088
512 (frag size = 128)	0.503	0.512	0.781	0.759
2304	0.906	0.860	1.720	1.624

11.6 CARRIER SENSE MULTIPLE ACCESS WITH COLLISION AVOIDANCE – (CSMA/CA)

The *Carrier Sense Multiple Access with Collision Avoidance* (CSMA/CA) Medium Access Control algorithm was designed for the popular WiFi wireless network technology [802.11]. CSMA/CA also senses the transmission channel before transmitting a frame. Furthermore, CSMA/CA tries to avoid collisions by carefully tuning the timers used by CSMA/CA devices.

CSMA/CA uses acknowledgements like CSMA. Each frame contains a sequence number and a CRC. The CRC is used to detect transmission errors while the sequence number is used to avoid frame duplication. When a device receives a correct frame, it returns a special acknowledgement frame to the sender. CSMA/CA introduces a small delay, named *Short Inter Frame Spacing* (SIFS), between the reception of a frame and the transmission of the acknowledgement frame. This delay corresponds to the time that is required to switch the radio of a device between the reception and transmission modes.

Compared to CSMA, CSMA/CA defines more precisely when a device is allowed to send a frame. First, CSMA/CA defines two delays : *DIFS* and *EIFS*. To send a frame, a device must first wait until the channel has been idle for at least the *Distributed Coordination Function Inter Frame Space* (DIFS) if the previous frame was received correctly. However, if the previously received frame was corrupted, this indicates that there are collisions and the device must sense the channel idle for at least the *Extended Inter Frame Space* (EIFS), with . The exact values for SIFS, DIFS and EIFS depend on the underlying physical layer.

The figure below shows the basic operation of CSMA/CA devices. Before transmitting, host *A* verifies that the channel is empty for a long enough period. Then, its sends its data frame. After checking the validity of the received frame, the recipient sends an acknowledgement frame after a short SIFS delay. Host *C*, which does not participate in the frame exchange, senses the channel to be busy at the beginning of the data frame. Host *C* can use this information to determine how long the channel will be busy for. Note that as, even a device that would start to sense the channel immediately after the last bit of the data frame could not decide to transmit its own frame during the transmission of the acknowledgement frame.

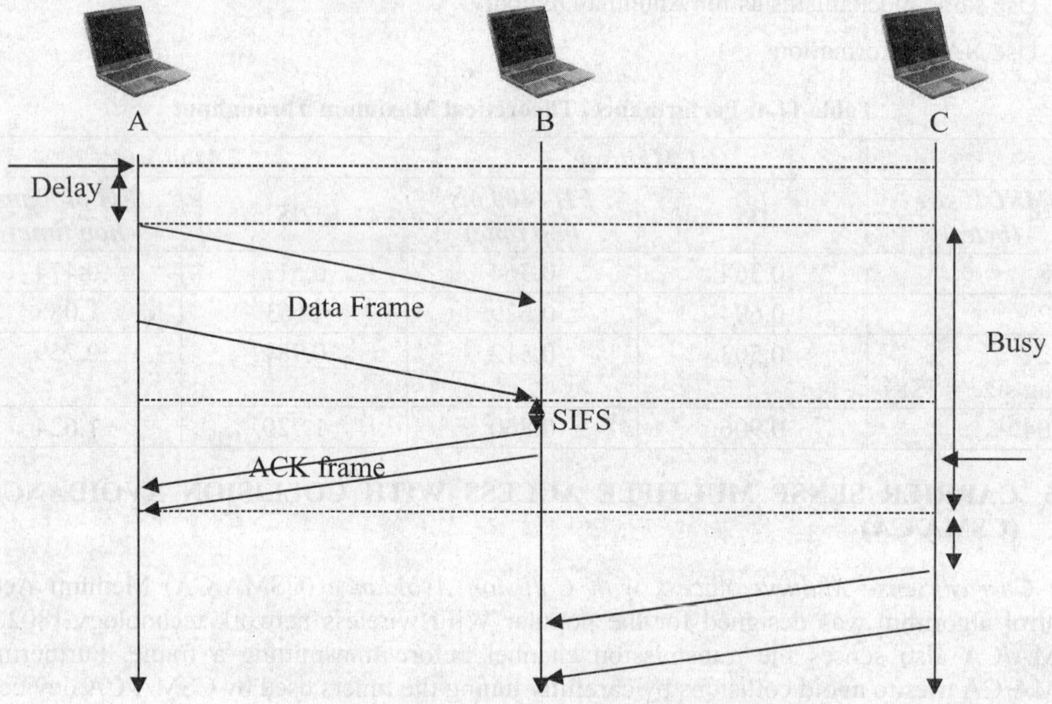

Fig. 11.8: Operation of a CSMA/CA Device

11.6.1 Operation of a CSMA/CA device

The main difficulty with CSMA/CA is when two or more devices transmit at the same time and cause collisions. This is illustrated in the figure below, assuming a fixed timeout after the transmission of a data frame. With CSMA/CA, the timeout after the transmission of a data frame is very small, since it corresponds to the SIFS plus the time required to transmit the acknowledgement frame.

To deal with this problem, CSMA/CA relies on a backoff timer. This backoff timer is a random delay that is chosen by each device in a range that depends on the number of retransmissions for the current frame. The range grows exponentially with the retransmissions as in CSMA/CD. The minimum range for the backoff timer is where the *slotTime* is a parameter that depends on the underlying physical layer. Compared to CSMA/CD's exponential backoff, there are two important differences to notice. First, the initial range for the backoff timer is seven times larger. This is because it is impossible in CSMA/CA to detect collisions as they happen. With

A
B
C
DIFS
DIFS
Busy
Data frame
Data frame
Busy
Timeout
Timeout
Data frame
Data frame
Busy

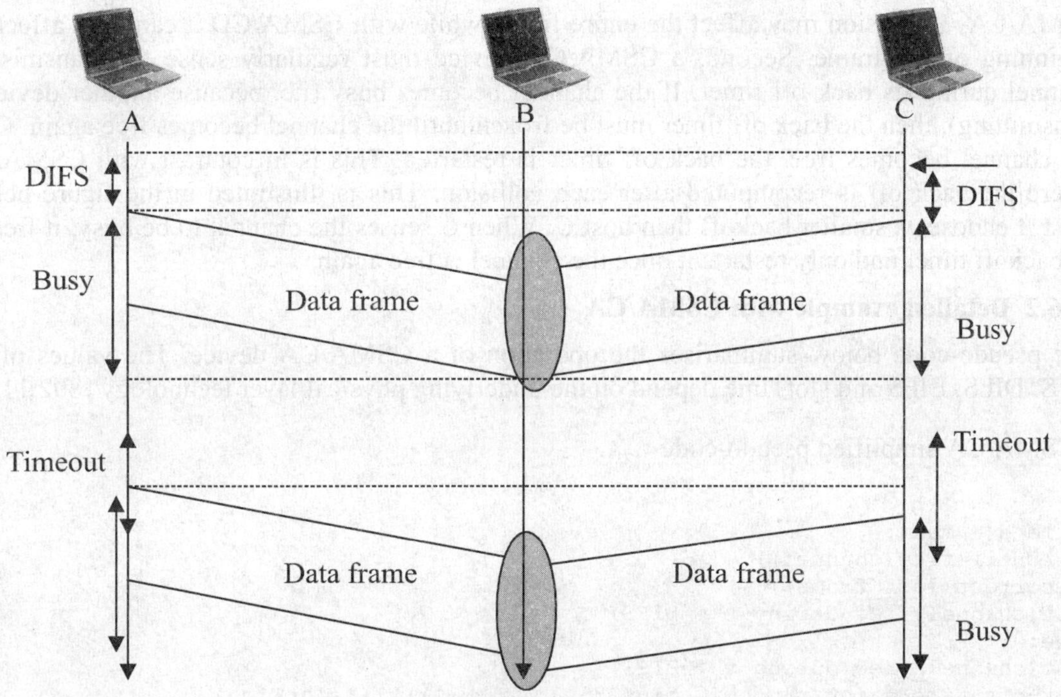

Fig. 11.9: Collision with CSMA/CA

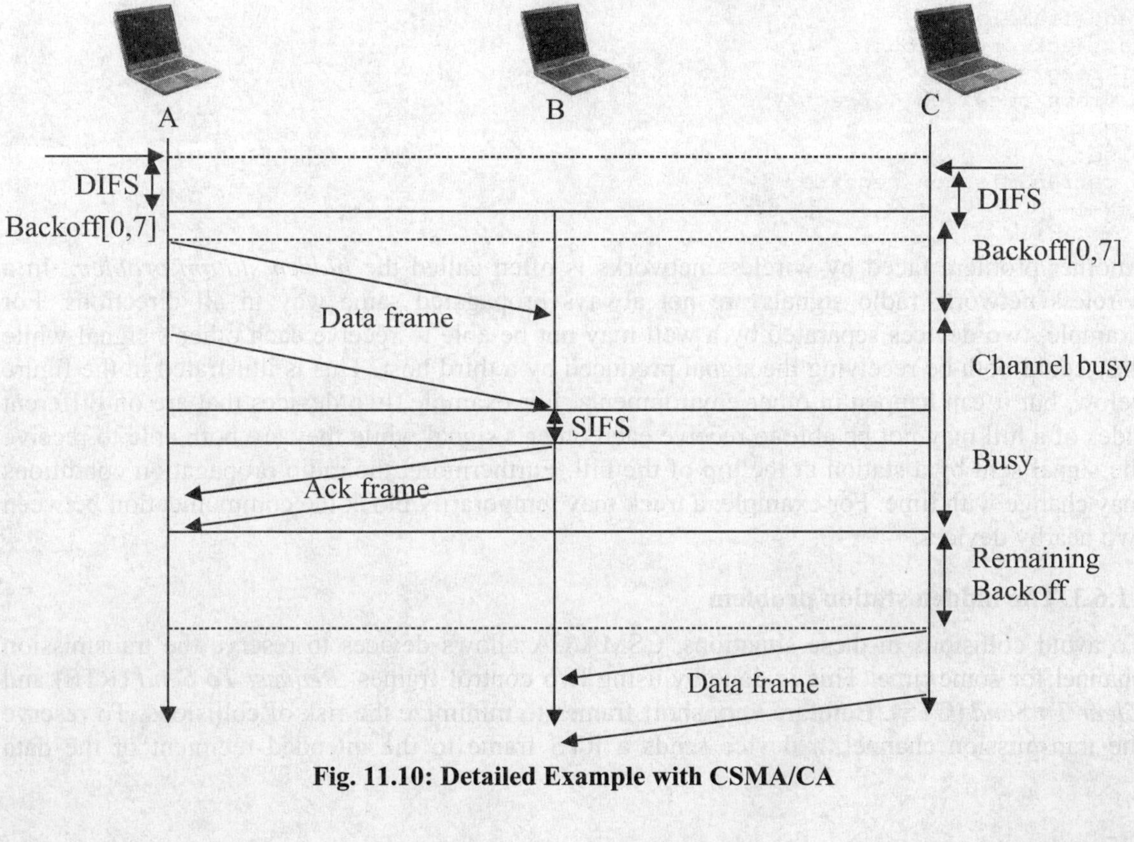

A
B
C
DIFS
Backoff[0,7]
DIFS
Backoff[0,7]
Data frame
Channel busy
SIFS
Busy
Ack frame
Remaining
Backoff
Data frame

Fig. 11.10: Detailed Example with CSMA/CA

CSMA/CA, a collision may affect the entire frame while with CSMA/CD it can only affect the beginning of the frame. Second, a CSMA/CA device must regularly sense the transmission channel during its back off timer. If the channel becomes busy (i.e. because another device is transmitting), then the back off timer must be frozen until the channel becomes free again. Once the channel becomes free, the back off timer is restarted. This is in contrast with CSMA/CD where the back off is recomputed after each collision. This is illustrated in the figure below. Host *A* chooses a smaller backoff than host *C*. When *C* senses the channel to be busy, it freezes its backoff timer and only restarts it once the channel is free again.

11.6.2 Detailed example with CSMA/CA

The pseudo-code below summarises the operation of a CSMA/CA device. The values of the SIFS, DIFS, EIFS and slotTime depend on the underlying physical layer technology [802.11]

CSMA/CA simplified pseudo-code

```
N=1
while N<= max :
waitUntil(free(channel))
if correct(last_frame) :
wait(channel_free_during_t >=DIFS)
else:
wait(channel_free_during_t >=EIFS)
back-off_time = int(random[0,min(255,7*(2^(N-1)))])*slotTime
wait(channel free during backoff_time)
# backoff timer is frozen while channel is sensed to be busy
send(frame)
wait(ack or timeout)
if received(ack)
# frame received correctly
break
else:
# retransmission required
N=N+1
```

Another problem faced by wireless networks is often called the *hidden station problem*. In a wireless network, radio signals are not always propagated same way in all directions. For example, two devices separated by a wall may not be able to receive each other's signal while they could both be receiving the signal produced by a third host. This is illustrated in the figure below, but it can happen in other environments. For example, two devices that are on different sides of a hill may not be able to receive each other's signal while they are both able to receive the signal sent by a station at the top of the hill. Furthermore, the radio propagation conditions may change with time. For example, a truck may temporarily block the communication between two nearby devices.

11.6.3 The hidden station problem

To avoid collisions in these situations, CSMA/CA allows devices to reserve the transmission channel for some time. This is done by using two control frames :*Request To Send* (RTS) and *Clear To Send* (CTS). Both are very short frames to minimize the risk of collisions. To reserve the transmission channel, a device sends a RTS frame to the intended recipient of the data frame. The RTS frame contains the duration of the requested reservation. The recipient replies, after a SIFS delay, with a CTS frame which also contains the duration of the reservation. As the duration of the reservation has been sent in both RTS and CTS, all hosts that could collide with either the sender or the reception of the data frame are informed of the reservation. They can compute the total duration of the transmission and defer their access to the transmission channel until then. This is illustrated in the figure below where host *A* reserves the transmission channel to send a data frame to host*B*. Host *C* notices the reservation and defers its transmission.

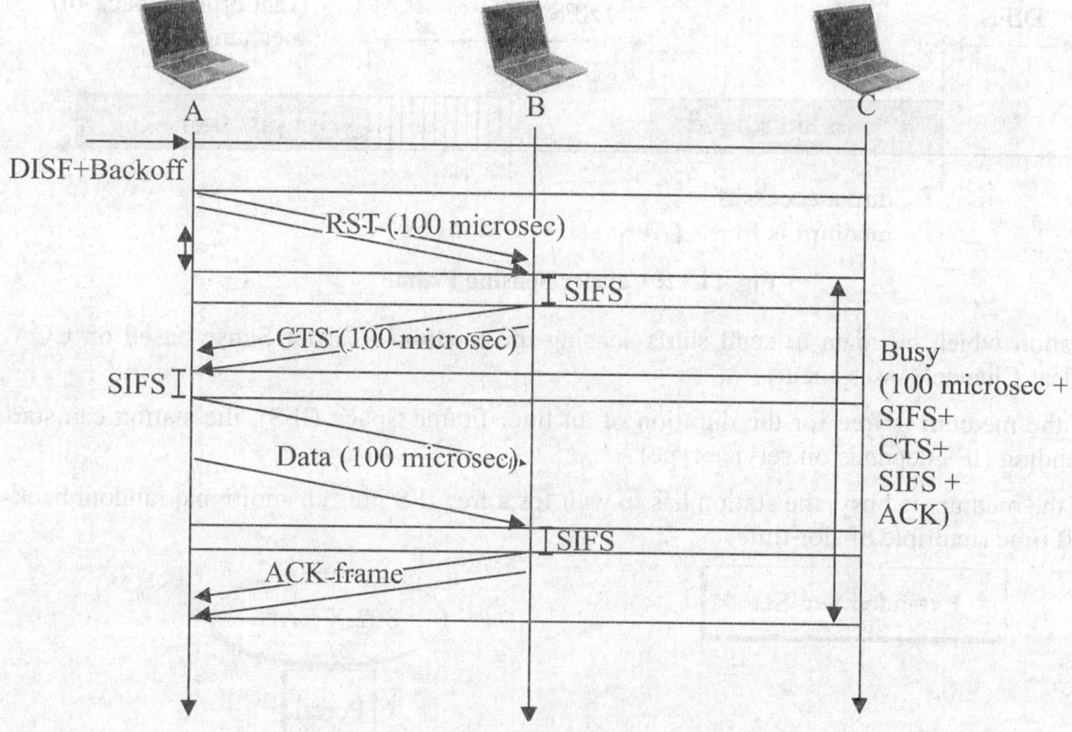

Fig. 11.11: Reservations with CSMA/CA

11.6.4 Reservations with CSMA/CA

The utilization of the reservations with CSMA/CA is an optimization that is useful when collisions are frequent. If there are few collisions, the time required to transmit the RTS and CTS frames can become significant and in particular when short frames are exchanged. Some devices only turn on RTS/CTS after transmission errors.

11.6.5 802.11 – Synchronization

- All STAs within a BSS are synchronized to a common clock
  - ✓ Infrastructure mode— AP is the timing master
    - periodically transmits Beacon frames containing Timing Synchronization function (TSF)
    - Receiving stations accepts the timestamp value in TSF

✓ Ad hoc mode— TSF implements a distributed algorithm

– Each station adopts the timing received from any beacon that has TSF value later than its own TSF timer

- This mechanism keeps the synchronization of the TSF timers in a BSS to within 4 µs plus the maximum propagation delay of the PHY layer.

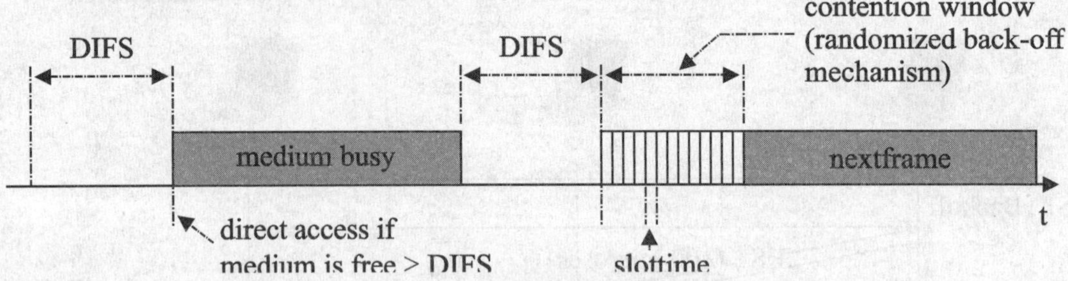

Fig. 11.12: Carrier Sensing Frame

- station which has data to send starts sensing the medium (Carrier Sense based on CCA, Clear Channel Assessment)
- if the medium is free for the duration of an Inter-Frame Space (IFS), the station can start sending (IFS depends on service type)
- if the medium is busy, the station has to wait for a free IFS plus an additional random back-off time (multiple of slot-time)

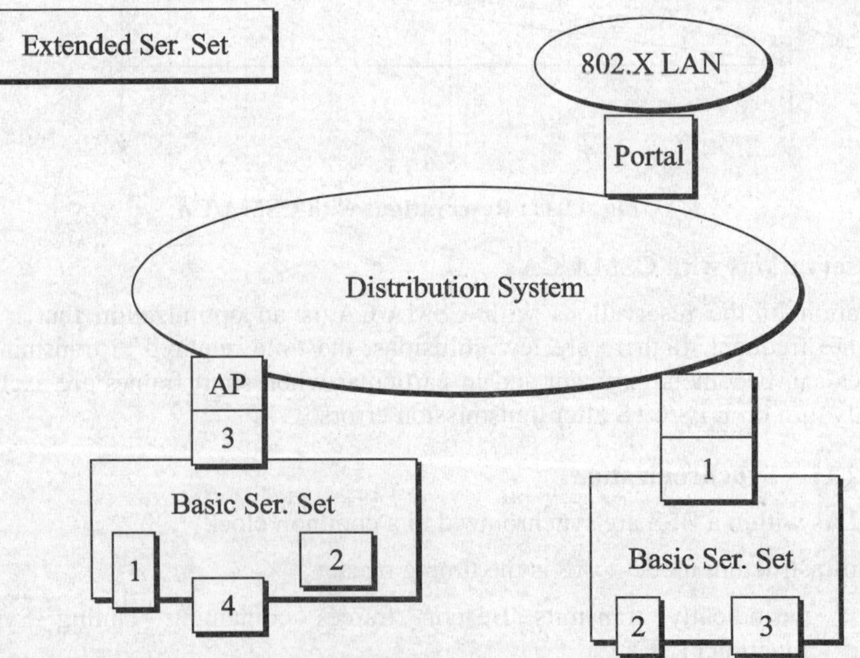

Fig. 11.13: 802.11 Architecture - BSS

- if another station occupies the medium during the back-off time of the station, the back-off timer stops (fairness)

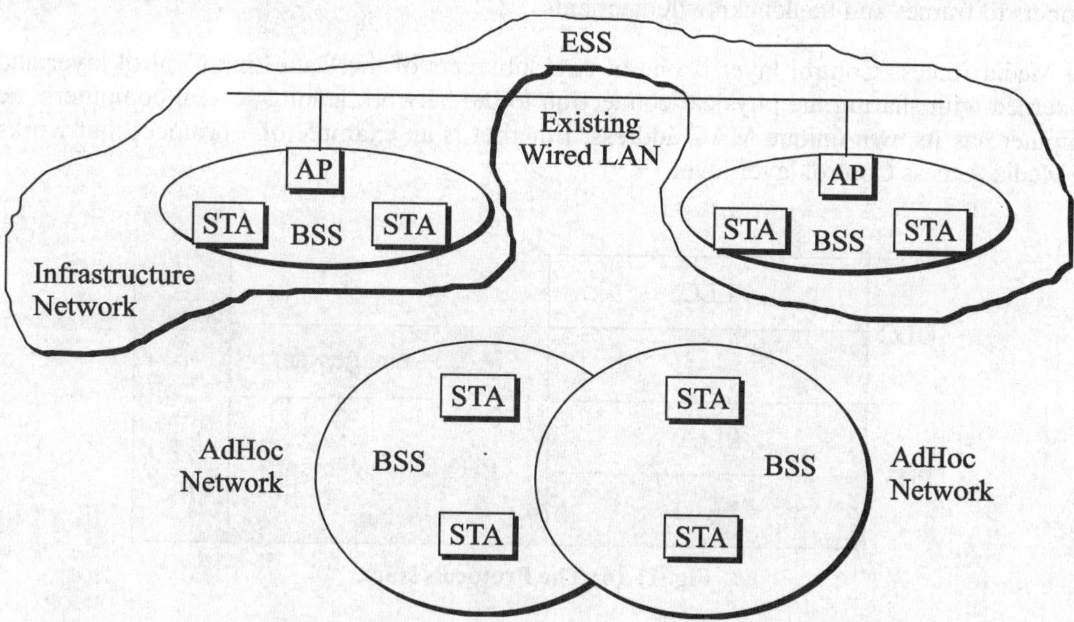

Fig. 11.14: 802.11 WiFi Networking BSS and ESS

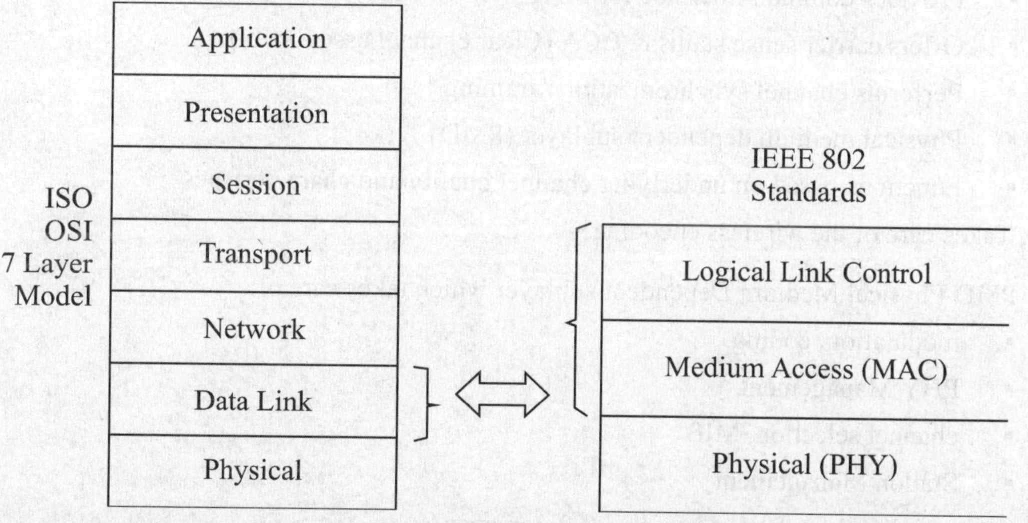

Fig. 11.15: Data Link Layer Format

11.7 802.11 - LAYERS AND FUNCTIONS

The Logical Link Control (LLC) layer is one of two sublayers of the Data-Link layer in the Open Systems Interconnection (OSI) model of communication. The LLC layer is concerned with managing traffic (flow and error control) over the physical medium. The LLC layer also identifies a line protocol, such as SDLC, NetBIOS, or NetWare, and may also assign sequence numbers to frames and track acknowledgements.

The Media Access Control layer is one of two sublayers of the Data Link Control layer and is concerned with sharing the physical connection to the network among several computers. Each computer has its own unique MAC address. Ethernet is an example of a protocol that works at the Media Access Control layer level.

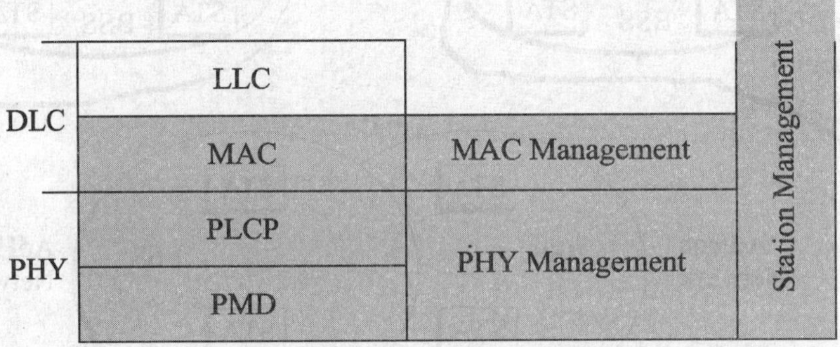

Fig. 11.16: The Protocols stack

11.7.1 PHY Sublayers

I. Physical layer convergence protocol (PLCP) and the functions are:

- Provides common interface for MAC
- Offers carrier sense status & CCA (Clear channel assessment)
- Performs channel synchronization / training
- Physical medium dependent sublayer (PMD)
- Functions based on underlying channel quality and characteristics

E.g., Takes care of the wireless encoding

II. PMD Physical Medium Dependent sublayer which takes care of:

- modulation, coding
- PHY Management
- channel selection, MIB
- Station Management
- coordination of all management functions

III. MAC Management

- Synchronization
  - ✓ try to find a LAN, try to stay within a LAN
  - ✓ timer etc.

PLCP (802.11b)

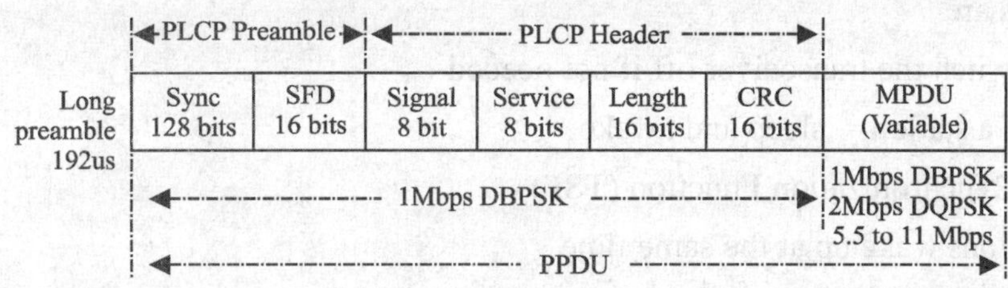

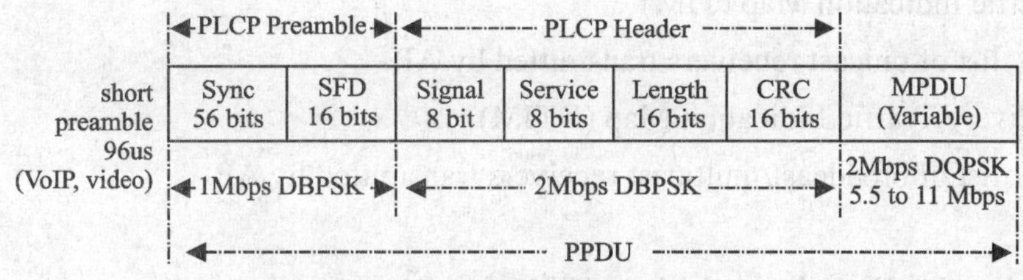

Fig. 11.17: PLCP (802.11b)

- Power management
  - ✓ sleep-mode without missing a message
  - ✓ periodic sleep, frame buffering, traffic measurements
- Association/Reassociation
  - ✓ integration into a LAN
  - ✓ roaming, i.e. change networks by changing access points
  - ✓ scanning, i.e. active search for a network
- MIB - Management Information Base
  - ✓ managing, read, write

11.7.2 Synchronization

- All STAs within a BSS are synchronized to a common clock

  a) Infrastructure mode— AP is the timing master, which
  - ✓ periodically transmits Beacon frames containing Timing Synchronization function (TSF)
  - ✓ Receiving stations accept the timestamp value in TSF

  b) Ad hoc mode— TSF implements a distributed algorithm
  - ✓ Each station adopts the timing received from any beacon that has TSF value later than its own TSF timer
- This mechanism keeps the synchronization of the TSF timers in a BSS to within 4 μs plus, the maximum propagation delay of the PHY layer

Power Management

The functions are

- Idle— switch the transceiver off if not needed
- States of a station— sleep and awake
- Timing Synchronization Function (TSF)
  - ✓ stations wake up at the same time

a) Infrastructure
  - ✓ Traffic Indication Map (TIM)
    - – list of unicast receivers transmitted by AP
  - ✓ Delivery Traffic Indication Map (DTIM)
    - – list of broadcast/multicast receivers transmitted by AP

b) Ad-hoc
  - ✓ Ad-hoc Traffic Indication Map (ATIM)
    - – announcement of receivers by stations buffering frames
    - – more complicated - no central AP
    - – collision of ATIMs possible (scalability?)

Other MAC Operations

a) Fragmentation
  - Sequence control field
  - In burst
  - Medium is reserved
  - NAV is updated by ACK

b) Privacy
  - WEP bit set when encrypted.
  - Only the frame body.
  - Medium is reserved
  - NAV is updated by ACK
  - Symmetric variable key

c) WEP Details
  - Two mechanism
    - ✓ Default keys
    - ✓ Key mapping

- WEP header and trailer
  - ✓ KEYID in header
  - ✓ ICV in trailer
- dot11UndecryptableCount
  - ✓ Indicates an attack.
- dot11ICVErrorCount
  - ✓ Attack to determine a key is in progress.

11.7.3 Frame Format

- Types
  - ✓ control frames, management frames, data frames
- Sequence numbers
  - ✓ important against duplicated frames due to lost ACKs
- Addresses
  - ✓ receiver, transmitter (physical), BSS identifier, sender (logical)
- Miscellaneous
  - ✓ sending time, checksum, frame control, data

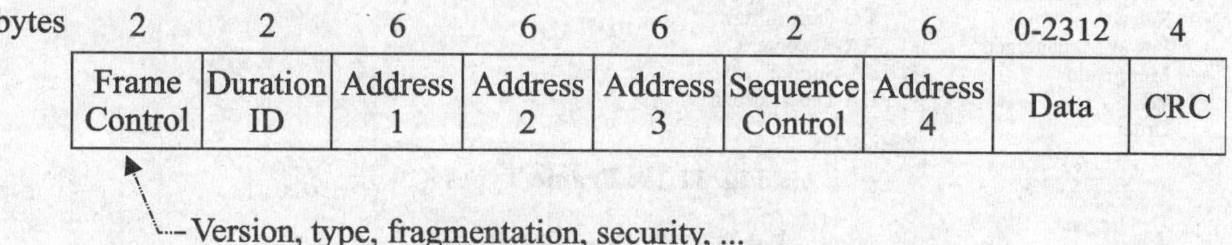

Fig. 11.18: MAC Frame Format

Types of Frame

a) Control Frames
- RTS/CTS/ACK
- CF-Poll/CF-End

b) Management Frames
- Beacons
- Probe Request/Response
- Association Request/Response
- Dissociation/Reassociation
- Authentication/Deauthentication
- ATIM

c) Data Frames

d) PCF Operation
- Poll – eliminates contention
- PC – Point Coordinator
  - ✓ Polling List
  - ✓ Over DCF
  - ✓ PIFS

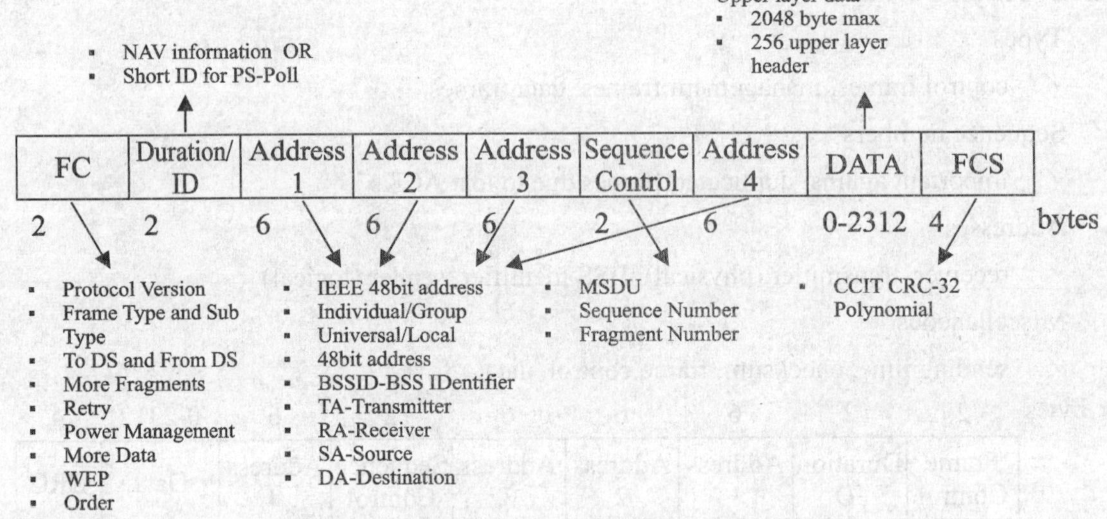

Fig. 11.19: Frame Types

Table 11.5: Frame Subtypes

Control	*Data*	*Management*
▪ RTS	▪ Data	▪ Beacon
▪ CTS	▪ Data+CF-ACK	▪ Probe Request & Response
▪ ACK	▪ Data+CF-Poll	▪ Authentication
▪ PS-Poll	▪ Data+CF-ACK+CF-Poll	▪ Deauthentication
▪ CF-End & CF-End ACK	▪ Null Function	▪ Association Request & Response
	▪ CF-ACK(nodata)	▪ Reassociation Request & Response
	▪ CF-Poll (nodata)	▪ Disassociation
	▪ CF-ACK+CF+Poll	▪ Announcement Traffic Indication Message (ATIM)

- CFP – Contention Free Period
  - ✓ Alternate with DCF
- Periodic Beacon – contains length of CFP
- CF-Poll – Contention Free Poll
- NAV prevents during CFP
- CF-End – resets NAV

11.7.4 Coexistence of PCF and DCF

- A Point Coordinator (PC) resides in the Access Point and controls frame transfers during a Contention Free Period (CFP)
- A CF-Poll frame is used by the PC to invite a station to send data. Stations are polled from a list maintained by the PC
- The CFP alternates with a Contention Period (CP) in which data transfers happen as per the rules of DCF
- This CP must be large enough to send at least one maximum-sized packet including RTS/CTS/ACK
- CFPs are generated at the CFP repetition rate
- The PC sends Beacons at regular intervals and at the start of each CFP
- The CF-End frame signals the end of the CFP

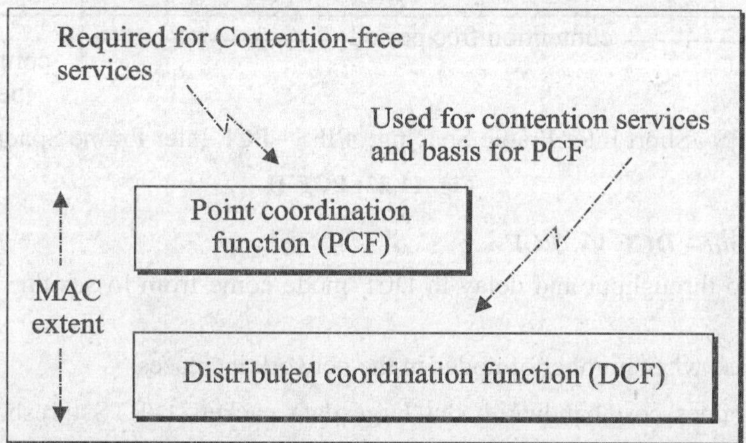

Fig. 11.20: Point Co Ordination Function and Distributed Coordination Function (PCF and DCF)

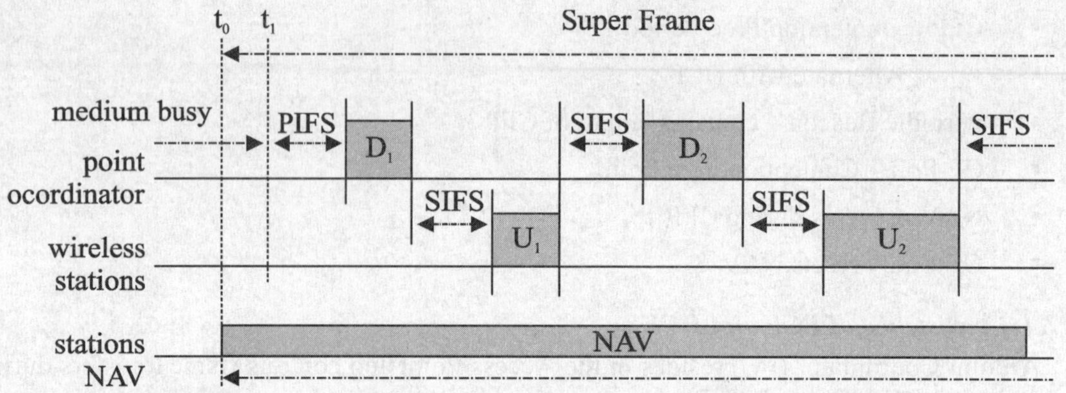

SIFS - Short Inter Frame Spacing; PIFS - PCF Inter Frame Spacing

Fig. 11.21: PCF -I

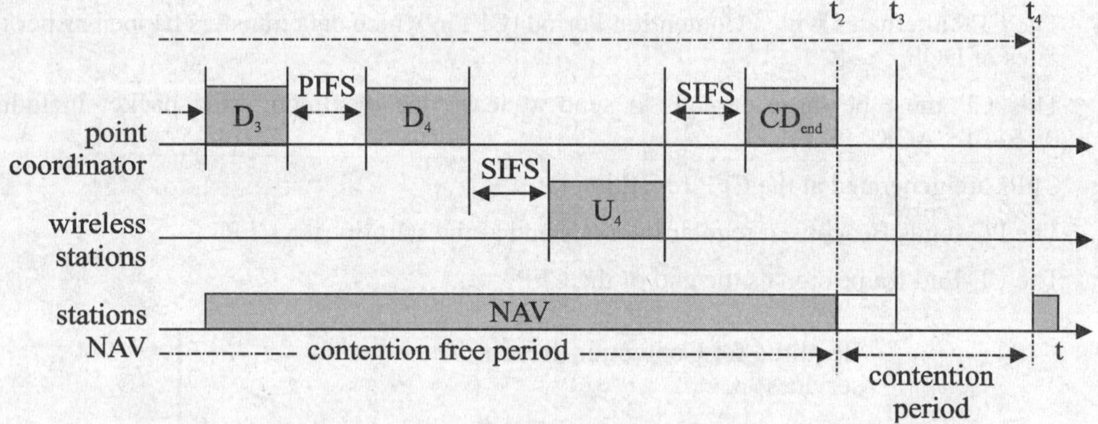

SIFS - Short Inter Frame Spacing; PIFS - PCF Inter Frame Spacing

Fig. 11.22: PCF-II

11.7.5 Throughput – DCF Vs. PCF

- Overheads to throughput and delay in DCF mode come from losses due to collisions and backoff
- These increase when number of nodes in the network increases
- RTS/CTS frames cost bandwidth but large data packets (>RTS threshold) suffer fewer collisions
- RTC/CTS threshold must depend on number of nodes
- Overhead in PCF modes comes from wasted polls
- Polling mechanisms have large influence on throughput
- Throughput in PCF mode shows up to 20% variation with other configuration parameters – CFP repetition rate

- Saturation throughput of DCF less than PCF in all studies presented here ('heavy load' conditions)

11.8 WiFi NETWORK COMPONENTS

- Station
- BSS - Basic Service Set
  - ✓ IBSS : Infrastructure BSS : QBSS
- ESS - Extended Service Set consistsof
  - ✓ A set of infrastructure BSSs.
  - ✓ Connection of APs
  - ✓ Tracking of mobility
- DS – Distribution System
  - ✓ AP communicates with another ad-hoc network

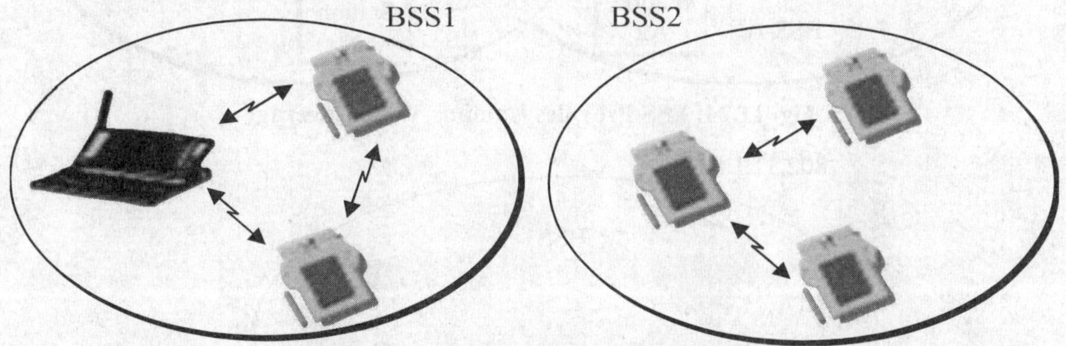

Fig. 11.23: WiFi Network Components

11.8.1 Elements of a Wi-Fi Network

- *Access Point (AP)*— The AP is a wireless LAN transceiver or "base station" that can connect one or many wireless devices simultaneously to the Internet.
- *Wi-Fi cards*— They accept the wireless signal and relay information. They can be internal and external. (e.g PCMCIA Card for Laptop and PCI Card for Desktop PC)
- *Safeguards*— Firewalls and anti-virus software protect networks from uninvited users and keep information secure.

11.8.2 How a Wi-Fi Network Works

- Basic concept is same as Walkie talkies.
- A Wi-Fi hotspot is created by installing an access point to an internet connection.
- An access point acts as a base station.
- When Wi-Fi enabled device encounters a hotspot the device can then connect to that network wirelessly.

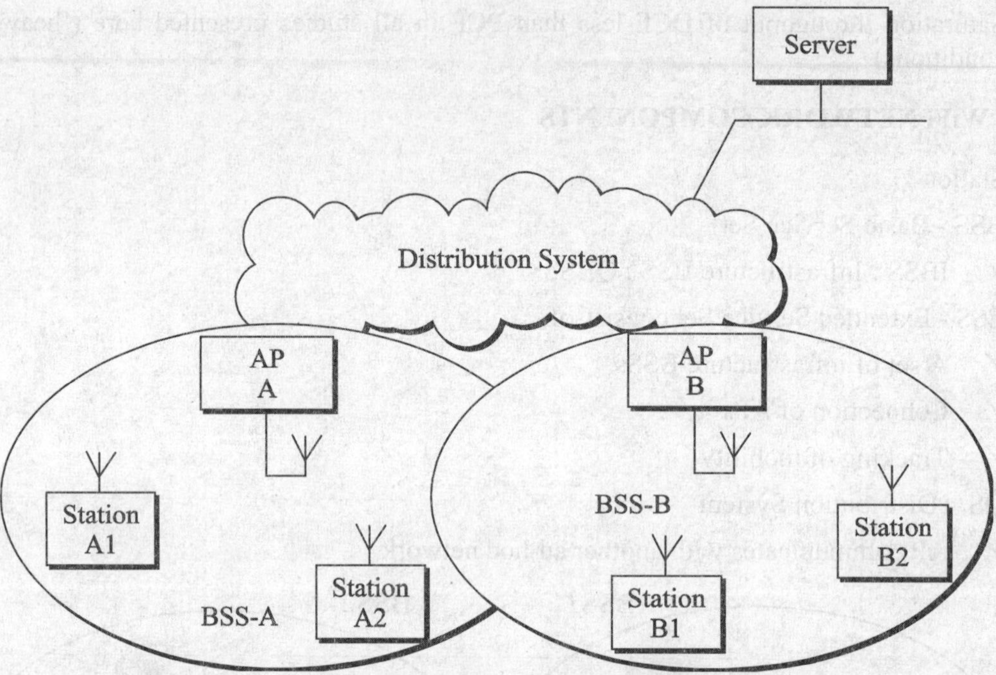

Fig. 11.24: ESS Provides Campus-Wide Coverage

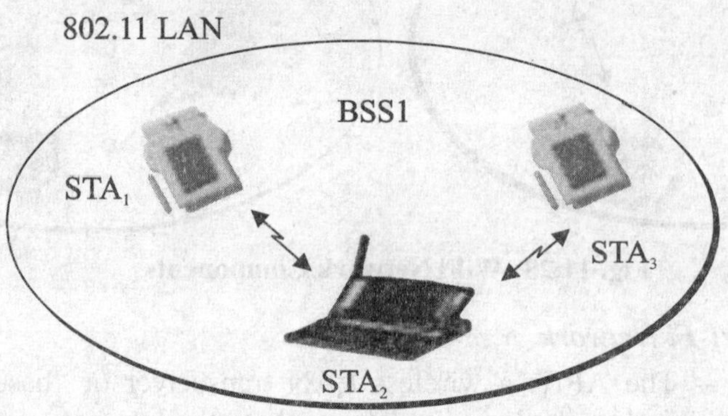

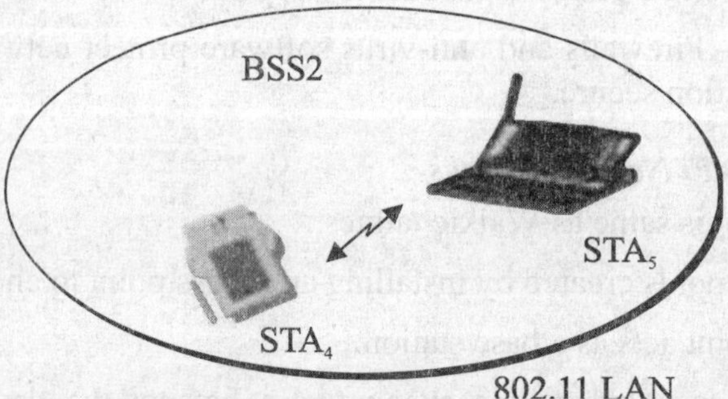

Fig. 11.25: WiFi Network Components

- A single access point can support up to 30 users and can function within a range of 100 – 150 feet indoors and up to 300 feet outdoors.
- Many access points can be connected to each other via Ethernet cables to create a single large network.

Direct communication within a limited range is also possible

✓ *Station (STA)* is a terminal with access mechanisms to the wireless medium

✓ *Basic Service Set (BSS)* is a group of stations using the same radio frequency

✓ Interconnection network is formed from one logical network (EES: Extended Service Set) based on several BSS

11.9 WLAN INFRASTRUCTURE NETWORK

802.11 – WLAN Infrastructure Network

- Station (STA)

  ✓ terminal with access mechanisms to the wireless medium and radio contact to the access point

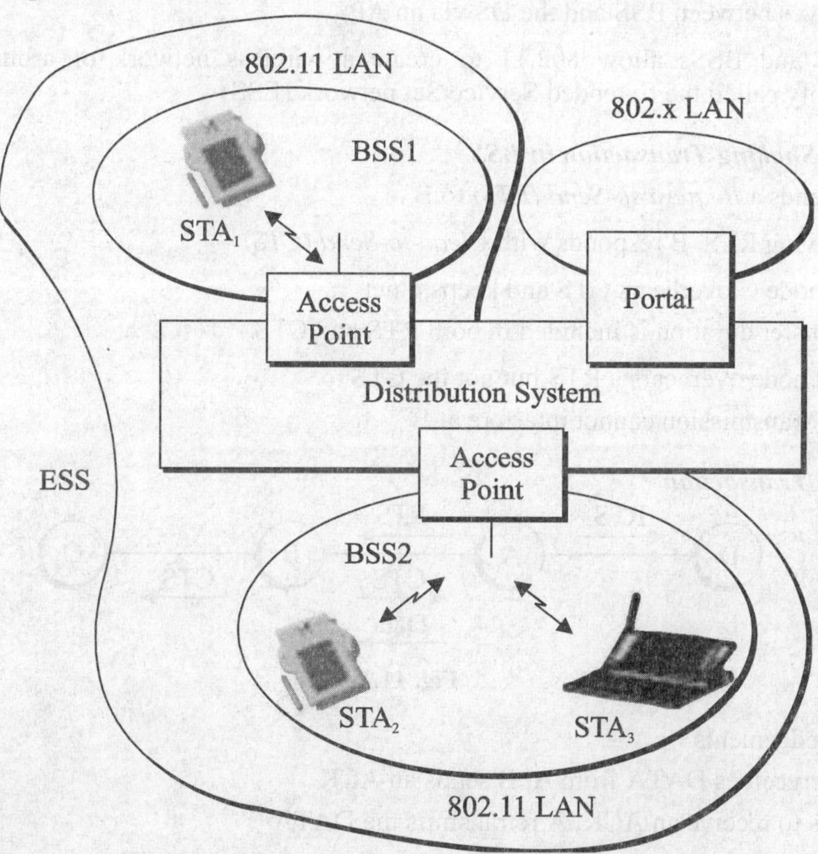

Fig. 11.26: Interconnecting Network

- Basic Service Set (BSS)
  - ✓ group of stations using the same radio frequency
- Access Point
  - ✓ station integrated into the wireless LAN and the distribution system
- Portal
  - ✓ bridge to other (wired) networks
- Distribution System

11.9.1 Distribution System (DS) Concepts

- The Distribution system interconnects multiple BSSs
- 802.11 standard logically separates the wireless medium from the distribution system – it does not preclude, nor demand, that the multiple media be same or different
- An Access Point (AP) is a STA that provides access to the DS by providing DS services in addition to acting as a STA.
- Data moves between BSS and the DS via an AP
- The DS and BSSs allow 802.11 to create a wireless network of arbitrary size and complexity called the Extended Service Set network (ESS)

11.9.2 Hand Shaking Transaction in BSS

- A first sends a *Request-to-Send (RTS)* to B
- On receiving RTS, B responds with *Clear-to-Send (CTS)*
- Hidden node C overhears CTS and keeps quiet
  - ✓ Transfer duration is included in both RTS and CTS
- Exposed node overhears a RTS but not the CTS
  - ✓ D's transmission cannot interfere at B

Reliability in Transaction

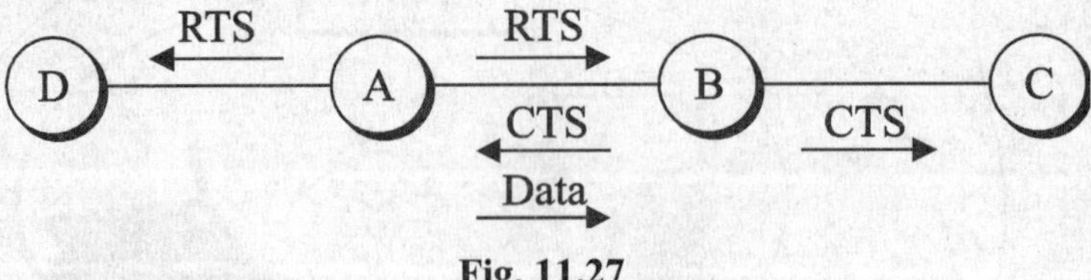

Fig. 11.27

Use acknowledgements

- When B receives DATA from A, B sends an ACK
- If A fails to receive an ACK, A retransmits the DATA
- Both C and D remain quiet until ACK (to prevent collision of ACK)
- Expected duration of transmission+ACK is included in RTS/CTS packets

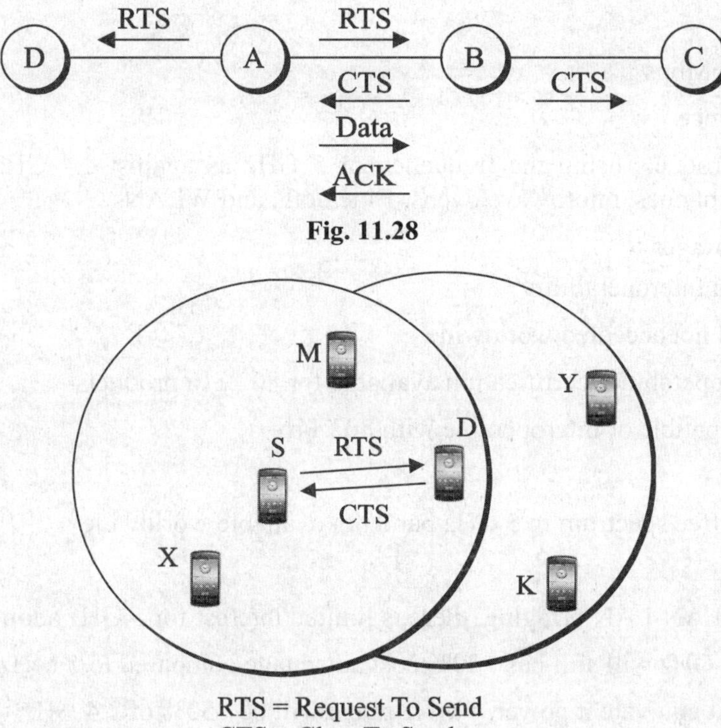

Fig. 11.28

RTS = Request To Send
CTS = Clear To Send

Fig. 11.29: IEEE 802.11

Enhancements in IEEE 802.11 Standard

- *802.11a* offers speeds with a theoretically maximum rate of 54Mbps in the 5 GHz band
- *802.11b* offers speeds with a theoretically maximum rate of 11Mbps at in the 2.4 GHz spectrum band
- *802.11g* is a new standard for data rates of up to a theoretical maximum of 54 Mbps at 2.4 GHz

11.10 802.11a STANDARD

Employs Orthogonal Frequency Division Multiplexing (OFDM)

- Offers higher bandwidth than that of 802.11b, DSSS (Direct Sequence Spread Spectrum) technology used for transmission
- 802.11a MAC (Media Access Control) is same as 802.11b
- Operates in the 5 GHz range

11.10.1 Advantages of 802.11a

- Ultra-high spectrum efficiency
  - ✓ 5 GHz band gives 300 MHz bandwidth (vs. 83.5 MHz @ 2.4 GHz)
  - ✓ More data can travel over a smaller amount of bandwidth

- High speed
  - ✓ Up to 54 Mbps
- Less interference
  - ✓ Fewer products using the frequency of 5 GHz as against 2.4 GHz band shared by cordless phones, microwave ovens, Bluetooth, and WLANs

11.10.2 Disadvantages

- Standards and Interoperability
  - ✓ Standard not accepted worldwide
  - ✓ No interoperability certification available for 802.11a products
  - ✓ Not compatible or interoperable with 802.11b
- Legal issues
  - ✓ License-free spectrum in 5 GHz band not available worldwide
- Market
  - ✓ Beyond LAN-LAN bridging, there is limited interest for 5 GHz adoption
  - ✓ Cost-2.4 GHz will still has >40% cost advantage compared to 5 MHz which is costly
  - ✓ Range-At equivalent power, 5 GHz range will be ~50% of 2.4 GHz
  - ✓ Power consumption-Higher data rates and increased signal require more power
  - ✓ OFDM is less power-efficient then DSSS

11.10.3 Application

- Building-to-building connections
- Video, audio conferencing/streaming video, and audio
- Large file transfers, such as engineering CAD drawings
- Faster Web access and browsing
- High worker density or high throughput scenarios
- Numerous PCs running graphics-intensive applications

11.11 IEEE 802.11g STANDARD

The New Mainstream Wireless LAN Standard

Today's popular IEEE 802.11b (802.11b) for wireless local area networks (WLANs) has changed the face of networking, providing tremendous flexibility for mobile workers and hassle-free Internet sharing for home users. The next milestone in the evolution of WLANs is the introduction of IEEE 802.11g (802.11g). This new IEEE standard will dramatically improve the performance of WLANs, while providing compatibility with the existing installed base of 802.11b networks. In this chapter we will learn how to,

- Provide an explanation of existing WLAN standards
- Describe 802.11g specification requirements
- Set expectations for 802.11g performance
- Discuss the high performance implementation of the 802.11g standard
- 802.11g is a high-speed extension to 802.11b
    - ✓ Compatible with 802.11b
    - ✓ High speed up to 54 Mbps
    - ✓ 2.4 GHz (vs. 802.11a, 5 GHz) Spectrum used
    - ✓ Using OFDM for backward compatibility
    - ✓ Adaptive Rate Shifting

11.11.1 Advantages

- Provides higher speeds and higher capacity requirements for applications
    - ✓ Wireless Public Access
- Compatible with existing 802.11b standard
- Leverages Worldwide spectrum availability in 2.4 GHz
- Likely to be less costly than 5 GHz alternatives
- Provides easy migration for current users of 802.11b WLANs
    - ✓ Delivers backward support for existing 802.11b products
- Provides path to even higher speeds in the future

11.11.2 Performance and Characteristics

Data rate, range, throughput, and compatibility vary among the three WLAN standards. These variations are caused by differences in frequency, modulation schemes, and number of data rates.

11.11.3 Data Rates

The 802.11 standard technologies all support multiple data rates to allow clients to communicate at the best possible speed. Data rate selection is a tradeoff between obtaining the highest possible data rate while trying to minimize the number of communication errors. Whenever there is an error in the data, the systems must spend time to retransmit the data until it is error free. Each 802.11 client performs a procedure to select the best data rate. The 802.11g clients can select from the widest possible range of both OFDM data rates of 54, 48, 36, 24, 18, 12, 9, and 6 Mbps, and the CCK rates of 11, 5.5, 2, and 1 Mbps.

11.11.4 Throughput

Throughput is not the same as data rate for networking systems, because of overhead, environment, and network composition. The throughput of 802.11g products can depend on whether there are 802.11b products nearby. Performance is best in environments where an 802.11g access point (AP) is only communicating with 802.11g clients in a homogeneous WLAN. In these environments, the data rate within 75 feet is 54 Mbps and the throughput is 22–24 Mbps when using Transmission Control Protocol (TCP). In the interest of maximizing performance in the presence of 802.11b products, the 802.11g APs coordinate the use of the transmission medium with protection mechanisms (see sidebar). Because the protection mechanisms require overhead communication, compatibility is provided at the expense of throughput. The CTS-to-self protection mechanism lowers the maximum TCP throughput to approximately 15 Mbps, as shown in the following table.

11.11.5 Compatibility

Because 802.11g uses the same radio signaling (CCK) as 802.11b at the lower four 802.11g data rates, it is fully backward compatible with 802.11b. This enables networks to continue supporting 802.11b enabled devices when migrating to the higher performance standard.

11.11.6 Range and Data Rate

As distance from the access point increases, 802.11 based products provide reduced data rates to maintain connectivity. The 802.11g standard has the same propagation characteristic as 802.11b, because it transmits in the identical 2.4-GHz frequency band. Because 802.11b and 802.11g products share the same propagation characteristics, implementations provide roughly the same maximum range at the same data rate. Because 5-GHz radio signals do not propagate as 2.4-GHz radio signals, the 802.11a product range is limited compared to the 802.11b or 802.11g product range.

The table 11.6 illustrates the expected data rate of each technology at different ranges.

Table 11.6: Wireless LAN Standards

Standard	*Data Rate (Max.)*	*Distance*	*Frequency*
IEEE 802.11a	54 Mbps	50 Meters	5.0GHz
IEEE 802.11b (Wi-Fi)	11 Mbps	100 Meters	2.4GHz
IEEE 802.11g (Backward compatible with 802.11b)	54 Mbps	100 Meters	2.4GHz
HiperLAN2 (ETSI Standard)	54 Mbps	50 Meters	5.0 GHz

11.12 IEEE 802.11e STANDARD

- EDCF - Enhanced DCF
- HCF - Hybrid Coordination Function
- QBSS

- HC – Hybrid Controller
- TC – Traffic Categories
- TXOP – Transmission Opportunity
  - ✓ granted by EDCF-TXOP or HC- poll TXOP
- AIFS – Arbitration Interframe Space

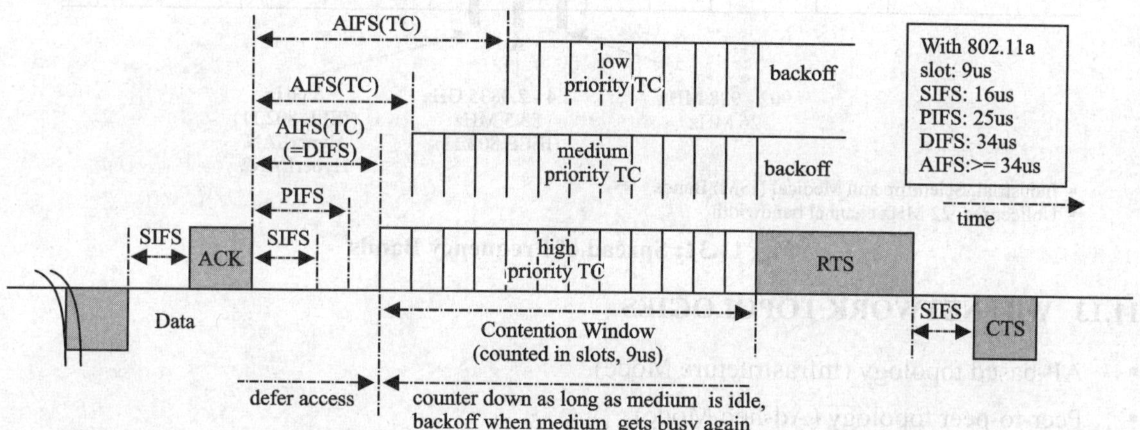

Fig. 11.30

11.12.1 IEEE 802.11 Protocols

- *IEEE 802 11a*— PHY Standard: 8 channels : 54 Mbps Products are available
- *IEEE 802.11b*— PHY Standard: 3 channels : 11 Mbps Products are available
- *IEEE802.11d*— MAC Standard: operate in variable power levels : ongoing
- *IEEE 802 11e*—MAC Standard QoS support: Second half of 2002
- *IEEE 802 11f*— Inter-Access Point Protocol: 2nd half 2002
- *IEEE 802 11g*— PHY Standard 3 channels : OFDM and PBCC 2nd half 2002
- *IEEE 802 11h*— Supplementary MAC Standard: TPC and DFS: 2nd half 2002
- *IEEE802.1H*— Supplementary MAC Standard: Alternative WEP : 2nd half 2002

Frequency Bands - ISM

- Industrial, Scientific and Medical (ISM) bands
- Unlicensed, 22MHz channel bandwidth

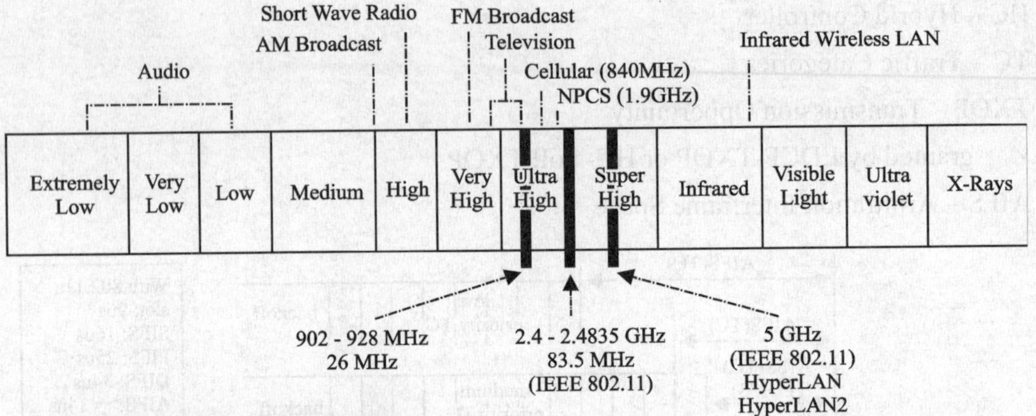

Fig. 11.31: Spread of Frequency Bands

11.13 WiFi NETWORK TOPOLOGIES

- AP-based topology (Infrastructure Mode)
- Peer-to-peer topology (Ad-hoc Mode)
- Point-to-multipoint bridge topology

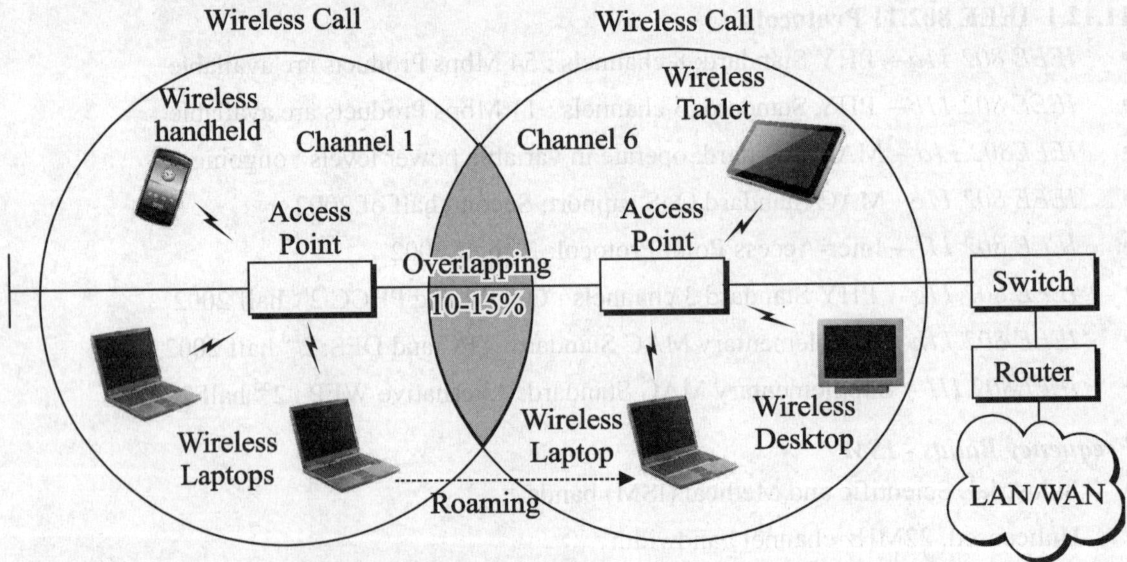

- The client communicate through Access Point
- BSA-RF coverage provided by an AP
- ESA - It consists of 2 or more BSA
- ESA cell includes 10-15% overlap to allow roaming

Fig. 11.32: Typical WLAN

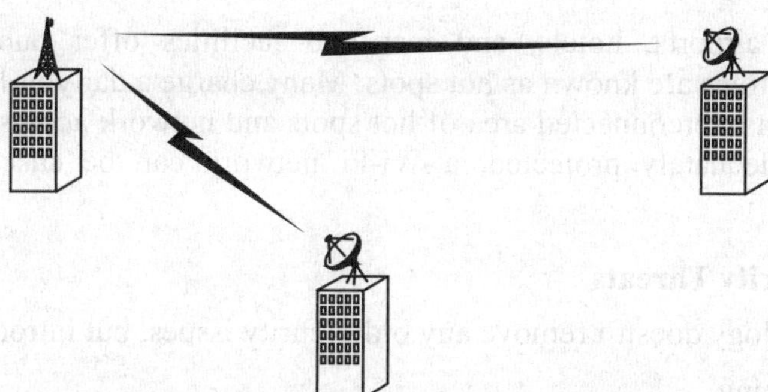

Fig. 11.33: WiFi with external connectivity

AP-based topology

- The client communicate through Access Point.
- BSA-RF coverage provided by an AP.
- ESA-lt consists of 2 or more BSA.
- ESA cell includes 10-15% overlap to allow roaming.

Point-To-Multipoint Bridge Topology

This is used to connect a LAN in one building to a LANs in other buildings even if the buildings are miles apart These conditions receive a clear line of sight between buildings. The line-of-sight range varies based on the type of wireless bridge and antenna used as well as the environmental conditions.

Wi-Fi Applications

- Home
- Small Businesses or SOHO
- Large Corporations & Campuses
- Health Care
- Wireless ISP (WISP), Travellers

11.13.1 Wi-Fi Certification

Wi-Fi (short for "wireless fidelity") is a term for certain types of wireless local area network (WLAN) that use specifications in the 802.11 family. The term Wi-Fi was created by an organization called the Wi-Fi Alliance, which oversees tests that certify product interoperability. A product that passes the alliance tests is given the label "Wi-Fi certified" (a registered trademark).

Originally, Wi-Fi certification was applicable only to products using the 802.11b standard. Today, Wi-Fi can apply to products that use any 802.11 standard. The 802.11 specifications are part of an evolving set of wireless network standards known as the 802.11 family. The particular specification under which a Wi-Fi network operates is called the "flavor" of the network. Wi-Fi has gained acceptance in many businesses, agencies, schools, and homes as an alternative to a wired LAN. Many airports, hotels, and fast-food facilities offer public access to Wi-Fi networks. These locations are known as hot spots. Many charge a daily or hourly rate for access, but some are free. An interconnected area of hot spots and network access points is known as a hot zone. Unless adequately protected, a Wi-Fi network can be susceptible to access by unauthorized users.

11.13.2 Wi-Fi Security Threats

- Wireless technology doesn't remove any old security issues, but introduces new ones
  - ✓ Eavesdropping
  - ✓ Man-in-the-middle attacks
  - ✓ Denial of Service

a) Eavesdropping

- Easy to perform, almost impossible to detect
- By default, everything is transmitted in clear text
  - ✓ Usernames, passwords, content ...
  - ✓ No security offered by the transmission medium
- Different tools available on the internet
  - ✓ Network sniffers, protocol analysers . . .
  - ✓ Password collectors
- With the right equipment, it's possible to eavesdrop traffic from few kilometers away

b) MITM Attack

A man-in-the-middle (MITM) attack is an exploit in which an intruder intercepts communications between two parties, usually an end user and a website. The attacker can use the information accessed to commit identity theft or other types of fraud. Users can protect themselves from a traditional man-in-the-middle attack by refraining from logging into sites where sensitive data is maintaned while on a public network. However, a variation on that exploit, called an "active man-in-the-middle attack" makes it possible for an intruder to access information for any site that the user logs into at other times.

1. Attacker spoofes a disassociate message from the victim
2. The victim starts to look for a new access point, and the attacker advertises his own AP on a different channel, using the real AP's MAC address
3. The attacker connects to the real AP using victim's MAC address

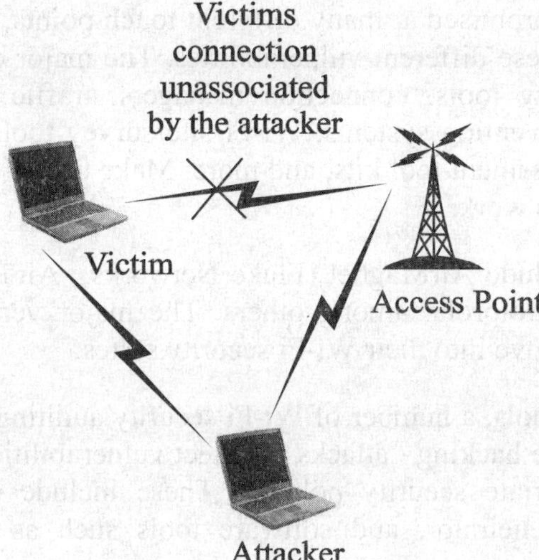

Fig. 11.34: MITM Attack

c) ***Denial of Service***

- Attack on transmission frequecy used
  - ✓ Frequency jamming
  - ✓ Not very technical, but works
- Attack on MAC layer
  - ✓ Spoofed deauthentication / disassociation messages
  - ✓ can target one specific user
- Attacks on higher layer protocol (TCP/IP protocol)
  - ✓ SYN Flooding

d) ***Authentication***

- Keeping unauthorized users off the network
- User Authentication
  - ✓ Authentication Server is used
  - ✓ Username and password
    - Risk— Data (username & password) send before secure channel established Prone to passive eavesdropping by attacker

11.13.3 Wi-Fi Security Tools

- Establishing a encrypted channel before sending username and password
- Server Authentication, Digital Certificate and Validation of digital certificate which occurs automatically within client software are some of the tools.

Wi-Fi security can be compromised at many different touch points, and a number of tools have been developed to guard these different vulnerabilities. The major categories of Wi-Fi security tools include AP discovery tools, connection managers, traffic analyzers, packet sniffers, intrusion detection and prevention systems, Wi-Fi site survey tools, endpoint security clients, vulnerability scanners, assessment tool kits, and more. Make use of appropriate options to make your Wi-Fi security policies work.

Wi-Fi security vendors include AirMagnet (Fluke Networks), AirTight Networks, Bluesocket, Cisco Systems, HP, and Motorola, among others. The major vendors package many of the security tools mentioned above into their Wi-Fi security suites.

Apart from these security tools, a number of Wi-Fi security auditing or penetration testing tools are available. They simulate hacking / attacks to detect vulnerabilities in a given Wi-Fi network to help frame the appropriate security policies. These include devices such as the Silica Immunity and Portable Penetrator, and software tools such as CORE IMPACT Pro and Ethereal.

Common Wi-Fi encryption terms

AES— Advanced encryption standard. Used in WAP2

CCMP— Counter mode with cipher block chaining message authentication code protocol (A derivative of AES).

EAP— Extensible authentication protocol. A number of variations

LEAP— Lightweight extensible authentication protocol, a variation of EAP developed by CISCO Systems.

RADIUS— Remote authentication dial in user service.

TKIP— Temporal key integrity protocol

11.13.4 WI-FI Security Techniques

- Service Set Identifier (SSID)
- Wired Equivalent Privacy (WEP)
- 802.1X Access Control
- Wireless Protected Access (WPA)

11.13.5 Service Set Identifier (SSID)

A service set identifier (SSID) is a sequence of characters that uniquely names a wireless local area network (WLAN). An SSID is sometimes referred to as a "network name." This name allows stations to connect to the desired network when multiple independent networks operate in the same physical area. Each set of wireless devices communicating directly with each other is called a basic service set (BSS). Several BSSs can be joined together to form one logical WLAN segment, referred to as an extended service set (ESS). A Service Set Identifer (SSID) is simply the 1-32 byte alphanumeric name given to each ESS. For example, a departmental WLAN (ESS) may consist of several access points (APs) and dozens of stations, all using the same SSID. Another organization in the same building may operate its own departmental WLAN, composed of APs and stations using a different SSID. The purpose of SSID is to help stations in department A find and connect to APs in department A, ignoring APs belonging to department B. Each AP advertises its presence several times per second by broadcasting beacon frames that carry the ESS name (SSID). Stations can discover APs by passively listening for beacons, or they can send probe frames to actively search for an AP with the desired SSID.

- SSID is used to identify an 802.11 network
- It can be pre-configured or advertised in beacon broadcast
- It is transmitted in clear text
    - ✓ Provide very little security

11.13.6 Wired Equivalent Privacy (WEP)

Wired Equivalent Privacy (WEP) is a security protocol, specified in the IEEE Wireless Fidelity (Wi-Fi) standard, 802.11b, that is designed to provide a wireless local area network (WLAN) with a level of security and privacy comparable to what is usually expected of a wired LAN. WEP seeks to establish similar protection to that offered by the wired network's physical security measures by encrypting data transmitted over the WLAN. Data encryption protects the vulnerable wireless link between clients and access points; once this measure has been taken, other typical LAN security mechanisms such as password protection, end-to-end encryption, virtual private networks (VPNs), and authentication can be put in place to ensure privacy.

Provide same level of security as by wired network

- Original security solution offered by the IEEE 802.11 standard
- Uses RC4 encryption with pre-shared keys and 24 bit initialization vectors (IV)
- key schedule is generated by concatenating the shared secret key with a random generated 24-bit IV
- 32 bit ICV (Integrity check value)
- No. of bits in keyschedule is equal to sum of length of the plaintext and ICV
- 64 bit preshared key-WEP
- 128 bit preshared key-WEP2
- Encrypt data only between 802.11 stations.once it enters the wired side of the network (between access point) WEP is no longer valid
- Security Issue with WEP
- Short IV
- Static key
- Offers very little security at all

11.13.7 802.1x Access Control

- Designed as a general purpose network access control mechanism
  - ✓ Not Wi-Fi specific
- Authenticate each client connected to AP (for WLAN) or switch port (for Ethernet)
- Authentication is done with the RADIUS server, which "tells" the access point whether access to controlled ports should be allowed or not
  - ✓ AP forces the user into an unauthorized state
  - ✓ user send an EAP start message
  - ✓ AP return an EAP message requesting the user's identity
  - ✓ Identity send by user is then forwarded to the authentication server by AP
  - ✓ Authentication server authenticate user and return an accept or reject message back to the AP
  - ✓ If accept message is return, the AP changes the client's state to authorized and normal traffic flows

11.13.8 WiFi Security Protocols

802.1x is an extensible authentication framework for port-based access control. This framework can be used with a number of authentication methods, including:

EAP-TLS (Transport Layer Security)— RFC 2716, implemented in Windows XP, requires mutual certificate-based authentication.

EAP-TTLS (Tunneled Transport Layer Security)— An Internet draft, implemented by Funk Odyssey, that extends TLS to securely tunnel further information - notably, client sub-authentication based on legacy passwords.

LEAP (Lightweight EAP)— Cisco's own variation on EAP, implemented by AiroNet products, that provides mutual authentication based on password challenge-response.

PEAP (Protected EAP Protocol)— A new Internet draft designed to overcome some of the vulnerabilities that exist in other EAP methods, providing secure mutual authentication and legacy subauthentication.

In a recent INT Media Research survey of 300 companies with active WLANs, less than a quarter of those surveyed expect to deploy 802.1x by the end of 2003. WEP shared key authentication and higher-layer (VPN or SSL) authentication are being used far more often than 802.1x. From this, We conclude that 802.1x and related EAP methods have not yet matured to the point where consumers can plan to use it.

Nonetheless, 802.1x plays a central role in emerging IEEE 802.11i standards for enhanced WLAN security, enabling authentication and key distribution. Key vendors like Cisco and Microsoft have announced intent to support 802.1x with PEAP in future WLAN products. If PEAP materializes, I expect LEAP to fade away. But this race is still a bit early to call.

There is another critical ingredient in WLAN security: confidentiality. The IEEE 802.11i fix for WEP-based products, known as the Temporal Key Integrity Protocol (TKIP), should begin appearing in firmware upgrades by the end of 2002. In 2003, a more robust AES-based Wireless Robust Authenticated Protocol (WRAP) will emerge in next generation WLAN hardware. TKIP fixes the most glaring weaknesses in WEP, while WRAP provides a stronger, faster privacy solution from scratch.

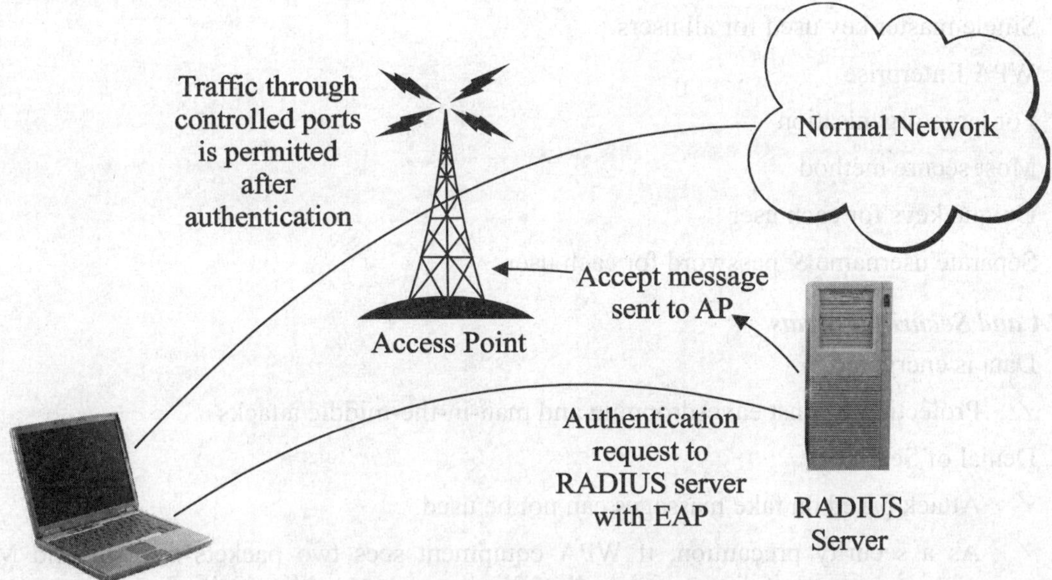

Fig. 11.35: 802.1x Access Control

11.13.9 Wireless Protected Access (WPA)

- WPA is a specification of standard based, interoperable security enhancements that strongly increase the level of data protection and access control for existing and future wireless LAN system.
- User Authentication
  - ✓ 802.1x
  - ✓ EAP
- TKIP (Temporal Key Integrity Protocol) encryption
  - ✓ RC4, dynamic encryption keys (session based)
    - – 48 bit IV
    - – per packet key mixing function
  - ✓ Fixes all issues found from WEP
- Uses Message Integrity Code (MIC) Michael
  - ✓ Ensures data integrity

- Old hardware should be upgradeable to WPA
- WPA comes in two flavors
- WPA-PSK
- use pre-shared key
- For SOHO environments
- Single master key used for all users
- WPA Enterprise
- For large organisation
- Most secure method
- Unique keys for each user
- Separate username & password for each user

WPA and Security Threats

- Data is encrypted
  - ✓ Protection against eavesdropping and man-in-the-middle attacks
- Denial of Service
  - ✓ Attack based on fake massages can not be used.
  - ✓ As a security precaution, if WPA equipment sees two packets with invalid MICs within a second, it disassociates all its clients, and stops all activity for a minute
  - ✓ Only two packets a minute enough to completely stop a wireless network

11.14 IEEE 802.11i STANDARD

- Provides standard for WLAN security
- Authentication
  - ✓ 802.1x
- Data encryption
  - ✓ AES protocol is used
- Secure fast handoff-This allow roaming between APs without requiring client to fully reauthenticate to every AP.
- Will require new hardware

Advantages

- Mobility
- Ease of Installation
- Flexibility

- Cost
- Reliability
- Security
- Use unlicensed part of the radio spectrum
- Roaming
- Speed

Limitations

- Interference
- Degradation in performance
- High power consumption
- Limited range

Table 11.7: IEEE 802.11i Enhanced Security

Description	Enhancements to the 802.11 MAC standard to increase the security; addresses new encryption methods and upper layer authentication
Importance	High: weakness of WEP encryption is damaging the 802.11 standard perception in the market
Related standards	This applies to 802.11b. 802.11a and 802.11g systems. 802.1x is key reference for upper layer authentication
Status + Roadmap	Enhanced encryption software will replace WEP software; This is on a recommended best practice /voluntary basis; development in Tgl: first draft Mar 2001; next draft due Mar 2002; stable draft: July 2002; final standard: Jan 2003
Products affected	Client and AP cards (Controller chip. Firmware, Driver) AP kernel, RG kernel, BG kernel
Agere's activity	Actively proposing WEP improvement methods, participating in all official/interim meetings
Key players	Agere / Microsoft / Agere / Cisco / Ather os / Intel / 3Com / Inter sil / Symbol / Certicom /RSA / Funk
Key issues	Mode of AES to use for encryption (CTR/CBC [CBC MIC] or OCB [MIC and Encryption function])

Table 11.8: IEEE 802.1x - Port Based Control

Description	Enhancements to the 802.11 MAC standard to increase the security; addresses new encryption methods and upper layer authentication
Importance	High: weakness of WEP encryption is damaging the 802.11 standard perception in the market
Related standards	This applies to 802.11b. 802.11a and 802.11 g systems. 802.1x is key reference for upper layer authentication
Status + Roadmap	Enhanced encryption software will replace WEP software; This is on a recommended best practice / voluntary basis; development in Tgl: first draft Mar 2001; next draft due Mar 2002; stable draft: July 2002; final standard: Jan 2003
Products affected	Client and AP cards (Controller chip. Firmware, Driver) AP kernel, RG kernel, BG kernel
Agere's activity	Actively proposing WEP improvement methods, participating in all official/interim meetings
Key players	Agere / Microsoft / Agere / Cisco / Ather os / Intel / 3Com / Inter sil / Symbol / Certicom / RSA / Funk
Key issues	Mode of AES to use for encryption (CTR/CBC [CBC MIC] or OCB [MIC and Encryption function])

Table 11.9: IEEE 802.1p - Traffic Class

Reference	IEEE 802.1p (Traffic Class and Dynamic Multicast Filtering)
Description	A method to differentiate traffic streams in priority classes in support of quality of service offering
Importance	Medium: forms a key part of the 802.11e proposals for QoS at the MAC level
Related standards	This applies to 802.11b. 802.11a and 802.11g systems; is an addition to the 802.1d Bridge standard (annex H).
Status + Roadmap	Final standard; incorporated in 1998 edition of 802.1d (annex H)
Products affected	Client and AP cards (Driver); AP kernel. RG kernel. BG kernel
Agere's activity	Investigating implementation options
Key players	N/A
Key issues	N/A

11.15 IEEE 802.15 - BLUE TOOTH

802.15 is a communications specification that was approved in early 2002 by the Institute of Electrical and Electronics Engineers Standards Association (IEEE-SA) for wireless personal area networks (WPANs). The initial version, 802.15.1, was adapted from the Bluetooth specification and is fully compatible with Bluetooth 1.1.

Bluetooth is a well-known and widely used specification that defines parameters for wireless communications among portable digital devices including notebook computers, peripherals, cellular telephones, beepers, and consumer electronic devices. The specification also allows for connection to the Internet.

11.15.1 IEEE 802.15 Bluetooth Standard

- Regulatory Range-2.4 to 2.4835 GHz
- RF Channels 0 to 78
- Carrier spacing is 1 MHz
- *Technology*— FHSS
- *RF Bandwidth*— 200 KHz
- *Transmit Power*— 0.1w
- Operates in 2.4 GHz ISM (industrial, scientific and medical) band
- 79 channels are there totally
- frequency hopping spread spectrum technique used
- transmitter uses two-level GFSK
- up to 8 devices can communicate in a small network called piconet

Error Correction

Three types of Error Correction schemes are used

1) 1/3 rate Forward Error Correction
2) 2/3 rate FEC
3) Automatic repeat request (ARQ)

Bluetooth Applications

- *Data and voice access point*— instant real time voice and data transmission over wireless connection.
- *Cable Replacement*— eliminates proprietary cable attachments

Adhoc networking— devices can establish contact with one another when within the range.

The IEEE 802.15 Working Group proposes two general categories of 802.15, called TG4 (low rate) and TG3 (high rate). The TG4 version provides data speeds of 20 Kbps to 250 Kbps. The TG3 version supports data speeds ranging from 11 Mbps to 55 Mbps. Additional features include the use of up to 254 network devices, dynamic device addressing, support for devices in which latency is critical, full handshaking, security provisions, and power management. There will be 16 channels in the 2.4-GHz band, 10 channels in the 915-MHz band, and one channel in the 868-MHz band.

The IEEE plans to refine the 802.15 specification to work with the Specification and Description Language (SDL), particularly SDL-88, SDL-92, and SDL-2000 updates of the International Telecommunication Union (ITU) recommendation Z.100.

11.16 IEEE 802.11n HIGH DATA RATES

Initial Situation: Antenna Diversity

WLAN radio networks, working according to IEEE 802.11abg are usually equipped with antenna diversity. This can be quickly recognized at equipment with external antennas because 2 antennas are attached to the device. With this technology the negative consequences of the multipath propagation of the radio wave are reduced considerably. Multipath propagation is typical for radio waves in the GHz frequency band (microwave) where radio waves reach the receiver via different ways, run different distances and change their phase and polarization. The WLAN receiver must be high quality because he has to separate this mixture of different wave fronts to decode the original information. The receiver gets support from a switch which helps to choose one out of those two antennas. If he has decided in favour of one, then he will receive the following data packet (frame) from this antenna and transmits his answer via this antenna. This decision must be drawn again and again. It is important to know that radio chipsets own exactly one sending path and exactly one receive path. Both are connected to the two antennas via a switch. If the system has decided to select one antenna during reception, both the sending path and the other antenna will be switched off. During the consecutive sending both the receive path and one antenna will be deactivated. This mechanism is true for both access points and clients. It is also called "switched antenna diversity".

Diversity Becomes MIMO

At IEEE 802.11abg systems at one point of time there is exactly one reception or one transmission path active. The IEEE 802.11n offers an improvement with MIMO. MIMO means *multiple in multiple out* and is the reception or transmission via several independent sending and reception paths (spatial streams). By means of this separation a higher data rate is achieved but also a more robust signal transmission. This separation of streams is also called spatial multiplexing. Unfortunately, it comes along with more computing effort of the signal processor chip. Furthermore it requires more space (and therefore costs) by several transmission and reception paths on the chip set and in addition increased efforts for the antenna technology. This is compensated by the trend of silicon vendors who integrate more chips of the chipset into one package and reduce costs.

Increased Data Rate by Means of Multipath Propagation (Spatial Multiplexing)

Spatial multiplexing is a technology which converts the disadvantage (IEEE 802.11abg) of multipath propagation into an advantage (IEEE 802.11abgn). By the separation of the data stream into several streams it is possible to distribute the data on several transmitters and afterwards on several (spatially separated) antennas. By this spatial separation the transmitted signals may select different paths, gets reflected at different obstacles and reaches the receiver at different points of time. For an optimized usage of the technology at least the same number of antennas and receivers is necessary. The data rate increases almost linearly with the number of data streams and antennas used. If a cost reduced client owns only 2 antennas and 2 spatial streams, e.g. an access point with 3 antennas and 3 spatial streams must adjust to this situation. The access point will transmit via his third antenna a redundant signal. A participant in an IEEE 802.11n radio network is therefore described by the number of antennas for transmission and the number of antennas for reception. In addition, the number of spatial streams should be mentioned. So, a system 3×3 with 2 streams is a WLAN unit with, 3 transmit and 3 receive antennas (in this order) and it is supported by 2 spatial streams in the radio chip set (e.g. because the radio chip set is optimized pricewise).

Modulation with HT-OFDM

In general, Orthogonal Frequency Division Multiplex (OFDM) modulation is well known from IEEE 802.11a and g and it is used in the Physical layer (PHY). But several optimizations are implemented to be used in IEEE 802.11n. For example the frequency spectrum of a 20 MHz channel is divided up in a more optimized way into sub channels. Additional optimizations increase the throughput by approx. 30% compared to OFDM known from IEEE 802.11a and g. However, a real improvement is achieved by channel bonding of two 20 MHz channels to a 40 MHz channel. Only this improvement boosts the gross data up to 150 Mbps for one stream (instead of 54 Mbps of IEEE 802.11a and g). It has to be taken into account, that merely 3 such non overlapping 20 MHz channels are available in the 2.4 GHz frequency band. At 5 GHz there are between 11 and 19 (dependent on the country) available. In general, it can be said that IEEE 802.11n leverages the frequency spectrum in a better way and offers a higher data rate.

For a description of the performance of a WLAN unit according to IEEE 802.11n it is important to check exactly the specification, because lot optimizations are optional. Furthermore it must be measured, which net data rate can be actually achieved, because both chip set and the implementation of the software protocol offer a lot room for optimization.

Improvements in the MAC Layer

Known weaknesses in the MAC Layer of IEEE 802.11a and g are also improved and optimize the net throughput. E.g. distances between data packets (interframe space) can be shortened for long data packets. Furthermore single data packets (frames) can be aggregated to increase the density and avoid overhead. As MIMO offers several transmit and receive streams, energy consumption is an important topic. If a participant is inactive, at IEEE 802.11n it is allowed to switch off all its receive streams except for one. This one listens to the data traffic in the air interface and wakes up the other receivers in case of an incident.

Downward Compatibility

Configured for legacy mode an IEEE 802.11n unit acts equal to an IEEE 802.11abg unit. Advantages derive from MIMO, where several transmit and receive streams work together at the same point of time. This results in a higher coverage and more reliable data traffic, for the same data rate.In mixed mode the first data of a frame, the preamble, is transmitted according to IEEE802.11ag. Afterwards, the payload is transmitted according the agreed mode, very fast with IEEE 802.11n or as hitherto with IEEE 802.11abg. In this mode, an IEEE 802.11n radio network can integrate IEEE 802.11ag units.

Finally, there is the green field mode, which defines a pure IEEE 802.11n traffic and exploits in the best way the advantages of IEEE 802.11n.

Standardization

Today (2009), IEEE 802.11n is finally approved. Since 2007, there is a version "Draft 2.0" available which is already implemented in lot products. This version was pushed by customers who required higher data rates and it was supported by Wi-Fi. An advantage of Draft 2.0 is the fact that the Wi-Fi has defined the interoperability tests for a mixed installation of units from different vendors and runs already the certification. Therefore, this Draft is wide spread. It can be expected that future products will support both Draft 2.0 and the final version.

Note: Several times IEEE and Wi-Fi have already practiced this process in the past, e.g. at security with IEEE 802.11i / WPA or multimedia with IEEE 802.11e / WMM.

Applications and Advantages in Home, Enterprise and Industry

The well known standards IEEE 802.11abg offer (gross) data rates of 54 Mbps which correspond with a net data rate of approx. 27 Mbps. However, a WLAN radio link with this performance represents a bottle neck in today's Fast Ethernet data networks. This kind of network expects data rates up to 100 Mbps (or even 1000 Mbps). Therefore, the higher data rates of IEEE 802.11n are more than appreciated. Video is one of the killer applications in home networks which have big benefit from the improvements of IEEE 802.11n. Professional installations at enterprise customers expect the connection of as many workers as possible in the smallest area (e.g. conference room). This density requires a high data rate per square meter. In industry applications a high reliability is the most important feature of a radio network. There, MIMO offers a stable radio link (at the same transmission rate). The usually disturbing multipath propagation favours even the data transmission because the original data stream is separated into several streams and transmitted in parallel. Furthermore, in industrial applications there is also the trend to higher data rates. Not seldom video data can be found, too because e.g. live pictures from the process can be monitored in the control room. To guarantee a continuous data stream, a minimal data rate may not be fallen below. Finally, WLAN is frequently used in point-to-point connections to link to a remote production site. This connection represents the bottle neck of the system and the highest possible net throughput is very important.

11.17 IEEE 802.11S MESHED WIRELESS LANS

The term meshed or mesh network means literally what it says. The basic idea behind mesh networks is based on redundant paths for the transfer of data from one node to the next. If one path is disrupted, the network automatically finds a new one. In many case, the declared aim is also to be able to add additional nodes in a mesh network with little effort. Ideally, the network should manage itself. In conjunction with wireless LAN networks, the idea of a mesh network has become reality in the meantime although previously implemented meshed MANs were always based on proprietary developments.

Systems Today

There are many types of mesh networks. Some providers call a Wireless Distribution System (WDS) together with the Rapid Spanning Tree Protocol (RSTP) a mesh network. There are versions with only one or multiple gateways to other cable networks or the Internet. Other providers, on the other hand, consider that a pure mesh network completely does without the use of any backbone infrastructure. In this case, the data is sent over several nodes to a recipient without any routers in between. The clients also function as routers for other clients.

Wireless Meshed in Automation

In automation, mesh networking allows redundant data paths with which the loss of individual connections (meshes) can be compensated fully automatically. The use of wireless LAN technology in conjunction with meshed networking can allow operation in environments where cable trays would be difficult or uneconomical to install. A further scenario for the use of such networks could be in ad hoc wireless LANs that (equipped with meshed networking technology) could be set up quickly with little administrative effort, for example for trade fairs, festivals or military applications in the field.

Standardisation

An IEEE working group is aiming to establish a heterogeneous standard for wireless mesh networks by spring 2011. This is known as IEEE 802.11s. The aims of this standard are simple extensibility up to and including large distributed wireless LANs, flexibility in production facilities and in similar fast changing environments, the possibility of setting up networks for crisis management, for example in the case of catastrophes, and the formation of highly redundant networks that can be used by the military and in safety-oriented environments. The future standard currently envisages three basic infrastructure elements for setting up meshed wireless LAN structures. Mesh points establish and expand a wireless backbone; mesh access points have the same function with the additional option of linking clients over a second wireless module. Mesh portals function as backbone providers and acting as a bridge also provide access to different network types. Figure 2 illustrates how the components could be arranged.

Setup of a Mesh Network

The standard IEEE 802.11s standard describes the capabilities of a mesh point. It should be capable of recognizing its neighbours and of finding the correct route using a path selection protocol. The routing should be very hardware-oriented, in other words, optimized for speed. Data security is based on IEEE 802.11i for which an enhancement is necessary compared with normal wireless LAN environments to implement secure connections with clients over several hops.

The mesh points must, of course, establish secure connections among themselves for which suitable mechanisms must be included for two-way authentication. To allow roaming from one mesh access point to the next, fast reauthentication must also be possible (seamless roaming) to avoid disrupting time-critical applications or sessions relevant for security. A further point is management in mesh networks to avoid overload. An expansion of the IEEE 802.11e standard is planned for management packets (for example flow control). Since the mesh points are located very close to each other, there is inevitably a strong mutual influence due to overlapping of the RF fields and mutual interference. It is therefore important that techniques such as beam forming are used to ensure that the same radio channels are used "at the earliest" in the next but one cell to avoid the channels in immediately neighbouring cells from overlapping. The risk of collisions is also greater.

11.18 IEEE 802.22 STANDARD FOR WIRELESS REGIONAL AREA NETWORKS

This new standard for Wireless Regional Area Networks (WRANs) takes advantage of the favorable transmission characteristics of the VHF and UHF TV bands to provide broadband wireless access over a large area up to 100 km from the transmitter. Each WRAN will deliver up to 22 Mbps per channel without interfering with reception of existing TV broadcast stations, using the so-called white spaces between the occupied TV channels. This technology is especially useful for serving less densely populated areas, such as rural areas, and developing countries where most vacant TV channels can be found.

IEEE 802.22 incorporates advanced cognitive radio capabilities including dynamic spectrum access, incumbent database access, accurate geolocation techniques, spectrum sensing, regulatory domain dependent policies, spectrum etiquette, and coexistence for optimal use of the available spectrum.

The IEEE 802.22 Working Group started its work following the Notice of Inquiry issued by the United States Federal Communications Commission on unlicensed operation in the TV broadcast bands.

11.19 PLANNING THE NETWORK

With any network technology, there are tradeoffs between performance and cost. With wireless technologies, other factors such as range and capacity should also be considered. Table summarizes typical user requirements and the characteristics of WLAN technology. In most cases, 802.11g provides the correct mix of characteristics for the different categories of user requirements. Upgrading to 802.11gis the easiest and least expensive choice, because it can be done gradually, without sacrificing the current WLAN infrastructure. The 802.11g APs automatically support existing 802.11b clients while providing increased speed to 802.11g clients.

Planning Network Migration

As network managers plan upgrades from existing wireless 802.11b networks, the two basic technologies to consider are 802.11g and 802.11a/g. An upgrade to 802.11g is a simple proposition. Users equipped with802.11g-enabled notebooks will gain immediate access to the 802.11b network. These users will experience a throughput boost as APs are upgraded to 802.11g. As budget allows, dual-band 802.11a/g products can be deployed to meet the demand for more network capacity while remaining backward compatible. The dual-band APs may need to be more closely spaced to ensure coverage for 802.11a clients. Transmit power control can be enabled in the 802.11gnetwork to optimize performance of closely spaced access points. Because 802.11g is forecast to rapidly replace 802.11b, a dual-band a/b AP solution becomes immediately obsolete.

Public Access—Hotspots (Wi-Fi Zone™)

Compatibility and range matter most to Hotspot operators and public access WLAN customers. Public WLAN Hotspots must be certain that their APs can communicate using mainstream standards that offer connectivity to the widest possible range of subscribers. Today, nearly all Hotspot traffic is 802.11b. Public access operators remain in the 2.4-GHz band because it offers twice the range and four times the coverage area of the 5-GHzalternative, and public access customers continue to use the 2.4-GHz spectrum to maximize connectivity. As Hotspots upgrade, they will add 802.11g to their networks to add range and preserve interoperability.

Capacity, Coverage, and Deployment Considerations for IEEE 802.11g

Few technologies have received as much anticipation as 802.11g, the IEEE standard for wireless local area networking that operates in the 2.4 GHz band with a top data rate of 54 Mbps. It is easy to understand why-802.11g provides performance that can be comparable to that of the 802.11a WLAN standard that operates in the 5-GHz band, while providing backward compatibility with the legacy 11-Mbps 802.11b standard. This combination of higher performance and backward compatibility is similar in concept to the wildly successful and now-ubiquitous 100-Mbps Fast Ethernet standard from the wired LAN world. Network professionals naturally expect similar ubiquity for products based on the 802.11g standard, sometimes to the exclusion of 802.11b- and 802.11a-based products. This document outlines the capabilities of 802.11g, highlighting both its advantages and its deficiencies. The information provided will enable network professionals to achieve an understanding of the performance and capacity capabilities of 802.11g, range and coverage area expectations, and other information that will help to result in a successful 802.11g deployment.

802.11g in Brief

The IEEE 802.11g WLAN standard can be thought of as an intersection between the 802.11b and 802.11a standards. Like 802.11b, 802.11g operates in the same 2.4-GHz portion of the radio frequency spectrum that allows for license-free operation on a nearly worldwide basis. 802.11g is also limited to the same three nonoverlapping channels as 802.11b. An important mandatory requirement of 802.11g is full backward compatibility with 802.11b, which both provides investment protection for the installed base of 802.11b clients and extracts a substantial performance penalty when operating in this mode.

Table 11.10: 802.11g Data Rates, Transmission Types, and Modulation Schemes

Data Rate (Mbps)	*Transmission Type*	*Modulation Scheme*
54	OFDM	64 QAM
48	OFDM	64 QAM
36	OFDM	16 QAM
24	OFDM	16 QAM
18	OFDM	QPSK1
12	OFDM	QPSK
11	DSSS	CCK2
9	OFDM	BPSK3
6	OFDM	BPSK
5.5	DSSS	CCK
2	DSSS	QPSK
1	DSSS	BPSK

QPSK quadrature amplitude modulation; CCK complementary code keying; BPSK biphase shift keying

Like 802.11a, 802.11g uses Orthogonal Frequency Division Multiplexing (OFDM) for transmitting data. OFDM is a more efficient means of transmission than Direct Sequence Spread Spectrum (DSSS) transmission, which is used by 802.11b. When coupled with various modulation types, 802.11g (like 802.11a) is capable of supporting much higher data rates than 802.11b. As noted in Table 1, 802.11g uses a combination of OFDM and DSSS transmission to support a large set of data rates-in fact, all of the data rates supported by both 802.11a and 802.11b.

11.20 802.11g PERFORMANCE AND CAPACITY

Within the context of WLANs, network capacity is roughly the product of throughput multiplied by the number of available channels. As stated above, like 802.11b, 802.11g devices are limited to no more than three nonoverlapping channels. The result is that any increase in network capacity relative to 802.11b will result from increases in throughput alone. The throughput provided by 802.11g networks is dependent upon a number of environmental and application factors, chief amongst them being whether or not the 802.11g network is supporting legacy 802.11b clients.

802.11 networks use Carrier Sense Multiple Access with Collision Avoidance (CSMA/CA), a media access method similar to that of shared Ethernet. Also, 802.11b devices, which share the same 2.4 GHz band as 802.11g, have no means of detecting OFDM transmissions. Although 802.11b devices can sense “noise” in the 2.4-GHz band via their Clear Channel Assessment (CCA) capabilities, they cannot decode any data, management, or control packets sent via OFDM. Given this, the 802.11g standard includes protection mechanisms to provide for coexistence and backward compatibility.

When 802.11b clients are associated to an 802.11g access point, the access point will turn on a protection mechanism called Request to Send/Clear to Send (RTS/CTS). Originally a mechanism for addressing the “hidden node problem” (a condition where two clients can maintain a link to an access point but, due to distance cannot hear each other), RTS/CTS adds a degree of determinism to the otherwise multiple access network. When RTS/CTS is invoked, clients must first request access to the medium from the access point with an RTS message. Until the access point replies to the client with a CTS message, the client will refrain from accessing the medium and transmitting its data packets. When received by clients other than the one that sent the original RTS, the CTS command is interpreted as a “do not send” command, causing them to refrain from accessing the medium. One can see that this mechanism will preclude 802.11b clients from transmitting simultaneously with an 802.11g client, thereby avoiding collisions that decrease throughput due to retries. One can see that this additional RTS/CTS process adds a significant amount of protocol overhead that also results in a decrease in network throughput.

In addition to RTS/CTS, the 802.11g standard adds one other significant requirement to allow for 802.11b compatibility. In the event that a collision occurs due to simultaneous transmissions (the likelihood of which is greatly reduced due to RTS/CTS), client devices “back off” the network for a random period of time before attempting to access the medium again. The client arrives at this random period of time by selecting from a number of slots, each of which has a fixed duration. For 802.11b, there are 31 slots, each of which are 20 microseconds long. For 802.11a, there are 15 slots, each of which are nine microseconds long. 802.11a generally provides shorter backoff times than does 802.11b, which provides for better performance than 802.11a, particularly as the number of clients in a cell increases. When operating in mixed mode (operating with 802.11b clients associated) the 802.11g network will adopt 802.11b backoff times. When operating without 802.11b clients associated, the 802.11g network will adopt the higher-performance 802.11a backoff times.

When 802.11g-based networks are operating in the absence of legacy 802.11b clients, network throughput is similar to that of 802.11a. With its OFDM means of transmission and 802.11a backoff scheme, 802.11g can essentially be viewed as 802.11a applied to the 2.4-GHz band. Table 2 illustrates throughput comparisons for 802.11a, 802.11b, and 802.11g. Note that the throughput increase for 802.11g when in mixed-mode operation is relatively modest when compared to 802.11b, and is a fraction of the throughput provided by 802.11g when not supporting legacy clients.

Table 11.11: Approximate Throughput Comparison for 802.11a, 802.11b, and 802.11g

	Data Rate (Mbps)	*Approximate Throughput (Mbps)*	*Throughput as a Percentage of 802.11b Throughput*
802.11b	11	6	100%
802.11g-with 802.11b clients in cell (CTS/RTS)	54	8	133%
802.11g-with 802.11b clients in cell (CTS-to-self)	54	13	217%
802.11g (no 802.11b clients in cell)	54	22	367%
802.11a	54	25	417%

The 802.11g standard provides an option called CTS to Self, which is able to provide greater throughput when in mixed-cell mode. As the name suggests, CTS to Self dispenses with the RTS and relies upon the 802.11b client's clear channel assessment capabilities to check for an open medium. Cisco Systems® intends to provide CTS to Self capabilities, which will provide for increased performance for future products as well as the installed base via a firmware upgrade.

Having established the throughput capabilities of 802.11g in both modes, one can now examine its overall capacity capabilities. Remember, as a result of operating in the same 2.4 GHz band as 802.11b, 802.11g is similarly limited to three nonoverlapping channels. This compares to the 12 unlicensed channels that are available in many parts of the world for 802.11a. With the inclusion of radar detection capabilities that are part of the 802.11h standard, the number of available 5 GHz channels for 802.11a will increase from 12 to 24 on a nearly worldwide basis. Cisco intends to support 802.11h in future 802.11a products that will become available in 2004. Even when not supporting 802.11b clients, 802.11g still provides a fraction of the network capacity provided by 802.11a. Table 3 illustrates a comparison of 802.11b, 802.11g, and 802.11a network capacity.

Table 11.12: Network Capacity Approximations for 802.11b, 802.11g, and 802.11a

	Throughput (Mbps)	*Channels*	*Capacity (Mbps)*
802.11b	6	3	18
802.11g (mixed mode operation)	8	3	24
802.11g (no legacy support)	22	3	66
802.11a	25	12	300
802.11a (with 802.11h support)	25	24	600
802.11g Range and Coverage			

As a matter of physics, there is an inverse relationship between wavelength and range. All other things being held equal, a signal transmitted in a lower portion of the frequency spectrum will carry further than a signal transmitted in a higher band. Additionally, a longer waveform (from lower in the spectrum) will tend to propagate better through solids (like walls and trees) than a shorter waveform. Because 802.11g operates in the same 2.4 GHz portion of the radio frequency spectrum as does 802.11b, it will share its fundamental advantage over the 5 GHz-based 802.11a. With 802.11b and 802.11g all things are not, however, held equal. Another fundamental rule is that as data rates increase, range decreases. 802.11b uses DSSS to support data rates of 11, 5.5, 2, and 1 Mbps each, with correspondingly longer ranges as the data rates decrease. 802.11g uses OFDM to support data rates of 54, 48, 36, 24, 18, 12, 9, and 6 Mbps each, with correspondingly longer ranges as the data rates decrease. The higher data rates supported by 802.11g result in shorter range than the range supported by the maximum 802.11b data rate. Still, OFDM is a more efficient means of transmission than is DSSS, meaning that at a given range, higher OFDM-based data rates will be supported than DSSS-based data rates (all other things being held constant).

Other factors to consider are transmit power and receive sensitivity. The selection of either DSSS or OFDM transmission type has an effect on the maximum power the transmitter can use, as well as the capability of the receiver, particularly at higher data rates. The reason for this is that higher-order modulation schemes such as the 64 quadrature amplitude modulation (QAM) used to support 54 and 48 Mbps data rates requires a high degree of acuity on the part of the receiver. High power coming from the radio's transmitter tends to desensitize the receiver, a phenomenon known as Error Vector Magnitude (EVM). This leads to a counterintuitive effect, whereby increasing transmit power tends to decrease the range of the device at these higher data rates. Radios operating in 802.11g mode therefore use lower transmit power than when operating in 802.11b mode.

The result of differing waveforms, data rates, transmission types, and transmission characteristics are numerous ranges for the three 802.11 technologies. Of course, any stated ranges are no more than approximations, as several environmental factors can have a dramatic impact on range and resulting coverage area. Still, one can discern the relative ranges the different technologies provide from Table 4 below. Note the significant range differences for 802.11a relative to 802.11g. Also note the superior range of OFDM data rates relative to DSSS data rates in 802.11g, as illustrated by the greater range at 18 Mbps than at 11 Mbps.

Table 11.13: Comparative Ranges in an Open Indoor Office Environment through Cubicle Walls

Data Rate (Mbps)	*802.11a (40 mW with 6 dBi gain diversity patch antenna) Range*	*802.11g (30 mW with 2.2 dBi gain diversity dipole antenna)*	*802.11b (100 mW with 2.2 dBi gain diversity dipole antenna)*
54	45 ft (13 m)	90 ft (27 m)	-
48	50 ft (15 m)	95 ft (29 m)	-
36	65 ft (19 m)	100 ft (30 m)	-
24	85 ft (26 m)	140 ft (42 m)	-
18	110 ft (33 m)	180 ft (54 m)	-
12	130 ft (39 m)	210 ft (64 m)	-
11	-	160 ft (48 m)	160 ft (48 m)
9	150 ft (45 m)	250 ft (76 m)	-
6	165 ft (50 m)	300 ft (91 m)	-
5.5	-	220 ft (67 m)	220 ft (67 m)
2	-	270 ft (82m)	270 ft (82m)
1	-	410 ft (124 m)	410 ft (124 m)

Because 802.11g operates in the same frequency band as 802.11b, it may share a common set of antennas. Cisco currently offers an extensive selection of 2.4 GHz antennas to achieve a variety of coverage patterns. Because WLAN operation in the 5-GHz range is a relatively new phenomenon and because 802.11a volumes are currently far lower than those of 802.11b, there is not nearly as wide a selection of antennas available. As a result, today one has a greater ability to shape a coverage area through the use of specialized antennas with 802.11g than 802.11a. Additionally, the more limited propagation characteristics of the 5 GHz waveform can further restrict the shape of a coverage area due to obstructions that would represent far less an impediment to a 2.4 GHz-based technology.

11.21 DEPLOYMENT CONSIDERATIONS FOR 802.11g

802.11g can be regarded as a superset of 802.11b, providing all the functionality of, and backward compatibility with, 802.11b, plus the higher performance associated with OFDM transmission. With 802.11g-based products, there are other reasons to consider these devices outside of the advantages specific to 802.11g itself:

802.11b-based products provide an integrated RC4 encryption engine to provide Wired Equivalent Privacy (WEP) and WPA security without significant performance degradation. Cisco 802.11g-based products provide an encryption engine that supports both the RC4 and the Rijndael algorithm for WEP, WPA, and Advanced Encryption Standard (AES) encryption to provide high-speed support for the upcoming 802.11i standard and FIPS-140 compliance.

802.11g radio represents a fifth generation in 2.4 GHz technology building upon earlier 802.11 and 802.11b radios. Even when operating in 802.11b DSSS mode, the Cisco 802.11g radio provides superior range performance relative to the previous generation 802.11b-only radio. For applications where 802.11g is not a requirement, one should still consider the 802.11g radio for its 802.11b performance.

Because 802.11g heavily relies on earlier 2.4-GHz technology, it takes advantage of the significant cost reduction engineering and economies of scale that have resulted from the increasing volumes of 802.11b products. As such, the build cost of an 802.11g is similar to that of an 802.11b radio.

With the above facts, there is little reason not to purchase 802.11g-based devices over 802.11b. It is equally apparent, however, that 802.11g alone does not provide anything approaching the sort of capacity provided by 802.11a. An answer to this dilemma can be summed up in two words-dual band.

11.22 DUAL-BAND DEPLOYMENTS

In the same way that 802.11g leverages 802.11b technology, 802.11a leverages 802.11g technology. At a high level, an 802.11 radio can be considered to have three major parts-a MAC, a physical layer controller (PHY), and a radio frequency (RF) front end. The MAC, where functions such as the encryption engine discussed above reside, is common across 802.11a, 802.11b, and 802.11g. Support for OFDM and DSSS transmission types resides in the PHY. As the name implies, the RF Front end is the portion of the radio that actually transmits and receives signals, and as such is specific to the frequency band in which it operates. As a result, an 802.11a radio can re-use the same MAC and PHY as an 802.11g radio. The incremental difference between an 802.11g radio and a dual-band radio supporting the 802.11a or 802.11g standard is the addition of a 5 GHz RF Front end, which adds a relatively small and decreasing amount of incremental build cost. It is expected that for mainstream client devices like notebooks and desktop PCs, neither 802.11a nor 802.11g will exist as a standalone client-side radio to any great degree. Rather, by the end of 2004, the great majority of client radios in form factors like Mini-PCI (for embedded use), CardBus, PCI, and USB will provide dual-band 802.11a/g support.

Vendors participating in the 802.11 market recognize that this incremental cost buys a substantial amount of additional capacity for a relatively small price. Most industry experts agree that the predominant client-side radio shipping in 2004 will be a dual-band 802.11a/g radio. When associating in a WLAN infrastructure, these dual-band client radios will typically look first for an 802.11a access point, followed by 802.11g, and finally 802.11b. In this way, they take the fullest advantage of whatever capacity is available, while providing for backward compatibility.

Given the absence of incremental cost and the upcoming availability of supporting clients, networking professionals should begin the process of migrating their infrastructures from 802.11b to 802.11g. Customers need not "forklift upgrade" their current 802.11b infrastructures-they can choose to either upgrade only the radios within the access points or simply mix in new 802.11g access points with existing 802.11b access points for a heterogeneous, yet interoperable, 2.4-GHz infrastructure.

Customers need not perform a new site survey when deploying 802.11g access points. As stated above, the standard provides for several data rates with inversely proportional supported ranges. To be specific, at its 802.11b, 11-Mbps range, the same radio will provide for an approximately 18 Mbps, 802.11g data rate. Also, this fifth-generation 2.4 GHz radio will outperform the previous generation 802.11b-only radio, meaning that the 802.11g radio will provide for an approximate 24 Mbps data rate at the 11 Mbps range of installed 802.11b access points (which have previous-generation radios).

While the initial performance increase provided by 802.11g will be modest, this is likely to improve over time. First, a firmware upgrade scheduled for the first half of 2004 is planned to include CTS to Self capabilities, which are understood to improve performance when operating in mixed-mode environments. Moreover, new 802.11b devices will become increasingly less common as vendors migrate to 802.11g and 802.11a. This will, over time, decrease the incidence of 802.11b devices in the installed base and decrease the incidence of mixed-mode operation. By selecting OFDM as the transmission type for access point management beacons, customers can configure 802.11g access points such that they specifically exclude 802.11b client associations. This will, of course, dramatically improve the performance of associated 802.11g clients. It does, however, complicate channel reuse patterns and 802.11b coverage, given the small number of 2.4 GHz channels that one has available.

In the same way that one can install 802.11g access points without necessarily performing a new site survey, one can similarly provide 802.11a support. 1200 Series Access Point simultaneously support both a 2.4 GHz 802.11b or 802.11g radio and a 5 GHz 802.11a radio. By adding the 802.11a radio to access points that are deployed based upon an 802.11g (or for that matter, 802.11b) site survey, some amount of 802.11a coverage will be provided. 802.11a radios can be added to 1200 Series access points at time of purchase or as a field upgrade. As discussed previously, this 802.11a coverage will not provide nearly the same data-rate support as the 802.11g "side" of the access point, and it is likely that there will even be areas known as "nulls" that are completely without 802.11a coverage. Still, upcoming dual-band 802.11a/g clients have the intelligence to switch between 5 GHz and 2.4 GHz, taking advantage of 802.11a capacity in areas where it is available and switching to 802.11g (or even 802.11b) when it is not. Client devices will endeavor to maintain data rate over frequency band. For example, a client associated to an 802.11a radio at 54 Mbps will seek out an 802.11g radio supporting 54 Mbps before it "downshifts" from 54 Mbps to a lower data rate on the 802.11a radio.

As the number of WLAN-enabled client devices on the network increases and the network evolves to more commonly support 802.11a through dual-band clients, customers can begin to add single-band 802.11a-only access points to their infrastructures. In so doing, they can cover any null areas and generally bring 802.11a coverage up to data-rate parity with 802.11g coverage. The very large number of 802.11a channels (particularly when coupled with 802.11h) will tend to make the process of site surveying for this follow-on deployment far more quick, easy, and less expensive than an initial 802.11b or 802.11g site survey.

802.11g is an exciting new technology that offers additional performance, while providing investment protection for 802.11b clients through backward compatibility. By using previous technologies and economies of scale, 802.11g devices are available at little or no additional cost relative to 802.11b. As such, there are many reasons to begin migrating from 802.11b to 802.11g.

802.11g is not, however, a panacea for WLAN capacity issues. When operating in mixed-mode environments, the throughput and capacity improvements are very modest. Even with advances like CTS to Self and when operating in 802.11g-only mode, capacity will be limited by the small number of available 2.4 GHz channels. Recognizing this, vendors will soon begin providing dual-band 802.11a/g clients at attractive prices. Vendors today provide dual radio access points that simultaneous support 5 GHz 802.11a and 2.4 GHz 802.11g for association with almost any type of 802.11 client. As WLAN capacity needs increase, network professionals are well-advised to begin deploying a dual-band infrastructure to access the far greater capacity available with 802.11a. As such, 802.11g should be viewed as a portion of an overall WLAN architecture, not a substitute for 802.11a. 802.11g is a "bridge" technology and an ideal means for migrating from low-capacity 802.11b networks to the high-capacity, dual-band WLANs of the very near future.

11.23 IEEE STANDARD 802.16 FOR WiMAX

WiMAX (Worldwide Interoperability for Microwave Access) is based on the IEEE 802.16 standard for Metropolitan Area Networks (MAN). Its goal is to deliver wireless broadband access to customers using base stations with coverage distances in the order of miles. Originally, the standard considered only fixed and nomadic links (802.16-2004) that could be used for "last mile" connectivity providing an alternate to T1 and DSL wired lines or as a backhaul for cellular or Wi-Fi networks. In order to address mobile subscribers, WiMAX was expanded to include portable devices (802.16e) such as personal digital assistants (PDAs), laptops, or phones. Supporting mobility required including provisions for roaming and inter-cell handoff and incorporating more flexibility into the standard to sustain multiple users demanding various types of services. In mobile WiMAX, the system's resources are dynamically allocated to deliver high data rates seamlessly to terminals traveling at vehicular speeds. The frequencies allocated for WiMAX span the 2-66 GHz range. The exact frequency of operation for any given system is dependent on the propagation conditions that are encountered during its use. The frequencies higher than 10 GHz are practical only for fixed line-of-sight (LOS) type services. Non-line of sight (NLOS) communications perform better when the frequencies of operation are kept under 10 GHz. The frequencies below 6 GHz have better propagation properties and are better suited for mobile communications because they most likely guarantee service to all the niches of the coverage area.

The WiMAX standard enables system vendors to create many different types of WiMAX-based products, including various configurations of base stations and customer premise equipment (CPE). WiMAX supports a variety of wireless broadband connections:

- High-bandwidth metropolitan-area networks (MANs) to home and small-business users, replacing DSL and cable modems;

- Backhaul networks for cellular base stations, bypassing the public switched telephone network;
- Backhaul connections to the Internet for WiFi hotspots.

Where they exist today, these applications use expensive proprietary methods for broadband wireless access. This expense can be dramatically reduced by using interoperability-tested WiMAX silicon solutions based on the IEEE 802.16d standard. The WiMAX Forum promotes interoperability of products and technologies.

deployment of broadband wireless access networks by using a global standard and certifying

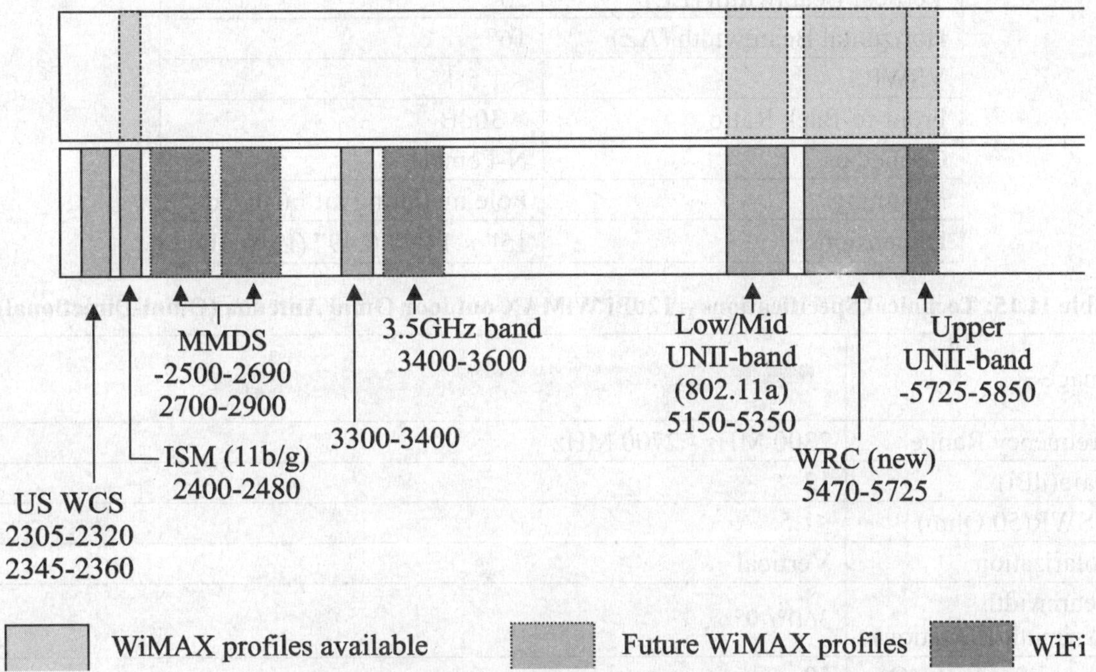

Fig. 11.36: WiMAX RF Spectrum Choices Range from 2 to 11 GHz and Overlap Wi-Fi Bands as Shown here. Within This Range, the WiMAX Forum Will Initially Focus on Equipment.

11.23.1 WiMAX Antennas' Configuration

Outdoor antenna kits for Clear/ Sprint 4G WiMAX. Includes support for Clear 4G USB modem (PXU1900), Clear Series G CPE modem (WIXB-175), Sierra 250U 3G/4G modem, Sprint 4G USB U1901, Zyxel MAX-206M2, Samsung SWC-E100 Express Card, Clear Hub Express (Gemtek WIXFBR-131) etc. This Clearwire Modem Antenna Kit includes *One* antenna, low-loss LMR-400 coaxial cable and pigtail for connection to USB or CPE modem. Use drop-down list below to select cable lengths, modem type etc.

Table 11.14: Technical Specifications – 18dbi WiMAX Outdoor Panel Antenna (Directional)

Image	
Frequency Range	2.5-2.7 GHz
Gain	18.3 dBi
Vertical Beamwidth (EL)	23°
Horizontal Beamwidth (AZ)	16°
VSWR	< 1.5:1
Front-to-Back Ratio	> 30dB
Connector	N-Female
Mounting	Pole mounting kit included
Dimensions	15" × 15" × 0.49" (L×W×D)

Table 11.15: Technical Specifications – 12dBi WiMAX outdoor Omni Antenna (Omni-Directional)

Image	
Frequency Range	2300 MHz - 2700 MHz
Gain(dBi)	12
VSWR(50 Ohm)	≤1.5
Polarization	Vertical
Beamwidth (Azimuth/Elevation)	360°/ 9°
Input impedance(Ω)	50
Size(inches)	ø1.4" × 45" Height
Construction	ABS Plastic
Cable/ Connector	N-Female (no cable)
Mount	Comes standard with a pole mount for 2" OD Poles (contact us if you need mount for larger 6" OD poles)

Table 11.16: Technical Specifications – 8dBi Cellular/WiMAX Outdoor LPDA Antenna (Directional)

Image	
Frequency Range	824-960, 1710-2190, 2500-2690 MHz
Gain(dBi)	8.0 dBi
Polarization	Vertical or Horizontal
HorBeamwidth (AZ BW)	70°
VertBeamwidth (EL BW)	50°
Maximum Input Power	200W (53dBm)
VSWR	<1.5:1
F2B	>15dB
Input Impedance(Ω)	50
Size(inches)	11.6" × 8.27" × 2.52"
Connector	N-Female

Table 11.17: Technical Specifications – Other Antenna Selections

	WMM-7-27— 3G/ 4G Multiband Outdoor MIMO Diversity Antenna (2.5dBi) Note: ▪ *Covers*— 698-960 MHz, 1710-2700 MHz (LTE Band13, Cellular, PCS, AWS, WiFi, WiMax) ▪ this is a dual-antenna for MIMO diversity. Contains two cables connectors one for the Primary Antenna Port and one for auxiliary antenna port. ▪ note that this is a low-gain antenna (unity gain) and as such should be used where the outdoor signal is relatively strong. ▪ note that this comes with a 16FT cable (we will provide appropriate connectors). If you need longer runs just add cable from dropdown list. ▪ select your modem pigtail below (we will include dual pigtails when you add pigtails together with this antenna)
	VA25-16-NF— 2.5 - 2.7 GHz 16 dBi Yagi Antenna. Use as primary or secondary antenna when a low-profile is desired/required.

	*HG2609U*— 2.5 - 2.7 GHz WiMax 8.5 dBi Omni Antenna Replaces the 12dBi omni when not as much gain is needed and when a shorter antenna is required. This is 20" long vs 45" for the 12dBi.
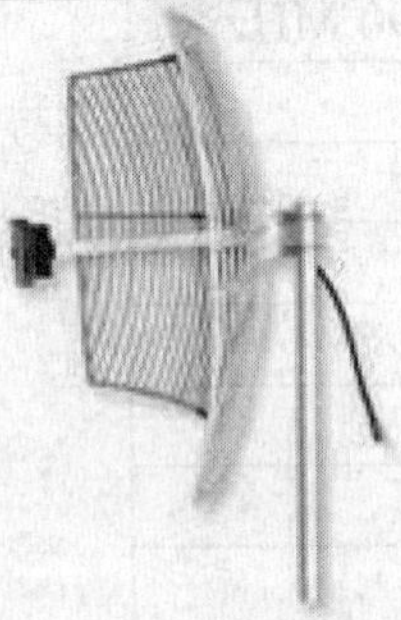	*RFWAT2P5GDNF*— 2.3 GHz - 2.7 GHz 24dBi WiMax Grid Antenna Used primarily to overcome cable losses for long cable runs ~100ft+
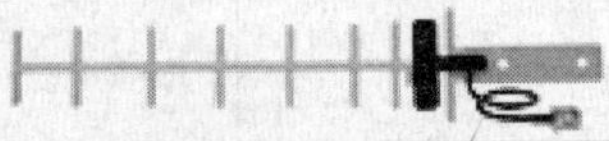	*301124*— 1800-1990 MHz 13dBi 3G PCS Yagi Antenna 3G Only.
	295-PW— 9dBi Multi-Band Omni-Directional Cellular Antenna 3G Only.
▪ Contact us to replace with other WiMax band antennas ▪ For other Cellular band (850MHz/1900MHz/AWS) antennas see out cellular-antenna selection page. ▪ For 4G LTE pigtails & antennas see our LTE page.	

WiMAX antennas, just like the antennas for car radio, cell phone, FM radio, or TV, are designed to optimize performance for a given application. The figure above illustrates the three main types of antennas used in WiMAX deployments. From top to bottom are an omni directional, sector and panel antenna each has a specific function.

Omni Directional Antenna

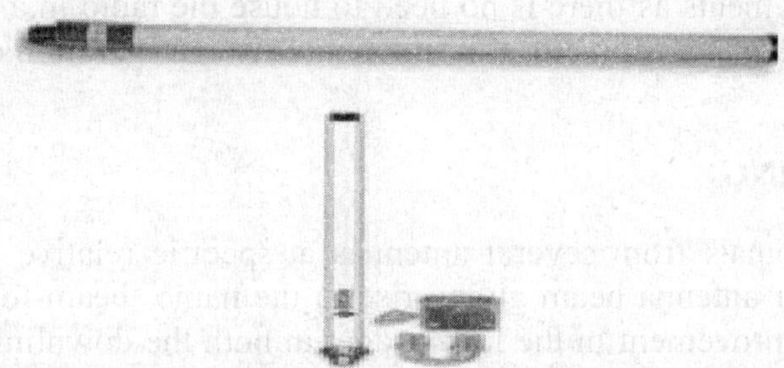

Fig. 11.37: An Omni-Directional Antenna Broadcasts 360 Degrees from the Base Station

Omni directional antennas are used for point-to-multipoint configurations. The main drawback to an omni directional antenna is that its energy is greatly diffused in broad-casting 360 degrees. This limits its range and ultimately signal strength. Omni directional antennas are good for situations where there are a lot of subscribers located very close to the base station. An example of omni directional application is a WiFi hotspot where the range is less than 100 meters and subscribers are concentrated in a small area.

Sector Antennas

Fig. 11.38: Sector Antennas are Focused on Smaller Sectors

A sector antenna, by focusing the beam in a more focused area, offers greater range and throughput with less energy. Many operators will use sector antennas to cover a 360-degree service area rather than use an omni directional antenna due to the superior performance of sector antennas over an omni directional antenna.

Panel Antennas

Fig. 11.39: Panel Antennas are Most Often used for Point-to-Point Applications

Panel antennas are usually a flat panel of about one foot square. They can also be a configuration where potentially the WiMAX radio is contained in the square antenna enclosure. Such configurations are powered via the Ethernet cable that connects the radio/antenna combination to the wider network. That power source is known as Power over Ethernet (PoE). This streamlines deployments as there is no need to house the radio in a separate, weatherproof enclosure if outdoors or in a wiring closet if indoors. This configuration can also be very handy for relays.

11.24 BEAM-FORMING

The transmission of signals from several antennas at specific relative phases can be used to create a much narrower antenna beam giving rise to the name 'beam-forming'. Beam-forming provides substantial improvement in the link budget in both the downlink and uplink directions by increasing the effective antenna gain in addition to reducing fade margin requirements due to interference. Beam-forming does require knowledge of a subscriber's location making it more challenging to implement for subscribers in moving at high speeds. According to cellular network statistics however, the majority of subscribers are either stationary or only moving at pedestrian speeds thus enabling beam-forming to provide significant benefits for most usage models

A 4-antenna beam-forming configuration for example, can provide a 6 dB signal enhancement while significantly improving the transmission fade margin. As a result, beam-forming delivers more range,higher throughput, and improved indoor coverage. With the potential for fewer base stations to achieve specific system-wide capacity, beam-forming can provide a savings of as much as 50% on capital expenses (CAPEX) and 30% on operating expenses (OPEX). Beam-forming is the third 'smart antenna'technology that has been incorporated in the WiMAX specification to improve system capacity andsperformance in broadband mobile networks.

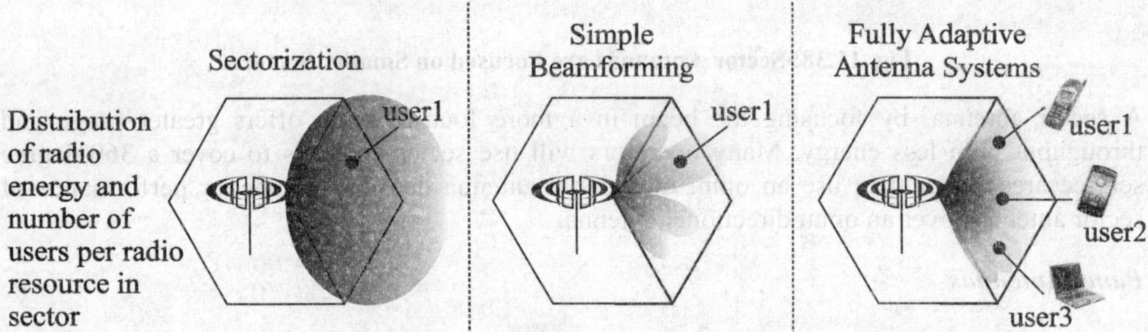

Fig. 11.40: Beam Forming Improving Capacity

Higher-Order Modulation

In contrast to existing analog (AM, FM) and low efficiency digital modulation schemes (PSK, BPSK, and QPSK) widely used in today's networks, broadband wireless requires the use of higher order modulation schemes with better spectral efficiency. These higher order modulation schemes however, are more sensitive to interference and multi-path, both of which are prevalent in wireless deployments where ubiquity is required and large numbers of users are present.

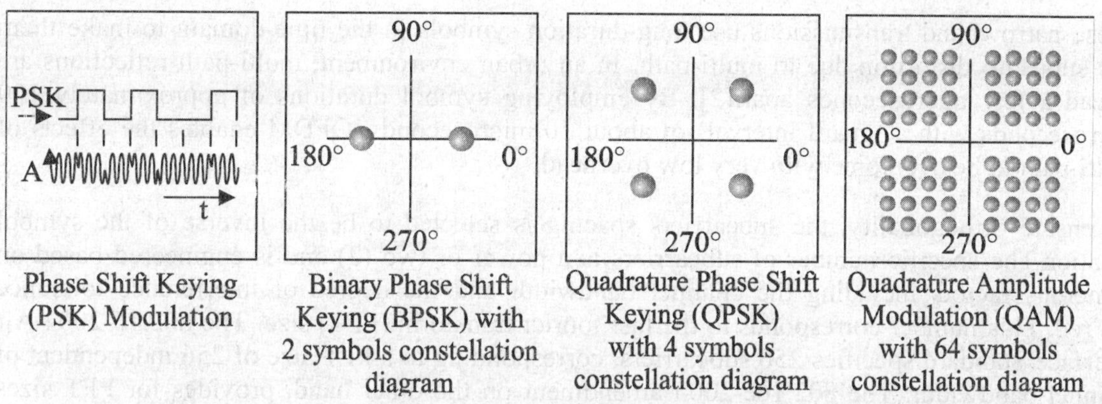

Fig. 11.41: Examples of Different Order Modulation Schemes

Providing carrier-class mobile broadband services and ensuring a winning business model for the service provider.

To counter these effects, OFDM, OFDMA, and S-OFDMA are new advanced access technologies that provide the necessary channel robustness for the support of higher spectral efficiency and higher channel throughput. These new access technologies are the basis for mobile WiMAX and other next generation mobile broadband systems.

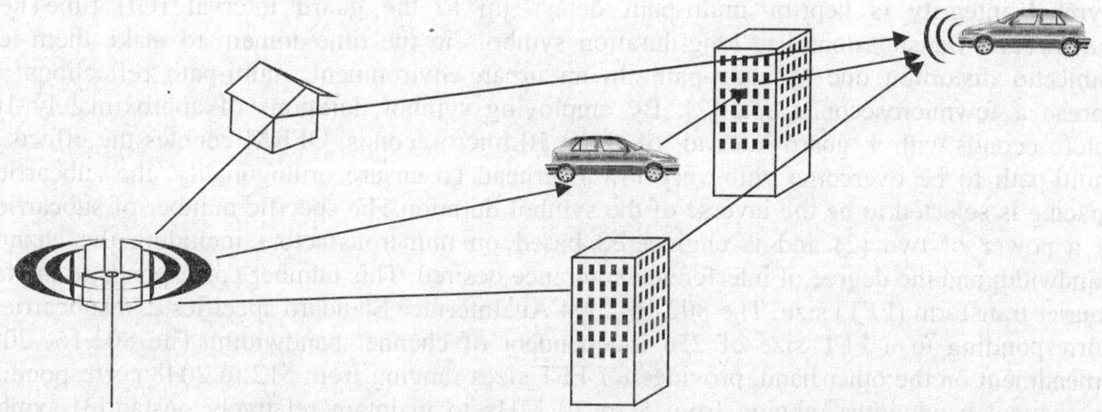

Fig. 11.42: Typical Example of Multi-Path Problem

11.25 OFDM

The need for reliable broadband services in an on-line-of-sight (NLOS) wireless environment, typically riddled by severe multi-path, and interference from other wireless service providers, has driven the wireless industry to the wide spread adoption of Orthogonal Frequency Division Multiplexing (OFDM) in standards and products.

For robustness, OFDM partitions the data stream in to multiple narrow band transmissions in the frequency domain using subcarriers that are orthogonal to one another. These subcarriers are then assembled into frequency channels for over the air transmission.

These narrowband transmissions use long-duration symbols in the time-domain to make them less subjectto distortion due to multi-path. In an urban environment, multi-path reflections are spread a few microseconds apart[2]. By employing symbol durations of approximately 100 microseconds with a 'guard interval' of about 10 microseconds, OFDM enables the effects of multi-path to be overcome with very low overhead.

To ensure orthogonality, the subcarriers spacing is selected to be the inverse of the symbol duration.The specific number of subcarriers is a power of two (2) and is engineered based on numerous factors including the channel bandwidth and the degree of interference tolerance desired. This number corresponds to the fast fourier transform (FFT) size. The 802.16-2004 Air Interface Standard specifies 256 subcarriers, corresponding to a FFT size of 256 independent of channel bandwidth. The 802.16e-2005 amendment on the other hand, provides for FFT sizes ranging from 512 to 2048 corresponding to channel bandwidths ranging from 5 to 20 MHz to maintain relatively constant[3] symbol duration and subcarrier spacing independent of channel bandwidth. With OFDM therefore, the combination of multiple orthogonal subcarriers transmitted in parallel with long duration symbols ensures that the overall broadband throughput is immune to constraints due to NLOS environments and multi-path interference.

[3] The mobile WiMAX Release-1 system profiles include channel bandwidths of 7.0 and 8.75 MHz with a specified FFT size of 1024 resulting in slightly longer symbol durations than the 10 MHz channel bandwidth which also specifies a 1024 FFT size.

Symbol integrity is keptfor multi-path delays up to the guard interval (GI) timeThese narrowband transmissions use long-duration symbols in the time-domain to make them less subjectto distortion due to multi-path. In an urban environment, multi-path reflections are spread a fewmicroseconds apart[2]. By employing symbol durations of approximately 100 microseconds with a 'guard interval' of about 10 microseconds, OFDM enables the effects of multi-path to be overcome with very low overhead.To ensure orthogonality, the subcarriers spacing is selected to be the inverse of the symbol duration.The specific number of subcarriers is a power of two (2) and is engineered based on numerousfactors including the channel bandwidth and the degree of interference tolerance desired. This number corresponds to the fast fourier transform (FFT) size. The 802.16-2004 Air Interface Standard specifies 256 subcarriers, corresponding to a FFT size of 256 independent of channel bandwidth. The 802.16e-2005 amendment on the other hand, provides for FFT sizes ranging from 512 to 2048 corresponding to channel bandwidths ranging from 5 to 20 MHz to maintain relatively onstant[3] symbol duration and subcarrier spacing independent of channel bandwidth. With OFDM therefore, the combination of multiple orthogonal subcarriers transmitted in parallel with longduration symbols ensures that the overall broadband throughput is immune to constraints due to NLOS environments and multi-path interference.

The mobile WiMAX Release-1 system profiles include channel bandwidths of 7.0 and 8.75 MHz with a specified FFT sizeof 1024 resulting in slightly longer symbol durations than the 10 MHz channel bandwidth which alsospecifies a 1024 FFT size.

By assigning subchannels to specific subscribers, transmissions from several subscribers can occur simultaneously without interfering, thus minimizing an effect known as multiple access interference (MAI).

Furthermore, subchannelization enables the concentration of transmit power over a reduced number of subcarriers. This results in increased link margins which in turn, lead to improved range and coverage. The IEEE 802.16e-2005 amendment was developed to extend the 802.16 Air Interface Standard to cover mobile applications. This amendment adopted OFDMA to provide the flexibility to deal with varied usage scenarios and the challenges associated with rapidly moving mobi:e users in a NLOS environment. The802.16e-2005 standard provides three subchannel allocation alternatives that can be selected based on the usage scenario as follows:

- Subcarriers can be scattered throughout the frequency channel range. This is referred to as fully used sub-channelization or FUSC.
- Several scattered clusters of subcarriers can be used to form a subchannel. This is referred to as partially used sub-channelization or PUSC.
- Subchannels can be composed of contiguous groups of subcarriers. This is referred to as adaptive modulation and coding or AMC.

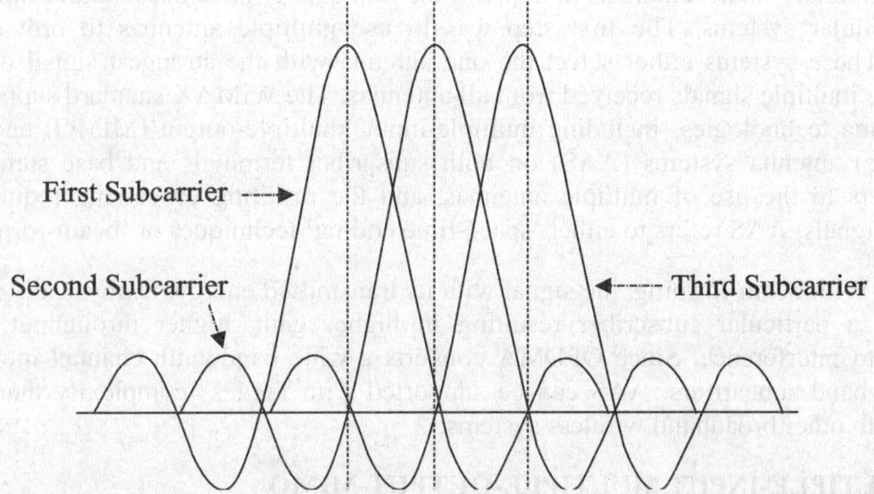

Fig. 11.43: Subcarrier Spacing is Carefully Selected So That Each Subcarrier is Orthogonal to the Other Subcarriers. Subcarrier Spacing is Equal to the Reciprocal of the (Useful) Symbol Duration

With FUSC and PUSC, the allocation of subcarriers to subchannels is done in a pseudorandom fashion such that the subcarriers for a given subchannel in a certain cell are different than subcarriers for that same subchannel in another cell (for example the subcarriers in subchannel 1 in cell 1 will be different than the subcarriers in subchannel 1 in cell 2). This pseudorandom permutation provides an interference averaging effect further reducing the adverse effects of cell to cell interference. In general, FUSC and PUSC are the best alternatives for mobile applications, whereas AMC is well suited for stationary, portable, and low mobility applications.

S-OFDMA— Scalable OFDMA (S-OFDMA) provides the ability to adjust OFDMA in accordance with the bandwidth of the channel being used. As regulators assign varying amounts of spectrum to different service providers, the OFDMA parameters can be optimized in proportion to the bandwidth granted to a specific service provider. With S-OFDMA, the FFT size varies with the channel bandwidth based on parameters called out in 802.16e-2005. In a 5 MHz channel an FFT size of 512 subcarriers is specified, whereas in a 10 MHz channel an FFT size of 1024 is specified. This ensures that both the 5 MHz and 10 MHz systems have the same symbol duration and hence similar robustness to multi-path distortion even though they vary in size.

Smart Antenna Systems

Smart antenna systems refer to a class of antenna technologies designed to improve the received signal strength in a wireless access network. The intent is to improve the carrier-to-interference plus noise ratio (CINR). The use of 'smart' antenna technologies can both increase received signal strength and decrease interference levels to greatly enhance performance in a mobile communication network.

Received signal strengths fluctuate as subscribers move throughout the coverage area and the use of multiple or 'smart' antennas to improve the link quality have been studied since the days of early cellular systems. The first step was to use multiple antennas to provide 'receive diversity'. These systems either select the one antenna with the strongest signal or optimally combine the multiple signals received from all antennas. The WiMAX standard supports several smart antenna technologies, including multiple-input, multiple-output (MIMO) and advanced (or adaptive) antenna systems (AAS) on both subscriber terminals and base stations. While MIMO refers to the use of multiple antennas, and the resulting processing required for the additional signals; AAS refers to either 'space-time coding' techniques or 'beam-forming'.

With beam-With beam-forming, the signal with its transmitted energy, is physically formed and directed to a particular subscriber resulting in higher gain, higher throughput, and more robustness to interference. Since OFDMA converts a wide bandwidth channel into numerous flat, narrowband subcarriers, AAS can be supported with far less complexity than would be required with other broadband wireless systems.

11.26 MULTIPLE-INPUT MULTIPLE-OUTPUT-MIMO

Multiple-Input, Multiple-Output (MIMO) describes systems that use more than one radio and antenna system at each end of the wireless link. In the past it was too costly to incorporate multiple antennas and radios in a subscriber terminal. Recent advances in radio miniaturization and integration technology now makes it feasible and cost effective. Combining two or more received signals has the most immediate benefit of improving received signal strength, but MIMO also enables transmission of parallel data streams for greater throughput. For example, in a 2×2 MIMO (two transmit and two receive elements), dual polarization point-to-point system, the carrier's allocated frequency can be used twice, effectively doubling the throughput data rate. In point-to-multipoint systems employing MIMO, each base station antenna transmits a different datastream and each subscriber terminal receives various components of the transmitted signals with each of its subscriber antennas as illustrated in the figure below. By using appropriate algorithms, the subscriber terminal is able to separate and decode the parallel simultaneously received data streams. The mobile WiMAX standard covers a suite of MIMO encoding techniques for up to four antennas at each end of the link, (4×4 MIMO).

11.27 SPACE-TIME CODING-STC

Space-time coding (STC) is a family of techniques for implementing transmission diversity. Mobile WiMAX uses transmit diversity in the downlink direction to provide spatial diversity that enhance the signal quality to a specific subscriber located anywhere within the range of the antenna beam. Although providing less signal gain than beam-forming, transmit diversity is more robust for mobile users since it does not require prior knowledge of the path characteristics of a subscriber's particular frequency channel. One such STC technique, known as the Alamouti Code, was published in 1998[4] and has been incorporated in the WiMAX standard.

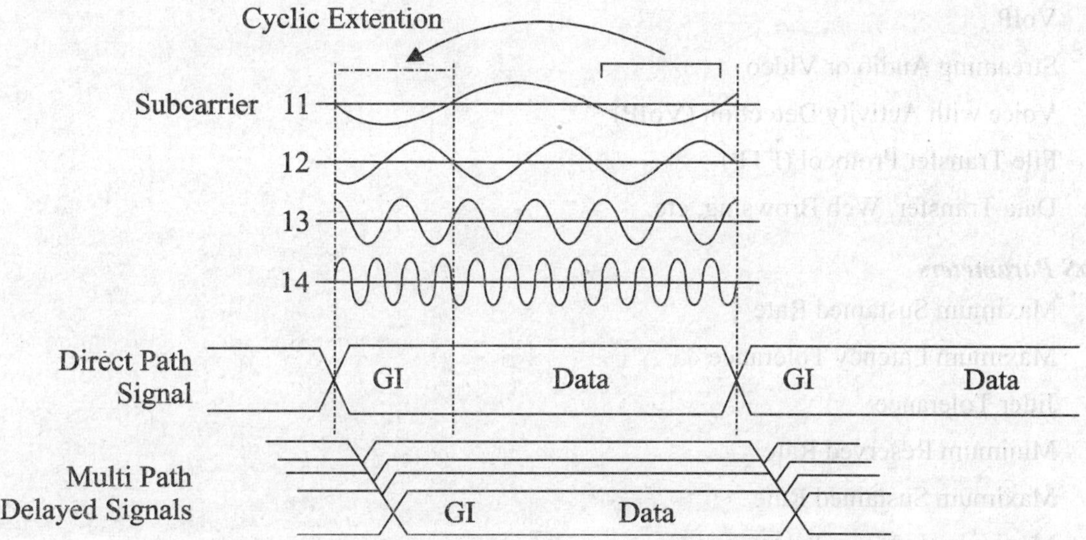

Fig. 11.44: Symbol Integrity is Kept for Multi-Path Delays Up to the Guard Interval (GI) Time

Quality of Service Support

Support for quality of service (QoS) is essential for broadband wireless systems with channels designed to simultaneously carry a combination of voice, video, and data services. QoS algorithms are required to ensure that the shared use of the channel does not result in service degradation or failure. Examples include jerky or abrupt video streams, latency levels in a voice call that interfere with natural conversation or the download of an Internet page that is unacceptably delayed or freezes. Despite the fact that subscribers are sharing the broadband link with others, they expect an acceptable level of performance from the service provider under all conditions.

The mobile WiMAX standard provides a suite of tools to support QoS for multiple applications. The WiMAX base station allocates all uplink and downlink airtime resources using a traffic scheduling proceduret hat reflects traffic demand and the subscription parameters of individual subscribers. Comprehensive algorithms are then employed to ensure that the application-specific QoS parameters are met. The following table provides a summary of the QoS categories, applications and QoS parameters to be controlled as delineated in the 802.16e-2005 standard.

11.28 QoS CATEGORY

- UGSUnsolicited Grant Service
- rtPSReal-Time Polling Service
- ErtPSExtended Real-Time Polling Service
- nrtPSNon-Real-Time Polling Service
- BEBest-Effort Service

Applications

- VoIP
- Streaming Audio or Video
- Voice with Activity Detection (VoIP)
- File Transfer Protocol (FTP)
- Data Transfer, Web Browsing, etc.

QoS Parameters

- Maximum Sustained Rate
- Maximum Latency Tolerance
- Jitter Tolerance
- Minimum Reserved Rate
- Maximum Sustained Rate
- Maximum Latency Tolerance
- Traffic Priority
- Minimum Reserved Rate
- Maximum Sustained Rate
- Maximum Latency Tolerance
- Jitter Tolerance
- Traffic Priority
- Minimum Reserved Rate
- Maximum Sustained Rate
- Traffic Priority
- Maximum Sustained Rate
- Traffic Priority

Radio Resource

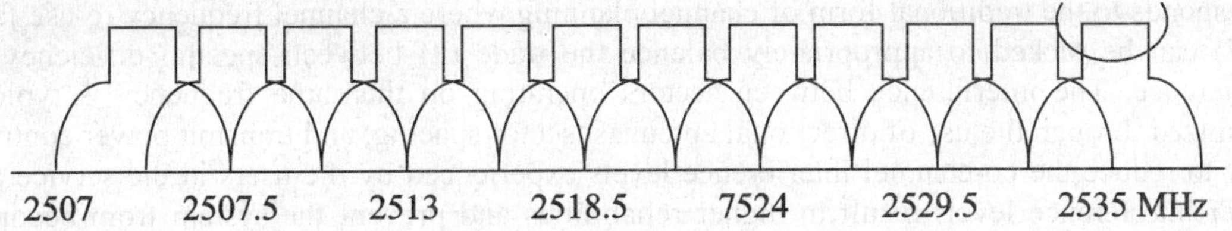

1024 Carriers total

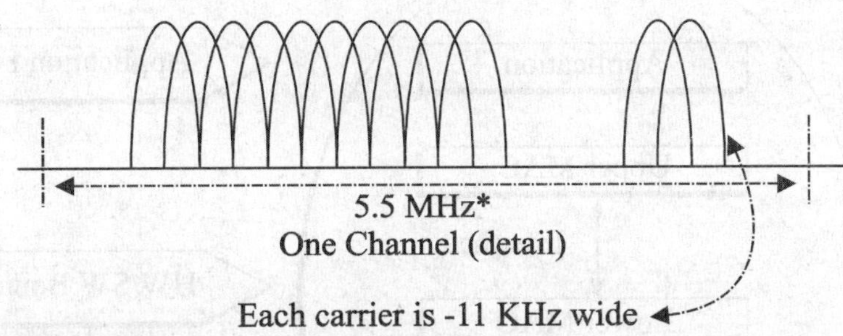

* In this example, 5.5 MHz channels are allocated.
WiMAX channel bandwidth is 5 MHz so in this case there is a guard band of 0.5 MHz.

Fig. 11.45: Subcarrier Spacing is Carefully Selected so that each Subcarrier is Orthogonal to the Other Subcarriers. Subcarrier Spacing is Equal to the Reciprocal of the (Useful) Symbol Duration

11.29 INTERFERENCE IN WiMAX SYSTEMS

Before addressing the interference of a deployed WiMAX system it is best to review how the sub-channels are divided among users in the uplink (UL) and downlink (DL). More specifically, the Time Division Duplex (TDD) transmission scheme of the 802.16e standard will be considered. In the initial working group release, the standard supports 5 and 10 MHz bandwidth allocations for each radio frequency channel. The available channel bandwidth is made up of sub-carriers each of which can be modulated individually with information. WiMAX uses Orthogonal Frequency Division Multiple Access (OFDMA) to assign sub-carriers to different users. The number of sub-carriers available for assignment in the UL and DL are a function of the channel bandwidth, the frame size, and the UL/DL transmit ratio. In mobile WiMAX, the smallest unit of frequency-time allocation available is a slot which contains 48 data sub-carriers. The sub-carriers comprising a slot can be made up of adjacent sub-carriers or can be allocated in a distributed fashion throughout the available carrier space. In general, distributed carrier allocations perform better in mobile environments, while adjacent sub-carriers are better suited for fixed links. The number of slots assigned to a particular user per frame is a function of their data needs.

Channel planning in WiMAX systems can be performed in several ways. Channel allocation is left up to the service providers and is based upon the amount of available spectrum and the density of the users requiring service. When enough bandwidth is at hand, the channels (5 or 10 MHz portions of spectrum) can be allocated and reassigned among the available sectors in such a way as to minimize the co-channel interference at neighboring sites. This procedure corresponds to the traditional form of channel planning where a channel frequency re-use factor (FRF) can be picked to appropriately balance the trade off between spectral efficiency and interference. The interference between sectors operating on the same frequency is typically minimized through the use of directional antennas, sector spacing, and transmit power control in order to reduce the co-channel interference levels experienced by the users in the service area. Lower interference levels result in higher reliabilities and prevent the system from becoming unduly interference limited.

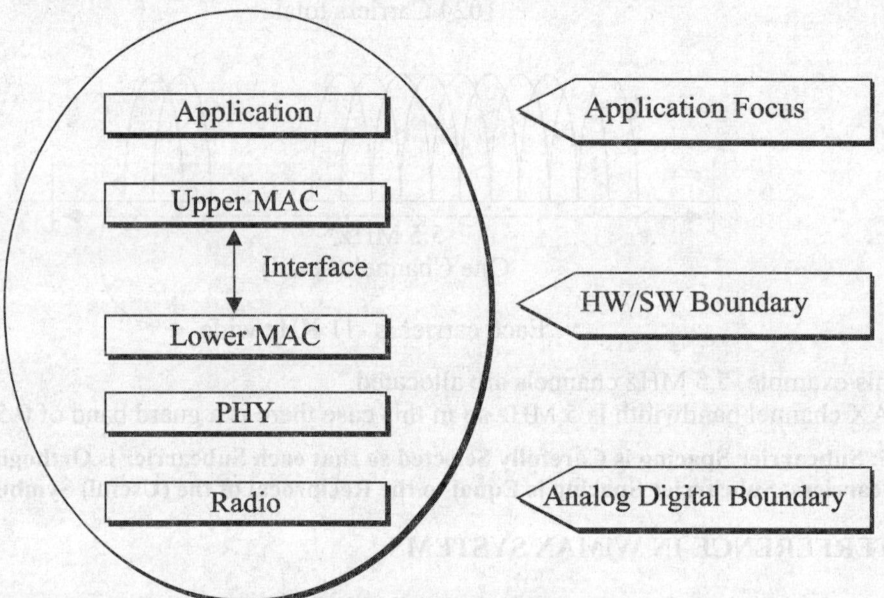

Fig. 11.46: WiMAX System Components Include Dedicated Hardware such as the PHY and "Lower" MAC in Addition to MAC-Related Software Functions. The Radio and PHY are Distinguished Here According to Analog and Digital Functionality, Respectively.

Implementing subscriber stations with this same type of customized hardware

11.30 CAPACITY OF WiMAX SYSTEMS

Another important factor affecting the performance of a WiMAX system is capacity. Capacity determines the amount of data that can be delivered to and from the users. There is a limit on how much data can be reliably sent through any given channel. There are several ways of quantifying the capacity of a wireless system. The traditional way of quantifying capacity is by calculating the data rate per unit bandwidth that can be delivered in a system. An alternate way of looking at capacity is by quantifying the number of users that can be supported by a system, by a sector, or per channel to name a few. A channel can also be defined in several ways; it can be defined as a frequency range, a time slot, or as a frequency-time combo slot.

In a WiMAX system, not all users are of the same type. Browsing the web, emailing, sending/receiving video, downloading files, or using VoIP are all activities that might be performed simultaneously within the population of users. Each of these operations places varying demands on the system. Some might require a higher data rate on download than on upload, while others are about evenly distributed. In order to predict capacity users should be classified based on their demands and how much load they place on the system. For example, streaming video requires considerably more data rate than VOIP so a user receiving video uses up more system resources. At any given time there will be a mixture of services that are being requested and the system is able to support several voice users with the same resources it takes to serve one video user. An alternate way of looking at capacity is to establish the load that a typical number of users place on a system and then determine at what point the load surpasses each sector's ability to deliver. The number of system resources that are consumed in a given area depends on its demographics and the type of users that are present in that location (factors such as terrain and time of day can also affect demand).

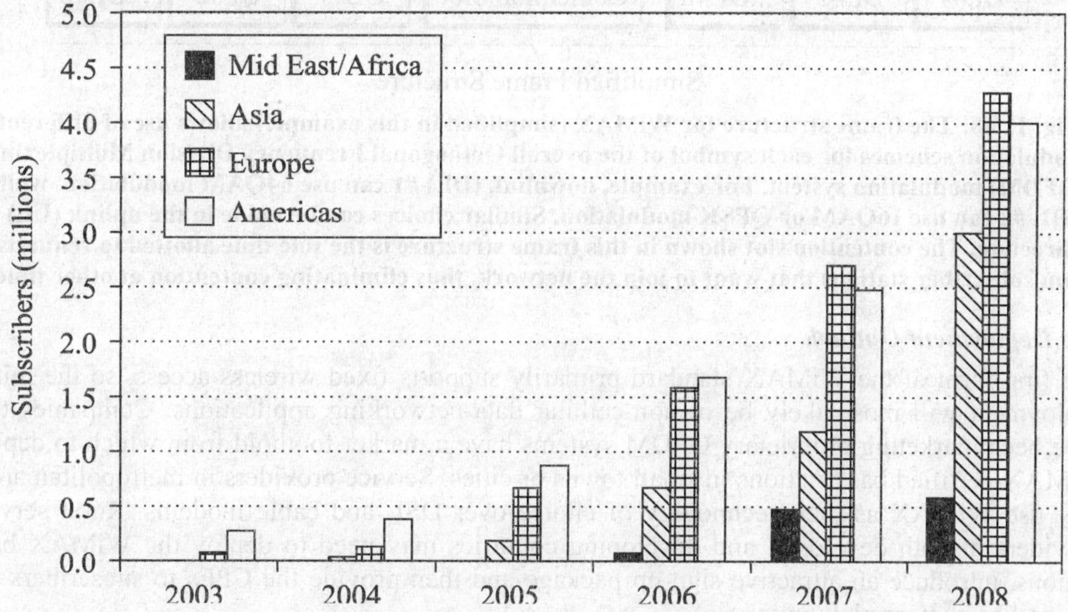

Fig. 11.47: Worldwide Sub-11GHz Subscriber Base - 802.16a and Proprietary
(Source: Intel Capital)

It can be useful to examine capacity in the extreme cases where a sector can achieve the maximum or minimum of both the number of supported users and spectral efficiency (bits/second/Hz) in a sector. The worst case occurs when all the users are at the edge of the coverage area of the cell and are only reachable by the lowest order modulation (QPSK with ½ rate coding) and at the same time have the greatest demand on the system (all demand high resolution video). On the other hand, the most number of supported users and the best spectral efficiencies occur when all users are close to the base station (and can attain the highest order modulations; 64QAM with 5/6 rate coding) and demand low data rate services like email. Both of these cases are possible scenarios and all other cases that achieve varying numbers of sustained users and spectral efficiencies will fall in between these two extremes. The data rate that a sector should be able to deliver is therefore a random variable that is dependent on the distribution of the type of users in the service area as well as their achievable modulations. A similar argument can be made about the number of supported users in a sector which is also stochastic and is a function of the achievable modulation order as well as the distribution of the type of users over the coverage area

WiMAX enables optimization of each subscriber's data rate by allowing the base station to set modulation schemes on a link-by-link basis. A subscriber station close to the base station could use 64QAM modulation, while the weaker signal from a more remote subscriber might only permit the use of 16QAM or QPSK. The 802.16 MAC can even use a different modulation method for each subscriber's downlink and uplink bursts. As shown in Figure 2, the minimum granularity of a DL or UL burst is one OFDM symbol

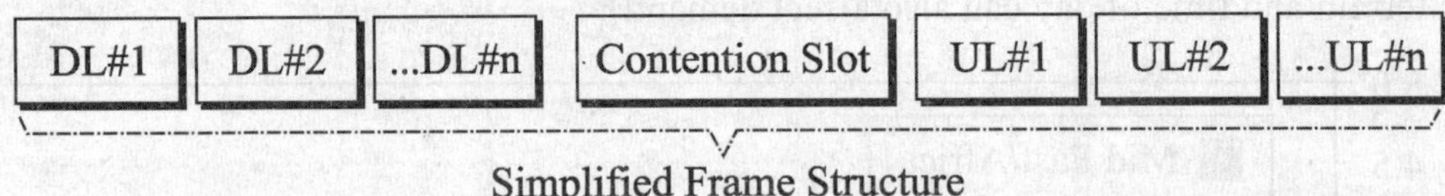

Fig. 11.48: The frame structure for WiMAX (simplified in this example) allows use of different modulation schemes for each symbol of the overall Orthogonal Frequency Division Multiplexing (OFDM) modulation system. For example, downlink (DL) #1 can use 64QAM modulation, while DL #2 can use 16QAM or QPSK modulation. Similar choices can be made in the uplink (UL) direction. The contention slot shown in this frame structure is the sole time allotted to requests from subscriber stations that want to join the network, thus eliminating contention at other times.

The Deployment Outlook

The first form of the WiMAX standard primarily supports fixed wireless access, so the initial deployment will most likely be in non-cellular data-networking applications. Companies that have been marketing proprietary OFDM systems have a market foothold from which to deploy WiMAX-certified base stations in small towns or cities. Service providers in metropolitan areas may use WiMAX as their technology of choice over DSL and cable modems. Rural service providers in both developed and developing countries may need to deploy the WiMAX base stations, introduce an attractive sign-up package and then provide the CPEs to subscribers via the mail or in-store pick-up.

Other WiMAX players will include WiFi product vendors, pure-play CPE companies and traditional networking equipment manufacturers. The WiFi product vendors can leverage their existing sales channels by incorporating WiMAX into their products as a way to backhaul hotspot traffic to the public WAN.

Because WiMAX deployment requires the push of service providers, the WiFi product vendors must work with these providers for product launch. The pure-play CPE companies will most likely either partner with base station companies that have service provider ties or solicit the service providers to evaluate their products.

Understanding the enormous potentials of the fixed wireless networking market, networking equipment makers have shown great interests in WiMAX. Like the WiFi product vendors, the networking equipment makers will have to work with the service providers for deployment.

As the 802.16d standard evolves, a variety of wireless products such as WiMAX-enabled internet access cards may appear. Similarly, as 802.16e becomes the mobile standard for the wireless MAN, products such as laptops, PDAs and cell phones will be the revenue drivers.

In the early days of deployment, trial networks will be scattered around the globe. Once users understand WiMAX's benefits, the adoption rate could spread like wildfire—a possible scenario for 2006 and beyond. Toward that goal, the companies participating in WiMAX product development are establishing a foundation of high-performance, affordable silicon and systems that customers will find irresistible.

Review Points

IEEE 802 Standard comprises a family of networking standards that cover the physical layer specifications of technologies from Ethernet to wireless. 802.11 is an evolving family of specifications for wireless local area networks (WLANs) developed by a working group of the Institute of Electrical and Electronics Engineers (IEEE). There are several specifications in the family and new ones are occasionally added. *Wireless Ethernet standards defined are,* IEEE 802.11- capable of transmissions of 1 to 2 Mbps and operates in 2.4 GHz band using either frequency hopping spread spectrum (FHSS) or direct sequence spread spectrum (DSSS). IEEE 802.11a-upto 54 Mbps and operates in 5 GHz band and uses OFDM encoding scheme. IEEE 802.11b -upto 11 Mbps and operates in 2.4 GHz band and uses only DSSS encoding scheme. IEEE 802.11g- upto 54 Mbps and operates in 2.4 GHz band.

802.11 - Physical Layer

Physical (PHY) layer is of three categories viz, Infra red, Frequency Hopping Spread Spectrum and Direct Sequence Spread Spectrum(IR , FHSS, DSSS) The DS systems use a carrier that remains fixed to a specific frequency band. The data signal is spread onto a much larger range of frequencies and achieve much higher throughput with better range. FH systems use a radio carrier that "hops" from frequency to frequency in a pattern known to both transmitter and receiver. Infrared system uses 850-950 nm, and 10 m range having carrier detection, energy detection, synchronization.

Carrier Sensing

CSMA/CA (Carrier Sense Multiple Access/Collision Avoidance) is a protocol for carrier transmission in 802.11 networks. In CSMA/CA, as soon as a node receives a packet that is to be sent, it checks to be sure the channel is clear (no other node is transmitting at the time). If the channel is clear, then the packet is sent. If the channel is not clear, the node waits for a randomly chosen period of time, and then checks again to see if the channel is clear.

PHY Sublayers

This includes

1) Physical layer convergence protocol (PLCP),

2) PMD Physical Medium Dependent

3) PHY Management and

4) Station Management and MAC Management functions are Synchronization, Power management, Association/Reassociation and MIB - Management Information Base.

Other MAC Operations include –Fragmentation, Privacy and WEP Details

Point Co ordination Function (PCF) and Distributed Coordination Function (DCF) A Point Coordinator (PC) resides in the Access Point and controls frame transfers during a Contention Free Period (CFP) . Overheads to throughput and delay in DCF mode come from losses due to collisions and backoff. Overhead in PCF modes comes from wasted polls. Saturation throughput of DCF less than PCF in all studies presented here ('heavy load' conditions),

- **WiFi Network Components - they are,** Station BSS - Basic Service Set, IBSS: Infrastructure BSS, QBSS, ESS - Extended Service Set, Portal, Access Point and DS – Distribution System

802.11a Advantages - Ultra-high spectrum efficiency, High speed, and Less interference, Fewer products using the frequency (2.4 GHz band shared by cordless phones, microwave ovens, Bluetooth, and WLANs) 802.11a Disadvantages are Standards and Interoperability not as required , Legal issues and less market

IEEE 802.11g is the New Mainstream Wireless LAN Standard - Provides higher speeds and higher capacity requirements for applications, compatible with existing 802.11b standard and Leverages Worldwide spectrum availability in 2.4 GHz. The 802.11g clients can select from the widest possible range of both OFDM data rates of 54, 48, 36, 24, 18, 12, 9, and 6 Mbps, and the CCK rates of 11, 5.5, 2, and 1 Mbps. Performance is best in environments where an 802.11g access point (AP) is only communicating with 802.11g clients in a homogeneous WLAN.

Wi-Fi Network Topologies

- AP-based topology (Infrastructure Mode)
- Peer-to-peer topology (Ad-hoc Mode)
- Point-to-multipoint bridge topology

Wi-Fi (short for "wireless fidelity") is a term for certain types of wireless local area network (WLAN) that use specifications in the 802.11 family. Wi-Fi can apply to products that use any 802.11 standard. The 802.11 specifications are part of an evolving set of wireless network standards known as the 802.11 family. The particular specification under which a Wi-Fi network operates is called the "flavor" of the network. Wi-Fi has gained acceptance in many businesses, agencies, schools, and homes as an alternative to a wired LAN. Many airports, hotels, and fast-food facilities offer public access to Wi-Fi networks. These locations are known as hot spots. Many charge a daily or hourly rate for access, but some are free. An interconnected area of hot spots and network access points is known as a hot zone. Unless adequately protected, a Wi-Fi network can be susceptible to access by unauthorized users.

Wi-Fi Security Threats— Wireless technology introduces new ones which are ,Eavesdropping, Man-in-the-middle attacks, and Denial of Service.

Wi-Fi security tools— Establishing a encrypted channel before sending username and password, Server Authentication, Digital Certificate and Validation of digital certificate which occurs automatically within client software are some of the tools.

Wi-Fi Security Techniques use are, Service Set Identifier (SSID), Wired Equivalent Privacy (WEP), 802.1X Access Control and Wireless Protected Access (WPA).

WiFi Security Protocols are, EAP-TLS (Transport Layer Security), EAP-TTLS (Tunneled Transport Layer Security), PEAP (Protected EAP Protocol), and LEAP (Lightweight EAP).

Bluetooth, Standard - IEEE-802.15

802.15 is a communications specification that was approved by the Institute of Electrical and Electronics Engineers Standards Association (IEEE-SA) for wireless personal area networks (WPANs). Bluetooth is a well-known and widely used specification that defines parameters for wireless communications among portable digital devices including notebook computers, peripherals, cellular telephones, beepers, and consumer electronic devices. The specification also allows for connection to the Internet. Regulatory Range-2.4 to 2.4835 GHz is used, the no. of RF Channels are 0 to 78, Carrier spacing is 1 MHz, Technology: FHSS, RF Bandwidth : 200 KHz and Transmit Power : 0.1w.

IEEE 802.11n (high data rates) Multipath propagation is typical for radio waves in the GHz frequency band (microwave)where radio waves reach the receiver via different ways, run different distances and change their phase and polarization. IEEE 802.11n offers an improvement with MIMO. MIMO means *multiple in multiple out* and is the reception or transmission via several independent sending and reception paths (spatial streams).

Increased data rate by means of multipath propagation (spatial multiplexing) by the separation of the data stream into several streams it is possible to distribute the data on several transmitters and afterwards on several (spatially separated) antennas. Orthogonal Frequency Division Multiplex (OFDM) modulation is from IEEE 802.11a and g and it is used in the Physical layer (PHY).

IEEE 802.11s (Meshed Wireless LANs)

This method to facilitate that network should manage itself. In conjunction with wireless LAN networks, the idea of a mesh network has become reality in the meantime. Meshed MANs were always based on proprietary developments. Some providers call a Wireless Distribution System (WDS) together with the Rapid Spanning Tree Protocol (RSTP) a mesh network. Mesh networking allows redundant data paths with which the loss of individual connections (meshes) can be compensated fully automatically.

IEEE Standard 802.16WiMAX

WiMAX (Worldwide Interoperability for Microwave Access) is based on the IEEE 802.16 standard for Metropolitan Area Networks (MAN). Its goal is to deliver wireless broadband access to customers using base stations with coverage distances in the order of miles. Originally, the standard considered only fixed and nomadic links (802.16-2004) that could be used for "last mile" connectivity providing an alternate to T1 and DSL wired lines or as a backhaul for cellular or Wi-Fi networks. In order to address mobile subscribers, WiMAX was expanded to include portable devices (802.16e) such as personal digital assistants (PDAs), laptops, or phones. Supporting mobility required including provisions for roaming and inter-cell handoff and incorporating more flexibility into the standard to sustain multiple users demanding various types of services.

IEEE 802.22 Standard for Wireless Regional Area Networks in TV Whitespaces is already completed and is being implemented in several countries. IEEE 802.22 incorporates advanced cognitive radio capabilities including dynamic spectrum access, incumbent database access, accurate geolocation techniques, spectrum sensing, regulatory domain dependent policies, spectrum etiquette, and coexistence for optimal use of the available spectrum.

Review Questions

1. List a few major networking standards specifications as per IEEE.
2. Explain 802.11 with respect to physical layer concept used.
3. What is spread spectrum?
4. Write detailed note on FHSS and DSSS.
5. Compare the performance of FHSS and DSSS systems.
6. Explain the principle of working in CSMA/CA.
7. Write note on PCF and DCF and explain how both co-exist.
8. Explain with sketch, what are BSS and ESS.
9. What are the main components in WLAN infrastructure?
10. Explain functionality in RTS and CTS in WiFi.
11. Detail the major advantages of 802.11g.
12. Compare 11a, 11b and 11g in 802 standard.
13. What is meant by ISM band and what is the Frequency used there in?
14. Discuss WiFi Network Topologies.
15. What are major security threats in WiFi? Discuss about MITM.
16. Explain the working of SSID, WEP and WPA - the WiFi Security Techniques.
17. Explain the blue tooth standard 802.15 and its working.
18. How to plan your WLAN network for full efficiency in working?
19. What is WiMAX standard? What are the major advantages of WiMAX?
20. What is the Beam Forming concept?
21. Write note on OFDM Technology used in WiMAX.
22. What are advantages of using MIMO technology in Wireless Network?
23. How the interference in WiMAX is dealt with efficiently?

Beyond 3G - Long Term Evolution – LTE (3GPP Release 8)

12.1 INTRODUCTION

Initiated in 2004, the Long Term Evolution (LTE) project focused on enhancing the Universal Terrestrial Radio Access (UTRA) and optimizing 3GPP's radio access architecture. The aim was to increase average user throughput four-times the Release 6 HSDPA levels in the Downlink (100Mbps), and three times the HSUPA levels in the Uplink (50Mbps). In 2007, the LTE of the 3rd generation radio access technology – "E UTRA" – progressed from the feasibility study stage to the first issue of approved Technical Specifications. By the end of 2008, the specifications were sufficiently stable for commercial implementation. Orthogonal Frequency Division Multiplexing (OFDM) was selected for the Downlink and Single Carrier-Frequency Division Multiple Access (SC-FDMA) for the Uplink. The Downlink supporting data modulation schemes QPSK, 16QAM, and 64QAM and the Uplink BPSK, QPSK, 8PSK and 16QAM. LTE's E UTRA uses a number of defined channel bandwidths between 1.25 and 20 MHz (contrasted with UTRA's fixed 5 MHz channels).

12.1.1 Motivation for 3GPP Release 8 - the LTE

- Need to ensure the continuity of competitiveness of the 3G system for the future
- User demand for higher data rates and quality of service
- Packet Switch optimized system
- Continued demand for cost reduction (CAPEX and OPEX)
- Low complexity
- Avoid unnecessary fragmentation of technologies for paired and unpaired band operation

12.1.2 LTE Release 8 Key Features

- OFDM in Downlink, robust against multipath interference & high affinity to advanced techniques such as frequency domain channel-dependent scheduling &
- DFTS-OFDM ("Single-Carrier FDMA") in Uplink, Low PAPR,
- User orthogonality in frequency domain
- Multi-antenna application
- Very low latency
- Short setup time & Short transfer delay
- Short HO latency and interruption time; Short TTI, RRC procedure, Simple RRC states

- Support of variable bandwidth 1.4MHZ, 3, 5, 10, 15 and 20 MHz
- Simple protocol architecture
- Shared channel based
- PS mode only with VoIP capability
  - ✓ e Node B as the only E-UTRAN node
  - ✓ Smaller number of RAN interfaces, eNodeB « MME/SAE-Gateway (S1), eNodeB « eNodeB (X2)
- Compatibility and inter-working with earlier 3GPP Releases
- Inter-working with other systems, e.g. cdma2000
- FDD and TDD within a single radio access technology
- Efficient Multicast/Broadcast
  - ✓ Single frequency network by OFDM
- Support of Self-Organising Network (SON) operation

12.1.3 Spectral Efficiency

Spectral efficiency is increased by up to four-fold compared with UTRA, and improvements in architecture and signalling reduce round-trip latency. Multiple Input / Multiple Output (MIMO) antenna technology should enable 10 times as many users per cell as 3GPP's original W CDMA radio access technology.

To suit as many frequency band allocation arrangements as possible, both paired (FDD) and unpaired (TDD) band operation is supported. LTE can co-exist with earlier 3GPP radio technologies, even in adjacent channels, and calls can be handed over to and from all 3GPP's previous radio access technologies.

In the same time frame as the development of LTE, 3GPP's core network has been undergoing System Architecture Evolution (SAE), optimizing it for packet mode and in particular for the IP-Multimedia Subsystem (IMS) which supports all access technologies

12.1.4 LTE Release 8 Major Parameters

Table 12.1

Access Scheme	UL	DFTS-OFDM
	DL	OFDMA
Bandwidth		1.4,3, 5, 10, 15, 20MHz
Minimum TTI		1msec
Sub-carrier spacing		15kHz
Cyclic prefix length	Short	4.7μsec
	Long	16.7μsec
Modulation		QPSK, 16QAM, 64QAM
Spatial multiplexing		Single layer for UL per UE Up to 4 layers for DL per UE MU-MIMO supported for UL and DL

Table 12.2

Category		*1*	*2*	*3*	*4*	*5*
Peak rate Mbps	DL	10	50	100	150	300
	UL	5	25	50	50	75
Capability for physical functionalities						
RF bandwidth		20MHz				
Modulation	DL	QPSK, 16QAM, 64 QAM				
	UL	QPSK, 16QAM		QPSK, 16QAM, 64QAM		
Multi-antenna						
2 Rx diversity		Assumed In performance requirements				
2x2 MIMO		Not	Mandatory supported			
4x4 MIMO		Not supported		Mandatory		

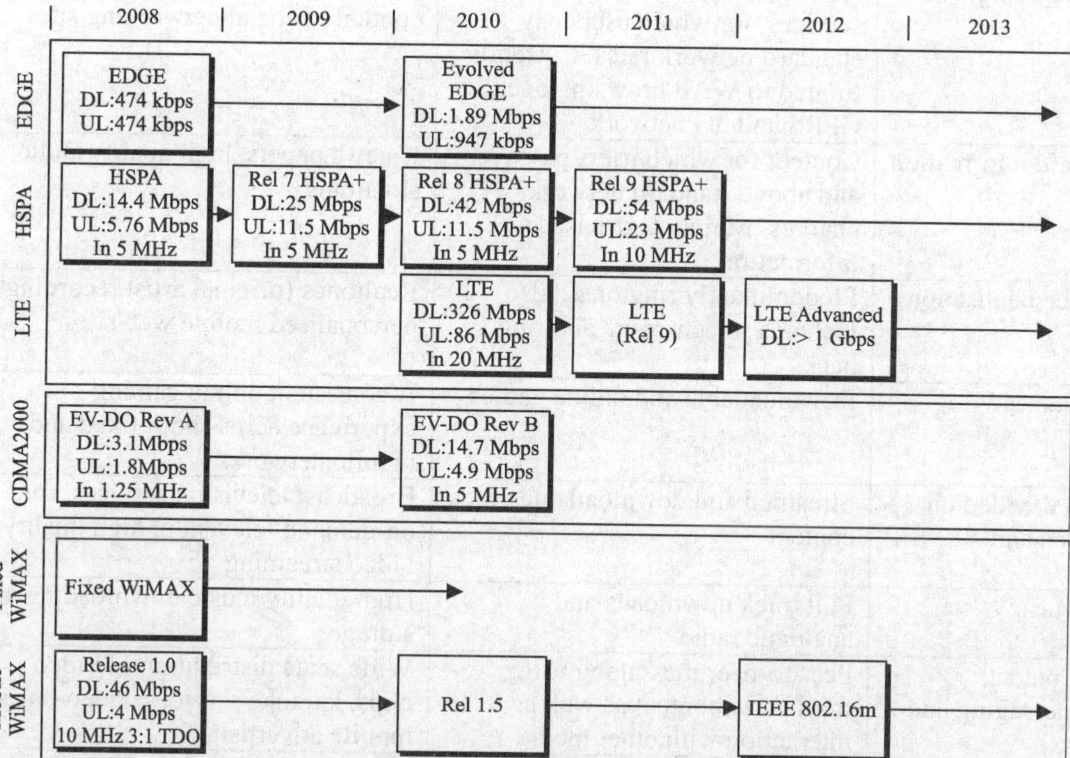

Fig. 12.1: Evolution of TDMA, CDMA and OFDMA Systems

12.2 3GPP EVOLUTION

- *Release 99 (2000)*— UMTS/WCDMA
- *Release 5 (2002)*— HSDPA

- *Release 6 (2005)*— HSUPA, MBMS (Multimedia Broadcast/Multicast Services)
- *Release 7 (2007)*— DL MIMO, IMS (IP Multimedia Subsystem), optimized real-time services (VoIP, gaming, push-to-talk).
- *Release 8 (2009)*— LTE (Long Term Evolution)

12.3 MAIN FEATURES OF LONG TERM EVOLUTION (LTE)

Table 12.3: Services (Source: Analysys Research/UMTS Forum 2007)

Service Category	*Current Environment*	*LTE Environment*
Rich voice	Real-time audio	VoIP, high quality video conferencing
P2F messaging	SMS. MMS. low priority e-mails	Photo messages, 1M, mobile e-mail, video messaging
Browsing	Access to online information services, for which users pay standard network rates. Currently limited to WAP browsing over GPRS and 3G networks	Super-fast browsing, uploading content to social networking sites
Paid information	Content for which users pay over and above standard network charges- Mainly text-based information.	E-news papers, high quality audio streaming
Personalisation	Predominantly ringtones, also includes screensavers and ring backs	Realtones (original artist recordings), personalised mobile web sites
Games	Downloadable and online games	A consistent online gaming experience across both fixed and mobile networks
TV/ video on demand	Streamed and downloadable video content	Broadcast television services, true on-demand television, high quality video streaming
Music	Full track downloads and analogue radio	High quality music downloading and storage
Content messaging and	Peer-to-peer messaging using third party content as well as interaction with other media	Wide scale distribution of video clips, karaoke services, video-based mobile advertising
M-commerce	Commission on transactions (including gambling) and payment facilities undertaken over mobile networks	Mobile handsets as payment devices, with payment details carried over high speed networks to enable rapid completion of transactions
Mobile data networking	Access to corporate intranets and databases, as well as the use of applications such as CRM	P2P file transfer, business applications, application sharing, M2M communication, mobile intranet/extranet

Need for higher data rates and greater spectral efficiency was achieved with HSDPA/HSUPA and/or new air interface defined by 3GPP LTE

Need for Packet Switched optimized system was realized with evolved UMTS towards packet only system

Need for high quality of services were achieved by use of licensed frequencies to guarantee quality of services, always-on experience (reduce control plane latency significantly) and reduce round trip delay

By simplifying architecture and reducing number of network elements a planned cheaper infrastructure is possible in LTE

4x Data Rate is realized with instantaneous downlink peak data rate of 100Mbit/s in a 20MHz downlink spectrum (i.e. 5 bit/s/Hz) and instantaneous uplink peak data rate of 50Mbit/s in a 20MHz uplink spectrum (i.e. 2.5 bit/s/Hz).

12.3.1 Other Important Features of LTE

Cell range— 5 km - optimal size and 30km sizes with reasonable performance and up to 100 km cell sizes supported with acceptable performance

Cell capacity— up to 200 active users per cell(5 MHz) (i.e., 200 active data clients)

Mobility— Optimized for low mobility (0-15km/h) but supports high speed

Latency— user plane < 5ms and control plane < 50 ms

Spectral Efficiency— Improved spectrum efficiency-the number bits per hertz per second increased 10 times.

Migration— Cost-effective migration from 3GPP Release 6 Universal Terrestrial Radio Access (UTRA) radio interface and architecture is realized.

Improved broadcasting— The inbuilt IP Multimedia Subsystem with IP-optimized component allows efficient Multimedia Broadcast Multicast System to group of subscriber bases within different geographics.

Bandwidth— Scalable bandwidth with dynamic allocation of 20MHz, 15MHz, 10MHz, 5MHz and 5MHz depending on the actual requirement enables judicious and economical utilization of the spectrum.

Co-existence with legacy standards (users can transparently start a call or transfer of data in an area using an LTE standard, and, when there is no coverage, continue the operation without any action on their part using GSM/GPRS or W-CDMA-based UMTS)

12.3.2 Multiple Access Scheme

- *Downlink*— OFDMA
- *Uplink*— Single Carrier FDMA (SC-FDMA)

12.3.3 Adaptive Modulation and Coding

- *DL modulations*— QPSK, 16QAM, and 64QAM
- *UL modulations*— QPSK and 16QAM
- *Rel-6 Turbo code*— Coding rate of 1/3, two 8-state constituent encoders, and a contention-free internal interleaver.
- Bandwidth scalability for efficient operation in differently sized allocated spectrum bands
- Possible support for operating as single frequency network (SFN) to support MBM
- Multiple Antenna (MIMO) technology for enhanced data rate and performance.
- ARQ within RLC sublayer and Hybrid ARQ within MAC sublayer.
- Power control and link adaptation
- Implicit support for interference coordination
- Support for both FDD and TDD
- Channel dependent scheduling & link adaptation for enhanced performance.

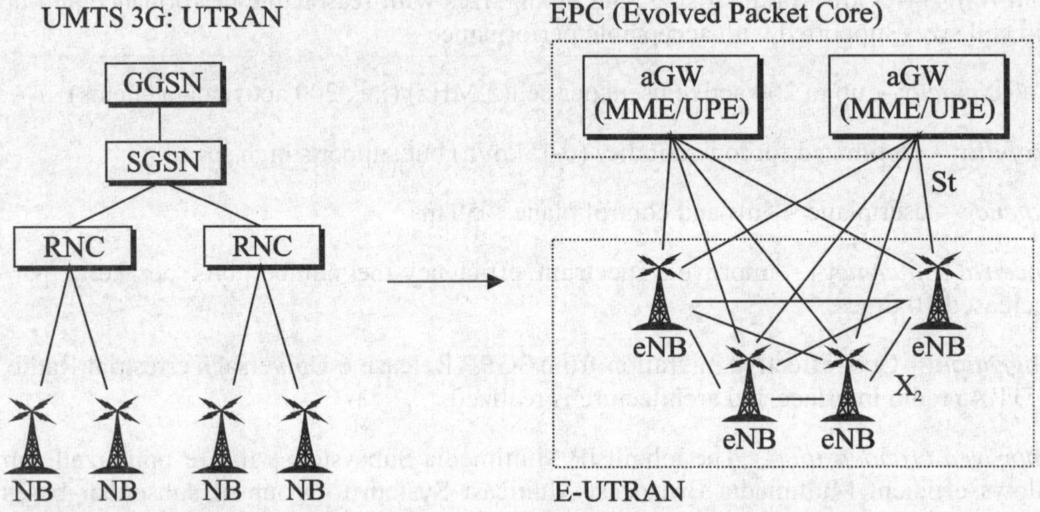

Fig. 12.2

- Reduced radio-access-network nodes to reduce cost, protocol-related processing time & call set-up time

Table 12.4: Carrier Aggregation Focus Scenarios According to 3GPP

Infra-band contiguous carrier aggregation			
FDD	UL/DL: 40 MHz in Band 3		
TDD	UL/DL: 50 MHz in Band 40		
Inter-band non-contiguous carrier aggregation			
Region 1 (Europe)	UUDL	40 MHz	20 MHz CC (Band 7) and 20 MHz CC (Band 20)
	UL/DL	40 MHz	20 MHz CC (Band 3] and 20 MHz CC (Band 20)
	UL/DL	40 MHz	20 MHz CC (Band 7] and 20 MHz CC (Band 3)
Region 2 (US)	UL/DL	20 MHz	10 MHz CC (Band 5) and 10 MHz CC (Band 12)
	UL/DL	10 MHz	5 MHz CC (Band 17) and 5 MHz CC (Band 4)
Region 3 (Asia)	UL/DL	20 MHz	10 MHz CC (Band 1)and 10 MHz CC (Band 18/19)
	UL/DL	40 MHz	20 MHz CC (Band 38) and 20 MHz CC (Band 40)
Intra-band non-contiguous carrier aggregation			
FDD/TDD	None		

12.4 SYSTEM ARCHITECTURE EVOLUTION (SAE)

It is the core network architecture of 3GPP's future LTE wireless communication standard. SAE is the evolution of the GPRS Core Network, with some differences.

12.4.1 The Main Principles and Objectives of the LTE-SAE Architecture

- A common anchor point and gateway (GW) node for all access technologies
- IP-based protocols on all interfaces;
- Simplified network architecture
- All IP network
- All services are via Packet Switched domain
- Support mobility between heterogeneous RATs, including legacy systems as GPRS, but also non-3GPP systems (say WiMAX)

12.4.2 System Architecture Evolution SAE

MME (Mobility Management Entity)—Manages and stores the UE control plane context, generates temporary Id, provides UE authentication, authorization, mobility management

UPE (User Plane Entity)— Manages and stores UE context, ciphering, mobility anchor, packet routing and forwarding, initiation of paging

3GPP anchor— Mobility anchor between 2G/3G and LTE

SAE anchor— Mobility anchor between 3GPP and non 3GPP (I-WLAN, etc) creased

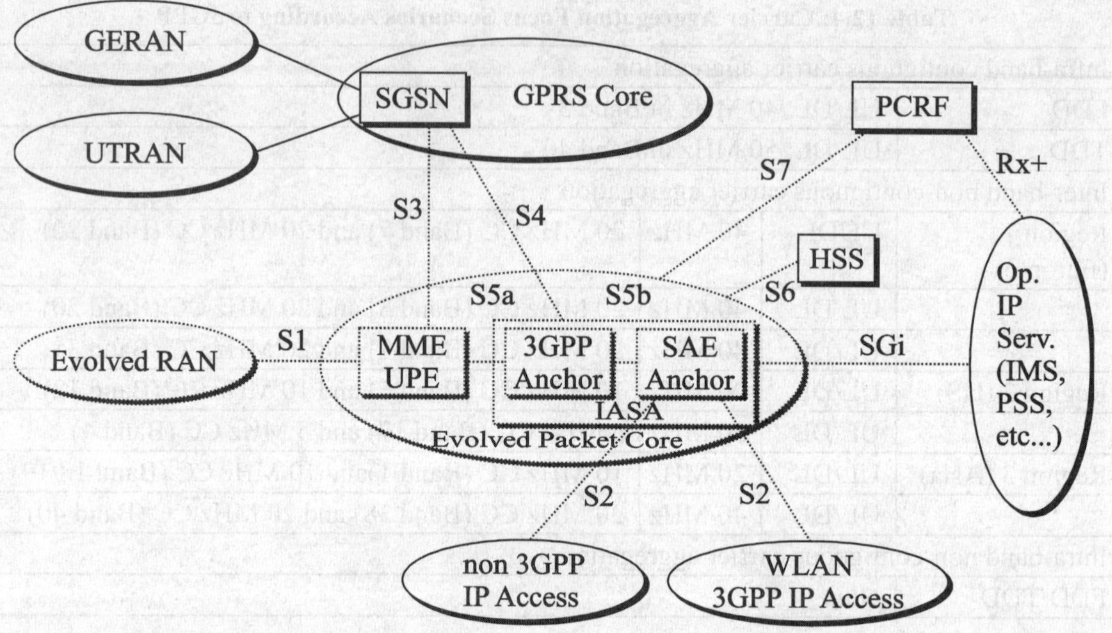

.... **New Functional Element / interface**

S1 : provides access to Evolved RAN radio resources for the transport of user plane and control plane traffic. The S1 reference point enables MME and UPE separation and also deployments of a combined MME and UPE

S2 : mobility support between WLAN 3GPP IP access or non 3GPP IP access and Inter AS Anchor

S3 : Enables user and bearer information exchange for inter 3GPP access system

S4 : Mobility support between GPRS Core and Inter AS Anchor

S5a : Provides the user plane with related control and mobility support between MME/UPE and 3GPP anchor.

Fig. 12.3: System Architecture

Evolved Packet Core

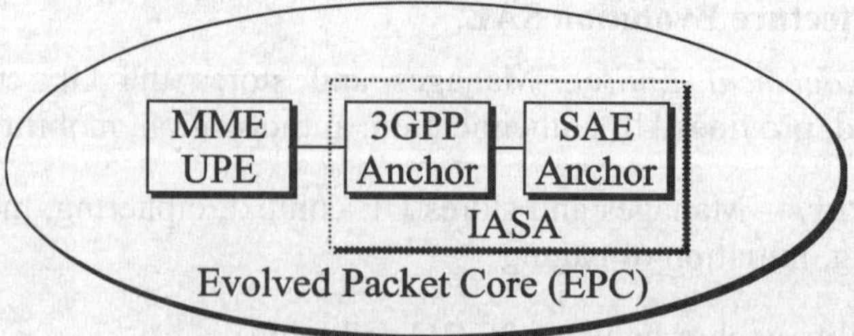

Fig. 12.4: Evolved Packet Core

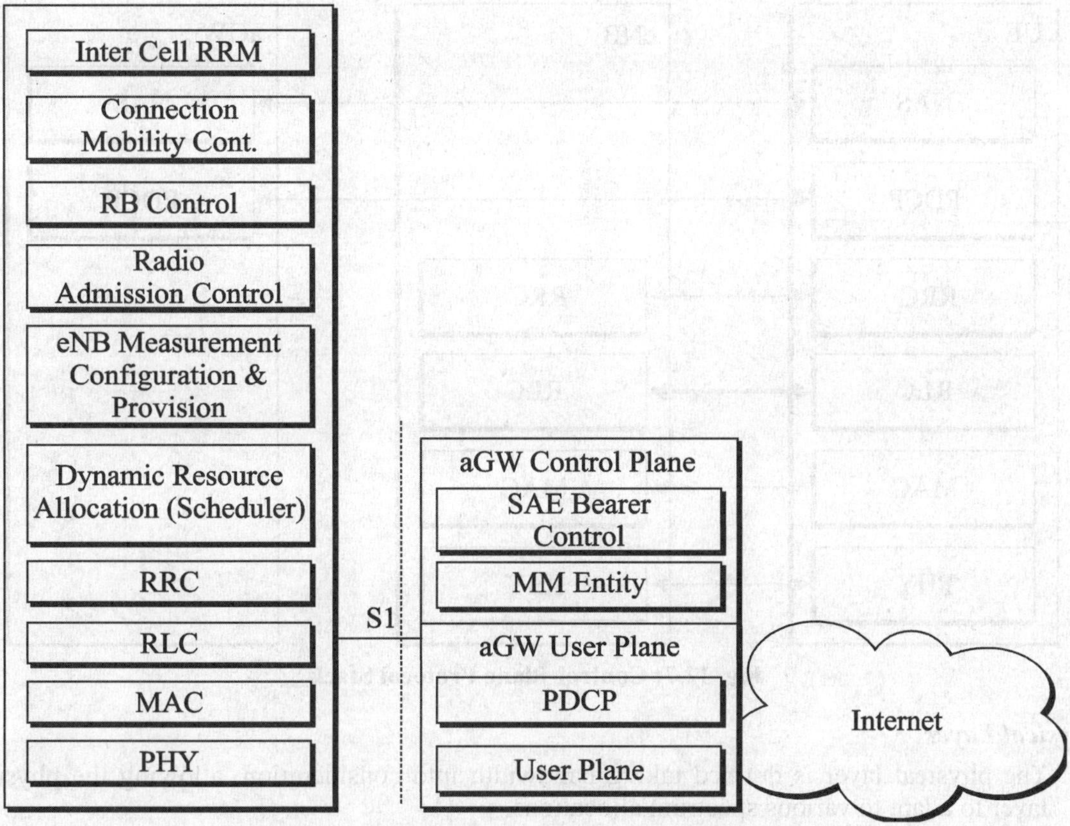

Inter Cell RRM
Connection Mobility Cont.
RB Control
Radio Admission Control
eNB Measurement Configuration & Provision
Dynamic Resource Allocation (Scheduler)
RRC
RLC
MAC
PHY
S1
aGW Control Plane
SAE Bearer Control
MM Entity
aGW User Plane
PDCP
User Plane
Internet

Fig. 12.5: E-Utran Architecture — Layered Structure

UE
PDCP
RLC
MAC
PHY
eNB
RLC
MAC
PHY
aGW
PDCP

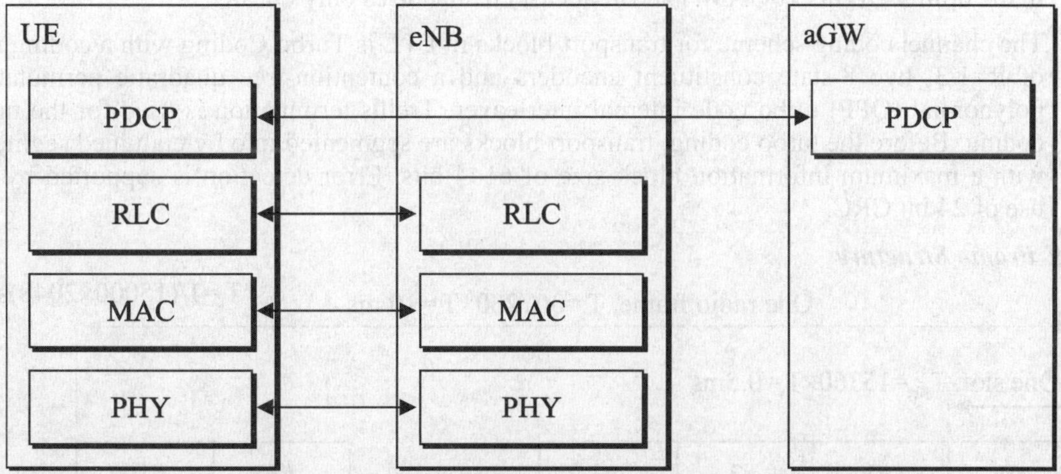

Fig. 12.6: User-Plane Protocol Stack

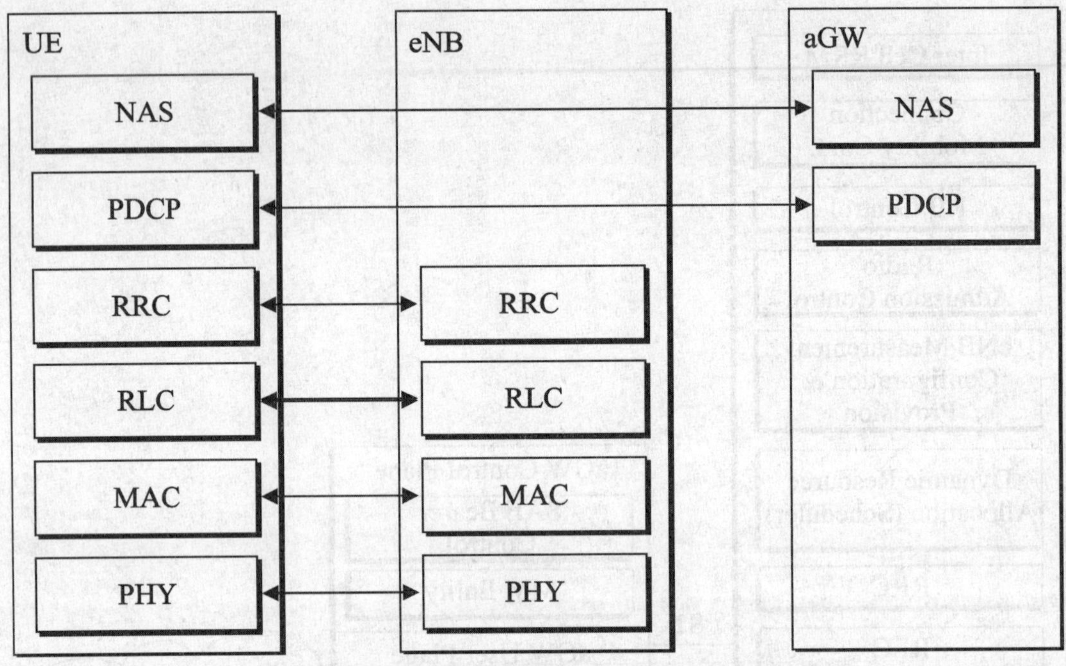

Fig. 12.7: Control-Plane Protocol Stack

Physical Layer

- The physical layer is defined taking bandwidth into consideration, allowing the physical layer to adapt to various spectrum allocations.
- The modulation schemes supported in the downlink are QPSK, 16QAM and 64QAM, and in the uplink QPSK, 16QAM.The Broadcast channel uses only QPSK.
- The channel coding scheme for transport blocks in LTE is Turbo Coding with a coding rate of R=1/3, two 8-state constituent encoders and a contention-free quadratic permutation polynomial (QPP) turbo code internal interleaver. Trellis termination is used for the turbo coding. Before the turbo coding, transport blocks are segmented into byte aligned segments with a maximum information block size of 6144 bits. Error detection is supported by the use of 24 bit CRC.

LTE Frame Structure

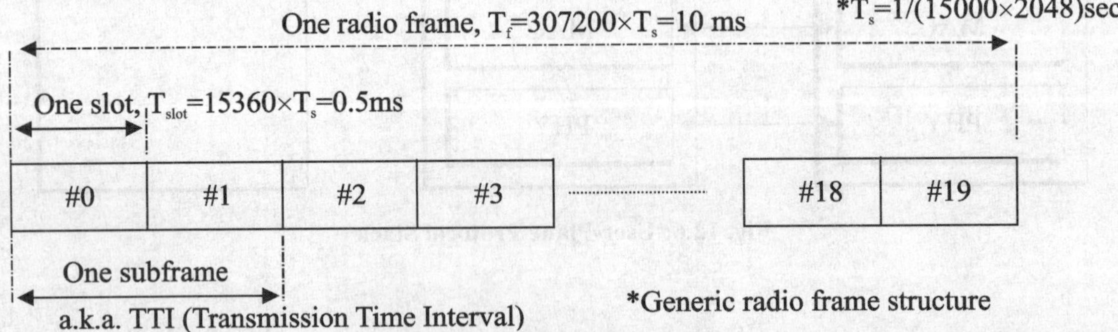

Fig. 12.8: LTE Frame Structure

One element that is shared by the LTE Downlink and Uplink is the generic frame structure. The LTE specifications define both FDD and TDD modes of operation. This generic frame structure is used with FDD. Alternative frame structures are defined for use with TDD.

LTE frames are 10 msec in duration. They are divided into 10 subframes, each subframe being 1.0 msec long. Each subframe is further divided into two slots, each of 0.5 msec duration. Slots consist of either 6 or 7 ODFM symbols, depending on whether the normal or extended cyclic prefix is employed

12.5 OFDM

LTE uses OFDM for the downlink – that is, from the base station to the terminal. OFDM meets the LTE requirement for spectrum flexibility and enables cost-efficient solutions for very wide carriers with high peak rates. OFDM uses a large number of narrow sub-carriers for multi-carrier transmission.

The basic LTE downlink physical resource can be seen as a time-frequency grid. In the frequency domain, the spacing between the subcarriers, Δf, is 15kHz. In addition, the OFDM symbol duration time is 1/Δf + cyclic prefix. The cyclic prefix is used to maintain orthogonality between the sub-carriers even for a time-dispersive radio channel.

One resource element carries QPSK, 16QAM or 64QAM. With 64QAM, each resource element carries six bits.

The OFDM symbols are grouped into resource blocks. The resource blocks have a total size of 180kHz in the frequency domain and 0.5ms in the time domain. Each 1ms Transmission Time Interval (TTI) consists of two slots (Tslot).

In E-UTRA, downlink modulation schemes QPSK, 16QAM, and 64QAM are available.

12.5.1 Downlink Physical Layer Procedures

For E-UTRA, the following downlink physical layer procedures are especially important:

- Cell search and synchronization:
- Scheduling:
- Link Adaptation:
- Hybrid ARQ (Automatic Repeat Request)

Uplink Physical Layer Procedures

For E-UTRA, the following uplink physical layer procedures are especially important:

- Random access
- Uplink scheduling
- Uplink link adaptation
- Uplink timing control
- Hybrid ARQ

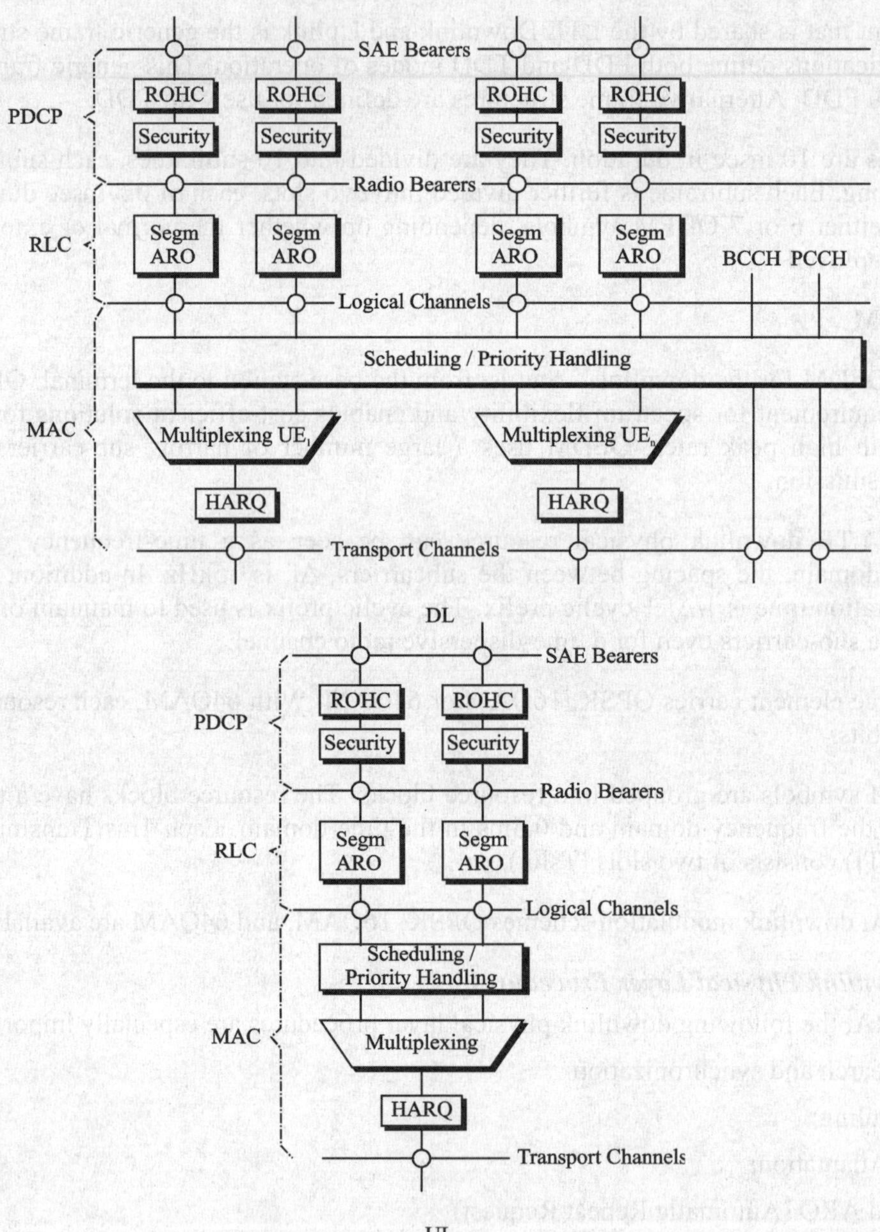

Fig. 12.9: Downlink Physical Layer Procedure

The three sublayers are

- Medium access Control (MAC)
- Radio Link Control (RLC)
- Packet Data Convergence Protocol(PDCP)

Layer 2

MAC (media access control) protocol

- handles uplink and downlink scheduling and HARQ signaling.
- Performs mapping between logical and transport channels.

RLC (radio link control) protocol

- focuses on lossless transmission of data.
- In-sequence delivery of data.
- Provides 3 different reliability modes for data transport. They are
  - ✓ Acknowledged Mode (AM)-appropriate for non-RT (NRT) services such as file downloads.
  - ✓ Unacknowledged Mode (UM)-suitable for transport of Real Time (RT) services because such services are delay sensitive and cannot wait for retransmissions
  - ✓ Transparent Mode (TM)-used when the PDU sizes are known a priori such as for broadcasting system information.

PDCP (packet data convergence protocol)

- handles the header compression and security functions of the radio interface

RRC (radio resource control) protocol

- handles radio bearer setup
- active mode mobility management
- Broadcasts of system information, while the NAS protocols deal with idle mode mobility management and service setup

SC-FDMA

The LTE uplink transmission scheme for FDD and TDD mode is based on SC-FDMA (Single Carrier Frequency Division Multiple Access).

This is to compensate for a drawback with normal OFDM, which has a very high Peak to Average Power Ratio (PAPR). High PAPR requires expensive and inefficient power amplifiers with high requirements on linearity, which increases the cost of the terminal and also drains the battery faster.

SC-FDMA solves this problem by grouping together the resource blocks in such a way that reduces the need for linearity, and so power consumption, in the power amplifier. A low PAPR also improves coverage and the cell-edge performance.

Still, SC-FDMA signal processing has some similarities with OFDMA signal processing, so parameterization of downlink and uplink can be harmonized.

The random access may be used to request initial access, as part of handover, or to re-establish uplink synchronization. 3GPP defines a contention based and a non-contention based random access procedure.

Scheduling of uplink resources is done by eNodeB. The eNodeB assigns certain time/frequency resources to the UEs and informs UEs about transmission formats to use. Scheduling grants for the uplink are communicated to the UEs via the PDCCH in the downlink. The scheduling decisions may be based on QoS parameters, UE buffer status, uplink channel quality measurements, UE capabilities, UE measurement gaps, etc.

As uplink link adaptation methods, transmission power control, adaptive modulation and channel coding rate, as well as adaptive transmission bandwidth can be used.

Uplink timing control is needed to time align the transmissions from different UEs with the receiver window of the eNodeB. The eNodeB sends the appropriate timing-control commands to the UEs in the downlink, commanding them to adapt their respective transmit timing.

Uplink Hybrid ARQ protocol is already known from HSUPA. The eNodeB has the capability to request retransmissions of incorrectly received data packets. ACK/NACK information in downlink is sent on Physical Hybrid ARQ Indicator Channel (PHICH).

Table 12.5: Parameters for Downlink Transmission Scheme

Transmission BW		1.25 MHz	2.5 MHz	5 MHz	10 MHz	15 MHz	20 MHz
Sub-frame duration		0.5 ms					
Sub-carrier spacing		15 kHz					
Sampling frequency		1.92 MHz (1/2 × 3.84 MHz)	3.84 MHz	7.68 MHz (2 × 3.84 MHz)	15.36 MHz (4 × 3.84 MHz)	23.04 MHz (6 × 3.84 MHz)	30.72 MHz (8 × 3.84 MHz)
FFT size		128	256	512	1024	1536	2048
Number of occupied sub-carriers*,**		76	151	301	601	901	1201
Number of OFDM symbols per sub frame (Short/Long CP)		7/6					
CP length (μs/samples)	Short	(4.69/9) × 6, (5.21/10) × 1*	(4.69/18) × 6, (5.21/20) × 1	(4.69/36) × 6, (5.21/40) × 1	(4.69/72) × 6, (5.21/80) × 1	(4.69/108)×6, (5.21/120)×1	(4.69/144) ×6 (5.21/160) ×1
	Long	(16.67/32)	(16.67/64)	(16.67/128)	(16.67/256)	(16.67/384)	(16.67/512)

12.6 CHANNELS IN LTE

Transport Channels

In order to reduce complexity of the LTE protocol architecture, the number of transport channels has been reduced. This is mainly due to the focus on shared channel operation, i.e. no dedicated channels are used any more.

Downlink Transport Channels are

- Broadcast Channel (BCH)
- Downlink Shared Channel (DL-SCH)
- Paging Channel (PCH)
- Multicast Channel (MCH)

Uplink Transport Channels are

- Uplink Shared Channel (UL-SCH)
- Random Access Channel (RACH)

Logical Channels

- Logical channels can be classified in control and traffic channels.

Control Channels are

- Broadcast Control Channel (BCCH)
- Paging Control Channel (PCCH)
- Common Control Channel (CCCH)
- Multicast Control Channel (MCCH)
- Dedicated Control Channel (DCCH)

Traffic Channels are

- Dedicated Traffic Channel (DTCH)
- Multicast Traffic Channel (MTCH)

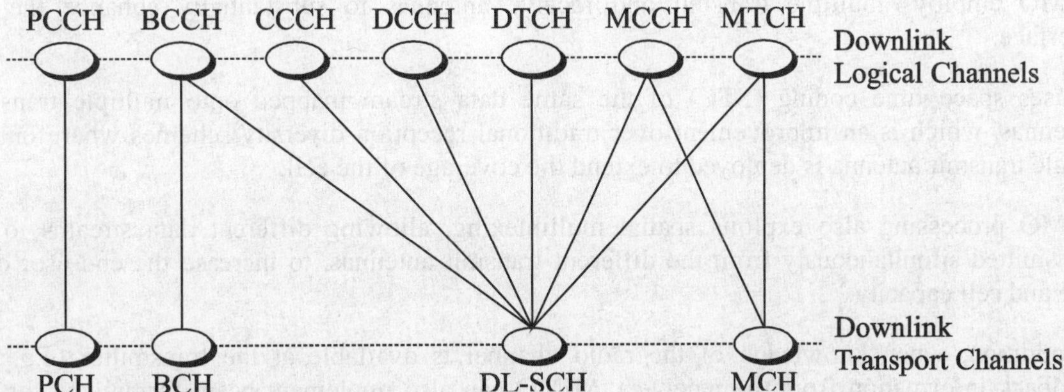

Fig. 12.10: Mapping between Downlink Control and Transport Channels

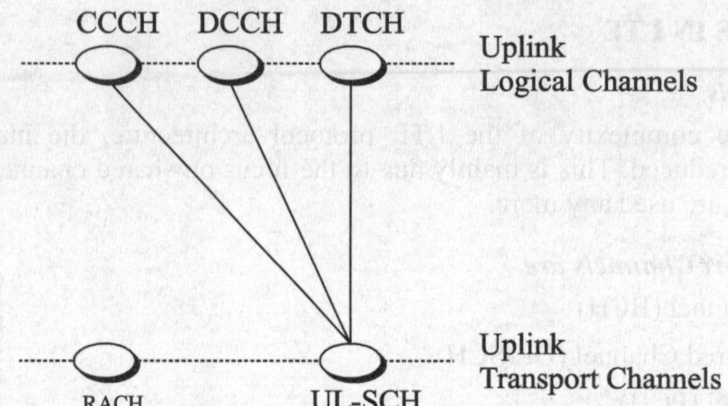

Fig. 12.11: Mapping between Uplink Control and Transport Channels

12.7 LTE MBMS CONCEPT

- MBMS (Multimedia Broadcast Multicast Services) is an essential requirement for LTE. The so-called E-MBMS will therefore be an integral part of LTE.
- In LTE, MBMS transmissions may be performed as single-cell transmission or as multi-cell transmission. In case of multi-cell transmission the cells and content are synchronized to enable for the terminal to soft-combine the energy from multiple transmissions.
- The superimposed signal looks like multipath to the terminal. This concept is also known as Single Frequency Network (SFN).
- The E-UTRAN can configure which cells are part of an SFN for transmission of an MBMS service. The MBMS traffic can share the same carrier with the unicast traffic or be sent on a separate carrier.
- For MBMS traffic, an extended cyclic prefix is provided. In case of subframes carrying MBMS SFN data, specific reference signals are used. MBMS data is carried on the MBMS traffic channel (MTCH) as logical channel.

12.8 MULTIPLE ANTENNA TECHNIQUES IN LTE

MIMO employs multiple transmit and receive antennas to substantially enhance the air interface.

It uses space time coding (STC) of the same data stream mapped onto multiple transmit antennas, which is an improvement over traditional reception diversity schemes where only a single transmit antenna is deployed to extend the coverage of the cell.

MIMO processing also exploits spatial multiplexing, allowing different data streams to be transmitted simultaneously from the different transmit antennas, to increase the end-user data rate and cell capacity.

In addition, when knowledge of the radio channel is available at the transmitter (e.g. via feedback information from the receiver), MIMO can also implement beam-forming to further increase available data rates and spectrum efficiency

12.8.1 Advanced Antenna Techniques in LTE

Single data stream / user

- *Beam-forming*— Coverage, longer battery life
- *Spatial Division Multiple Access (SDMA)*— Multiple users in same radio resource
- *Multiple data stream / user Diversity*— Link robustness
- *Spatial multiplexing*— Spectral efficiency, high data rate support

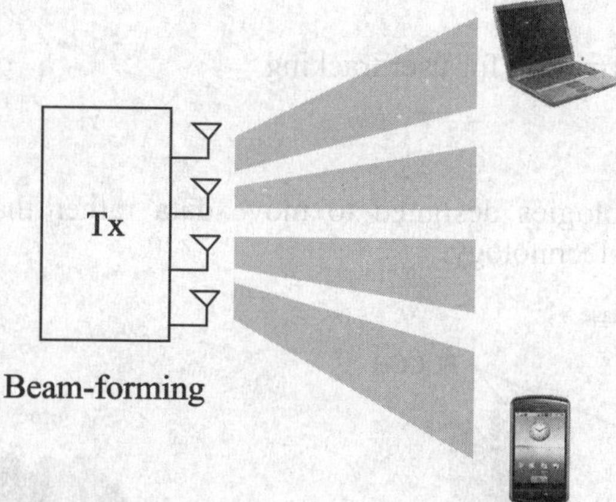

Fig. 12.12: Beam Forming

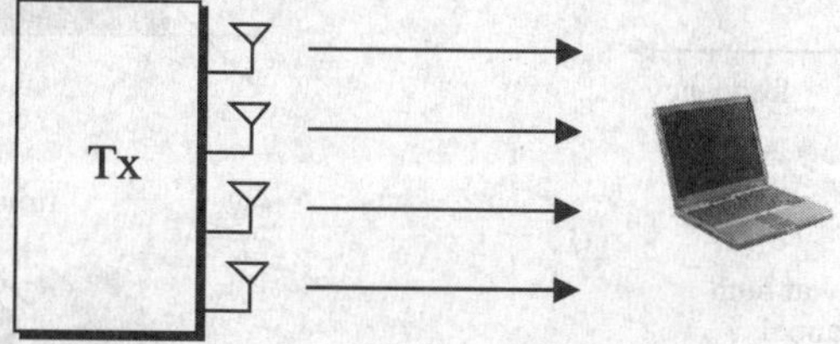

Fig. 12.13: Multiple Antennas

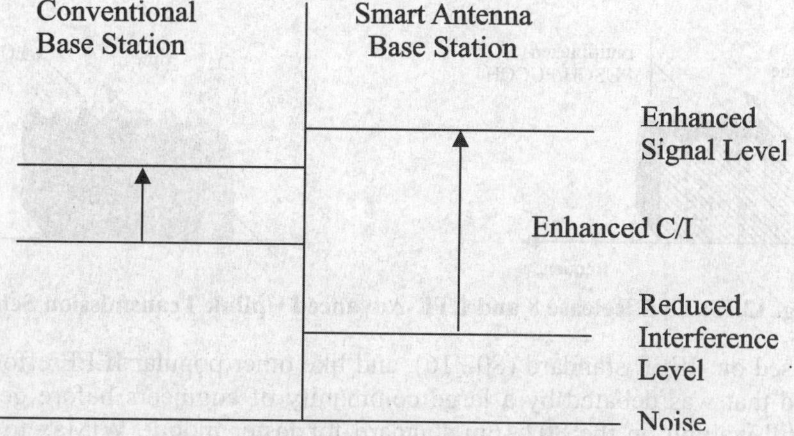

Fig. 12.14: Effect of Smart Antenna

12.8.2 Beam Forming and SDMA

- Enhances signal reception through directional array gain, while individual antenna has omni-directional gain
- Extends cell coverage
- Suppresses interference in space domain
- Enhances system capacity
- Prolongs battery life
- Provides angular information for user tracking

12.9 LTE Vs WiMAX

First, both are 4G technologies designed to move data rather than voice and both are IP networks based on OFDM technology.

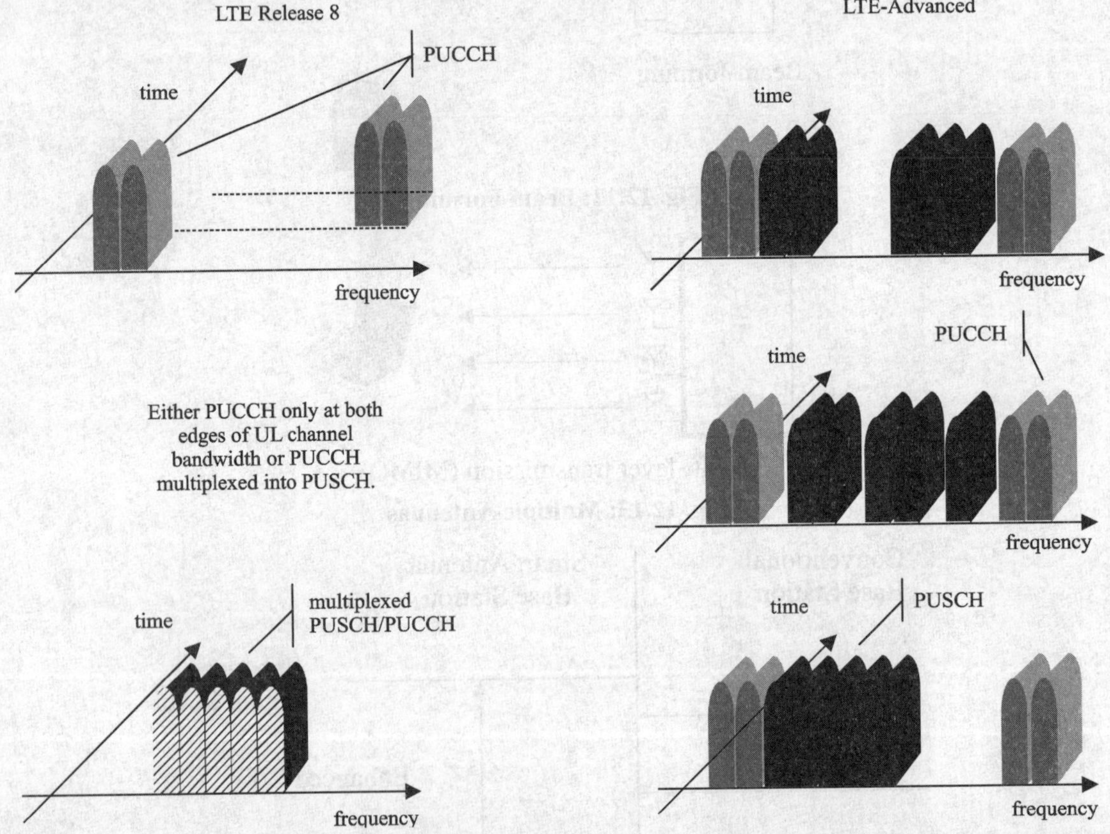

Fig. 12.15: LTE Release 8 and LTE-Advanced Uplink Transmission Schemes

WiMax is based on IEEE standard (802.16), and like other popular IEEE effort, Wi-Fi, it's an open standard that was debated by a large community of engineers before getting ratified. In fact, we're still waiting on the 802.16m standard for faster mobile WiMax to be ratified. The level of openness means WiMax equipment is standard and therefore cheaper to buy — sometimes half the cost and sometimes even less. Depending on the spectrum alloted for WiMax deployments and how the network is configured, this can mean a WiMax network is cheaper to build.

As for speeds, LTE will be faster than the current generation of WiMax, but 802.16m that should be ratified is fairly similar in speeds.

Table 12.6: Parameters of HSPA and WiMAX

Parameter	***HSPA[1]***			***WiMAX***	
	Rel-7		***Rel-8***	***Rel 1.5***	
Frequency	2000 MHz			2500 MHz	
Duplex	FDD			FDD	TDD
Channel BW	2x5 MHz			2x5 MHz	10 MHz
BS Antenna	(1x2) SIMO	(2x2) MIMO		(2x2) MIMO	
MS Antenna	(1x2) SIMO			(1x2) SIMO	
DL Mod-Coding[2]	64QAM-5/6	16QAM-3/4	64QAM-5/6	64QAM-5/6	64QAM-5/6
UL Mod-Coding[2]	16QAM-3/4			64QAM-5/6	64QAM-5/6
DL Peak User Rate	17.5 Mbps	21 Mbps	35 Mbps	36 Mbps	48 Mbps[3]
UL Peak User Rate	8.3 Mbps	8.3 Mbps	8.3 Mbps	17 Mbps	24 Mbps[4]

Table 12.7: Radio Perspective WiMAX Vs LTE

	WiMax 802.16e	***LTE***	***Comments***
Network Architecture	Flat IP based BS ASN GW	Very Flat IP Based eNodeB and GW	Reduction of nodes as Compared to 2G/3G
Services	Packet data VOIP	Packet data VOIP	
Mobility	<120 km	Upto 350km 2G/3G handover global roaming	LTE-Embedded in 3GPP wrld
Access Technology	Scalable OFDMA in UL & DL	DL: OFDMA UL : SCFDMA	SC FDMA reduces PAPR by-5dB

Table 12.8: LTE Vs WiMAX Comparision (Radio Perspective)

	WiMax	*LTE*	*Comments*
MIMO, #Antennas	BS: 1, 2, 4 ; MS: 1,2 Closed + open Loop	eNodeB: 1, 2, 4 ; UE: 2 Closed + open Loop	LTE working assumption is 2 DL Antennas per UE
MIMO Modes	Diversity + Spatial Multi.	Diversity + Spatial MULTI.	
HARQ	Chase Comb + IR; stop & wait	Chase Comb. + IR; N=S stop & wait; UL Sync, DL Async	
Subchannel/ Physical Resource Block	24x2 Constellation Points in PUSC Mode	12x14 Constellation Points	
Interleaving / Mapping	Adjacent AMC 2x3 or PUSC/FUSC Permutation; Focus Permutation	Localized + Distributed; Focus Localized	LTE prefers frequency selective Packet Scheduling, WiMax focuses on interference averaging.
Pilot Assisted Channel Estimation (PACE)	DL Preamble + distributed permuted Pilots depending on # Antennas	Distributed Pilots depending on # Antennas	
Overall Overhead @ MAC Layer	VolP+ Data Mixture typically - 25 %	VolP+ Data Mixture typically - 15-20%	LTE is more efficient, e.g. VoIP optimizations
L1/L2 Signalling	Flexible FCH + MAP following the Preamble; Sync. by Ranging CH	Signaling Channels in max first 3 Symbols; Separate BCH, SCH	LTE provides optimized and more efficient L1/L2 Signaling also utilizing CDM components
User Multiplexing	Flexible arbitrary Rectangles in T-F-Domain	Stripe-wise Allocation in F-Domain	LTE with less complex Resource Signaling

Table 12.9: Radio Perception WiMAX Vs LTE

Channel Bandwidth	1.25,3.5,5,7,10,1 5,20MHz	1.2,52.5,5, 10,15,20MHz	Both very flexible
FFT Size and sub carrier spacing	128-2048 variable dF:7-20kHz	128-2048 fixed dF:15kHz	Large dF to overcome Doppler shift
Spectrum	Licensed & unlicensed:2.3, 2.5,3.5,5.8GHz	Licensed IMT-2000 MHz bands	LTE Low frq band-coverage adv
Duplex mode	TDD+FDD TDD focus	TDD+FDD FDD focus	FDD asyn. adv
frame	5 ms	1 ms	Latency reduced in LTE
Modulation & Coding	BPSK..64-QAM	QPSK..64-QAM	

Table 12.10: LTE Vs WiMAX

Parameter	***LTE***	***Mobile WiMAX Rel 1.5***
Duplex	FDD and TDD	FDD and TDD
Frequency Band for Performance Analysis	2000 MHz	2500 MHz
Channel BW	Up to 20 MHz	Up to 20 MHz
Downlink	OFDMA	OFDMA
Uplink	SC-FDMA	OFDMA
DL Spectral Efficiency[1]	1.57 bps/Hz/Sector (2x2) MIMO[2]	1.59 bps/Hz/Sector (2x2) MIMO
UL Spectral Efficiency[1]	0.64bps/Hz/Sector (1x2) SIMO[2]	0.99 bps/Hz/Sector (1x2) SIMO
Frame Size	1 millisec	5 millisec
HARQ	Incremental Redundancy	Chase Combining
Link Budget	Typically limited by Mobile Device	Typically limited by Mobile Device
Advanced Antenna Support	DL: 2x2, 2x4, 4x2, 4x4 UL:1x2, 1x4,2x2, 2x4	DL: 2x2, 2x4, 4x2, 4x4 UL: 1x2, 1x4, 2x2, 2x4

Table 12.11: LTE Projections & Mobile WiMAX – FDD 2 × 20 MHz Channel BW

Parameter	*Reported LTE Results*				*WiMAX Rel 1.5*	
	Motorola[1]		*T-Mobile*[2]	*Qual-comm*[3]		
BS Antenna	2×2	4×4	2×4	4×2	2×2	4×4
Channel BW	2 × 20 MHz				2 × 20 MHz	
Mod-Code Rate	64QAM-5/6		64QAM-5/6	64QAM-?	64QAM-5/6	
DL Peak User Rate	117 Mbps	226 Mbps	144 Mbps	277 Mbps	144.6 Mbps	289 Mbps
MS Antenna			1x2	1x2	1x2	
Mod-Code Rate			64QAM[4]-?	16QAM[4]-?	64QAM-5/6	
UL Peak User Rate			50.4 Mbps	75 Mbps	69.1 Mbps	

However, LTE will take time to roll out, with deployments reaching mass adoption by 2012. WiMax is out now, and more networks should be available later this year.

The crucial difference is that, unlike WiMAX, which requires a new network to be built, LTE runs on an evolution of the existing UMTS infrastructure already used by over 80 per cent of mobile subscribers globally. This means that even though development and deployment of the LTE standard may lag Mobile WiMAX, it has a crucial incumbent advantage.

LTE is a highly optimized, spectrally efficient, mobile OFDMA solution built from the ground up for mobility, and it allows operators to offer advanced services and higher performance for new and wider bandwidths.

LTE is based on a flattened IP-based network architecture that improves network latency, and is designed to interoperate on and ensure service continuity with existing 3GPP networks. LTE leverages the benefits of existing 3G technologies and enhances them further with additional antenna techniques such as higher-order MIMO.

12.10 MIMO TECHNIQUES IN 3GPP

Wireless System Designers have a number of Challenges;

1) Limited availability of RF Spectrum
2) Complex Time-varying Wireless Environment
3) Fading and Multipath

There is a Need on Increasing demands like Higher Data Rate (LTE: DL-100Mbps, UL:50Mbps), Better QoS and Fewer Dropped Calls

Objective of improving spectral efficiency and link reliability is met by innovative system design like using MIMO and OFDM.

Tx
Rx
SISO
Tx
Rx
SIMO
Tx
Rx
MISO
Tx
Rx
MIMO
Single User
Multi-user
Multi-cell
Interference user

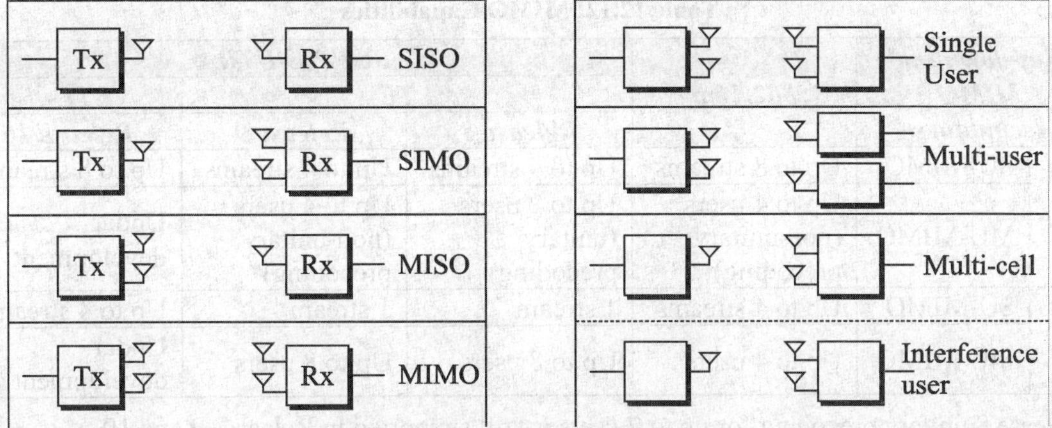

Fig. 12.16: Multiple Antenna

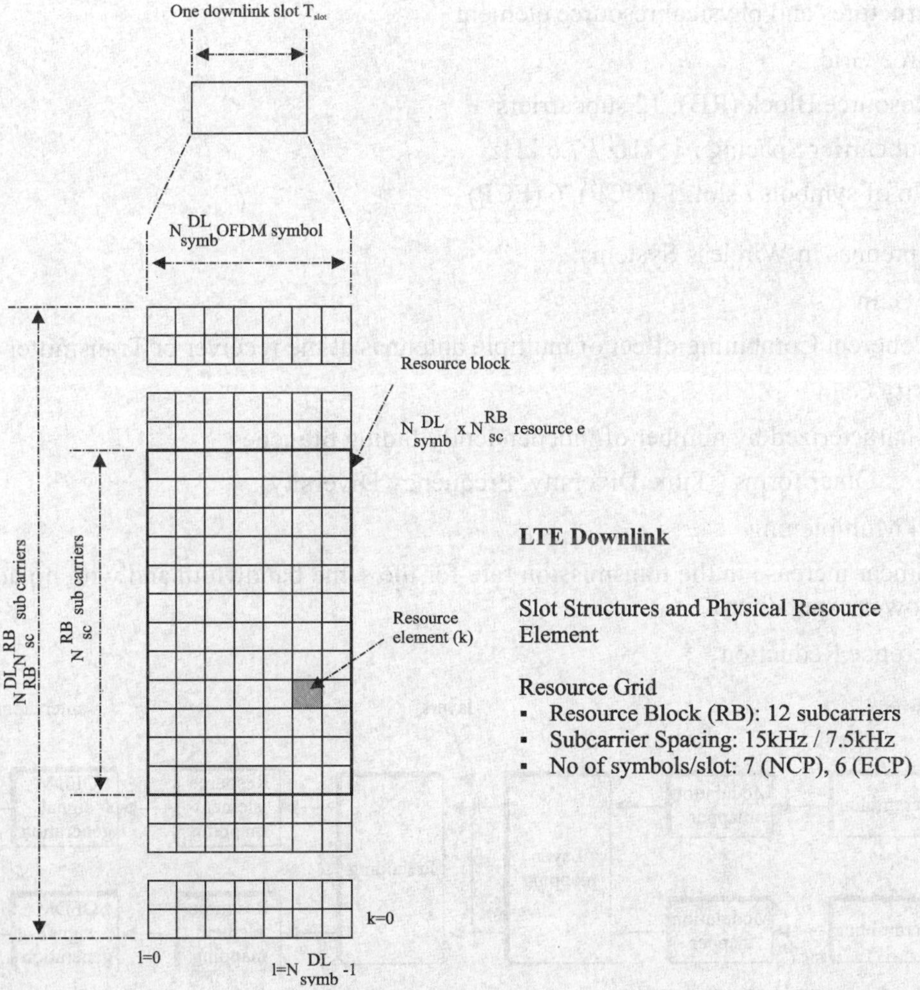

One downlink slot T_{slot}
N_{symb}^{DL} OFDM symbol
Resource block
$N_{symb}^{DL} \times N_{sc}^{RB}$ resource e
$N_{RB}^{DL} N_{sc}^{RB}$ sub carriers
N_{sc}^{RB} sub carriers
Resource element (k)
k=0
l=0
$l=N_{symb}^{DL}-1$
LTE Downlink
Slot Structures and Physical Resource Element
Resource Grid
Resource Block (RB): 12 subcarriers
Subcarrier Spacing: 15kHz / 7.5kHz
No of symbols/slot: 7 (NCP), 6 (ECP)

Fig. 12.17: DL Carrier

Table 12.12: MIMO Capabilities

Key downlink MIMO techniques		*802.16m*	*3GPP E-UTRA*		
			LTE		*LTE-A*
			Release 8	*Release 9*	*Release 10*
DL	SU-MIMO	Up to 8 streams	Up to 4 streams	Up to 4 streams	Up to 8 streams
	MU-MIMO	Up to 4 users (non-unitary precoding)	Up to 2 users (unitary precoding)	Up to 4 users (non-unitary precoding)*	Under development
UL	SU-MIMO	Up to 4 streams	1 stream	1 stream	Up to 4 streams
	MU-MIMO	Up to 4 users	Up to 8 users	Up to 8 users	Under development

*Release 8 unitary precoding for up to 2 users is still supported in Releases 9 and 10.

LTE Downlink

- Slot structures and physical resource element
- Resource Grid
  - ✓ Resource Block (RB): 12 subcarriers
  - ✓ Subcarrier Spacing : 15kHz / 7.5 kHz
  - ✓ No of symbols / slot: 7 (NCP), 6 (ECP)

Multiple Antennas in Wireless Systems:

- Array Gain
  - ✓ Coherent Combining effect of multiple antennas at the receiver or Transmitter or both
- Diversity Gain
  - ✓ Characterized by number of independently fading branches
    - – Other forms (Time Diversity, Frequency Diversity)
- Spatial Multiplexing
  - ✓ Linear increase in the transmission rate for the same bandwidth and with no additional power expenditure
- Interference Reduction

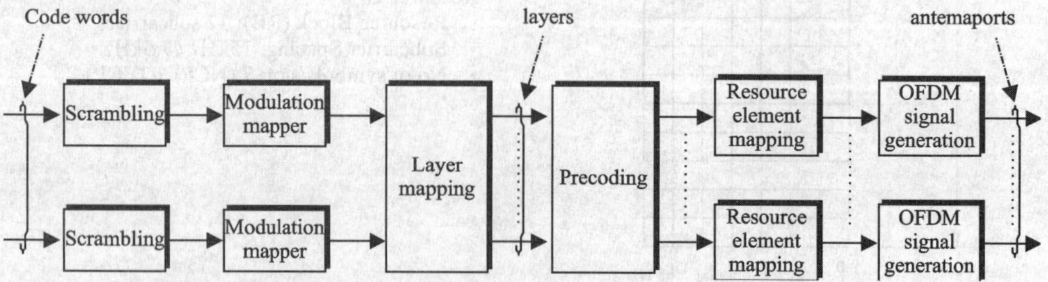

Fig. 12.18: LTE Downlink — Downlink Channel Processing

LTE Downlink — Downlink Channel Processing

- Scrambling of coded bits in each of the code words Generating complex-valued modulation symbols from scrambled bits
- Mapping modulation symbols onto one or several Tx. layers
- Precoding modulation symbols on each layer for
- transmission on the antenna ports
- Mapping of modulation symbols for each antenna port to RE
- Generating complex-valued time-domain OFDM signal for each antenna port

Intra-LTE Handover

In this network controlled handover the decision is taken by Source eNode B. There are three phases before actual hand over takes place

- Preparation phase
  - ✓ preparation of Target eNodeB by context transfer prior to HO command
  - ✓ Break before make approach
  - ✓ core network not involved during preparation phase
  - ✓ Temporary forwarding of UP data from Source eNode B to Target ENB
- Path switching at AGW
  - ✓ after establishment of new connection between UE and Target ENB
  - ✓ no temporary buffering at AGW

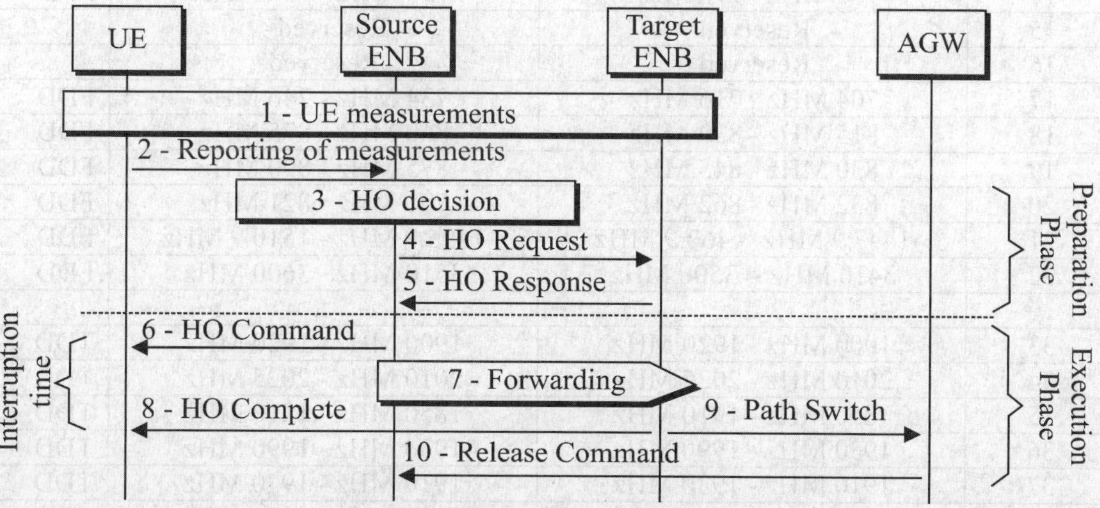

Fig. 12.19: Intra LTE Hand Over

- Performance
  - ✓ short interruption time in the range of 10 ms
  - ✓ same handover procedure applicable for real-time (delay sensitive) and non real-time (non delay sensitive) services
  - ✓ suitable for lossless and seamless handovers

12.11 LTE ADVANCED OPERATING BANDS

Table 12.13

Operating Band	*Uplink (UL) operating band BS receive/UE transmit*	*Downlink (DL) operating band BS transmit /UE receive*	*Duplex Mode*
	$F_{UL\ low}$ - $F_{UL\ high}$	$F_{DL\ low}$ - $F_{DL\ high}$	
1	1920 MHz - 1980 MHz	2110 MHz - 2170 MHz	FDD
2	1850 MHz - 1910 MHz	1930 MHz - 1990 MHz	FDD
3	1710 MHz - 1785 MHz	1805 MHz - 1880 MHz	FDD
4	1710 MHz - 1755 MHz	2110 MHz - 2155 MHz	FDD
5	824 MHz - 849 MHz	869 MHz - 894MHz	FDD
6	830 MHz- - 840 MHz-	865 MHz - 875 MHz-	FDD
7	2500 MHz - 2570 MHz	2620 MHz - 2690 MHz	FDD
8	880 MHz - 915 MHz	925 MHz - 960 MHz	FDD
9	1749.9 MHz - 1784.9 MHz	1844.9 MHz - 1879.9 MHz	FDD
10	1710 MHz - 1770 MHz	2110 MHz - 2170 MHz	FDD
11	1427.9 MHz - 1447.9 MHz	1475.9 MHz - 1495.9 MHz	FDD
12	698 MHz - 716 MHz	728 MHz - 746 MHz	FDD
13	777 MHz - 787 MHz	746 MHz - 756 MHz	FDD
14	788 MHz - 798 MHz	758 MHz - 768 MHz	FDD
15	Reserved	Reserved -	
16	Reserved	Reserved	
17	704 MHz - 716 MHz	734 MHz - 746 MHz	FDD
18	815 MHz - 830 MHz	860 MHz - 875 MHz	FDD
19	830 MHz - 845 MHz	875 MHz - 890 MHz	FDD
20	832 MHz - 862 MHz	791 MHz - 821 MHz	FDD
21	1447.9 MHz - 462.9 MHz	1495.9 MHz - 1510.9 MHz	FDD
22	3410 MHz - 3500 MHz	3510 MHz - 3600 MHz	FDD
...	...	...	...
33	1900 MHz - 1920 MHz	1900 MHz - 1920 MHz	TDD
34	2010 MHz - 2025 MHz	2010 MHz - 2025 MHz	TDD
35	1850 MHz - 1910 MHz	1850 MHz - 1910 MHz	TDD
36	1930 MHz - 1990 MHz	1930 MHz - 1990 MHz	TDD
37	1910 MHz - 1930 MHz	1910 MHz - 1930 MHz	TDD
38	2570 MHz - 2620 MHz	2570 MHz - 2620 MHz	TDD
39	1880 MHz - 1920 MHz	1880 MHz - 1920 MHz	TDD
40	2300 MHz - 2400 MHz	2300 MHz - 2400 MHz	TDD
41	3400 MHz - 3600 MHz	3400 MHz - 3600 MHz	TDD

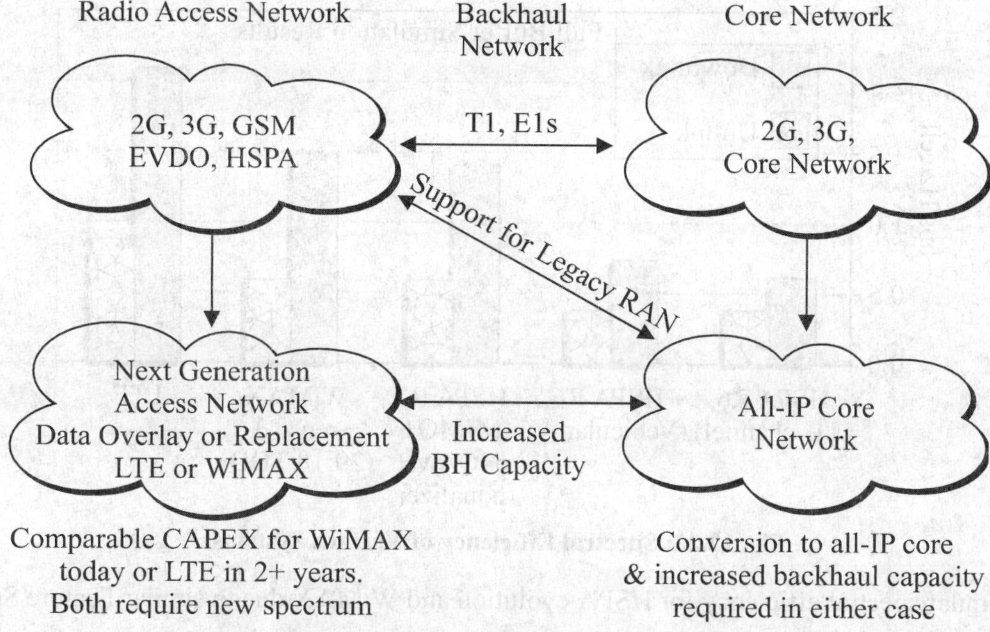

Fig. 12.20: Upgrade path for existing operators

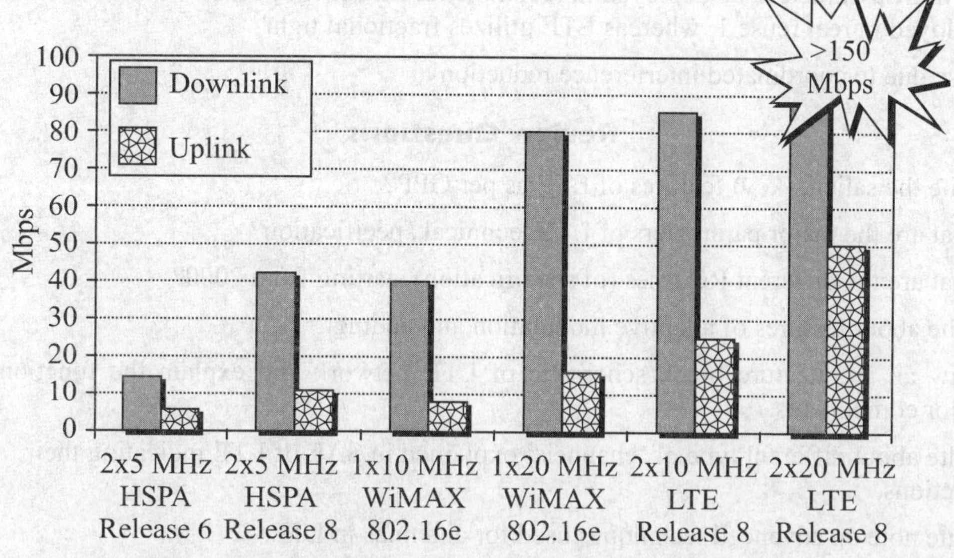

Fig. 12.21: Throughput Comparison of Different Systems

- Rather similar Peak Data Rates for HSPA evolution and WiMAX
- LTE provides outstanding Data Rates beyond 150 Mbps in 2 × 20 MHz Bandwidth due to less overhead
- WiMAX uses asymmetric 29:18 TDD in 10/20 MHz, whereas HSPA and LTE use FDD with 2 × 5 and 2 × 10/20 MHz
- Prerequisite: 2 × 2 MIMO with 64-QAM Downlink

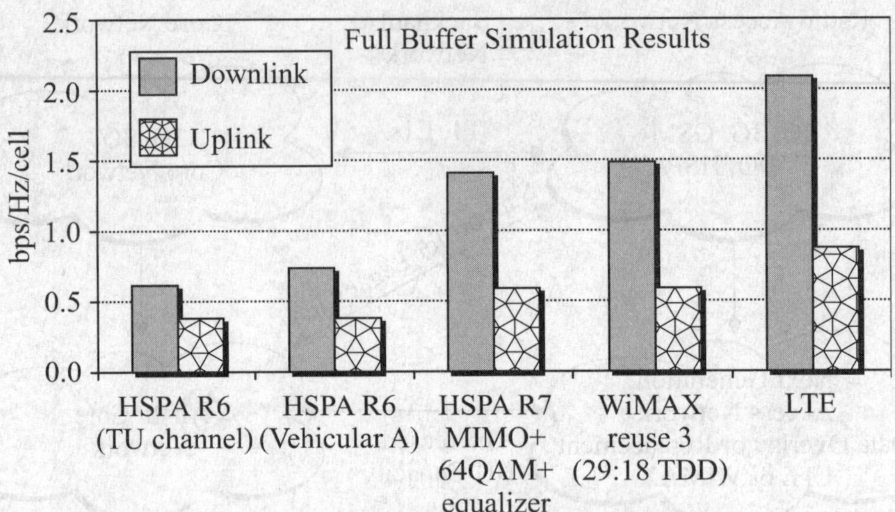

Fig. 12.22: Spectral Efficiency of Various Systems

- Similar spectral efficiency for HSPA evolution and WiMAX due to similar Feature Set
- LTE is expected to provide higher efficiency than HSPA or WiMAX
- WiMAX assumed to be deployed in recommended frequency reuse 1/3, HSPA is definitely deployed in real reuse 1, whereas LTE utilizes fractional tight
- reuse due to coordinated interference reduction

Review Questions

1. Write the salient (key) features of LTE as per GPP?
2. What are the major parameters of LTE technical specification?
3. What are the different Releases (of specification) starting from 2000?
4. Write about features of adaptive modulation and coding.
5. Draw an architecture block schematic of LTE network and explain the functions of all major components.
6. Write about different type of 'channels' explained in SAE of LTE indicating their functions.
7. Write note on advanced techniques used for antennas in LTE.
8. Make a comparative statement of LTE Vs WiMAX.
9. What are OFDM and MIMO? How they are deployed in LTE?
10. Compare throughput and spectral efficiency of HSPA, LTE and WiMAX.

13 FOURTH GENERATION NETWORK (4G) LTE - ADVANCED

13.1 INTRODUCTION

LTE (Long Term Evolution) standardization within the 3GPP (3rd Generation Partnership Project) has reached a mature state. Since the end of 2009, LTE mobile communication systems have been deployed as a natural evolution of GSM (Global system for mobile communications) and UMTS (Universal Mobile Telecommunications System). The ITU (International Telecommunication Union) has coined the term IMT-Advanced to identify mobile systems whose capabilities go beyond those of IMT 2000 (International Mobile Telecommunications). Specifically data rate requirements have been increased. In order to support advanced services and applications 100Mbps for high and 1Gbps for low mobility scenarios must be realized. Throughout 2009, 3GPP has worked on a study with the purpose of identifying the LTE improvements required to meet IMT-Advanced requirements. In September 2009 the 3GPP Partners made a formal submission to the ITU proposing that LTE Release 10 & beyond (LTE-Advanced) should be evaluated as a candidate for IMT-Advanced. Beyond achieving technical requirements, a major reason for aligning LTE with the call for IMT-Advanced is that IMT conformant systems will be candidates for future new spectrum bands that are still to be identified. This ensures that today's deployed LTE mobile networks provide an evolutionary path towards many years of commercial operation. This Chapter summarizes LTE-Advanced features.

13.2 LTE-ADVANCED REQUIREMENTS

The requirements for IMT-Advanced systems as created by 3GPP technical report on technologies are given below:

- a high degree of commonality of functionality worldwide while retaining the flexibility to support a wide range of services and applications in a cost efficient manner.
- compatibility of services within IMT and with fixed networks;
- capability of interworking with other radio access systems;
- high quality mobile services;
- user equipment suitable for worldwide use;
- user-friendly applications, services and equipment;
- worldwide roaming capability; and
- enhanced peak data rates to support advanced services and applications

(100 Mbps for high and 1 Gbps for low mobility were established as targets for research).

Peak Data Rate

The system should target a downlink peak data rate of 1 Gbps and an uplink peak data rate of 500 Mbps.

Latency

C-Plane— The target for transition time from idle mode (with internet protocol (IP) address allocated) to connected mode should be less than 50 ms including the establishment of the user plane (excluding the S1 interface transfer delay). The target for the transition from a "dormant state" to connected mode (i.e. discontinuous reception (DRX) substate in connected mode) should be less than 10 ms (excluding the DRX delay).

U-Plane— LTE-Advanced should allow for reduced U-plane latency compared to LTE Release 8.

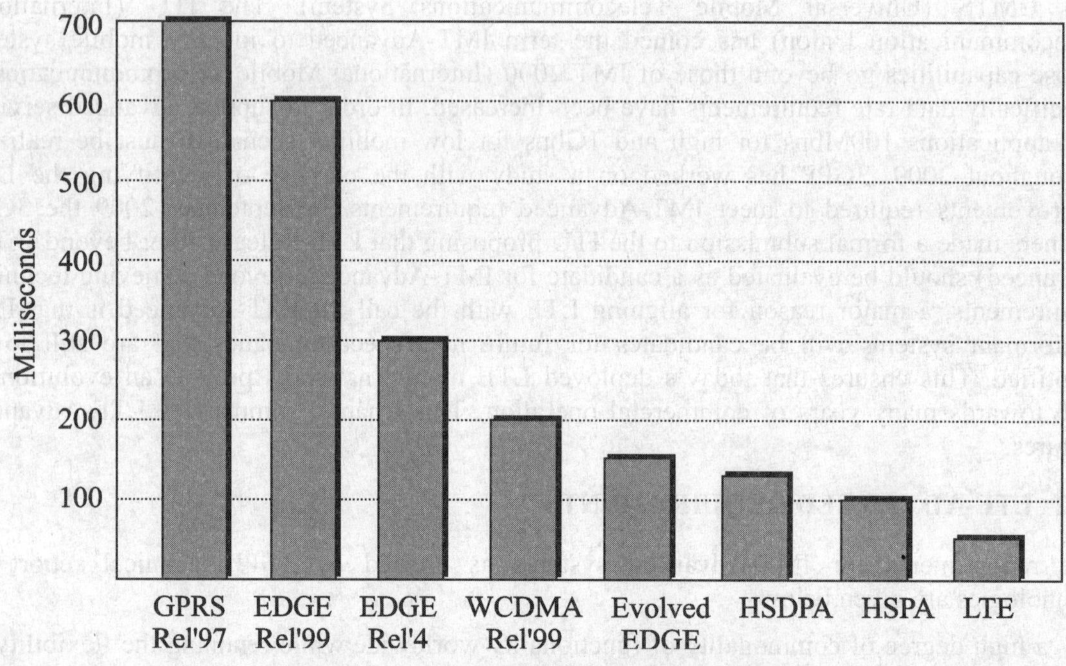

Fig. 13.1: Latency of Different Technologies

Spectrum Efficiency

LTE-Advanced aims to support downlink (8x8 antenna configuration MIMO) peak spectrum efficiency of 30 bps/Hz and uplink (4x4 antenna configuration) peak spectrum efficiency of 15 bps/Hz. Additionally average spectrum efficiency targets have been set according to Table 13.1. Average spectrum efficiency is defined as the aggregate throughput of all users (the number of correctly received bits over a certain period of time) normalized by the overall cell bandwidth divided by the number of cells.

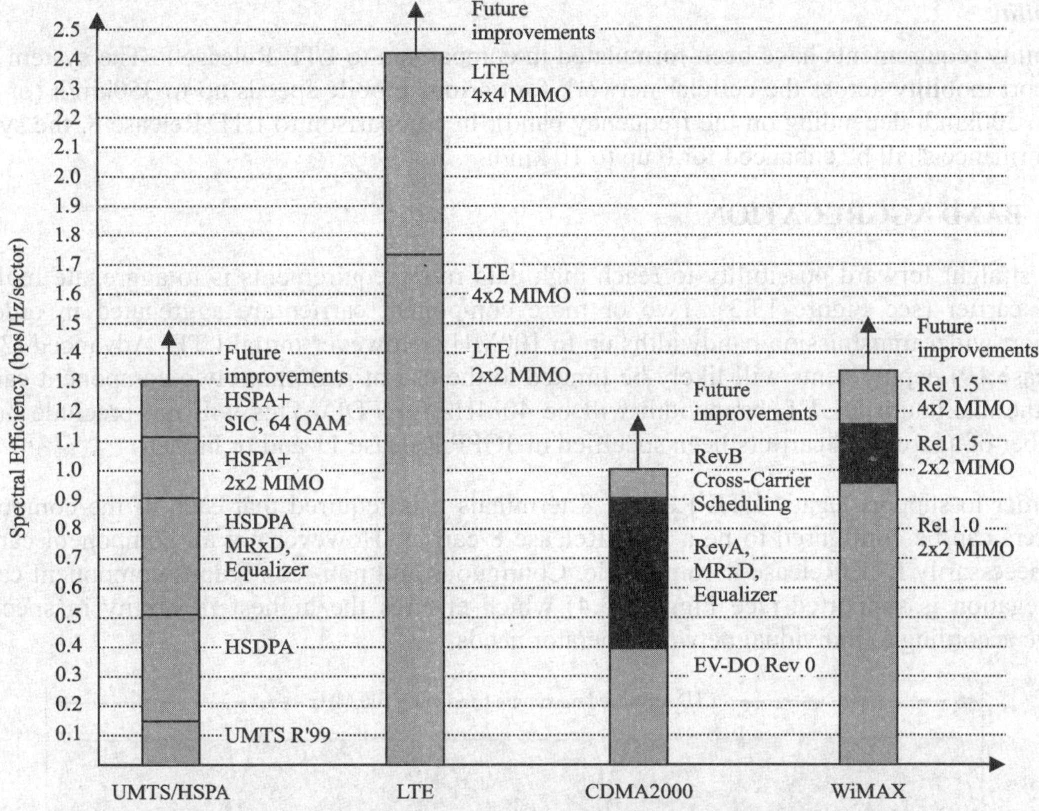

Fig. 13.2: Comparison of Downlink Spectral Efficiency

Table 13.1: Targets for Average Spectrum Efficiency

	Antenna configuration	*Target [bps/Hz/cell]*
Uplink	1x2 / 2x4	1.2 / 2.0
Downlink	2x2 / 4x2 / 4x4	2.4 / 2.6 / 3.7

Cell User Throughput

LTE-Advanced should allow cell edge user throughput to be as high as possible. The cell edge user throughput is defined as the 5% point of the cumulative density function (CDF) of the user throughput normalized with the overall cell bandwidth. Requirements for cell edge performance are given in Table 13.2 below.

Table 13.2: Targets for Cell Edge User Throughput

	Antenna configuration	*Target [bps/Hz/cell/user]*
Uplink	1x2 / 2x4	0.04 / 0.07
Downlink	2x2 / 4x2 / 4x4	0.07 / 0.09 / 0.12

Mobility

Mobility requirements have been formulated in comparison to LTE Release 8. The system shall support mobility across the cellular network for various mobile speeds up to 350km/h (or even up to 500km/h depending on the frequency band). In comparison to LTE Release 8, the system performance shall be enhanced for 0 up to 10 km/h.

13.3 BAND AGGREGATION

One straight forward possibility to reach high data ratés requirements is to aggregate multiple LTE carrier (see Figure 13.3). Two or more component carrier are aggregated in order to support wider transmission bandwidths up to 100MHz. However initial LTE- Advanced (3GPP Release 10) deployments will likely be limited to the use of maximum two component carrier, i.e. the maximum DL/UL bandwidth will be 40MHz for FDD. This will not preclude higher number of aggregated carriers been specified in 3GPP Release 11 and/or higher.

In order to support legacy LTE Release 8 terminals it is required that each of the component carriers can be configured to be a LTE Release 8 carrier. However not all component carriers are necessarily LTE Release 8 compatible. Contiguous and non- contiguous component carrier aggregation is supported (see Figure 13.4) which ensures the highest flexibility in spectrum usage according to individual network operator needs.

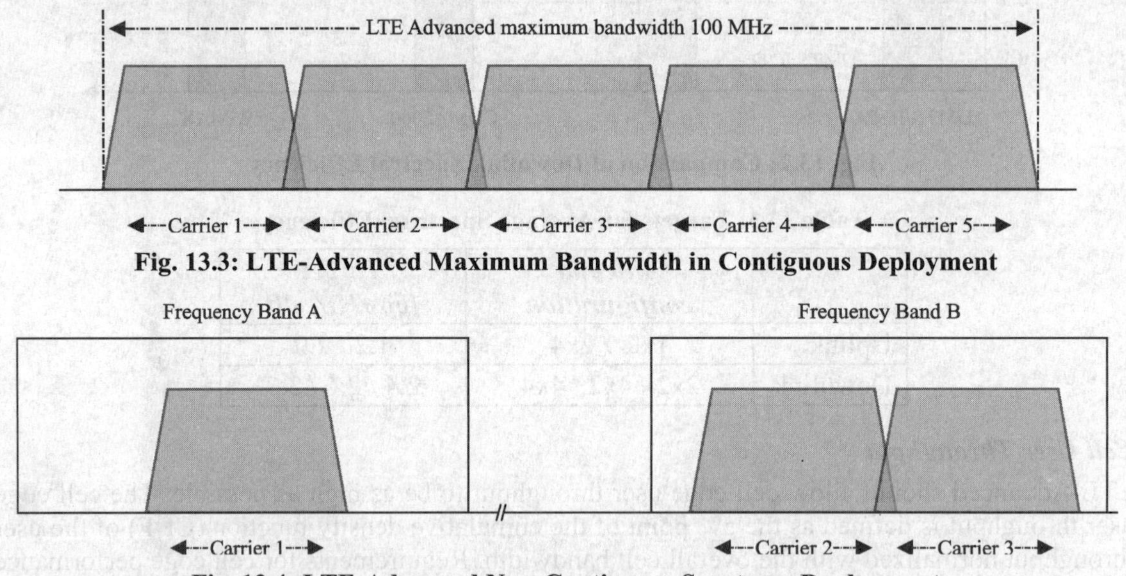

Fig. 13.3: LTE-Advanced Maximum Bandwidth in Contiguous Deployment

Fig. 13.4: LTE-Advanced Non-Contiguous Spectrum Deployment

Spectrum Flexibility

The initial identified frequency bands in addition to the already allocated bands in LTE

- 2.3I2.4 GHz
- 3.4I4.2 GHz
- 4.4-4.99 GHz

LTE-Advanced shall operate in spectrum allocations of different sizes including wider spectrum allocations than those of LTE Release 8. The main focus for bandwidth solutions wider than 20MHz should be on consecutive spectrum. However aggregation of the spectrum for LTE-Advanced should take into account reasonable user equipment (UE) complexity. Frequency division duplex (FDD) and time division duplex (TDD) should be supported for existing paired and unpaired frequency bands, respectively.

LTE Release 8 allows a 100 kHz frequency raster placing the LTE channel within the operator owned bandwidth. The 15kHz subcarrier spacing in combination with contiguously aggregated component carriers requires a 300kHz carrier spacing in order to preserve the orthogonality in the downlink transmission scheme. Each component carrier is limited to a maximum of 110 resource blocks in the frequency domain using the LTE Release 8 numerology. Certainly component carriers transmitted by the same eNodeB need to provide the same cell coverage. It is envisaged that different terminal categories will be defined supporting simultaneous transmission and reception of one or more component carriers.

13.4 LTE DOWNLINK THROUGHPUT

Figure 13.6 provides additional insight into LTE downlink throughput, showing layer 1 throughput measured at 10 MHz bandwidth using the Extended Vehicular A 3 km/hour channel model. The figure shows the increased performance obtained with the addition of different orders of MIMO.

For typical and average throughputs, it is reasonable to expect an order of magnitude higher performance than HSPA, which one can anticipate from radio channels that are four times wider (20 MHz vs. 5 MHz) and at least a doubling of spectral efficiency.

Actual throughput rates that users will experience will be lower than the peak rates and will depend on a variety of factors including:

1) RF Conditions and User Speed. Peak rates depend on optimal conditions. Under suboptimal conditions, such as being at the edge of the cell or if the user is moving at high speed, throughput rates will be lower.
2) Network Loading. Like all wireless systems, the throughput rates will go down as more users simultaneously use the network. This is largely a linear degradation.
3) Protocol Overhead— Peak rates are generally stated for the physical layer. Due to overhead at other layers, actual data payload throughput rates may be lower by an approximate 5% to 20% amount. The precise amount depends on the size of packets. Larger packets (e.g., file downloads) result in a lower overhead ratio.

Figure shows how throughput rates can vary by number of active users and radio conditions. The higher curves are for better radio conditions.

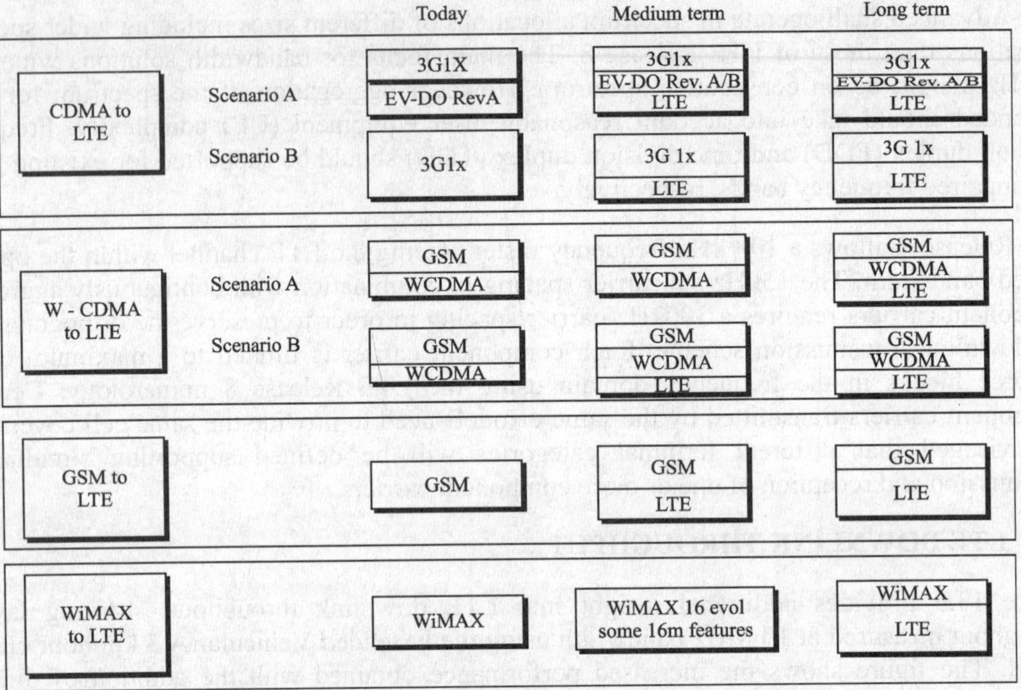

Fig. 13.5: Different Deployment Scenarios for LTE

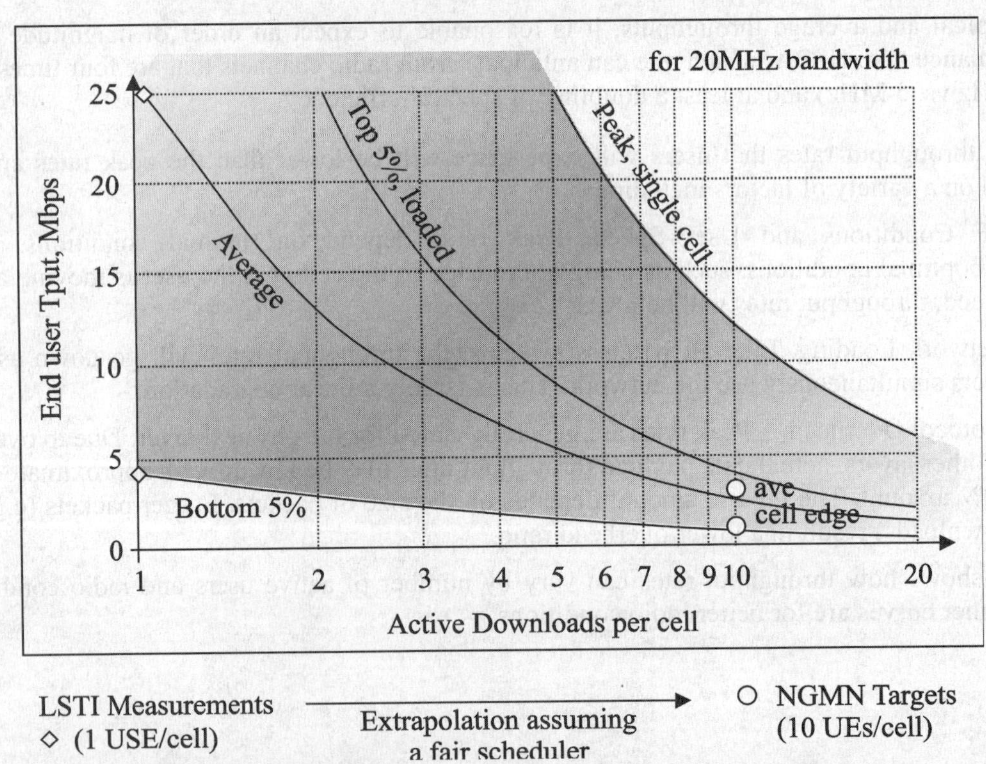

Fig. 13.6: LTE Actual Throughput Rates Based on Conditions

13.5 DEPLOYMENT OF MULTIPLE TECHNOLOGIES - A COMPARISION

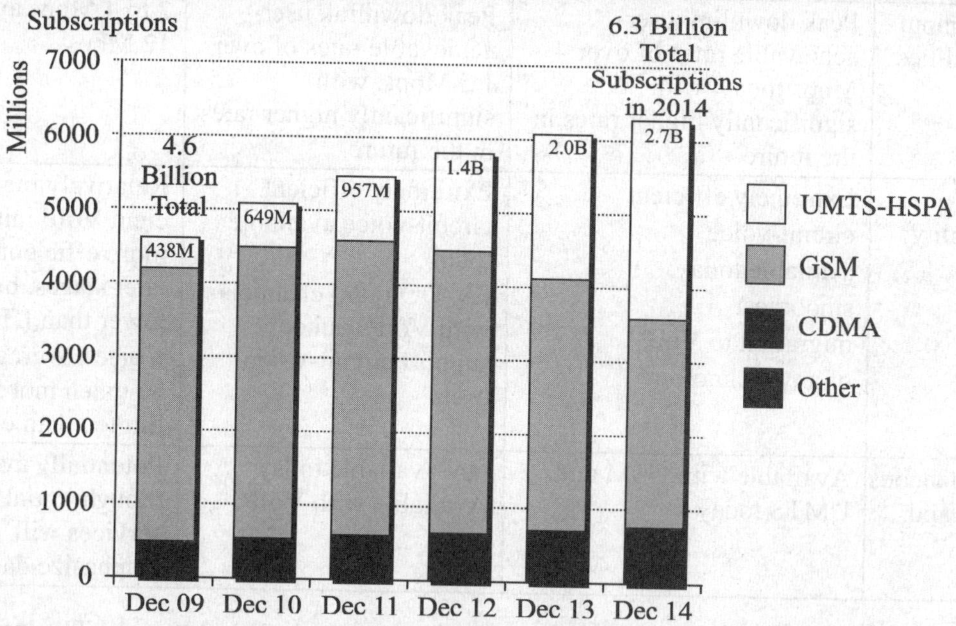

Fig. 13.7: Relative Volume of Subscribers Across Wireless Technologies

Table 13.3: Comparison Table

Technology	*EDGE/ HSPA/ LTE*	*CDMA2000*	*WiMAX*
Adoption	Cellular operators globally	Cellular operators globally.	Limited to date
Coverage/ Footprint	Global	Global with the general exception of Western Europe	Very limited
Deployment	Fewer cell sites required at 700 and 850 MHz.	Fewer cell sites required at 700 and 850 MHz.	Many more cell sites required at 2.5 GHz.
Devices	Broad selection of GSM/EDGE/UMTS/ HSPA devices	Broad selection of 1xRTT/EV-DO devices	Initial devices emphasize data
Radio Technology	Highly optimized TDMA for EDGE, highly optimized CDMA for HSPA, highly optimized OFDMA for LTE	Highly optimized CDMA for Rev 0/A/B, highly optimized OFDMA for Rev C	Optimized OFDMA in Release 1.0. More optimized in Release 1.5
Spectral Efficiency	Very high with HSPA, matches OFDMA approaches in 5 MHz with HSPA+	Very high with EV-DO Rev A/B	Very high, but not higher than HSPA+ for Release 1.0, and not higher than LTE for Release 1.5

Technology	*EDGE/ HSPA/ LTE*	*CDMA2000*	*WiMAX*
Throughput Capabilities	Peak downlink user-achievable rates of over 4 Mbps today, with significantly higher rates in the future	Peak downlink user-achievable rates of over 1 5 Mbps, with significantly higher rates in the future	2 to 4 Mbps average, 12 Mbps
Voice Capability	Extremely efficient circuit-voice available today; smoothest migration to VolP of any technology	Extremely efficient circuit-voice available today EV-DO radio channels with VolP cannot support circuit-voice users	Relatively ineffi-cient VolP initially: more efficient in later stages, but lower than LTE. Voice coverage will be much more limited than cellular
Simultaneous Voice and Data	Available with GSM and UMTS today	Not available today Available with VoIP	Potentially available, though initial services will emphasize data

In the chart above, the small "Other" category represents both WiMAX and LTE. Information projections on HSPA, LTE and WiMAX in millions of subscribers are as follows:

Table 13.4: Growth of Subscriber base (Millions)

	2008	*2009*	*2010*	*2011*	*2012*	*2013*	*2014*
WiMAX	0.5	2.8	7.5	16.7	37.1	82.1	.
LTE	0.0	0.0	0.5	3.5	13.1	44.5	131.5
HSPA	304	438	649	057	1400	200 0	2700

Table 13.5: Competitive Position of Major Wireless Technologies

Technology	*EDGE/ HSPA/ LTE*	*CDMA2000*	*WiMAX*
Subscribers	Over 3.7 billion today; 4 billion expected by 2010	455 million today; slower growth expected than GSM-HSPA	82 million anticipated by 2013
Maturity	Extremely mature	Extremely mature	Emerging/immature

Review Questions

1. List out the main requirements as per GPP for an Advanced LTE system.
2. Explain the enhancement in respect of peak data rate, latency, spectrum efficiency and throughput in the LTE advanced system.
3. Write about spectrum feasibility in GPP Release 10.
4. How the data rate of Downlink is enhanced to higher level?

14 Global Standardization of IMT-2000

14.1 INTRODUCTION

Many mobile operators are now providing nation- wide commercial services with a Wideband Code Division Multiple Access (W-CDMA) system, taking the global lead in deployment of 3rd generation mobile systems. The successful deployment of the W-CDMA and cdmaOne systems is due to the enormous time and effort spent not only for research and development of their equipment but also the contentious but constructive discussions that have taken place in the standardization process for more than one and a half decades.

The most fundamental requirement for standardization of IMT-2000 is to create a standard that provides capabilities to facilitate worldwide roaming and mobile multimedia applications as defined in Recommendation ITU-R M.1455[1)] "Key Characteristics for the IMT-2000 Radio Interfaces." In order to meet these requirements, the ITU has been playing a centripetal role in creating harmonized recommendations backed up by practical work carried out in parallel by such technical forums as the 3GPPs, which comprise regional standard development organizations (SDOs) in Europe, North America, and Asia. This centripetal role has led to the creation of five radio interfaces that are referred to as family members of IMT-2000 as defined in Recommendation ITU-R M.1457, "Detailed Specifications of the Radio Interfaces of IMT-2000."

Among the five family members, W-CDMA is categorized as a CDMA Direct Sequence (CDMA-DS) and cdmaOne is categorized as a CDMA Multi-Carrier (CDMA-MC). Both of these members have been allocated a spectrum of 120 MHz in Japan, and consequently Fujitsu has been making continuous technical contributions to these two systems. This chapter mainly focuses on standardization activities for the CDMA-DS and CDMA-MC systems.

Because of the many abbreviations in this chapter, an explanation of these abbreviations is given in Table 14.1 for better readability.

14.2 HISTORY OF STANDARDIZATION OF IMT-2000

The overall history of the standardization of IMT-2000 is shown in Table 14.2 in chronological order from the perspective of three regional standardization activities as well as those in the ITU. The dawn of the standardization process can be traced back to the middle of the 1980s, when IMT-2000 used to be called in the ITU-R by its former name of "Future Public Land Mobile Telecommunications System" (FPLMTS).

Table 14.1: Abbreviations

1XEV DO	1X Evolution Data Only
1XEV DV	1X Evolution Data and Voice
3G	3rd Generation
3GPP	3rd Generation Partnership Project
3GPP2	3rd Generation Partnership Project 2
ACTS	Advanced Communication Technologies and Services
AMC	Adaptive Modulation and Coding
ANSI	American National Standards Institute
ARIB	Association of Radio Industries and Businesses
ATDMA	Advanced TDMA Mobile Access
CBC	Cell Broadcast
CDMA	Code Division Multiple Access
CDMA-DS	CDMA Direct Sequence
CDMA-MC	CDMA Multi-Carrier
CODIT	Code Division Testbed
CPM	Conference preparatory meeting
CR	Change Request
CWTS	China Wireless Telecommunication Standard group
DECT	Digital Enhanced Cordless Telecommunications
EDGE	Enhanced Data rate for GSM Evolution
EIA	Electronic Industries Alliance
ETSI	European Telecommunications Standards Institute
FCS	Fast Cell Selection
FDD	Frequency Division Duplex
FMA	FRAMES Multiple Access
FPLMTS	Future Public Land Mobile Telecommunications System
FRAMES	Future Radio Wideband Multiple Access System
GLR	Gateway Location Register
GPRS	General Packet Radio Service
GSM	Global System for Mobile Communications
GSMA	GSM Association
GTP	GPRS Tunneling Protocol
HARQ	Hybrid Automatic Repeat Request
HRPD	High Rate Packet Data

HSDPA	High Speed Downlink Packet Access
IETF	Internet Engineering Task Force
IMS	IP Multimedia Subsystem
IMT-2000	International Mobile Telecommunication 2000
IP^2	IP-based IMT Platform
IPR	Intellectual Property Rights
IPv6	Internet Protocol Version 6
ISD	International Standard Development Sub-committee
ITU-R	International Telecommunication Union, Radio communication Sector
ITU-T	International Telecommunication Union, Telecommunication Standardization Sector
LCS	Location Services
MAP	Mobile Application Part
mITF	Mobile IT Forum
MPHPT	Ministry of Public Management, Home Affairs, Posts and Telecommunications
MVCE	Mobile VCE (Virtual Centre of Excellence in Mobile and Personal Communications)
ODMA	Opportunity Driven Multiple Access
OFDM	Orthogonal Frequency Division Multiple Access
OHG	Operators Harmonization Group
PDNR	Preliminary Draft New Recommendation
RACE	Research of Advanced Communication Technologies in Europe
RAN	Radio Access Network
RCR	Research and Development Center far Radio Systems
Rel	Release
REVAL	ITU-R Recommendation on Evaluation
RS EL	ITU-R Recommendation on Selection Procedure
RSPC	ITU-R Recommendation on Specification of IMT-2D00
RTT	Radio Transmissions Technologies
SDO	Standards Development Organization
SMG	Special Mobile Group
SSDT	Site Selection Diversity Transmission
T1	Committee T1
T1P1	Technical Subcommittee T1P1
TDD	Time Division Duplex

TDMA-SC	TDM A Single Carrier
TD-SCDM A	Time Division Synchronous Code Division Multiple Access
TG8/1	Task Group 8/1
TIA	Telecommunications Industry Association
TSG	Technical Specification Groups
TSG-3A	TSG Service and System Aspects
TSG-T	TSG Terminals
TTA	Telecommunications Technology Association
TTC	Telecommunication Technology Committee
UE	User Equipment
UMTS	Universal Mobile Telecommunication System
URL	Uniform Resource Locator
UTRA	UMTS Terrestrial Radio Access/Universal Terrestrial Radio Access
UTRAN	Universal Terrestrial Radio Access Network
UWC-136	Universal Wireless Communications-136
VoIP	Voice Over Internet Protocol
WARC	World Administrative Radio Conference
WCDMA	Wideband CDMA
WCDM A-N7A	North American WCDMA
WG	Working Group
WIMS CDMA	Wireless Multimedia and Messaging Services WCDMA
WP	Working Party
WRC	World Radio communication Conference
WTDMA	Wideband TDM A
WWRF	Wireless World Research Forum

CDMA-MC; CDMA-TDD (Time Division Duplex), which is sometimes referred to as TD- SCDMA (Time Division Synchronous Code Division Multiple Access); TDMA-SC (TDMA) Single Carrier); and FDMA/TDMA. Regarding CDMA-DS, CDMA-TDD, and CDMA-MC, it was suggested that practical development of the relevant technical specifications be commendations hyperlinks by which each specification can be reached. Fortunately, the 3GPP and 3GPP2 successfully completed the first set of global specifications resulting in the best use of the specifications for commercial deployment worldwide.

Table 14.2: Overall History of IMT-2000 Standardization

Year	*Fujitsu's Activities*	*ITU (ITU-R/ITU-T)*	*Europe (ETSI)*	*Japan (ARIB/TCC)*	*US (TIA/T1) and other regions*
1985		SG8IWP8/13 established in ITU CCIR for initial study of FPLMTS.			
1986					
1987					
1988			ETSI established. RACE I program started.		
1989					
1990			UMTS Ad Hoc established.		
1991		ITU-R TG8/1 established.			
1992	Commenced initial study of FPLMTS.	WARC'92 allocated 230 MHz for IMT-2000 in 2 GHz band: - 1885 to 2025 MHz - 2110 to 2200 MHz	RACE II started with CODIT and ATDMA.		
1993	Conducted experiment on propagation characteristics.			FPLMTS study committee established in RCR.	TIA TR46 established.
1994	Proposed WCDMA to ARIB for RTT of FPLMTS.			24 candidates for RTT of FPLMTS were proposed.	
1995	Conducted field experiment using WCDMA air interface.	RSEL and REVAL completed.	ACTS started. FRAMES project was set up.	RCR changed its name to ARIB. Evaluation of RTT candidates.	

Year	Fujitsu's Activities	ITU (ITU-R/ITU-T)	Europe (ETSI)	Japan (ARIB/TCC)	US (TIA/T1) and other regions
1996	Prototyping of WCDMA.		Two harmonized modes were defined as UMTS candidates: -FMA1 WTDMA -FMA2 WCDMA	Merging process was conducted to consolidate as WCDMA FDD and TDD.	
1997	Proposed WCDMA concept to ETSI. resulting in creation of α-concept group.	FPLMTS was renamed to IMT-2000. Study of introduction of family concept was started.	Five concept groups were formed: - α-concept WCDMA - β-concept OFDM -γ concept WTDMA - δ-concept TDMA/CDMA - ε-concept ODMA In MVCE, the Core-1 Program was formally commenced for new technology development for next-generation mobile communication systems.	WCDMA was selected for FDD and TDD operation as a unique proposal to ITU-R TG8/1.	

Year	Fujitsu's Activities	ITU (ITU-R/ITU-T)	Europe (ETSI)	Japan (ARIB/TCC)	US (TIA/T1) and other regions
1998	Presented experimental results to ETSI SMG2.	10 candidates for terrestrial component and 6 candidates for satellite component were approved.	ETSI decided to select WCDMA for UTRA FDD band and WTDMA/CDMA for TDD band. 3GPP inaugurated with ETSI, ARIB, TTC,TTA and T1 in December. UTRA was proposed to 3GPP.	WCDMA was proposed to ITU-R TG8/1.	TR45.5 submitted to ITU-R cdma2000 based on IS-95. Proposal is similar to CDMA1 proposal from TTA. TR46.1 submitted to ITU-R WIMS CDMA. T1P1 submitted to ITU-R WCDMA-N/A. Proposal has commonality with WCDMA proposal from ARIB and ETSI. WCDMA-N/A and WIMS WCDMA are merged into WP-CDMA and submitted to ITU-R. TTA submitted CDMA 1 and CDMA 2. CDMA 1 is similar to proposals from ETSI and ARIB. CDMA 2 is similar to proposal cdma2000.

Year	Fujitsu's Activities	ITU (ITU-R/ITU-T)	Europe (ETSI)	Japan (ARIB/TCC)	US (TIA/T1) and other regions
1999	Elected as an official of 3GPPTSG RAN WG4.	IPR concerns about CDMA technology were resolved. "Family of systems" concept was defined in Q. 1701 (framework for IMT-2000 networks). Network and terminal functions for support of IMT-2000 services were identified in Q.1711 (network functional model for IMT-2000).	Work in ETSI SMGs on UTRA transferred to 3GPP. The first set of specifications of UTRA. Rel-99 was released in December. Core-2 program started in MVCE.	ISD established to work with 3GPPS. Report on introduction of IMT-2000 was submitted by Telecommunications Technology Council of MPT Japan	3GPP2 inaugurated. CWTS in China joined 3GPP and proposed TD-SCDMA. OHG studied the possibility of harmonizing between CDMA-DS (WCDMA) and CDMA-MC (cdma2000). This resulted in the chip rate being changed to 3.84 Mcps for CDMA-DS and to 3.6864 Mcps for SDMA-MC.
1999		Extensive harmonization activities result in merging of RTTs into 5 IMT-2000 family members: - CDMA-D5 (WCDMA) - CDMA-MC (Cdma2000) -CDMA-TDD (TD-SCDMA) -TDMA-SC (UWC-136) - FDMA/TDMA (DECT) * IMT RKEY (key parameters of IMT- 2000) approved.			

Year	*Fujitsu's Activities*	*ITU (ITU-R/ITU-T)*	*Europe (ETSI)*	*Japan (ARIB/TCC)*	*US (TIA/T1) and other regions*
2000	Continued to work with 3GPF and 3GPP2 to stabilize specifications. - Proposed SSDT to 3GPP RAN Hosted several 3GPP meetings	IMT RSPC (M.1457) detailed specification of five IMT-2000 family members were approved by RA2000. WRC2000 identified additional frequency bands for IMT-2000: -806 to 960 MHz 1710 to 1885 MHz -2500 to 2690 MHz * Discussions about vision of systems beyond IMT-2000 were started.	A tremendous amount, of CRs were discussed and approved by 3GPP to stabilize Rel99 specifications	Based on the report from the Telecommunications Technology Council, the relevant legislation process was completed. ISD works closely with 3GPPS. A vision of systems beyond IMT-2000 was proposed to ITU-R WP3F.	

Year	*Fujitsu's Activities*	*ITU (ITU-R/ITU-T)*	*Europe (ETSI)*	*Japan (ARIB/TCC)*	*US (TIA/T1) and other regions*
2001	Elected as officials of TSG-RAN, RAN4, 5A2 andT1 of 3GPP, and 3GPP2 TSG-P. * Presented a scenario for UTRAN Future Evolution workshop of 3GPP. Presented OFDM as a possible candidate for future evolution. Drafted PDNR on measurement uncertainty, global circulation, and spurious emissions for ITU-R WP8F	CDMA2000 1X-DO (HDR) and HSDPA were approved for inclusion in the revised version of M.14 57. Discussions of vision of systems beyond IMT-2 000 were continued.	3-GPP released Rel4. WWRF was founded to formulate visions for future strategic research directions.	MITF was founded to study 4th generation mobile communication systems led by MPMHPT. A vision of systems beyond IMT-2000 was proposed to ITU-R WPSF. IP^2 was established in TTC to study a future IP-based core network.	
2002		Preparations were made for CPM about vision of systems beyond IMT-2 000.	3GPP released Rel5. Long-term evolution ad hoc meeting is established	Contributions are made to ITU-R WP8F for CPM.	

14.3 FRAMEWORK OF STANDARDIZATION IN THE ITU

Successful development of specifications of IMT-2000 would not have been achieved without the extensive and substantial harmonization activities performed by the ITU with its centripetal force and ability to achieve a global consensus. In particular, the ITU-R and ITU-T are the main bodies that produce recommendations for IMT-2000. The ITU-R is responsible for creating recommendation related to radio transmission aspects (Figure 14.1). The Working Party 8F (WP8F) under an umbrella of SG8 of the ITU-R has been especially active in creating all of the international standards and recommendations of IMT-2000. Regarding regulatory issues such as frequency allocation and its re-farming for the IMT-2000 spectrum, the World Radio communication Conference (WRC) is held every three years to provide solutions that are based on global consensus.

On the other hand, the ITU-T is studying other aspects of the core network of IMT-2000. Specifically, the SG3 is creating a recommendation on tariffs and accounting principles, and the SG11 is creating signaling requirements and protocols (Figure 14.2). In addition, the Special Study Group "IMT-2000 and Beyond," has been established to investigate service and interface requirements for IMT-2000 and beyond, application and interworking of IMT-2000 systems, and harmonization and convergence of IMT-2000 systems.

Figure 14.3 shows the relations between the ITU and technical forums such as the 3GPPs and regional SDOs. As can be seen, there is a circular process in which the practical work of specifications development is carried out in the 3GPPs. The outcome of this work is submitted in the form of hyperlink references to the ITU through the member SDOs of the 3GPPs, and the SDOs adopt the relevant recommendations for their regional use.

14.4 3GPP ORGANIZATION

In April 1998, the ARIB and Telecommunication Technology Committee (TTC) of Japan had a preliminary meeting with the ETSI in Sophia US and the Telecommunications Technology Association (TTA) of Korea joined the meeting and these four SDOs started substantial discussions on how the standardization work should fulfill the requirements of the mobile market, users, vendors, and operators. Through their discussions, a collaborative agreement regarding the partner- ship project for the 3rd generation mobile system was reached with the ARIB, ETSI, T1, TTA, TTC, and China Wireless Telecommunication Standard group (CWTS) of China. This agreement led to the

14.5 SCOPE AND OBJECTIVES

The original scope of the 3GPP was to provide globally applicable technical specifications for the 3rd generation mobile system based on an enhanced GSM core network and UTRA (Universal Terrestrial Radio Access) using W-CDMA FDD and TDD. The scope was later expanded to maintenance and development of GSM-related technical specifications, including enhancements of GSM radio access technologies such as GPRS and EDGE. This expansion was done to ensure handover between UMTS and GSM, which was an essential requirement in Europe.

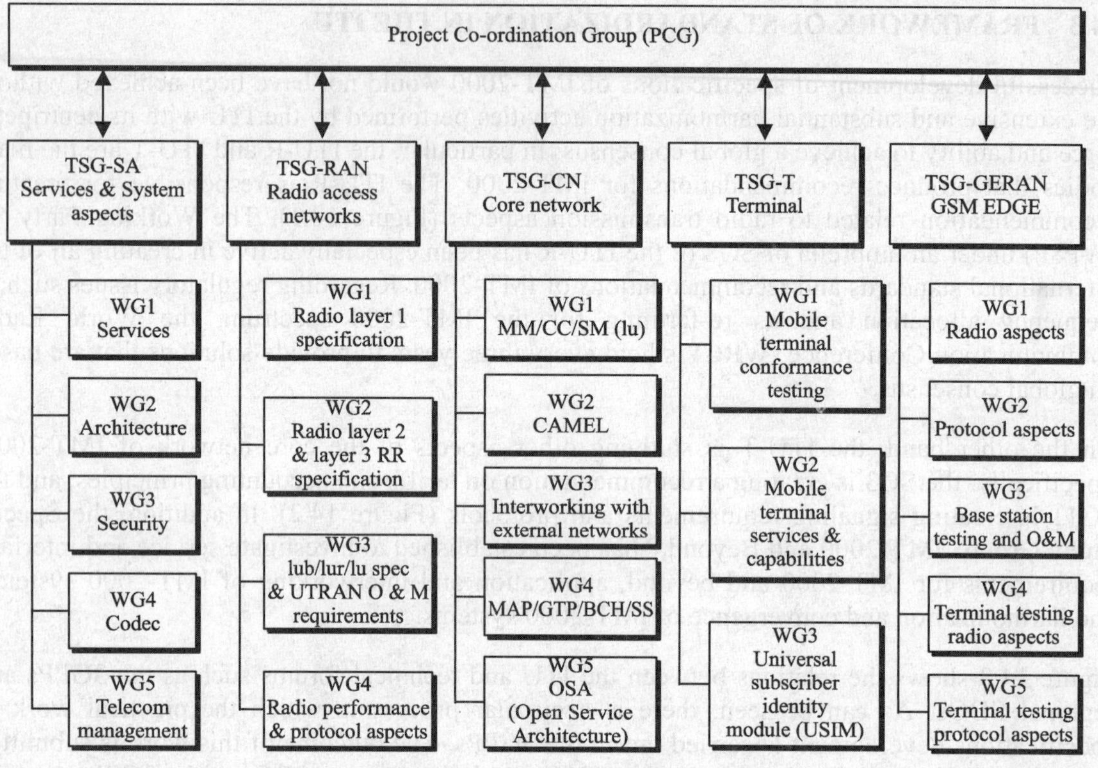

Fig. 14.1: Structure of 3GPP

The objective of the 3GPP was to develop a set of global specifications for UTRA to facilitate global circulation of mobile terminals and it is responsible for the creation of a basic specification of standards.

14.6 ORGANIZATIONAL PARTNERS

The OPs include six SDOs: ARIB, CWTS, ETSI, T1, TTA, and TTC. The MRPs include the GSM Association) and the UMTS Forum) both of which represent the European mobile market and industry. The OPs retain authority to define, publish, and set regional standards, while the MRP identifies consolidated views of mobile market requirements. The individual members are tasked with making technical contributions within the scope of the 3GPP in close cooperation with other entities such as the Internet Engineering Task Force, (IETF) and IPv6 Forum

14.7 ENHANCEMENT OF FEATURES (REL99/REL4/ REL5)

Table 14.3 shows the main features defined in the three major specification sets that the 3GPP has so far released: Release-99, Release-4, and Release-5. Release-99 includes the basic capabilities and functionalities of UMTS. In Release-4, one of the new features was contributed by CWTS of China and incorporated as W-CDMA TDD.

In March 2002, most of Release-5 was frozen and the IP Multimedia Subsystem (IMS) as shown in Figure 14.2 was incorporated to enable the operation of cost-effective and high-quality IP-based multimedia services, including VoIP. The IMS adds new features to IP-based services, for example, security, content-based charging, and location related-services.) These new features help operators to quickly and flexibly find new sources of revenue that are not available in existing circuit- switched services and packet-switched services.

Table 14.3: Main features defined in 3GPP specification sets

Release '99 *December 1999*	*Release 4* *March 2001*	*Release 5* *March 2002*
▪ Basic capability of UTRA (W-CDMA FDD) ▪ UTRAN architecture (lu/lur/lub interfaces and protocols) ▪ UMTS AMR (Adaptive Multi-Rate codec for UMTS) ▪ Enhanced Call Control ▪ GLR (Gateway Location Register) ▪ Advanced QoS for UMTS (4 QoS classes were defined, as "Conversation", "Streaming", "Interactive" and "Background")	Features in Rel99 plus: ▪ UTRA (W-CDMA-TDD) ▪ UTRAN architecture (TDD part of lu/lur/lub interface and protocols) ▪ Transport and Control Separation in CS CN domain ▪ Introducing 1.28 Mcps TDD mode ▪ LCS (Location Service)	Features in Rel4 plus: ▪ IMS (IP Multimedia service Sub-system) ▪ HSDPA (High Speed Data Packet Access) ▪ End to End QoS ▪ Extended Transparent End-toEnd Packet Switched Mobile Streaming Applications ▪ Wideband AMR ▪ Security Enhancements ▪ Intra Domain Connection of RAN Nodes to Multiple CN Nodes

In addition, a significant improvement in radio access technology called High Speed Data Packet Access (HSDPA) was included to improve the throughput of downlink packet transmission to 8 Mb/s. HSDPA provides this improvement because it uses Adaptive Modulation and Coding (AMC), Hybrid ARQ (HARQ), and Fast Cell Se- lection (FCS) technologies.

14.7.1 Enhancement of Features toward Release-6

Now that Release-5 is almost completed, the 3GPP is moving toward the next release, Release-6, to further improve performance and to enhance capabilities. Some of the new features that are on the table are Multimedia Broadcast Multicast Service (MBMS), interworking between Wireless LAN (WLAN) and UMTS, and Orthogonal Frequency Division Multiple Access.

Study of MBMS as an enhanced form of Cell Broadcast (CBC) with a larger message size has been started. MBMS may pioneer a new service which allows broadcast of multimedia messaging and video/music streaming capabilities as one of its major applications. The interworking between WLAN and UMTS has been identified as one of the keys for providing flexibility when accessing multiple radio resources and for providing service mobility between WLAN and the 3G system in various mobile environments. Initial work has been started under the TSG SA, and the first draft on its architecture has already been completed.

Orthogonal Frequency Division Multiple Access (OFDM) is being studied as a radio access technology which may drastically increase data rates by using a large number of orthogonal frequencies that are mutually spaced apart. Because of its potential for realizing high-bit-rate data transfer, an OFDM feasibility study that will complete its initial phase in 2003 is about to be started. It is also foreseen that OFDM could be a promising candidate for what is called the 4th generation mobile system.

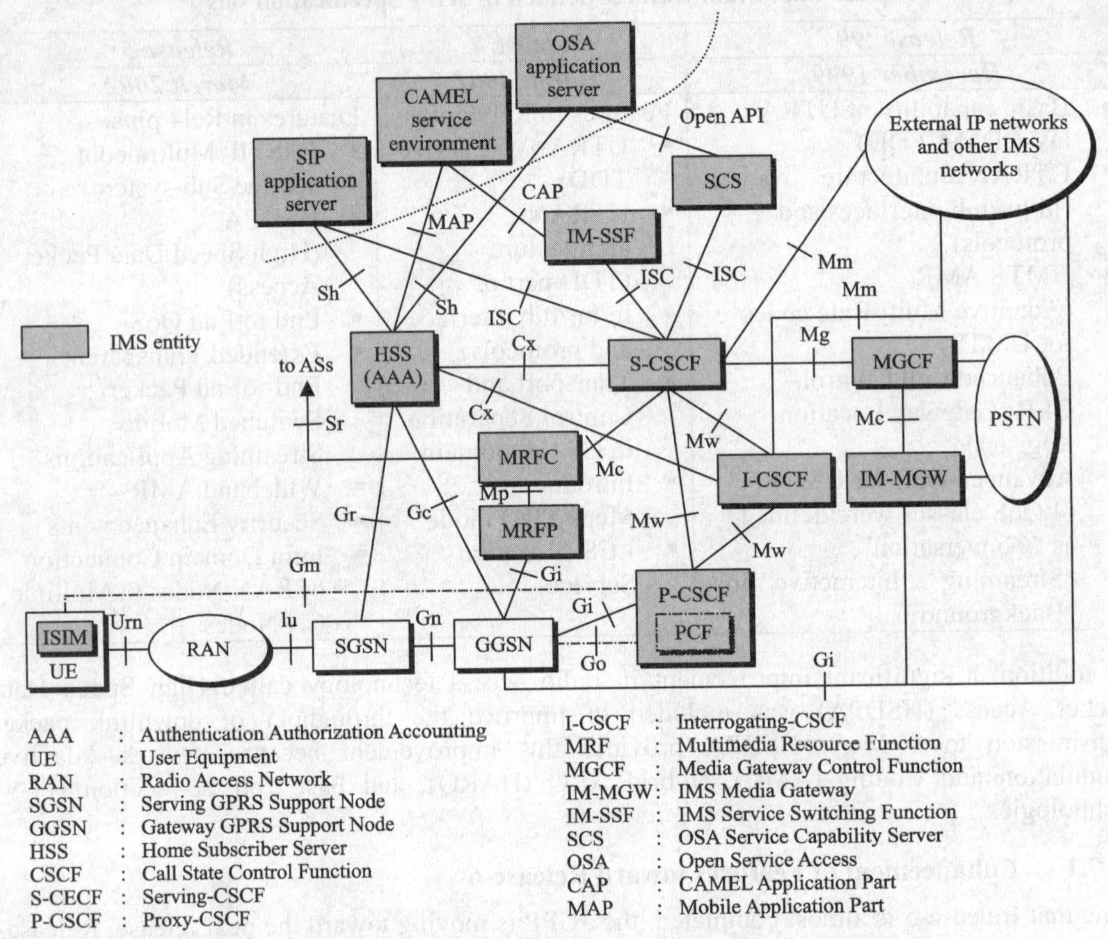

Fig. 14.2: Architecture of IP Multimedia Subsystem (IMS)

14.8 GPP2 FORMATION

Immediately after the 3GPP was inaugurated in Europe, the 3GPP2 was established as a counterpart of the CDMA-MC camp supporting the ANSI/TIA/EIA-41 and IS-95 specifications. The 3GPP2 specifies an air interface based on a cdma One technology called IS-95 and the cdma2000 interface, which is an evolved form of the IS-95 interface, to increase capacity and al- low faster data communication. It also specifies a core network based on an ANSI-41 specification developed to support cellular and cdmaOne net- works. Furthermore, the 3GPP2 is studying an IP-based core network for IMT-2000 to support various kinds of communications. The 3GPP2's relationship with the ITU-R is similar to the one between the 3GPP and the ITU-R. The 3GPP2 is responsible for developing technical specifications to which each SDO refers and are endorsed as regional standards by the ITU-R.

14.8.1 Organization

1) Internet Forum (IF), and IPv6 Forum are included as MRPs.

2) Organizational structure

The 3GPP2 has a structure similar to that of the 3GPP (Figure 14.3). It has five Technical Specification Groups (TSGs) for corresponding technical areas, led by the Steering Committee (SC). Cover- age of technical areas of the 3GPP2 is also similar to that of the 3GPP, including the service capability requirements (TSG-S), interfaces between the radio access network and core network (TSG-A), functions and interfaces between the cdma2000 infrastructure and user terminal equipment for the radio access part (TSG-C), Internet and IP multimedia core network (TSG-P), and core net- work internal interfaces for call associated and non-call associated signaling (TSG-N).

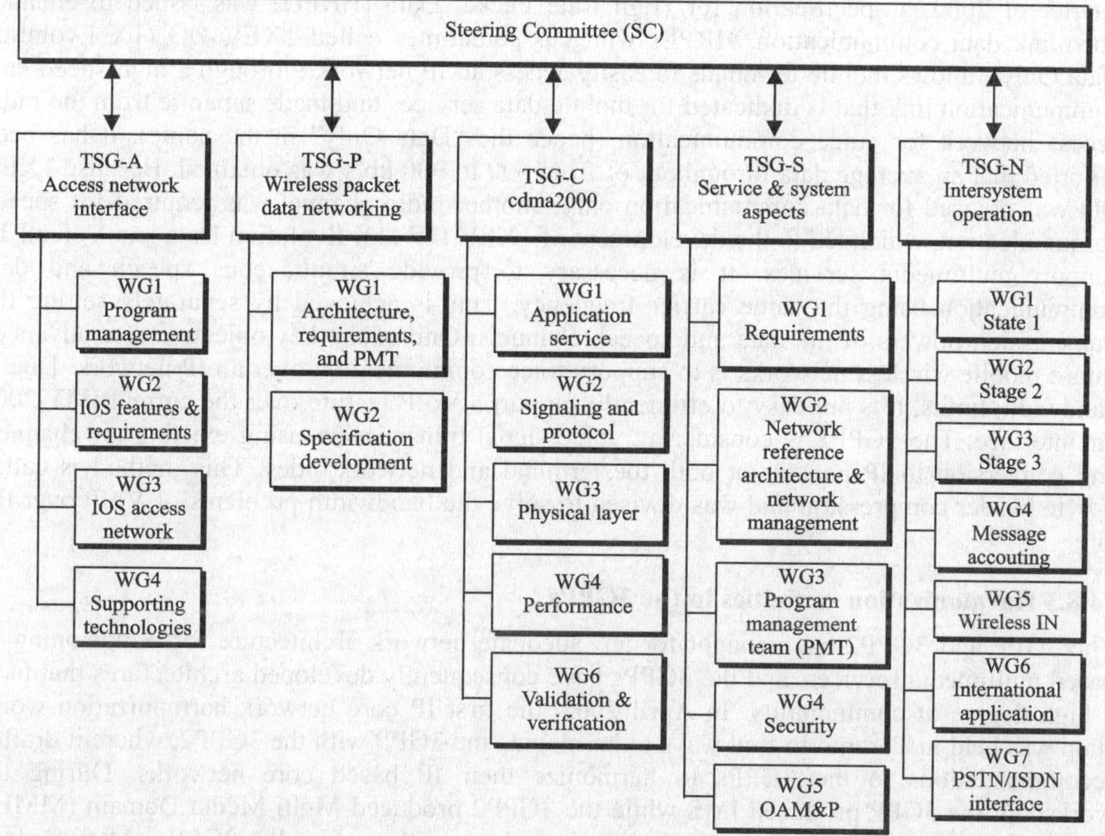

Fig. 14.3: Structure of 3GPP2

14.8.2 Specification Document

Each TSG issues a set of specifications based on its study. The structure of these specifications is organized and issued by each TSG. Unlike the 3GPP, no particular numbering scheme is applied to the specification documents.

In 1999, IS-2000 Release-0 was defined as the first step toward an IMT-2000 system based on cdmaOne technology to support the following features:

1) Quick power control for the downlink traffic channel,
2) turbo coding,
3) transmission diversity, and
4) a high-speed supplemental channel for up to 144 kb/s data communication.

In 2000, Release-A was issued to enhance data communication services supporting the following:

The 3GPP2 has also been working to enhance its capability. Typical new features for this purpose include 1XEV DO, 1XEV DV, and support of IP multimedia services. In the fourth quarter of 2000, a specification for High Rate Packet Data (HRPD) was issued to enhance downlink data communication. HRPD, which is sometimes called 1XEV DO (1X Evolution Data Only), allows mobile terminals to easily access an IP network thorough a high-speed data communication link that is dedicated for mobile data services and made separate from the radio access network for voice communication (hence the "Data Only" in the name). It has been reported that an average data throughput of from 600 to 900 kb/s was obtained. Because 1XEV DO was devised for data communication only, another radio channel was required for speech communication, which led to the development of 1XEV DV (1X Evolution Data and Voice). To support multimedia services, it is necessary to provide simultaneous speech and data communication using the same carrier frequency. This is achieved by separately setting the transmission powers of the data and speech channels. One of the key objectives for advanced future mobile wireless networks is to support voice communication over an IP network. Due to bandwidth limits, it is not easy to efficiently support a VoIP feature over the current IMT-2000 air interface. The 3GPP2 is considering voice signal transmission using existing air channels and conversion to IP packets at both the terminal and network sides. This method is called 0-byte header compression and was devised to solve the bandwidth problems of VoIP over the air.

14.8.3 Harmonization Activities in the 3GPPs

The 3GPP and 3GPP2 have sought for an adequate network architecture for provisioning IP based multimedia services, and the 3GPPs have consequently developed architectures that have a high degree of commonality. In April 2002, the first IP core network harmonization workshop was held in Toronto to find ways to harmonize the 3GPP with the 3GPP2, where it drafted recommendations to the 3GPPs to harmonize their IP based core networks. During the workshop, the 3GPP produced IMS while the 3GPP2 produced Multi Media Domain (MMD), and both of these sets of recommendations have been endorsed by the 3GPPs. Afterwards, a new study on interoperability between IP-based core networks and WLAN systems was initiated in the 3GPP TSG-SA, and Fujitsu has contributed to this study.

14.8.4 Fujitsu's Activities in the Standardization Process

In 1993, in the early stage of R&D for IMT-2000, Fujitsu commenced studies on CDMA. In those studies, Fujitsu conducted field experiments using a frequency band of 2 GHz to determine whether the CDMA air interface was a candidate RTT for proposal to the ITU-R.

Based on the experimental results, Fujitsu proposed a W-CDMA with a chip rate of 4.096 Mcps to the ARIB in 1994 and to the ETSI in 1997. Through discussions within the group, Fujitsu agreed to change the chip rate to 3.84 Mcps for harmonization with other proposals. In the first stage of the establishment of the 3GPP, Fujitsu contributed a great deal by making proposals regarding its structure and working procedures and decided to send some officials to the forum. As one of the representatives of ARIB and TTC, Fujitsu has also helped to create the requisite amendments to the scope of the 3GPP. example, the MAP/GTP enhancement for GPRS, the protocol between the UE and core network, GLR, development of the Iu/Iur/Iub interface, SSDT in UTRAN, and the charging aspects of MBMS.

In parallel with these activities, Fujitsu has been a long-time participant in the ITU-R and ITU-T, making not only technical contributions to promote stabilization of technical recommendations but also strategic contributions to ensure that recommendations comply with Japanese laws under the guidance of the Ministry of Public Management, Home Affairs, Posts and Telecommunications.

14.9 ENHANCEMENTS AND EVOLUTION OF IMT-2000

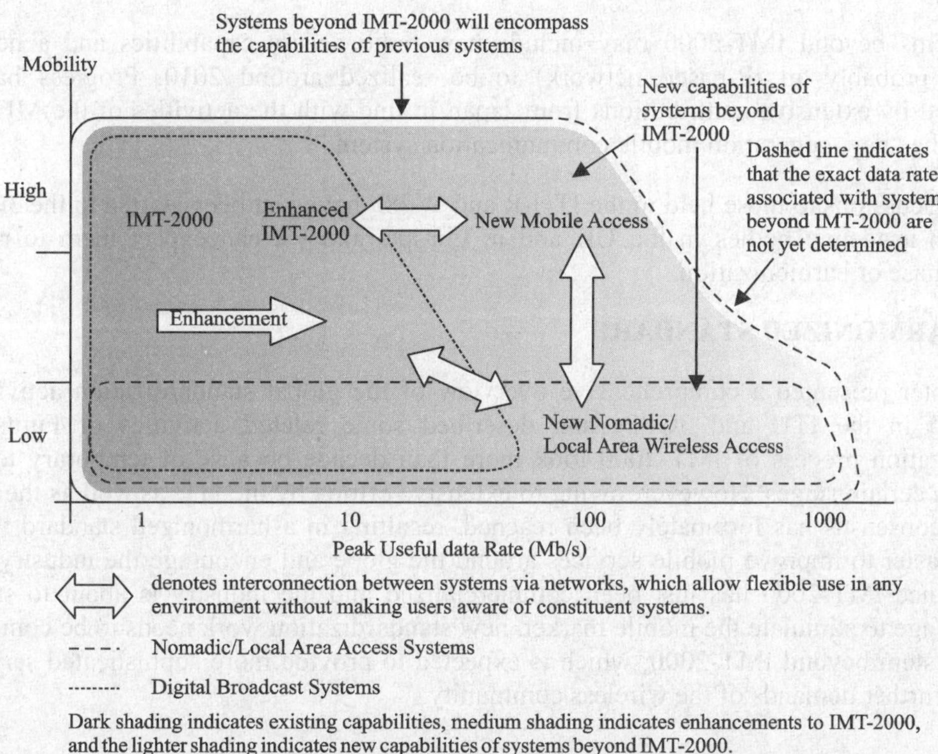

Fig. 14.4: IMT Enhancements

As mentioned in the previous sections, the first sets of IMT-2000 specifications, based on Release-99 developed by the 3GPP and Release-0 by the 3GPP2, have been produced in the form of Recommendation ITU-R M.1457. However, there have been further demands such as faster data rates for users and an IP-based multimedia sub- system to enhance the performance and capability of current IMT-2000 systems. These demands have encouraged the ITU-R to revise the current M.1457 to include new features such as HSDPA, LCS, IMS, 1XEV-DO, and 1XEV-DV. Continuous and regular revision in the ITU-R is being carried out for technical enhancement within the scope of IMT-2000 8.2 Systems beyond IMT-2000.

Having seen that the specifications for the first releases of IMT-2000 systems have been competed, the ITU-R has undertaken studies on the future development of IMT-2000 and systems beyond IMT-2000 to cope with the need for enhancements of technical capabilities, the range of available services, and the breadth of applications. Capabilities of systems beyond Fujitsu has also actively contributed to the development of the technical specifications of, for IMT-2000 were intensively discussed in the ITU-R WP8F (Fig. 14.4), which came from the ITU-R document, "Preliminary Draft New Recommendation (PDNR): Vision, framework and overall objectives of the future development of IMT-2000 and of systems beyond IMT-2000."

The systems beyond IMT-2000 may include new radio access capabilities and a new core network (probably an IP-based network) to be realized around 2010. Progress has been accelerated by extensive contributions from Japan in line with the activities of the MITF16 to promote the "new-generation mobile communication system."

Similar discussions to those held in the ITU-R and WP8F have just been started in the 3GPPs as well as in academic bodies in the UK and in Europe, and we can expect them to result in another phase of harmonization.

14.10 HARMONIZED STANDARD

This chapter presented a comprehensive overview of the global standardization activities for IMT-2000 in the ITU and 3GPPs and described some related activities of Fujitsu. The standardization process of IMT-2000 took more than decade because of temporary technical turmoil in certain stages. However, owing to extensive efforts by the ITU as well as the 3GPPs, a global consensus has fortunately been reached, resulting in a harmonized standard that will make it easier to improve mobile services around the globe and encourage the industry for the future. Since IMT-2000 has just been commercialized and the industry is about to step into another stage to stimulate the mobile market, new standardization work needs to be commenced for the system beyond IMT-2000, which is expected to provide more sophisticated services to meet the further demands of the wireless community.

Review Questions

1. What is IMT2000 standard and mention the key characteristics?
2. What are the scope and objectives of 3GPP?
3. Write about the enhancements in features in the release 6.
4. What is IMS? Draw a schematic of IP Multimedia Network.
5. What are the organizations represented by 3GPP2?
6. What are the new enhancements achieved in IMT-2000?

15 IMT-2000 Network Architecture

15.1 INTRODUCTION

Mobile telephone and data transmission services are mainly provided by that second-generation mobile systems that are the domestic standards worldwide. In Japan, the major digital mobile networks are based on the Personal Digital Cellular (PDC) system. On the other handin America a mobile telecommunication service vendor has started a commercial service based on the CDMAOne system, which is a North America standard. In other countries, mobile networks are constructed with one of two systems, viz Global Systems for Mobile (GSM) communications, which has shown the best results so far, and the other is the CDMAOne system, which is based on the latest technology.

There is a limit to the data communication speed in second-generation mobile networks. Also, it has been pointed out that there is a limit to the supply of high-speed IP packet services, for which there will be an explosive increase in demand. In network being discussed at international standards organizations to overcome the weak points of second-generation mobile networks. IMT-2000 is expected to consist of multi-vendor networks and to advance the standardization of the interface between the functional elements of networks.

IMT-2000 networks can be functionally classified into Core Networks (CNs), Radio Access Networks (RANs), Intelligent Networks (INs), and other networks installed in central offices.

The IMT-2000 standards are being discussed by two organizations: the 3rd Generation Partnership Project (3GPP) and the 3rd Generation Partnership Project2 (3GPP2). The participants of the 3GPP are ARIB, ETSI, TI, TTA, and TTC, and the participants of the 3GPP2 are ANTI, ARIB, ETSI, TTA, and TTC. The 3GPP aims to construct an IMT-2000 network based on the GSM network. On the other hand, the 3GPP2 aims to develop standards for the IMT-2000 network by enhancing the cdmaOne system. In the 3GPP, IMT-2000 is referred to as the Universal Mobile Telecommunication System (UMTS) or Wideband CDMA (W-CDMA). In Japan, the ARIB and TTC have advanced the domestic standardization of W- CDMA and cdma2000.

However, although the network configurations of W-CDMA/UMTS and cdma2000 are similar, there is a difference in the packet processing method. This chapter outlines the IMT-2000 networks and the differences between the two network technologies.

15.2 SERVICES IN IMT-2000 NETWORKS

One of the main purposes of IMT-2000 is to provide global roaming services. In order to offer worldwide communication services that include access to fixed networks and the Internet, IMT- 2000 is designed to connect not only land mobile networks but also fixed networks and satellite mobile networks.

Another major purpose of IMT-2000 is to provide broadband services for mobile terminals. Of course, seamless handover is required to provide quality of service (QoS) in high-speed transfer services. The services that IMT-2000 is designed to provide are described below.

15.2.1 Multimedia Communication Service

A multimedia service offers the service qualities (transmission rate, line quality, delay time, etc.) required for voice communication and data communication (including video communication). For example, notebook personal computers equipped with a mobile terminal offer a service quality that is equivalent to that offered by fixed networks. As a result, it is now possible to access the World Wide Web, e-mail, electronic commerce services (e.g., electronic bank services), and information services such as electronic newspapers and education courses outdoors.

Moreover, a highly accurate location information service using mobile networks has been examined. For example, traffic information and sightseeing guides for a specific area and navigation services can be provided based on terminal location information.

15.2.2 Global Service

A global service allows a user to communicate anywhere, both indoors and outdoors, regardless of the user's moving speed and location (e.g., city, suburb, or countryside). One of the major achievements of a global service is that it enables global roaming: that is, users can use the same mobile terminal in any country without having to change any of its settings.

To realize a global service, three levels of mobility are required: terminal mobility, user mobility, and service mobility. Terminal mobility means independence from the location and radio conditions. User mobility means that any mobile terminal can be used. Service mobility means that the service environment of the home network can be reproduced in another network.

One of the major technical issues in these global services is how to provide the high levels of security and privacy that are required.

15.2.3 Seamless Service

A seamless service allows a user to connect to a conventional network and the Internet with the same quality regardless of the wireless environment, location, and communication service vendor.

15.3 STANDARDIZATION TREND

The 3GPP and 3GPP2 were established to discuss the IMT-2000 from the end of 1998 to the beginning of 1999. The 3GPP makes mobile net- work system specifications based on the GSM communications/General Packet Radio Service (GPRS), and the 3GPP2 is based on the ANSI-41. The standardization work of Release1999 (the 1999 edition recommendation, or R99 for short) was completed by the 3GPP in December 1999.

R99 basically follows the functions of GSM and GPRS that have already been recommended. In the 3GPP2, the standardization work of Release A was completed in December 1999. Release A basically follows the functions of cdmaOne that have already been recommended.

Both the 3GPP and 3GPP2 have included the achievement of high-speed data transfer in all of their recommendations. The speeds they recommend are 64 kb/s or more in circuit switching mode and 384 kb/s or more in packet switching mode (2 Mb/s for a stationary terminal).

15.4 MOBILE NETWORK STRUCTURE

The migration from conventional networks is the most important issue for realizing IMT-2000 mobile networks. In this section, we describe the architecture of IMT-2000 networks. Then, we introduce the node group needed to construct a mobile network.

15.4.1 Realization of IMT-2000 Networks

To construct IMT-2000 networks from conventional networks, network venders can use either of the following two network construction methods.

1) *New installation of IMT-2000 networks*— The IMT-2000 network can be installed without influencing conventional operating networks. However, the initial capital investment required to install IMT-2000 is high.

2) *Construction of IMT-2000 networks through effective use of existing networks*— In this method, the facilities of the conventional networks are used as much as possible to construct IMT-2000 networks economically. For example, the RAN part of IMT-2000, including the voice circuit-switching, can be connected with conventional core networks. As described above, the standardization of the IMT-2000 network is done based on the existing networks. This method to the IN in the conventional networks can be connected to IMT-2000 networks.

Compared to the first method, this method requires a lower initial capital investment and makes it easier to construct an IMT-2000 network. However, this method requires changes to be made to the conventional networks.

15.4.2 Necessary Nodes for Construction of IMT-2000 Networks

As mentioned above, an IMT-2000 network basically consists of the RAN, CN, IN, and other elements (Figure 15.1). This section introduces each of these nodes in the W-CDMA/UMTS system.

1) *Radio Access Network*— The RAN is a wireless network located between the user terminal and the CN. It is composed of Radio Network Controllers (RNCs), Node-Bs, OMC-Rs, and other components.

2) *Core Network*— The CN is a network located between the RAN and another network (e.g., a Public Switched Telephone Network [PSTN]). It is composed of circuit switches (Mobile Switch Center [MSC]/ Gateway Mobile Switch Center [GMSC]), packet switches (Serving GPRS Support System [SGSN]/ Gateway GPRS Support System [GGSN]), sub- scriber databases (Home Location Register [HLR]/ Visitor Location Register [VLR]), address resolution servers for packet processing (Domain Name Server [DNS]), and the authentication and security centers (Authentication Center [AuC]/ Equipment Identity Register [EIR]).

3) *IN*— The intelligent network is a node group for achieving enhanced services (number portability, freephone, credit card calls, etc.). It is composed of Service Control Points (SCPs).

4) *Other devices*— Some of the other IMT-2000 network components have a lot on the usability of existing technologies.

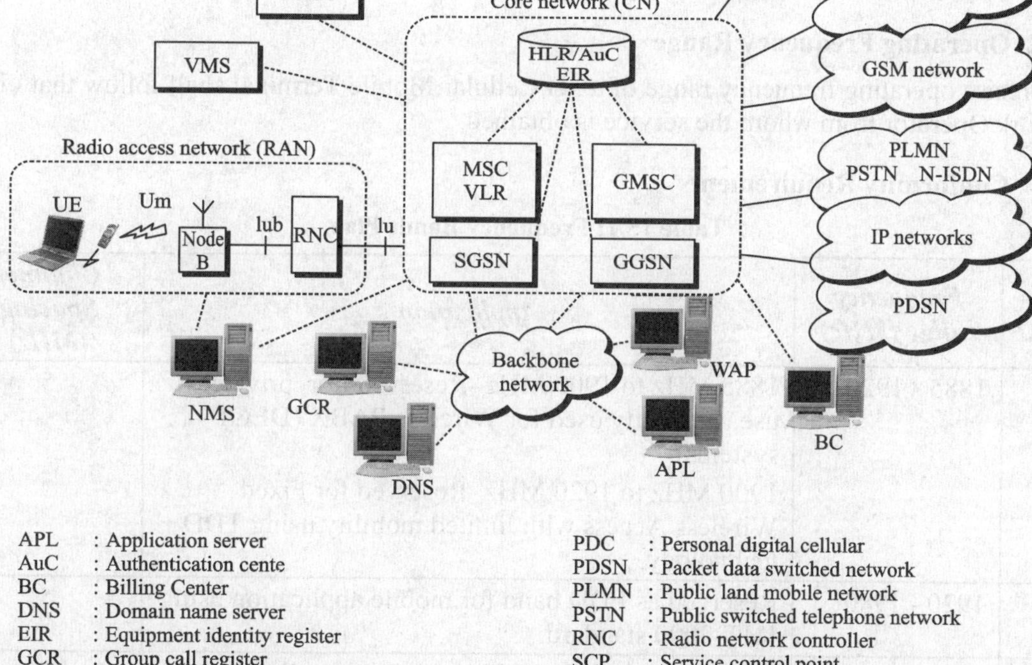

APL : Application server
AuC : Authentication cente
BC : Billing Center
DNS : Domain name server
EIR : Equipment identity register
GCR : Group call register
GGSN : Gateway GPRS support node
GMSC : Gateway mobile switching center
GSM : Global system for mobile
HLR : Home location register
MSC : Mobile switching center
N-ISDN: Narrowband ISDN
NMS : Network management system
PDC : Personal digital cellular
PDSN : Packet data switched network
PLMN : Public land mobile network
PSTN : Public switched telephone network
RNC : Radio network controller
SCP : Service control point
SGSN : Serving GPRS support node
SMSC : Short message center
UE : User equipment
VLR : Visitor location register
VMS : Voice mail system
WAP : Wireless application protocol

Fig. 15.1: IMT-2000 (UMTS) Network Structure

- Voice Mail System (VMS). This has voice re- Moreover, subscriber databases (e.g., the Home cording and replay functions such as an Location Register [HLR]) and the devices related answer phone. There is also a component for receiving and re-sending faxes Short Message Center (SMSC). This component is used for transmitting and receiving character information. The SMSC can be used, for example, to notify subscribers that there is a message for them in the VMS Group Call Register (GCR). This is a data HLR. When the subscriber moves, the location base for group call services. Wireless Application Protocol (WAP) server. This is a server that offers subscribers various information using the Wireless Application Protocol.

15.5 TECHNICAL SPECIFICATION FOR IMT 2OOO

15.5.1 Radio Frequency Requirements

3G Cellular Mobile Terminal shall operate within the following frequency bands and channel spacing as defined in Table 15.1.

Comprehensive information pertaining to frequency bands plan may be referred to MCMC SRSP-524M.

15.5.2 Operating Frequency Range

The precise operating frequency range of a 3G Cellular Mobile Terminal shall follow that of the Network Operator from whom the service is obtained.

15.5.3 Conformity Requirements

Table 15.1: Frequency Bands Plan

Sub-band	*Frequency range (MHz)*	*Application*	*Channel Spacing (MHz)*
A	1885 - 1920	1885 MHz to 1900 MHz -Reserved for private use. Currently used for Wireless PABX (DECT systems). 1900 MHz to 1920 MHz -Reserved for Fixed Wireless Access with limited mobility using TDD technology.	5
B	1920 - 1980	Reserved as FDD band for mobile application using IMT-2000 standard.	5
C	1980 - 2010	Reserved for IMT-2000 Mobile Satellite services.	5
D	2010 - 2025	Reserved as a TDD band for indoor application using IMT-2000 standard.	5
E	2110 - 2170	Reserved as a FDD band for mobile application using IMT-2000 standard.	5
F	2170 - 2200	Reserved for IMT-2000 Mobile Satellite Service.	5

Note— Comprehensive information pertaining to frequency bands plan may be referred to MCMC SRSP-524M.

a) Supplier shall demonstrate that the 3G Cellular Mobile Terminals have been tested and certified for operating in the frequency bands stated in Table 14.1 and conforms to the following standards.

   i) ETSI EN 301 908-01

   ii) ETSI EN 301 908-02

   iii) ETSI EN 301 908-6

   iv) ETSI TS 134 121

   v) ETSI TS 134 122

   iv) MCMC SRSP-524M

b) If the 3G Cellular Mobile Terminal also supports the Global System for Mobile Communications (GSM) and wireless local area network (WLAN) modes of operation, suppliers shall demonstrate that the 3G Cellular Mobile Terminal has been tested and certified for conformance to the following standards.

   1) ETSI EN 301 511

   2) ETSI EN 301 419-2

   3) ETSI EN 300 328-02

15.5.4 Electromagnetic Compatibility (EMC) Requirements

Supplier shall demonstrate that the 3G Cellular Mobile Terminal have been tested and certified according to EMC requirements to ensure an adequate level of compatibility for 3G Cellular Mobile Terminal intended to be used Malaysia.

The equipment shall comply with the EMC emissions requirements as defined in the ETSI EN 301 489-1. The requirements shall cover radiated and conducted emission.

15.6 SAFETY AND HEALTH REQUIREMENTS

15.6.1 Electrical Safety and Health

The equipment shall comply with the safety requirements defined in MS IEC 60950-1. The supplier shall submit full type test report to MS IEC 60950-1 or equivalent standards.

15.6.2 Specific Absorption Rate (SAR)

Suppliers shall demonstrate that the 3G Cellular Mobile Terminal has been tested and certified for conformance to the following International Commission on Non-Ionizing Radiation Protection (ICNIRP) recommendations.

a) EN 50360:2001

b) EN 62209-1:2006

A plugs, socket-outlets, adaptors and connection units - Part 1: Specification for rewirable and non-rewirable 13 A fused plugs

Electric cables Flexible cords rated up to 300/500 V, for use with appliances and equipment intended for domestic, office and similar environments

Specification for flat non-wirable two-pole plugs 2.5 A 250 V, with cord, for the connection of class II-equipment for

15.7 W-CDMA/UMTS PACKET PROCESSING

The specifications for the packet system of W-CDMA/UMTS are the same as those for the GPRS system that has been used with conventional GSM networks. Currently, mobility management of the subscriber is done using the information in the HLR is renewed. When the packet arrives, the location information in the HLR is referenced and the packet is transmitted to the switch node to which the target mobile terminal is registering (Figure 15.2).

15.7.1 Packet Switching in IMT-2000

It was mentioned above that there are two kinds of IMT-2000 systems: W-CDMA/UMTS and cdma2000. This section outlines the packet processing of these two systems.

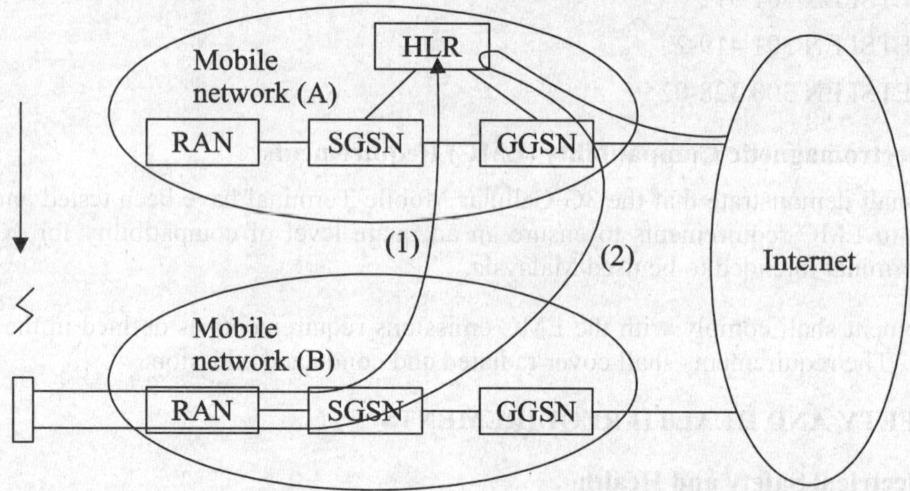

(1) The location information in HLR is updated along with the subscriber movement.
(2) SGSN is specified by the location information in HLR.

Fig. 15.2: UMTS Packet Processing

15.7.2 cdma2000 Packet Processing

Because the specifications for the packet processing method were not standardized in cdmaOne, they have been standardized in its re- placement, cdma2000. The packet processing method of cdma2000 adopts the Mobile IP system, which differs from the HLR system in W-CDMA/ UMTS and is being discussed by the IETF. When a user moves to a foreign network, a care-of address is sent from the Foreign Agent (FA) in the foreign network to the Home Agent (HA) in the user's home network. As shown in Figure 15.3, the packets for a moving user are re-forwarded to the FA by the HA according to the care-of address. roaming is done, the pre-paid card service available in the home network can be made available in other networks. To realize a VHE, the intelligent network centrally manages the service logic at a Service Control Point (SCP) and the SCP controls the Service Switching Point (SSP) to offer the subscriber service as shown in Figure 4.

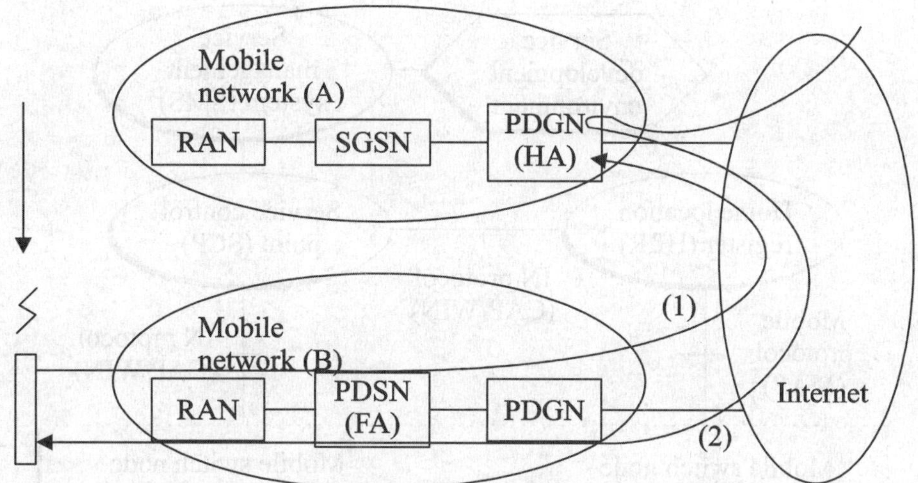

(1) The core-of-address (CoA) of mobile terminal is updated in HA along with the subscriber movement..
(2) In coming packets are re-forwarded by the CoA in HA.

Fig. 15.3: cdma2000 Packet Processing

The different protocols of SCP and SSP/HLR were standardized by the 3GPP and 3GPP2. The 3GPP applied the Customized Application or Mobile network Enhanced Logic (CAMEL), and the 3GPP2 applied the Wireless Intelligent Network (WIN).

CAMEL is based on the Intelligent Network realizing a Virtual Home Environment (VHE).

15.8 INTELLIGENT NETWORK (IN)

The IMT-2000 IN is the key component for Intelligent network for mobile network. Application Protocol (INAP) that is being recommended by the ITU-T/ETSI. CAMEL implements a part of the GSM Mobile Application Protocol (MAP) for interconnection between the SCP and HLR and was recommended in the form of the CAMEL Application Protocol (CAP).

On the other hand, for cdma2000 networks, the Wireless IN (WIN) was recommended. The WIN was enhanced from the ANSI-41 MAP, which the Telecommunication Industry Association (TIA)/Electronic Industry Association (EIA) standardized for the CDMA recommendations. New operations for SCP and HLR communication were recommended for the WIN. Also, the existing MAP was changed to accommodate the introduction of the WIN.

In the future, intelligent networks will occupy the most important positions in networks and will become indispensable for offering a seamless service in mobile and also fixed networks. Intelligent networks integrate the functions of the service control and management and can provide various services between different networks a user moves to a foreign network, a care-of address is sent from the Foreign Agent (FA) in the foreign network to the Home Agent (HA) in the user's home network. As shown in Figure 15.3, the packets for a moving user are re-forwarded to the FA by the HA according to the care-of address.

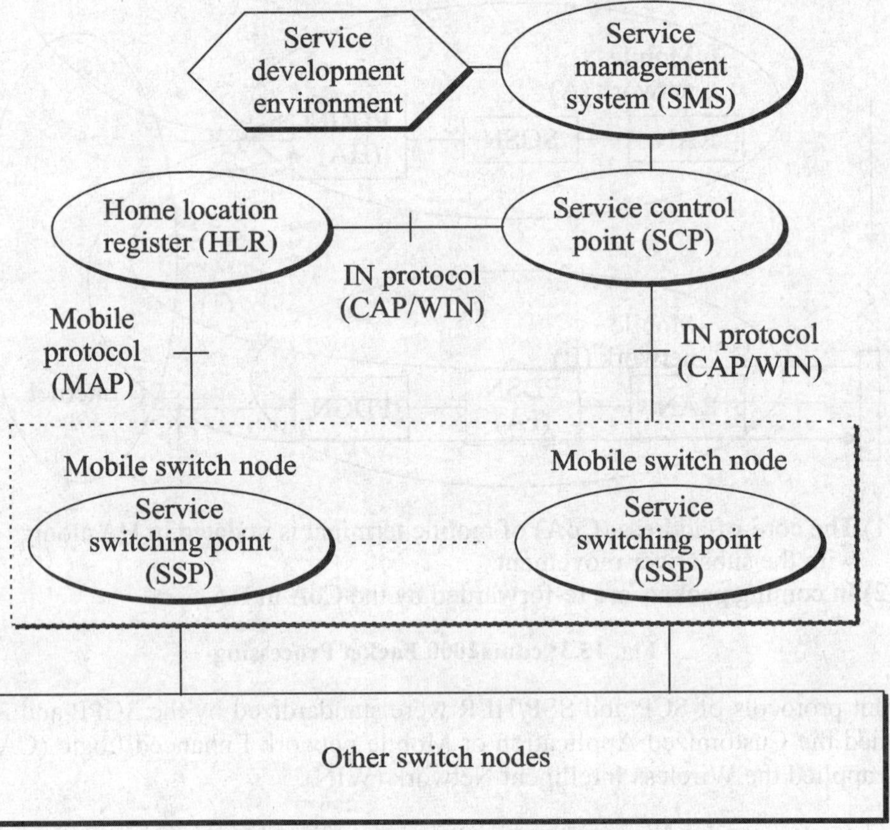

Fig. 15.4: Intelligent Network for Mobile Network

Review Points

Standardization

There is a limit to the data communication speed in second-generation mobile networks. Also, it has been pointed out that there is a limit to the supply of high-speed IP packet services, for which there will be an explosive increase in demand in network being discussed at international standards organizations to overcome the weak points of second-generation mobile networks. IMT-2000 is expected to consist of multi-vendor networks and to advance the standardization of the interface between the functional elements of networks. IMT-2000 networks can be functionally classified into Core Networks (CNs), Radio Access Networks (RANs), Intelligent Networks (INs), and other networks installed in center offices.

Services

Major purpose of IMT-2000 is to provide broadband services for mobile terminals. Of course, seamless handover is required to provide quality of service (QoS) in high-speed transfer services. The services that IMT-2000 provides are,- multimedia service which offers the service qualities (transmission rate, line quality, delay time, etc.) required for voice communication and data communication (including video communication) and highly accurate location information service using mobile networks like, traffic information and sightseeing guides for a specific area and navigation services.

Realization of IMT-2000 Networks

Requires a lower initial capital investment and makes it easier to construct an IMT-2000 network by effective use of existing networks. In this method, the facilities of the conventional networks are used as much as possible to construct IMT-2000 networks economically. Necessary nodes for construction of IMT-2000 networks include-Radio Access Network (RAN),Core Network (CN), intelligent network (IN) and Other devices

Packet Switching in IMT-2000

The packet processing method of cdma2000 adopts the Mobile IP system, which differs from the HLR system in W-CDMA/ UMTS and is being discussed by the IETF. When a user moves to a foreign network, a care-of address is sent from the Foreign Agent (FA) in the foreign network to the Home Agent (HA) in the user's home network. The packets for a moving user are re-forwarded to the FA by the HA according to the care-of address, roaming is done, the pre-paid card service available in the home network can be made available in other networks.

Intelligent Network (IN)

The IMT-2000 IN is the key component for Intelligent network for mobile network. Application Protocol (INAP) that is being recommended by the ITU-T/ETSI. CAMEL implements a part of the GSM Mobile Application Protocol (MAP) for interconnection between the SCP and HLR and was recommended in the form of the CAMEL Application Protocol (CAP). In the future, intelligent networks will occupy the most important positions in networks and will become indispensable for offering a seamless service in mobile and also fixed networks.

Review Questions

1. Write about multimedia communication service in IMT2000.
2. What are the new nodes in IMT2000 and explain their functions?
3. Draw a network block diagram and mention all the components.
4. Write about the frequency plans deployed in IMT2000.
5. What is SAR? Write a note on SAR.
6. Explain how packet switching is adapted.
7. Write a note on intelligent network in mobile configuration.

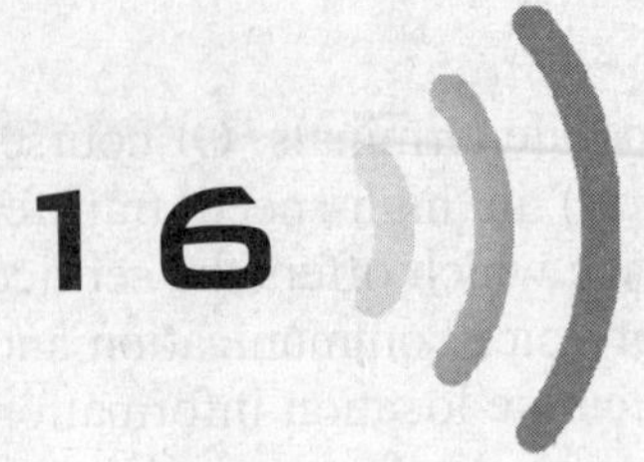

16 Wireless Technology Migration Path

16.1 INTRODUCTION

This section discusses 1G to 4G designs, the evolution and migration of wireless-data technologies from EDGE to LTE, as well as the evolution of underlying wireless approaches. Progress in 3GPP has occurred in multiple phases, first with EDGE, and then UMTS, followed by today's enhanced 3G capabilities such as HSPA, HSPA+ and now, LTE, which itself is evolving to LTE-Advanced. Meanwhile, underlying approaches have evolved from Time Division Multiple Access (TDMA) to CDMA, and now from CDMA to OFDMA, which is the basis of LTE.

16.2 MIGRATION PATH 1G TO 4G

There is some confusion in the industry as to what technology falls into which cellular generation. 1G refers to analog cellular technologies and became available in the 1980s. 2G denotes initial digital systems, introducing services such as short messaging and lower speed data. CDMA2000 1xRTT and GSM are the primary 2G technologies, although CDMA2000 1xRTT is sometimes called a 3G technology because it meets the 144 kbps mobile throughput requirement. EDGE, however, also meets this requirement. 2G technologies became available in the 1990s.

3G requirements were specified by the ITU as part of the International Mobile Telephone 2000 (IMT-2000) project, for which digital networks had to provide 144 kbps of throughput at mobile speeds, 384 kbps at pedestrian speeds, and 2 Mbps in indoor environments. UMTS-HSPA and CDMA2000 EV-DO are the primary 3G technologies, although recently WiMAX was also designated as an official 3G technology. The ITU has recently issued requirements for IMT-Advanced, which constitutes the official definition of 4G. Requirements include operation in up to 40 MHz radio channels and extremely high spectral efficiency. The ITU recommends operation in up to 100 MHz radio channels and peak spectral efficiency of 15 bps/Hz, resulting in a theoretical throughput rate of 1.5 Gbps. Previous to the publication of the requirements, 1 Gbps was frequently cited as a 4G goal.

No technology meets these requirements yet; none is even close. It will require new technologies such as LTE-Advanced (with work already underway) and IEEE 802.16m. Some have tried to label current versions of WiMAX and LTE as "4G", but this is only accurate to the extent that such designation refers to the general approach or platform that will be enhanced to meet the 4G requirements. With WiMAX and HSPA significantly outperforming 3G requirements, calling these technologies 3G clearly does not give them full credit as they are a generation beyond current technologies in capability. But calling them 4G is not correct.

Unfortunately, the generational labels do not properly capture the scope of available technologies and have resulted in some amount of market confusion. Some people have even called technologies such as HSPA 3.5G and LTE 3.9G, although these are not official designations.

16.3 EVOLUTIONARY APPROACH BY 3GPP

Rather than emphasizing any one wireless approach, 3GPP's evolutionary plan is to recognize the strengths and weaknesses of every technology and to exploit the unique capabilities of each one accordingly. GSM, based on a TDMA approach, is mature and broadly deployed. Already extremely efficient, there are nevertheless opportunities for additional optimizations and enhancements. Standards bodies have already defined "Evolved EDGE," which will be available for deployment in the 2009 to 2010 timeframe. Evolved EDGE more than doubles throughput over current EDGE systems, halves latency, and increases spectral efficiency. By the end of the decade, because of sheer market momentum, the majority of worldwide subscribers will still be using GSM/EDGE technologies.

Meanwhile, CDMA was chosen as the basis of 3G technologies including WCDMA for the frequency division duplex (FDD) mode of UMTS and Time Division CDMA (TD-CDMA) for the time division duplex (TDD) mode of UMTS. The evolved data systems for UMTS, such as HSPA and HSPA+, introduce enhancements and simplifications that help CDMA-based systems match the capabilities of competing systems, especially in 5 MHz spectrum allocations.

Innovations such as dual-carrier HSPA,are already explained in detail "Evolution of HSPA (HSPA+)," is to coordinate the operation of HSPA on two adjacent 5 MHz carriers for higher throughput rates. In combination with MIMO, dual-carrier HSPA will achieve peak network speeds of 84 Mbps.

16.4 PERFORMANCE LEVEL

Given some of the advantages of an OFDM approach, 3GPP has specified OFDMA as the basis of its Long Term Evolution effort. LTE incorporates best-of-breed radio techniques to achieve performance levels beyond what will be practical with CDMA approaches, particularly in larger channel bandwidths. In the same way that 3G coexists with Second Generation (2G) systems in integrated networks, LTE systems will coexist with both 3G systems and 2G systems. Multimode devices will function across LTE/3G or even LTE/3G/2G, depending on market circumstances. Beyond radio technology, EPC/SAE provides a new core architecture that enables both flatter architectures and integration of LTE with both legacy GSM-HSPA networks, as well as other wireless technologies. The combination of EPC and LTE is referred to as the Evolved Packet System (EPS).

LTE is of crucial importance to operators since it provides the efficiencies and capabilities being demanded by the quickly growing mobile broadband market. The cost for operators to deliver data (e.g., cost per Mbyte) is almost directly proportional to the spectral efficiency of the technologies. LTE has the highest spectral efficiency of any specified technology, making it an essential technology as the market matures. LTE is available in both FDD and TDD modes. Many deployments will be based on FDD in paired spectrum. The TDD mode, however, will be important in enabling deployments where paired spectrum is unavailable. To address ITU's IMT-Advanced requirements, 3GPP is developing LTE-Advanced, a technology that will have peak rates of more than 1 Gbps. See the appendix section "4G, IMT-Advanced and LTE-Advanced" for a detailed explanation.

The earlier chapters summarize the key 3GPP technologies and their characteristics.

16.5 VARIOUS RELEASES OF 3GPP

The development of GSM and UMTS-HSPA happens in stages referred to as 3GPP releases, and equipment vendors produce hardware that supports particular versions of each specification. It is important to realize that the 3GPP releases address multiple technologies. For example, Release 7 optimized VoIP for HSPA, but also significantly enhanced GSM data functionality with Evolved EDGE. A summary of the different 3GPP releases is as follows:

- *Release 99*— Completed. First deployable version of UMTS. Enhancements to GSM data (EDGE). Majority of deployments today are based on Release 99. Provides support for GSM/EDGE/GPRS/WCDMA radio-access networks.
- *Release 4*— Completed. Multimedia messaging support. First steps toward using IP transport in the core network.
- *Release 5*— Completed. HSDPA. First phase of IMS. Full ability to use IP-based transport instead of just Asynchronous Transfer Mode (ATM) in the core network.
- *Release 6*— Completed. HSUPA. Enhanced multimedia support through Multimedia Broadcast/Multicast Services (MBMS). Performance specifications for advanced receivers. WLAN integration option. IMS enhancements. Initial VoIP capability.
- *Release 7*— Completed. Provides enhanced GSM data functionality with Evolved EDGE. Specifies HSPA Evolution (HSPA+), which includes higher order modulation and MIMO. Provides fine-tuning and incremental improvements of features from previous releases. Results include performance enhancements, improved spectral efficiency, increased capacity, and better resistance to interference. Continuous Packet Connectivity (CPC) enables efficient "always-on" service and enhanced uplink UL VoIP capacity, as well as reductions in call set-up delay for PoC. Radio enhancements to HSPA include 64 QAM in the downlink DL and 16 QAM in the uplink. Also includes optimization of MBMS capabilities through the multicast/broadcast, single-frequency network (MBSFN) function.
- *Release 8*— Completed. Comprises further HSPA Evolution features such as simultaneous use of MIMO and 64 QAM. Includes work item for dual-carrier HSPA (DC-HSPA) wherein two WCDMA radio channels can be combined for a doubling of throughput performance. Specifies OFDMA-based 3GPP LTE. Defines EPC.
- *Release 9*— Under development. Likely 2010. Will include HSPA and LTE enhancements including HSPA multi-carrier operation.
- *Release 10*— Under development. Likely 2011. Will specify LTE-Advanced that meets the requirements set by ITU's IMT-Advanced project.

Whereas operators and vendors actively involved in the development of wireless technology are heavily focused on 3GPP release versions, most users of the technology are more interested in particular features and capabilities such as whether a device supports HSDPA. For this reason, the detailed discussion of the technologies in this paper emphasizes features as opposed to 3GPP releases.

16.6 SPECTRUM

Another important aspect of UMTS-HSPA deployment is the expanding number of available radio bands, as shown in Table 16.1, and the corresponding support from infrastructure and mobile-equipment vendors. The fundamental system design and networking protocols remain the same for each band; only the frequency-dependent portions of the radios have to change.

As other frequency bands become available for deployment, standards bodies are adapting UMTS for these bands as well. This includes 450 and 700 MHz. UMTS-TDD equipment is already available for 450 MHz. The 1710-1770 uplink was matched with 2110-2170 downlink to allow for additional global harmonization of the 1.7/2.1GHz band. Meanwhile, the Federal Communications Commission auctioned the 700 MHz band in the United States in January 2008. The availability of this band, the Advanced Wireless Services (AWS) band at 1710-1755 MHz with/2110-2155 MHz in the US, and the forthcoming 2.6 GHz frequency band in Europe are providing operators with wider deployment options. An increasing number of operators are also deploying UMTS at 900 MHz, a traditional GSM band.

As the total amount of available spectrum increases and as technologies simultaneously become spectrally more efficient, total capacity rises rapidly, supporting more subscribers and making many new types of applications feasible.

16.6.1 FDD Bands Defined for 3GPP Technologies

Table 16.1: FDD Bands for 3GPP Technologies

Operating Band	*Band Name*	*Total Spectrum*	*Uplink (MHz)*	*Downlink (MHz)*
Band 1	2.1 GHz	2 × 60 MHz	1920-1980	2110-2170
Band 2	1900 MHz	2 × 60 MHz	1850-1910	1930-1990
Band 3	1800 MHz	2 × 75 MHz	1710-1785	1805-1880
Band 4	1.7/2.1 GHz	2 × 45 MHz	1710-1755	2110-2155
Band 5	850 MHz	2 × 25 MHz	824-849	869-894
Band 6	800 MHz	2 × 10 MHz	830-840	875-885
Band 7	2.6 GHz	2 × 70 MHz	2500-2570	2620-2690
Band 8	900 MHz	2 × 35 MHz	880-915	925-960
Band 9	1700 MHz	2 × 35 MHz	1749.9-1784.9	1844.9-1879.9
Band 10	Ext 1.7/2.1 GHz	2 × 60 MHz	1710-1770	2110-2170
Band 11	1500 MHz	2 × 25 MHz	1427.9-1452.9	1475.9-1500.9
Band 12	Lower 700 MHz	2 × 18 MHz	698-716	728-746
Band 13	Upper 700 MHz	2 × 10 MHz	777-787	746-756
Band 14	Upper 700 MHz Public Safety / Private	2 × 10 MHz	788-798	758-768

It should be noted that although the support of a new frequency band may be introduced in a particular release, the 3GPP standard also specifies ways to implement devices and infrastructure operating on any frequency band, according to release anterior to the introduction of that particular frequency band. For example, although band 5 (US Cellular Band) was introduced in Release 6, the first devices operating on this band were compliant with the release 5 of the standard.

16.6.2 TDD Bands Defined for 3GPP Technologies

Table 16.2: TDD Bands for 3GPP Technologies

Operating Band	*Total Spectrum*	*Frequencies (MHz)*
Band 33	20 MHz	1900-1920
Band 34	15 MHz	2010-2025
Band 35	60 MHz	1850-1910
Band 36	60 MHz	1930-1990
Band 37	20 MHz	1910-1930
Band 38	50 MHz	2570-2620
Band 39	40 MHz	1880-1920
Band 40	100 MHz	2300-2400

16.6.3 Spectrum for Next Generation

Different countries have regulated spectrum more loosely than others. For example, operators in the United States can use either 2G or 3G technologies in cellular, Personal Communications Service (PCS), and 3G bands, whereas in Europe there are greater restrictions—although efforts are underway that are resulting in greater flexibility including the use of 3G technologies in current 2G bands.

With the projected increase in the use of mobile-broadband technologies, the amount of spectrum required by the next generation of wireless technology (that is, after 3GPP LTE in projects such as International Mobile Telecommunications (IMT) Advanced) could be substantial given the desire to operate radio channels as wide as 100 MHz. Ideally, this spectrum would fall below 5 GHz. This search for new spectrum is a long-term undertaking, and it may be well into the next decade before any such new spectrum becomes available. Given the expanding size and economic significance of the mobile- computing industry, however, decisions made on new spectrum—especially with respect to global harmonization—will have profound consequences.

As regulators make more spectrum available, it is important that such spectrum be:

1) Harmonized on a regional or global basis.
2) Unencumbered by spectrum caps and other legacy voice-centric spectrum policies.
3) Made available in as wide radio channels as possible (i.e., 10 MHz, 20 MHz and more).
4) Utilized efficiently without causing interference to existing spectrum holders.

Emerging technologies such as LTE benefit from wider radio channels. These wider radio channels are not only spectrally more efficient, but offer greater capacity, an essential attribute because typical broadband usage contributes to a much higher load than a voice user. For instance, watching a YouTube video consumes 100 times as many bits per second on the downlink as a voice call.

16.6.4 LTE Spectral Efficiency

Figure 16.1 shows increasing LTE spectral efficiency obtained with wider radio channels, with 20 MHz showing the most efficient configuration.

To better understand the reasons for deploying the different data technologies and to better predict the evolution of capability, it is useful to examine spectral efficiency. The evolution of data services will be characterized by an increasing number of users with ever-higher bandwidth demands. As the wireless-data market grows, deploying wireless technologies with high spectral efficiency will be of paramount importance. Keeping all other things equal such as frequency band, amount of spectrum, and cell site spacing, an increase in spectral efficiency translates to a proportional increase in the number of users supported at the same load per user—or, for the same number of users, an increase in throughput available to each user. Delivering broadband services to large numbers of users can best be achieved with high spectral-efficiency systems, especially because the only other alternatives are using more spectrum or deploying more cell sites.

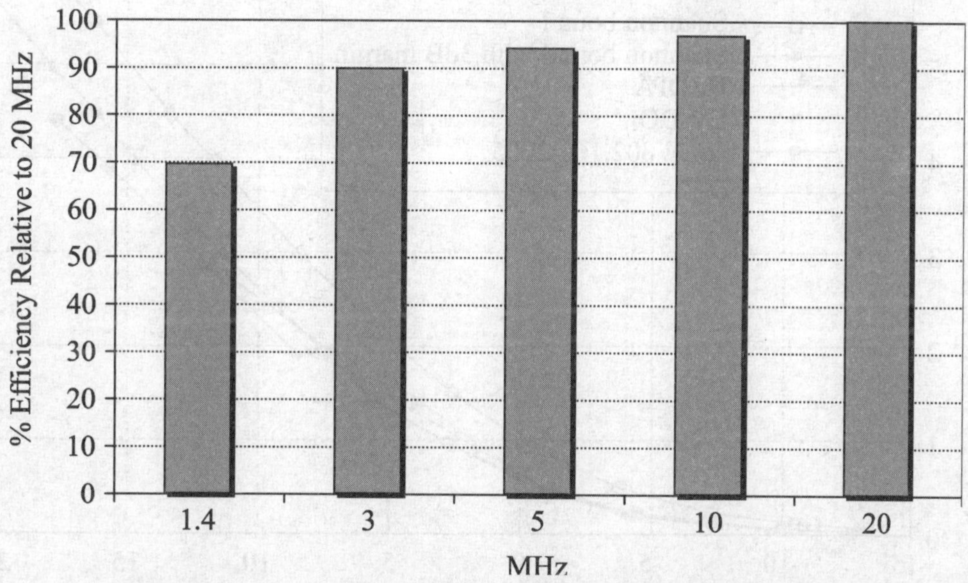

Fig. 16.1: LTE Spectral Efficiency as Function of Radio Channel Size

Increased spectral efficiency, however, comes at a price. It generally implies greater complexity for both user and base station equipment. Complexity can arise from the increased number of calculations performed to process signals or from additional radio components. Hence, operators and vendors must balance market needs against network and equipment costs. One core aspect of evolving wireless technology is managing the complexity associated with achieving higher spectral efficiency. The reason technologies such as OFDMA are attractive is that they allow higher spectral efficiency with lower overall complexity; thus their use in technologies such as LTE and WiMAX.

The roadmap for the EDGE/HSPA/LTE family of technologies provides a wide portfolio of options to increase spectral efficiency. The exact timing for deploying these options is difficult to predict, because much will depend on the growth of the wireless data market and what types of applications become popular.

When determining the best area on which to focus future technology enhancements, it is interesting to note that HSDPA, 1xEV-DO, and IEEE 802.16e-2005 all have highly optimized links—that is, physical layers. In fact, as shown in Figure 16.3, the link layer performance of these technologies is approaching the theoretical limits as defined by the Shannon bound. (The Shannon bound is a theoretical limit to the information transfer rate [per unit bandwidth] that can be supported by any communications link. The bound is a function of the Signal to Noise Ratio [SNR] of the communications link.) Figure 16.2 also shows that HSDPA, 1xEV-DO, and IEEE 802.16e-2005 are all within 2 to 3 decibels (dB) of the Shannon bound, indicating that there is not much room for improvement from a link layer perspective. Note that differences do exist in the design of the MAC layer (layer 2), and this may result in lower than expected performance in some cases as described previously.

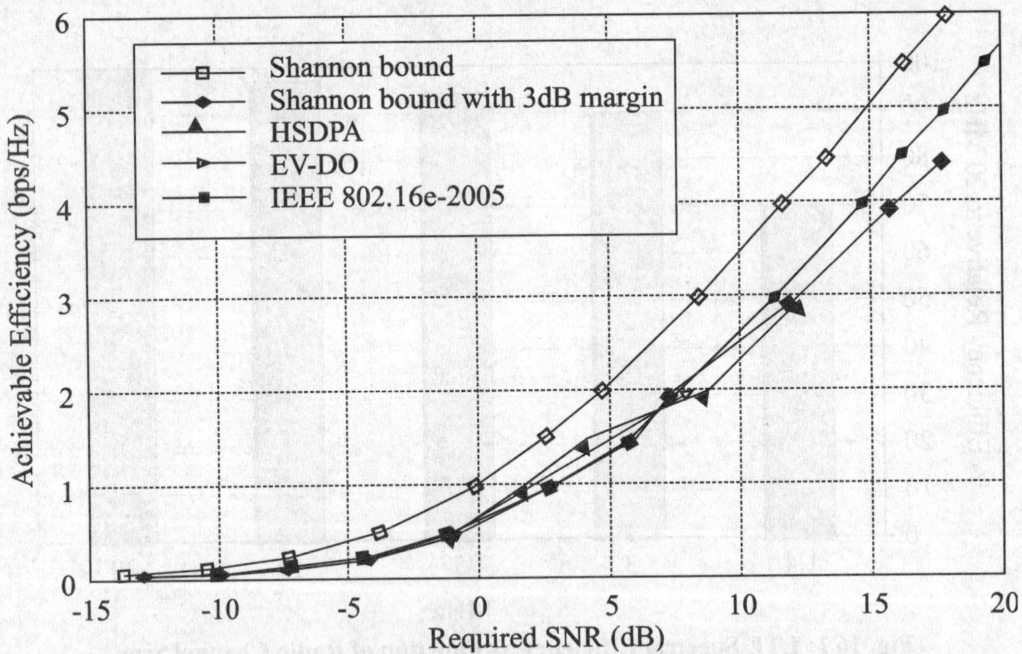

Fig. 16.2: Performance Relative to Theoretical Limits for HSDPA, EV-DO and IEEE 802.16e - 2005

The curves in Figure 16.2 apply to an Additive White Gaussian Noise Channel (AWGN). If the channel is slowly varying and the effect of frequency selectivity can be overcome through an equalizer in either HSDPA or OFDM, then the channel can be known almost perfectly and the effects of fading and non-AWGN interference can be ignored—thus justifying the AWGN assumption. For instance, at 3 km per hour, and fading at 2 GHz, the Doppler spread is about 5.5 Hz. The coherence time of the channel is thus 1 sec/5.5 or 180 msec. Frames are well within the coherence time of the channel, because they are typically 20 msec or less. As such, the channel appears "constant" over a frame and the Shannon bound applies. Much more of the traffic in a cellular system is at slow speeds (for example, 3 km/hr) rather than at higher speeds. Thus, the Shannon bound is relevant for a realistic deployment environment.

As the speed of the mobile station increases and the channel estimation becomes less accurate, additional margin is needed. This additional margin, however, would impact the different standards fairly equally.

The Shannon bound only applies to a single user; it does not attempt to indicate aggregate channel throughput with multiple users. It does indicate, however, that link layer performance is reaching theoretical limits. As such, the focus of future technology enhancements should be on improving system performance aspects that maximize the experienced SNRs in the system rather than on investigating new air interfaces that attempt to improve the link layer performance.

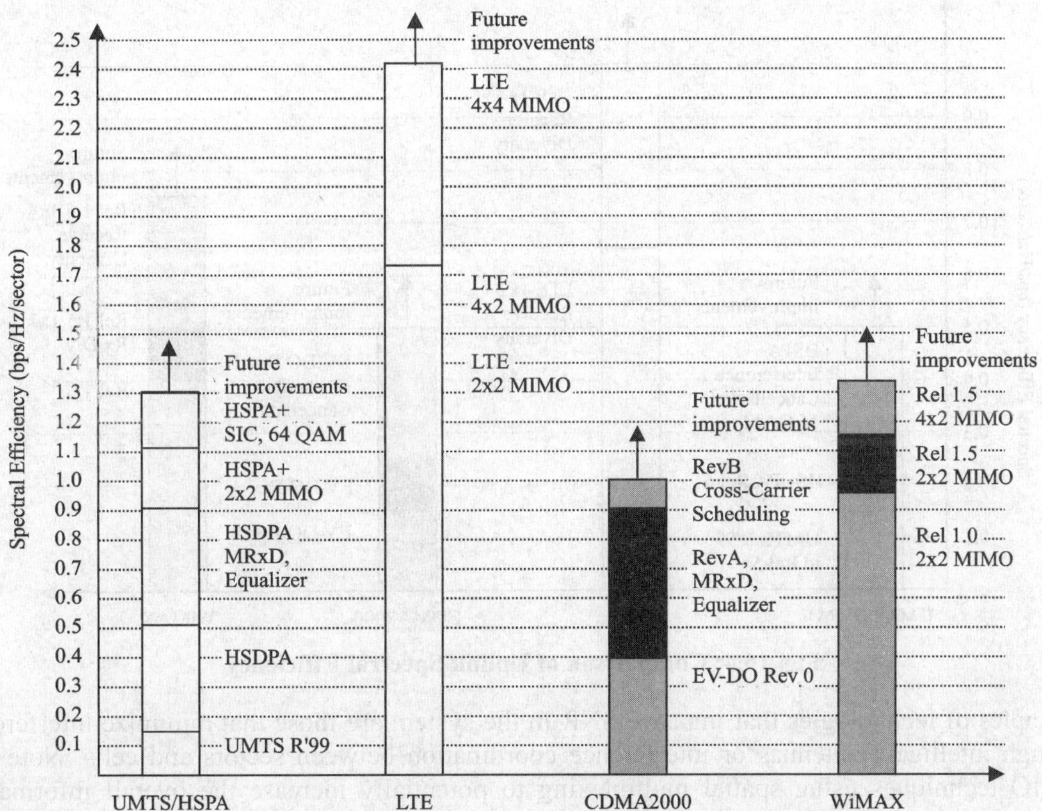

Fig. 16.3: Comparison of Downlink Spectral Efficiency

Table 16.3: Compares the Uplink Spectral Efficiency of the Different Systems

Feature	*LTE*	*WiMAX Release 1 .0*	*WiMAX Release 1 .5*	*Impact*
Hybrid Automatic Repeat Request (ARQ)	Incremental redundancy	Chase combining	Chase combining	Incremental redundancy is more efficient (lower SNR required (or given error rate)
Frame Duration	1 m sec subframes	5 msec subframes	5 msec subframes	Shorter subframes yield lower user plane delay and reduced channel quality feedback delays
Overhead / Control Channel Efficiency	Relatively low overhead	Relatively high overhead	Relatively high overhead apart from reduction in pilots	Lower overhead improves performance

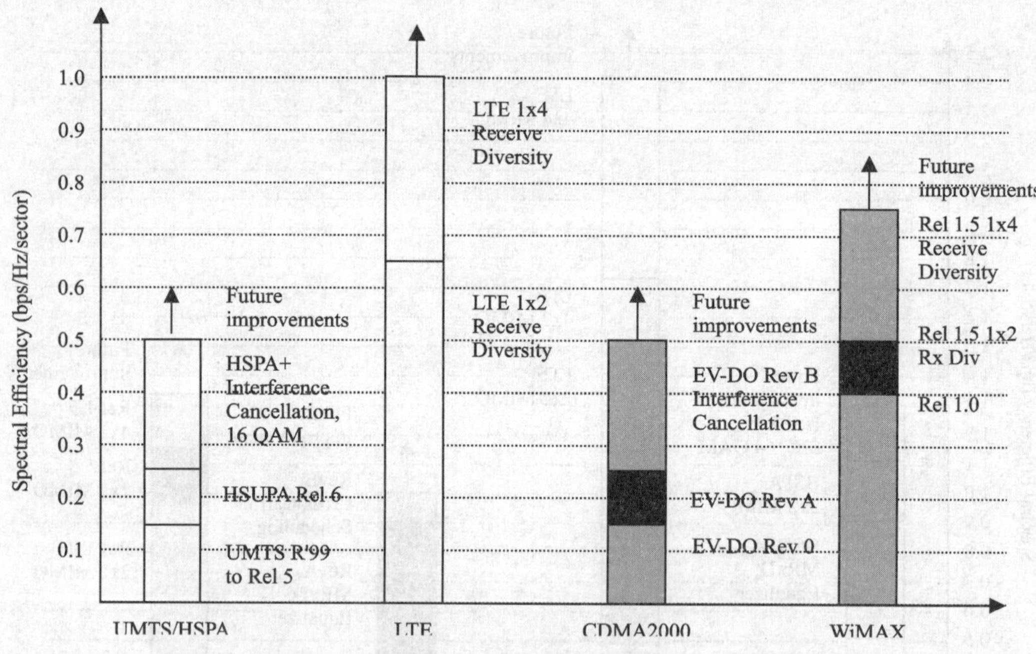

Fig. 16.4: Comparison of Uplink Spectral Efficiency

Examples of technologies that improve SNR in the system are those that minimize interference through intelligent antennas or interference coordination between sectors and cells. Note that MIMO techniques using spatial multiplexing to potentially increase the overall information transfer rate by a factor proportional to the number of transmit or receive antennas do not violate the Shannon bound, because the per-antenna transfer rate (that is, the per-communications link transfer rate) is still limited by the Shannon bound.

Figure 16.4 compares the spectral efficiency of different wireless technologies based on of some concern in this regard is that spectrum for LTE is becoming available in different frequency bands in different countries. For instance, initial US deployments will be at 700 MHz, in Japan at 1500 MHz and in Europe at 2.6 GHz. Thus, with some many varying spectrum bands, it will most likely necessitate that roaming operation be based on GSM or HSPA on common regional or global bands.

16.7 CORE-NETWORK EVOLUTION

3GPP is defining a series of enhancements to the core network to improve network performance and the range of services provided, and to enable a shift to all-IP architectures. One way to improve core-network performance is by using flatter architectures. The more hierarchical a network, the more easily it can be managed centrally; the tradeoff, however, is reduced performance, especially for data communications, because packets must traverse and be processed by multiple nodes in the network. To improve data performance and, in particular, to reduce latency (delays), 3GPP has defined a number of enhancements in Release 7 and Release 8 that reduce the number of processing nodes and result in a flatter architecture.

In Release 7, an option called one-tunnel architecture allows operators to configure their networks so that user data bypasses a serving node and travels directly via a gatewaynode. There is also an option to integrate the functionality of the radio-network controller directly into the base station.

For Release 8, 3GPP has defined an entirely new core network, called the Evolved Packet Core, previously called System Architecture Evolution. The key features and capabilities of EPC/SAE include:

- Reduced latency and higher data performance through a flatter architecture.
  - ✓ Support for both LTE radio-access networks and interworking with GSM-HSPA radio-access networks.
- The ability to integrate non-3GPP networks such as WiMAX.
- Optimization for all services provided via IP.

This paper provides further details in the sections on HSPA Evolution (HSPA+) and EPC/SAE.

16.8 SERVICE EVOLUTION

Not only do 3GPP technologies provide continual improvements in capacity and data performance, they also evolve capabilities that expand the services available to subscribers. Key service advances include Fixed Mobile Convergence (FMC), IMS, and broadcasting technologies. This section provides an overview of these topics, and the appendix provides greater detail on each of these items.

FMC refers to the integration of fixed services (such as telephony provided by wireline or WiFi) with mobile cellular-based services. Though FMC is still in its early stages of deployment by operators, it promises to provide significant benefits to both users and operators. For users, FMC will simplify how they communicate making it possible for them to use one device (for example, a cell phone) at work and at home where it might connect via a Wi-Fi network or a femto cell. When mobile, users connect via a cellular network. Users will also benefit from single voice mailboxes and single phone numbers, as well as the ability to control how and with whom they communicate. For operators, FMC allows the consolidation of core services across multiple-access networks. For instance, an operator could offer complete VoIP-based voice service that supports access via DSL, Wi-Fi, or 3G. FMC also offloads the macro network from data-intensive applications such as movie downloads.

There are various approaches for FMC, including Generic Access Network (GAN), formerly known as Unlicensed Mobile Access (UMA), femtocells, and IMS. With GAN, GSM-HSPA devices can connect via Wi-Fi or cellular connections for both voice and data. UMA/GAN is a 3GPP technology, and it has been deployed by a number of operators, including T-Mobile in the United States. An alternative to using Wi-Fi for the "fixed" portion of FMC is femtocells. These are tiny base stations that cost little more than a Wi- Fi access point and, like Wi-Fi, femtocells leverage a subscriber's existing wireline- broadband connection (for example, DSL). Instead of operating on unlicensed bands, femtocells use the operator's licensed bands at very low power levels. The key advantage of the femtocell approach is that any single-mode, mobile-communications device a user has can now operate using the femtocells.

16.9 IMS CONCEPT

IMS is another key technology for convergence. It allows access to core services and applications via multiple-access networks. IMS is more powerful than GAN, because it supports not only FMC, but also a much broader range of potential applications. In the United States, AT&T has committed to an IMS approach and has already deployed an IMS-based video sharing service. Although defined by 3GPP, the Third Generation

Partnership Project 2 (3GPP2), CableLabs and WiMAX have adopted IMS. IMS is how VoIP will (or could) be deployed in CDMA 2000 EV-DO, WiMAX, HSPA and LTE networks.

IMS allows the creative blending of different types of communications and information, including voice, video, IM, presence information, location, and documents. It provides application developers the means to create applications that have never before been possible, and it allows people to communicate in entirely new ways by dynamically using multiple services. For example, during an interactive chat session, a user could launch a voice call. Or during a voice call, a user could suddenly establish a simultaneous video connection or start transferring files. While browsing the Web, a user could decide to speak to a customer-service representative. IMS will be a key platform for all-IP architectures for both HSPA and LTE.

A new initiative called Rich Communications Suite (RCS), supported by many operators and vendors, builds upon IMS technology to provide a consistent feature set, as well as implementation guidelines, use cases, and reference implementations. RCS uses existing standards and specifications from 3GPP, OMA and GSMA.

Core features include:

- An enhanced phone book (device and/or network based) that includes service capabilities and presence-enhanced contact information.

- Enhanced messaging (supporting text, instant messaging and multimedia) with chat and messaging history.
- Enriched calls that include multimedia content (e.g., video sharing) during voice calls.

Another important new service is support for mobile TV through what is called multicast or broadcast functions. 3GPP has defined multicast/broadcast capabilities for both HSPA and LTE.

16.10 NETWORK INTERFACES FOR APPLICATIONS

Another important development related to service evolution is operators making interfaces available to external applications for information and control. Two widely deployed capabilities today include location queries and short message service. With location, mobile devices or external applications (e.g., applications operating on computers outside of the network) can query the location of a user, subject to privacy restrictions. This can significantly enhance many applications including navigation, supplying location of nearby destinations (e.g., restaurants, stores), location of friends for social networking, and worker dispatch. With SMS, external applications can send user requested content such as flight updates.

Until now, the interfaces for such functions have either been proprietary, or specific to that function. However, there are now interfaces that span multiple functions using a consistent set of programming methods. One set is the Parlay X Web Services, a set of functions specified through a joint project of the Parlay Group, the European Telecommunications Standards Institute (ETSI) and 3GPP. The Open Mobile Alliance (OMA) now manages the Parlay X specifications. Parlay X Web Services include support for location and SMS, as well as many other functions with which developers will be able to build innovative applications.

Table 16.4 summarizes the available Parlay X specifications. Operators are beginning to selectively deploy these functions. The advantage of this approach is that developers can build applications that are compatible with multiple operator networks.

A related project is GSMA OneAPI, a GSM Association project to also define network interfaces, but that prioritizes implementation based on expected market demand. OneAPI defines a simplified Web service for most functions that is essentially a subset of the related Parlay X Web service. It also defines a REST (Representational State Transfer) interface for most functions as an alternative to using the Web service. RESTful interfaces are simpler for developers to work with and experiment with than Web services.

Regardless of whether operators deploy with Parlay X or OneAPI, these are mainstream interfaces that will open wireless networks to thousands of Internet programmers who will be able to build applications that leverage the latent information and capabilities of wireless networks.

16.11 MOBILE APPLICATION ARCHITECTURES

Many applications used over wireless connections will be the same as those used over the Internet with desktop/laptop PCs. An increasing number of applications, however, will be developed specifically for mobile devices. This can be a challenge for developers, because there are a number of different mobile platforms now available including Android, Apple iPhone, LiMo, Palm Pre, RIM BlackBerry, Symbian and Windows Mobile. Unlike the desktop market, the mobile device market has become quite fragmented. Each of the device platforms comes with its own application development environment, and developers must face a learning curve to become adept at programming for any specific platform. Some developers may be content targeting specific platforms. Others, however, may need their applications to operate across multiple platforms.

Fortunately, there are various developments that address the fragmentation challenge.

These include:

- *Mobile Middleware*— These are software infrastructures that consist of a client component that operates on the mobile device, and a server component that acts as a proxy for the client. Vendors provide tools with which developers can develop an application in a platform-neutral manner, and which then operates on multiple device types. Mobile middleware is mostly used for business applications.
- *Mobile Web 2.0*— Mobile browsers are adopting many of the same sophisticated capabilities as desktop browsers. Combined with networks that have higher throughputs and lower latency, an increasing number of applications can be Web hosted, making the applications available from diverse platforms. Mobile Web 2.0 technologies include items such as Ajax, offline operation, video capabilities, fast JavaScript execution, and mashups (combining data from multiple Web sources). Cloud computing, enabled by Mobile Web 2.0, will play as important a role for mobile systems as for desktops.
- *Java Developments*— Though Java itself has presented a challenge through inconsistent implementation on devices, there are new capabilities that will result in more consistent, as well as more powerful, device execution environments. Examples include Mobile Service Architecture (MSA) for predictable capability and Mobile Information Device Profile 3 for multi-tasking.

16.12 BROADBAND-WIRELESS DEPLOYMENT CONSIDERATIONS

Much of the debate in the wireless industry is on the merits of different radio technologies, yet other factors are equally important in determining the services and capabilities of a wireless network. These factors include the amount of spectrum available, backhaul, and network topology.

Spectrum has always been a major consideration for deploying any wireless network, but it is particularly important when looking at high-performance broadband systems. HSPA and HSPA+ can deliver high throughput rates on the downlink and uplink with low latency in 5 MHz channels when deployed in single frequency (1/1) reuse. By this, we mean that every cell sector (typically three per cell) in every cell uses the same radio channel(s).

As previously discussed, an OFDMA approach in a 5 MHz radio channel yields only a small performance advantage. To achieve higher data rates requires wider radio channels, such as 10 or 20 MHz wide channels, in combination with emerging OFDMA radio technologies. Very few operators today, however, have access to this much spectrum. It was challenging enough for

GSM operators to obtain UMTS spectrum. If delivering very high data rates is the objective, then the system must minimize interference. This result is best achieved by employing looser reuse, such as having every sector use only one-third of the available radio channels (1/3 reuse). The 10 MHz radio channel could now demand as much as 30 MHz of available spectrum.

Backhaul is another factor. As the throughput of the radio link increases, the circuits connecting the cell sites to the core network must be able to handle the increased load. With many cell sites today serviced by just a small number of T1/E1 circuits, each able to carry only 1.5/2.0 Mbps, operators will have to significantly upgrade backhaul capacity to obtain the full benefit of next-generation wireless technologies. An OFDMA system with 1.5 bps per hertz (Hz) of spectral efficiency in 10 MHz on three sectors has up to 45 Mbps average cell throughput.

Additionally, any technology's ability to reach its peak spectrum efficiency is somewhat contingent on the system's ability to reach the instantaneous peak data rates allowed by that technology. For example, a system claiming spectrum efficiency of 1.5 bps/Hz (as described above) might rely on the ability to reach 100 Mbps instantaneously to achieve this level of spectrum efficiency. Any constraint on the transport system below 100 Mbps will restrict the range of achievable throughput and, in turn, impact the spectral efficiency of the system.

The mismatch between backhaul capabilities and radio performance in some networks is one reason that user rates on some 3G systems are lower than theoretical rates. Operators are actively enhancing their backhaul approaches, and there are many available and emerging wireline technologies such as VDSL and optical Ethernet, as well as competitive point-to-point microwave systems that make this possible.

Finally, the overall network topology also plays an important role, especially with respect to latency. Low latency is critical to achieving very high data rates, because of the way it affects TCP/IP traffic. How traffic routes through the core network—how many hops and nodes it must pass through—can influence the overall performance of the network. One way to increase performance is by using flatter architectures, meaning a less hierarchical network with more direct routing from mobile device to end system. The core EPC/SAE network for 3GPP LTE emphasizes just such a flatter architecture.

In summary, it can be misleading to say that one wireless technology outperforms another without a full understanding of how that technology will be deployed in a complete system that also takes spectrum into account.

16.13 FEATURE AND NETWORK ROADMAP

GSM operators first enhanced their networks to support data capability through the addition of GPRS infrastructure with the ability to use existing cell sites, transceivers, and interconnection facilities. Since installing GPRS, GSM operators have largely upgraded data service to EDGE, and any new GSM network includes EDGE capability.

Operators have deployed UMTS-HSPA worldwide. Although UMTS involves a new radio-access network, several factors facilitate deployment. First, most UMTS cell sites can be collocated in GSM cell sites enabled by multi-radio cabinets that can accommodate

GSM/EDGE, as well as UMTS equipment. Second, much of the GSM/GPRS core network can be used. This means that all core-network elements above the Serving GPRS Support Node (SGSN) and Mobile Switching Center (MSC)—the Gateway GPRS Support Node (GGSN), the Home Location Register (HLR), billing and subscriber administration systems, service platforms, and so forth—need, at most, a software upgrade to support 3G UMTS-HSPA. And while early 3G deployment used separate 2G/3G SGSNs and MSCs, all-new MSC and/or SGSN products are capable of supporting both GSM and UMTS-HSPA radio-access networks. Similarly, new HSPA equipment will be upgradeable to LTE through a software upgrade.

New features such as HSDPA, HSUPA, and MBMS are being designed so that the same zIn other words, a network supporting Release 5 features (for example, HSDPA) can support Release 99, Release 5, and Release 6 terminals (for example, HSUPA) operating in a Release 5 mode. Alternatively, a network supporting Release 6 features can support Release 99, Release 5, and Release 6 terminals. This flexibility assures the maximum degree of forward- and backward- compatibility. Note also that most UMTS terminals today support GSM, thus facilitating use across large coverage areas and multiple networks.

Once deployed, operators can minimize the costs of managing GSM/EDGE and UMTS networks, because these networks share many of the same aspects including:

- Packet-data architecture
- Cell sites
- Antenna systems
- Backhaul circuits
- Subscriber account management
- Service platforms

Users largely don't even need to know to what type of network they are connected, because their multimode GSM-HSPA devices can seamlessly hand off between networks.

The changes being planned for the core network are another aspect of evolution. Here, the intent is to reduce the number of nodes that packets must traverse. This will result in both reduced deployment costs and reduced latency. The key enabling technology is EPC/SAE, which is described in detail later in this paper.

The upgrade to LTE will be relatively straightforward, with new LTE infrastructure having the ability to reuse a significant amount of the UMTS-HSPA cell site and base station including using the same shelter, tower, antennas, power supply and climate control. Different vendors have different so-called "zero-footprint" solutions allowing operators to use empty space to enable re-use of existing sites without the need for any new floor space.

An operator can add LTE capability simply by adding an LTE baseband card. New multi-standard radio units (HSPA and LTE), as well as LTE-only baseband cards, are mechanically compatible with older building practices, so that operators can use empty space in an old base station for LTE baseband cards, thus enabling re-use of existing sites without the need for any new floor space, as mentioned previously.

Base station equipment is available for many bands including the 1.7/2.1 GHz AWS band and the recently auctioned 700 MHz bands in the US. Vendors and operators are planning LTE commercial deployments beginning in 2010.

On the device side, multi-mode chipsets will enable devices to easily operate across UMTS and LTE networks. For example, one chipset vendor has announced a series of chips that support the following combination of technologies: UMTS, HSPA+ and LTE; EV-DO Rev B; and UMTS, HSPA+, EV-DO Rev B and LTE.[33]

One important and interesting aspect of technology deployment is that an advanced technology such as LTE enables operators to upgrade prior technologies, such as HSPA.

Examples include:

- *VoIP for HSPA*— Since LTE uses an IP core, once it is deployed, supporting voice on HSPA via VoIP will be a much simpler task as it can share the same core IP network as LTE.
- *Device processing power*— Supporting the high throughput rates with LTE (e.g., 50 Mbps or higher) will provide sufficient processing in the device to also support very high HSPA rates (e.g., 30 Mbps or higher).

16.14 ROLLOUT OF EDGE/HSPA/LTE FEATURES OVER TIME

Table 16.4: Expected UMTS/LTE Feature and Capability Availability

Year	*Features*
2009	Networks and devices capable of Release 7 HSPA+, including MIMO, boosting HSPA peak speeds to 28 Mbps Enhanced IMS-based services (for example, integrated voice/ multimedia /presence/location)
2010	Evolved EDGE capabilities available to significantly increase EDGE throughput rates HSPA+ peak speeds further increased to peak rates of 42 Mbps based on Release 8 LTE introduced for next-generation throughput performance using 2×2 MIMO Advanced core architectures available through EPC/SAE, primarily for LTE but also for HSPA+, providing benefits such as integration of multiple network types and flatter architectures for better latency performance Most new services implemented in the packet domain over HSPA+ and LTE
2011 and later	LTE enhancements such as 4×2 MIMO and 4×4 MIMO LTE-Advanced specifications completed
2012	LTE-Advanced potentially deployed in initial stages

Over time, the separate GSM/EDGE Access Network (GERAN), UMTS Access Network (UTRAN), and core-infrastructure elements will undergo consolidation, thus lowering total network cost and improving integrated operation of the separate access networks. For actual users with multimode devices, the networks they access will be largely transparent. Today, nearly all UMTS phones and modems support GSM /EDGE.

16.15 ADVANCES IN HSPA AND LTE

Figure 16.5 presents the continuing advances in HSPA and LTE, plotted over time, showing an approximate doubling of throughput per year.

Despite rapid UMTS deployment, market momentum means that even by the end of the decade, most worldwide subscribers will still be using GSM. By then, however, most new subscribers will be taking advantage of UMTS. Only over many years, as subscribers upgrade their equipment, will most network usage migrate to UMTS. Similarly, even as operators start to deploy LTE networks at the end of this decade and the beginning of the next, it will probably be the middle of the next decade before a large percentage of subscribers are actually using LTE. During these years, most networks and devices will be tri-mode—supporting GSM, UMTS, and LTE. The history of wireless-network deployment provides a useful perspective. GSM, which in 2009 is still growing its subscriber base, was specified in 1990 with initial networks deployed in 1991. The UMTS Task Force established itself in 1995, Release 99 specifications were completed in 2000, and HSPA+ specifications were completed in 2007. Although it's been more than a decade since work began on the technology, only now is UMTS deployment and adoption starting to surge.

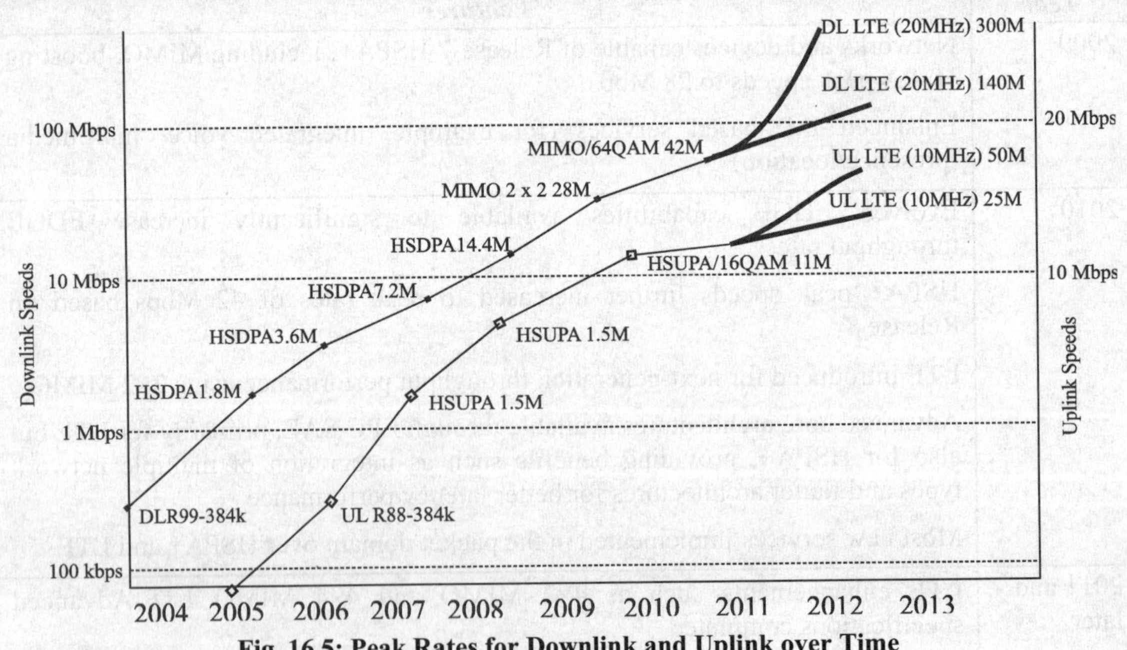

Fig. 16.5: Peak Rates for Downlink and Uplink over Time

16.16 ADOPTION OF TECHNOLOGIES

Figure 16.5 shows the relative adoption of technologies over a multi-decadal period and the length of time it takes for any new technology to be adopted widely on a global basis.

One option for GSM operators that have not yet committed to UMTS, and do not have an immediate pressing need to do so, is to migrate directly from GSM/EDGE or Evolved EDGE to LTE with networks and devices supporting dual-mode GSM-EDGE/LTE operation.

16.17 DEPLOYMENT SCENARIOS

Table 16.5

	Downlink		***Uplink***	
	Peak Net work Speed	***Peak and/ or Typical User Rate***	***Peak Network Speed***	***Peak and/ or Typical User Rate***
		peak 700 kbps to 1.7 Mbps typical		peak 500 kbps to 1.2 Mbps typical
HSPA Current Implementation	7.2 Mbps		5.76 Mbps	
HSPA	14.4 Mbps		5.76 Mbps	
HSPA+ (DL 64 QAM, UL 16 QAM)	21.6 Mbps	1.5 Mbps to 7 Mbps 13 Mbps peak	11.5 Mbps	1 Mbps to 4 Mbps
HSPA+ (2×2 MIMO, DL 16 QAM, UL 16 QAM)	28 Mbps		11.5 Mbps	
HSPA+ (2×2 MI MO, DL 64 QAM,UL 16 QAM)	42 Mbps		11.5 Mbps	
HSPA+ (2×2 MI MO. DL 64 QAM, UL 16 QAM, Dual Carrier)	84 Mbps		23 Mbps	
LTE (2×2 MIMO)	173 Mbps	4 Mbps to 24 Mbps (in 2 × 20 MHz)	58 Mbps	
LTE (4×4 MIMO)	326 Mbps		86 Mbps	
CDMA2000 1 XRTT	153 kbps	130 kbps peak	153 kbps	130 kbps peak
CDMA2000 1XRTT	307 kbps		307 kbps	
CDMA2000 EV-DO Rel 0	2.4 Mbps	> 1 Mbps peak	153 kbps	150 kbps peak
CDMA20QO EV-DO Rev A	3.1 Mbps	> 1 5 Mbps	1.8 Mbps	> 1 Mbps

There are many different scenarios that operators will use to migrate from their current networks to future technologies such as LTE. Figure 16.9 presents various scenarios including operators who today are using CDMA2000, UMTS, GSM and WiMAX. For example, as shown in the first bar, a CMDA2000 operator in scenario A could in the medium term deploy a combination of 1xRTT, EV-DO Rev A/B and LTE and, in the long term, could migrate EV-DO data traffic to LTE. In scenario B, a CDMA2000 operator with just 1xRTT could introduce LTE as a broadband service and, in the long term, could migrate 1xRTT users to LTE including voice service.

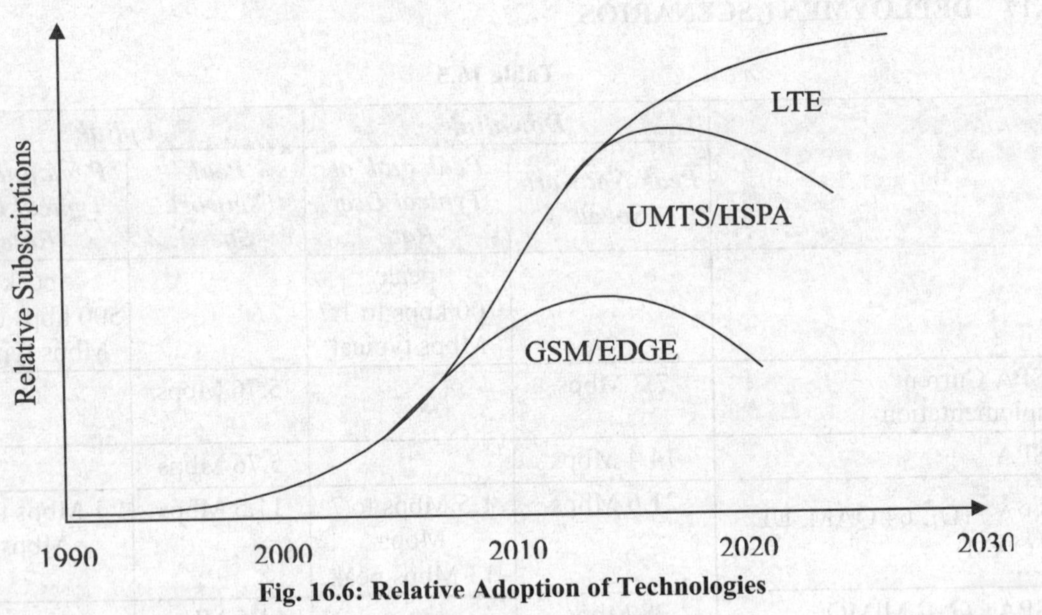

Fig. 16.6: Relative Adoption of Technologies

16.18 LATENCY

Just as important as throughput is network latency, defined as the round-trip time it takes data to traverse the network. Each successive data technology from GPRS forward reduces latency, with HSDPA networks having latency as low as 70 milliseconds (msec). HSUPA brings latency down even further, as will 3GPP LTE. Ongoing improvements in each technology mean all these values will go down as vendors and operators fine tune their systems.

16.19 MIGRATION OPTIONS

3GPP and 3GPP2 both have specified detailed migration options for current 3G systems (UMTS-HSPA and EV-DO) to LTE. Due to economies of scale for infrastructure and devices, 3GPP operators are likely to have a competitive cost advantage over 3GPP2 operators.

Table 16.6: Data Rates

	Downlink		*Uplink*	
	Peak Network Speed	***Peak and/ or Typical User Rate***	***Peak Network Speed***	***Peak and/or Typical User Rate***
		peak 600 kbps to 1.4 Mbps typical[60]		peak 300 to 500 kbps typical
CDMA2000 EV-DO Rev B (3 radio channels MHz)	9.3 Mbps		5.4 Mbps	
CDMA2000 EV-DO Rev B Theoretical (1 5 radio channels)	73.5 Mbps		27 Mbps	
WiMAX Release 1 .0 (1 0 MHz TDD, DL/ UL=3, 2×2 MIMO)	46 Mbps	2 to 4 Mbps average	4 Mbps	
WiMAX Release 1 .5	TBD		TBD	
IEEE 802.1 6m	TBD		TBD	

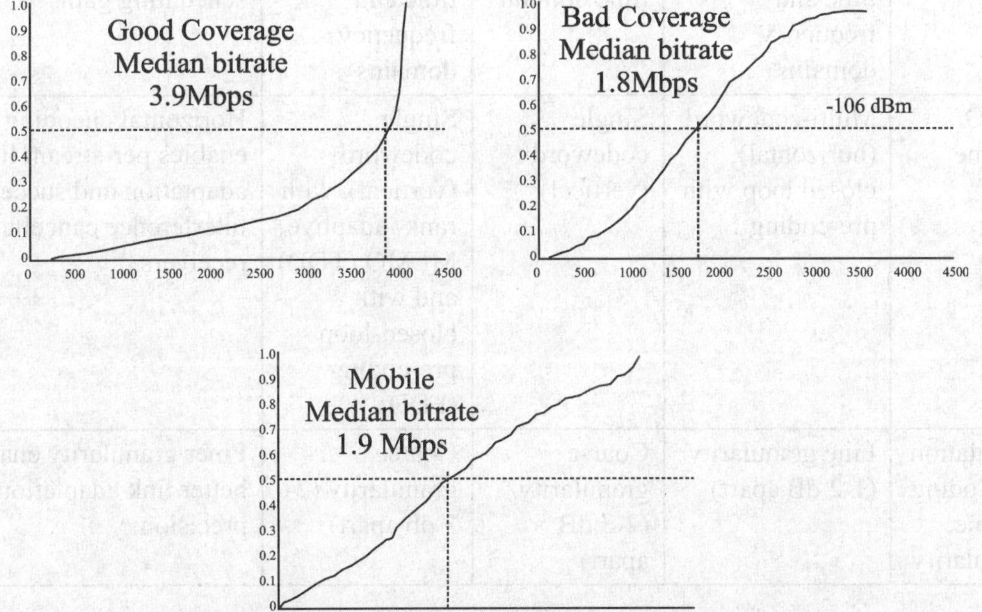

Fig. 16.7: HSDPA Performance of a 7.2Mbps Device in a Commercial Network

Table 16.7: LTE and WiMAX Features

Feature	*LTE*	*WiMAX Release 1.0*	*WiMAX Release 1.5*	*I m pact*
Multiple Access	OFDM in downlink. Discrete Fourier Transform (DFT)-spread OFDM in uplink	OFDM in downlink and uplink	OFDM in downlink and uplink	DFT-spread OFDM reduces the peak-to-average power ratio and reduces terminal complexity, requires one-tap equalizer in base station receiver.
Uplink Power Control	Fractional path-loss compensation	Full path-loss compensation	Full path-loss compensation	Fractional path-loss compensation enables flexible tradeoff between average and cell-edge data rates
Scheduling	Channel dependent in time and frequency domains	Channel dependent in time domain	Channel dependent in time and frequency domains	Access to the frequency domain yields larger scheduling gains
MIMO Scheme	Multi-codeword (horizontal), closed loop with pre-coding	Single codeword (vertical)	Single codeword (vertical), with rank- adaptive MEMO (TDD) and with closed-loop pre-coding (FDD)	Horizontal encoding enables per-stream link adaptation and successive interference cancellation receivers.
Modulation and Coding Scheme Granularity	Fine granularity (1-2 dB apart)	Coarse granularity (2-3 dB apart)	Coarse granularity (2-3 db apart)	Finer granularity enables better link adaptation precision.

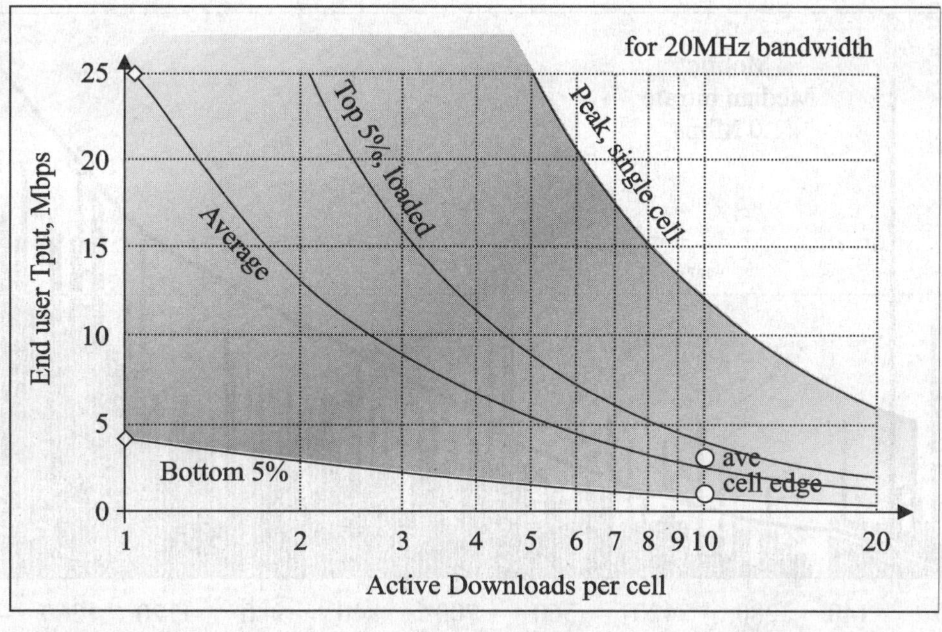

Fig. 16.8: LTE Actual Throughput Rates based on Conditions

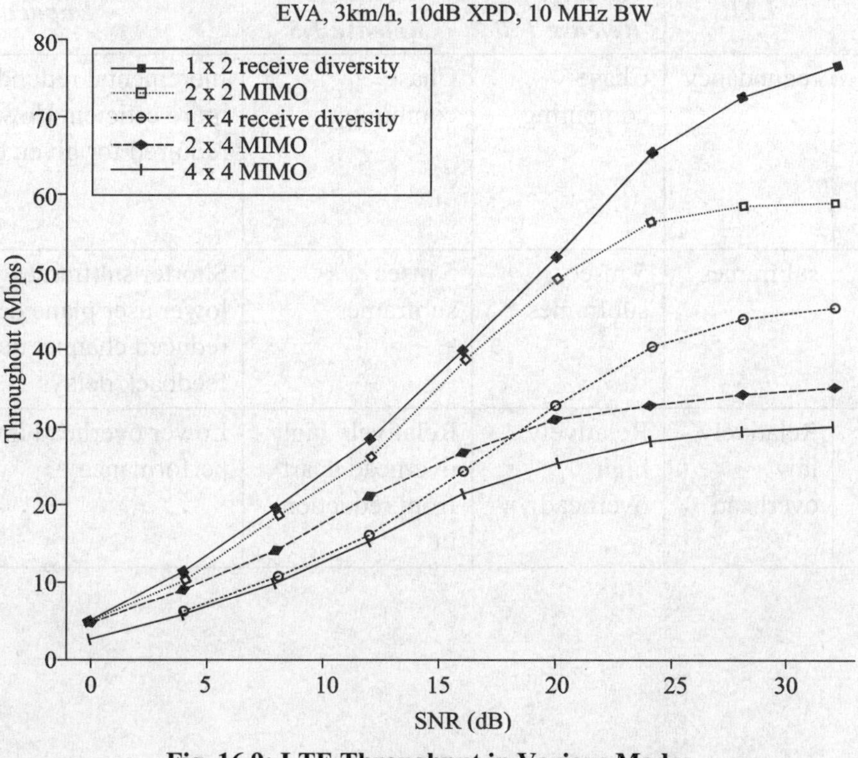

EVA, 3km/h, 10dB XPD, 10 MHz BW

1 x 2 receive diversity
2 x 2 MIMO
1 x 4 receive diversity
2 x 4 MIMO
4 x 4 MIMO

Throughout (Mbps)

SNR (dB)

Fig. 16.9: LTE Throughput in Various Modes

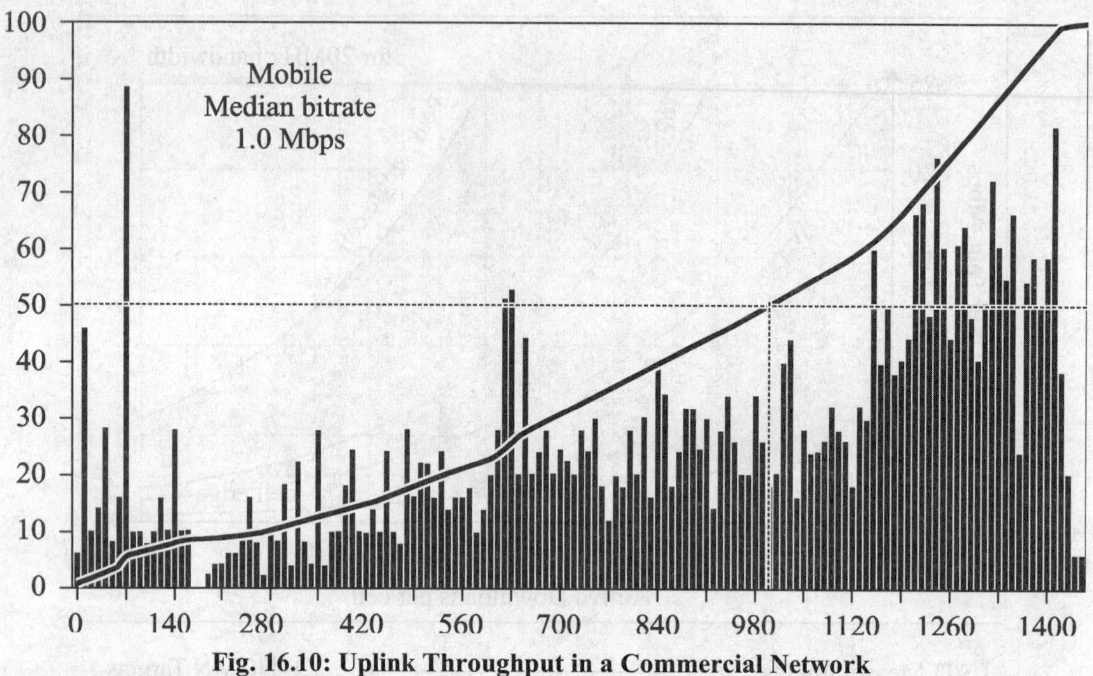

Fig. 16.10: Uplink Throughput in a Commercial Network

Table 16.8: Compares the Uplink Spectral Efficiency of the Different Systems

Feature	*LTE*	*WiMAX Release 1 .0*	*WiMAX Release 1.5*	*Impact*
Hybrid Automatic Repeat Request (ARQ)	redundancy	Chase combining	Chase combining	Incremental redundancy is more efficient (lower SNR required for given error
Duration	subframes	5 msec subframes	5 msec subframes	Shorter subframes yield lower user plane delay and reduced channel quality feedback delays
Overhead / Control Channel Efficiency	Relatively low overhead	Relatively high overhead	Relatively high overhead apart from reduction in	Lower overhead improves performance

Table 16.9: Throughput Performance of Different Wireless Technologies

	Downlink		***Uplink***	
	Peak Network Speed	***Peak and/ or Typical User Rate***	***Peak Network Speed***	***Peak and/or Typical User Rate***
EDGE (type 2 MS)	473.6 kbps		473.6 kbps	
EDGE (type 1 MS) (Practical Terminal)	236.8 kbps	200 kbps peak 70 to 135 kbps typical	236 8 kbps	200 kbps peak 70 to 135 kbps typical
Evolved EDGE (type 1 MS)	11 84 kbps	1 Mbps peak 350 to 700 kbps typical expected (Dual Carrier)	473.6 kbps	400 kbps peak 150 to 300 kbps typical expected
Evolved EDGE (type 2 MS)	1894.4S" kbps		947.2 kbps	
UMTS WCDMA Release 99	2.04S Mbps		768 kbps	
UMTS WCDMA Release 99 (Practical Terminal)	384 kbps	350 kbps peak 200 to 300 kbps typical	384 kbps	350 kbps peak 200 to 300 kbps typical
HSDPA Initial Devices (2006)	1.8 Mbps	> 1 Mbps peak	384 kbps	350 kbps peak
HSDPA	14.4 Mbps		384 kbps	
HSPA Initial implementation	7.2 Mbps	> 5 Mbps	2 Mbps	> 1.5 Mbps

Review Questions

1. What are the data rates stipulated for 3G for different environments?
2. List out various releases of 3GPP in a progressive order.
3. List out frequency bands defined for TDD in 3GPP.
4. Write a note on spectral efficiency of LTE system and the uplink spectral efficiency.
5. What are the main features of IMS?
6. Write a note on Wireless Broadband.
7. Explain how upgradation to LTE is cost effective and inexpensive.
8. What is Latency, explain how that is minimised in LTE?

17 WIRELESS NETWORKS - COMPETING TECHNOLOGIES

17.1 INTRODUCTION

Although GSM-HSPA networks are dominating global cellular-technology deployments, operators are deploying other wireless technologies to serve both wide and local areas. This chapter looks at the relationship between GSM/UMTS/LTE and some of these other technologies.

17.2 CDMA2000

CDMA2000, consisting principally of 1xRTT and One Carrier-Evolved, Data-Optimized (1xEV-DO) versions, is the other major cellular technology deployed in many parts of the world. 1xRTT is currently the most widely deployed CDMA2000 version. A number of operators have deployed or are deploying 1xEV-DO where a radio carrier is dedicated to high-speed data functions. In June 2009, there were 106 EV-DO Rel. 0 networks and 62 EV-DO Rev. A networks deployed worldwide.

Currently deployed network versions are based on either Rel. 0 or Rev. A radio-interface specifications. EV-DO Rev. A incorporates a more efficient uplink, which has spectral efficiency similar to that of HSUPA. Operators started to make EV-DO Rev. A system which is commercially available in 2007.

EV-DO uses many of the same techniques for optimizing spectral efficiency as HSPA including higher order modulation, efficient scheduling, turbo-coding, and adaptive modulation and coding. For these reasons, it achieves spectral efficiency that is virtually the same as HSPA. The 1x technologies operate in the 1.25 MHz radio channels, compared to the 5 MHz channels UMTS uses, resulting in lower theoretical peak rates, although average throughputs for high level network loading are similar. Under low- to medium-load conditions, because of the lower peak achievable data rates, EV-DO or EV- DO Rev. A achieves a lower typical performance level than HSPA. Operators have quoted 400 to 700 kilobits per second (kbps) typical downlink throughput for EV-DO Rev. 0 and between 600 kbps and 1.4 Mbps for EV-DO Rev. A.

One challenge for EV-DO operators is that they cannot dynamically allocate their entire spectral resources between voice and high-speed data functions. The EV-DO channel is not available for circuit-switched voice, and the 1xRTT channels offer only medium- speed data. In the current stage of the market, in which data only constitutes a small percentage of total network traffic, this is not a key issue. But as data usage expands, this limitation will cause suboptimal use of radio resources. Figure 12 illustrates this severe limitation. Another limitation of using a separate channel for EV-DO data services is that it currently prevents users from engaging in simultaneous voice and high-speed data services, whereas this is possible with UMTS and

HSPA. Many users enjoy having a tethered data connection from their laptop—by using Bluetooth, for example—and being able to initiate and receive phone calls while maintaining their data sessions.

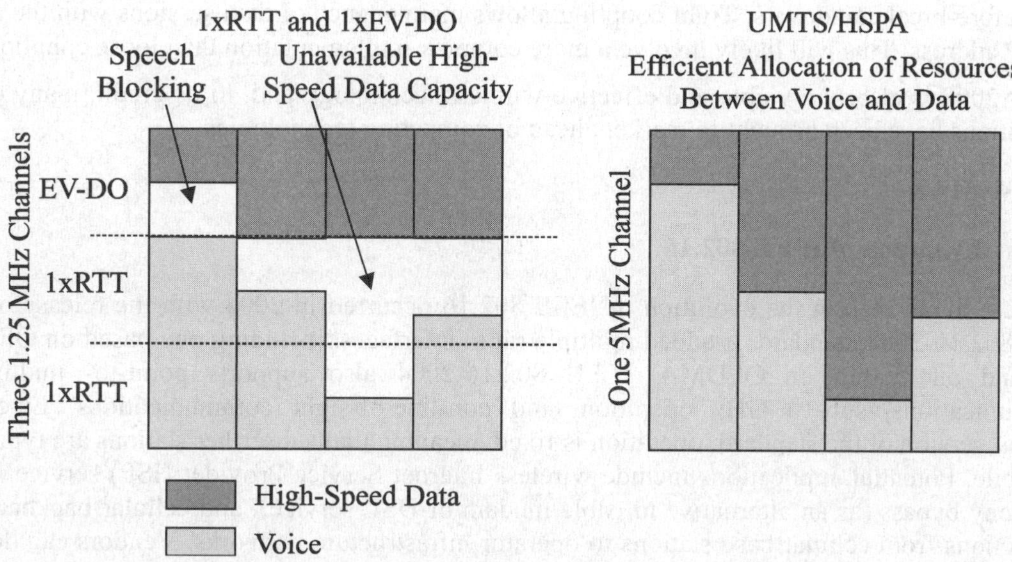

Fig. 17.1: Radio Resource Management 1 X RTT / 1 X EV-DO Versus UMTS-HSPA

EV-DO will eventually provide voice service using VoIP protocols through EV-DO Rev. A, which includes a higher speed uplink, QoS mechanisms in the network, and protocol optimizations to reduce packet overhead, as well as addressing problems such as jitter.

Even then, however, operators will face difficult choices: How many radio channels at each base station should be made available for 1xRTT to support legacy terminals versus how many radio channels should be allocated to EV-DO. In contrast, UMTS allows both circuit-switched and packet-switched traffic to occupy the same radio channel, where the amount of power each uses can be dynamically adjusted. This makes it simple to migrate users over time from circuit-switched voice to packet-switched voice.

Beyond Rev. A, 3GPP2 has defined EV-DO Rev. B, which can combine up to 15 1.25 MHz radio channels in 20 MHz—significantly boosting peak theoretical rates to 73.5 Mbps. More likely, an operator would combine three radio channels in 5 MHz. Such an approach by itself does not necessarily increase overall capacity, but it does offer users higher peak-data rates. Other enhancements are planned for EV-DO, including femtocell support, MIMO and 64 QAM in the downlink, and 16 QAM in the uplink. There are also a number of planned improvements for CDMA2000 1xRTT that will result in increased voice capacity.

3GPP2 had defined an OFDM-based technology called Ultra Mobile Broadband (UMB), with performance characteristics similar to LTE. This work item, however, has been terminated as the standard had no commercial support, and many CDMA2000 operators including Verizon have announced their intentions to migrate to LTE. 3GPP2 has defined technical means to integrate CDMA2000 networks with LTE along two available approaches:

1. *Loose coupling*— This involves little or no inter-system functionality, and resources are released in the source system prior to handover execution.

2. *Tight coupling*— The two systems intercommunicate with network-controlled make-before-break handovers. Tight coupling allows maintenance of data sessions with the same IP address. This will likely involve a more complex implementation than loose coupling.

CDMA2000 is clearly a viable and effective wireless technology and, to its credit, many of its innovations have been brought to market ahead of competing technologies.

17.3 WiMAX

17.3.1 Evolution of IEEE 802.16

The next major step in the evolution of IEEE 802.16 occurred in 2004 with the release of the IEEE 802.16-2004 standard. It added multiple radio interfaces, including one based on OFDM-256 and one based on OFDMA. IEEE 802.16-2004 also supports point-to- multipoint communications, sub-10 GHz operation, and non-line-of-sight communications. Like the original version of the standard, operation is fixed, meaning that subscriber stations are typically immobile. Potential applications include wireless Internet Service Provider (ISP) service, local telephony bypass (as an alternative to cable modem or DSL service), and cellular backhaul for connections from cellular base stations to operator infrastructure networks. Vendors can design equipment for either licensed or unlicensed bands.

Vendors are now delivering IEEE 802.16-2004-certified equipment. This standard does not compete directly with cellular-data and private Wi-Fi networks; thus, it can provide complementary services. In addition to operator-hosted access solutions, private entities such as municipal governments, universities, and corporations will be able to use this version of WiMAX in unlicensed bands (for example, 5.8 GHz) for local connectivity, although there has been little or no development in this area.

The IEEE has also completed a mobile-broadband standard—IEEE 802.16e-2005—that adds mobility capabilities including support for radio operation while mobile, handovers across base stations, and handovers across operators. Unlike IEEE 802.16-2004, which operates in both licensed and unlicensed bands, IEEE 802.16e-2005 (referred to as mobile WiMAX) makes the most sense in licensed bands. Operators have begun limited mobile WiMAX network deployments in 2009. Current WiMAX profiles emphasize TDD operation. Mobile WiMAX networks are not backward-compatible with IEEE 802.16-2004 networks.

17.3.2 Version 1, 1.5 and 2.0

Initial mobile WiMAX networks will be deployed using 2X2 MIMO, TDD and 10 MHz radio channels in a profile defined by the WiMAX Forum known as WiMAX Wave 2 or, more formally, as WiMAX System Profile 1.0. Beyond Release 1.0, the WiMAX Forum has defined a new profile called WiMAX Release 1.5 with product certification expected by the end of 2009. Mobile WiMAX release 1.5 includes various refinements intended to improve efficiency and performance and could be available for deployment in a similar timeframe as LTE.

Release 1.5 enhancements include MAC overhead reductions for VoIP (persistent scheduling), handover optimizations, load balancing, location-based services support, FDD operation, 64 QAM in the uplink, downlink adaptive modulation and coding, closed- loop MIMO (FDD mode only), and uplink MIMO. A subsequent version, Mobile WiMAX 2.0, will be designed to address the performance requirements being developed in the ITU IMT-Advanced Project and will be standardized in a new IEEE standard, IEEE 802.16m. According to Sprint Nextel, IEEE 802.16m will be available in 2011. WiMAX has been introduced in the earlier chapters with more details.

WiMAX employs many of the same mechanisms as HSPA to maximize throughput and spectral efficiency, including high-order modulation, efficient coding, adaptive modulation and coding, and Hybrid Automatic Repeat Request (HARQ). The principal difference from HSPA is IEEE 802.16e-2005's use of OFDMA. As discussed in the section "Technical Approaches (TDMA, CDMA, OFDMA)" above, OFDM provides a potential implementation advantage for wide radio channels (for example, 10 to 20 MHz). In 5 to 10 MHz radio channels, there is no evidence indicating that WiMAX will have any performance advantage compared to HSPA+.

It should be noted, however, that IEEE 802.16e-2005 contains some aspects that may limit its performance, particularly in scenarios in which a sector contains a large number of mobile users. The performance of the MAC layer is inefficient when scheduling large numbers of users, and some aspects—such as power control of the mobile station—are provided using MAC signaling messages rather than the fast power control used in WCDMA and other technologies. Thus, while WiMAX uses OFDMA, the performance will likely be somewhat less than HSPA due to increased overhead and other design issues.

WiMAX is a new powerful technical innovation to bridge the digital divide. WiMAX is a broadband wireless technology that is largely supported by the computer and the telecom industry, cost-effective and standard base. It is engineered to deliver the latest type of ubiquitous fixed and mobile services such as VoIP, Information Technology and Video at very low cost. WiMAX systems are able to cover a large geographical area, up to 50 km and to deliver significant bandwidth to end-users up to 72 Mbps. This chapter intends to highlight some points that make WiMAX the most appropriate technology to reduce digital divide.

WiMAX can be summarized as follows:

- WiMAX stands for Worldwide Interoperability for Microwave Access.
- WiMAX/IEEE 802.16 is a global standard-based technology for Broadband Wireless Access
- WiMAX is Equivalent to Wi-Fi Alliance for IEEE 802.11
- WiMAX forum will certify Interoperability of IEEE 802.16 and ETSI HiperMAN

17.3.3 Broadband ICT Access

Compared with other wired solution such as ADSL, or any other wireless or satellite system, WiMAX based access networks will enable operators and service providers to cost-effectively reach millions of new potential customers providing them with broadband ICTs access. This is even truer for developing countries and rural areas for which the cost/profitability and the demand factors are essential. This obviously includes adequate coverage, reliability, performances (throughput), capacity and applications.

Ease of installation is one of the key issues to lower deployment costs in developing countries or rural areas. In rural areas, the consequences of the long distances from the core network access point and the scattered location of villages, farms... in the countryside makes any deployment very costly. In developing countries, the lack of main infrastructure (electricity, roads.), and environmental condition (temperature, humidity.) adds on the difficulty. Thanks to the NLOS/LOS coverage advantage, the operator/service provider can easily plans a 95% predictability coverage ensuring high installation success rates and controls deployment costs.

A quicker and simpler installation with a much greater rate of success means operators spend less money rolling out their networks. WiMAX NLOS capability also allows indoors self install CPEs within several Km radius.

Even more important than the range limitation, the coverage, i.e. the capability to reach any potential customer within the base station covering area, is essential for the operator/service provider. While many currently available wireless broadband solutions can only provide Line-Of-Site (LOS) coverage, WiMAX, thanks to its OFDM technology, has been optimized to provide excellent Non-Line-Of- Site (NLOS) coverage (up to 15 Km around the base station) and long range transmission up to 50Km in LOS conditions. Combining both LOS and NLOS coverage, WiMAX is the ideal solution for getting the exact requested coverage in the most economical way. Wireless is more flexible and thus easier to deploy according to the market demand (Capex follows the needs).Although most of the existing wireless technologies suffer from limited range and coverage (usually a few hundred meters around the base station) resulting in very costly combination of technologies (wired and/or wireless), WiMAX technology benefits of a wide coverage and can be deployed as a Point MultiPoint last mile. connection but also as part of the backhaul to the PSTN and Internet access points.

The WiMAX role in an access network is illustrated in following scheme. With potential range of 30 to 50 kilometers in Line Of Site (LOS) conditions, WiMAX offer a huge improvement over all existing broadband wireless technology. With the addition of the capability for the operator to adapt its network configuration to his marketing strategy (coverage, throughput, services, and grade of service) WiMAX provides a very powerful solution to meet the operators objective for profitability.

17.3.4 A Multi-Application Technology

Following the normal trend of digitalization and packet transmission and switching, WiMAX uses the Internet protocol and thus supports all multimedia services from Voice over IP (VoIP) to high speed internet and video transmission. WiMAX allows service providers to offer all the latest generation of services and beyond, thanks to a throughput up to tens of Mbps. With regard to the potential users, this means that WiMAX have the capacity to deliver services from households to SME.s, SOHO.s, Cybercafés, Multimedia Telecentres, Schools and Hospital.

17.3.5 The Worldwide Standardization Benefits

Developed and supported by the WiMAX forum (more than 300 members), WiMAX will become the worldwide technology based standard for broadband and will guaranty interoperability (i.e. multivendor CPEs), reliability and evolving technology, but also, thanks to high volumes and integration, will ensure equipments with very low cost. With CPEs under 100 $ as one of the first objective, business model can easily be profitable even in developing countries.

17.3.6 The Spectrum Flexibility

In line with the objective to become the worldwide standard based technology for broadband, WiMAX will use a single radio covering all licensed and unlicensed frequency bands allocated by the ITU for such services i.e.:

- The two licensed bands 3.3-3.8 GHz and 2.3-2.7 GHz
- One license exempt band 5.725-5.85 GHz.

In addition to the flexibility offered to address all national spectrum situations, this single radio, thanks to the volume effect, will makes base stations and customer premises equipment costs very attractive

17.3.7 The Financial Solution

WiMAX technology flexibility allows a great variety of services, type of users and progressive deployment in any geographical locations. This means that the same network can support private and public services and thus favor financial partnerships.

17.3.8 A Solution That Allows Strong Competition

WiMAX is part of an Internet ecosystem. It is cost effective for a few or for a million subscribers, it is easy to deploy, to install, it is transparent and secured and thus allows strong healthy dynamic competition among different types of service providers. It is an adequate solution for ILEC, Wireless Internet Service Providers, Local community, Government. Allowing competition in developing country is the fastest way to provide services in unserved areas.

17.3.9 Fixed and Mobile Access and More

The WiMAX networks will be able to support fixed, nomadic, portable and mobile wireless broadband connectivity on the same network.

Looking back to the barriers, WiMAX appears clearly as the solution to favor the broadband access in developing countries with the following advantages, viz.,. Deployment cost, Low Demand, Subscriber loop length, Lack of cost effective equipment Regulatory issues and Other Barriers like Wireless flexibility, LOS+NLOS coverage, OFDM modulation, WiMAX is a new powerful broadband wireless technology aiming at providing a universal ubiquitous and equitable and affordable access to ICTs infrastructure and services and thus highly contributing to bridge the Digital Divide WiMAX has emerged as a potential alternative to cellular technology for wide-area wireless networks. Based on OFDMA and recently accepted by the

International Telecommunications Union (ITU) as an IMT-2000 (3G technology) under the name OFDMA TDD WMAN (Wireless Metropolitan Area Network), WiMAX is trying to challenge existing wireless technologies—promising greater capabilities and greater efficiencies than alternative approaches such as HSPA. But as WiMAX, particularly mobile WiMAX, has come closer to reality, vendors have continued to enhance HSPA, and perceived WiMAX advantages are no longer apparent. Instead, WiMAX has gained the greatest traction in developing countries as an alternative to wireline deployment. In the United States, Clearwire, Sprint Nextel and others (Intel, Google, Comcast, Time Warner Cable, and Bright House Networks) have created a joint venture to deploy a nationwide WiMAX network. In June 2009, this network was available in Atlanta, Baltimore and Portland.

17.3.10 Interoperable Technologies

Like GSM-HSPA, WiMAX is not a single technology; it is a family of interoperable technologies. The original specification, IEEE 802.16, was completed in 2001 and intended primarily for telecom backhaul applications in point-to-point, line-of-sight configurations using spectrum above 10 GHz. This original version of IEEE 802.16 uses a radio interface based on a single-carrier waveform.

17.3.11 Technical Advantages and Disadvantages

Relative to LTE, WiMAX has the following technical disadvantages: 5 msec frames instead of 1 msec frames, Chase combining instead of incremental redundancy, coarser granularity for modulation and coding schemes and vertical coding instead of horizontal coding. One deployment consideration is that TDD requires network synchronization. It is not possible for one cell site to be transmitting and an adjacent cell site to be receiving at the same time. Different operators in the same band must either coordinate their networks or have guard bands to ensure that they don't interfere with each other. This may introduce problems as more operators introduce networks in the same spectrum band; for example, the 2.5 GHz band in the United States may be used for both TDD and FDD operation.

Although IEEE 802.16e exploits significant radio innovations similar to HSPA+ and LTE, it faces challenges such as economies of scale and technology maturity. Very few operators today have access to spectrum for WiMAX that would permit them to provide widespread coverage.

In reference to economies of scale, GSM-HSPA subscribers number in the billions. Even over the next five years, the number of WiMAX subscribers is likely to be quite low. For example, Informa projects 82.1 million by 2013 while Maravedis predicts a lower 75 million WiMAX subscribers by the end of 2014.

Finally, from a technology standpoint, mobile WiMAX on paper may be slightly more capable than today's available versions of HSPA. But by the time it becomes widely available, mobile WiMAX will actually have to compete against evolved HSPA systems that will offer largely similar capabilities. Further, by then, LTE will not be that far from deployment.

One specific area in which WiMAX has a technical disadvantage is cell size. In fact, 3G systems have a significant link budget advantage over mobile WiMAX because of soft- handoff diversity gain and an FDD duplexing advantage over TDD. Arthur D. Little reports that the radii of typical HSPA cells will be two to four times greater than typical mobile WiMAX cells for high-throughput operation. One vendor estimates that for the same power output, frequency, and capacity, mobile WiMAX requires 1.7 times more cell sites than HSPA. Given that many real world deployments of HSPA will occur at frequencies such as 850 MHz, and LTE at 700 MHz, WiMAX deployments at 2.5 GHz will be at a significant disadvantage.

With respect to spectral efficiency, WiMAX is comparable to HSPA+, as discussed in the section "Spectral Efficiency" that follows. As for data performance, HSPA+ in Release 8—with a peak rate of 42 Mbps—exceeds mobile WiMAX in 10 MHz in TDD 2:1 DL:UL using 2X2 MIMO with a peak rate of 40 Mbps. The sometimes-quoted peak rate of 63.4 Mbps for mobile WiMAX in 10 MHz assumes no bandwidth applied to the uplink.

Some have cited intellectual property rights as an area in which WiMAX has an advantage. There is little substantial, publicly available information, however, to support such claims. First, the large HSPA vendors have invested heavily in these technologies— hopefully giving them significant leverage with which to negotiate reasonable intellectual property rights (IPR) rates with other vendors. Second, the mobile WiMAX industry is in its infancy, and there is considerable lack of clarity when it comes to how different companies will assert and resolve IPR issues.

17.4 TODAY'S CELLULAR NETWORKS

Today's networks can finance the deployment of data capabilities through a successful voice business. Building new networks for broadband wireless mandates substantial capacity per subscriber. Consumers who download 1 gigabyte of data each month represent a ten times greater load on the network than a 1,000-minute-a-month voice user. And if the future is in multimedia services such as movie downloads, it is important to recognize that downloading a single DVD-quality movie—even with advanced compression— consumes approximately 2 gigabytes. It is not clear how easily the available revenue per subscriber will be able to finance large-scale deployment of network capacity. Despite numerous attempts, no terrestrial wireless-data-only network has ever succeeded as a business. Although there is discussion of providing voice services over WiMAX using VoIP, mobile-voice users demand ubiquitous coverage—including indoor coverage. Matching the cellular footprint with WiMAX will require national roaming arrangements, complemented by new dual-technology devices or significant operator investments. LTE - WiMAX competency has already been familiar to readers from chapter 16.

Review Points

Currently deployed network versions are based on either Rel. 0 or Rev. A radio-interface specifications. EV-DO Rev. A incorporates a more efficient uplink, which has spectral efficiency similar to that of HSUPA. Operators started to make EV-DO Rev. A system which is commercially available in 2007.

3GPP2 has defined EV-DO Rev. B, which can combine up to 15 1.25 MHz radio channels in 20 MHz—significantly boosting peak theoretical rates to 73.5 Mbps. More likely, an operator would combine three radio channels in 5 MHz. Such an approach by itself does not necessarily increase overall capacity, but it does offer users higher peak-data rates. Other enhancements are planned for EV-DO, including femtocell support, MIMO and 64 QAM in the downlink, and 16 QAM in the uplink. There are also a number of planned improvements for CDMA2000 1xRTT that will result in increased voice capacity.

WiMAX is a new powerful technical innovation to bridge the digital divide. And it is a broadband wireless technology that is largely supported by the computer and the telecom industry, cost-effective and standard base. It is engineered to deliver the latest type of ubiquitous fixed and mobile services such as VoIP, Information Technology and Video at very low cost. WiMAX systems are able to cover a large geographical area, up to 50 km and to deliver significant bandwidth to end-users up to 72 Mbps.

WiMAX can be summarized as follows:

- WiMAX stands for .World Interoperability for Microwave Access..
- WiMAX/IEEE 802.16 is a global standard-based technology for Broadband Wireless Access
- WiMAX is Equivalent to Wi-Fi Alliance for IEEE 802.11
- WiMAX forum will certify Interoperability of IEEE 802.16 and ETSI HiperMAN

WiMAX will use a single radio covering all licensed and unlicensed frequency bands allocated by the ITU for such services i.e.: The two licensed bands 3.3-3.8 GHz and 2.3-2.7 GHz and one license exempt band 5.725-5.85 GHz.

Initial mobile WiMAX networks will be deployed using 2X2 MIMO, TDD and 10 MHz radio channels in a profile defined by the WiMAX Forum known as WiMAX Wave 2 or, more formally, as WiMAX System Profile 1.0. Beyond Release 1.0, the WiMAX Forum has defined a new profile called WiMAX Release 1.5 with product certification. Mobile WiMAX release 1.5 includes various refinements intended to improve efficiency and performance.

Release 1.5 enhancements include MAC overhead reductions for VoIP (persistent scheduling), handover optimizations, load balancing, location-based services support, FDD operation, 64 QAM in the uplink, downlink adaptive modulation and coding, closed- loop MIMO (FDD mode only), and uplink MIMO. A subsequent version, Mobile WiMAX 2.0, will be designed to address the performance requirements being developed in the ITU IMT-Advanced Project and will be standardized in a new IEEE standard, IEEE 802.16m.

Review Questions

1. Write note on radio resource management in 1xRTT and HSPA.
2. What is the system profile of WiMAX version 1.0?
3. What is the spectrum flexibility in WiMAX?
4. What are the different types of broadband connectivity WiMAX can support?
5. What is the non-LOS coverage provided by WiMAX system?
6. Explain the advantages of WiMAX as per IEEE 802.16e.
7. Write a comparative statement for WiMAX Release 1.0 and Release 1.5.

18 MIMO-OFDM Technology for Wireless Networks

18.1 INTRODUCTION

This chapter describes how MIMO-OFDM (Multiple Input Multiple Output -Orthogonal Frequency Division Multiplexing) technology delivers significant performance improvements for wireless LANs, enabling them to serve existing applications more cost-effectively as well as making new, more demanding applications possible. It also explains how manufacturers and end-users can profit by deploying MIMO-OFDM products today without sacrificing any benefits of the anticipated IEEE 802.11n standard tomorrow. There are three basic parameters that completely describe the quality and usefulness of any wireless link: speed, range and reliability. Prior to the development of MIMO-OFDM, the three parameters were interrelated according to strict rules. Speed could be increased only by sacrificing range and reliability. Range could be extended at the expense of speed and reliability. And reliability could be improved by reducing speed and range. MIMO OFDM has redefined the tradeoffs, clearly demonstrating that it can boost all three parameters simultaneously. While MIMO will ultimately benefit every major wireless Industry including mobile telephone, the wireless LAN industry is leading in exploiting MIMO innovations.

18.1.1 Constraints of Wireless LANs

The market for wireless LANs, particularly in the consumer and small business segments, has skyrocketed. By all accounts, annual growth in wireless LAN device shipments has increased from threefold to fivefold since 2001. With huge opportunities for wireless LANs looming in home entertainment, Voice over IP (VoIP), and public access, the biggest market growth may yet lie ahead.

Products based on existing wireless LAN standards often fail to meet the range requirements encountered in homes, small businesses, retail stores, and other business locations. For example, a consumer may be frustrated to discover that a wireless LAN cannot reach both an upstairs bedroom and a home office in a corner of the basement. A small business may be disappointed to discover that it needs three or four access points interconnected via a wire backbone to cover its modest-sized premises. And an enterprise may learn that a location beyond the reach of wire is also difficult to reach wirelessly. Existing wireless LAN standards also lack the throughput levels required by emerging and potentially huge applications such as home entertainment. For example, a single High Definition TV (HDTV) stream requires at least 20-24 Mbps of sustained throughput throughout the home. A wireless LAN's advertised data speed is usually the "raw" link rate—a significant fraction of which is reserved for protocol overhead (commands, status messages, and error control mechanisms). Plus, the capacity of a wireless LAN may be shared between multiple users and applications. Though today's wireless LAN standards promise speeds up to 54 Mbps, actual user throughput often drops into the single digits near the edge of the home coverage area—if a connection can even be maintained—making "wired quality" streaming video impractical using wireless LAN devices based on existing standards.

18.1.2 Pre-Standard Solutions

Fortunately, these limitations are surmounted using a combination of MIMO and OFDM technologies. That is why MIMO-OFDM is the foundation of all proposals for the IEEE 802.11n standard. However, the standard is not expected to be finalized until 2006; the first products conforming to the standard probably won't appear until 2007. Several commentators advise manufacturers and end-users to avoid the MIMO-OFDM solutions available now and wait for products based on the upcoming standard. Some argue that end-users should always reject solutions that are not based on recognized industry standards—no matter how innovative or beneficial. Others suggest "pre-standard" solutions may prove financially injurious to end users, could disrupt the operation of existing wireless LANs, and may be misrepresented as compliant with or easily upgraded to the yet-to-be-defined 802.11n standard. However, it's possible to support standards and also recognize that "pre-standard" solutions often possess time-to-market advantages. The "pre-standard" solution may be the best choice for customers with immediate needs. Plus, pre-standard products may be fully compatible with, or even enhance the performance of, products based on existing standards. As long as device manufacturers don't promise more than they can guarantee (such as software upgrades to the not-yet defined 802.11n standard and interoperability tests), there is little risk of sowing confusion among consumers (see "What Pre-Standard, MIMO-Enhanced Wi-Fi Products Can and Can't Guarantee," below.)

18.1.3 Multipath Signal and MIMO

Multipath propagation is a feature of all wireless communication environments. There is usually a primary (most direct) path from a transmitter at point "A" to a receiver at point "B." Inevitably, some of the transmitted signal takes other paths to the receiver, bouncing off objects, the ground, or layers of the atmosphere. Signals traversing less direct paths arrive at the receiver later and are often attenuated. A common strategy for dealing with weaker multipath signals is to simply ignore them—in which case the energy they contain is wasted. The strongest multipath signals may be too strong to ignore, however, and can degrade the performance of wireless LAN equipment based on existing standards. Radio signals can be depicted on a graph with the vertical axis indicating amplitude and the horizontal axis indicating time as sine waves. See Figure 18.1a. When a multipath signal arrives slightly later than the primary signal, it peaks and troughs. They are not quite aligned with those of the primary signal, and the (combined) signal seen by the receiver is somewhat blurred. See Figure 18.1b. If the delay is sufficient to cause the multipath signal's peaks to line up with the primary signal's troughs, the multipath signal will partially or totally cancel out the main signal. See Figure 18.1c.

Traditional radio systems either do nothing to combat multipath interference, relying on the primary signal to out-muscle interfering copies, or they employ multipath mitigation techniques. One mitigation technique uses multiple antennas to capture

a) A radio signal may be represented as a sine wave

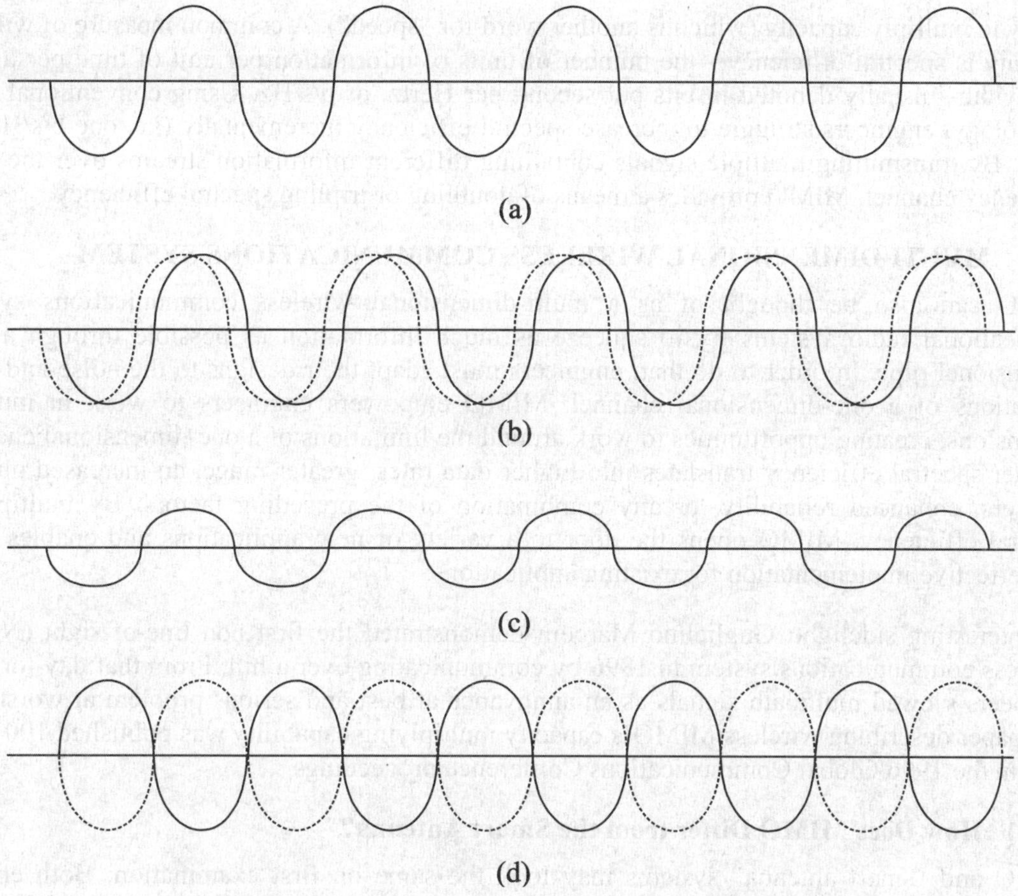

Fig. 18.1: How Multipath Propagation Affects Radio Signals

b) Multipath signals arriving slightly out-of-phase combine at the receiver to create a somewhat weaker and less distinct signal

c) In the extreme case, multipath signals arriving 180° out-of-phase will cancel each other out Time the strongest signal at each moment in time. Another technique adds different delays to received signals to force the peaks and troughs back into alignment. Whatever the mitigation technique, all assume multipath signals are wasteful and/or harmful and strive to limit the damage.

18.1.4 Increased Throughput

MIMO, in contrast, takes advantage of multipath propagation to increase throughput, range/coverage, and reliability. Rather than combating multipath signals, MIMO puts multipath signals to work carrying more information. This is accomplished by sending and receiving more than one data signal in the same radio channel at the same time. The use of multiple waveforms constitutes a new type of radio communication—communication using multi-dimensional signals—which is the only way known to improve all three basic link performance parameters (range, speed and reliability). Because MIMO transmits multiple signals across the communications channel (rather than the conventional system's single signal), MIMO has the ability to multiply capacity (which is another word for "speed"). A common measure of wireless capacity is spectral efficiency—the number of units of information per unit of time per unit of bandwidth—usually denoted in bits per second per Hertz, or b/s/Hz. Using conventional radio technology, engineers struggle to increase spectral efficiency incrementally (i.e. one b/s/Hz at a time). By transmitting multiple signals containing different information streams over the same frequency channel, MIMO provides a means of doubling or tripling spectral efficiency.

18.2 MULTI-DIMENSIONAL WIRELESS COMMUNICATIONS SYSTEM

MIMO can also be thought of as a multi-dimensional wireless communications system. Conventional radio systems try to squeeze as much information as possible through a one-dimensional pipe. In order to do that, engineers must adapt their designs to the noise and other limitations of a one-dimensional channel. MIMO empowers engineers to work in multiple dimensions, creating opportunities to work around the limitations of a one-dimensional channel. Greater spectral efficiency translates into higher data rates, greater range, an increased number of users, enhanced reliability, or any combination of the preceding factors. By multiplying spectral efficiency, MIMO opens the door to a variety of new applications and enables more cost-effective implementation for existing applications.

An interesting sidelight: Guglielmo Marconi demonstrated the first non line-of-sight (NLOS) wireless communications system in 1896 by communicating over a hill. From that day forward, engineers viewed multipath signals as an annoyance at best and serious problem at worst. The first paper describing wireless MIMO's capacity multiplying capability was published 100 years later in the 1996 Global Communications Conference proceedings

18.2.1 How Does MIMO Differ from the Smart Antenna?

MIMO and "smart antenna" systems may look the same on first examination: Both employ multiple antennas spaced as far apart as practical. But look under the hood, and you will see that MIMO and smart antenna systems are fundamentally different.

Smart antennas enhance conventional, one-dimensional radio systems. The most common smart antenna systems use beamforming (a.k.a. beam switching) to concentrate the signal energy on the main path and receive combining (a.k.a. diversity) to capture the strongest signal at any given moment. Note that beamforming and receive combining are only multipath mitigation techniques, and do not multiply data throughput over the wireless channel. (Figure 18.2)

That's not to say beamforming and receive combining aren't useful. Both have demonstrated an ability to improve performance incrementally in point-to-point applications (e.g., outdoor wireless backhaul applications). However, while beamforming and receive combining are valuable enhancements to conventional radio systems, MIMO is a paradigm shift, dramatically changing perceptions of and responses to multipath propagation. While receive combining and beamforming increase spectral efficiency one or two b/s/Hz at a time; MIMO multiplies the b/s/Hz.

a) Beamforming (beam steering) employs two transmit antennas to deliver the best multipath signal

b) Diversity (receive combining) uses two receive antennas to capture the best multipath signal

c) There may be a physical resemblance between radio systems using a combination of beam steering and diversity and MIMO systems. Note, however, that with the beam steering/diversity approach, only one signal is sent over the channel.

d) MIMO uses multiple transmitters, receivers and antennas to send multiple signals over the same channel, multiplying spectral efficiency.

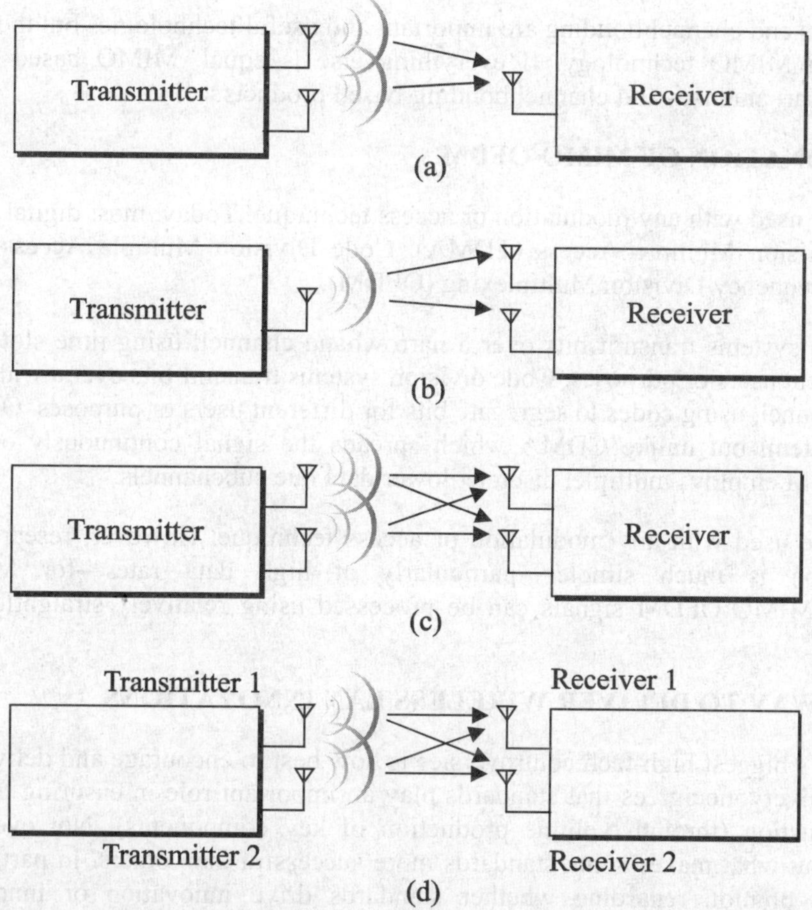

Fig. 18.2: Comparing Smart Antenna Schemes (a, b, and c) with MIMO (d)

18.2.2 Channel Bonding

Another performance-enhancing technique is channel bonding. Channel bonding multiplies throughput by combining two or more radio channels. Assuming the channels are available, channel bonding is one of the most direct methods of increasing throughput. But there is a significant price associated with channel bonding: increased bandwidth consumption. In some cases, channel bonding may not be an option because the target frequencies have been allocated to other users or services. In other cases, the performance benefits may not outweigh the technical challenges. In all cases, channel bonding must be implemented carefully to minimize the interference problems that may arise when using more bandwidth.

Both MIMO and channel bonding can multiply throughput. But there are two key differences between the approaches. Though channel bonding increases throughput and capacity, it may reduce range slightly. MIMO enhances all three performance attributes simultaneously. And while channel bonding increases throughput by consuming more bandwidth, MIMO increases spectral efficiency, multiplying throughput in the same bandwidth.

Smart antennas and channel bonding are important and useful technologies but they must not be confused with MIMO technology. If everything else is equal, MIMO based products will outperform smart antenna- and channel bonding-based products.

18.3 COMBINATION OF MIMO-OFDM

MIMO can be used with any modulation or access technique. Today, most digital radio systems use Time Division Multiple Access (TDMA), Code Division Multiple Access (CDMA), or Orthogonal Frequency Division Multiplexing (OFDM).

Time division systems transmit bits over a narrowband channel, using time slots to segregate bits for different users or purposes. Code division systems transmit bits over a wideband (spread spectrum) channel, using codes to segregate bits for different users or purposes. OFDM is also a wideband system, but unlike CDMA which spreads the signal continuously over the entire channel, OFDM employs multiple, discrete, lower data rate subchannels.

MIMO can be used with any modulation or access technique. However, research shows that implementation is much simpler—particularly at high data rates—for MIMO-OFDM. Specifically, MIMO-OFDM signals can be processed using relatively straightforward matrix algebra.

18.4 BEST WAY TO DELIVER WIRELESS LAN INNOVATIONS

One of today's biggest high-tech controversies is how best to encourage and deliver technology innovations. Everyone agrees that standards play an important role in ensuring interoperability and cost reduction (through volume production of key components). Not everyone agrees, however, about what makes some standards more successful than others. In particular, there is difference in opinion regarding whether standards drive innovation or innovation drives standards.

Each year, thousands of standards are published. Some standards are extremely successful; many achieve limited success. But the majority are simply overtaken by events. The Global Systems for Mobile Communications (GSM) is an example of an extremely successful standard. Internet Protocol Version 6 (IPv6) is almost universally recognized as the Internet's next generation protocol, but it has made little headway in replacing IPv4. The Internet was built on TCP/IP, a protocol developed by two engineers, instead of the highly-touted Open Systems Interconnection (OSI) protocol developed by the International Standards Organization (ISO).

Successful standards often codify market-proven innovations. Ethernet, like Token Ring, began life as a proprietary local area networking (LAN) standard. Vendors have learned over time that it's better to control 20% of a very large market than © 2005 Datacomm Research Company 100 % of a small market with a doubtful future. That's why most vendors are anxious to offer a proprietary innovation as the foundation for an open standard. To wit, most successful standards start with a technology that has gained market traction and open it to wider participation. Standards for proven markets deserve and receive more attention and urgency. Participants are more amenable to compromise, recognizing that neither vendors nor users benefit from lengthy delays.

Today, there are many successful standards that started as proprietary innovations with clear end-user benefits. But there are few if any examples of markets that failed to develop simply because such innovations were introduced prematurely.

Standards usually take a minimum of 1-2 years to develop, and products conforming to those standards usually require another year before they are commercially available; many customers routinely replace computer and communications equipment every few years to take advantage of further developments.

More importantly, vendors have become more sophisticated about introducing innovative technology. For example, wireless LAN products incorporating MIMO-OFDM technology (often called "pre-standard, MIMO-enhanced Wi-Fi" because MIMOOFDM is central to the forthcoming 802.11n standard) are fully compatible and interoperable with existing 802.11b,802.11g, and 802.11a devices on the same network at the same time. (In fact, MIMO-OFDM products enhance the performance of the existing standards as we explain in the next section.)

18.5 MIMO-OFDM BENEFITS

The fact that products incorporating pre-standard MIMO-enhanced Wi-Fi look the same on the outside as products with smart antennas hints at another benefit. The pre-standard MIMO products have the antennas and other circuitry needed to provide smart antenna functionality when operating in a mode based on existing standards.

In fact, this smart antenna functionality boosts performance even when present on just one end of a link. Thus, pre-standard MIMO products are not only fully compatible with existing Wi-Fi standards; they also enhance the performance of those standards.

18.6 MIMO-OFDM ENABLES NEW WIRELESS LAN APPLICATIONS AND MARKETS

Wireless LANs scored their first major success in vertical industrial applications— primarily warehouse and retail floor inventory management. The market exploded as wireless LANs were embraced for PC networking and sharing broadband access in small businesses and homes. This success has positioned wireless LANs to drive the development of three new markets with huge growth potential: home entertainment networking, cordless Voice over IP (VoIP), and a variety of machine-to-machine (M2M) applications.

Cordless VoIP represents an even greater prospect. Assuming a significant fraction of private and public wireless LANs are modified to handle VoIP traffic, a market for integrating Wi-Fi with mobile phones will emerge. There are currently 1.5 billion mobile phone subscribers, with more than 500 million handsets sold annually.

And there is more to cordless VoIP than first meets the eye; for example, cordless VoIP could enable strategic alliances between mobile phone and cable network operators. Major cable operators are entering local phone markets, creating opportunities for mobile carriers to offer handsets that serve as cordless phones in the home—a single phone for all of users' telephone service needs.

The potential number of wireless LAN nodes needed for machine-to-machine applications is mind boggling. For example, the average home security system could easily use a dozen nodes for door and window sensors, motion detectors, and video cams. Other major wireless M2M applications include telematics, asset monitoring, mobile commerce, healthcare, real-time enterprise communications, and homeland security

MIMO-OFDM could prove to be a key enabler in all of these markets. Home entertainment will require wireless networks capable of transmitting high-speed data (actual user data rates of 50 Mbps and higher) throughout the entire home. Cordless VoIP calls for low latency, wide coverage, and reliable operation while walking about. Wireless M2M applications require both high-speed and excellent coverage. High-speed will be critical as imaging becomes a preferred data gathering method in specific market segments, and coverage will be a requirement as many remote nodes are embedded in other devices or machines.

18.7 MIMO-Based Wireless LAN Products

A number of individuals, university research labs, and corporate R&D departments have contributed to the development of MIMO technology. Some of the earliest work was performed at Lucent Technology's Bell Labs and Stanford University during the 1990s.

Airgo Networks, Inc. (Palo Alto, California) was first to enable MIMO based wireless LAN products priced within reach of consumers. Airgo's "True MIMO" chipset solution has been adopted by top wireless LAN manufacturers including Belkin, Buffalo Technology, Linksys (the market leader), Netgear, and SOHO ware.

Meanwhile, the consensus in the wireless LAN industry is that MIMO is the core technology For the next generation standard being developed by the IEEE 802.11n working group. With MIMO-based products already on the market—and more models no doubt on the way—the working group needs to expedite development of a specification that is both Acceptable to the majority of vendors and harmonious with the rapidly growing installed base of MIMO-based products.

At every step of the 802.11n standards process—starting with the draft standard vote, continuing with incorporation of comments, and ending with the final standard ratification—changes will be made that are likely to require hardware modifications in the MIMO chipsets. Even after the final standard is fully ratified, any supplier's chipsets may require further hardware changes to ensure interoperability. Today, many WFA tests require features that are not specified in the relevant 802.11 standard because, realistically, such standards are almost never sufficient to ensure that any two devices will interoperate. Thus, it is impossible for a chipset supplier to guarantee that a software or firmware upgrade to an OEM product will be sufficient to achieve 802.11n interoperability with devices based on other suppliers' chipsets. It will be approximately two years before the WFA is able to certify 802.11n interoperability. In the meantime, OEMs and consumers should not make purchase decisions based on claims concerning a notyet-defined standard and set of interoperability tests.

MIMO-enhanced Wi-Fi devices should be based on the application requirements, the performance and cost of the MIMO-enhanced products, and the investment protection afforded by backwards compatibility with existing 802.11a/b/g standards. Customers contemplating purchase of pre-standard, MIMO-enhanced Wi-Fi products also Want to consider whether the vendor promises that its future, certified interoperable 802.11n standard products Will be backwards-compatible with its current pre-standard MIMO products. Unlike promises of easy upgrades to future, not-yet-defined standards, the backwards compatibility of future products with existing products is something vendors can guarantee. Such guarantees serve as an investment protection program, allowing customers to continue using pre-standard client devices alongside future 802.11n standard client devices by replacing only the access points with dual-mode models.

18.7.1 MIMO: A Technical Improvement

MIMO-OFDM technology is more than the latest technical improvement for wireless LANs. MIMO-OFDM is a major technology upgrade enabling demanding new applications with huge market potential and facilitating significant growth in existing applications. Though the IEEE 802.11n task group is developing a standard for MIMO-OFDM wireless LAN devices around which the entire industry should rally, the delivery of pre-standard MIMO enhanced Wi-Fi devices today can only boost development of a robust market for MIMO-OFDM wireless LAN devices.

18.8 MIMO-OFDM IN THE TDD MODE

Data rates for wireless cellular and local area networks have been steadily increasing in recent years, with an approximate five-fold increase in throughput every four years. With new applications such as wireless multimedia and the replacement of cables for communication purposes in home, office and public access scenarios, we can anticipate this trend to continue. Three challenging requirements arise from the call for higher data rates in next generation wireless systems: we have to increase spectral efficiency, design systems for larger bandwidths, and we shall reduce the costs per bit as well.

Exploiting the rich scattering typical for indoor and urban environments ,multiple-input multiple output (MIMO) systems allow for sound gains in the spectral efficiency, thus facilitating the Transmission at high data rates in a spectrum which is usually limited by regulation and other factors. With increasing bandwidth, more and more echoes are resolved in the channel, calling for efficient equalization techniques. Orthogonal frequency-division multiplex (OFDM) is a very attractive option to solving this problem, and the combination of MIMO and OFDM allows a substantially reduced complexity of the spatio-temporal processing. This is due to the fact that the OFDM pre- and post processing transforms the multi-path channel into multiple flat fading channels for which well-known MIMO detection schemes can be used.

But we still have to exploit the plethora of diversity offered by the multi-path MIMO channel, which is not trivial with MIMO-OFDM. Note that the maximal diversity order in the multi-path MIMO channel is given as the product of the numbers of receive antennas and resolved echoes, when the spatial multiplexing technique is used. In general, space-frequency codes must be designed to realize this diversity, which may be different from the well-known designs for space-time codes.

Alternatively, one may attain the capacity by water-filling and related methods, based on channel state information (CSI) available at the transmitter. With channel-aware pre-processing and adaptive modulation, data are loaded onto the sub-carriers and spatial channels according to the post-processing signal-to-interference-and-noise ratio (SINR). The error bursts typical for fading channels can such be avoided already prior to the transmission. Channel coding is no longer required to realize the multipath diversity.

Consequently, the interleaver size and the corresponding delay can be reduced. The basic challenge is to make CSI available at the transmitter. This could be achieved by sending feed-back information over the reverse link, but there is a more efficient method in the time-division duplex (TDD) mode. The latter uses the same carrier frequency alternately for transmission and reception. Due to channel reciprocity, we may transmit training sequences in the up-link direction before the data transmission in the down-link. The reciprocal CSI is then used to pre-process the transmitted data, as well as for optimal scheduling in the space-frequency domain (See Fig. 18.3). From the system point-of-view, we must consider what is the ultimate gain for the whole system. In the above example, the CSI obviously helps in the downlink optimization. But at the same time, the training sequences eat up valuable resources in the uplink (capacity in the channel, battery power). There is an optimal trade-off point somewhere which needs to be assessed in future research.

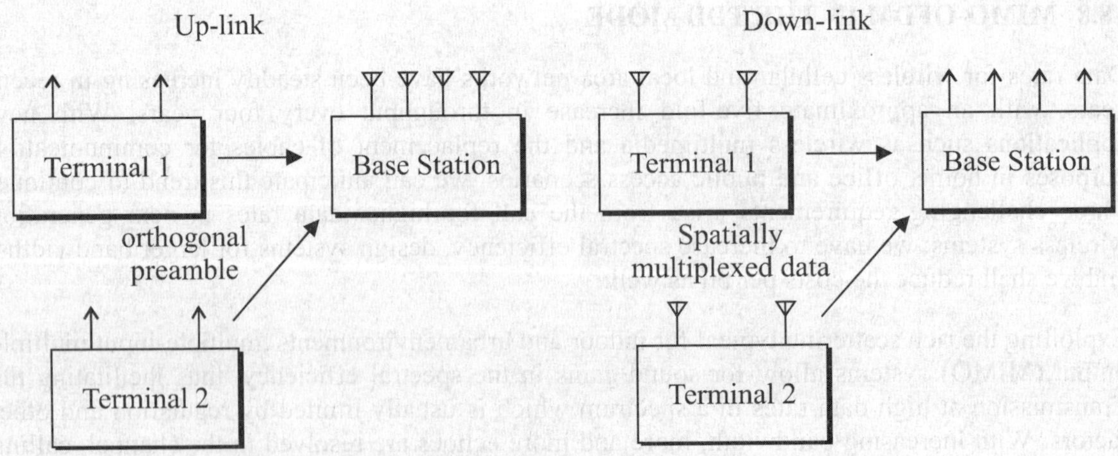

Fig. 18.3: MIMO in TDD mode

Figure In the time-division duplex mode, the channel information for the down-link can be made available at the transmitter by using the reciprocal channel information from the up-link, or vice versa.

We feel that this simple principle is the key to realizing the above requirement to reduce the costs per bit while providing a high data rate. With CSI at the transmitter, we gain the flexibility to shift the signal processing effort almost completely to the base station in both, up- and down-link. This allows a simple terminal design. Alternatively, we can share the effort between two mobile terminals in the adhoc mode. For each carrier, a simple matrix-vector multiplication at both stations, combined with rate and power control, is sufficient to attain the full capacity (This is called "eigenmode signaling")

18.8.1 Challenges

This is aimed to identify open research challenges concerning the combination of MIMO, OFDM and TDD which have not been previously addressed, to be able to eventually realize the system concept. The paper is organized as follows: In section 2, application scenarios and **base station** requirements for future wireless systems are described. The system concept for the physical layer is introduced in section 3. The following sections 4-6 summarize the state of the art and analyze open research items in the three component technologies of the combined approach proposed here. Section 7 highlights that a cross-layer optimization is required to achieve the optimal system performance and it addresses the optimal space-frequency scheduling strategy. Section 8 is concerned with the real-time implementation. Finally, conclusions are drawn in Section 9.

18.9 OFDM

Proposals for bandwidth usage in current research and standardization efforts as well as large amounts of spectrum allocation for unlicensed operation in the high GHz range are a clear indicator that future wireless systems will use bandwidths ranging from several tens of MHz up to several hundreds of MHz, for wireless broadband applications (i.e., "Gigabit Wireless"). However, increasing the transmission bandwidth simultaneously increases the sampling frequency of the channel. As the sampling interval becomes shorter, the paths impinging from different scatterers are eventually temporally resolved – the (discrete sampled) channel impulse response is in this case no longer a single Dirac impulse ("tap") but a sequence of taps – a tapped delay line (TDL), usually described by a power delay profile (PDP) . Traditional single carrier (SC) systems will suffer from strong inter symbol interference (ISI) when transmitting over a frequency selective channel, which makes equalization at the receiver cumbersome. For complexity reasons, it is therefore advantageous to perform equalization in the frequency domain. Two Fourier transforms are required – one of which is done at the transmitter, the other one at the receiver. The aim of this *multi carrier (MC) modulation* is to have a number of parallel sub-carriers high enough such that the bandwidth of one sub-carrier is significantly lower than the channel's coherence bandwidth and the frequency selective channel is hence transformed into several narrowband frequency flat fading channels. In the time domain, this means that for each individual sub-carrier the symbol time is raised much above the maximum channel delay such that the effects of ISI are negligible.

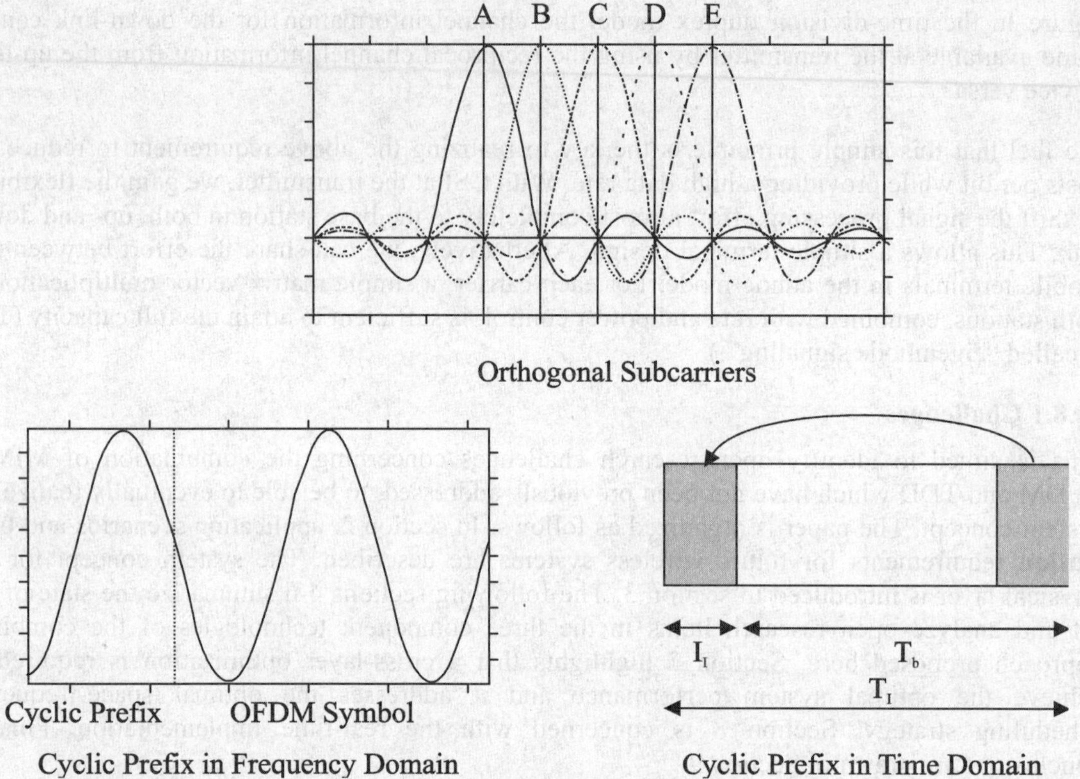

Fig. 18.4: OFDM Basics

A commonly used and spectrally efficient technique arising in this context is Orthogonal Frequency Division Multiplexing (OFDM). By means of an Inverse Fast Fourier Transform (IFFT), the transmitter transforms the frequency domain data samples on several sub-carriers (which are equidistantly distributed in frequency domain) into the time domain, adds a prefix/postfix and transmits the resulting signal over the channel. The receiver cancels the prefix/postfix and uses a Fast Fourier Transform (FFT) to transform the received signal back into the frequency domain. We will dwell on the details of pre-/postfixes in the following section. The number of sub-carriers is usually a power of 2, to allow for efficient implementation of the IFFT/FFT.

18.9.1 OFDM System Design

Narrow bandwidth →long symbol times
→ all significant multipaths arrive within a symbol time minimizing ISI
→ no equalization →low complexity

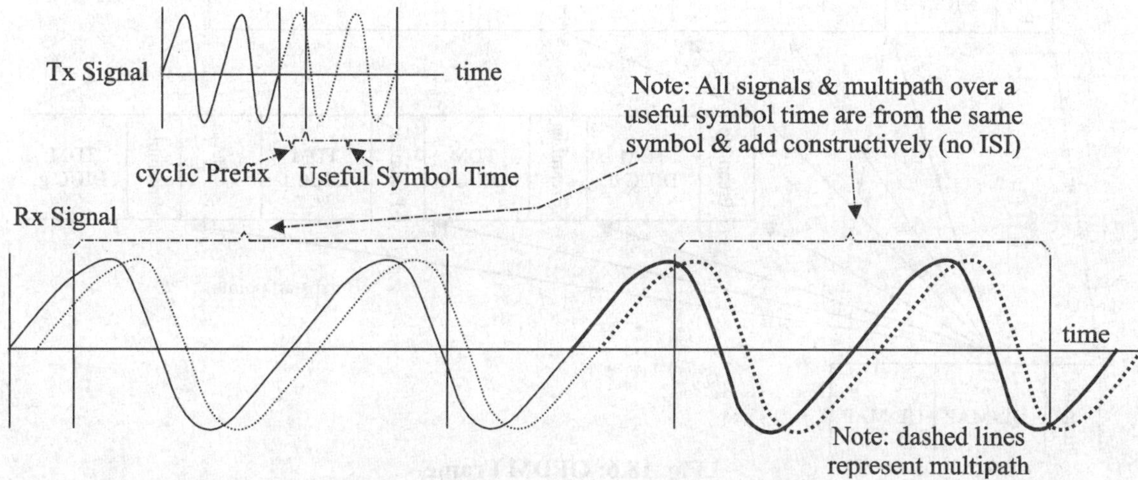

Fig. 18.5: Equalizers are Avoided in OFDM

18.9.2 FFT Size

Tradeoffs of FFT Size

- The FFT size determines the number of sub-carriers in the specified bandwidth
- Larger FFT sizes lead to narrower subcarriers and smaller inter-subcarrier spacing
  - ✓ More susceptibility to ICI, particularly in high Doppler

(*Note*: Doppler shift for 125 km/hr for operation at 3.5 GHz is v/λ = 35 m/sec/0.086 m = 408 Hz)

  - ✓ Narrower subcarriers lead to longer symbol times → less susceptibility to delay spread
- Smaller FFT sizes the opposite is true

Table 18.1: FFT Size for Different Bandwidth

Parameters	*Values*				
System bandwidth (MHz)	1.25	2.5	5	10	20
Sampling frequency	1.429	2.85 7	5.714	11.429	22.857
Sample time ($1/F_s$, nsec)	700	350	175	88	44
FFT size (N_{FFT})	128	256	512	1024	2048
Subcarrier frequency spacing	11.16071429 kHz				
Useful symbol time (T_b=1/f)	89.6 μs				
Guard time ($T_g = T_s/8$)	11.2 μs				
OFDMA symbol tune ($T_s = T_b + T_g$)	100.8 μs				

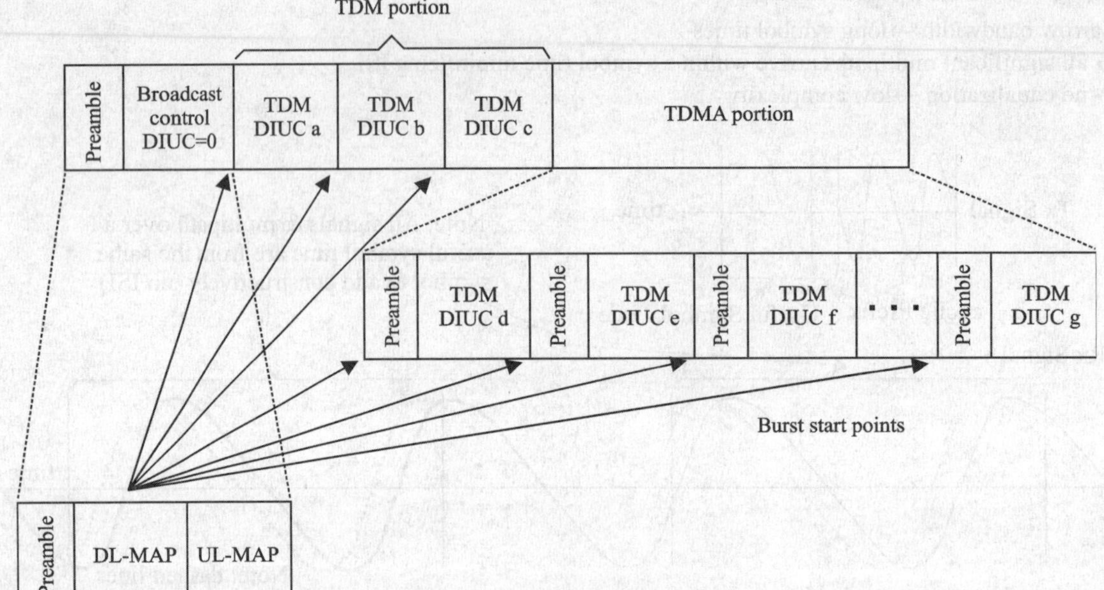

Fig. 18.6: OFDM Frame

18.10 MOBILE MULTIPATH CHANNEL

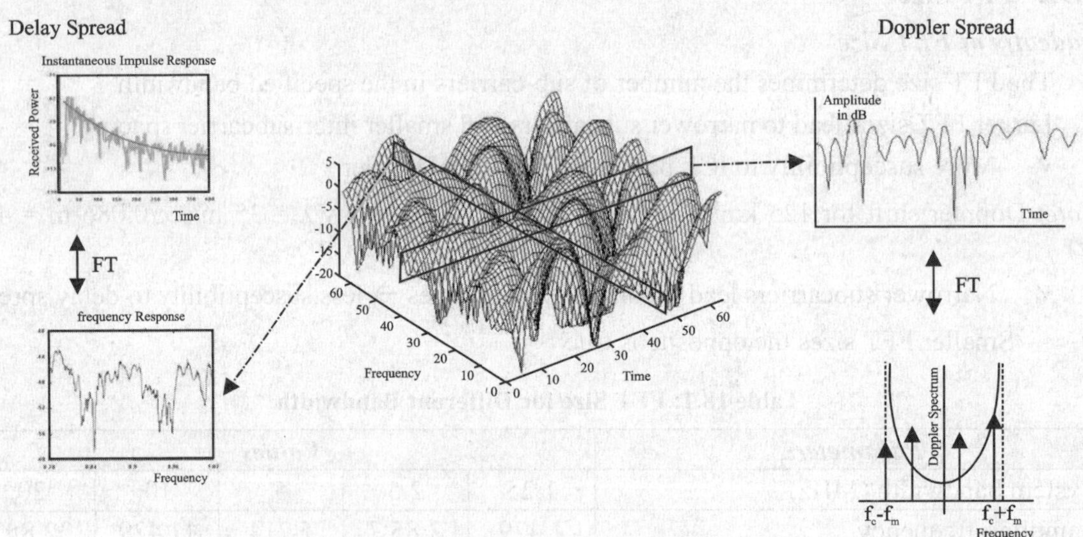

Fig. 18.7: The Mobile Multipath Channel

One major challenge for the design of an OFDM system is the selection of an appropriate FFT size (number of sub-carriers). In order to avoid OFDM inter-symbol-interference, the length of the guard interval *T* must be larger than the maximum channel impulse response *GI* is an additional overhead that should not exceed a certain threshold 1 max . However, the guard interval (usually, 25% of the OFDM symbol length). Otherwise, the spectral efficiency would be reduced too much. On the other hand, the OFDM symbol must be short enough such that the temporal variations resulting from relative movements of the transmitter, receiver and/or scatterers do not result in a time-varying channel within one OFDM symbol, which would result in inter-carrier-interference (ICI) and thus significantly deteriorate system performance. Since sub-carrier spacing and symbol duration are inversely proportional, the former requirement sets a lower bound on the number of sub-carriers: *NBT*η>, where *B* is the bandwidth of the channel. It is independent of both carrier frequency and user mobility. The latter requirement sets an */*sc* *GI* max upper bound on the number of sub-carriers since at any fixed bandwidth, the OFDM symbol length scales linearly with the number of sub-carriers. If we assume for example a Jakes spectrum and design the OFDM symbol to be shorter than the 99% channel coherence time, then the number of sub-carriers is upper bounded by ( ) () ,max max *NBf*η<+, where 0.032 / 1 *sd* *f fv c*= is the maximum, max /*dc* Doppler frequency.

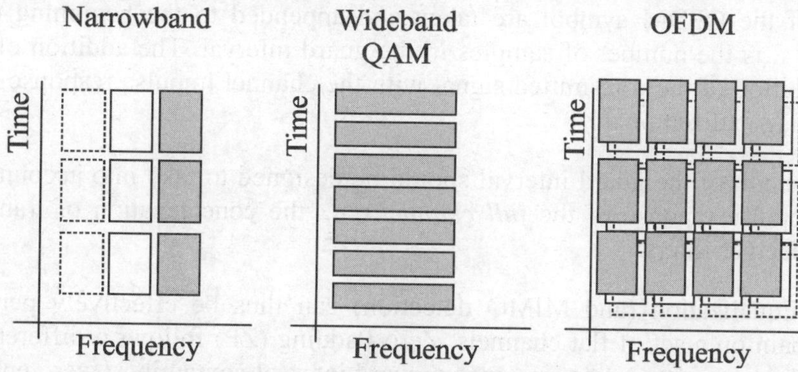

Fig. 18.8: Effects of Multipath Delay and Doppler

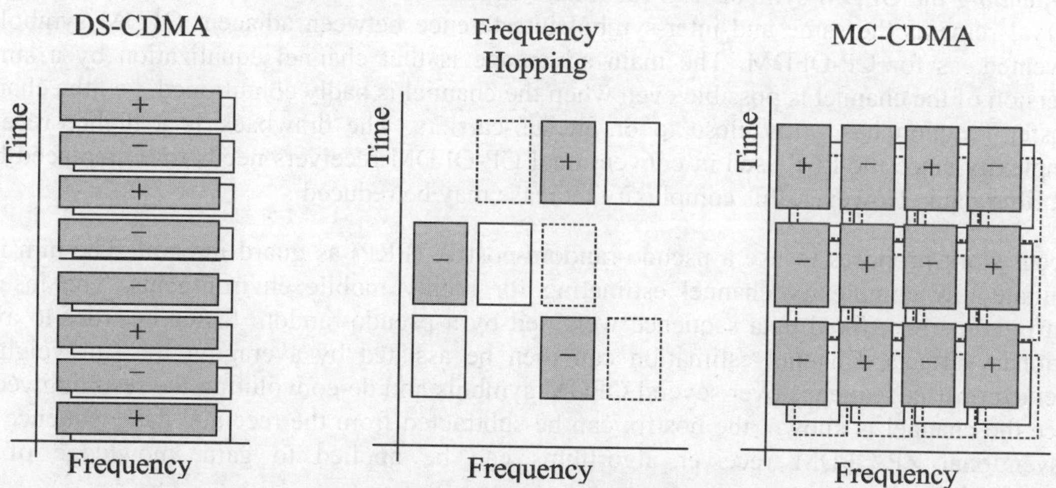

Fig. 18.9: Effects of Multipath (II)

The upper bound obviously depends on the carrier frequency as well as on the user mobility. While OFDM carriers are orthogonal, their spectrums do overlap. Doppler shift or, equivalently, insufficient frequency synchronization thus introduce inter-carrier interference (ICI). Doppler spread, or phase noise introduce ICI as well (the effect is a sum of shift effects). Concerning the effect of synchronization on the OFDM performance, the reader is referred to [29]. Usually, a Doppler spread (or phase noise) equivalent to 3%-5% of the carrier spacing may be acceptable. This gives another lower bound on the carrier spacing (and hence an upper bound on the number of subcarriers).

In WiFi, the carrier spacing is rather high to account for cheap oscillators. For future wireless LAN systems in the 60 GHz range, Doppler spread and phase noise considerations may put different requirements.

18.11 PREFIX/POSTFIX DESIGN

After fixing the FFT size and the guard interval length, one needs to decide which type of prefix/postfix should be used. The "standard" approach is the use of a Cyclic Prefix (CP). The L last samples of the OFDM symbol are taken and appended to the beginning of the OFDM symbol, where L is the number of samples in the guard interval. The addition of a CP ensures that the convolution of the transmitted signal with the channel impulse response is circular and can hence be diagonalized on a

Note that the length of the guard interval should be designed to take into account the length of the channel impulse reponse of the *full channel*, i.e., the concatenation of transmitter filters, channel, and receiver filters.

FFT basis— Equalization (and MIMO detection) can thus be effectively performed in the frequency domain on a set of flat channels. Zero Padding (ZP) follows a different approach by *appending* to the transmitted data sequence a guard interval containing L zero entries instead of *pre-pending* the OFDM symbol with redundant signal copies. Note that the length of the guard interval remains the same and inter-symbol interference between adjacent OFDM symbols is prevented, as for CP-OFDM. The main advantage is that channel equalization by a simple inversion of the channel is possible even when the channel is badly conditioned, i.e., the channel transfer function has zeros close to or on sub-carriers. The drawback is a higher receiver complexity since the FFT used in conventional CP-OFDM receivers needs to be replaced by a FIR filter bank. However, this complexity increase may be reduced .

Recent work proposes to use a pseudo-random-postfix (PRP) as guard interval. The aim is to facilitate low complexity channel estimating for highly mobile environments. The inserted postfix contains a fixed data sequence weighted by a pseudo-random factor in order to avoid stationary effects. Channel estimation can then be assisted by averaging the (un-weighted) received postfix sequence over several OFDM symbols and de-convoluting the resulting vector. Once the channel is known, the postfix can be subtracted from the received data sequence and conventional ZP-OFDM receiver algorithms can be applied to gain knowledge of the transmitted data.

18.12 PULSE SHAPING

A first drawback of the standard OFDM waveform is the rectangular pulse shape in the time domain. The corresponding sinc-Spectrum has a bad localization in the frequency domain. This waveform can be modified by an appropriate windowing. But in a conventional OFDM setup, this leads either to the need for either a post-processing equalizer or to the addition of an extra guard interval, in order to remove the resulting ISI. Another way to introduce a windowing leading to good frequency localization is to use over-sampled filter banks. The over-sampling increases the spacing between the sub-carriers, and it produces the equivalent of the time-domain guard interval in the frequency domain. So again we have, as for the standard OFDM, a loss in the spectral efficiency.

Another way to introduce the pulse shaping without loss of orthogonality is to include a time-offset when modulating each sub-carrier. For instance, the Offset-QAM (OQAM) modulation format has been used in to get, in the real field, a set of orthogonal waveforms named IOTA (Isotropic Orthogonal Transform Algorithm). IOTA has the nice property to be nearly optimal with regard to the time-frequency localization criterion, i.e. an appropriate criterion when considering transmission over time and frequency dispersive channels. As any OFDM/OQAM scheme, IOTA can reach a maximum spectral efficiency, which is not the case of standard OFDM with CP or ZP. Furthermore, as any modulated transforms, it can be easily and efficiently implemented, thanks to fast Fourier transform (FFT) algorithms. However, compared to classical OFDM, an extra cost is required in order to implement poly-phase pre- and post-filters to generate a waveform that is longer than the simple rectangular window. However, as shown in the filter bank implementation described in nearly optimal results can be obtained with very short waveforms.

Based on a theoretical analysis it appears that, for transmission over time and frequency dispersive channels, orthogonal waveforms are no longer the best choice and that non orthogonal waveforms have to be used instead. A bi-orthogonal generalization of OFDM/OQAM has already been investigated, that could be a candidate for the fourth generation of mobile communication systems.

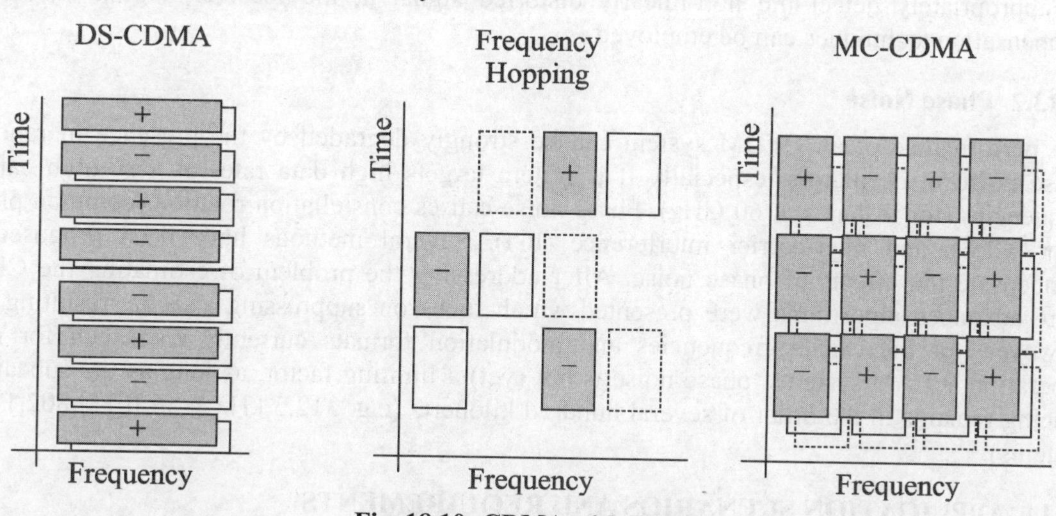

Fig. 18.10: CDMA with FHSS

18.13 IMPLEMENTATION

18.13 .1 Peak-To-Average Power Ratio (PAPR)

The time-domain signal in an OFDM system is the superposition of the signals of a large number of sub-carriers. This results in an approximately Gaussian distribution of the I- and Q-components of the complex base-band signal. Consequently, OFDM systems require transmit and receive signal processing blocks with a high dynamic range. This leads to more costly RF components sincem amplifiers with a larger linear dynamic range are less efficient than the "switching" amplifiers used in the previous mobile systems, for any given supply voltage level, There are two approaches to reduce this problem: we can either avoid large PAPRs (PAPR reduction) or live with the clipping effects that otherwise occur in the high power amplifier (HPA) of the transmitter. The latter effect is twofold – on the one hand, it distorts the transmitted signal waveforms and thus leads to an increased bit error rate, especially for higher order modulation schemes. On the other hand, the clipping leads to a broadened spectrum of the transmitted OFDM signal – which is the far more damaging effect, since the emission is usually restricted by a spectrum mask. There has been active research in recent years in the area of pre-processing the OFDM signals for PAPR reduction by coding. However, the additional redundancy of PAPR reduction coding causes a reduction in user data rate and most schemes also lack flexibility. Another approach is to avoid "bad" OFDM words by changing them for equivalent ones. The equivalence is given by changing pseudorand omly the transmitted word – which however requires channel side information, at least intrinsically. An extensive overview of PAPR reduction schemes is given in.

Whenever a broadened spectrum of the OFDM signal is acceptable, one may relax the requirements on RF front-end components, allowing for cheaper power-amplifiers to be used. To appropriately detect the non-linearly distorted signal at the receiver, digital base-band compensation techniques can be employed.

18.13.2 Phase Noise

The performance of an OFDM system can be strongly degraded by the presence of random phase noise in oscillators, especially if a system targets high data rates at very high carrier frequencies (for instance at 60 GHz). Phase noise causes constellation rotation (common phase error, CPE), and inter-carrier interference (ICI). Several methods have been proposed to compensate the effects of phase noise. After addressing the problem of estimating the CPE , more advanced algorithms were presented which focus on suppressing also the resulting ICI However, for the carrier frequencies and modulation formats currently envisaged for next generation WLAN systems, phase noise is not (yet) a limiting factor, as long as the subcarrier spacing remains in the order of several hundred kilohertz (e.g. 312.5 kHz as in IEEE 802.11a/n systems).

18.14 APPLICATION SCENARIOS AND REQUIREMENTS

Seamless interoperation with other communication infrastructure will facilitate user mobility by providing the desired information anywhere at any time. This trend is already visible in the rapidly rising number of Wireless LAN access points in hotels, lounges and offices around the world.

Example applications in this context comprise access to email, intranet and internet, the distribution of multimedia content in home and hot spot environments, replacement of Ethernet networks in offices, and wireless peripheral interfaces for digital equipment. Naturally, customers expect the same high quality of service and ease of use as known from wire based solutions. This translates into a multitude of challenges: high capacity reserves, in order to support the extreme peak data rates, reconfigurability and multi-band operation in order to provide service in a heterogeneous environment, and plug-and play network configuration in order to enable fast and flexible set-ups.

Home Environment: The massive use of high quality multimedia applications (streaming audio and video, with data rates in excess of several tens of Mbit/s) for numerous users is one reason for the anticipated need of very high bit rates. Other key requirements in this area are self configuration and zero maintenance features as well as low transmit powers, to minimize exposure of humans to electromagnetic radiation. Office and Enterprise Environment: WLAN solutions available to date already enabled office staff to work detached from its desk. However, with high numbers of users accessing a single access point and 100MBit/s Ethernet being state of the art, peak data rates can be expected to be in the order of 1 GBit/s. Moreover, core business applications such as Voice over IP and video conferencing demand very high Quality of Service (including encryption features). Hot Sport / Public Access Environment: Large scale coverage in a future heterogeneous wireless access network will be provided by next generation cellular networks whereas high data rate access in urban and hot spot environments will be provided by short range wireless systems. Expected high variations in user data rates and differing service requirements call for a highly flexible MAC. In order to enable user mobility, the system will have to interoperate with other B3G standards.

18.14.1 Operating Principle of the Air Interface

From the information-theoretic point of view, there are two approaches with almost equivalent performance limits: There is the classical "blind" transmission scheme, which sometimes overloads the wireless fading channel and repairs the resulting error bursts at the receiver by interleaved channel coding, which unfortunately introduces additional delay between transmission and reception. The second concept is an adaptive scheme based on channel side information at the transmitter avoiding these errors already in advance. We feel that the adaptive scheme fits better to the above requirements, and it has another interesting impact. From the core network perspective it is desired that only error free data may enter through the wireless-to-wired gateway.

With the classical scheme, there is an unavoidable possibility of error over the wireless link. With the adaptive scheme, the throughput may vary in time, according to the time-varying capacity of the wireless channel. Provided that the channel variation can be tracked sufficiently fast at the transmitter, it can be guaranteed that the variable-rate data are free of error when entering the gateway, Even under extreme bit error rate constraints in the core network. The physical and MAC layer are shown in Fig. 18.11, in the up-link of the infrastructure mode. We assume that each mobile terminal (MT) as well as the access point (AP) feature multiple antennas.

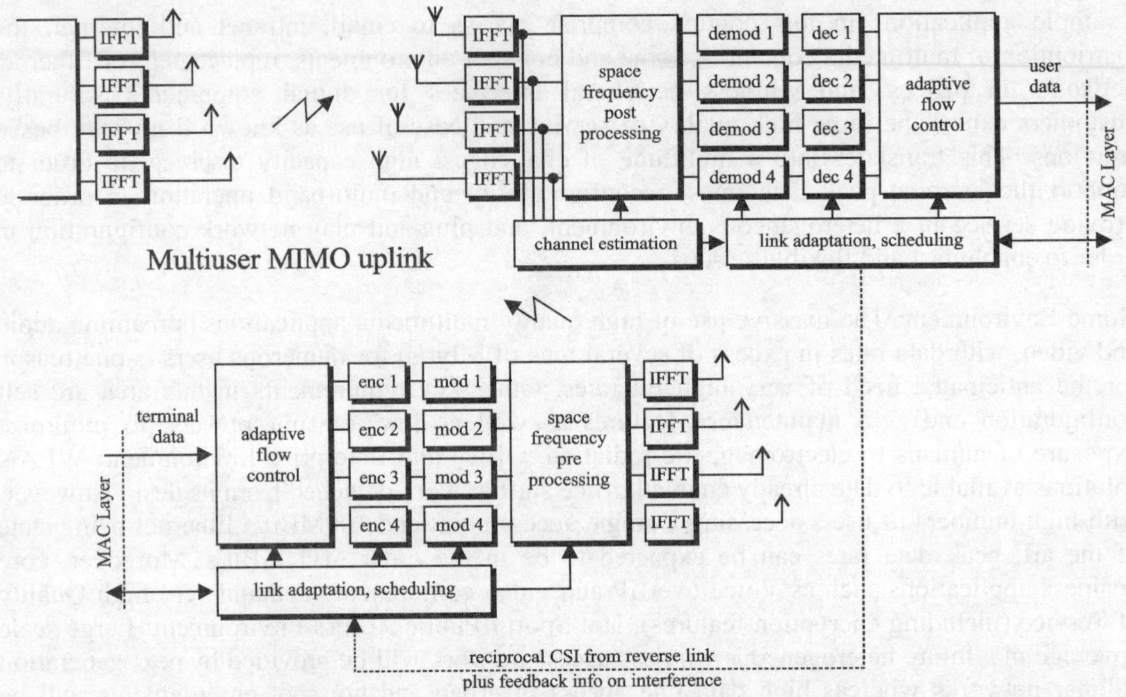

Fig. 18.11: Concept for the PHY and MAC Layers

Up-link— The MT starts by transmitting pilot sequences for the channel estimation. According to the channel and interference situation at the AP, the scheduler in the AP assigns the required resources in the space-frequency domain to the MT such that the desired quality-of-service requirements (error rates, delay) can be met. The adaptive flow control distributes the data accordingly. Each spatial and frequency channel should at least have individual modulation, steered by the link adaptation unit. Individual coding could be used as well, as indicated, but might be too complex, eventually. Power control is realized using the joint space-frequency pre-processing after modulation. Finally, the signals are passed through an IFFT, modulated onto the carrier and transmitted over the air. In principle, the corresponding units are used in reversed order at the AP. As in the classical system, it is easy to shift the signal processing effort almost completely to the AP in the up-link, except for power and rate control, which are performed at the terminal but steered from the AP. The (usually complex) MIMO signal processing is performed at the AP.

Down-link— At first, the AP requests the MT to transmit pilot sequences for the channel estimation in the up-link direction and additional information of the current interference scenario at the MT. Using channel reciprocity, the channel state information from the up-link is then correspondingly used to steer the space-frequency pre-coding and to schedule the data transport in the space-frequency domain at the AP, to maximize the throughput and to minimize the latency of the individual users. The data are pre-coded, which means that the MIMO processing is already done at the AP, so that only minor post-processing is required at the MT, such as scaling, demodulation and decoding. The data streams to be multiplexed in space shall already arrive spatially separated at the MT antennas.

Ad-hoc mode— Here the effort is shared between the stations, based on the eigenmode signaling, which results in the minimal total effort for the MIMO processing as well. Initially, the MTs exchange pilot signals for the channel estimation. The space-frequency pre-processing at the transmitting MT is then used to couple the data optimally into the MIMO channel and the post-processing at the receiving MT is used to couple them out. The throughput is optimized by the channel-adaptive space-frequency power and rate control.

Summarizing the above statements, we see that the TDD mode offers the freedom to shift the signal processing effort to wherever it is desired, since it allows us to reuse the channel state information from the UL for the DL, and vice versa, due to channel reciprocity. This particularly enables the design of mobile terminals at reasonable costs, even for very high data rates. Moreover, optimal link adaptation becomes feasible since near-perfect channel side information is available at the transmitter.

18.15 BROADBAND MIMO CHANNELS AND CHANNEL PROPAGATION ISSUES

The mean capacity of an independent and identically distributed (i.i.d.) Rayleigh fading MIMO channel is well known to scale linearly with the minimum of the numbers of transmit and receive antennas. This is perfectly confirmed by the measurement data for an indoor non-line-ofsight (NLOS) scenario. When the line-of-sight (LOS) is added, a minor degradation is observed at large numbers of antennas, indicating a minor rank loss of the channel matrix. The huge measured capacities (more than 80 bps/Hz with 16 antennas at 20 dB SNR) are related to the observation that the LOS component is normally not as important compared to the scattered signal, at least indoor swith omni-directional antennas. In the general case of MIMO rice channels and non-omni-directional antennas, one has to take into account the trade-off between the multiplexing gain (due to the NLOS scattering environment) and the path loss gain due to the LOS component. The trade-off is mainly a function of the eigen value distribution of the mean matrix and the Tx-Rx Distance.

Future wireless systems may occupy bandwidths ranging from several 10 MHz to even 100 MHz. With increasing bandwidth, more and more taps are resolved and the channel offers a high degree of multi-path diversity. When spatial multiplexing is used, the achievable diversity order is equal to the product of the numbers of receive antennas and taps. Broadband spatial multiplexing has then two implications on the channel capacity: Firstly, the mean capacity increases with the number of antennas. Secondly, the more taps are resolved, the sharper becomes the capacity distribution which is a result of the huge amount of diversity offered by the channel. Therefore, broadband MIMO systems not only provide a higher capacity, they also have higher link reliability and promise almost wire-like quality of service (QoS). If we anticipate that the slope of the capacity which is simulated over 10 random i.i.d. channel realizations) can be continued (dashed blue line), then the outage probability becomes negligible even when it is measured against figures of merit in the core network.

On the other hand, the spatial structure of the MIMO channel may change as we go from indoor to outdoor scenarios. In Fig. 18.12, the ordered singular values (SVs) for three scenarios (plotted versus frequency) are compared to the theoretical distributions for the i.i.d. Rayleigh fading channel (The SVs can be considered as the amplitude gains of the spatially multiplexed streams). The random matrix theory predicts an almost equal spacing between the mean SVs. Indoor data agree fairly well with this expectation, and a similar distribution is found at an urban crossing, as well. But on an almost empty parking lot, which is a rather extreme outdoor scenario where the scattering is significantly reduced, the two largest SVs values start to separate from the others. Note that different field directions are addressed in these measurements by four sets of triple antennas addressing different field directions. The two channels with significantly enhanced SVs are due to the polarization, offering multiple spatial channels also in the worst-case line-of-sight scenario.

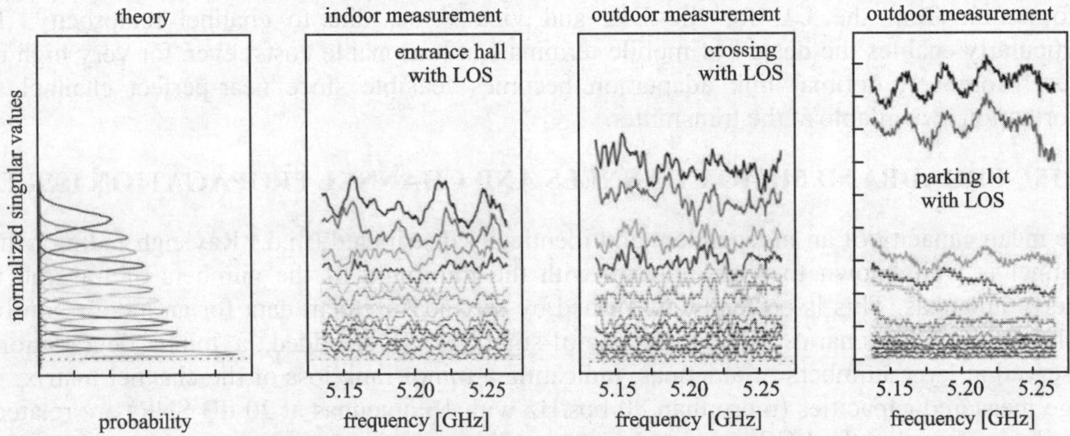

Fig. 18.12: Singular Value Distributions in Three Scenarios, Compared to the Theory

Note that the gains of the spatial channels change from frequency to frequency, which is obvious from Fig. 18.12, and sometimes they become zero for one or more spatial channels at certain frequencies. In order to transmit the data optimally over such arbitrarily conditioned MIMO channels, we need an individual link adaptation at each frequency bin and on each spatial channel. Such a concept may be realistic if we exploit the channel knowledge from the reverse link direction, and when the channel is not too rapidly changing. Of course, we need to signal what transmission mode is used in order to reduce receivers processing load. Then the granularity of this adaptation (in frequency domain, # of different modulations, coding rates etc.) becomes an issue as too fine granularity consumes too much capacity. A proper trade-off between adaptation and signaling granularity is required here.

18.16 CHANNEL MODELING ISSUES

The above results point out the necessity of developing a better understanding of the underlying propagation conditions, and more generally the features of the channel critical to communication systems operating in the broadband MIMO OFDM setting for short range and long range scenarios. Of particular importance among these features are the parameters characterizing the eigenmodes/singular modes of the propagation channel, the time-frequency variant structure, the effect of polarization and correlation. In a broadband MIMO model nicknamed Maxent MIMO Model based on information theoretic considerations (maximum entropy principle) was developed and shown to be capacity complying. It includes the time-variant structure as well as the angles of arrival and departure The maximum entropy principle is a general method which is consistent with one's state knowledge to construct maximum entropy based models. One of the interesting features of the models is their ability to take into account one's state of knowledge and leave in an unconstrained space all the information not provided. The resulting models are mainly based on product of random matrices with Gaussian entries (due to information based on the mean and the variance, otherwise this is not the case) with some pattern mask depending on the relations in the environment. The Maxent model encompasses Sayeed's virtual representation, the Kronecker model and the so-called keyhole channels as special cases. However, the effect of polarization, path loss (for the link budget), the effect of transmit and receiver filters, the effect of the antenna pattern and correlation are still open issues and need to be addressed in light of the transmission techniques to be used in MIMO-OFDM TDD mode.

18.17 MIMO ALGORITHMS FOR TDD

One basic advantage of MIMO-OFDM is that we can reuse the well-known algorithms from the flat fading channel on each carrier. In general, we wish to shift as much signal processing as possible to the AP, to allow economic MTs at high data rates. Next we distinguish between the infrastructure and ad-hoc mode.

Infrastructure up-link— Linear MIMO detection schemes, as the MMSE detector, may have the worst performance at first sight, but they have the proven potential to be implemented in real time for larger numbers of antennas, using parallel multiply-and-accumulate structures realizable in FPGAs and ASICs. The loss of capacity is not as large when a suitable link adaptation is used, which is surprisingly efficient also with linear schemes. These adaptive linear algorithms may be extended to the case of MIMO-OFDM where the gap to the optimal schemes reduces further, eventually due to the multi-path diversity. Hence, the linear schemes may serve as a good basis to introduce the new technique in the field. Later, the detectors may be replaced by better schemes, as successive interference cancellation (SIC), lattice-aided detection, sphere decoding or maximum-likelihood detection (MLD). Note that for each of these schemes, a suitable link adaptation must be developed in order to satisfy quality-of-service requirements.

Infrastructure down-link— Recent information theory shows that the down-link capacity region is the same as in the up-link, provided that the channel coefficients are known at the transmitter. This fundamental result is called the up-link/down-link duality. So it is not surprising that the well known up-link processing schemes have corresponding for the down-link.

For instance, the down-link scheme for the well-known zero-forcing algorithm in the up-link is called channel inversion. Similarly, there are dual algorithms based on the SIC (Tomlinson-Harashima pre-coding on modulo-lattice reduction and also the sphere pre-coding has recently been reported .The dual scheme for the MLD is the classical "dirty paper" pre-coding which states in principle that known interference signals are not relevant for the channel capacity. But the realization is not yet known. As for the up-link, the better the performance, the higher is the effort.

Ad-hoc mode— Here, the optimal eigenmode signaling can be directly used. It requires simple matrixvector operations both at the transmitter and at the receiver. There are hints that the eigenmode signaling is sensitive in time-varying channels, since the CSI at transmitter and receiver may differ from each other and this could eventually lead to a confused stream assignment . These effects can be avoided by passing the pilot signals through the pre-coder, which is then considered as a part of the effective channel. So the stream assignment can be restored at the receiver .

18.18 MIMO IN TDD

Reciprocity

Personal Handyphone System (PHS) in Japan already operates in the TDD mode, and it exploits the channel reciprocity for the array processing at the base station. Unfortunately, the technology is driven by a single company (Arraycom) and PHS is no internationally supported standard. Moreover, the PHS is a narrowband system and it does not apply multiple antennas at the MT. Many questions concerning the antenna calibration must be reconsidered for the broadband case until the reciprocity-based technique is applicable to OFDM signals. For dealing with reciprocity, we must consider two points: Firstly, it requires special (calibrated) RF front-ends to be realized. Secondly, the reciprocity may get lost due to the terminal movement, so that the CSI taken over from the reverse link becomes outdated. Both issues must be considered, separately.

Transceiver calibration The major advantage of the TDD system is the inherent channel reciprocity, and the presented system concept is fully based on it. But the reciprocity holds only at the antennas, and normally it gets lost in the base-band after the IQ mixer. One usually uses different IQ mixers, amplifiers and path lengths in the separate RF chains at the transmitter and at the receiver. There has been previous work concerning the calibration of the PHS base station array antennas in order to exploit the channel reciprocity. In principle, one of the base station antennas is used as a reference transmitter, and the test signal transmitted from that antenna over the air is measured at the receivers of all other base station antennas for the purpose of calibration. Based on the results of such measurements, a calibration procedure is developed which allows the desired reciprocal processing of the base-band signals of all antenna elements.

Papers from the scientific community recently propose self-calibration techniques. For instance, a noise source is used as a reference in [3], while the antenna is disconnected from the transceiver. But then the effort in the RF chain is increased, due to additional switches and directional couplers, which all must be perfectly matched. This is likely to increase the costs of the terminal (note that reciprocity is also required at the terminal, at least in the ad-hoc mode).

More recently, a reciprocal transceiver structure has been proposed. In principle, one may re-use the IQ mixer and the low-noise and power amplifiers in the TDD mode, since the terminal does not transmit and receive simultaneously. By using an RF transfer switch, the link direction of the in-line low-noise and power amplifiers can be reversed. Moreover, the IQ mixer is reused, both as a modulator and demodulator. In a hybrid setup, which has already been tested in the lab, a calibration procedure is still required. It directly estimates all the parameters contributing to the residual non-reciprocity (phase errors, amplitude imbalances), based on a precise transceiver model. From the estimated parameters, individual calibration matrices are formed for the transmitter and receiver modes. The error vector magnitude of the residual non-reciprocity has such been reduced down to -30 dB. Currently, the calibration is narrow-band, and it is useful in a 20 MHz bandwidth. But we like to point out that a careful integration of the amplifier and the transfer switch, combined with digital up- and down-conversion or an analogue IQ mixer with negligible imbalance could make these transceivers calibration-less. This is desirable, at least at the mobile terminal .

18.19 TIME-VARIANT CHANNELS

Of course, the wireless channel must itself be reciprocal as well. It is easy to prove this with two antennas and a network analyzer in the lab, by alternately measuring the channel in both directions. The reciprocity is given even in indoor scenarios, where the scattering is rich. But as soon as antennas move faster than the channel is updated, time variation destroys the channel reciprocity. Hence, time variation must be negligible while the channel coefficients are estimated in the up-link and the precoded data are then transmitted in the down-link. At low mobility, this requires a simple change in the OFDM burst structure, where the pilot signals for the channel estimation are initially transmitted from the MT to the BS. At higher mobility, the changes in the link direction must be realized very fast. The challenge is then to still identify the signals from different antennas, to estimate the channel with good quality and still to transmit a useful amount of data in a fraction of the channel coherence time. But these requirements may not be much stricter than in conventional wireless systems which use the channel information only at the receiver. We need to transmit the pilot signals only from the terminal towards the base station, either in the up-link (as in the conventional system) or prior to the down-link and receive the data within the coherence time. Such a roundtrip needs two times the propagation delay (2 μs for a distance of 300 m), which is shorter than one OFDM symbol if the number of sub-carriers and the length of the guard interval are properly designed as described.

18.20 INTERFERENCE

Interference is the true headache in cellular TDD systems. It arises from many reasons (uplink downlink synchronization, intra- and inter-cell interference) and it is handled with additional interference management functionality.

Synchronization-related interference— A major promise of the TDD mode in UTRA is the flexible load distribution between up-link and down-link. However, the results in clearly indicate that the switching point between up- and downlink must be synchronized in adjacent cells, particularly in the down-link, while the up-link is less affected.

Intra-cell interference— When a continuous CDMA signal is transmitted over a multi-path fading channel, the spreading codes are no longer orthogonal, which causes multiple-access interference as well as interference between consecutive CDMA symbols. Both can be removed with rather complex receiver structures which is critical at the mobile terminal.

The OFDM signaling waveforms remain orthogonal also in multi-path channels. provided that a suitable guard interval is used, and that the synchronization of the MTs is well established, there may be no intra-cell interference, at least in the down-link. In the up-link, each terminal must be individually synchronized. This is straightforward, when the terminals are operated in the TDMA mode, as in the Hiper Lan 2 standard. With OFDMA in the uplink, the synchronization becomes an issue to be addressed, in particular when multiple users must be supported at a single carrier, as suggested by the information theory.

Inter-cell interference— Reusing the carrier frequency in adjacent cells became popular with the CDMA systems where it was claimed that all interference can be suppressed by the processing gain. But the exemplary results in indicate that this approach might be wrong, since no cooperation between adjacent base stations is realized. The performance in a given cell depends strongly on the load in the adjacent cells, and it is obvious that the inter-cell interference is a limiting factor when the system load is high, even with optimal receiver structures.

18.21 CROSS-LAYER DESIGN

Multiple Access for MIMO: Single Vs. Multiple Link Optimization

In wireless single user links, one applies multiple antennas in order to increase the spectral efficiency and the performance. Many results and techniques are well known that can achieve a certain performance and that can guarantee a certain spectral efficiency . Furthermore, the properties of the multiple antenna channel and their impact on the performance was analyzed .

On the other hand, in multiuser scenarios, the MIMO multiple access channel (MAC) appears in the uplink transmission from multiple users to the multi-antenna base station. In general, the optimal transmit strategies depend crucially on the applied performance metric. Different power constraints can be imposed: The sum power of all users can be constrained to limit inter-cell interference. The transmit powers of each user can be constrained or the transmit power of each antenna of each user can be bounded. In addition to the power constraint, the type of channel state information (CSI) at the mobiles and at the base plays an important role. In the proposals for High Speed Uplink or Downlink Packet Access (HSDPA, HSUPA), the multiuser transmit as well as receive strategy depend on the channel quality and on the quality-of-service (QoS) requirements of the users.

18.21.1 Queuing Theoretic Analysis: Stability and Capacity

With the expected increasing proliferation of new services, which require low delay and high-rate uplinks, like e.g. image/video-upload, is associated a need for flexible uplink transmission design. Hence, the issue of efficient uplink scheduling is gaining increasing importance in the design of e.g. HSUPA radio link scheme proposed for future use. Recently, a number of multiple access scheduling policies based on combined optimization of the bursty data-packet traffic of the data-link layer and the information flow of the PHY has been presented [16]. Such scheduling design constitutes a distinct field of cross-layer design of the network communication stack [2]. The idea behind cross-layer design is to allow for the combined optimization of different objectives throughout the communication stack, which can result in increased network efficiency.

18.21.2 Minimizing Dependency towards Channel State Information

Optimal multi access transmission strategies require a complete channel state information to be available at the transmitter/scheduler to form the correct precoding matrices, power allocation. In view of the uncertainty surrounding the channel estimation at the transmitter due to the non-full reciprocity of the TDD channel, it is of interest to investigate scheduling techniques which either are more robust to errors in transmit channel state information (TCSI) or reduce the need for it. Recently, it was proposed a reduced feedback scheme for multiuser diversity in single transmit antenna systems which reduces the feedback needs by as much as 90% while maintaining 90% of the system capacity. The technique is based on a channel quality thresholding principle used to discard certain users from the competition in accessing the channel. This type of techniques is currently being investigated for extension to the MIMO case with SDMA.

18.21.3 Dynamic Resource Allocation for Deterministic Channel use

A key advantage of wideband OFDM(A) systems is the possibility of performing multiuser Water filling both in time and frequency. Although the ergodic capacity region is not increased by the wideband resources, the additional dimensions potentially allow for a more fair use of the channel due to the increased randomness in the system. This randomness can be beneficial if constraints are placed in order to guarantee a certain instantaneous bandwidth. As mentioned earlier, the latter are particularly important for today's circuit-switched applications (e.g. voice, real-time video) if they are to be run effectively on wireless packet networks. In the context of a cross-layer view, we are interested in wideband resource allocation strategies guaranteeing the peak queue length as opposed to average queue length for a given link. In orthogonal allocation and power control strategies guaranteeing a deterministic channel use (i.e. guaranteed instantaneous bit-rate) are considered for parallel (e.g. OFDMA) slowly fading channels with multiple-antennas. These strategies are thus very appealing for slowly-fading TDD systems since exploiting amplitude Reciprocity does not pose significant constraints on electronics design. The achievable rates approach those of the ergodic sum-rate, however with strict guarantees on channel use.

18.22 REAL-TIME IMPLEMENTATION

The system concept is based on full channel information at the transmitter. Since the wireless channel may change rapidly, in particular when the terminal is moving, we need to adapt to the current channel realization already prior to transmission. The long-term channel variation is not predictable in rich scattering scenarios. This might be possible only in cases where the LOS component is dominant.

So the adaptation to the channel must take place in a fraction of the coherence time. Typical values both for Wireless LANs and cellular systems are in the order of a few ms, even though a higher mobility is required for cell phones. Note that the proper frame length depends on the SNR at which a system operates. After an initial estimate of the channel, the time variation causes an interference rising with a slope of 20 dB per decade in time. Once this interference becomes comparable to the noise, a new estimate is needed. Wireless LANs operate at much lower noise and interference levels than cellular systems, and so they may be similarly sensitive to the time variation of the channel, even if the mobility is much lower.

All operations concerning the transmitted signal (spaced-frequency pre-coding and scheduling) must be properly adapted in this short time. So the algorithms must strictly satisfy real-time constraints while performing close to optimal, which is the basic challenge in the system concept considered here. Most principle problems in the real-time implementation of MIMO-OFDM have already been solved separately, but the system integration has not yet been fully finished. Regarding the up-link, the definition of orthogonal pre-ambles, the corresponding low-complexity channel estimation, the fast weight calculation and at least the linear data reconstruction have already been integrated and successfully tested over the air in a number of prototypes, almost simultaneously. In the following, we refer to [2]. Figure (left) shows part of the reconstructed BPSK data signals (I and Q signals for two antennas) after the spatially multiplexed transmission over the air at 5.2 GHz, estimating the channels for all 48 used sub-carriers, calculating the weight matrices and reconstructing the data signals using the linear MMSE algorithm, which all is done in real time. The minor cross-talk between the I and Q branches is due to the IQ imbalance in the three receiver chains. The right part of Figure shows the effect of the multi-path fading, which is resolved in the frequency domain with OFDM. Using the channel-aware MIMO-OFDM concept described above, the corrupted carriers in the upper side-band would not be loaded with data, while the lower side-band will carry most of the traffic. Concerning the complexity, the 3-antenna receiver for 2 transmitted data streams fits into a Virtex II/8000 FPGA, where the channel estimation and data reconstruction are performed. The limitation comes from the dedicated BlockRAMs needed to store the channel and weight coefficients close to either the correlation circuits for the channel estimation or to the multipliers in the matrix vector multiplication unit used for the data reconstruction, respectively. The combination of adaptive modulation and linear MIMO detection has recently been demonstrated with a flat-fading MIMO detector. It may be straight forward to implement the adaptation for multiple carriers as well . The down-link is in principle very similar. For a single carrier, the linear pre-coding and the interference-free signal reception at multiple mobile terminals has already been demonstrated, based on the channel side information obtained over a perfect feed-back link.

Review Points

There are three basic parameters that completely describe the quality and usefulness of any wireless link: speed, range and reliability. Prior to the development of MIMO-OFDM, the three parameters were interrelated according to strict rules. Speed could be increased only by sacrificing range and reliability. Range could be extended at the expense of speed and reliability. And reliability could be improved by reducing speed and range. MIMO OFDM has redefined the tradeoffs, clearly demonstrating that it can boost all three parameters simultaneously. While MIMO will ultimately benefit every major wireless Industry.

Multipath propagation is a feature of all wireless communication environments. There is usually a primary (most direct) path from a transmitter at point “A” to a receiver At point “B.” Signals traversing less direct Paths arrive at the receiver later and are often attenuated. A common strategy for dealing with weaker multipath signals is to simply ignore them—in which case the energy they contain is wasted. The strongest multipath signals may be too strong to ignore, however, and can degrade the performance of wireless LAN equipment based on existing standards.

MIMO, in contrast, takes advantage of multipath propagation to increase throughput, range/coverage, and reliability. This is accomplished by sending and receiving more than one data signal in the same radio channel at the same time. MIMO transmits multiple signals across the communications channel (rather than the conventional system's single signal), MIMO has the ability to multiply capacity.

MIMO can also be thought of as a multi-dimensional wireless communications system. MIMO empowers engineers to work in multiple dimensions, creating opportunities to work around the limitations of a one-dimensional channel. Greater spectral efficiency translates into higher data rates, greater range, an increased number of users, enhanced reliability.

MIMO enhances all three performance attributes simultaneously. And while channel bonding increases throughput by consuming more bandwidth, MIMO increases spectral efficiency, multiplying throughput in the same bandwidth. Smart antennas and channel bonding are important and useful technologies but they must not be confused with MIMO technology.

OFDM is a multi carrier channel and the aim of this *multi carrier (MC) modulation* is to have a number of parallel sub-carriers high enough such that the bandwidth of one sub-carrier is significantly lower than the channel's coherence bandwidth and the frequency selective channel is hence transformed into several narrowband frequency flat fading channels. In the time domain, this means that for each individual sub-carrier the symbol time is raised much above the maximum channel delay such that the effects of ISI are negligible. The FFT size determines the number of sub-carriers in the specified bandwidth Larger FFT sizes lead to narrower subcarriers and smaller inter-subcarrier spacing

Application environment— The massive use of high quality multimedia applications (streaming audio and video, with data rates in excess of several tens of Mbit/s) for numerous users is one reason for the need of very high bit rates. Other key requirements in this area are self configuration and zero maintenance features as well as low transmit powers, to minimize exposure of humans to electromagnetic radiation.

Future wireless systems may occupy bandwidths ranging from several 10 MHz to even 100 MHz. When spatial multiplexing is used, the achievable diversity order is equal to the product of the numbers of receive antennas and taps. The mean capacity increases with the number of antennas and more taps are resolved, the sharper becomes the capacity distribution which is a result of the huge amount of diversity offered by the channel. Therefore, broadband MIMO systems not only provide a higher capacity, they also have higher link reliability and promise almost wire-like quality of service (QoS).

TDD application— A key advantage of wideband OFDM(A) systems is the possibility of performing multiuser Water filling both in time and frequency. These strategies are thus very appealing for slowly-fading TDD systems since exploiting amplitude Reciprocity does not pose significant constraints on lectronics design.. In the context of a cross-layer view, we are interested in wideband resource allocation strategies guaranteeing the peak queue length as opposed to average queue length for a given link.

In real time implementation all operations concerning the transmitted signal (spaced-frequency pre-coding and scheduling) must be properly adapted in this short time. So the algorithms must strictly satisfy real-time constraints while performing close to optimal, which is the basic challenge in the system concept considered here. Most principle problems in the real-time implementation of MIMO-OFDM have already been solved separately, but the system integration has not yet been fully finished.

Review Questions

1. State three basic parameters of wireless link and how they are interrelated?
2. Explain the feature - multipath signal propagation and mention its ill-effects on signal which is degraded.
3. Define Spectral Efficiency.
4. Explain how MIMO antennas differ from smart antenna?
5. Write about MIMO-OFDM benefits.
6. What is CSI and state how to make it available at the transmitter?
7. Explain the salient features of OFDM.
8. What are IFFT and FFT?
9. What is PAPR and mention its effects on signal?
10. Write note on operating principle of the Air-interface and explain the operations with respect ot UL and DL.
11. Write note on MIMO algorithms for TDD.
12. Explain (i) Intra-cell interference, (ii) inter-cell interference.
13. Explain how to minimize dependency towards CSI.
14. What are the issues (challenges) in real time implementation of MIMO-OFDM.

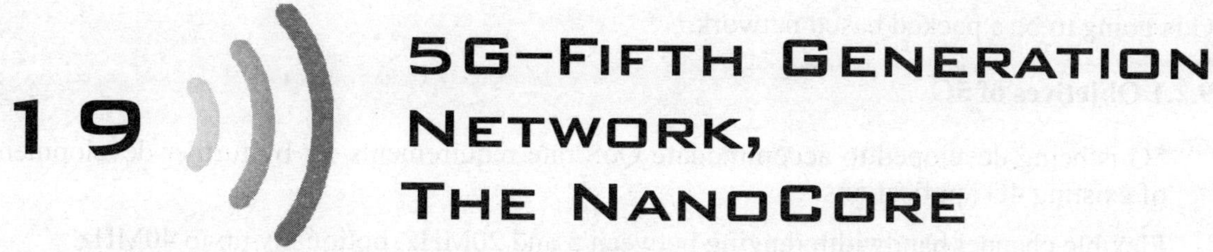

19 5G–Fifth Generation Network, The NanoCore

19.1 CONVERGENCE OF TECHNOLOGIES

5G will be more about reliability and convergence of technologies. Imagine a phone with upto 8 MIMO's and simultaneously it using different technologies. So a user is connected to the web using multiple technologies and at any instant of time he is getting multiple streams from different sources. When one of these sources fail then the other technology can simply take over and provide the connection. In a simple case if we map this to today's technology then we would have one antenna connected to HSPA, one to WiMAX, one to WiFi, one to UWB, etc., etc.

Hopefully IMS (or another similar technology) will become reality much earlier but even if it doesn't by the time 5G will arrive its already operational. Multiple devices can be connected by the same contact and present rules can control them. It can help with other services like Messaging and PoC.

Television streaming should become completely seamless and it should be possible to provide 100's of channels without any spectrum limitations.

The cell sizes can become extremely large and cells can have say 80% overlap but there would be no interference. This would even give opportunity to have Femtocell like devices that can provide coverage for say upto a kilometre and it would cause no interference. This should also help get rid of cell-edge rate problem and can help avoid congestion, capacity crunch, etc. Cloud computing can hit the mobile technology as well and the phones can do amazing things without much of the power required. A bit like the 'sixth-sense' technology case where the computation power is in the cloud and the phone is just a device to connect to the web. In fact the cloud concept could be extended where different gadgets can become part of the cloud so maybe your refrigerator can be processing your data if you are near it or maybe you television is if you are near it. The end user should not be aware and shouldn't care as long as his job is getting done. When these many features will be available in a technology then the applications can do amazing stuff, only creative developers will be required to come up with new and amazing innovative ideas.

19.2 WHAT IS 5G?

5G is a packet switched wireless system with wide area coverage and high throughput.

5G wireless uses OFDM and millimeter wireless that enables data rate of 20 mbps and frequency band of 2-8 GHz.

5G is going to be a packed based network.

19.2.1 Objetives of 5G

- 5G is being developed to accommodate QoS rate requirements set by further development of existing 4G applications.
- Flexible channel bandwidth ranging between 5 and 20MHz, optionally up to 40MHz.
- Data rate of at list 1Gb/s between any two points in the world is to be realised.
- Increase system spectral efficiency of up to 15 bit/s/Hz/cell in the downlink and 12 bit/s/Hz/cell for indoor usage.

19.2.2 IPv6 Support in 5G

- IPv6 increases the IP addresses size from 32bit to 128 bits, to support more levels of addressing hierarchy and much greater number of addressable node.
- IPv6 support large number of wireless enabled devices.
- IPv6 Extend the IP address space enough to offer a unique IP address to any device.
- IPv6 Improve support for IP Mobility.

19.2.3 Benefits of 5G

- High speed, high capacity, and low cost per bit.
- Support interactive multimedia, voice, streaming video, Internet, and other broadband services, more effective and more attractive, bi directional, accurate traffic statistics.
- Global access, service portability, and scalable mobile services.
- The high quality services of 5G technology based on policy to avoid error.
- 5G technology is providing large broadcasting of data in Gigabit which is supporting almost 65,000 connections.
- 5G technology offer transporter class gateway with unparalleled consistency.

Through remote management offered by 5G technology a user can get better and fast solution

19.2.4 What is to be Achieved in 5G

- Migration to 5G networks ensures convergence of networks, technologies, applications and services.
- 5G can serve as a flexible platform.
- Wireless carriers have an opportunity to shorten Investment return, improve operating efficiency and increase revenues.
- 5G - a promising Generation of wireless communication that will change people's lives.

19.3 CONVERGENCE TO SINGLE PLATFORM

What we have today as Nanotechnology, All IP, Cloud computing, LTE etc. are some of the technologies used by human to balance his needs. However further modernization will be on convergence of this existing technology in to a single platform. This chapter deals the same, here we have tried to converge some of the existing technologies (i.e) Nanotechnology, Cloud Computing, All IP, and LTE in to a single core network "The NanoCore" which could be a possible 5G Wireless network.

Moore's Law— Future wireless mobile communications will be shifted from today's traditional transmission-specific radio technology to an interface-based technology in order to be more compatible with computer system architecture. The future mobile device will therefore be first and foremost a computer and till today wireless Telecommunication is bounded by Moore's law. Moore's law describes a long-term trend in the history of computing hardware. The number of transistors that can be placed inexpensively on an integrated circuit has doubled approximately every two years. The trend has continued for more than half a century and is not expected to stop until 2015 or later. This law sounds well up to LTE Advanced which is considered as a latest wireless trend. But next generation wireless communication will certainly break Moore's law. Hence Moore's law is no more and it is not going to be valid in the new generation of wireless.

At this point nanotechnology comes in to picture. Nanotech is often defined as the manipulation and control of matter at the nanometer scale (critical dimensions of 1-100nm).The primary contender for the post-silicon computation paradigm is molecular electronics, a nano-scale alternative to the CMOS transistor. Eventually, molecular switches will revolutionize computation by scaling into the third dimension – overcoming the planar deposition limitations of CMOS. Nantero employs carbon nanotubes suspended above metal electrodes on silicon to create high-density nonvolatile memory chips. Carbon nanotubes are small (~10 atoms wide), 30x stronger than steel at 1/6 the weight, and perform the functions of wires, capacitors and transistors with better speed, power, density and cost.

19.4 TECHNOLOGICAL DEVELOPMENT

1G— The 1st generation was pioneered in early 1980's. First generation cellular mobile telephones developed around the world using different, incompatible analogue technologies. It support speed up to 2.4kbps. Major contributors were AMPS, NMT, and TACS. In terms of overall connection quality, 1G compares unfavorably to its successors. It has low capacity, unreliable handoff, poor voice links, and no security at all since voice calls were played back in radio towers, making these calls susceptible to unwanted eavesdropping by third parties.

2G— The 2nd generation was accomplished in later 1990's. 2G mobile telephones used digital technology. Group Special Mobile (GSM) was first developed in the 1980s and was the first2G system. Mainly used for Voice communication and supports speed up to 64kbps. In term "2.5G" usually describes a 2G cellular system combined with General Packet Radio Services (GPRS), or other services not generally found in 2G or 1G networks. A 2.5G system may make use of 2G system infrastructure, but it implements a packet-switched network domain in addition to a circuit- switched domain..It can support data rate up to 144kbps.GPRS, EDGE, & CDMA 2000 were the focal 2.5G technologies. This does not necessarily give 2.5G an advantage over 2G in terms of network speed, because bundling of timeslots is also used for circuit- switched data services (HSCSD).

3G— An attempt to establish an international standard for 3G mobile is being moderated through the ITU, under the auspices of its IMT-2000 program. It was inveterate in late 2000.It provides transmission speed up to 2Mbps. Third generation (3G) services combine high speed mobile access with Internet Protocol (IP)-based services. Apart from transmission speed innovative enhancement was made in Quality of services. Add on services such as global roaming, better voice quality, always on made 3G as a significant generation. In addition to being more expensive, 3G handsets also require more power than most 2G models. The major disadvantage for 3G network plans centers around pricing. Generally, 3G network price points are much higher than 2G networks with comparable features.

4G— Mobile operators face a decision: Their 3G networks will soon be overwhelmed by the amount of data traffic they are handling. And demand is growing faster and faster as customers become accustomed to "anywhere, anytime" access to the Internet. One common characteristic of the new services to be provided by 4G, is their demanding requirements in terms of QoS. Applications such as wireless broadband access, Multimedia Messaging Service (MMS), video chat, mobile TV, HDTV content and Digital Video Broadcasting (DVB) are being developed to use a 4G network.

19.4.1 4G Architecture

We believe that the future of mobile data services lies with Long-Term Evolution technology, or LTE. Offering vastly improved network performance at just a fraction of the cost of 3G technology, LTE has the capabilities to greatly expand network capacity and offer a large number of customers the ability to access a wide range of high-speed services such as video-on-demand, peer-to-peer file sharing, and complex Web services. At the same time, additional spectrum is becoming available that will enable operators to manage their networks more flexibly, offering greater coverage and better performance for less money. 4G usually refers to the successor of the 3G and 2G standards. In fact, the 3GPP is currently standardizing LTE Advanced as future 4G standard. A 4G system may upgrade existing systems in parallel with the LTE radio access, packet Core networks are also evolving to the flat SAE architecture. This new architecture is designed to optimize network performance, improve cost efficiency and facilitate the uptake of mass market IP-based services.

The Evolved Packet Switched System (EPS) provides IP connectivity between a UE and an external packet data network using the Evolved Universal Terrestrial Radio Access Network (E-UTRAN) consisting of an Evolved Packet Core (EPC) and Evolved UTRAN (E-UTRAN). E- UTRAN consists of eNBs, providing the E-UTRA user plane and control plane protocol terminations towards the UE.

The goals for LTE include improving spectral efficiency, lowering costs, improving services, making use of new spectrum and reformed spectrum opportunities, and better integration with other open standards.

19.4.2 LTE Advanced Requirements

The requirement specification TR 36.913 has already been approved in TSG-RAN#40. Detailed Technical proposals will be investigated within the working groups. Current agreements on the requirements for LTE Advanced:

- *Peak data rate DL*— 1 Gbps, UL: 500 Mbps
- *Transmission bandwidth*— Wider than approximately 70 MHz in DL and 40 MHz in UL
- *Latency*— C-plane from Idle (with IP address allocated) to Connected in <50 ms and U plane latency shorter than 5 ms one way in RAN taking into account 30% retransmissions (FFS)
- Cell edge user throughput 2 times higher than that in LTE
- Average user throughput 3 times higher than that in LTE
- Capacity (spectrum efficiency) 3 times higher than that in LTE
- *Peak spectrum efficiency DL*— 30 bps/Hz, UL: 15 bps/Hz
- *Spectrum flexibility*— Support of scalable bandwidth and spectrum aggregation
- *Mobility*— Same as that in LTE
- Coverage should be optimized in a micro cell environments with ISD up to1 km
- Backward compatibility and interworking with LTE with 3GPP legacy systems

LTE is not a revolutionary technology, nor is it meant to be. The goal of the technology is to be able to meet the future demand of wireless broadband access, and thus satisfy customer expectations of improved data transmission performance, as well as voice transmission, without having to pay more money. Ultimately, every operator has a choice: Move now to begin the transition to LTE and capture the early cost advantage, or wait until demand rises to the point where LTE investments become necessary.

19.5 NEED FOR 5G

Mobile broadband is becoming a reality, as the internet generation grows accustomed to having broadband access wherever they go and not just at home or in the office. Of the estimated 3.4 billion people who will have broadband by 2014, about 80 percent will be mobile broadband subscribers – and the majority will be served by High Speed Packet Access (HSPA) and Long Term Evolution (LTE) networks. There is strong evidence supporting predictions of increased mobile broadband usage.

But we have an uncertainty at this movement (i.e) all the above requirements are expected to be satisfied by LTE advanced itself. Then why there is a need for 5G? Yes of course LTE might support peak data rate of DL: 1Gbps, UL: 500Mbps within a scalable bandwidth where the user can gratify his requirement. In turn LTE advanced provides beyond the demand. The actual dilemma starts here…

As per the present status all over the world WCDMA is commercially launched .Some nations has planned to launch LTE within next quarter. Operator is looking ahead for wide-scale deployment of LTE in 2012. Operators will also find that the timing is right to make the switch because much of the first generation of 3G equipment will need to be upgraded soon. LTE networking equipment and handsets, already under development, will become available in 2010, and should be rolled out in large quantities in Europe by 2012.

This clearly shows that within 2020 LTE will become the latest trend for wireless communication all over the world. But yet our question remains unanswered. Why there is a need for 5G? Though LTE provides wide range of growth for present wireless telecommunication, people are not in a circumstance to make use of those benefits in an effective manner. LTE might be rigorously used in commercial/Industrial areas. But think of a common man who utmost utilize LTE for downloading a movie or make a video call. Fact is that there is no such ground-breaking application exists in real world to be utilized by a common man. We may doubt how this verdict is applicable for current innovative world, where we have enormous splendid real time applications. Concern is that our present wireless telecommunications is bottlenecked to use those applications in an effective manner.

We will now mainly focus on how a 5G network can provide more approach to a common man to utilize his available possessions in an immense way to make him to feel the real progress. While considering a 5G network now it is very obvious that the access network is almost frozen and there will not be any further modification. Current OFDMA is appropriate for at least next half a century. Then what could be the amendment for 5G? Furthermore their won't be any alter in the wireless infrastructure as it happened from 1G to 4G instead there could be add-on application or up gradation done at the core network to satisfy customer needs. This will make the operators/Service providers to sense preeminent to migrate for a 5G as soon as possible once 4G is commercially deployed.

While considering a smooth migration for 5G it is apparent that it should be valid for all sorts of radio access technologies. So that it could make better revenue for current global operators as well as interoperability will become more feasible. To make 5G practical for all sorts of radio access technologies there should be a common platform unique for all the technologies. One of those unique platforms is Flat IP network.

19.6 FLAT IP NETWORK

Certainly Flat IP network is the key concept to make 5G acceptable for all kind of technologies. To meet customer demand for real-time data applications delivered over mobile broadband networks, wireless operators are turning to flat IP network architectures. Flat IP architecture provides a way to identify devices using symbolic names, unlike the hierarchical architecture such as that used in "normal" IP addresses. This is of more interest to mobile broadband network operators.

With the shift to flat IP architectures, mobile operators can:

- Reduce the number of network elements in the data path to lower operations costs and capital expenditure

- Partially decouple the cost of delivering service from the volume of data transmitted to align infrastructure capabilities with emerging application requirements
- Minimize system latency and enable applications with a lower tolerance for delay; upcoming latency enhancements on the radio link can also be fully realized.
- Evolve radio access and packet core networks independently of each other to a greater extent than in the past, creating greater flexibility in network planning and deployment
- Develop a flexible core network that can serve as the basis for service innovation across both mobile and generic IP access networks
- Create a platform that will enable mobile broadband operators to be competitive, from a price/performance perspective, with wired networks Flat network architecture removes that voice-centric hierarchy from the network. Instead of overlaying a packet data core on the voice network, separate and much- simplified data architecture can be implemented that removes the multiple elements from the network chain.

That's why the developers of the next generation of mobile networks are trying to build security in from the star for prevailing 5G networks. And what all the technologies incorporated in it to craft it as a global server.5G networks make use of this flat IP concept to make it easier for different RAN to upgrade in to a single Nano Core network. Our 5G network uses Nanotechnology as defensive tool for security concern that arises due to flat IP.

19.7 RADIO ACCESS NETWORK (RAN)

Radio resource management which is more important is provided by these :

RAN- Radio Access Network in GSM GPRS/EDGE, UMTS, IP Network, The Nano Core Communication, Medical/Health/Education, Nanotechnology, Morph, Graphene Nanosensor Satellite GPS, Quantum cryptography EV-DO, CDMA ONE, IS 95 and ISP AIPN

MultiCore Technology is provided by,

- ✓ NE - Nano Equipment (UE)
- ✓ AIPN –All IP Network
- ✓ NanoCore - Server

Nanotechnology faids a place firmly in,

- Quantum Computing, Nano Dots, Optoelectronics, Quantum cryptography
- Cloud Computing-Application Platform Infrastructure-Business Cloud
- Government-Private Portal-Public Portal and Banking

Incorporated Technologies

Sophisticated technology has enabled an age of globalization. Technological convergence is the tendency for different technological systems to evolve towards performing similar tasks. What Nicholas Negroponte labeled the transformation of "atoms to bits," the digitization of all media content is the recent development. When words, images and sounds are transformed into digital information, we expand the potential relationships between them and enable them to flow across platforms.

19.8 NANO-AIPN-CLOUD - CONVERGENCE

The Nano Core-The 5G Nancore is a convergence of below mention technologies. These technologies have their own impact on existing wireless network which makes them in to 5G

Table 19.1: Compare 4G with 5G

	4G(2000-10)	*5G(2010-15)*
Switching	All packets	All packets
Service	Dynamic information access, wearable devices	Dynamic information access, wearable devices with AI capabilities
Data rate	Up to 20Mbps	Up to 1 Gbps
Technology	combination of broadband, LAN/WAN/PAN/WLAN and wwww	combination of broadband, LAN/WAN/PAN/WLAN and wwww
Standards	Single unified standards	Single unified standards
Multiplexing	CDMA	CDMA

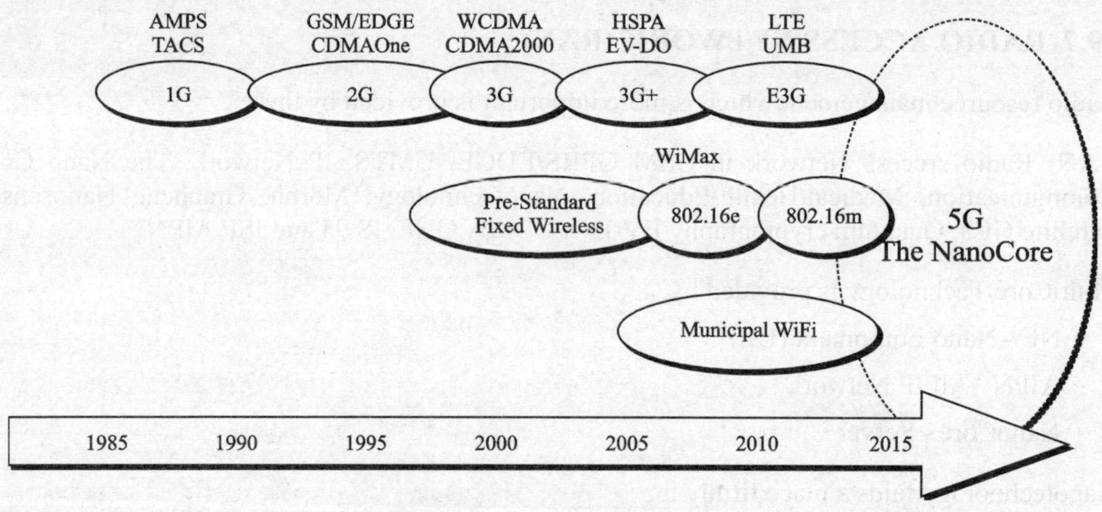

Fig. 19.1: Evolution path to 5G

19.9 NANOTECHNOLOGY

Nanotechnology is the application *of* nano science to control process on nano meter scale. i.e between 0.1 and 100nm.The field is also known as molecular nanotechnology(MNT).MNT deals with control of the structure of matter based on atom-by-atom and molecule by molecule engineering. The term nanotechnology was introduced by Nori Taniguchi in 1974 at the Tokyo international conference on production engineering.

Nanotechnology is the next industrial revolution, and the telecommunications industry will be radically transformed by it in a few years. Nanotechnology has shown its impact on both mobile as well as the core network. Apart from this it has its own impact on sensor as well as security. This is considered as a most significant in telecommunication. We will be discussing the same in our further slides.

19.9.1 Nano Equipment (NE)

Mobile phone has become more than a communication device in modern world but it has turned into an identity of an individual. In 5G NanoCore these mobile are referred as NanoEquipment as they are geared up with nanotechnology. One of the central visions of the wireless industry aims at ambient intelligence: computation and communication always available and ready to serve the user in an intelligent way. This requires that the devices are mobile. Mobile devices together with the intelligence that will be embedded in human environments – home, office, public places – will create a new platform that enables ubiquitous sensing, computing, and communication

Specification of Nano Equipments

Self Cleaning – the phone cleans by itself

Self powered – the phone derives its energy/power from the sun, water, or air.

Sense the environment – the phone will tell you the weather, the amount of air pollution present, etc.

Flexible – bend but not break Transparent – "see through" phones

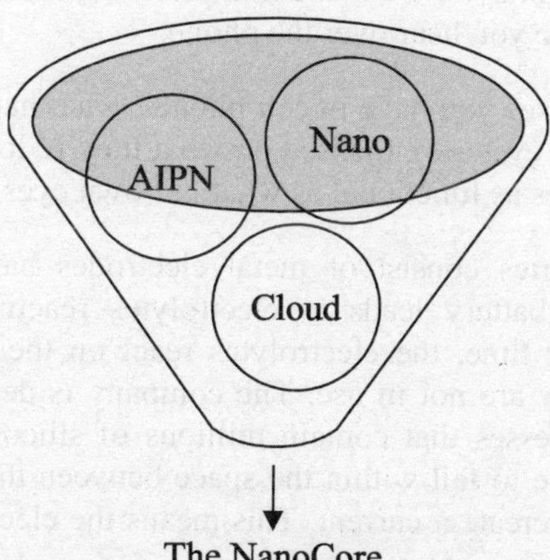

Fig. 19.2: The Nano Core

Concept of Morph— Nokia together with the University of Cambridge (UK), has developed this concept called Morph. Morph is from the Greek morphe meaning shape or form Morph is a concept that demonstrates how future mobile devices might be stretchable and flexible, allowing the user to transform their mobile device into radically different shapes. It demonstrates the ultimate functionality that nanotechnology might be capable of delivering: flexible materials, transparent electronics and self-cleaning surfaces.

Graphene's Transistor— The IBM scientists, sponsored by DARPA (the U.S. Defense Advanced Research Projects Agency), have built prototype transistors with the new material, called graphene. It is a form of graphite that consists of a single layer of carbon atoms arranged in a honeycomb pattern. Graphene's structure allows electrons to travel through it very quickly and gives it greater efficiency than existing transceiver chip materials. IBM announced Thursday the researchers have achieved a frequency of 26GHz on prototype graphene transistors. Those frequencies are far above what cellular networks use today. There may be military and medical uses for frequencies above 1THz, such as seeing concealed weapons or doing medical imaging without using harmful x-rays.

But at conventional frequencies, graphene-based transceivers could make both cell phones and base stations more sensitive and better able to pick up weak signals. The key is signal-to-noise ratio, or being able to distinguish the radio signal from the other waves around it. At a given distance, a phone with a better signal-to-noise ratio can take better advantage of the signal available from the nearest cell tower. A more sensitive phone might even work in areas where today's phones can't.

GPS— Nanotechnology soon could enhance cell phones with carbon- nano tube vacuum tubes, microscopic microphones, liquid lenses, compasses linked with global positioning system satellites and even electronic noses.

Micro-Micro Phones— "We have two ears to help locate sounds in space. This helps us focus in on a single conversation in a noisy room. Having multiple microphones would allow us to be maximally sensitive to the sounds we want and minimally sensitive to the sounds we don't. This would help cut down the noise you hear over the phone.

Liquid lens— In the fixed lenses you have in cell phones, what happens is there is a lot of jitter, the image is a mess, but your eyes stay focused on what they're looking at -- do jitter reduction. So we want to make our optics as functional as what our own eyes have.

Intelligent Batteries— Batteries consist of metal electrodes bathed in chemicals known as electrolytes. Plugging in a battery leads to electrolytes reacting, with electrons streaming through the electrodes. Over time, the electrolytes react on their own, which is why battery power drains even when they are not in use. The company is developing a battery crafted via semiconductor industry processes that contain millions of silicon nanotubes, atop each sits a droplet of electrolyte. If made to fall within the space between the tubes by applying a voltage change, the droplets react to create a current. This means the electrolytes activate only when in use.

Nanosensor— Impact of nanotechnology over mobile phones has made them to act as intelligent sensors. Nanosensors and nano-enabled sensors have applications in many industries, among them transportation, communications, building and facilities, medicine, safety, and national security, including both homeland defense and military operations.

Few sensors today are based on pure nano science, and the development of nano-enabled sensors is in the early stages; yet we can already foresee some of the possible devices and applications.

Physical Sensors— This approach may allow the mass of individual biomolecules to be measured. Electrometers - This device has demonstrated charge sensitivity below a single electron charge per unit bandwidth (~0.1 electrons/ Hz at 2.61 MHz), better than that of state-of-the-art semiconductor devices. Chemical Sensors - Various nano tube-based gas sensors have been described in the past few years. Biosensors - DNA detection with these nano-scale coded particles has been demonstrated.

At present further more researches are going on to realize nanotechnology for future mobile communication in different aspects. We can expect more enhancements in potential existence.

19.10 NANOTECHNOLOGY OVER CORE NETWORK

The requirement of Nano core evidently shows that it requires high speed and a reliable capacity to manipulate such a mammoth task as a single entity and to maintain a poise in security aspects as perceptive data will be transferred over air. Our most recent core (WiMAX, LTE) can't be able to accomplish these requirements. But ingress of Nano Core with Nanotechnology will fulfill the above requirements.

Creating platforms to support the necessary Nano Core elements requires performance, flexibility and extensibility in the underlying hardware/software infrastructure. DSP farms are required for media conversion and transcoding while the latest high performance computing processors take care of all the control and signaling functions. The need to combine these functions within a highly available and "network ready" chassis make Advanced TCA the ideal architecture. Advanced TCA enables the appropriate connectivity as well as the infrastructure to support high density DSP cards. Now a day□s nanotechnologies are used in DSP Fabrication. Much more new perceptions are introduced in DSP designing which increases the overall system speed & capacity.

19.11 QUANTUM COMPUTING

Quantum computing is the area of study focused on developing computer technology based on the principles of quantum theory, which explains the nature and behavior of energy and matter on the quantum (atomic and subatomic) level.

In modern digital computers, information is transmitted by flowing electricity in the form of electrons, which are negatively charged subatomic particles. Transistors in computers are electrical switches that store data as "bits," in which "off" (no electrical charge) and "on" (charge is present) represent one bit of information: either 0 or1.

For example, with three bits, there are eight possible combinations of 1 or 0: 1-1-1, 0-1-1, 1-0-1, 1-1-0, 0-0-0, 1-0-0, 0-1-0 and 0-0-1. But three bits in a digital computer can store only one of those eight combinations at a time. Quantum computers, which have not been built yet, would be based on the strange principles of quantum mechanics, in which the smallest particles of light and matter can be in different places at the same time. In a quantum computer, one "qubit" – quantum bit – could be both 0 and 1 at the same time. So with three qubits of data, a quantum computer could store all eight combinations of 0 and 1 simultaneously. That means a three-qubit quantum computer could calculate eight times faster than a three-bit digital computer. Typical personal computers today calculate 64 bits of data at a time. A quantum computer with 64 qubits would be 2 to the 64th power faster, or about 18 billion billion times faster. (Note: billion billion is correct.).

Quantum computers have the potential to perform certain calculations significantly faster than any silicon- based computer. Improved Storage capability: One of the major requirements of NanoCore is that ability to store large amount of data. More and more modern electronic devices need larger memories. Current technology makes these demands very difficult to meet, but nanotechnology offers the solution.

Nanodots— One such new data-storage device in R&D is the use of nanosized „dots□ of nickel which it is hoped could be used to store terabytes of data, even for home and personal users. Considering the relatively large (physically) storage devices we have now, and the fact we tend to currently refer to size in terms of gigabytes, the amazing potential is plain to see. Each "nanodot" consists of a discrete ball of several hundred nickel atoms and can have one of two magnetic states. This allows them to hold a single bit of information - a '1' or a '0' - as is the computing convention. In current hard drives, bits (of information) must be placed far enough apart so as not to interfere with each other.

Nanodots operate as complete units which are not structurally linked, therefore allowing them to be packed closer together. They arrange themselves at such a density that should allow anything up to 5 terabytes (5000GB) of data to be stored in a space the size of a postage stamp. Work still has to be carried out to allow these nanodots to operate and interact with other computing devices, such as silicon chips, but the technology is definitely showing promise. The Nanodot is appropriate for both NE as well as NanoCore. It will be implemented in both the part.

19.11.1 Improved Speed

To please its customers 5G needs to comprise a fast access to its services, NanoCore requires a far-fetched speed to process those multiple requirements.

Optoelectronics: Faster transfer of data within and between devices can be achieved using nanotechnology. A major limitation in transfer speeds is the use of electrical wiring and contacts. The use of optical fibres revolutionized the telecommunications industry by increasing the rate of data transfer between components. Optoelectronics can dramatically increase data transfer rates within devices such as pc's by replacing copper wiring. In the future for example, it could be possible to use quantum dot based lasers to transfer information between components within devices at the speed of light, with each piece of information 'coded' by being a unique wavelength of light.

Externally, by increasing the number of nodes in information networks, data can be transferred more rapidly between two points. This will become possible through the development of cheap ambient sensor networks based on nanotechnology. Nanotechnology is certain to improve

NanoCore network and be a strong force in developing new ones. The field is progressing, but considerable work must be done before we see its full impact.

19.11.2 Improved Security

While considering NanoCore as a global server where user can access his real time applications, there should be a special anxiety given to the security. Security of data which being transmitted should be protected all the way.

Quantum cryptography: Critical component of quantum communication device may enable cryptography. Quantum cryptography is an emerging technology currently used by both military and financial organizations to send information as entangled particles of light. In theory, anyone who tries to tap into this information changes it in a way that reveals their presence. This type of technology can be used in particular cases like when the military needs to send the key to encrypted data across the world, it can't necessarily rely on today's communication lines.

However in 5G networks were user will be accessing all kinds of significant messages from different platforms, can make use of this quantum cryptography to avoid harmful hazards.

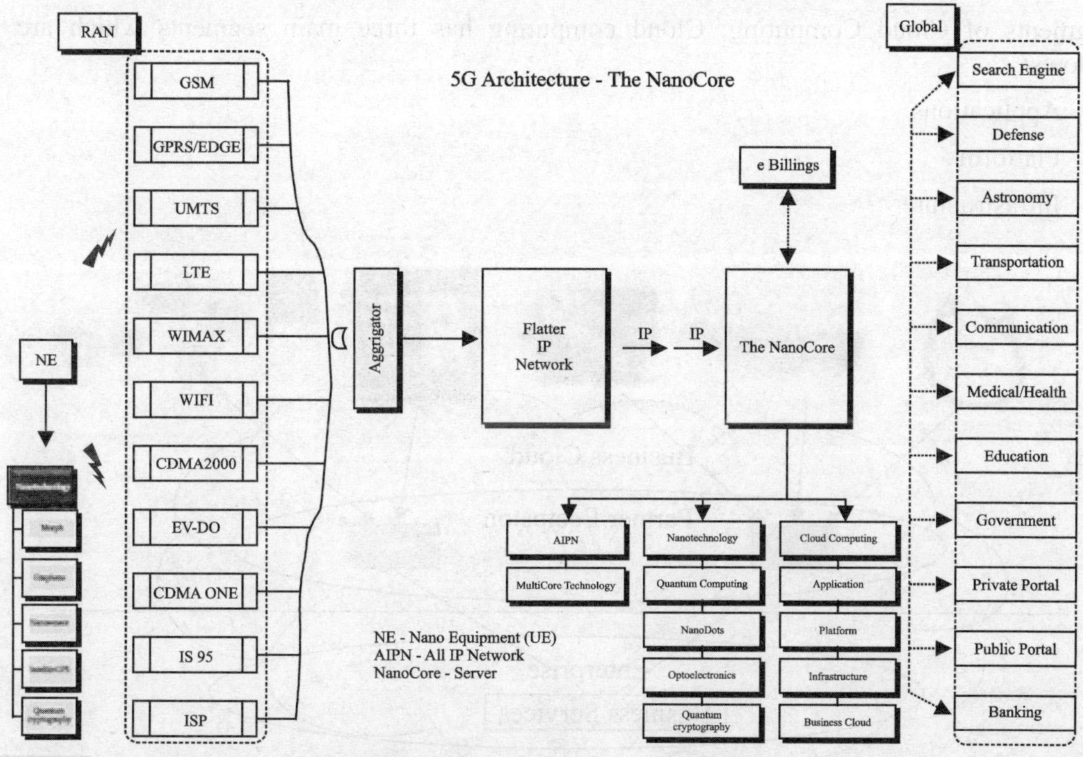

Fig. 19.3: 5G Architecture - The NanoCore

19.12 CLOUD COMPUTING

Cloud computing is a technology that uses the internet and central remote server to maintain data and applications. In 5G network this central remote server will be our content provide. Cloud computing allows consumers and business to use applications without installation and access their personal files at any computer with internet access. The same concept is going to be used in NanoCore where the user tries to access his private account form a global content provider through NanoCore in form of cloud.The development of cloud computing provides operators with tremendous opportunities. Since cloud computing relies on the networks, it shows the significance of networks and promotes network development. It also requires secure and reliable service providers, capabilities that operators have deep expertise in. Operators can enter the cloud computing market and create new value-added services and experiences by integrating industry content and applications in the digital supermarket model.This could make our user to obtain much more real-time application to utilize his 5G network efficiently. Secure and reliable service can be provided with the help of quantum cryptography. Cloud computing customer avoids capital expenditure for the Nanocore thereby also reducing the cost of purchasing physical infrastructure by renting the usage from a third party Provider(Content Provider). The NanoCore devours the resources and pay for what it uses.

Segments of Cloud Computing: Cloud computing has three main segments which are as follows:

1. Applications
2. Platform
3. Infrastructure

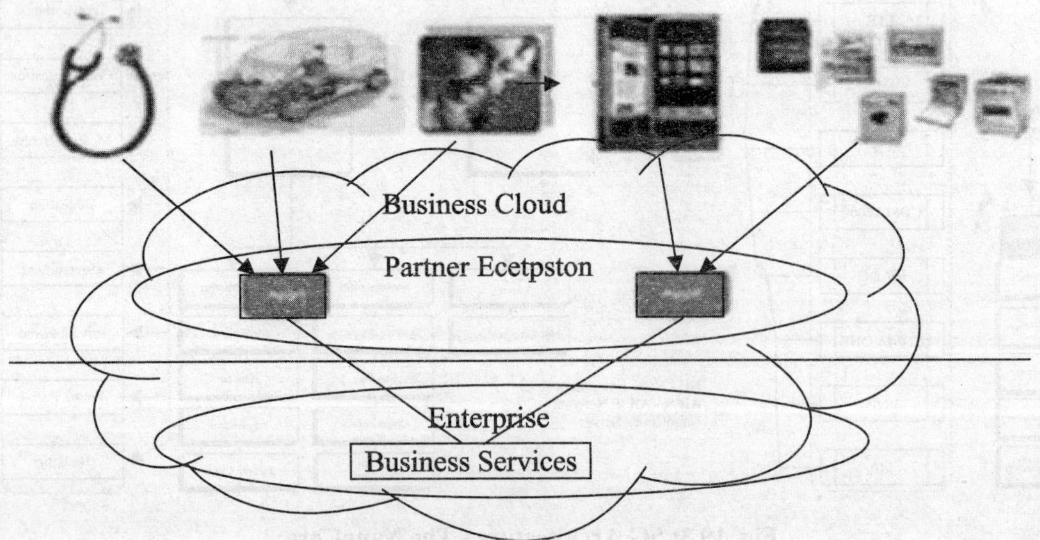

Fig. 19.4: Cloud Computing

Each segment serves different products for businesses and individuals with different purpose and applications. It is based on, on demand software services. On demand software services come in different varieties. They vary in their pricing scheme and how the software is delivered to the end users. In the past, the end-user would purchase a server that can be accessed by the end user over the internet.

Platform— The platform segment of cloud computing refers to products that are used to deploy internet. Net Suite, Amazon, Google, and Microsoft have also developed platforms that allow users to access applications from centralized servers. Google, Net Suite, Rack space cloud, amazon.com and sales force are some of the active platforms.

Infrastructure— The third segment in cloud computing, known as the infrastructure, is the backbone of the entire concept. Infrastructure vendors' environments such as Google gears allow users to build applications. Cloud storage, such as Amazon's S3, is also considered to be part of the infrastructure segment.

The 5G NanoCore will efficiently utilizes all the above 3 segments to satisfy his customer demands. The concept of cloud computing will reduce the CAPEX of 5G network deployment. In turn this will create a less billing to the end user for all kinds of services that he utilizes through NanoCore.

19.13 ALL IP NETWORK

As already discussed for converging different technologies to form a single 5G NanoCore. We require a common platform to interact. Flat IP architecture act as an essential part of 5G network. The All-IP Network (AIPN) is an evolution of the 3GPP system to meet the increasing demands of the mobile telecommunications market. To meets customer demand for real-time data applications delivered over mobile broadband networks, wireless operators are turning to flat IP network architectures. Primarily focused upon enhancements of packet switched technology, AIPN provides a continued evolution and optimization of the system concept in order to provide a competitive edge in terms of both performance and cost.

The key benefits of flat IP architectures are-lower costs, universal seamless access improved user experience, reduced system latency and decoupled radio access and core network evolution

The drive to all IP-based services is placing stringent performance demands on IP-based equipment and devices, which in turn is growing demand for multicore technology. There is strong growing demand for advanced telecommunications services on wired and wireless Next Generation Network (NGN) infrastructures, and fast growing demand for the same in the enterprise too. Data will flow more freely as mobile communications networks move toward a "flat IP" model, but developers and operators will face new security challenges. This kind of security challenges can be trounced by nanotechnology.

19.13.1 The Key Aspects of the all IP

Support for a variety of different access systems, Common capabilities provided independent to the type of service provided with convergence to IP technology considered from the perspective of the system as a whole, High performance mobility, management that provides end-user, terminal and session mobility, Ability to adapt and move sessions from one terminal to another

Ability to select the appropriate access system based on a range of criteria

Provision of advanced application services as well as seamless and ubiquitous services

Ability to efficiently handle and optimally route a variety of different types of IP traffic including user-to-user, user-to- group and ubiquitous service traffic models

High level of security and support for user privacy e.g. location privacy, identity privacy Methods for ensuring QoS within and across AIPNs

Appropriate identification of terminals, subscriptions and users

Federation of identities across different service providers

19.13.2 Multicore Technology

To support IP based architecture NanoCore should incorporate multi core technology in it. The shift to multi core technology to run advanced IP-based applications and services is well underway. Multi core technology has certainly introduced the hardware required for powerful processing demanded by converged telecommunications and enterprise applications running on IP-based architectures.

19.14 NANOCORE –AS MANAGED SERVICES

Sharing of infrastructure is becoming more general among telecom operators now days as they can give fine revenue. Noramally there are two types of infra sharing viz., Active Infra sharing and Passive Infra sharing.

Commercial deployment of NanoCore approach's a passive infra sharing where several operators can have a single shared NanoCore for their network enhancement. This could reduce their initial CAPEX requirements. NanoCore can be governed by a solitary global vendor or it can be shared among small vendors as managed services. This could make better sense in terms of Quality aspects. In rare cases, NanoCore can be oversee by the government itself. Everything depends on its enthusiastic. If this happens, all our existing operators will become Mobile Virtual Network Operator (MVNO).

19.14.1 Future Enhancement

The future enhancement of NanoCore will be incredible as it combines with Artificial intelligent (AI).One can able to control his intelligent Robot using his mobile phone. Human life will be surrounded by artificial sensors which could be communicating with your mobile phones. Your Mobile can automatically type the message what your brain thinks. We might get a circumstance where we don't require any spectrum for communication. We might be communicating with people on other planets using mobile phone December 1,2010es. We might have a single Nano Core common for all the nations. This might improve mobility of user as well as a smaller amount of billing to end user. Who knows some times we may communicate with the supernatural things with our mobile phones. Everything depends on how human being is going to utilize these technologies in an innovative manner.

19.14.2 Risk & Challenges

Each technology has its own risks & challenges. One of the major risks is that when things get globalized chance of fraudulent will be uncomplicated. Main challenge for 5G network is security concern. There should be stability between technologies which is incorporated in NanoCore to form as 5G. Even though 5G core is a miniaturized version. Cost of Nano Core will be more as it incorporates Nano devices in it, which are of high cost. Operator should realize the massive applications of 5G when he thinks for CAPEX.HW/SW specification of Nano Core could be one of the major challenges of 5G.Special care should be taken such that usage of novel technologies should not harm human health.

While the future is becoming more difficult to predict with each passing year, we should expect an accelerating pace of technological change. That it is a great time to invest in startups. As in evolution and the explosion, many will become extinct. But some will change the world. So we pursue the strategy of a diversified portfolio.

19.15 BEAM DIVISION MULTIPLE ACCESS (BDMA) FOR 5G

19.15.1 Concept of BDMA

When a base station communicates with mobile stations, an orthogonal beam is allocated to each mobile station. The BDMA technique of the present invention divides an antenna beam according to locations of the mobile stations to allow the mobile stations to give multiple accesses, thereby significantly increasing the capacity of the system. Mobile stations and a base station are in an LOS (Line of Sight) state, when they exactly know each other's positions; they can transmit beams which direct to each other's position to communicate without interfering with mobile stations at cell edge.

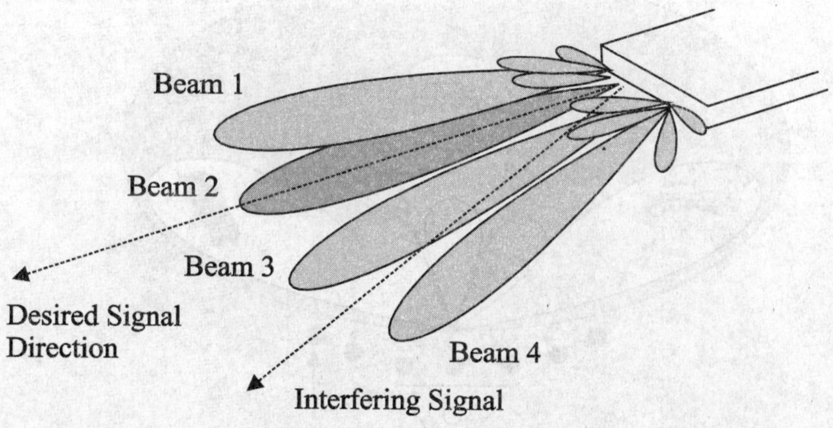

Fig. 19.5: Beam Division Access

It is an object of the present invention to provide a beam division multiple access system and a method thereof for a mobile communication system as a new space division method using a phase array antenna. Which use beam forming technology and uses multiple beam forming pattern simultaneously in a cell, allowing to give multiple access.

When mobile stations are positioned at different angles with respect to a base station, the base station transmits beams at different angles to simultaneously transmit data to multiple mobile stations.

One mobile station does not use one beam exclusively, but mobile stations positioned at a similar angle share one beam to communicate with the base station.

The mobile stations sharing the same beam divide same frequency/time resources and use orthogonal resources.

A base station can change direction, the number, and widths of the beams adaptively and easily according to a mobile communication environment.

The beams can be three-dimensionally divided; a spatial reuse of frequency/time resources can be maximized.

In initial communication step, because a base station and mobile stations do not know each other's positions, the mobile stations detect their positions and moving speeds, and omnidirectionally transmit the detected positions and moving speeds information thereof to the base station. Next, the base station calculates a direction and a width of a downlink beam based on the position and moving speed information of the mobile station received from the mobile station Subsequently, the base station transmits the downlink beam to the mobile station with the calculated direction and width. When the mobile station receives the calculated direction and width of the downlink beam, it tracks a direction of the downlink beam to set a direction of an uplink beam, and transmits the uplink beam in the set direction.

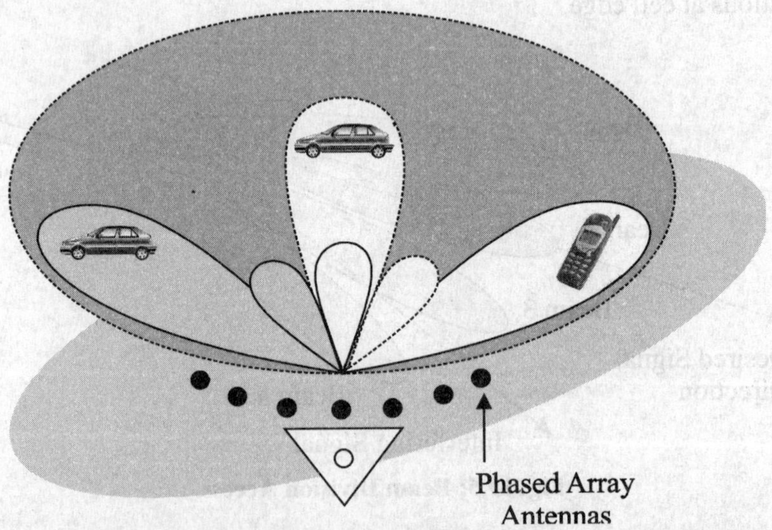

Fig. 19.6: Beam Forming

After the mobile station sets the uplink beam, a beam update is periodically performed between the mobile station and the base station.

The FDD-BDMA frame is almost the same as that of the TDD-BDMA. The difference is that the initial mobile station information slot is allocated by dividing a frequency resource, and not by dividing a time resource. A further difference is that there is a base station broadcast in the FDD-BDMA instead of a preamble of the TDD-BDMA.

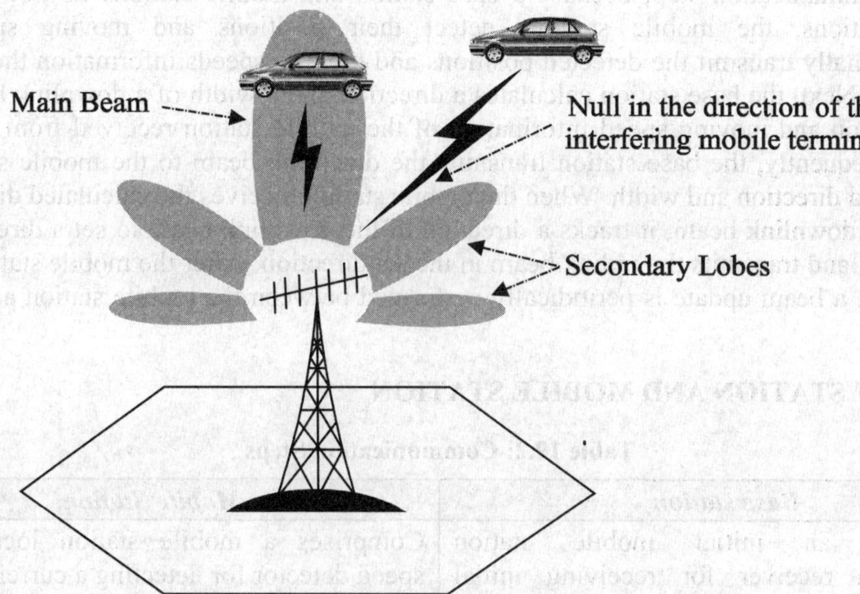

Fig. 19.7: FDD-BDMA

19.15.2 Advantages

The mobile communication system may maximize spatial use of frequency/time resources and a system capacity of a base station by the number of beams in the base station, by efficiently dividing a space resource as well as frequency/time resources, and allotting orthogonal beams to mobile stations so that the mobile stations can give multiple accesses.

It may solve an inter-cell interference problem to solve performance deterioration problems of users at cell edge occurring in a cellular system.

Radiation pattern of an antenna of the base station and radiation pattern of an antenna of the mobile station are designed to match each other; radiation efficiency of the antennas can be maximized.

In addition, since mobile stations existing at a similar position share one beam to communicate, a lower MCS level problem or PAPR (Peak-to-Average Power Ratio) problems of a control channel occurring because mobile stations having good channels and mobile stations having bad channels simultaneously use the same base station, can be solved. The BDMA is applicable to a design of cellular wireless communication systems for the next generation mobile

An uplink beam generator for tracking a direction of the downlink beam received by the downlink beam receiver and generating an uplink beam. An uplink beam transmitter for transmitting the uplink beam generated by the uplink beam generator to the base station. The uplink beam transmitter periodically transmits the current location and moving speed of the mobile station detected by the mobile station location and speed detector to the base station. At least two of the mobile stations using the same beam give multiple access To the base station.

In initial communication step, because a base station and mobile stations do not know each other's positions, the mobile stations detect their positions and moving speeds, and omnidirectionally transmit the detected positions and moving speeds information thereof to the base station. Next, the base station calculates a direction and a width of a downlink beam based on the position and moving speed information of the mobile station received from the mobile station Subsequently, the base station transmits the downlink beam to the mobile station with the calculated direction and width. When the mobile station receives the calculated direction and width of the downlink beam, it tracks a direction of the downlink beam to set a direction of an uplink beam, and transmits the uplink beam in the set direction. After the mobile station sets the uplink beam, a beam update is periodically performed between the mobile station and the base station.

19.16 BASE STATION AND MOBILE STATION

Table 19.2: Communication Steps

Base station	*Mobile Station*
Comprises an initial mobile station information receiver for receiving initial mobile station information that a mobile station omnidirectionally transmits in an initial communication	Comprises a mobile station location and speed detector for detecting a current location and moving speed of a mobile station
A mobile station location and speed detector for detecting a location and a moving speed of the mobile station from the initial mobile-station information of the initial mobile station information receiver	An initial mobile station information transmitter for omnidirectionally transmitting initial mobile station information comprising the current location and moving speed of the mobile station to a base station
A downlink beam generator for generating a downlink beam based on the location and line moving speed of the mobile station transferred from the mobile station location and speed detector The downlink beam generator adjusts a width of the downlink beam when the mobile station moves.	A downlink, beam receiver for receiving a downlink beam from the base station An uplink beam generator for tracking a direction of the downlink beam received by the downlink beam receiver and generating an uplink beam
The downlink beam generator adjusts a direction of the downlink beam when the mobile station moves.	An uplink beam transmitter for transmitting the uplink beam generated by the uplink, beam generator to the base station.

Base station	*Mobile Station*
A downlink beam transmitter for transmitting the downlink beam generated by the downlink beam generator to the mobile station through a phase array antenna.	The uplink beam transmitter periodically transmits the current location and moving speed of the mobile station detected by the mobile station location and speed detector to the base station.
A periodic mobile station information receiver for receiving and transferring periodic information in which the mobile station transmits during a beam division multiple-access communication between the base station and the mobile station, to the mobile station location and speed detector.	At least two of the mobile stations using the same beam give multiple-access to the base station.

The FDD-BDMA frame is almost the same as that of the TDD-BDMA. The difference is that the initial mobile station information slot is allocated by dividing a frequency resource, and not by dividing a time resource. A further difference is that there is a base station broadcast in the FDD-BDMA instead of a preamble of the TDD-BDMA.

Review Questions

1. Explain what is meant by convergence of Technologies.
2. What are the chief objectives of 5G?
3. What are the key benefits of 5G system?
4. What do you understand by nanotechnology?
5. Write note on Flat IP Network.
6. Explain the workign of RAN in 5G architecture.
7. What do you call NE or Nano Equipment and explain its features?
8. How quantum computing help improve the data speed as well as the security aspects?
9. Write about cloud computing in the context of 5G.
10. Write note on All IP Network.
11. Explain the concept of BDMA.
12. Write the advantages of Beam Division Multiple Access.

ABBREVIATIONS

1G	First Generation
2G	Second Generation
3GPP	3rd Generation Partnership Project
3GPP2	3rd Generation Partnership Project 2
ACCH	Associated Control Channel
ACK	Acknowledge
ACL	Access Control List
ACM	Address Complete Message
ADSL	Asymmetric Digital Subscriber Line
AES	Advanced Encryption Standard
AFRCN	Absolute Radio Frequency Chl Numbers
AI	Artificial Intelligent
AIF	Antenna Interface Frame
AM	Acknowledged Mode
AMC	Adaptive Modulation and Coding
AMPS	Advanced Mobile Phone System
ANM	Answer Message
AP	Access Point
ARIB	Association of Radio Industries and Business
ARQ	Automatic Repeat Request
ARR	Automatic Repeat Request
ATM	Asynchronous Transfer Mode
AuC	Authentication Center
BB	Building Blocks
BCCH	Broadcast Control Channel
BCH	Broadcast Channel
BDMA	Beam Division Multiple Access
BEP	Bit-Error Probability
BG	Border Gateway
BICC	Bearer Independent Call Control
BPSK	Binary Phase Shift Keying
BQTF	Bluetooth Qualification Test Facility
BSIC	The Base Station Identification code
BSS	Basic Service Set
BTS	Base Transceiver Station
CAMEL	Customized Application or Mobile network Enhanced Logic
CAP	CAMEL Application Protocol

CBC	Cell Broadcast
CCCH	Common Control Channel
CCK	Complementary Code Keying
CCU	Channel Codec Unit
CDMA	Code Division Multiple Access
CDMA-DS	CDMA Direct Sequence
CDMA-MC	Multi-Carrier
CEIR	Central Equipment Identity Register
CF	Compact Flash
CFP	Contention Free Period
CG	Charging Gateway
CLIP	Calling Line Identification Presentation
CNs	Core Networks
CP	Cyclic Prefix
CP	Communications Processor
CPC	Continuous Packet Connectivity
CPE	Common Phase Error
CSI	Channel State Information
CSMA/CA	Carrier Sense Multiple Access with Collision Avoidance
CSMA/CD	Carrier Sense Multiple Access with Collision Detection
CS-MGW	Circuit Switched Media Gateway
CT2	Cordless Telephony 2
CTS	Clear To Send
CWTS	China Wireless Telecommunication Standard group
DAMPS	Digital Advanced Mobile Phone Services
DAP	Dynamic A-bis Pool
DCCH	Dedicated Control Channel
DCF	Discrete Coordinated Function
DC-HSPA	Dual-Carrier HSPA
DDE	Dynamic Data Exchange
DECT	Digital Enhanced Cordless Technology
DFS	Dynamic Frequency Selection in the 5 GHz band
DL-SCH	Downlink Shared Channel
DNS	Domain Name Server
DO	Data Optimized
DSSS	Direct Sequence Spread Spectrum (IEEE 802.11b)
DTCH	Dedicated Traffic Channel
DTE	Data Terminal Equipment
DVB	Digital Video Broadcasting
ECSD	Enhanced Circuit-Switched Data
EDGE	Enhanced Data rates for GSM Evolution
EDGE	Enhanced Data Rates for Global Systems for Mobile
EIA	Electronic Industry Association
EIR	Equipment Identity Register

EIRP	Equivalent Isotropic Radiated Power
EPS	Evolved Packet System
ESN	Electronic Serial Numbers
ESS	Extended Service Set
ETSI	European Telecommunications Standardization Institute
EU	European Union
E-UTRAN	Evolved Universal Terrestrial Radio Access Network
FA	Foreign Agent
F-CACH	Forward Common Access Channel
FCC	Federal Communications Commission
F-CCCH	Forward Common Control Channel
FCS	Fast Cell Selection
F-DCCH	Dedicated Control Channel
FDD	Frequency Division Duplex
FDMA	Frequency Division Multiple Access
FEC	Forward Error Correction
FFT	Fast Fourier Transform
FHSS	Frequency Hopping Spread Spectrum
FITB	Fibre to The Building
FITC	Fibre to The Curb
FITH	Fibre to The Home
FMC	Fixed Mobile Convergence
FOC	Fiber-Optic Cable
F-SCH	Supplemental Channel
FSU	Support Sub Telephones
FTEG	Law regarding wireless equipment and Telecommunications installations in Germany
FWD	Fixed Wireless Terminal
GAN	Generic Access Network
GCR	Group Call Register
GERAN	GSM/EDGE Access Network
GPSK	Gaussian Phase Shift Keying
GGSN	Gateway GPRS Support Node
GMSC	Gateway Mobile Switch Center
GMSK	Gaussian Minimum Shift Keying
GPRS	General Packet Radio Services
GPS	Global Positioning System
GSM	The Global Systems for Mobile Communications
GTA	Global Title Address
GW	Gateway
HA	Home Agent
HARQ	Hybrid Automatic Repeat Request
HD	High Definition
HDSL	High Birates Digital Subscriber Line

HDTV	High Definition TV
HIPERLAN	High-performance Radio LAN in the 5 GHz band
HLR	Home Location Register
HLR.	Home Location Register
HPA	High Power Amplifier
HPLMN	Home Public Land Mobile Network
HRPD	High Rate Packet Data
HSCSD	High Speed Circuit Switched Data
HSDPA	High Speed Data Packet Access
HSDPA,HSUPA	High Speed Uplink or Downlink Packet Access
HSPA	High Speed Packet Access
HT-OFDM	High throughput OFDM, optimized version of OFDM for
IAM	Initial Address Message
IBSS	Independent Basic Service Set
ICI	Inter-Carrier-Interference
ICNIRP	International Commission on Non-Ionizing Radiation Protection
IE	Industrial Ethernet
IEEE	Institute of Electrical and Electronics Engineers
IETF	Engineering Task Force
IFFT	Inverse Fast Fourier Transform
IMEI	International Mobile Equipment Identity
IMS	IP-Multimedia Subsystem
IMSI	International Mobile Subscriber Identity
IMT	International Mobile Telecommunications
IMT2000	International Mobile Telecommunications 2000
IN	Intelligent Network
IOTA	Isotropic Orthogonal Transform Algorithm
IP	Internet Protocol
IPR	Intellectual Property Rights
IPTV	IP Television
IPv6	Internet Protocol Version 6
IR	Incremental Redundancy
IS	Intrinsically Safe (protected against explosion)
ISDN	Integrated Service Digital Network
ISM	Industrial, Scientific and Medical Band
ISO	International Standards Organization
ISP	Internet Service Provider
IT	Information Technology
ITU	International Telecommunications Union
Kc	Session Key
Kc	ciphering key
Ki	Authentication Key
LA	Link Adaptation
LAI	Location Area Identity

LAN	Local Area Networking
LCD	Liquid Crystal Display
LIG	Legal Interception Gateway
LMSI	International Mobile Subscriber Identity
LOS	Line-of-sight
LTE	Long Term Evolution
M2M	Machine-to-machine
MAC	Media Access Control
MAHO	Mobile-Assisted Handover
MAP	Mobile Application Protocol
MAP	Mobile Application Part
MB	Mobile to Base
MBMS	Multimedia Broadcast/Multicast Services
MBSFN	Multicast/Broadcast, Single-Frequency Network
MC	Multi Carrier
MCC	Mobile Country Code
MCCH	Multicast Control Channel
MCH	Multicast Channel
ME	Mobile Equipment
MEID	Mobile Equipment Identifiers
MGC	Media Gateway Controller
MGW	Media Gateway
MIC	Message Integrity Protocol Technique for increasing the integrity of data in WLANs
MID	Mobile Internet devices
MIMO	Multiple Input Multiple Output
MLD	Maximum-Likelihood Detection
MMD	Multi Media Domain
MME	Mobility Management Entity
MMS	Multimedia Messaging Service
MMSE	The Multimedia Message Service Environment
MNC	Mobile Network Code
MS	Mobile Station
MSA	Mobile Service Architecture
MSAs	Metropolitan Statistical Areas
MSC	Mobile Switching Center
MSIN	Mobile Subscriber Identity Number
MSISDN	Mobile Subscriber ISDN Number
MSISDN	Mobile Station I operation SDN Number
MSO	mobile Switching Office
MSRN	Mobile Station Roaming Number
MSS	Mobile Satellite Service within UMTS
MT	Mobile Terminal
MTCH	Multicast Traffic Channel

MTSO	Mobile Telephone System Office
MVNO	Mobile Virtual Network Operator
NAMPS	Narrow-Band AMPS
NE	Nano Equipment
NGN	Next Generation Network
NLOS	Non-Line-Of Site
NMS	Network Management System
NMT	Nordic Mobile Telephone
OFDM	Orthogonal Frequency Division Multiplexing
OFDM	Orthogonal Frequency Division Multiplex
OFDM/CCK	Orthogonal Frequency Division Multiplex/complimentary code
OMA	The Open Mobile Alliance
OMTP	Open Mobile Terminal Platform
OQAM	Offset-QAM
OS	Open Systems Interconnection
OTD	Orthogonal Transmit Diversity
PA	Power Amplifier
PAN	Personal Area Network
PAPR	Peak-to-Average Power Ratio
PCCH	Paging Control Channel
PCF	Point Coordinated Function
PCH	Paging Channel
PCMCIA	Personal Computer Memory Card International Association
PCS	Personal Communications Service
PCU	Packet Control Unit
PDA	Personal Digital Assistant
PDC	Personal Digital Cellular
PDCP	Packet Data Convergence Protocol
PDNR	Preliminary Draft New Recommendation
PHS	Personal Handyphone System
PHY	Physical Layer
PIN	Personal Identification Number
PN	Pseudo-Random Noise
PoC	Push-to-Talk over Cellular
PRN	Prol.'ide Roaming Number
PRP	Pseudo-Random-Postfix
PSS	Packet-switched Streaming Service
PSTN	Public Switched Telephone Network
QAM	Quadrate Amplitude Modulation
QoS	Quality of Service
QPP	Quadratic Permutation Polynomial
QPSK	Quadrate Phase Shift Keying
R&TTE	Radio and Telecommunications Terminal Equipment
R_DCCH	Reverse Dedicated Control Channel

RACH	Random Access Channel
RADIUS	Remote Authentication Dial
RAM	Random Access Memory
RAN	Radio Access Network
RAND	Random Number
RANs	Radio Access Networks
R-CCCH	Reverse Common Control Channel
RCM	Radio Client Module
RCS	Rich Communications Suite
R-EACH	Reverse Enhanced Access Channel
REST	Representational State Transfer
RF	Radio Frequency
R-FCH	Fundamental Channel
RLC	Radio Link Control
RLM	Radio Link Module
RNCs	Radio Network Controllers
ROM	Read Only Memory
RR	Radio Resource
RRC	Radio Resource Control
RSAs	Rural Statistical Areas
R-SCH	Reverse Supplemental Channel
RSTP	Rapid Spanning Tree Protocol
RT	Real Time
RTS	Request To Send
SACCH	Associated Control Channel
SAE	System Architecture Evolution
SAS	Security Accreditation Scheme
SAT	Supervisory Audio Tone
SC	Steering Committee
SCDMA	Synchronous Code Division Multiple Access
SC-FDMA	Single Carrier-Frequency Division Multiple Access
SCHs	Supplemental Channels
SCM	Station Class Mark
SCPs	Service Control Points
SDMA	Spatial Division Multiple Access
SDOs	Standard Development Organizations
SFN	Single Frequency Network
SGSN	Support Node
SGSN	Serving GPRS Support Node
SIC	Successive interference cancellation
SID	System Identification
SIG	Special Interest Group-The user organization for Bluetooth
SIM	Subscriber Identity Module
SMR	Specialized Mobile Radio

SMS	Short Message Service
SMSC	Short Message Center
SNMP	Simple Network Management Protocol
SON	Self-Organizing Network
SRES	Signed Response
SSID	Service Set Identifier Address
STC	Space Time Coding
STS	Space-Time Spreading
TACS	Total Access Communication Services
TCH	Traffic Channel
TCSI	Transmit Channel State Information
TD-CDMA	Time Division CDMA
TDD	Time Division Duplex
TDMA	Time Division Multiple Access
TIA	Telecommunication Industry Association
TIMSI	Temporary IMSI
TKIP	Temporal Key Integrity Protocol
TM	Transparent Mode
TMSI	Temporary Mobile Subscriber Identity
TPC	Transmission Power Control
TRAU	Transcoder/Rate Adapter Unit
TSGs	Technical Specification Groups
TTA	Telecommunications Technology Association
TTC	Telecommunication Technology Committee
TTI	Transmission Time Interval
UE	User Equipment
UL-SCH	Uplink Shared Channel
UM	Unacknowledged Mode
UMA	Unlicensed Mobile Access
UMB	Ultra Mobile Broadband
UMS	Unified Messaging System
UMTS	Universal Mobile Telecommunications System.
UNII	Unlicensed National Information Infrastructure
UPE	User Plane Entity
URAN	UMTS Radio Access Network
UTC	Universal Coordinated Time
UTRA	Universal Terrestrial Radio Access
UTRAN	UMTS Terrestrial Radio Access Network
VDSL	Very High Speed Digital Subscriber Line
VHE	Virtual Home Environment
VLR	Visitor Location Register
VMS	Voice Mail System
VoIP	Voice over IP
W3C	World Wide Web Consortium

WAP	Wireless Application Protocol
W-CDMA	Wideband Code Division Multiple Access
WDS	Wireless Distribution System
WECA	Wireless Ethernet Compatibility Alliance
WEP	Wired Equivalent Privacy-Encryption scheme for WLANs
Wi-Fi	Wireless Fidelity
WIN	Wireless Intelligent Network
WLAN	Wireless Local Area Network
WLANA	The Wireless LAN Association
WLL	Wireless in Local Loop
WMAN	Wireless Metropolitan Area Network
WMM	Wi-Fi Multimedia
WP8F	Working Party 8F
WPA	Wireless Protected Access
WRC	World Radio communication Conference
ZP	Zero Padding

BIBILIOGRAPHY

GSM System Engineering, Artech House Mobile Communications Series, Asha K.

GSM system for mobile communication, Michel Mouly & Marie- Bernadette Pautet.

GSM system Engineering, Asha Mehrotra (Artech House Publisher).

GSM 03.22 function related to Mobile Station (MS) in idle mode and group receive mode, by Mehrotra

SIMATIC NET White Paper V.1.1 Industrial Wireless LAN – Industrial Features and Current Standards, November 2009 Siemens AG 2009

"Air Interface for Fixed and Mobile Broadband Wireless Access Systems," IEEE P802.16e/D8, May, 2005.

"Mobile WiMAX – Part I: A Technical Overview and Performance Evaluation," Gartner, Wireless LAN Semiconductors: Worldwide 2002-2007 (1/30/04);

IDC, Worldwide WLAN Semiconductor Forecast and Analysis 2004-2008 (July 2004); and

The Linley Group, A Guide to Wireless LAN Chipsets (June 2004)

IEEE 802.11n High Throughput Study Group Publication

IEEE 802.11-03/940r2 "IEEE P802.11 Wireless LANs, TGn Channel Models", January 9, 2004.

B. Muquet, Z. Wang, G. B. Giannakis, M. de Courville, P. Duhamel , "Cyclic- prefixed or Zero-padded Multicarrier Transmissions?", IEEE Transactions on Communications - December 2002.

R. W. Lowdermilk, "Design and performance of fading insensitive orthogonal frequency division multiplexing (ofdm) using polyphase filtering techniques", Asilomar Conference, November 1996.

M. Pauli and P. Kuchenbecker, "On the reduction of the out-of-band radiation of OFDM signals", ICC'98, June 1998.

P. Siohan, C. Siclet and N. Lacaille, "Analysis and design of ofdm/oqam systems based on filterbank theory," IEEE Trans. on Signal Processing, vol. 50, pp. 1170-1183, May 2002.

D. Petrovic, W. Rave, and G. Fettweis, "Common Phase Error due to Phase Noise in OFDM - Estimation and Suppression," in Proc. PIMRC, 2004.

W. Keusgen, B. Rembold, "KonzeptezurRealisierung von MIMO-Frontends", Frequenz, ZeitschriftfürTelekommunikation", vol. 55, Nov./Dec. 2001.

W. Eberle, J. Tubbax, B. Côme, S. Donnay, H. De Man, G. Gielen, „OFDM-WLAN Receiver Performance Improvement using Digital Compensation Techniques,", IEEE RAWCON 2002.

A. Bordoux, B. Come, N. Khaled, "Non-reciprocal transceivers in OFDM-SDMA Systems: Impact and Mitigation," IEEE RAWCON 2003.

E. Telatar, ``Capacity of multi-antenna Gaussian channels," European Transactions on Telecommunications, vol. 10, no. 6, pp. 585--595, Nov/Dec 1999.

A. J. Goldsmith and S.B. Wicker, ``Design challenges for energy-constrained ad Hoc wireless networks," IEEE Wireless Communications, vol. 9, no. 4, pp. 8--27, August 2002.

A. J. Goldsmith, S. A. Jafar, N. Jindal, and S. Vishwanath, "Capacity limits of MIMO channels" IEEE Journ. Selected Areas in Communications, vol. 21, no.5, pp. 684--702, 2003.

P. Viswanath, D. Tse, and R. Laroia, "Opportunistic beamforming using dumb antennas," IEEE Transactions on Information Theory , vol. 48, no. 6, 2002.

E. A. Jorswieck and H. Boche, "Transmission Strategies for the MIMO MAC with MMSE Receiver: Average MSE Optimization and Achievable Individual MSE Region", IEEE Trans. on Sig. Proc., Vol. 51, No. 11, pp. 2872-2881, 2003.

Achievable Rate and the Optimal Length of the Training and Data Phase," 2003, accepted for publication in IEEE Transactions on Wireless Communications, 2003.

V. Jungnickel, T. Haustein, A. Forck, S. Schiffermueller, H. Gaebler and C. von Helmolt, W. Zirwas, J. Eichinger and E. Schulz, "Real-time concepts for MIMO-OFDM,", Proc.CIC/IEEE Global Mobile Congress, 11-13 Oct. 2004, Shanghai, China.

MaryseWouters, Andre Bourdoux, StefaanDerore, Sven Janssens, VeerleDerudder, "An approach for real-time Prototyping of MIMO Systems," 12th European Signal Processing Conference (EUSIPCO), September 6-10, 2004, Vienna, Austria.

S. T. Chung, A. Lozano, H. C. Huang, "ApproachingEigenmode BLAST channel capacity using V-BLAST with rate and power feedback" Proc. VTC Fall, Atlantic City, 2001.

V. Jungnickel, T. Haustein, E. Jorswieck and C. von Helmolt, "A MIMO WLAN based on linear channel inversion,", IEE Professional Network on Antennas and Propagation, Dec. 2001.

R. Fischer, C. Windpassinger, A. Lampe, J.HuberProc. 4th ITG Conference on Source and Channel Coding, pp. 139-147, Berlin, 2002.

Broadcast and Multicast Services in cdma2000 by Jun Wang, RagulanSinnarajah, Tao Chen, Yongbin Wei, and Edward Tiedemann QUALCOMM Incorporated

Multimedia Broadcast Multicast Service – Technology Overview and Service Aspects by A. Boni, E. Launay, T. Mienville, P. Stuckmann

MBMS service provision and its challenges by J. Ogunbehn and A. Mendjeli Fujitsu Laboratories Europe UK

Paper on "IMT-2000 Network Architecture" by Toshio Shimoe and Takamichi Sano, May 31, 2002

Technical Specification For IMT-2000 Third-Generation (3G) Cellular Mobile Terminal SKMM WTS IMT-MT Rev. 1.01:2007 Suruhanjaya Komunikasi dan Multimedia Malaysia Off Pesiaran Multimedia, 63000

Overview of Global Standardization of IMT-2000 and Its Evolution by Eisuke Fukuda, Akishige Noda and Mamoru Higuchi June 3, 2002)

IEEE 802.16 Broadband Wireless Access Working Group

IMT-2000 Standardization by José Costa ITU-R Task Group 8/1 Region 2 Special Rapporteur 15 September 1999 E-mail: costa@nortelnetworks.com

HSPA to LTE-Advanced, Rysavy Research / 3G Americas, September 2009

Rohde & Schwarz, LTE-Advanced Technology Introduction

LTE NETWORK ARCHITECTURE EVOLUTION by Ville Eerola, Helsinki University of Technology

3GPP LTE-SAE Overview by U.Barth Sept. 06

3GPP TS 23.246 V7.1.1 (2006-12

Analysis OF MC-DS-CDMA Systems in Doubly Spread Channels Thad B. Welcht and Rodger E. Ziemer$ tUnited States Naval Academy $University of Colorado at Colorado Springs

Using MIMO-OFDM Technology to Boost Reless LAN Performance Today

DATACOMM Research Company, St. Louis, Missouri 63132 USA

H. Bölcskei, A.J. Paulraj, "Space-frequency coded broadband OFDM systems," Proc. IEEE WCNC, Sept. 2000, vol.1, pp. 1-6.

H. R. Karimi, M. Sandell, J. Salz, "Comparison between transmitter and receiver array processing to achieve interference nulling and diversity," Proc. PIMRC, 1999, pp. 997-1001.

H.Boche and M. Schubert. "A general duality theory for uplink and downlink beamforming," Proc. IEEE Vehicular Techn. Conf. (VTC) fall, Vancouver, Canada, September 2002.

J. H. Sung and J. R. Barry, "Bit-Allocation Strategies for Closed-Loop MIMO OFDM," Vehicular Technology Conference, Orlando, October 4-9, 2003.

R. Fischer, C. Windpassinger, A. Lampe, J.Huber Proc. 4th ITG Conference on Source and Channel Coding, pp. 139-147, Berlin, 2002

IEEE 802.11-03/940r2 "IEEE P802.11 Wireless LANs, TGn Channel Models", January 9, 2004.

H. Bölcskei, "Orthogonal frequency division multiplexing based on offset QAM", in advances in Gabor theory , Birkhäuser, Boston, 2002

J. Stott, "the effect of phase noise in COFDM", EBU technical review, Summer 1998.

Introduction to WiMAX Technology by Wonil Roh and Vladimir Yanover

IEEE (2006b) IEEE P802.16. IEEE Standard for Local and Metropolitan Area Networks – Part 16:

Air Interface for Fixed Broadband Wireless Access Systems – Amendment: Advanced Air Interface, December.

IEEE (2007) IEEE 802.16m. System Requirements,

IEEE (2008) IEEE P802.16Rev2. Revision of IEEE Std 802.16-2004 and consolidates material from IEEE Std 802.16e-2005, IEEE Std 802.16-2004/Cor1-2005, IEEE Std 802.16f-2005 and IEEE Std802.16g-2007, June.

ITU (2007) Recommendation ITU-R M.1457. Detailed Specifications of the Radio Interfaces of International Mobile Telecommunications-2000 (IMT-2000).

WiMAX Forum (2008c) WiMAX Technology Forecast,

WIMAX An Efficient Tool to Bridge the Digital Divide Prepared by Guy Cayla, Stephane Cohen and Didier Guigon, on behalf of WiMAX Forum November, 2005

WiMAX Forum white paper: iComplete guide to WiMAX, the business case for service provider deployment.

IEEE 802.16-2005: IEEE Standard for Local and Metropolitan Area Networks – Part 16: Air Interface for Fixed and Mobile Broadband Wireless Access Systems – Amendment 2: Physical Layer and Medium Access Control Layers for Combined Fixed and Mobile Operation in Licensed Bands, February 2006

WiMAX Forum white paper: iIEEE 802.16 Standard and WiMAX igniting Broadband Wireless Access.

Research Paper On 5G by Imthiyaz Ali and Next Generation by Imthiyaz Ali

Mobile Broadcast/Multicast Service (MBMS) White Paper from MediaLab, TeliaSonera Finland www.medialab.sonera.fi

3G Wireless Networks by Clint Smith P.E and Daniel Collins,Tata McGraw-Hill

www.umts-forum.org/component/option,com_docman/task,cat_view/gid,327/Itemid,214/

www.sorin-schwartz.com

www.wimaxforum.org and www.ieee802.org/16. 2004 Fujitsu Microelectronics America, Inc.

www.wigwam-project.com/;

www.ist-winner.org/

www.5gthenanocore.com Research Paper On 5G by Imthiyaz Ali

www.3g4g.co.uk

www.datacommresearch.com

WIGWAM project: http://www.wigwam-project.com/;

WINNER Project: http://www.ist-winner.org/

www.iaf-bs.de/downloads/iqmod-demod_eng.pdf

www.wirelessman.org/tgm/docs/80216m-07_002r4.pdf, October.

www.wimaxforum.org/technology/downloads/wimax_forum_wimax_forecasts_6_1_08.pdf.

www.5gthenanocore.com

INDEX

D

E

F

PREVIOUS TITLES BY THE AUTHOR

- **VALUE ADDED SERVICES IN TELECOM**

  Published in 1999

  This book covers topics such as ISDN, Digital Signaling, Intelligent Networks, Wireless in local Loop (WLL) and emerging scenario of Internet Service Providers. This volume is a collection of articles written by the author and published in Science and Technology Magazine of THE HINDU during the years 1996-1999. In his Foreword Sri. C.V.Rajan CGM Chennai Telephones has remarked "***It is a useful introductory book for the students and trainees of telecommunication***"

- **TELECOM NETWORK AND SERVICES IN THE NEW MILLENNIUM**

  Published in 2001

  This book describes many new and useful topics in telecom field like Access Technoloies,High bit-rate Digital subscriber line (HDSL),National Internet Backbone (NIB),VoIP,e-Commerce,Communication Protocols,ATM,SDH and International Mobile Telecommunication-2000.Sri. S. Satagopan, Advisor (Operations) Department of Telecommunication New Delhi writes in his foreword "***I recommend that this book must be with every Telecom Engineer/Student to get to know the recent development in the Telecom Field***"

- **MOBILE NETWORKS AND NEW SERVICES**

  Published in 2004

  A guide to understand fundamentals of advanced wireless network concepts. Basic principles and essential features of GSM, GPRS, WAP, CDMA, cor-DECT are dealt with in detail. Multi Protocol Label switching (MPLS) and Managed Leased Line Network are covered with respect to actual implementation. Concept of Call Centre and Telecom Management Network (TMN) are also explained. Sri. K. B. Brahmadathan, Chief General Manager BSNL writes "***I am sure,this book will be of immense use to all.....has an uncanny knack of explaining complicated subjects in a simple way.The method of presentation,the lucidity and clarity and content deserve to be lauded...***"